THE MAX KADE RESEARCH INSTITUTE SERIES: GERMANS BEYOND EUROPE

Series Editors

A. Gregg Roeber and Daniel Purdy

The Max Kade Research Institute Series is an outlet for scholarship that examines the history and culture of German-speaking communities in America and across the globe, from the early modern period to the start of the First World War. Books in this series examine the movements of the German-speaking diaspora as influenced by forces such as migration, colonization, war, research, religious missions, or trade. This series explores the historical and cultural depictions of the international networks that connect these communities, as well as linguistic relations between German and other languages within European global networks.

This series is a project of the Max Kade German-American Research Institute located on Penn State's campus. This institute, co-directed by A. Gregg Roeber and Daniel Purdy, was founded in 1993 thanks to a grant from the Max Kade Foundation, New York.

THE FRANCIS DANIEL PASTORIUS READER

The

FRANCIS DANIEL PASTORIUS READER

Writings by an Early American Polymath

EDITED BY PATRICK M. ERBEN

ASSOCIATE EDITORS: ALFRED L. BROPHY AND MARGO M. LAMBERT

The Pennsylvania State University Press
University Park, Pennsylvania

Library of Congress Cataloging-in-Publication Data

Names: Pastorius, Francis Daniel, 1651–1719, author. | Erben, Patrick M. (Patrick Michael), editor. | Brophy, Alfred L., editor. | Lambert, Margo M., editor.

Title: The Francis Daniel Pastorius reader : writings by an early American polymath / Patrick M. Erben, editor ; Alfred L. Brophy and Margo M. Lambert, associate editors.

Description: University Park, Pennsylvania : The Pennsylvania State University Press, [2019] | Series: The Max Kade Research Institute series: Germans beyond Europe | Texts are reproduced in Pastorius' own English or in original translations from German, Latin, French, and Dutch. | Includes bibliographical references and index.

Summary: "A comprehensive overview of the writings of Francis Daniel Pastorius, founder of Germantown, lawyer, educator, and early modern polymath. Includes many of Pastorius's unpublished manuscripts as well as new translations of German-language tracts printed in his lifetime"—Provided by publisher.

Identifiers: LCCN 2019007781 | ISBN 9780271083285 (cloth : alk. paper)

Subjects: LCSH: Pastorius, Francis Daniel, 1651–1719—Knowledge and learning. | Pastorius, Francis Daniel, 1651-1719—Books and reading. | American poetry—Colonial period, ca. 1600–1775. | German Americans—Pennsylvania—Philadelphia. | Quakers—Pennsylvania—Philadelphia. | Germantown (Philadelphia, Pa.)—History.

Classification: LCC F152.P267 A25 2019 | DDC 973.2092—dc23

LC record available at https://lccn.loc.gov/2019007781

The Pennsylvania State University Press is a member of the Association of University Presses.

It is the policy of The Pennsylvania State University Press to use acid-free paper. Publications on uncoated stock satisfy the minimum requirements of American National Standard for Information Sciences—Permanence of Paper for Printed Library Material, ANSI Z39.48–1992.

Contents

Illustrations

Preface

WHO WAS FRANCIS DANIEL PASTORIUS AND WHY DOES HE MATTER?

Francis Daniel Pastorius (1651–1719) has been called the pioneer of German immigration to America in the seventeenth and eighteenth centuries. Some have even called him the "German William Bradford," likening Pastorius to the famous founder of Plymouth Colony. In fact, overeager, nationalistic German American historians compared the *Concord*, which carried the first German settlers—represented by Pastorius—to Germantown, to the *Mayflower* in their attempt to elevate German culture in the United States through commemoration and pageantry that focused on a glorified image of him. In 1883 and 1933, German Americans in the United States organized celebrations to commemorate the 200th and 250th anniversary of his arrival and the founding of Germantown in 1683, and in 1951, even after the events of World War II, "Pastorius Day" was celebrated in remembrance of the 300th anniversary of his birth.[1] Created by German immigrant Albert Jaegers in 1917 and dedicated in 1920, the Pastorius Monument still graces Mount Vernon Park in Germantown and features Pastorius leading a group of immigrants.[2] Such mythologizing of German immigrant culture and history has justifiably fallen out of favor, but it has also guaranteed Pastorius's disappearance from American literary and cultural history. Our reader aims at presenting Pastorius and his work on its own terms and within its own religious, literary, and intellectual contexts.

Pastorius was a seventeenth-century German-born immigrant to Pennsylvania, the founder of Germantown, a lawyer, educator, early modern polymath, community leader, and one of the most prolific writers and collectors of contemporary knowledge in early North America.[3] In Europe, Pastorius had received a superior education and was trained to become a lawyer and, like his father, a leading government official. Yet he soon rejected the haughtiness, wastefulness, and impiety of elite European society. While working as a lawyer in Frankfurt, Pastorius joined a group of Lutheran Pietists who were part of a reform movement attempting to lead Protestantism toward deeper piety and inwardness of faith. When the Frankfurt Pietists purchased land in Pennsylvania, Pastorius traveled there to represent their interests and begin a life dedicated to personal and communal renewal. He shepherded Germantown through its infancy. After the Frankfurt Pietists failed to follow him to Pennsylvania, he joined the Society of Friends (Quakers), who had been persecuted in England for their radical religious beliefs. Yet he and three other Germantown residents challenged the Quakers' stance toward slavery by lodging a formal protest against the institution in 1688. Pastorius also put his education to good use, teaching in Philadelphia and Germantown schools. He held a variety of public offices, ranging from bailiff, clerk, recorder, treasurer, and justice of the peace to member of the Pennsylvania Provincial Assembly. The legacy of his teaching, public service, and religious reform would last far beyond his death in late 1719.

Notwithstanding his public roles and historical significance, Pastorius was, above all, a writer and a collector of contemporary knowledge from many subject areas, including religion, linguistics, history, geography, philosophy, medicine, botany, and horticulture. His writings were first intended to convey his newly gained knowledge of America to family and friends. Yet when he experienced several crises of confidence in Pennsylvania's ability to transform the religious and social intolerance its settlers brought with them from Europe, Pastorius turned toward a more private endeavor of collecting knowledge—especially in his many commonplace books, encyclopedic collections, and poetic miscellanies. Rather than merely following the Renaissance ideal of the polymath, Pastorius fashioned these knowledge collections as idealized expressions of his frequently frustrated hopes for harmony. In his manuscript collections, Pastorius sought to create blueprints of the kind of intellectual and spiritual communities (represented by a multiplicity of languages, authors, texts, excerpts, and his original compositions) that so often remained beyond reach in his day-to-day life.

Yet Pastorius's personal and public writings transcend the simple dichotomy between utopian hopefulness and dystopian disappointment that structures stereotypical perceptions of early America. Rather, we see a neglected but compelling drama unfold: the work of rebuilding a dream, adapting and remolding it, creating a new community and new ideals by continually testing which Old World ideals, knowledge, and practices were worth reproducing in America. At first glance, Pastorius's almost excessive pursuit of collecting knowledge in his commonplace books—such as the 800-page "Bee-Hive" manuscript—seems like a desperate attempt to salvage the vestiges of European erudition and privilege. But, on closer examination, the careful weighing of what to discard and what to preserve for later evaluation that characterizes Pastorius's encyclopedic collections, the bibliographies that capture his extensive reading, his multilingual poetry, and his correspondence with some of the most prominent members of Pennsylvania's community can be seen for the larger purpose they serve: helping family and community cultivate the all-important skill of discernment.

Pastorius's work is so valuable today because of the unique path he took both to his experience in America and to the clash between old and new knowledge systems. His desire to enable himself, his community, and his descendants to make informed choices grants readers today a panoramic vision of the influx of ideas to early America and their circulation throughout the Atlantic world. His writings encompass changing approaches to knowledge in the transitional period between the humanism of the late Renaissance and the rationalism and empiricism of the early Enlightenment. Like Renaissance scholars before him, Pastorius sought precedents among the writers of Greek and Roman antiquity such as Seneca and Pliny the Elder and among the Church Fathers such as Augustine and Thomas Aquinas; yet he also valued Enlightenment philosophers such as Francis Bacon and John Locke. The books he owned, read, and excerpted from (as captured in his extensive bibliographies) represent a broad overview of the transmission of ideas and knowledge in this period. His practice of collecting, culling, ordering, and reflecting on the available information and ideas thus opens insights into the changing nature of information storage, retrieval, and processing in early modern Europe and America.

Pastorius's project of knowledge collection pursued four primary goals and concerns, all surprisingly germane to our so-called Information Age. First, he wrestled with the question of which ideas, knowledge, and knowledge systems of Europe could be applied in the changed social, religious, political, and natural settings of America and should thus be transferred there. Second, Pastorius cultivated the practice of discernment in his writings: confronting a surplus of information and ideas, he strove to make wise choices based on spiritual, ethical, and intellectual standards. Third, he asked how best to store information, order it, and make it accessible. And, fourth, Pastorius was concerned with how his collections of knowledge, personal library, and poetic compositions might best serve the mutual edification of a larger community of readers and writers. Probing Pastorius's approach to the origin, reliability, transfer, storage, organization, and, especially, the social and political functions of knowledge will help us in evaluating our own preoccupation with these concerns.

In spite of the shifting relationship to knowledge in the early modern age, Pastorius was firmly rooted in the spiritual awakenings of the seventeenth and early eighteenth centuries and the search for religious truth, guided specifically by the Quaker concept of an indwelling divine spirit. The encyclopedic section of his "Bee-Hive" manuscript book covers multiple viewpoints on any given subject in order to entertain the possibility that truth might emerge from the cumulative consideration of ideas, guided by underlying moral and ethical principles such as the Golden Rule. Indeed, for Pastorius, the multiplicity of ideas, viewpoints, religious beliefs, and languages could only be sustained and brought into harmony if all members of his community accepted that a greater knowledge of God and service to fellow human beings was the ultimate goal of learning. He held fast to basic principles championed by Quakers and Pietists alike: the brotherhood of all believers, the superiority of personal faith over theological doctrine and religious ritual, hope for a fundamental renovation of human society, and an inward conviction of faith translated into an outward change of manners and actions—all resulting in a practical piety bent on serving humanity. These principles run like a thread throughout all of Pastorius's writings: from his early descriptions of Pennsylvania, his religious tracts, and his educational works to his manuscript gatherings of all types of knowledge. Living and working at the end of the seventeenth and the beginning of the eighteenth century, Pastorius witnessed and participated in radical changes from earlier, spiritually or magically inspired views, to more "modern" rationally or empirically grounded paradigms. Even as his writings seem to vacillate between both, his concepts of inwardly accessible truth and practical piety for the good of humanity and the glorification of God remain unwavering.

Pastorius's endeavor to grasp divine truth and his various accumulations of knowledge also tie him to two distinct forms of elitism in the intellectual history of the West. In the late Renaissance, esoteric and mystically inclined reformers of knowledge and faith, represented by figures such as Athanasius Kircher, Jan Amos Comenius, and the anonymous writers of the Rosicrucian manifestos, claimed privileged insight into the divine scriptures allegedly governing both the physical and the spiritual worlds. But, throughout the seventeenth century, there emerged a new brand of thinkers who anticipated and initiated the Enlightenment, including the pioneer of the modern scientific method Francis Bacon, chemists like Robert Boyle, knowledge collectors like Thomas Browne, and philosophers like John Locke and René Descartes. Historians of ideas commonly ascribe to the former worldview a greater social and educational exclusiveness and even a quasi-medieval clinging to superstition and magic, while seeing in the latter a more equalizing spirit of universal access to knowledge through the power of human ingenuity and scientific observation. But, in their steadfast championing of a spiritual and intellectual elite, Pastorius's writings provide a connective bridge between both modes of thinking.

Pastorius rejected the snobbish culture of European universities because it perpetuated unmerited privilege without truly serving humanity or the glorification of God. Nevertheless, he subscribed to an ideal encapsulated in the concept of the "universal college"—that exceptional individuals would deploy their intellectual capabilities and social standing for the overall reformation of knowledge and social relations. In this vein, as an educational complex that included an orphanage, schools, a college, and a seminary, together with facilities for practical training in horticulture, agriculture, and mechanics, the Franckesche Stiftungen (Francke Foundations), established by the Pietist theologian and clergyman August Hermann Francke in Halle, Saxony, supported the selection and training of exceptionally qualified individuals who would then be sent out into the world to rejuvenate the totality of human affairs. Although in their endeavors these individuals and institutions were spurred by Christian faith, retained a Neoplatonist idealism, and even dabbled in a theo-mystical esotericism that smacked of alchemy, they helped create a religious, intellectual, and social elite who participated in the scientific revolution, with its emphasis on impartial inquiry and the creation of useful knowledge. In short, readers should avoid interpreting Pastorius's writings and thought in simplistic historical terms in which earlier spiritualist worldviews were suddenly and radically overturned by newer skeptical and empiricist models. Pastorius sought to reconcile the seemingly opposing currents of faith and science as well as elite erudition and universal education.

Certainly, Pastorius was not immune to the temptations of privilege; he sometimes lamented the loss of preferment and ease that a life in government service in Germany could have provided. Indeed, his command of Latin, his legal training, his vast knowledge of classical writers and precepts, and his genteel command of upper-class norms of conduct enabled him to act the social equal of William Penn and his secretary, James Logan, and thus advance the development of social and cultural institutions in early Pennsylvania. In spite of those advantages, however, Pastorius probed the pitfalls of status and privilege, especially the degeneration of spiritual acuteness that came with wealth and ease. Although he echoed the classical tropes of rural simplicity in his paeans on the homely life he led with his garden and bees in Germantown, Pastorius also harnessed Quaker ideals—antimaterialism, charity, and social welfare—for concrete moments of social critique, such as his protest against slavery and his championing of women's voices within Quaker society. In his lifelong collecting, storing, and evaluating of knowledge, he grappled with the burden of privilege: how could knowledge collection and production be transformed from a token of exclusivity into a conduit for truth, morality, and spiritual inclusiveness? *The Francis Daniel Pastorius Reader* invites readers to embrace the apparent contradictions and conflicting intellectual points of view that Pastorius attempted to reconcile in his writings—and to appreciate the similarities of the challenges he faced to those we face today. How do we wrestle with the varieties of new knowledge, the ethical conundrums they pose, and the proliferation of new media and means of disseminating information—without losing our sense of identity, community, and value?

The *Pastorius Reader* gathers for the first time a comprehensive selection from Pastorius's wide-ranging works, with a detailed and thorough introduction to contextualize his historical, intellectual, and religious backgrounds as well as shorter introductions to the selected texts themselves, a biographical chronology, an explanatory listing of the significant people and places in his life, and copious notes. English-speaking readers now have access to translations of Pastorius's multilingual writings in poetry and prose. Beginning with his printed works, the *Reader* includes a new translation of his first description of Pennsylvania; his defense of the Quakers against rumors and misunderstandings among European Protestants; his pamphlet defending the mainstream Quakers against the attacks of the Keithians;[4] and his primer of the English language for use in teaching. The majority of Pastorius's writings and intellectual efforts remain in manuscript, including his various notebooks and commonplace books as well as the vast bibliographies of the works he read or consulted, his epigrams, poetry, and various encyclopedic collections of the knowledge of his time; his correspondence with individuals in America and Europe; his advice manuals on agriculture, gardening, beekeeping, and medicine; and, finally, his writings on law and civil administration.[5] Pastorius did not seek to have these works printed but instead circulated them as manuscripts within appreciative circles of family members, friends, neighbors, Quakers, and other bibliophiles—a form of scribal publication.[6] Doing so helped Pastorius and others come together in an intellectual and spiritual community that allowed for ideas to be tested and shared, piety to be advanced, and reason to be sharpened without the partisan public debates that print publication often gave rise to. The *Pastorius Reader* presents selections from his hitherto unpublished writings—one of the largely overlooked treasures of early American literature.

The structure and underlying rationale of the *Reader* reflect Pastorius's favorite image and model for his collection and storage of knowledge (and the title of his largest manuscript book): the beehive. Pastorius embraced the beehive model because of the many similarities between the activities of readers and collectors and those of bees in a hive: many individuals, living in a complex society or community, individually pursuing the collecting, depositing, and refining of a precious substance, yet joining their efforts in an elaborate and collaborative enterprise that ultimately produces a highly valued product. Pastorius's work had many compartments or spaces in which knowledge, insight, experience, and thought could be deposited. We invite readers to explore Pastorius's manifold interests and occupations, expressed in various genres and modes, always returning to common themes and concerns of spiritual unity and moral regeneration. The model of the beehive exemplifies Pastorius's ultimate vision for the project of reading and writing, and, by extension, for the building of an ideal community in America: an ongoing and collaborative process that would evaluate all knowledge and ideas, subjecting them to open-ended scrutiny, arrangement, and evaluation. Just as bees roam wide to collect the raw materials to make honey, so Pastorius roamed wide for ideas and intellectual stimulation in his collection of knowledge, but he assiduously subjected everything he read and knew to a crucial query: how did each item and each larger pursuit serve both God and humanity? Striving for perfection yet remaining ever mindful of the potential for error and misjudgment, Pastorius followed a motto that he implicitly and explicitly repeated throughout his writings: "Test everything. Hold on to the good" (1 Thess. 5:21).

Acknowledgments

I wish to acknowledge co-editor Al Brophy for introducing me to Pastorius; Alison Games, my dissertation advisor for all of her support throughout my research into Pastorius's life and world; and my husband, Chris Bryant, for his unfailing and loving support as well.

—MARGO LAMBERT

I would like to thank Associate Dean Holning Lau of the University of North Carolina School of Law and Dean Mark Brandon of the University of Alabama School of Law for arranging for generous subsidies for this reader. Susannah Loumiet and Marc Korngay provided excellent research assistance on Pastorius's Quaker and non-Quaker bibliographies.

—AL BROPHY

More than twenty years ago, I first came to "meet" Francis Daniel Pastorius by reading the several descriptions he wrote of his journey to and settlement in Pennsylvania. Being a recent immigrant from Germany myself, I found that Pastorius's hopes, successes, and losses deeply resonated with me. He has accompanied me throughout my academic career so far, and studying his work has opened many doors for me. I thank him for this but even more for articulating a vision of a better world in which knowledge, truth, compassion, faith, and justice matter. I would also like to thank David Shields and Reiner Smolinski, who first introduced me to Pastorius, as well as my parents, Manfred and Brunhilde Erben, for taking me to see Pastorius's house in Sommerhausen (near Würzburg in Bavaria) so many years ago and supporting my endeavors along the way. After leaving Germany, Pastorius never saw his family again, and I am glad that I never had to experience such a profound separation.

Many individuals have my deepest gratitude for contributing to the completion of this book in ways great and small. The *Pastorius Reader* would not have been possible without the many contributions of my associate editors, Margo Lambert and Al Brophy, who shared my passion for all things Pastorius and who undertook the time-consuming work on textually difficult portions of the *Reader*, collaborated with a congenial spirit, and, most of all, remained patient when I took much longer than expected to gather and revise the final manuscript. Al has gone far beyond the most hopeful expectations in finding funds to support its publication.

I would further like to thank for their generous support the Department of English and Philosophy at the University of West Georgia, especially Chair Meg Pearson, as well as the Office of Research and Sponsored Project, particularly Vice President Denise Overfield. It is heartening that even when talk of financial scarcity has become the norm in higher education, humanities projects may still find support in word and deed.

The *Pastorius Reader* has received endorsements and critical as well editorial reviews from many scholars and editors, to whom I am profoundly grateful. At Penn State Press, I would like to thank Series Editors A. Gregg Roeber and Daniel Purdy for championing this project early on and for not losing faith in its completion. As outside reviewers, Hermann Wellenreuther and Rose Beiler cheered the project on while spending many hours sifting through the manuscript and making many useful suggestions for revision. The *Reader* is much better because of their expertise. That it has at last come to fruition is mostly due to the enduring patience and dedication of acquisitions editor Kathryn Yahner. Thank you, Kathryn, for your time, labor, professionalism, and kind yet insistent pursuit of seeing the *Pastorius Reader* through to publication. I also want to thank managing editor Laura Reed-Morrisson for overseeing the final stages of the book with great patience and grace and both business manager Tina Laychur and editorial assistant Hannah Hebert for assembling the nuts and bolts of this project. Copy editor Jeff Lockridge assiduously probed every "nook and cranny" of the manuscript; his diligence, skill, and perseverance have improved the *Pastorius Reader* in all ways possible.

Many individuals helped me navigate the mind-boggling details of Pastorius's many languages and writings. Nathan Michalewicz, then an M.A. student in history at West Georgia, provided all translations of Pastorius's often idiosyncratic Latin and French. Thank you, Nathan, for your immense contributions to this project. Also, Joanne van der Woude translated the Dutch, Chad Davidson the Italian, and Nadejda Williams the Greek passages. Several graduate research assistants—especially Brooke Sparks, Darin Medders, and Leeanne Hoovestol Kline—helped with a variety of indispensable tasks.

I would also like to express my gratitude to the archives that have granted permissions for the publication of texts and images: the Historical Society of Pennsylvania, the Quaker and Special Collections at Haverford College, the Kislak Center for Special Collections at the Rare Book and Manuscript Library of the University of Pennsylvania, especially the center's intrepid John Pollack, and the Zentralbibliothek Zürich.

Much closer to home, my family still believed in this book even when I no longer believed in it myself. They cheered me on, let me take my time brooding over obscure manuscript passages, and included Pastorius in our everyday conversations as if he were a member of the family. Samuel and Ruby have both been incredibly proud of their father's work and justifiably curious about how and why anyone could possibly have written so many words. Yet they are also growing up to become young scholars in their own right, and I am incredibly proud of *them*. And, best of all, Rebecca Harrison, my true love, you have been the most supportive, patient, helpful, and also persistent spouse I could ever imagine. I love how we understand and appreciate each other's work, and I imagine Francis Daniel Pastorius and Eudora Welty talking about us in the afterlife. I am excited about all of our future endeavors together as well as some time away from work.

This book is dedicated to Rebecca, Samuel, and Ruby.

—PATRICK ERBEN

How to Use This Book

☙ Readers may wish to save the volume introduction for later and directly delve into the selections of Pastorius's writings, each equipped with its own, briefer introduction outlining the principles of selection and the text's source as well as the circumstances of production, generic context, authorial purposes, mode of dissemination, and material and textual features. Notes provide additional information referring to specific names, titles, places, events, historical figures, and uncommon or archaic words. For the convenience of using this book both as a reader and as a reference tool, we include a detailed biographical chronology and a listing of significant people and places in Pastorius's life. While perusing the textual selections, readers may want to consult these tools to orient themselves within the general timeline of Pastorius's life and to understand the many connections among people in America and Europe he cultivated through his writings. In compiling this volume as a reader, we deliberately created some overlap or repetition between the thematic sections of the volume introduction and the introductions to the selected texts themselves. Whether sampling individual texts or reading the volume in its entirety, all readers should be able to grasp what each text is about, the context in which it is embedded, and how it speaks to recurring issues and questions in Pastorius's work.

In selecting and arranging texts, we have balanced a concern for genre and mode of dissemination with an attempt to highlight links among fields of knowledge, textual forms, and historical significance. Thus we divided the selected texts into printed and manuscript works—parts 1 and 2 of the *Reader*—reflecting the division between Pastorius's public and private endeavors, as well as the many connections between them. The printed works comprise the writings for which Pastorius was known both in his lifetime and in history. The *Reader* begins with his earliest description of Pennsylvania, followed by his two tracts on matters of religious dispute, and his English language primer. Although they have largely remained hidden until now, Pastorius's manuscript works form the bulk of his literary and intellectual accomplishments. Part 2 comprises selected manuscript texts from his commonplace books, bibliographies, poetic miscellanies, anniversary poems and tributes to his friends, letters, practical collections of horticultural, agricultural, apiary, and medicinal knowledge, and his legal and civic writings and manuals.

Alternatively, readers may wish to familiarize themselves with the background and contexts of Pastorius's work by first perusing the volume introduction, each of whose thematic sections highlights a key area of concern for Pastorius, such as religion, law, education, knowledge, community, and authorship. The conclusion to the introduction reflects on the ways in which Pastorius used writing in all modes and genres and on all occasions both to make sense of and to counteract the recurrence of the losses he experienced and the losses he feared. Overall, the volume introduction unpacks the multifaceted roles Pastorius played in his life, while emphasizing the connections between them. Pastorius aimed to keep no feature of his life and work separate from any other—whether it was his faith, his profession, his relationships to others, his search for knowledge, or his many languages—but hoped to bring all into harmony.

It is our hope that *The Francis Daniel Pastorius Reader* will entice a broad audience to delve into Pastorius's work and to appreciate both its merits and its relevance to understanding the early American past, the advent of modernity, and the many questions that continue to vex our own world. The writings selected here speak to a varied readership of scholars, students, and interested individuals in a variety of fields: American literature, German literature, comparative literature, American and Atlantic history, religious and church history, book history, the history of ideas, the history of law, translation studies, and especially the fields German American history and culture. Cognizant of its limitations, we see this edition as a starting point both for a comprehensive editorial preparation of Pastorius's writings and for a field of Pastorius studies. We hope that readers will pursue further research in the digitization projects of Pastorius's manuscripts undertaken by the Rare Book and Manuscript Library of the University of Pennsylvania and by the Historical Society of Pennsylvania. Pastorius admired books as vehicles of knowledge and enlightenment, but he also understood their limitations in making knowledge accessible and comprehensible. The *Reader* is both a paean to books and reading and a gateway to the many opportunities opened up by digital media.

Editorial Method

Pastorius's works, especially those writings preserved only in manuscript form, represent various challenges to editors and readers alike. The individual introductions to selected texts discuss specific material challenges and conditions, which differ greatly between Pastorius's printed works and his manuscripts. As a general rule, we have attempted to preserve the idiosyncrasies of Pastorius's writing style and have not normalized early modern spelling, grammar, and punctuation unless it was necessary to clarify the meaning or to avoid needless confusion for the readers. Thus what may appear as spelling mistakes in modern English or German are simply faithful reproductions of Pastorius's orthography.

Also, we are fully cognizant of the loss of content and potentially of meaning that can take place in transcribing into print manuscript books such as Pastorius's "Bee-Hive," whose material and visual arrangement contains many clues about Pastorius's composition process and revisions that cannot be reproduced in a printed book. We have tried to indicate in explanatory notes major decisions by Pastorius, such as his crossing out entire sections from his commonplace book "Alvearialia" because he had already transferred what he deemed relevant to their more permanent location, the "Bee-Hive." Nevertheless, after deciding when textual peculiarities in the manuscripts seemed primarily due to Pastorius's attempt to save space on preciously scarce paper and when they seemed to be his attempt to add information or references later on without always having space to do so, we championed readability over precise fidelity to the visual appearance of the original. Generally, therefore, we followed the "clear text" method described in Mary-Jo Kline and Susan Holbrook Perdue's *A Guide to Documentary Editing* (3rd edition; Charlottesville: University of Virginia Press, 2008) to make Pastorius's work accessible to readers unable or unwilling to avail themselves of digital facsimiles of his original printed and manuscript materials. Specific editorial practices (some of them deviating from the "clear text" method) are listed below.

Even as it introduces readers to his work, the *Pastorius Reader* also encourages further study using other sources available today, especially the digital facsimiles of his manuscript works available through the internet portals of the Historical Society of Pennsylvania's Digital Library (http://digitallibrary.hsp.org/), with its online versions of the Pastorius Papers, and of the University of Pennsylvania's Rare Book and Manuscript Library's digitization of the "Bee-Hive" (http://dla.library.upenn.edu/dla/medren/detail.html?id=MEDREN_2487547). Readers may compare our transcriptions and annotations with the online facsimiles of the original manuscripts, view the vast amount of materials that could not be included in this edition, and participate in the ongoing recovery process of Pastorius's writings. And, in doing so, they may come to appreciate the labor and difficult decisions involved in bringing Pastorius's manuscript work to the printed page.

The texts in the *Reader* are reproduced either in Pastorius's own English or in translations original to this edition; we have not included any previously published translated material. Translations from German are by Patrick M. Erben; from Latin and French, by Nathan Kirk Michalewicz; and from Dutch, by Joanne van der Woude; they hew as close as possible to the meaning, diction, and style of Pastorius's prose without trying to make it sound quaint or antiquated. Letters and poetry collected in the "Bee-Hive" in multiple languages are presented in their original and in translation (provided in the notes) to approximate the multilingual expression of similar ideas Pastorius intended rather than make the text appear like a uniform composition in English. Poetry in languages other than English is given in prose rather than verse translation to avoid confusing readers as to which versions are actually Pastorius's own and which are our current translations.

To make the text accessible to modern-day readers while preserving a useful amount of Pastorius's style and early modern practices,

1) We retained all readily comprehensible idiosyncratic spellings. For example, we retained "Pensilvania" and similar spellings of "Pennsylvania" frequently used by Pastorius.

2) We retained Pastorius's use of "ÿ" or "Ÿ" to represent the Dutch "y" sound, instead of the "ij" used in both early modern and current Dutch.

3) We spelled out contractions and abbreviations commonly used in early modern scribal practice to save space and time. For example, "Acc.ts" was rendered as "Accounts," "mo:" or "mo." as "month," "sd" and "abovesd" as "said" and "abovesaid," "wch" as "which," and "ye" or "ye" when it meant "the" as "the." Any exceptions to this practice are noted in the notes.

4) We retained all idiosyncratic capitalizations. (Pastorius capitalized many nouns in English, following the German practice of capitalizing all nouns.)

5) We deleted the periods Pastorius placed after numbers wherever appropriate.

6) We replaced double hyphens (similar to the mathematical equal signs) with single hyphens.

7) We replaced horizontal lines drawn over letters to indicate doubling with the double letters themselves.

8) We replaced superscript periods, followed by a virgule and a period (·/.), which Pastorius sometimes used to indicate paragraph breaks without actually making

them to save space, with regular periods and, wherever appropriate, with actual paragraph breaks.

9) We retained Pastorius's cross-references to other pages or entry numbers even when the entries or pages referred to are not included in the selected texts of this volume. (We hope these numbers will not be confusing to readers but will rather encourage them to use the *Reader* as a springboard for individual explorations of the online facsimiles of Pastorius's manuscript works.)

10) We used square brackets with an ellipsis—[...]—to indicate one or a few illegible words. If a word or several words were illegible but we could fill in a word or words through context clues, we indicated it or them with an insertion in square brackets (e.g., "[William] Penn").

11) We indicated illegible lines or sections, as well as sections omitted from the selected texts provided, with square brackets and an ellipsis stretching across the page: [. . . .]

12) We made biblical abbreviations and chapter-verse references consistent by adopting Pastorius's predominant usage throughout—both in our transcription of his writings and in our introductions, translations, notes, and annotations.

Biographical Chronology

1618 The Thirty Years' War, a conflict between various Catholic and Protestant powers, erupts and leads to huge population losses across the German states.[1]

1624 Melchior Adam Pastorius, FDP's father, is born in Erfurt.

1629 The home of FDP's paternal grandfather, Martin Pastorius (a Roman Catholic lawyer working in the Lutheran city of Erfurt), is burned down by Swedish troops. Fleeing, Martin Pastorius is seriously wounded and dies soon thereafter, leaving his widow, Brigitta, and their family to live in poverty.

1643–49 Melchior Adam studies law and travels throughout Europe; he lives in Rome for several years, where he attends the German College. Though, as told in his autobiography, he received only one ducat for his travels and studies from his mother, he profits from the patronage of several Roman Catholic princes and clerics.

1649 Melchior Adam attains a position at the court of Count Georg Friedrich of Limpurg in Sommerhausen, Franconia (present-day Bavaria); he converts from Catholicism to Lutheranism.

1650 Melchior Adam marries the widow Magdalena Dietz (born 1607).

1651 September 26. Franz (Francis) Daniel Pastorius is born in Sommerhausen; he will be the only child of Melchior Adam and Magdalena Pastorius.

1657 March 27. FDP's mother, Magdalena, dies on Good Friday.

1658 Melchior Adam marries Eva Margaretha Gelchsheimer.

1659 FDP's four-month-old sister dies. Upon the death of his father-in-law, Melchior Adam assumes his position as a government official and moves the family to the imperial city of Windsheim, some 30 miles from Sommerhausen. Over the following years, he will rise to the highest ranks of the city's government, including mayor and superior judge. He will also publish several books, including an account of the coronation of several German emperors, a book of spiritual poetry, and a description of Windsheim (1692), to which will be appended a description of Pennsylvania by FDP, based on *Sichere Nachricht* (1684; Certain News).

1659–68 FDP attends the Windsheim Gymnasium or Latin School (a humanist secondary school). He is deeply impressed by ethical teachings of the school's rector, Tobias Schumberg, who converses with his students primarily in Latin. FDP later composes a Latin poem, "De Mundi Vanitate" (Of the Vanity of the World), dedicated to Schumberg.[2]

1660 FDP's second infant sister dies only nine days after her birth.

1661	FDP's stepmother dies after the stillbirth of a third child.
1662	Melchior Adam marries the fifty-six-year-old widow Barbara Greulich, who will raise FDP. The couple will have no children of their own. Barbara will die in 1674.
1668	FDP leaves Windsheim to attend the University of Altdorf, near Nuremberg, where he studies liberal arts.
1670	FDP moves to Strasbourg (then a German city in the Alsace), where he studies law and the French language.
1672	FDP leaves Strasbourg as political tensions between France and the Holy Roman Empire rise. He briefly studies law at Altdorf but is unsatisfied with the faculty and transfers to the University of Jena in Thuringia, where he will study law under Heinrich Linck as well as the Italian language.
1674	FDP goes to Regensburg to witness a session of the Reichstag (Imperial Diet), the deliberative and legislative body of the Holy Roman Empire.
1674	Melchior Adam marries his fourth (and last) wife, Dorothea Esther Volckmann. They will have four children: Johann Samuel, Anna Catharina, Margaretha Barbara, and Augustin Adam.
1675	FDP returns to the University of Altdorf to complete his law degree under Linck, who has accepted a position there.
1676	FDP delivers his inaugural disputation in law and receives his doctorate in civil and canon law. In November, he returns to Windsheim to practice law.
1679	FDP moves to Frankfurt am Main on the recommendation of the Pietist pastor of Windsheim, Johann Heinrich Horb, who has married Sophie Cäcilia, the sister of the father of German Pietism, Philipp Jakob Spener. FDP is thus introduced to the Pietist circle in Frankfurt (known as the "Saalhof Pietists," after the hall where they have been meeting in a small religious gathering known as a "conventicle"). Here Pastorius meets prominent Pietists such as Spener, the merchant Jacob van de Walle, the lawyer Johann Jakob Schütz, and the mystics Johanna Eleonora von Merlau and Johann Wilhelm Petersen. This group of religious reformers met with William Penn and several other Quaker missionaries in 1677 and, in the 1680s, will become part of Penn's network promoting immigration to Pennsylvania.
1680	FDP departs for a grand tour as guide to the young German nobleman Johann Bonaventura von Bodeck. They visit Holland, England, France, Switzerland, and parts of Germany. Although his manuscript travel journal detailing the trip, "Itinerarium," appears to have been lost, FDP recounts some details from this journey in the preface (Vorrede) to his description of Pennsylvania (see chapter 1 of this reader). Pastorius increasingly comes to reject the vain courtly culture he experiences during his trip, which contributes to his later decision to seek a new social and spiritual beginning in Pennsylvania.
1682	FDP returns from his grand tour and reconnects with the Pietists in Frankfurt, who share with FDP several promotional pamphlets on Pennsylvania received through Penn's Quaker agent in Rotterdam, Benjamin Furly. The Pietists purchase a total of

25,000 acres of land in Pennsylvania in concert with other investors across Germany and plan to establish a spiritual community outside Philadelphia. For this purpose, they form the "German Society" (later renamed the "Frankfurt Land Company).

1683   April 2. The Pietists appoint FDP as their agent and representative in Pennsylvania. FDP visits a Quaker community in Kriegsheim (south of Mainz), which immigrates to Pennsylvania later that year. On his way down the Rhine, FDP stops at Krefeld, where he meets with a Quaker congregation that has also purchased several thousand acres in Pennsylvania and agrees to represent their interests upon his arrival in Philadelphia. FDP travels via Rotterdam, where he meets with Benjamin Furly, and London to Deal, England, which becomes his port of departure for America; he leaves Deal on June 7 on board the ship *America*. On his journey, FDP befriends the family of the Welsh Quaker (and later Lieutenant Governor) Thomas Lloyd. After Lloyd's death in 1694, FDP will revive his friendship with Lloyd's daughters through a series of yearly poems celebrating the anniversaries of their arrival in Philadelphia.

August 20. FDP arrives in Philadelphia. The Krefeld immigrants, constituting the first thirteen families to settle in Germantown, arrive on October 3. Pastorius negotiates personally with William Penn regarding the assignment of the purchased lands, including city lots in Philadelphia and a contiguous area for a German settlement. On October 12, Penn grants a 6,000-acre tract east of the Schuylkill River, surveyed by Thomas Holmes, for the settlement of Germantown. Pastorius lives in what he describes as a "cave" on one of the German Society's city lots in Philadelphia.

1684   FDP writes his first official report (dated March 7) to the Pietists' German Society, published later that year as *Sichere Nachricht auß America, wegen der Landschafft Pennsylvania, von einem dorthin gereißten Teutschen* (Certain News *from America, Concerning the Country of Pennsylvania, by a German Who Traveled There*). In the next years, additional immigrant families from Kriegsheim, Krefeld, and Mühlheim an der Ruhr will settle in Germantown, where they will establish a thriving linen-weaving industry. FDP serves as a justice of the peace for the County of Philadelphia until 1685.

1686   Having abandoned their goal to follow FDP to Pennsylvania, the Frankfurt Pietists reorganize the original German Society as the Frankfurt Land Company, which has as its exclusive purpose the administration and promotion of land sales. They retain FDP as their attorney, but he becomes increasingly dissatisfied with the now purely pecuniary mission of the company.

1687   FDP is elected to the Pennsylvania General Assembly.

1688   April 18. FDP and three other Germantown Quakers—Abraham op den Graeff, Dirck op den Graeff, and Gerret Hendericks—submit a protest against slavery to several Quaker Meetings; eventually, it is shelved by the Yearly Meeting at Burlington because no consensus can be reached among American Friends in Quaker Meetings at any level.

November 6. FDP marries Ennecke (Anna) Klostermanns, a recent German immigrant from Mühlheim.

1690   FDP's son Johann Samuel is born in Germantown.

| 1691 | FDP helps Germantown acquire a charter for self-government; appointed bailiff, he begins to record the proceedings of the newly established Germantown General Court in the "Rathsbuch" (Court Book). |

| 1692 | FDP is elected clerk of the Germantown Court. In the following years, he will rotate among the offices of justice of the peace, bailiff, and clerk for Germantown. |

FDP's son Heinrich (Henry) Pastorius is born in Germantown. Becoming embroiled in the Keithian controversy, instigated by Scottish Quaker George Keith over theology and church polity and resulting in a schism among Pennsylvania Quakers, FDP firmly supports more "orthodox" Quakers such as William Penn and Thomas Lloyd against Keith's attacks.

| 1696 | When four Keithian supporters disrupt a Quaker Meeting at Burlington, FDP issues a strongly worded rebuke in print, *Henry Bernhard Koster, William Davis, Thomas Rutter & Thomas Bowyer, four Boasting Disputers Of this World briefly REBUKED* (1697; published by William Bradford in New York). FDP begins his "Bee-Hive" manuscript, a commonplace book, encyclopedia, and poetic miscellany, and will continue his entries until his death. Increasingly, he shifts his time and efforts from public business to private scholarship and reading, excerpting and collecting the knowledge and wisdom of his and previous times. |

| 1697 | FDP writes a defense of the American Quakers, addressed to his former Pietist co-religionists, against rumors and accusations circulating in Germany. It is published in Amsterdam as *Ein Send-Brieff Offenhertziger Liebsbezeugung an die so genannte Pietisten in Hoch-Teutschland* (*A Missive of Sincere Affection to the So-Called Pietists in Germany*). |

| 1698 | FDP becomes a teacher at the Friends' Public School in Philadelphia, where he teaches until 1700. Adopting a rigorous curriculum for his American students, patterned on his European schooling, he nevertheless champions the importance of a practical education in letters to his father. FDP produces a number of schoolbooks in manuscript and publishes *A New Primmer or Methodical Directions to Attain the True Spelling, Reading & Writing of ENGLISH*. He becomes the subject of a complaint for the use of severe corporal punishment on a student, Israel Pemberton. |

| 1700 | The Frankfurt Land Company relieves FDP of his duties and transfers its power of attorney to the Pietist immigrants Daniel Falckner, Johannes Kelpius, and Johannes Jawert, none of whom possess any legal training. The Pietists, probably in collaboration with Melchior Adam Pastorius, publish FDP's *Umständige Geographische Beschreibung* (*Circumstantial Geographical Description*), printed by Andreas Otto in Frankfurt and Leipzig. The book includes a biographical preface by FDP, a revised and expanded version of his 1684 account to the Pietists (*Sichere Nachricht*), as well as personal letters written to his father and other German friends. |

| 1701 | Kelpius resigns from his post with the Frankfurt Land Company and Jawert moves to Maryland. On his own, Falckner begins to mismanage the company's assets, runs up personal debts, and starts drinking to excess. Despite FDP's repeated attempts to intercede, Falckner colludes with the Philadelphia attorney George Lowther to gain exclusive control of Frankfurt Land Company landholdings. |

1702   Melchior Adam Pastorius dies at age 77. FDP begins teaching at the Germantown Court school, where he will teach until shortly before his death in 1719.

1707   The Corporation of Germantown loses its charter.

1709   In collusion with Daniel Falckner and Quaker attorney David Lloyd, and unbeknownst to co-attorney Johannes Jawert and FDP (the only company investor actually living in Pennsylvania), recent German immigrant Johann Heinrich Sprögel defrauds the Frankfurt Land Company of more than 22,000 acres of land. It will take FDP until 1714 and much pleading with his influential Quaker friends Samuel Carpenter, James Logan, Richard Hill, and Isaac Norris to regain title to the lands he has lost. The drawn-out affair of the Frankfurt Land Company profoundly shakes FDP's trust in the ability of Pennsylvania to realize its spiritual potential.

1713   With his health deteriorating, FDP leaves his Germantown home less and less often, but carries on a lively correspondence with many notable Pennsylvanians, especially the young student Lloyd Zachary (later a successful physician). He also establishes an active exchange of letters and manuscripts with several Quaker literary women including Jane Fenn Hoskens, Lydia Norton, and Elizabeth Hill.

1714   FDP has a severe attack of fever.

1717   FDP suffers from a serious respiratory infection.

1719   Francis Daniel Pastorius dies of unspecified natural causes in the final days of the year.

Notes

PREFACE

1. The mythologizing of Pastorius as a pioneer of German immigration perhaps began with John Greenleaf Whittier's "The Pennsylvania Pilgrim" (1872), though Whittier's poem lacks the nationalistic excesses of German and German-American writers in the late nineteenth and early twentieth centuries; in fact, as an ardent abolitionist, Whittier primarily took interest in Pastorius's early opposition to slavery. On October 29, 1933, Albert Bernhardt Faust gave an address at the "Pastorius Celebration" in Cincinnati that attempted to place German immigrants on par with English-speaking settlers and elevated Pastorius and the founding of Germantown to an epic beginning: "The people of New England cherish the memory of the *Mayflower* and their William Bradford, Pilgrim governor of the Plymouth Colony. We venerate our ship *Concord* that brought the first body of German colonists to Philadelphia. Germantown is our Plymouth, and we also have a Bradford, our own leader second to none, a man of exceptional ability and devotion to a great cause, outstanding in rectitude, scholarship and humanity—Francis Daniel Pastorius." See Albert Bernhardt Faust, *Francis Daniel Pastorius and the 250th Anniversary of the Founding of Germantown* (Philadelphia: Carl Schurz Memorial Foundation, 1935), 5.

2. On the Pastorius Monument, see Hans A. Pohlsander, *German Monuments in the Americas: Bonds Across the Atlantic* (Bern: Peter Lang, 2010), 3–9.

3. The most comprehensive biographical work on Pastorius is Marion Dexter Learned, *The Life of Francis Daniel Pastorius* (Philadelphia: Campbell, 1908). Other reliable biographical scholarship on Pastorius includes Alfred L. Brophy, "Francis Daniel Pastorius," in *The Multilingual Anthology of American Literature: A Reader of Original Texts with English Translations*, ed. Marc Shell and Werner Sollors (New York: New York University Press, 2000), 12–15; Patrick M. Erben, "Francis Daniel Pastorius," in *Germany and the Americas: Culture, Politics, and History*, ed. Thomas Adam (Santa Barbara, Calif.: ABC-CLIO, 2005), 869–71; Margo M. Lambert, "Francis Daniel Pastorius: An American in Early Pennsylvania, 1683–1719/20" (Ph.D. diss., Georgetown University,

2007); John David Weaver, "Franz Daniel Pastorius (1651–c. 1720): Early Life in Germany with Glimpses of His Removal to Pennsylvania" (Ph.D. diss., University of California, Davis, 1985); and Marianne S. Wokeck, "Francis Daniel Pastorius," in *Lawmaking and Legislators in Pennsylvania: A Biographical Dictionary*, vol. 1, *1682–1709*, ed. Craig Horle et al. (Philadelphia: University of Pennsylvania Press, 1991), 586–90.

4. The "Christian Quaker" followers of Scottish missionary George Keith.

5. Much of Pastorius's time in Pennsylvania was occupied by his many leadership roles for the Corporation of Germantown and the Frankfurt Land Company. Most of the records, petitions, and legal manuscripts Pastorius wrote as bailiff, clerk, recorder, and treasurer are not included in this collection since they were meticulously edited and published in J. M. Duffin, ed., *Acta Germanopolis: Records of the Corporation of Germantown, Pennsylvania, 1691–1707* (Philadelphia: Genealogical Society of Pennsylvania, 2008).

6. On scribal publication and the role of manuscript circulation in the early modern age, see David D. Hall, *Ways of Writing: The Practice and Politics of Text-Making in Seventeenth-Century New England* (Philadelphia: University of Pennsylvania Press, 2008); and Anthony Grafton, *Worlds Made by Words: Scholarship and Community in the Modern West* (Cambridge, Mass.: Harvard University Press, 2009).

BIOGRAPHICAL CHRONOLOGY

1. This biographical chronology is based on J. M. Duffin, introduction to Duffin, *Acta Germanopolis*; Learned, *Life of Francis Daniel Pastorius*; Weaver, "Franz Daniel Pastorius"; and Wokeck, "Francis Daniel Pastorius."

2. "De Mundi Vanitate" was included in Pastorius's 1700 description of Pennsylvania, *Umständige Geographische Beschreibung Der zu allerletzt erfundenen Provintz Pensylvaniæ, In denen End-Gräntzen Americæ In der West-Welt gelegen* (Frankfurt and Leipzig: Andreas Otto, 1700), 62–63.

Introduction

The Lives and Letters of Francis Daniel Pastorius

Pastorius and the Search for Religious Community

In a letter to his father written in Deal, England, on June 7, 1683 (shortly before his departure for America), Pastorius explained his reasons for leaving Europe: "I have suffered myself to be moved by the special direction of the Most High to journey over to Pennsylvania, living in the hope that this my design will work out to my own good and that of my dear brothers and sisters, but most of all to the advancement of the glory of God (which is my aim above all else), especially as the audacity and sin of the European world are accumulating more and more from day to day, and therefore the just judgment of God cannot be long withheld."[1] Pastorius had gone through a period of religious crisis that left him exasperated about the chances for reaching salvation and a godly life in the Old World and that led him to seek out a new, radically changed situation in America. Apparently, his doubts about life in Europe set in during his days at various European universities: Pastorius rejected academic institutions; the immoral conduct of privileged students spending their time fencing, dancing, and drinking; the vain academic arguments of the scholars; and the superficial observation of religious rituals in the established churches—all seemed to hinder a true understanding of God. He sensed that something was morally and spiritually amiss in his life and the world around him, and he desperately sought an alternative.

Pastorius found inspiration first from the Lutheran minister Johann Heinrich Horb. Becoming pastor in Pastorius's hometown of Windsheim in 1679, Horb espoused the reformist religious ideals of his famous brother-in-law, Philipp Jakob Spener, defending him and his Pietist manifesto, *Pia Desideria* (1675)[2] and introducing Pastorius to Spener and his circle of Pietist followers in Frankfurt am Main. Increasingly, however, the Pietists in Frankfurt began to move away from Spener's moderate reformist ideas and toward a more radical, separatist Pietism, part of a movement sweeping through the Protestant territories of the Holy Roman Empire in the late seventeenth century.[3] Pietism arose from a dissatisfaction with the condition of the Protestant confessions, both Lutheran and Reformed, after the Thirty Years' War. For many reform-minded clergy and laypeople, Protestant churches seemed indistinguishable from their Catholic counterparts: both employed unregenerate preachers, both valued the letter of religious doctrine over the radical call of Scripture for a renewed Christianity, and both repressed congregants bent on renewal.

Pietism began not as a unified movement but as a simultaneous awakening among individual ministers and theologians, laypeople, and mystical visionaries who shared a desire for a greater inwardness of religious experience and for a practical, lived piety. An inward change of faith, they believed, should translate into a turn away from a worldly lifestyle, from pursuit of personal pleasure and financial gain, from jockeying for high office, and from proud disputes over church doctrines. Pietists promoted a religion of the heart through a personal and emotional relationship to Christ and thus also to the divine spirit. Moderate Pietists worked within established church structures to reform worship, faith, and piety.[4] Other groups, called "radical" by later critics and scholars, saw the orthodox Protestant churches as fallen and unregenerate, as "Babel" or "Babylon"—a scornful epithet Protestants once reserved for the Catholic Church. Among the so-called radical Pietists, some groups and individuals, including the Saalhof Pietists' eventual leader, Johann Jakob Schütz, and the mystic Johann Jakob Zimmermann, believed in the imminent arrival of the Millennium, portended by wars and celestial signs such as the Great Comet of 1680 and Halley's comet in 1682. When Pastorius referred to the potential destruction of Europe as a reason for his departure for America, he was echoing millennialist sentiments widely voiced in radical Pietist circles.

Pietist groups also differed in their views about church ordinances and the nature of Jesus Christ. Most Pietists distanced themselves from the mainstream Quakers' rejection of baptism and communion, as well as from their spiritualized notion of Christ and their apparent disregard for his physical suffering and the doctrine of atonement. Like the Quakers, however, Pietists criticized "orthodox" Protestants for attending church services and receiving the sacraments without an inward spiritual change and an outward change in behavior. Thus both movements advocated for the reflection of inner, spiritual conviction of faith in practical piety and for concrete acts of love toward fellow human beings. Pastorius's religious choices demonstrate the fluidity between related Protestant dissident movements like Quakerism and Pietism, on the one hand, and the distinctiveness of specific practices and ideas in each tradition, on the other.[5]

Both Pietists and Quakers probed how individuals and groups who were committed to a renovation of their faith should behave toward the society and the dominant church where they lived. Christians had the obligation to carry their cross in the face of persecution and to use their talents to serve their fellow human beings in the here and now. The question of emigration from Europe increasingly gained in importance as individuals and groups who shared common concerns for a fundamental renewal of Christianity pondered where and how their goal could be achieved. In the late seventeenth century, the emerging concept of Philadelphianism linked various Protestant groups in England and Germany in their common pursuit of Christian renewal and their common exodus from the societies and confessional churches they considered the Babel of the current age. Philadelphian notions—especially a common belief in universal spiritual renewal, the unity of Christian churches and believers, and the brotherhood of all human beings—gave Quakers and radical Pietists a common purpose. To cement this shared idealism and create a religious network, William Penn and several other prominent Quakers traveled to Germany and Holland twice during the 1670s, visiting the Frankfurt Pietists who were meeting at the Saalhof in 1677. When Penn received the Charter of the Province of Pennsylvania in 1681, he immediately promoted immigration to the colony as a spiritual enterprise and spread word of his plans to like-minded groups in Europe, like the Frankfurt Pietists.[6]

Pastorius quickly seized upon the promise of religious fellowship and the idea of building a Christian utopia in Pennsylvania. His decision to emigrate from Europe with the Pietists was thus spurred by his desire to live in a community based on principles of spiritual renewal, universal love, lived and practical piety, and an inward sense of redemption. For Pastorius, an inward experience of salvation was inextricably linked to the bonds of affection among fellow believers he had found among the Saalhof Pietists. This helps explain both his impetuous decision to immigrate to America as the Pietists' representative and his relatively quick involvement in the Society of Friends upon his arrival in Pennsylvania. In his earliest letters from Pennsylvania to the Frankfurt Pietists, Pastorius represented William Penn and the Quaker founders of Pennsylvania as an extension of the Christian fellowship and affection he had already experienced and was hoping to experience once again—without the moral distractions of Europe—in America. The Pietists needed to fulfill their promise of immigrating to Pennsylvania if they wanted to reach their true spiritual potential. When they chose not to follow Pastorius, he felt a sense of betrayal.

Although Pastorius continued as the legal representative and administrator for the Pietists (who would reorganize the German Society as the "Frankfurt Land Company" in 1686), his emigration from Europe led to a loss of spiritual and personal community. As a result, Pastorius began a lifelong project of assessing the spiritual potential and compatibility of groups and individuals he met, including those speaking a different language and those of a different religion, gender, or race. Soon after his arrival in Philadelphia in 1683, Pastorius encountered members of North America's First Peoples—the Delaware or Lenape of the mid-Atlantic region. Pastorius had little chance to interact with Native Americans since Penn quickly entered into treaties with the Lenape that resulted in the takeover of Native lands by the new Protestant settlers. Nevertheless, Pastorius was curious about the language, the customs, and especially the religious sensibilities of the Lenape. For him, the conduct of the Native Americans put to shame those Christians who were Christian in name only and whose conduct he had condemned in Europe. Indeed, Pastorius attributed negative behavior such as lying, stealing, or drinking among indigenous people to the influence of just such Christian settlers. Although his portrayal of the Lenape reflected Pastorius's own spiritual convictions more than actual Native beliefs and customs, his representations still revealed his heartfelt desire to find common religious ground with the people who were so deeply connected to America and who confirmed to Pastorius the Quaker and radical Pietist belief in a universal and indwelling divine spirit. Their apparent benevolence toward the newly arrived settlers validated the spiritual investment he and others made in the land.

On his trip down the Rhine in 1683, Pastorius had visited the Krefeld Quakers and agreed to transact their land purchases in Pennsylvania. After his arrival in America, he lived for a brief period in Philadelphia before settling in the new Germantown community, where he would deal closely with the Krefeld settlers and with other German- and Dutch-speaking immigrants who held both Quaker and Mennonite beliefs. He soon joined the Quaker Meetings at Germantown and Philadelphia, though he never publicly described his decision to do so as a conversion. When the mystical Pietists gathered around Johannes Kelpius in Pennsylvania in 1694 to await the arrival of Christ, Pastorius kept his distance, put off perhaps by their esoteric speculations and radical beliefs in celibacy and ascetic living. But, more important, he had moved on from his earlier affiliation with the Pietists in Frankfurt, and he had found a spiritual home and lasting friendships among the Quakers, whom he now defended against detractors both in Europe and in Pennsylvania.

The schism that occurred among Pennsylvania Quakers during the 1690s—caused by what came to be known as the "Keithian controversy"[7]—posed a serious threat to the peace and religious community Pastorius had so ardently pursued in America. Valuing a personalized faith over a set of doctrines, mainstream Quakers regarded any religious testimony as a reflection of an individual's experience of the indwelling spirit of God. But George Keith, one of the leading figures of late seventeenth-century Quakerism in Scotland and England, rose to publicly challenge that view soon after arriving in Pennsylvania. He was appalled by his fellow Quakers' supposed ignorance of Scripture and the basic tenets of Christianity. Although the Quaker elite objected to Keith's vociferous attacks, they at first refused to comment on the doctrinal issues he raised. Eventually, however, they would rebut his arguments, claiming that Keith denied the sufficiency of the "Inner Light" for Christian salvation. Keith and his followers responded by calling themselves "Christian Quakers" and establishing a separate meeting in 1692. The mainstream Quakers rejected the new meeting and disowned Keith, yet the controversy persisted. Spreading into print and dragging on for years, with opponents on one side accusing those on the other of libel, it deeply scarred Pennsylvania's Society of Friends.

Pastorius tried to remain neutral but was aghast at the deeply unsettling effect that Keith and his followers were having on the Quaker spirit of harmony and affection. So when recent Pietist immigrants sided with Keith and disrupted a Quaker Meeting at Burlington, he broke his silence and issued a strongly worded pamphlet against Heinrich Bernhard Köster and his three followers.[8] Although, after this outburst, Pastorius would withdraw from public involvement in the controversy, much of his poetry and correspondence demonstrates how profoundly it undermined his conviction that Pennsylvania would provide a utopian escape from the intolerant partisanship of Europe. Steadfastly defending his longtime Quaker friends, Pastorius relied on literary exchanges with other Friends to regain a sense of spiritual and social balance.

His religious convictions never rested on a deep investment in the theological doctrines of a specific group. Rather, he stood on a middle ground between the spiritualist Quakers and the orthodox Lutheran Pietists. In mediating between different theologies, he countered the confessional exclusivity that had led to the religious wars of the past. Although he continued to emphasize the authority of the Bible, at the same time, he followed the guidance of the Inner Light. Pastorius considered his work as a public figure in Germantown, his activism against slavery, and his efforts as an educator to be practical testimonies of his faith. A civic leader who strove to create spiritual harmony among the people of his community, he was also a lay theologian who probed the connections between the word of God, the workings of the Holy Spirit in individuals, and the presence of God in the daily lives of people in all communities.

Pastorius as Lawyer and Lawgiver

His early training as a lawyer would significantly shape Pastorius's life—as would his deep-seated opposition to lawsuits and lawyers.[9] Begun in Windsheim in April 1676, his formal practice of law lasted only two and a half years and left him dissatisfied. Reflecting on that experience later in life, Pastorius recalled that he spent his time "marching from one Nobleman's house in the Province [Franconia] unto the other . . . and in short making nothing but work for Repentance."[10] In 1679, Pastorius moved to Frankfurt, where he "still played the Lawyer," while making plans with the Pietists to immigrate to Pennsylvania. As with many other utopian ventures, there were plenty of practical details to attend to. Believing they needed a firm foundation in law, especially in landholding, the Pietists designated Pastorius as their agent in Pennsylvania. In April 1683, fortified with the Frankfurt Land Company's Articles of Incorporation and a power of attorney to act on its behalf, Pastorius departed for Pennsylvania, where he took on an important role in the development of the German community. As company agent, he was responsible for a 15,000-acre tract of land, which he purchased for the company in London, and for the distribution of the company's land to its members. Written some years after its Articles of Incorporation, the company's charter guided its economic development. Members were given the right to vote and to receive profits based on the number of shares they owned. The charter contemplated the purchase of a brick kiln, commodities, and cattle, to be owned jointly by the members; it also provided for the transportation of people (servants and tenants) and of products such as tools and food. Perhaps most important, it established the distribution of company land through sale and rental.

Pastorius negotiated with William Penn, the proprietor of the Pennsylvania colony, to obtain a charter for Germantown, which, being modeled on English borough charters, allowed the Germantown residents to set up their own court and to free themselves from at least some taxes. Named as bailiff, Pastorius presided over the court. The Germantown charter was an important accomplishment for Pastorius and the Frankfurt Land Company, one he proudly mentioned in his letters home encouraging immigration to Pennsylvania. William Penn recognized Pastorius's substantial talent and his importance in the German community by appointing him a justice of the Philadelphia County Court in 1686 and later also clerk of that court. Records for Pastorius's tenure on the County Court have not survived, but his copy of the colony's laws has. It reveals Pastorius's concern with fairness: he wrote the Golden Rule and "Salus Populi Supreme Lex est" (The Good of the People Is the Supreme Law) on the cover page. He was elected to the Pennsylvania General Assembly in 1687. Governor Benjamin Fletcher again appointed him County Court justice in 1693; meanwhile, Pastorius served as a *Vorsteher* (elder) of Germantown. The six elders distributed land in Germantown and established procedures for resolving disputes through "peacemakers." Although Pastorius in some ways rejected the practice of law, he continued to draw upon his legal training and experience, seeking to use the workings of the law to rebuild society. Pastorius and his associates wanted to create a godly community that would break free of the materialism and violence they had seen in Europe, but they needed to have a solid foundation in law as they remade their world.

Pastorius's legal treatise in manuscript, "The Young Country Clerk's Collection," and other writings such as the "Bee-Hive" give a picture of his legal ideas. Pastorius wanted a world of simple and humane dealings between neighbors, a world of simple justice that was summed up in the Golden Rule. In a 1692 letter to his father in Europe,

Pastorius wrote that he had identified what he called "Leges Concepirte" (Legal Ideas) drawn from the Old Testament to guide the Germantown Court in deciding cases. He included a set of aphorisms stressing the need to treat people fairly and to follow religious and moral norms. Besides the Old Testament, he often quoted George Fox's writings about the mistreatment of Quakers by English judges. The law should, he argued, ensure equal treatment without discrimination based on religious beliefs and should provide simple rules the average person could understand. Judges should act to protect rather than persecute members of the community. Pastorius's "Young Country Clerk's Collection" was, in effect, a guidebook to help ordinary landowners make contracts, transfer real estate, and prepare wills. Significantly, it did not have any forms for civil lawsuits, to which Pastorius was opposed, in keeping with the Quaker principle of "love and unity," which forbade such legal actions.[11] In place of forms for civil lawsuits, his guidebook had a form for arbitration of disputes. Pastorius's legal training and experience made him an ideal person to guide the Frankfurt Land Company and shape the legal culture of early Pennsylvania. His hope was to have a simple and accessible legal system guided by principles of Quakerism and Pietism. In his legal practice and thought, Pastorius attempted to remake the world in the image of a godly community.

Pastorius as Learner and Educator

Pastorius spent much of his life educating himself and others. After attending the Windsheim Latin School, he began his university studies in 1668 in Altdorf (close to Nuremberg) but also attended classes in Jena, Strasbourg, Basel, and Regensburg, in a typical peregrination for seventeenth-century university students. Earning his doctorate of law in 1676, he proceeded to practice law, first in Windsheim and then in Frankfurt am Main. During and after his formal education, Pastorius eagerly pursued his self-education, including several modern languages such as French and Italian. Interested in religious as well as classical works, he read voraciously, borrowing books whenever the opportunity arose. Eventually, Pastorius's elite training and his assiduous personal studies made him one of the best-educated individuals in early British North America. Yet he lived at a time of tremendous educational, intellectual, religious, and philosophical changes, changes that pulled him in many different directions of thought. He was conflicted about the worldliness and vanity of his own education, which compelled him to evaluate the dominant regimes of humanist education as it was practiced in seventeenth-century Europe. Pastorius wanted to follow the inward and emotional dedication to faith sought by Pietists and Quakers alike in the arena of education, faith that had been infused by the deeply utopian ideals of educational and linguistic reformer Jan Amos Comenius. Especially toward the end of his life, Pastorius also witnessed the beginnings of a movement we call, in hindsight, the "Enlightenment." As a learner, an educator, and a collector of knowledge, he found himself at the crossroads of older and newer ways of learning, teaching, and knowing.[12] In his work, mysticism and empiricism, humanism and rationalism, classicism and Christian utopianism would intersect in complex ways.

Pastorius's learning, teaching, and writing remained indebted to Renaissance humanism—both in its earlier, idealistic quest for rejuvenation and in its eventual calcification in the seventeenth century. The Renaissance broadened received Christian perspectives with the wide recovery of works by ancient Greek and Roman thinkers. Christian humanists like Erasmus of Rotterdam merged Christian ideals with pagan virtues such as courage, wisdom, and justice. Frequently reading and citing Erasmus, Pastorius championed the notion that education served a social function and that an ideal society had to be shaped by individuals steeped not only in Christian but also in classical virtues. In combining the two, Renaissance humanist education would gain renewed relevance for Pastorius in Pennsylvania.

Yet, for several reasons, the humanism of the Renaissance became stale, restricting, or corrupted. For one, the rediscovery of the classics turned memorization of classical precepts and quotations into the primary occupation of the schools, giving rise to printed commonplace books into which students could transfer (and then memorize) excerpts following preestablished categories of knowledge. When the humanist curriculum with its emphasis on classical languages, grammar, and rhetoric was transferred from elite tutor-student relationships to institutional settings, such as schools for the middle classes and sons of government officials, like Pastorius, the approach to knowledge and teaching became more pedantic, mechanical, and rule oriented. More shocking for the young idealistic Pastorius embarking on his university curriculum and grand tour across Europe, education had become dominated by the obsession of aristocrats and their lower-class emulators with etiquette and social skills like dancing and fencing. Latin was cultivated not as a lingua franca enabling communication among intellectuals and theologians from a wide range of different language communities but as a mere token of elite status and exclusivity among academics and government officials. Pastorius despaired of the ability of education to instill morality and piety. In hindsight, even the Reformation with its goal of stripping the Catholic Church of its elaborate rituals while directing congregants to the precepts of the faith and the truths of Scripture had accomplished too little for Pietists and other reformist critics. By the mid- to late seventeenth century, the principal legacy of the Reformation had become the teaching of doctrinal precepts in an attempt to clearly set believers of specific denominations apart from one another. Actual Bible reading was often replaced by memorization of the catechism, with its collection of articles of faith digested into formulas.

Hoping to revive the earlier spirit of Christian Renaissance humanism and to reform Protestant Christianity, Pastorius and other Pietists looked both backward to an esoteric-mystical past and forward to a more scientific future. Like most Pietists, Pastorius admired the writings of the Church Father Augustine, the late medieval German mystic Johannes Tauler, and the seventeenth-century German Lutheran pastor and reformer Johann Arndt, author of the perennial classic of Protestant spirituality *Wahres Christentum* (1612; *True Christianity*). Pastorius also embraced the ideas of Czech linguist and educational reformer Jan Amos Comenius, whose writings were well represented in Pastorius's library.[13] In his most popular textbooks, such as the *Janua Linguarum Reserata* (1631; The Door of Languages Unlocked) and the *Orbis Sensualium Pictus* (1659; The Visible World in Pictures), Comenius attempted to link languages to their presumed divine origin and thereby restore a harmony both between words and things and among individuals, peoples, and faiths. Comenius also advocated for a network of schools and universities governed by a Christian universalism devoid of denominational infighting. Pastorius's ideas on founding a new society in America, multilingual poetry, and his attempts at creating an open and free school system reflected Comenius's influence among educational reformers in both Europe and America.[14]

Yet Pastorius was also intrigued by ideas of the emerging "New Science," as put forth in the philosophical works of Francis Bacon and John Locke.[15] In his *Plan for the Advancement of Learning* (1605) and his *Novum Organum* (1620), Bacon championed inductive reasoning and the primacy of experience in creating knowledge, thus beginning a school of thought known as "empiricism";[16] he also called for knowledge that produced useful results for individuals and humankind. As Pastorius saw it, these ideas squared nicely with the focus of religious reformers like Pietists and Quakers, who advocated for a renewed faith that emphasized religious experience over doctrinal knowledge. Quakers like George Fox and William Penn preferred experiential learning and practical training to book knowledge and recitation. Arriving in Pennsylvania, Pastorius found the Quakers' rejection of both the heightened intellectualism of universities and the doctrinal wrangling of theologians much to his liking.[17]

Pastorius considered his emigration from Europe not only a flight from its religious and moral degeneration but also a specific rejection of the Aristotelian program prevailing at European universities,[18] and the fencing, riding, dancing, and excessive drinking adopted by most university students as extracurricular activities to the detriment of their actual studies. Instead, he pledged to apply his broad learning to the religious, cultural, and civic improvement of the new German settlement and to the even larger spiritual renewal of human society. Besides his role as the civic leader of Germantown, Pastorius stands out as one of the first teachers in the Pennsylvania colony. His educational work comprises three general areas: teaching at the Philadelphia and

Germantown schools; the writing and compiling of schoolbooks; and the collection of contemporary knowledge in extensive manuscript volumes.[19]

Despite their overall distrust of advanced education, the Quakers' emphasis on equality, practical training, and the individual's ability to read Scripture compelled them to place education at the forefront of their program of building a social structure and civic order in the new colony. Pennsylvania's 1683 Frame of Government stipulated that "all persons . . . having children . . . shall cause such to be instructed in Reading and writing . . . And that they be taught some useful trade or skill," charging the governor and Provincial Council to "erect and order all publick schools."[20] The council hired Enoch Flower as teacher for a primary school in 1683 and employed George Keith in 1689 to lead secondary education in the new colony, which he would do until his dismissal in 1691 during his quarrel with the Quaker establishment. When the Friends' Public School was established in Philadelphia in 1698, Thomas Makin and Francis Daniel Pastorius became its teachers.

Pastorius's education made him an obvious candidate for one of the two teaching positions at the Friends' School. Along with Makin, Pastorius taught Quaker and non-Quaker children, both boys and girls, using a curriculum that included reading and writing in English, arithmetic, and Latin. Pastorius's sons—also students at the Philadelphia school—reported in a letter to their grandfather in Germany that they went to school eight hours on weekdays and four on Saturdays.[21] A manuscript collection dedicated to the birth of Penn's son John and signed by several students, "Genetliacum or an hearty Congratulation" gives us a glimpse into Pastorius's teaching methods. The collection contains, as the title to its enlarged version tells us, "A few Onomastical Considerations," brief moral and religious reflections associated with a specific name, in this case, "John."[22] Although such exercises may have been tedious even by seventeenth-century standards, they reveal the intertwining of language learning with spiritual edification typical of both Pietist and Quaker education. Pastorius taught at the Philadelphia school from 1698 until 1700; in 1702, he began teaching at a newly established school in Germantown, where he remained as teacher until at least 1716, but possibly until his death in 1719. According to the "Raths-Buch" (general court records) of Germantown, "on 30 December 1701 it was agreed upon that here in Germantown a school should be established."[23] The Germantown Court school operated by subscription, followed no particular denomination, and apparently admitted both male and female students; an evening school was most likely established to allow working adults to continue their education.[24] Pastorius also fostered the education of the Philadelphia and Germantown communities by writing and compiling several schoolbooks. Only one appeared in print, *A New Primmer or Methodical Directions to attain the True Spelling, Reading & Writing of ENGLISH* (New York: William Bradford, [1698]), which is reprinted for the first time in this reader.[25]

Despite the Quakers' distrust of higher education and focus on basic literacy, Pastorius found that many of the most prominent members of Quaker society in Pennsylvania—such as William Penn, Thomas Lloyd, James Logan, and other prominent Quakers—were university educated and spoke the two languages of the educated European elites—French and Latin. Pastorius proudly commented that he and William Penn spoke French as a lingua franca upon his first arrival; even when Penn returned to Pennsylvania in 1699, Pastorius would write him a welcome poem in French. How, then, did Pastorius and other prominent and highly educated Pennsylvania Quakers reconcile the apparent tension between their faith's distrust of both advanced learning and the proliferation of books with their own appetite for reading and extensive personal libraries?[26]

Pastorius's educational efforts *outside* the institutionalized Quaker school setting reveal creative ways in which he and other Quakers embedded a world of putatively impious writings within personal interactions among fellow Friends. He circulated his books and many excerpts among other members of the Quaker community and commented on their use in many annotations and letters. Pastorius thus rendered extensive book knowledge acceptable by emphasizing the key role trusted readers played in interpreting texts and determining their meaning. At the same time, he also cautioned other Quakers against abandoning book learning and relying exclusively on an inner faith susceptible to delusion and corruption. Pastorius's "Bee-Hive" manuscript in particular argued that critical and informed reading practices could help readers distinguish "honey" from "venom." A closer look at Pastorius's intertwined roles as reader, writer, and collector of knowledge reveals more about the reconciliation between higher learning and Quaker spirituality he attempted to achieve in early America.

Pastorius as Thinker, Reader, and Collector of Knowledge

Although Pastorius's collections of knowledge in commonplace books and encyclopedic manuscripts such as the "Bee-Hive" arose in part from his role as educator at the Philadelphia and Germantown schools, their extent, depth, and erudition went far beyond the pedagogical and practical needs of early Pennsylvania. Filling thousands of pages with excerpts from and reflections on classical, Renaissance, humanist, Quaker and non-Quaker religious, secular, and even scientific books, Pastorius seemed to hold on to the erudite traditions of his elite European past in denial of his new life in what he once called an "uncouth land, & howling Wilderness."[27] Clearly, Pastorius's manuscript writings had one foot planted in Europe and the other in the concrete realities of early America. Yet such a split between old and new, learned and practical, makes Pastorius appear like an individual ever torn between two worlds, two ways of thinking, between his daily practical chores and his nighttime intellectual pleasures of reading, collecting, and writing. Where, then, did Pastorius stand in the history of ideas and in the momentous changes in thought occurring on the cusp of the eighteenth century?[28]

In many ways, Pastorius seems steeped in an earlier world of seeking knowledge through a mysterious discovery of a divine scripture, following the esoteric notions of Paracelsus, the alchemists of the Renaissance, and especially the Rosicrucians with their claims to have found or created a single book containing all knowledge. The Rosicrucian manifesto *Confessio Fraternitatis* (Kassel, 1615) teased its readers with such a possibility: "Wouldn't it be a precious thing if you could find, read, understand, and remember in one book everything contained in all the books that have ever been or will be written and published?"[29] Similarly, on one of its several title pages reflecting different stages of the project, Pastorius called his "Bee-Hive" "an Encyclopady of all that can be known." Yet understanding the different methods of gaining knowledge used by the Rosicrucians and by Pastorius helps us place his work in the transition from Renaissance esotericism to Enlightenment empiricism: whereas the Rosicrucians claimed a mysterious hidden knowledge disclosed in a moment of mystical revelation, Pastorius gained the knowledge contained in the "Bee-Hive" through a lifetime of reading, collecting, and storing.

Similarly, we might imagine Pastorius as one of the last remnants of a theo-mystical tradition dying with some of its paragons like Athanasius Kircher (who died in 1680, just before the Pennsylvanian "experiment" would take shape).[30] Even though Pastorius and Kircher have both been characterized as polymaths, to directly compare the two would be misleading. Pastorius collected existing knowledge and evaluated its applicability to life in a Christian utopia fundamentally guided by the principle of brotherly love, whereas Kircher claimed to produce new knowledge drawing on a variety of ancient sources, such as his alleged deciphering of Egyptian hieroglyphs. Rising philosophers and scientists of the Enlightenment, especially René Descartes, rejected Kircher. Did Pastorius belong more to the skeptical intellectual, philosophical, and scientific school of empiricists founded by Descartes? Although Pastorius apparently did not read the essays of Descartes, he did read and admire the works of another proponent of the intellectual revolution in the late seventeenth and early eighteenth centuries—the English philosopher John Locke (1632–1704).[31] Moreover, Pastorius's project of knowledge collection anticipates the work of Denis Diderot (1713–1784) and his fellow editors of the *Encyclopédie* (*Encyclopedia, or a Descriptive Dictionary of the Sciences, Arts and Trades*), published between 1751 and 1772, in their effort to "collect the knowledge dispersed on the surface of the earth, and to unfold its general system."[32] Whereas the encyclopedists explicitly attacked any kind of supernatural knowledge and dismissed religion as largely superstition, Pastorius fundamentally trusted that all knowledge came from and had to lead to a greater understanding of God and divine truth.

Beyond the general question of Pastorius's place in the history of ideas in European culture of the seventeenth and early eighteenth centuries, more specific questions arise about the significance and meaning of his intellectual work in early America. How could Pastorius reject the sterile wrangling and vain arguments of the academic elites in Europe, yet collect a range of opinions by authors and authorities from among those same elites in the encyclopedic section of his "Bee-Hive"? Why did he write in Latin and Greek, the classical languages of scholars, alongside his writings in English, German, and Dutch, the everyday languages spoken in Germantown and Philadelphia? Why did Pastorius declare that his "Bee-Hive" was meant for the stimulation and edification of his sons, even as he encouraged those sons to learn practical trades such as weaving and shoemaking? Did his private and domestic concerns and his personal and intellectual interests connect to his public and political roles in the colonial community? What did it mean for Pastorius to read and write among Quakers who distrusted book learning rather than labor among the European scholars and academics who had trained him? Finally, how did his voracious reading and collecting of knowledge serve his spiritual quest for religious renewal and community? Or were these only vanities, transplanted to America, which Pastorius could not resist?

THE TRANSFER OF KNOWLEDGE FROM THE OLD WORLD TO THE NEW

On one of the several "Bee-Hive" title pages (reflecting different stages of the manuscript's production), Pastorius alerts readers to the transfer of knowledge as a material process. He specifically mentions two commonplace collections that preceded the "Bee-Hive." The first, which Pastorius had brought over from Germany, is titled simply "F.D.P. Francis Daniel Pastorius"; like traditional commonplace books still in use in his day but with origins in the fifteenth century, it has predetermined divisions into which Pastorius has written alphabetically ordered terms; many boxes, however, have never been filled and many of the 400-odd pages—consisting of high-quality paper—have been left blank.[33] The second commonplace book, begun in Pennsylvania, is titled "Alvearialia, Or such Phrases and Sentences which in haste were Booked down here, before I had Time to Carry them to their respective proper Places in my English-Folio-Bee-hive."[34] Consigned to lower-quality paper, "Alvearialia" has sheets of different sizes stitched together. Pastorius referred to this manuscript volume as his "Waste-Book"; he used it to jot down passages from books he borrowed. As he transferred passages or information into specific places in the "Bee-Hive," he would cross them out in "Alvearialia."

The differences between the two commonplace books highlight the material and intellectual change in Pastorius's transfer of knowledge: in Europe, Pastorius had the luxury of using fine paper and outlining preconceived terms; learning and knowledge were given a structure, based on a commonplace tradition handed down by Renaissance scholars such as Erasmus, which avid young students were to fill in based on their reading. "Alvearialia" reflects the scarcity of both books and paper in Pennsylvania; it also demonstrates that the knowledge collected was not static but changed with the judgment of the collector. The "Bee-Hive" embodies the same transition. Pastorius used European paper given to him by Dutch merchant Jacob Telner to begin the "Bee-Hive" but continued it on the "courser, homely or home-spun Stuff" produced by William Rittenhouse, founder of the first paper mill in Pennsylvania. The discontinued commonplace book reflects the material and intellectual shifts in Pastorius's collecting activity: the prelined boxes of the "F.D.P" were inadequate for his American context.

Yet his rejection of European academic culture did not lead Pastorius to abandon advanced classical and humanist learning but, rather, to advocate a transformation of both learning and the way knowledge was produced that would make traditional European ideas applicable and useful in colonial America. Despite his radical shift in positioning and perspective, Pastorius signaled that he would continue to participate in two related forms of information production and transfer in early modern Europe and the Atlantic world: the Republic of Letters and the movement of arts and sciences from Europe to America in the wake of empire—known as the "translatio imperii et studii." The Republic of Letters, according to Ian McNeely and Lisa Wolverton, was an "international community of learning stitched together initially by handwritten letters in the mail and later by printed books and journals."[35] Calling attention to his own stitching together of European and American paper, Pastorius cleverly highlighted his blending of traditions, and he asserted his place in the fabric of the transatlantic Republic of Letters. Trading in the refined paper of his earlier commonplace books for the coarser paper of his later ones allowed Pastorius to disavow European elitism even as he promoted the notion that learning would flourish in America.[36]

Renaissance scholars' concern with the preservation and storage of information had been triggered by the loss of ancient knowledge during the Middle Ages. And the proliferation and dissemination of knowledge through print during the Renaissance necessitated efficient information storage systems; scholars grappled with the problem how they might have access to information even when the vehicle of knowledge—books—was not always at their disposal. Emigration posed a similar problem, with individuals leaving behind access to a vast number of books. Pastorius thus acknowledged the role of the "Bee-Hive" as an information storage and retrieval system: "For as much as our Memory is not Capable to retain all remarkable words, Phrases, Sentences or Matters of moment, which we do hear and read, It becomes every good Scholar to have a <u>Common-Place-Book</u>, & therein to Treasure up whatever deserves his Notice, &c."[37] His effort to maintain large bibliographies reflects his belief that the principal functions of the commonplace book were not only to store knowledge but also to link its excerpts and precepts to the larger, ever-growing number of books.

Of course, the reproduction and dissemination of European knowledge, moral precepts, and civility among immigrant populations in the American colonies were meant to stem what New England Puritans dubbed "Criolian Degeneracy"—the degeneration of European civilization under the influence of the harsh American climate and the supposedly savage peoples surrounding insular European settlements.[38] But Pastorius resisted the mindless reproduction of European patterns of learning, patterns Anthony Grafton explains in some detail: "The young men in the Renaissance, in the main, read their classics at first in a single way: not to search for ancient wisdom as it really was, naked and challenging, but to admire antique *sapientia* as set out in a sort of printed museum—divided into rooms, framed and labeled in ways that predetermined the meaning of the relics displayed."[39] Instead of fostering students' critical acumen, Grafton tells us, the categories and commentaries that served as precepts for the activity of reading and excerpting the classics "imprisoned and shaped the text as powerfully as the old ones [medieval models of reading] had."[40] Pastorius rejected the copying of pithy quotations or wise sayings into preestablished categories.

Instead, he urged his readers to develop their own standards for evaluating knowledge, deciding what to store and how to arrange it. On the title page of his "Alvearialia" commonplace book (page 2), Pastorius shifted the locus of intellectual decision making from patrons and intellectual authorities to the reader: "If any would have me Dedicate it [the book] to some Body, I herewith complementally consecrate the same To Himself, of what Quality Soever, provided nevertheless he be One of the Excellent-Spirited in this New English World." Far from rejecting the knowledge of the ancients or the teachers of his own age, Pastorius submits it to the critical ordering skills of those who will receive and make use of such knowledge. In Pennsylvania, he hoped, education and intellectual acumen would be a matter not of privilege but rather of the "Quality" of a learner's mind. He imagined readers and writers as "Excellent-Spirited" individuals who would evaluate and collect knowledge according to their own ethical, religious, social, and intellectual principles in this "New English World."

Two of Pastorius's most practical and, judging from their tattered appearance, most used manuscript collections demonstrate his expansive project of transferring European knowledge to an American context: "The Monthly Monitor," a collection of horticultural and agricultural advice, and "Talia Qualia Medicinalia, Artificialia & Naturalia," his handbook of medicine, herbal remedies, and physiological principles.[41] As the last words of its title clearly signal, this second collection brings together both chemiatric medicine (healing through the use of chemicals) in the tradition of the Renaissance Swiss physician Paracelsus and scholastic medicine in the tradition of the ancient Greek physician Galen and based on the "classical and medieval transmission of a [...] botanical reservoir of simples and *composita*."[42] Pastorius's manuscript handbook neither endorses nor rejects either approach but subordinates both to a Christian faith that places healing in the hands of God alone. Medicine and religion, healing and faith, were both parts of the same endeavor.[43]

For Pastorius, the secret of good health lay in a healthy diet and the availability of medicinal plants in one's own garden—the focus of "The Monthly Monitor." Beginning in 1701, he recorded monthly instructions for work to be done around the garden, field, house, and kitchen, along with observations on astrology, weather, and precepts for a healthy eating. He also included various sections on horticulture, aspects of land management such as fertilizing, beekeeping, and viticulture. In all of this, the connections between health, nutrition, and environment are omnipresent. Focusing on information crucial for well-being, "Talia Qualia Medicinalia" and "The Monthly Monitor" show that, in Pastorius's world of knowledge transmission, collection, and adaptation, no simple dichotomies between Old and New World, Old and New Science, and Enlightenment and early modern ways of knowing existed. Pastorius established a system of knowledge gathering and interpretation that provided internal cohesion between faith and science, book learning and empiricism, ancient and modern, tradition and innovation, local and global.

Pastorius also applied multilingualism to his new environment. Coupling language diversity with the use of a common language would, he hoped, build a society that accepted differences yet spoke in one coherent idiom. He valued Latin and French, the languages of the learned in Europe, as signs of an educated society;[44] in the letters he wrote to the children of some of Pennsylvania's most prominent citizens, such as Elizabeth Hill and Lloyd Zachary, Pastorius displayed his proficiency in both. But he wrote his printed works only in German and English, and his manuscript commonplace books, mostly in English, the dominant language of Pennsylvania.

Pastorius's use of English, German, and Dutch all in the same work and together with other European and ancient languages of the learned served practical and communal as well as spiritual and symbolic purposes that were specific to his experiences in and utopian vision for Pennsylvania. Pastorius considered himself to be a linguistic and cultural mediator between the English-, German-, and Dutch-speaking members of this Protestant community, and he considered his polyglot poetics and collecting of writings in many languages to be symbolic of the spiritual unity possible across many different language communities. Even though mainstream Quakers tended to regard excessive language learning as vanity, Pastorius insisted that his polyglot abilities could drive home an important point the Quakers often made: that the spirit mattered more than the words or any specific language aptitude.[45] Despite his polyglot vision of spiritual unity, however, Pastorius wrote the encyclopedic section of the "Bee-Hive"—the "Alphabetical Hive"—entirely in English, and, after mentioning a number of different languages, declared that his sons would "never attain to the Understanding of said Languages." For Pastorius, English was multilingual in itself, uniting influences and borrowings from many other languages.[46]

Somewhat naively, Pastorius tried to apply his belief in the spiritual unity of European peoples speaking many different languages and coming from many different cultures to the Native American people of early Pennsylvania, in particular, the Lenape. He idealized Lenape customs and culture and contrasted them to European vices. In describing Native religion, worship, and spirituality, Pastorius believed there to be a profound spiritual connection between the radical Protestant emphasis on an inward, intuitive faith and Native American spirituality, a connection that turned the Lenape people into a Christian community in waiting. Eventually, however, he would have to acknowledge that the rapid removal of the Lenape from lands they sold or ceded to William Penn and his agents had made realizing his Philadelphian aspirations impossible.[47] Pastorius's attempt to transfer Quaker concepts and ideals to the Lenape had failed almost certainly because of the actual differences between the European settlers and the Lenape and the true effects of European immigration on Native American peoples—something Pastorius did not or perhaps even could not recognize.

QUAKER SLAVERY AND THE PRINCIPLE OF DISCERNMENT

In his transfer and collection of knowledge, Pastorius's central practice was *discernment*—the selection and evaluation of knowledge and its application to the core principles of self and community. Pastorius took his motto for this process from 1 Thessalonians 5:21: "Test everything. Hold on to the good," which had already been the motto of Johann Arndt and then become one of the key ideals of radical Pietism.[48] Operating outside the realm of the orthodox Reformed and Lutheran churches, radical Pietists looked for inspiration and guidance in an eclectic array of sources. Because writers from across the religious spectrum had gathered divinely inspired ideas, their works deserved to be read and scrutinized.

Pastorius's two most important commonplace books, the "Alvearialia" and the "Bee-Hive," explicitly highlighted and explained the principle of discernment while concretely engaging in it. On the "Alvearialia" title page, Pastorius embedded a modified version of his motto from 1 Thessalonians 5:21—"Prove first and then Approve what's good"—in a larger instruction on the principle of discernment: "Assigning those, to whose hands they [the things he collected in the book] may come, that perhaps shall never have the Opportunity to behold mine abovesaid Alphabetical Hive, to minding always the h. Apostles wholsom[e] Admonition / 1 Thess. 5:20.[49] Omnia explorantes, Bonum tenete. / Read, Reader, read, Judiciously, / Shun Implicit Credulity: / Prove first and then <u>Approve what's Good</u>; / Judge not of things not understood."[50] Pastorius prized his readers' ability to think openly and make independent judgments based on evenhanded scrutiny and informed choice. But he also realized that not all opinions and judgments could be equally acceptable in all circumstances.

The best example for Pastorius's principle of discernment as the rigorous linking of critical thinking and reading skills to concrete, civic conduct was his treatment of Quakers engaging in slavery.[51] In 1688, Gerret Hendericks, Dirck op den Graeff, Francis Daniel Pastorius, and Abraham op den Graeff submitted the first public protest against the institution of slavery in North America to the Monthly, Quarterly, and Yearly Friends' Meetings.[52] In September of that year, however, the Yearly Meeting at Burlington shelved that protest: "A Paper being here presented by some German Friends Concerning the Lawfulness and Unlawfulness of Buying and keeping Negroes, It was adjudged not to be so proper for this Meeting to give a Positive Judgment in the Case, It having so General a Relation to many other Parts, and therefore at present they forbear It."[53]

Written as a collaboration by Pastorius and his co-signers, the "Quaker Protest Against Slavery" applied Pastorius's principles of discernment to a concrete moral, ethical, and social issue touching the community. Repeatedly, the "Protest" admonishes its readers to apply their own moral standards to the question at hand: "Oh! doe consider well this things [*sic*], you who doe it; if you would be done at this manner? and if it is done according to Christianity?" Essentially, Pastorius and his co-signers want their audience to act as critical interpreters of the situation and, consequently, "consider well this thing, if it is done good or bad?" In other words, the readers of the "Protest" should apply the skills of selecting good from bad writing that Pastorius demonstrated in his commonplace books to the social and moral question of slavery. Although Pastorius's fellow Quakers and Pennsylvanians refused to deal with the petition because no consensus on the issue of slavery could be reached, the "Protest" claims that the outside world has already formed a negative opinion of the colony's conduct: "Then [after slaves have been freed] is Pennsilvania to have a good report, instead it hath now a bad one for this sacke in other Countries." After criticizing the Quakers' poor discernment on this issue, Pastorius's "Bee-Hive" defined ideal readers and citizens as those who would select the "better sort of things, out of the best of Books, Who happily their Spears beat into Pruning hooks." Even though the "Quaker Protest Against Slavery in the New World" is now available online in digital facsimile through the Haverford College Quaker Collection, we include the text in chapter 8 of this reader for its historic value as one of the first antislavery petitions in North America and for its resonance with Pastorius's other practices of discernment in his systems of knowledge collection. Reading, culling, and collecting for Pastorius were crucial parts of critical decision making that applied to both intellectual and civic life.

A particularly good example of Pastorius's principle of discernment is his response to Cotton Mather's famous defense of Christians keeping slaves in Mather's 1706 book *The Negro Christianized*.[54] The "Bee-Hive" entry responding to Mather's book appears in the collection's poetic miscellany (entry 204, "Silvula Rhytmorum Germanopolitanorum"), where Pastorius has tried to capture in verse his ideas about books he has just read. For Mather, racial differences were a symptom of spiritual debasement and an obstacle to God's saving grace. He had argued for an embrace of African slaves as creatures in possession of a "rational soul" and thus capable and worthy of God's salvation—a mission field that fellow New Englanders would leave untilled at the jeopardy of their own souls. Since the supposed barbarism of black slaves was a result of their spiritually fallen state, Christianizing them would be a process of cultural and moral transformation. But, Mather insisted, Christian masters could help bring spiritual salvation to their slaves by converting them *without* having to free them as a result.

Pastorius's response to Mather exposes the ethical and theological fallacies at the core of a system of Christian slavery. Like Mather, Pastorius closely inspects the personal and spiritual interaction between master and slave but comes to very different conclusions. At the beginning of his "Bee-Hive" entry, he closely follows and more or less summarizes Mather's argument. Yet, even here, Pastorius already places more emphasis on spiritual equality by asserting sin as a universal condition, befalling members of "whatsoever Race." And then, in the next lines, Pastorius turns Mather's argument upside down: "Some Negroes are in heav'n glad, Their Masters sad in hell, / The which if they no Slaves had had, Might be for Ever well. / But having shewed No Mercy (to their poor Drudges here) shall have Judgment (hereafter) without Mercy, James 2:13."[55] Thus, rather than a divinely ordained instrument for the conversion of heathens, slavery is a sin that condemns slave owners to hell. Slavery itself, not missionary zeal, is Pastorius's primary target. He clearly believes that, rather than making slavery a more benevolent institution, "no Slaves" would be the far better path for Christians. Moreover, in the strongly worded "Bee-Hive" poem "Allermassen ungebührlich ist der Handel dieser Zeit" (Beyond all measure improper are practices of this age), Pastorius exposes economic self-interest as the true motivation behind the Christian justification of slavery and thus rejects altogether Mather's idea that Christianity and slavery are compatible.

Pastorius's opposition to slavery in the "Quaker Protest" and in the "Bee-Hive" demonstrates how he applied the principle of discernment. He took neither the Quakers' silent acceptance of slavery nor Mather's paternalistic advocacy of converting slaves without freeing them at face value. Rather, contrasting their positions with what he considered the core principle of the Gospels, the Golden Rule, and the core principles of Christian denominations such as the Quakers, he lambasted both Mather and Quakers for the gross inconsistencies between confession and conduct. Pastorius's collecting, selecting, and ordering knowledge in the "Bee-Hive" and his other manuscript books were thus not an isolated scholarly pleasure but rather an indispensable foundation for making informed judgments in everyday life.

CHANGING INFORMATION STORAGE SYSTEMS

Universal knowledge, though hopelessly utopian to us, seemed a lofty yet highly desirable goal to individuals in the seventeenth century; it promised a reformation of human society based on an enlightened readership and an end to human strife. Pastorius's commonplace collections, especially his "Bee-Hive," tapped into this aspiration, gathering all the knowledge humanly possible in a lifetime. On the title page of the "Bee-Hive's" external index, Pastorius wrote: "An <u>Encyclopedy</u> of all what can be known, / May very <u>well</u> be made by Common-placing down / The <u>Better</u> Sort of things out of the <u>Best</u> of Books." Although of the quest after universal knowledge may seem naive, encyclopedia projects begun in the eighteenth century (such as the French *Encyclopédie* under Denis Diderot or the *Encyclopædia Britannica*), as well as the internet today, constitute similar aspirations at comprehensive knowledge gathering. Even with the technological innovations at our disposal, we still face many of the same problems that Pastorius tackled in the "Bee-Hive" and other commonplace books: what information to collect, how to store it, how to order it, and how to *retrieve* it—in other words, how to grant people now and in the future access to that collected knowledge. Indeed, how best to mediate between collecting and retrieving knowledge was a chief concern for scholars like Pastorius.

The several information collection, storage, and retrieval methods and systems that Pastorius experimented with[56] are reflected in the structural organization of the "Bee-Hive": First, the title pages of its various sections are part of the information retrieval system. Each title page chronicles a different stage in the project, especially in the expanding or changing of how information is ordered and indexed; together, they articulate the philosophical and spiritual underpinnings, purposes, and practical, communal, and ethical applications of Pastorius's knowledge collecting. Second, Pastorius assembled vast bibliographies of the authors whose works he consulted for gathering the "Bee-Hive," with authors divided into "Quakers" and "no Quakers," each category having its own separate bibliography. Though Pastorius never dissolved this binary opposition, his author-focused system (and the group consciousness implied in it) would eventually give way to a keyword-focused one. Within these bibliographies, Pastorius distinguished books he actually excerpted (whose entries he marked with an asterisk) from those he merely consulted (no asterisk). Third, Pastorius collected short, pithy observations in his "Emblematical Recreations." Popular in the sixteenth and seventeenth centuries, emblem books combined images with an explanatory text that teased out some central wisdom or understanding, following the principle of moving from sight to insight. Fourth, Pastorius produced a large number of "onomastical devices"—witty or spiritual observations on the meaning of a person's name or on famous namesakes and their significance in history—and collected them in his "Bee-Hive." Fifth, Pastorius's "Silvula Rhytmorum Germanopolitanorum," the poetic miscellany embedded in the "Bee-Hive," is a collection not merely of poems but also of reflections on many topics. Pastorius used poetry to gather and develop his thoughts about a book and its ideas, a familiar person, or an event.

Sixth, Pastorius assembled an encyclopedic section, which he called the "Alphabetical Hive," and which formed the core and most prominent part of his collection of knowledge. Though based on his own and earlier humanist commonplace traditions, his "Alphabetical Hive" goes further. Written entirely in English, it demonstrates Pastorius's full adherence to the practicality of knowledge collection within his newly chosen home. Rather than copying verbatim or paraphrasing phrases from other authors, Pastorius strove to digest ideas on a specific subject, such as language or slavery, in one unified entry. Nevertheless, adjusting to his continued reading and the expansion of ideas and knowledge, Pastorius eventually abandoned his original alphabetical system for a numbered one. This strategy allowed him to expand the "Hive" endlessly; numbers added to the original alphabetical entries thus referred readers to the continuation of a subject.

Given the laborious efforts Pastorius made to have the "Bee-Hive" contain such an expansion of knowledge, why did he not simply adopt a system of loose leaves, which would have allowed him to flexibly add and move around new entries? Ultimately, Pastorius remained indebted and wedded to the format of the book and especially the manuscript book because it best met his fundamental concern for permanence and legacy. The "Bee-Hive" was handed down through generations, eventually reaching the University of Pennsylvania's Rare Book and Manuscript Library (where an online scan offers a different approach to accessibility but still does not replace the permanence of the physical book). Pastorius's collecting and indexing methods seemed to anticipate the internet's ascendancy toward universal knowledge storage. Yet what the "Bee-Hive" attempts—and the internet does not— is to make knowledge acquisition a more transparent process and to instill in readers the skills of critical reading and writing.

CIRCULATING KNOWLEDGE IN A COMMUNITY OF FRIENDS

Despite his diligent efforts in selecting and ordering information, traditional Quaker misgivings about higher education and the proliferation of books cast doubt on the expansive reading practiced by Pastorius and educated Quakers such as his close friend

James Logan. In response, Pastorius explored avenues for reconciling Quaker distrust of books (and the medium of print), his own voracious appetite for reading, and the increasing influx of new ideas to a New World on the cusp of the eighteenth century. Pastorius and his circle of Quaker friends included books in their reassuring system of personal communication and manuscript exchange. But the books these friends passed among themselves, instead of distracting them from inward reflection, only served to encourage them to add their own verdicts—assisted by meditation and the Inner Light—to the impersonal knowledge presented in print. Pennsylvania Quakers, with Pastorius as one of their most prominent practitioners, fashioned manuscript writing and exchange as an alternative form of literacy that was inextricably tied to their bonds of personal friendship as well as their intellectual and spiritual affinity. The exchange of manuscripts—such as Pastorius's "Bee-Hive" and poetic miscellanies, and his frequent inscriptions in books he borrowed or lent out—wed textuality to personal relationships and thus cultivated personal and communal bonding rather than distracting from it.[57]

Individuals facing the profusion of opinions and ideas presented in books were assisted by members of the community, who employed their own learning and wisdom for mutual edification. Pastorius's system of book exchange, personal commentary, trustworthy recommendation, and reciprocal dialogue about the meaning of books is best described in a letter dated December 20, 1718, to his young friend Lloyd Zachary,[58] with whom he had established a very lively correspondence over several years (one that would last until Pastorius's death in late 1719).[59]

Despite his role as Zachary's mentor, Pastorius does not present himself as an exclusive arbitrator of knowledge; rather, he reveals his own dependency on a larger circle of friends who are willing to lend their books. In turn, Pastorius believes that the much younger Zachary may enrich his mentor's wisdom. Through his correspondence with Pastorius, Zachary has become part of a select group of Pennsylvania Quakers, including some of the most prominent leaders of the Pennsylvania colony. Listing people who have lent books and enabled the expansion of his knowledge, Pastorius continues this system by lending books to his latest friend and correspondent. When Zachary solicits his mentor's assistance in choosing appropriate readings from the unwieldy plethora of printed works, he can rest assured that the three pieces Pastorius sends along with the December 20 letter have already passed the discerning eye of a trusted, experienced, and well-read friend. Along with the books recommended by Pastorius, Zachary gains a panoramic view of his mentor's principles of selecting useful sentences from other people's writings.

Accompanied by manuscript commentary and a compendium bearing the results of a trusted friend's collecting of knowledge, books lost their potential to distract from the Inner Light. Pastorius himself regularly borrowed books from Isaac Norris, Richard Hill, James Logan, and other prominent Pennsylvania Quakers, and he often added his own meditations before returning them. The whole system of book ownership and book circulation relied on a reciprocity that intimately resembled the ties of communal affection binding together members of the Quaker community.

Yet Pastorius's exchange of books and his literary, personal, intellectual, and spiritual advice were not restricted to other prominent men in the colony. A prime example of his inclusion of unprivileged Quaker women, for example, in his circle of textual exchange is Pastorius's correspondence with the itinerant Quaker preacher Lydia Norton from New England. Before departing for Barbados, Norton had spent some time preaching among the Quakers of the Philadelphia area, at which time Pastorius, who greatly admired her gifts as a minister, had borrowed the journal in which she recorded her missionary journeys and, within "4 days, (taking the Nights with it)," he had "Copied 44 Quart[o]-Leaves" from it.

As usual when returning a borrowed book, Pastorius attached a few verses, indicating his appreciation of Norton's journal as a valuable reflection of the workings of the Inner Light. But the letter he sent Norton when he did so (dated August 24, 1718, and recorded in his Letterbook)[60] also bespeaks Pastorius's appreciation of such autobiographical writings for the sake of aesthetic pleasure and intellectual stimulation. In other words, Pastorius's response to Norton's writings far exceeds his agreement with the spiritual notions of a fellow Quaker. The fact that he does not hesitate to criticize Norton's journal for lacking a rigorous organization and structural conciseness clearly indicates that Pastorius regarded his criticism as a serious contribution to improving her writing, not just her spiritual state. More important, he would not have voiced such criticism if he had expected Norton's journal to remain exclusively in private use. Thus his comments are meant to help Norton should she want to submit her writing to the public eye—whether in manuscript circulation or in print. As shown by Pastorius's mentoring of Quaker women—both elite (like the Lloyd daughters and granddaughters) and lower class (like Norton and the budding Quaker poet Jane Fenn)— teaching always depends on the guidance of the trained or highly educated teacher inculcating certain principles in students while ultimately helping them to leave such guidance behind. And underlying his apparent elite mentoring role is the principle of higher education training new generations of intellectuals that we still embrace today.

In his August 24, 1718, letter to Norton, Pastorius interweaves stylistic suggestions with more spiritual purposes: he emphasizes the relationship between text and audience in order to raise Norton's awareness of the public nature and communal significance of her writing. Thus her journal should not—as a diary might—merely chronicle every aspect of her life on her journeys, but should instead consider her readers' expectations and appeal to their sense of aesthetic pleasure. Pastorius argues that Norton's journal cannot effectively fulfill its ministerial mission if it lacks literary or rhetorical accomplishment. By the same token, he claims to express a general trend among readers, who "loath[e] Superfluities in all Sorts of Writings." Pastorius acts as a literary critic representing the tastes of a reading public—specifically the Society of Friends—to a writer of a popular Quaker genre. By no means disparaging Norton's more mundane experiences and daily routine as inconsequential, in trying to make her writing adhere to the conventions of a genre, Pastorius is actively seeking to improve its reception among her reading public.

The exchange of books, commentary, poetry, and religious as well as secular precepts among Quakers created an intellectual sphere that was at once more specific and more inclusive than the much-celebrated early modern Republic of Letters, in which membership largely depended on academic, educational, or scientific distinction. Indeed, members living on the periphery of that republic often complained that the arbiters of knowledge at the center—such as the members of the Royal Society in London—considered people in the colonies to be mere collectors rather than interpreters of knowledge. In Pastorius's Quaker community of letters, however, personal and spiritual affinities—mutual love and equality through the principle of the Inner Light—placed its members on a more level footing and also allayed any concern over the potentially corrupting influences of book learning.

Pastorius as Author

Scholarly commentary on Pastorius's published and unpublished writings has actually deterred students and researchers from considering his work from a literary perspective. Critiques by practitioners of the "New Criticism," the now-outdated notion of literary works as autonomous, highly original artifacts that serve as windows into an author's genius, have only served to hurt Pastorius's reputation as a writer. At the beginning of the "Bee-Hive," Pastorius himself claimed a lack of original vision: "I acknowledge with Macrobius, that in this Book all is mine, & nothing is mine" and announced his intentions to collect the "Marrow of other Men's Writings."[61] In a list preceding his "Silvula Rhytmorum," the poetic miscellany of the "Bee-Hive," he acknowledges having found its rhymes and poetic phrases in the widely known book *Emblemes* by English poet Francis Quarles (1592–1644);[62] he also prefaces the "Silvula" with a humility topos characteristic of the early modern age and especially of amateur writers who considered poetry writing appropriate only for a writer's unoccupied hours. In his Quaker environment, Pastorius had to ward off potential accusations of vanity or uselessness. Thus he justifies his poetic endeavors by first belittling them and then by claiming that he was trying to write poetry *only* while busy with practical work, such as spinning linen thread, and he introduces "Silvula" in a typically self-deprecating style: "Wheras now in the few next ensuing Leaves the Reader will find a Miscellany of my sorry Rimes, I would not have him think, that I made them with a purpose to be accounted a Poet [...] but only to try whether Versifying and Turning of the Spooling-wheel were things compatible at the same Time."[63]

Pastorius exposes what poets of the Romantic period would later want to hide: that we are all composites of ideas, thoughts, phrases, or *sententiae* (wise and pithy sayings) that are part not only of our specific cultural heritage but also of a collective intellectual and spiritual matrix that is continually being shared, reshaped, and redeployed. When reading Pastorius's poetry and other writings, we can find aesthetic, formal, and intellectual continuities, patterns, and reworkings of classical, medieval, Renaissance, humanist, and Baroque literary material alongside his personal, aesthetic, and original contributions to those traditions. Although readers may choose to focus more on the one than on the other, Pastorius's writings reward both kinds of readings. Here we highlight two main areas of his literary accomplishment: his promotional writings and his poetry.

WORKS OF SPIRITUAL PROMOTIONALISM

During the European discovery, exploration, and conquest of America, various descriptive genres flourished, most notably, the promotional account, an official report by a prominent member of an expedition, land investment company, or settlement that provided details of geographic locations and terrains, Native American populations, customs, natural resources and potential sources of wealth (especially precious metals and food sources), contact with indigenous populations, and the evaluation of the newly discovered or claimed land. Writers of these accounts used their literary craft not only to gain favor with sponsors and attract investors but often to promote themselves as well. They imbued their accounts of settlers in the new colonies with a sense of heroism and entrepreneurial acumen, kindling dreams of wealth and social advancement among the European reading public; their images of America uniquely blended European and Christian perspectives with vivid descriptions of natural settings.[64]

The promotional literature on Pennsylvania was different, however, appealing as it did to an international readership consisting primarily of English Quakers and Dutch- and German-speaking Mennonites, Anabaptists, and radical Pietists. A network of agents, promoters, translators, and editors in Europe—such as Benjamin Furly and Jacob Clauss—adapted Penn's accounts to the specific needs and sensibilities of these groups, some of whose members Penn had met on his missionary trips in the 1670s. They stressed even more than Penn had features of special appeal to those groups: freedom of conscience and worship, pacifism, the Philadelphian ideal of brotherly love and spiritual renewal, and a peaceful relationship not only between the different European immigrant groups but also between Europeans and Native Americans.[65]

Pastorius described the new colony of Pennsylvania in letters to his family and Pietist sponsors in Frankfurt. Some of these letters, such as *Sichere Nachricht* (1684; Certain News), were printed by the Frankfurt Pietists in a 1700 collection titled *Umständige Geographische Beschreibung* (*Circumstantial Geographical Description*), with a new preface by Pastorius as well as separate chapters. In his initial accounts, Pastorius emphasized his negotiations with Penn to arrange the land purchases and to lay out the future settlement of Germantown. Aesthetically and spiritually, Pastorius's letters stressed his friendship with Penn, relying on a common language (French) and their mutual knowledge of the classics. Above all, Pastorius encouraged the Pietists in Frankfurt to fulfill their promise to follow him to Pennsylvania; in addressing them, Pastorius made use of the stock features of promotional literature but adapted these for his intended audience and his particular relationship to them. He created a spiritual promotionalism that used the natural features of the land to exhort the Pietists to become spiritually fruitful. Immigration, Pastorius told the Pietists, was not a matter of physical comfort or economic gain but rather of suffering with Christ and fulfilling their spiritual potential.

Pastorius's *Umständige Geographische Beschreibung* includes seventeen core chapters that follow the basic scheme of promotional accounts, with a preface ("Vorrede") and a series of letters to friends and family in Europe. The chapters range in scope from a history of Pennsylvania's settlement, to a transcription of Penn's charter, to a history of Germantown and its laws, agriculture, and especially its three types of inhabitants: the European settlers from the Dutch and Swedish colonies on the Delaware River, new European immigrants (English Quakers and German- and Dutch-speaking Pietists), and Native Americans (especially the Lenape). The preface establishes the theme of a spiritual journey, a prominent trope in Protestant writings of the seventeenth and eighteenth centuries. Pastorius's travels and observations of worldly customs helped him turn inward and toward God. The preface thus asks its European readers to understand that the American colony described in the text offers immigrants a cure for the spiritual and moral afflictions besetting them in Europe. The main chapters and the appended letters stress quietness, rest, and contentment. Pastorius linked the decrease in worldly aspirations to his increase in spiritual fulfillment. The key word "rest [*Ruhe*]" appealed to radical Protestants in Europe since it meant both rest from financial or economic strife, religious persecution, uncertainty, and war and rest as an inward state of being. The rationale of the typical promotional account was thus turned on its head by Pastorius: the new colony became attractive to newcomers not because of the wealth and riches they might attain there but for the communities of religious affection they might find and for the lack of strife they would enjoy.

Pastorius wrote poetry for many different occasions and recorded that poetry in a variety of ways; much of it is collected in his "Silvula Rhytmorum Germanopolitanorum," the poetic miscellany that forms a substantial part of the "Bee-Hive," which contains poetry elsewhere as well, especially the pithy epigrams on the manuscript book's title pages announcing its purpose and philosophizing about the principles of knowledge collection. A short poem could often convey a point or insight in far fewer words than a prose treatise. Moreover, Pastorius enjoyed making smaller booklets that collected poetry for a specific purpose or occasion, of a particular poetic genre, or on a particular theme. His *Deliciæ Hortenses or Garden-Recreations* gathers poetry connecting observations Pastorius made in his garden with religious, moral, and intellectual insights.[66] In his "Ship-Mate-Ship" compilation, Pastorius collected poetry with a personal significance: beginning in 1714 and every year thereafter, he would write a long anniversary poem, addressed to three daughters of his late friend Thomas Lloyd (Hannah Hill, Mary Norris, and Rachel Preston) to commemorate the day in 1683 when Pastorius and Lloyd arrived together in Philadelphia on the *America*.

Poetry also played a prominent role in Pastorius's exchange of books with his friends. He often composed verses that responded to what he had just read and would write them in the book he had borrowed or would lend out, while copying these poems in the "Silvula" section of the "Bee-Hive." Entering a discussion with the lender or borrower of the book and with its content or author, these poems demonstrate the communal significance of his writings and the role that personal inspiration played in advancing the bonds between members of his community. Thus Pastorius's poetry, though always situated in the historical, religious, intellectual, communal, and interpersonal circumstances of his life, also devises intriguingly new formal and aesthetic treatments of each occasion or theme. As Oliver Scheiding has recently shown about Pastorius's "Epibaterium," a poem celebrating Penn's return to Pennsylvania from England in 1699, Pastorius's poetry blended German Baroque, classical, and contemporary English and American verse traditions and practices to create a style that was at once local and transnational.[67] His poetry rewards readers at home in a variety of national or aesthetic poetic traditions, and, given its often occasional nature, it satisfies both readers looking for clues to the historical and religious environment in which he worked and those more interested in literary and aesthetic qualities.

Although he transplanted himself to America, Pastorius was very much indebted to the style and intellect of German Baroque poetry, and especially to poets like Martin Opitz (1597–1639) and Friedrich Logau (1605–1655).[68] But Pastorius's peculiar wit and humor and his touching rhapsodies on friendships, the disappointments and rewards of immigrant life, and difficult concepts like faith, God, love, and time give his poems a distinctive flavor. Like many poets of his time, Pastorius strove to find new combinations to the Horatian formula of teaching *and* entertaining the reader. That his readers were almost always people he knew and who received his work in the personal medium of a manuscript permitted him to adapt both the message and the form of his poems to their specific needs. The intimacy of his poetic work allows us to learn more about the relationships between Pastorius and those in his circle, as well as his personal sensibilities and his experimentations with literary devices and poetic meter.

Although, in many ways, Pastorius is a transatlantic practitioner of German Baroque poetry, its excess and irregularity, its heaping of words for rhetorical effect, mannered technique, and penchant for ornamentation do not exactly square with his radical Pietist and Quaker desire for simplicity and moderation. In literary history, Pastorius's poetics stands closest to that of the early German Baroque poet Martin Opitz,[69] often called the "father of German poetry" because he insisted on writing and developing his craft in the neglected vernacular, thus countering the neo-Latin poetry of his late Renaissance contemporaries. Nevertheless, like Pastorius later in the seventeenth century, Opitz based his poetic innovations of German poetry on classical models, such as the alexandrine iambic hexameter; he even urged German poets to translate Greek and Latin models into German to improve their craft. Many of Opitz's watchwords for a new German poetry—formulated in his literary manifesto *Buch von der Deutschen Poeterey* (1624)—also apply to Pastorius: imitation was not a goal in itself but the first step toward innovation and invention; poetry was to be both edifying, even a form of philosophy, and educated, thus privileging the notion of the scholar-poet; and poetry was not a game but almost a science, with specific rules and traditions that privileged its learned practitioners. Opitz also emphasized themes Pastorius developed, such as the importance of learning over earthly wealth and exaltation of the quiet and contented country life.

Quaker sensibilities such as the high value placed on simplicity and the spiritual ends of learning squared well with Opitz's literary ideals and offered Pastorius an avenue for linking his German literary antecedents with the religious environment of his adult life in Pennsylvania. Like Opitz, Pastorius also favored poems on religious subjects, followed closely by occasional poems. Since his anniversary poems dedicated to Thomas Lloyd encapsulate both of these predilections, this introduction concludes with a detailed discussion of the poems Pastorius collected in his "Ship-Mate-Ship" volume. Rather than the more epigrammatic style that Pastorius often used in the "Silvula" section of the "Bee-Hive," all poems in "Ship-Mate-Ship" are lengthy; here Pastorius wished to match the format to the scope of his subject: the long history and friendship he shared with Lloyd and his family standing paradigmatically for the history of Pennsylvania and the changes occurring in Penn's "holy experiment." "Ship-Mate-Ship" thus constitutes the most prominent poetic treatment of the first thirty years of Pennsylvania's history, seen through the friendship between a Welsh Quaker and a German radical Pietist, finding spiritual and personal affinities and translating them onto the concept of community in early America.

THE "SHIP-MATE-SHIP" POEMS

On August 20, 1714, Pastorius began a series of anniversary poems commemorating the day thirty-one years earlier when he and his friend Thomas Lloyd (1640–1694) arrived in Philadelphia. Pastorius continued to write these poems until the year of his death. Addressing Lloyd's daughters Hannah Hill, Rachel Preston, and Mary Norris, Pastorius praised the role of friendship in his personal life in Pennsylvania and in the life of the Pennsylvania colony as a whole. For Pastorius, "Ship-Mate-Ship" means literally the condition of being shipmates and metaphorically the friendship or fellowship that might come from such an experience. The poems chronicle the camaraderie of the immigrant experience, along with its pitfalls—such as the disillusionment with society in America. Holding to the Quaker belief in suffering as the glue of religious community, Pastorius's poems redefine the notion of immigrant success and champion joint perseverance and mutual support as the primary virtues of society in America. One title page calls "Ship-Mate-Ship" "An Omer full of Manna";[70] Thomas Lloyd's name frames the acrostic and right-hand margin, while his daughters' and their husbands' names frame the top and bottom of the page. Pastorius thought of his poetry as a gift for the affection he had received from Lloyd and his family. These individuals and the special relationship in which they stand make them gifts; the poetry refashions the love already proffered among friends into a literary and physical memorial; ultimately, Jesus Christ transcends the "humane Friends" and the gifts they can give, for he is God's ultimate gift to humanity.

The first two poems of the collection in particular redefine the self through a redefinition of success and privilege, with Pastorius appearing resigned to the loss of his former identity. He interprets his marginal position as a non-English immigrant—an alien among his English-speaking shipmates—as an opportunity to explore spiritual rather than national consanguinity. In the first poem, written in 1714 and titled "A Token of Love and Gratitude," Pastorius constructs a series of confusions about the language of his shipmates that ironically highlight his own misunderstandings or even prejudices. The supreme irony for Pastorius was that Thomas Lloyd, the Welsh Quaker who, from his German speaker's point of view, spoke a confused or confusing language became the individual who made that German speaker feel most welcome. The lesson was clear: what seems most strange and alienating becomes most familiar and dear once hearts and minds open to true understanding. Pastorius and Lloyd became friends on the *America* because they already were Friends: they shared the Quaker belief in the universality of divine truth in every human being.

Similarly, Pastorius recognized that, even though his immigration to America meant the loss of prestige and wealth, it had opened the way for more spiritually potent forms of affiliation. His repeated mention of Lloyd and William Penn reflected Pastorius's acceptance into the political elite of the young colony, but he emphasized that their affection and their spiritual and intellectual qualities were the prime attraction for staying in Pennsylvania. Throughout the "Ship-Mate-Ship" poems, Pastorius repeats a pattern: personal disappointment and disillusionment force a turning both inward and toward congenial fellow beings who share spiritual and intellectual qualities. The loss of friends further spiritualizes the experience of friendship, suffering, and mutual affection. Memory and memorializing divert attention from loss to the qualities those friends exemplify, qualities that persist through time.

Pastorius's second redefinition in his anniversary poems—the redefinition of family—focuses on loss and a repeated transfer of family relationships to new acquaintances, co-religionists, friends, and fellow sufferers. The loss of family Pastorius experienced through emigration is repeated when his dearest friends, like Thomas Lloyd, die early, forcing him to repeat the process of creating, cultivating, and mourning intimate relationships akin to those within a family. Pastorius had lost his mother when he was six; he was raised by his father and stepmothers. The "Ship-Mate-Ship" poems advise readers accustomed to the loss of family—especially immigrants who left family behind in the Old World—to find intimate relationships resembling family bonds in their new land. Pastorius thus conceives of himself and the Lloyd daughters as an extended family who tested their faith through common trials and losses, such as the death of Rachel Preston, who is commemorated in the 1717 anniversary poem.

Framed as an extended meditation on past, present, and future, the anniversary poem for the year 1715 has Lloyd and Pastorius embarking on a common journey to "exile" themselves "towards the West, / And there to serve the Lord in stillness, Peace & Rest." Yet rather than the predicted "Utopia," both find another fallen world in America. The poem first sums up the disappointed quest but then goes back in time to narrate when, on the ship to Pennsylvania, Pastorius suffers potentially debilitating injuries, first from a falling lion figure and then from a fall on deck during a storm. Though these events serve as evidence for the fallen nature of humanity and the world, the crucial difference is made by Lloyd's assistance and healing—performed through the grace of God. For Pastorius, "Ship-Mate-Ship" means knowing and accepting one another's frailty and imperfection and thus alleviating one another's suffering. In more historical terms, Pennsylvania Quakers suffered together under the persecution by "apostates" like George Keith. References to the profound trauma the Keithian controversy caused Quakers like Thomas Lloyd and the larger Quaker community abound in the "Ship-Mate-Ship" poems.

Reminded at every anniversary of the loss of family and friends, Pastorius questioned the ability of language to make sense of the passing of time. The past, present, and future tenses create an almost despairing sense of the ephemeral. Although Lloyd's example serves as the guidepost for spending one's time wisely, Pastorius regards the future with a sense of trepidation. The answer to "what remains"?—"to read, write, toil & moil"—exemplifies his tireless reading, collecting, culling, and recording of knowledge and wisdom. Beside the seemingly frantic occupation with knowledge collection, Pastorius labored to ease the pain of loss by centering love ("charity") within the triad of "faith, hope, and charity" that opposed the morbid tread of time.[71]

The shift from writing the lives of earthly friends to honoring the Divine Grantor of eternal life is reflected in Pastorius's 1716 anniversary poem—a poetic biography of Christ. The year 1716 marked the thirty-third anniversary of Pastorius and Lloyd's landing in Philadelphia, which corresponded to Christ's age at the time of his death. Here Pastorius produced what he called something "of Consequence" and something he considered the most worthy subject for a significant anniversary.[72] Though he called it "A short Abridgement of the Sacred History," his poetic biography of Jesus Christ runs an impressive 466 lines, with hundreds of biblical references and fifty-two detailed footnotes.[73] The 1716 poem signaled for Pastorius and his correspondents the culmination in a progression from the acceptance of suffering and death of friends and family members to a complete immersion in the suffering and death of the Savior. Pastorius's anniversary poems thus both resemble and invert traditional martyrologies. Early modern martyr books, such as the Mennonite *Martyrs Mirror* (1660), began with Christ, moved to the Apostles and other early martyrs, and finally memorialized the blood witnesses of recent times. Pastorius first represents the martyrs in his own community and then culminates in the martyr of all martyrs. Pastorius's experience of "Ship-Mate-Ship"— suffering with and for other human beings—allows him to comprehend, appreciate, and ultimately believe in the sacrifice of the Redeemer. "Ship-Mate-Ship" is no longer just a metaphor for human community, spiritual fellowship, and the common sense of suffering; it is also a metaphor for faith itself. Pastorius and his friends have become Christ's shipmates, his Disciples. Pastorius's anniversary poems not only celebrate his arrival in Pennsylvania and more than thirty years of friendship with his shipmates; they also mark his acceptance of suffering, loss, and death as part of his condition of "Ship-Mate-Ship" with Christ.

Conclusion

Throughout his writings and community work, Pastorius strove to reconcile the many conflicting intellectual and religious currents of his time, his dual allegiances to German Pietists and English Quakers, and the diverse ethnic, linguistic, and religious components of early Pennsylvania and the Atlantic world, attempting to arrive at a common idiom or ethos that would further the prospects for a unified communal experiment. In his encyclopedic writings, his poetry, and his practical work in mediating between the different linguistic and religious constituencies of the colony, Pastorius linked the mystical search for divine truth, the Pietist emphasis on a language of the heart, and the Quaker quest to speak a pure and inspired language.

In all of Pastorius's writings, old and new knowledge had to submit to the scrutiny of a critical and well-educated reader, guided by the principle of brotherly love. His efforts to collect, select, and store knowledge sought to bridge the divide between human language and the divine meanings of the universe. Following in the footsteps of the pansophist Jan Amos Comenius, Pastorius held education, the storage and broad dissemination of knowledge, and the reformation of human language to be paramount in transforming human society. Though motivated by the Enlightenment desire to create and reflect order, Pastorius's writings remain anchored in the early modern mystical effort to rediscover hidden connections between human languages and the essence of things. His self-image as a translator, multilingual poet, and collector of knowledge striving for a spiritual core led him to invoke repeatedly the motto from Paul's first letter to the Thessalonians: "Test everything. Hold on to the good" (1 Thess. 5:21). In following this motto, Pastorius saw the multilingual environment of early Pennsylvania and the confluence of Quaker and non-Quaker writings on the pages of his manuscripts as an opportunity to undo at least some of the effects of Babel—not by championing any one language or knowledge system over any other but rather by refining, defining, and storing the spiritual essence of all language and knowledge.

Notes

1. Francis Daniel Pastorius, *Circumstantial Geographical Description of Pennsylvania*, trans. Gertrude Selwyn Kimball, in *Narratives of Early Pennsylvania, West New Jersey and Delaware*, ed. Albert Cook Myers, vol. 11 of *Original Narratives of Early American History*, ed. Franklin J. Jameson (New York: Scribner's, 1912), 411.

2. Philipp Jakob Spener, *Pia Desideria* (1675), trans. Theodore G. Tappert (Philadelphia: Fortress Press, 1964).

3. For recent overviews on Pietism in English, see Hans Schneider, *German Radical Pietism*, trans. Gerald MacDonald (Lanham, Md.: Scarecrow Press, 2007); Douglas A. Shantz, *An Introduction to German Pietism: Protestant Renewal at the Dawn of Modern Europe* (Baltimore: Johns Hopkins University Press, 2013); and Jonathan Strom, Hartmut Lehman, and James Van Horn Melton, *Pietism in Germany and North America, 1680–1820* (Burlington, Vt.: Ashgate, 2009). German-language scholarship on the subject is vast; a standard survey is Johannes Wallmann, *Der Pietismus* (Göttingen: Vandenhoeck & Ruprecht, 1990). See also the multivolume

Geschichte des Pietismus, ed. Martin Brecht (Göttingen: Vandenhoeck & Ruprecht, 1993–95). On the Frankfurt Pietists and Pastorius's involvement in particular, see Andreas Deppermann, *Johann Jakob Schütz und die Anfänge des Pietismus* (Tübingen: Mohr Siebeck, 2002); and Klaus Deppermann, "Pennsylvanien als Asyl des frühen deutschen Pietismus," in *Pietismus und Neuzeit: Ein Jahrbuch zur Geschichte des Neueren Protestantismus*, vol. 10 (Göttingen: Vandenhoeck & Ruprecht, 1984), 190–226.

4. Spener's student and founder of the Francke Foundations (Franckesche Stiftungen) in Halle, August Hermann Francke, for example, moved through a more radical Pietist phase during the 1690s but became more associated with church Pietism in his later career. See Veronika Albrecht-Birkner and Udo Sträter, "Die radikale Phase des frühen August Hermann Francke," in *Der Radikale Pietismus: Perspektiven der Forschung*, ed. Wolfgang Breul et al. (Göttingen: Vandenhoeck & Ruprecht, 2010), 57–84.

5. For general background literature on the Quakers (Society of Friends), especially their early period in England, see William Braithwaite, *The Beginnings of Quakerism*, 2nd ed. (Cambridge: Cambridge University Press, 1961); Braithwaite, *The Second Period of Quakerism*, 2nd ed. (Cambridge: Cambridge University Press, 1961); Richard Bauman, *Let Your Words Be Few: Symbolism of Speaking and Silence Among Seventeenth-Century Quakers* (Cambridge: Cambridge University Press, 1983); Melvin B. Endy, *William Penn and Early Quakerism* (Princeton: Princeton University Press, 1973); Rosemary Moore, *The Light in Their Consciences: Early Quakers in Britain, 1646–1666* (University Park: Pennsylvania State University Press, 2000); Kate Peters, *Print Culture and the Early Quakers* (Cambridge: Cambridge University Press, 2005); Nigel Smith, *Perfection Proclaimed: Language and Literature in English Radical Religion, 1640–1660* (Oxford: Clarendon Press, 1989). For Quakerism in North America and specifically in Pennsylvania, see James Bowden, *The History of the Society of Friends in America*, 2 vols. (1850; New York: Arno Press, 1972); Richard Bauman, *For the Reputation of Truth: Politics, Religion, and Conflict Among the Pennsylvania Quakers, 1750–1800* (Baltimore: Johns Hopkins University Press, 1971); Edwin B. Bronner, "The Quakers and Non-Violence in Pennsylvania," *Pennsylvania History* 35 (1968): 1–22; William I. Hull, *William Penn and the Dutch Quaker Migration to Pennsylvania* (1935; Baltimore: Genealogical Publishing Company, 1970); Rufus M. Jones, *The Quakers in the American Colonies* (1911; New York: Russell & Russell, 1962); Gary B. Nash, *Quakers and Politics, Pennsylvania, 1681–1726* (1968; Boston: Northeastern University Press, 1993); Frederick B. Tolles, *Meeting House and Counting House: The Quaker Merchants of Colonial Philadelphia, 1682–1763* (Chapel Hill: University of North Carolina Press, 1948); Tolles, "'Of the Best Sort but Plain': The Quaker Aesthetic," *American Quarterly* 9 (1959): 484–502; Tolles, *Quakers and the Atlantic Culture* (New York: Macmillan Company, 1960); Hermann Wellenreuther, *Glaube und Politik in Pennsylvania, 1681–1776: Die Wandlungen der Obrigkeitsdoktrin und des Peace Testimony der Quäker*, Kölner Historische Abhandlungen 20 (Cologne: Böhlau, 1972); Wellenreuther, "The Political Dilemma of the Quakers in Pennsylvania, 1681–1748," *Pennsylvania Magazine of History and Biography* 94, no. 2 (1970): 135–72; and Wellenreuther, "The Quest for Harmony in a Turbulent World: The Principle of 'Love and Unity' in Colonial Pennsylvania Politics," *Pennsylvania Magazine of History and Biography* 107 (1983): 537–76.

6. On William Penn's visits to Germany's Protestant dissenters during the 1670s, see Sünne Juterczenka, *Über Gott und die Welt: Endzeitvisionen, Reformdebatten und die europäische Quäkermission in der frühen Neuzeit* (Göttingen: Vandenhoeck & Ruprecht, 2008), 192–204.

7. For scholarship on the Keithian controversy, see Jon Butler, "'Gospel Order Improved': The Keithian Schism and the Exercise of Ministerial Authority in Pennsylvania," *William and Mary Quarterly*, 3rd ser., 31 (1974): 431–52; Butler, "Into Pennsylvania's Spiritual Abyss: The Rise and Fall of the Later Keithians, 1693–1703," *Pennsylvania Magazine of History and Biography* 101 (1977): 151–70; Butler, "Power, Authority, and the Origins of American Denominational Order: The English Churches in the Delaware Valley, 1680–1730," *Transactions of the American Philosophical Society* 68, no. 2 (1978): 32–39; Butler, "The Records of the First 'American' Denomination: The Keithians of Pennsylvania, 1694–1700," *Pennsylvania Magazine of History and Biography* 120 (1996): 89–105; Edward Cody, "The Price of Perfection: The Irony of George Keith," *Pennsylvania History* 39 (1972): 1–19; J. William Frost, *The Keithian Controversy in Early Pennsylvania* (Norwood, Pa: Norwood Editions, 1980); Frost, "Unlikely Controversialists: Caleb Pusey and George Keith," *Quaker History* 64, no. 1 (1975): 16–36; David L. Johns, "Convincement and Disillusionment: Printer William Bradford and the Keithian Controversy in Colonial Pennsylvania," *Journal of the Friends' Historical Society* (Great Britain) 57, no. 1 (1994): 21–32; Ethyn Williams Kirby, *George Keith, 1638–1716* (New York: Appleton-Century, 1942); Clare J. L. Martin, "Controversy and Division in Post-Restoration Quakerism: The Hat, Wilkinson-Story and Keithian Controversies and Comparisons with the Internal Divisions of Other Seventeenth-Century Non-Conformist Groups" (Ph.D. diss., Open University, 2003); and Andrew R. Murphy, *Conscience and Community: Revisiting Toleration and Religious Dissent in Early Modern England and America* (University Park: Pennsylvania State University Press, 2001).

8. Francis Daniel Pastorius, *Henry Bernhard Koster, William Davis, Thomas Rutter & Thomas Bowyer, four Boasting Disputers Of this World briefly REBUKED, And Answered according to their Folly, which they themselves have manifested in a late Pamphlet, entituled, Advice for all Professors and writers* (New York: William Bradford, 1697).

9. For a stand-alone treatment of Pastorius's legal training and thought, see Alfred L. Brophy, "'Ingenium est Fateri per quos profeceris': Francis Daniel Pastorius's *Young Country Clerk's Collection* and Anglo-American Legal Literature, 1682–1716," *University of Chicago Law School Roundtable* (1996): 637–734.

10. Francis Daniel Pastorius, "Genealogia Pastoriana," in "Bee-Hive: His Hive, Melliotrophium Alvear or, Rusca Apium, Begun Anno Domini or, in the year of Christian Account, 1696," UPenn MS Codex 726, Rare Book and Manuscript Library, University of Pennsylvania.

11. See Wellenreuther, "Quest for Harmony."

12. For educational changes in the Renaissance, early modern Europe, and colonial America, see Bernard Bailyn, *Education in the Forming of American Society* (Chapel Hill: University of North Carolina Press, 1962); James Bowen, *A History of Western Education* (New York: St. Martin's Press, 1975); T. D. Burridge, *What Happened in Education: An Introduction to Western Educational History* (Boston: Allyn and Bacon, 1970); Lawrence A. Cremin, *American Education: The Colonial Experience, 1607–1783* (New York: Harper & Row, 1970); S. E. Frost, *Historical and Philosophical Foundations of Western Education* (Columbus, Ohio: Merrill, 1966); Grafton, *Worlds Made*; Alyssa Magee Lowery and William Hayes, *The Heart and Mind in Teaching: Pedagogical Styles Through the Ages* (Lanham, Md.: Rowman & Littlefield, 2014); and Christopher Lucas, *Our Western Educational Heritage* (New York: Macmillan, 1972).

13. Francis Daniel Pastorius, "Res Propriæ," MS 8242, Pastorius Papers and Digital Library, Historical Society of Pennsylvania (from here on HSP). This manuscript lists all Pastorius's possessions including his library and makes multiple references to the works of Comenius, as does Pastorius's bibliography of non-Quaker authors in the "Bee-Hive" (see chapter 4 of this reader).

14. On Comenius and his educational and linguistic reforms, see Craig D. Atwood, *The Theology of the Czech Brethren from Hus to Comenius* (University Park: Pennsylvania State University Press, 2009); Raymond S. Haupert, *Pioneers in Moravian Education: John Amos Comenius and Count Nicholas von Zinzendorf* (Bethlehem, Pa.: Interprovincial Board of Christian Education, 1957); John Edward Sadler, *J. A. Comenius and the Concept of Universal Education* (New York: Barnes & Noble, 1966); Walter W. Woodward, *Prospero's America: John Winthrop, Jr., Alchemy, and the Creation of New England Culture, 1606–1676* (Chapel Hill: University of North Carolina Press, 2010); Robert Fitzgibbon Young, *Comenius in England* (New York: Arno Press, 1971); and Young, *Comenius and the Indians of New England* (London: King's College, University of London, 1929).

15. See Robin Briggs, *The Scientific Revolution of the Seventeenth Century* (London: Harlow, Longmans, 1969); Peter Dear, *Revolutionizing the Sciences: European Knowledge and Its Ambitions, 1500–1700*, 2nd ed. (Princeton: Princeton University Press, 2009); Lawrence M. Principle, *The Scientific Revolution: A Very Short Introduction* (New York: Oxford University Press, 2011); and Alan G. R. Smith, *Science and Society in the Sixteenth and Seventeenth Centuries* (London: Science History Publications, 1972).

16. Pastorius cites Bacon frequently in his manuscript books. One of his favorite quotations comes from Bacon's essay "Of Studies" (*The Essayes or Counsels, Civill and Morall*; 1625) and is repeated in various forms (with Pastorius's slight rephrasing or trimming): "Read not to contradict and confute; nor to believe and take for granted; nor to find talk and discourse; but to weigh and consider. Some books are to be tasted, others to be swallowed, and some few to be chewed and digested: that is, some books are to be read only in parts, others to be read, but not curiously, and some few to be read wholly, and with diligence and attention." Pastorius's bibliography of non-Quaker authors in the "Bee-Hive" (see chapter 4 of this reader) refers to several works by Bacon, including his *Essays*.

17. On Quaker educational principles, see John Burkhart and Ralph West, eds., *Better Than Riches: A Tricentennial History of William Penn Charter School, 1689–1989* (Philadelphia: William Penn Charter School, 1989); William C. Kashatus, *A Virtuous Education: Penn's Vision for Philadelphia Schools* (Wallingford, Pa.: Pendle Hill, 1997); Kashatus, "Franklin's Secularization of Quaker Education," in "*The Good Education of Youth*": *World of Learning in the Age of Franklin*, ed. John H. Pollack (New Castle, Del.: Oak Knoll Press, 2009), 55–71; Nancy Rosenberg, "The Sub-textual Religion: Quakers, the Book, and Public Education in Philadelphia, 1682–1800" (Ph.D. diss., University of Michigan, 1991); Tolles, *Meeting House*, esp. chap. 7, "A Taste for Books," and chap. 8, "Reading for Delight and Profit"; W. A. Campbell Stewart, *Quakers and Education: As Seen in Their Schools in England* (London: Epworth, 1953); Thomas Woody, *Early Quaker Education in Pennsylvania* (1918; New York: Arno Press, 1969). On education among Pennsylvania Germans, see Patrick M. Erben, "Educating Germans in Colonial Pennsylvania," in "*The Good Education of Youth*," ed. Pollack, 122–49.

18. The philosophy and teachings of the Greek philosopher Aristotle had been translated and reconciled with Christian doctrine by medieval theologians such as Albertus Magnus and Thomas Aquinas, thus exerting tremendous influence on medieval, Renaissance, and early modern thought. But Aristotelianism came under attack from the natural philosophers of the seventeenth century, especially for its insistence on deductive reasoning and its excessive use of the syllogism for all types of logical reasoning. Pastorius objected less to the specifics of Aristotelian thought than to the entrenchment of its principles at European universities. On the influence of Aristotle and Aristotelianism on early modern thought and education, see Anthony Kenny, *Essays on the Aristotelian Tradition* (Oxford: Oxford University Press, 2001); Richard E. Rubenstein, *Aristotle's Children: How Christians, Muslims, and Jews Rediscovered Ancient Wisdom and Illuminated the Middle Ages* (New York: Mariner Books, 2004); and Bertrand Russell, *A History of Western Philosophy* (New York: Simon & Schuster, 1967).

19. Though Pastorius's collecting in manifold commonplace books and notebooks relates to his overall educational activities, the extent and complexity of his collection process warrant a separate section of this introduction (see "Pastorius as Thinker, Reader, and Collector of Knowledge").

20. Pennsylvania's 1683 Frame of Government, as quoted in Kashatus, "Franklin's Secularization," 56.

21. In stark contrast to their father's university training, Pastorius's sons, John (Johann) Samuel and Henry (Heinrich), followed the Quaker call for practical training and became shoemaker and weaver, respectively. Although Pastorius seemed to embrace or even decide these choices of profession for his sons, he also dedicated his vast collections of knowledge—such as the "Bee-Hive"—to them and to their use.

22. Francis Daniel Pastorius, "A few Onomastical Considerations, enlarged From the Number of Sixty Six to that of One Hundred; and Presented or rather Re-presented to William Penn, Proprietary and Governour of Pennsilvania, & Territories thereunto belonging. Patri Patriæ, The Father of this Province, and lately also the Father of John Penn, an innocent & hopeful Babe, by whose Nativity & Names sake they were first contrived," MS, AM 1.3, German Society of Pennsylvania, Joseph Horner Memorial Library; photostat copy of original held at Friends' House, London.

23. "Den 30. Decemb. 1701 wurde vor gut befunden, hier in Germantown eine Schul aufzurichten," Francis Daniel Pastorius et al., "The General Court Records of the Corporation of Germantown, oder, Raths-Buch der Germantownischen Gemeinde," Germantown, 1691–1707, MS, Am 3711, HSP; no pagination. This entry is also written in Pastorius's hand. For a modern edition and translation of the General Court Records of Germantown, see Duffin, *Acta Germanopolis*.

24. The nineteenth-century German-American scholar Oswald Seidensticker consulted a "Cash-Book" kept by Pastorius, in which Pastorius recorded in 1702 the names of his evening students, who included Hanna Siverts and Agnes Kunders. Unfortunately, the "Cash-Book" is no longer extant, and only Seidensticker's notes from it remain in his essay "Pastorius und die Gründung von Germantown," *Der Deutsche Pionier* 3 (1871–72): 8–12, 56–58, 78–83. Here Seidensticker also claims that students of both sexes were admitted to the school but does not further support this assertion (58). If girls and women were indeed students at the school, they most likely were taught coeducationally since Pastorius was the only teacher.

25. Francis Daniel Pastorius, *A New Primmer or Methodical Directions To attain the True Spelling, Reading & Writing of ENGLISH. Whereunto are added, some things Necessary & Useful both for the Youth of this Province, and likewise for those, who from forreign Countries and Nations come to settle amongst us* (New York: William Bradford, [1698]). According to J. William Frost, "Pastorius's primer, issued in 1698, was the only textbook written by an American Friend before 1774." Frost, *The Quaker Family in Colonial America: A Portrait of the Society of Friends* (New York: St. Martin's Press, 1973), 100. For scholarship on colonial primers and literacy education, see Patricia Crain, *The Story of A: The Alphabetization of America from "The New England Primer" to "The Scarlet Letter"* (Stanford: Stanford University Press, 2000); and Jennifer E. Monaghan, *Learning to Read and Write in Colonial America* (Amherst: University of Massachusetts Press; Worcester, Mass.: American Antiquarian Society, 2005).

26. See Tolles, *Meeting House*, chap. 7 "The Taste for Books," and chap. 8, "Reading for Delight and Profit," 144–204; Edwin Wolf, *The Book Culture of a Colonial American City: Philadelphia Books, Bookmen, and Booksellers* (Oxford: Clarendon Press, 1988); Wolf, *The Library of James Logan, 1674–1751* (Philadelphia: The Library Company, 1974); and James N. Green, "The Book Trade in the Middle Colonies, 1680–1720," in *The Colonial Book in the Atlantic World*, ed. Hugh Amory and David D. Hall (Cambridge: Cambridge University Press, 2000), 199–223.

27. Francis Daniel Pastorius, "Ship-Mate-Ship. An Omer full of Manna, For Mary, Rachel, Hannah, The Daughters of brave Lloyd, By brave Men now enjoy'd" [Composition Book], MS 8846, Pastorius Papers and Digital Library, HSP, 4. Anthony Grafton, historian of the early modern age in Europe and the Atlantic world,

recently investigated Pastorius's use and modification of established European knowledge systems (or "regimes") in early America: "Pastorius and his friends created one such regime—and used its tools creatively and effectively, to build a local version of Enlightenment rooted not only in local empiricism and discovery, but also in cosmopolitan erudition and tradition." Grafton, in other words, finds that Pastorius's intellectual methods and ideals were both forward and backward looking. Anthony Grafton, "The Republic of Letters in the American Colonies: Francis Daniel Pastorius Makes a Notebook," *American Historical Review* 117, no. 1 (February 2012): 39. See also Grafton, "Jumping Through the Computer Screen," *New York Review of Books*, December 23, 2010.

28. For a succinct overview of changing knowledge systems or epistemologies in Western societies, see Ian F. McNeely and Lisa Wolverton, *Reinventing Knowledge: From Alexandria to the Internet* (New York: Norton, 2008), esp. chap. 4, "The Republic of Letters," 119–59.

29. Johann Valentin Andreæ, *Fama Fraternitatis* (1614); *Confessio Fraternitatis* (1615); *Chymische Hochzeit: Christiani Rosencreutz. Anno 1459* (1616), ed. Richard Van Dülmen (Stuttgart: Calwer, 1973), 35, as translated by Patrick M. Erben. The original German reads: "Wehre es nicht ein köstlich Ding, daß du also lessen kündtest in einem Buch, daß du zugleich alles, was in allen Büchern, die jemals gewesen, noch seyn oder kommen und außgehen warden, zu finden gewesen, noch gefunden wird und jemals mag gefunden warden, lessen, verstehen und behalten möchtest?" For further background on the mysterious Rosicrucian Society and its tremendous influence on the thought of the seventeenth century and beyond, see John Matthews et al., *The Rosicrucian Enlightenment Revisited* (Hudson, N.Y.: Lindisfarne Books, 1999); Christopher McIntosh, *The Rose Cross and the Age of Reason: Eighteenth-Century Rosicrucianism in Central Europe and Its Relationship to the Enlightenment* (Leiden: Brill, 1992); McIntosh, *The Rosicrucians: The History, Mythology and Rituals of an Occult Order* (Wellingborough, U.K.: Crucible, 1987); Hugh Ormsby-Lennon, "Rosicrucian Linguistics: Twilight of a Renaissance Tradition," in *Hermeticism and the Renaissance: Intellectual History and the Occult in Early Modern Europe*, ed. Ingrid Merkel and Allen G. Debus (Washington, D.C.: Folger Shakespeare Library, 1988), 311–41; Thomas Willard, "The Rosicrucian Manifestos in Britain," *Papers of the Bibliographical Society of America* 77 (1983): 489–95; Frances A. Yates, *The Rosicrucian Enlightenment* (London: Routledge & Kegan Paul, 1972).

30. Anathasius Kircher (1602–1680) was in many ways a polymath—one of the last so-called Renaissance men. Searching for knowledge of the natural world just before the advent of the modern scientific method, Kircher has been held up as a somewhat scurrilous example of a dying intellectual tradition before the embrace of a new paradigm. On Kircher in general, see John Glassie, *A Man of Misconceptions: The Life of an Eccentric in an Age of Change* (New York: Riverhead Books, 2012). For a brief assessment of Kircher's linguistic thought, see Umberto Eco, *Serendipities: Language and Lunacy*, trans. William Weaver (New York: Columbia University Press, 1998); Eco, *The Search for the Perfect Language*, trans. James Fentress (Oxford: Blackwell, 1995). For Kircher's status in the early modern Republic of Letters or scholarly community, see Grafton, *Worlds Made*, 14–16.

31. One of the most important philosophers of the early Enlightenment, John Locke exerted a tremendous influence on much of eighteenth-century thought. He is commonly accepted as one of the first English empiricists; his approach to human knowledge championed personal, especially sensory, experience. Pastorius cited two works by Locke in his extensive bibliographies: *A Common-Place Book to the Holy Bible* (1697) and *Essay Concerning Human Understanding* (1710). Entry 422 in Pastorius's "Silvula Rhytmorum," his poetic miscellany in the "Bee-Hive," concerns Locke's *Essay*. For concise introductions to John Locke and his work, see Michael Ayers, *Locke: Epistemology and Ontology* (New York: Routledge, 1996); Vere Chappell, ed., *The Cambridge Companion to Locke* (Cambridge: Cambridge University Press, 1994); and John Dunn, *Locke: A Very Short Introduction* (New York: Oxford University Press, 2003).

32. Denis Diderot et al., eds, *Encyclopedia, or a Descriptive Dictionary of the Sciences, Arts and Trades*, 5:1755, as quoted in "Encyclopedia," in *The Cambridge Dictionary of Philosophy*, 2nd ed., ed. Robert Audi (Cambridge: Cambridge University Press, 1999), 264.

33. Francis Daniel Pastorius, "F. D. P. Francis Daniel Pastorius [Commonplace Book]," MS 8864, Pastorius Papers and Digital Library, HSP. On the development of the commonplace tradition from the Middle Ages through the Renaissance, see Ann M. Blair, *Too Much to Know: Managing Scholarly Information before the Modern Age* (New Haven: Yale University Press, 2010); Ann Moss, "Commonplace-Rhetoric and Thought-Patterns in Early Modern Culture," in *The Recovery of Rhetoric: Persuasive Discourse and Disciplinarity in the Human Sciences*, eds. R. H. Roberts and J. M. M. Good (Charlottesville: University Press of Virginia, 1993), 49–60; and Moss, *Printed Commonplace-Books and the Structuring of Renaissance Thought* (Oxford: Clarendon Press, 1996).

34. Francis Daniel Pastorius, "Alvearialia, Or such Phrases and Sentences which in haste were Booked down here, before I had Time to Carry them to their respective proper Places in my English-Folio-Bee-hive," MS 8845, Pastorius Papers and Digital Library, HSP.

35. McNeely and Wolverton, *Reinventing Knowledge*, 122.

36. See David A. Boruchoff, "New Spain, New England, and the New Jerusalem: The 'Translation' of Empire, Faith, and Learning (*translatio imperii, fidei ac scientiae*) in the Colonial Missionary Project," *Early American Literature* 43, no. 1 (2008): 5–34.

37. Pastorius, "Bee-Hive," 55.

38. Concerning the importance of knowledge transfer to ensure the cultivation of civility in early America, see Cremin, *American Education*, "The Nurture of Civility," 58–79. On the fears of cultural degeneration among New England Puritans, see John Canup, "Cotton Mather and 'Criolian Degeneracy,'" *Early American Literature* 24, no. 1 (1989): 20–34; and Canup, *Out of the Wilderness: The Emergence of an American Identity in Colonial New England* (Middletown, Conn.: Wesleyan University Press, 1990).

39. Anthony Grafton, "The Humanist as Reader," in *A History of Reading in the West*, ed. Guglielmo Cavallo and Roger Chartier (Amherst: University of Massachusetts Press, 1999), 203.

40. Ibid., 204.

41. One of the few works that has taken notice of Pastorius's collections of knowledge in gardening, agriculture, and medicine is Shirley Hershey Showalter, "'Herbal Signs of Nature's Page': A Study of Francis Daniel Pastorius's View of Nature," *Quaker History* 71, no. 2 (1982): 89–99.

42. Renate Wilson, *Pious Traders in Medicine: A German Pharmaceutical Network in Eighteenth-Century North America* (University Park: Pennsylvania State University Press, 2000), 51.

43. On the intersections of medicine and religion in Pastorius's time, see Udo Benzendörfer and Wilhelm Kühlmann, eds., *Heilkunde und Krankheitserfahrung in der frühen Neuzeit* (Tübingen: Max Niemeyer, 1992); Jörg Jochen Berns, "Utopie und Medizin: Der Staat der Gesunden und der gesunde Staat: Utopische Entwürfe des 16. und 17. Jahrhunderts," in Benzendörfer and Kühlmann, *Heilkunde und Krankheitserfahrung*, 55–93; Thomas Royce Brendle and Claude W. Unger, *Folk Medicine of the Pennsylvania Germans: The Non-Occult Cures* (New York: Kelley, 1970); and Ole Peter Grell and Andrew Cunningham, eds., *"Religio Medici": Medicine and Religion in Seventeenth-Century England* (Aldershot, U.K.: Scolar Press, 1996).

44. In *Worlds Made by Words*, 9, Grafton identifies the use of Latin and French as the languages of Republic of Letters: "Its citizens agreed that they owed it loyalty, and almost all of them spoke its two languages—Latin, which remained the language of all scholars from 1500 to about 1650 and still played a prominent role thereafter, and French, which gradually replaced Latin in most periodicals and in almost all salons."

45. For a scholarly investigation of multilingualism and the rise of the vernaculars in European culture of the seventeenth century and the Baroque, see Leonard Foster, "Neo-Latin Tradition and Vernacular Poetry," in *German Baroque Literature: The European Perspective*, ed. Gerhart Hoffmeister (New York: Ungar, 1983), 87–108; and Foster, *The Poet's Tongues: Multilingualism in Literature* (Dunedin: University of Otago Press, 1970).

46. Francis Daniel Pastorius, "Alphabetical Hive," entry 1382, in "Bee-Hive."

47. Pastorius, *Circumstantial Geographical Description*, 385; Pastorius, *Umständige Beschreibung*, 29–30.

48. Hans Schneider, "Der radikale Pietismus im 17. Jahrhundert," in *Der Pietismus vom siebzehnten bis zum frühen achtzehnten Jahrhundert*, ed. Martin Brecht, vol. 1, *Geschichte des Pietismus* (Göttingen: Vandenhoeck & Ruprecht, 1993), 394.

49. Perhaps Pastorius was citing from memory here since he gives the wrong verse: 20 instead of 21.

50. Pastorius, "Alvearialia," 2.

51. On the Germantown Protest against slavery, see Katharine Gerbner, "Antislavery in Print: The Germantown Protest, the *Exhortation*, and the Seventeenth-Century Quaker Debate on Slavery," *Early American Studies* 9, no. 3 (2011): 552–75; and Gerbner, "'We Are Against the Traffik of Men-Body': The Germantown Quaker Protest of 1688 and the Origins of American Abolitionism," *Pennsylvania History: A Journal of Mid-Atlantic Studies* 74, no. 2 (2007): 149–72. For the Quaker practice of and eventual rejection of slavery, see Brycchan Carey, *From Peace to Freedom: Quaker Rhetoric and the Birth of American Antislavery, 1657–1761* (New Haven: Yale University Press, 2012); and Jean Soderlund, *Quakers and Slavery: A Divided Spirit* (Princeton: Princeton University Press, 1985).

52. Gerret Hendericks, Derick up de Graeff, Francis Daniell [*sic*] Pastorius, [and] Abraham up den Graef, "Quaker Protest Against Slavery in the New World, Germantown (Pa.) 1688," Manuscript Collection 990 B-R, Quaker and Special Collections, Haverford College. Even though Abraham and Dirck (Derick) were brothers, they spelled their names differently on these documents.

53. Pastorius, "Bee-Hive," as quoted in Learned, *Life of Francis Daniel Pastorius*, 263.

54. Concerning Cotton Mather's notions about slavery, see Margot Minardi, "The Boston Inoculation Controversy of 1721–1722: An Incident in the History of Race," *Willian and Mary Quarterly*, 3rd ser., 61, no. 1 (2004):

47–76; and Mark A. Peterson, "The Selling of Joseph: Bostonians, Antislavery, and the Protestant International, 1689–1733," *Massachusetts Historical Review* 4 (2002): 1–22.

55. James 2:13: "For judgment is without mercy to him who has shown no mercy; mercy triumphs over judgment."

56. The following sketch of Pastorius's collection, storage, and retrieval systems relies largely on Brooke Palmieri, "'What the Bees Have Taken Pains For': Francis Daniel Pastorius, The Beehive, and Commonplacing in Colonial Pennsylvania," Undergraduate Humanities Forum 2008–9: Change (University of Pennsylvania, 2009), http://repository.upenn.edu/uhf_2009/7/. Palmieri's painstaking description and analysis of Pastorius's systems is brilliant and authoritative.

57. On Quaker book ownership, libraries, and circulation, see Louisiane Ferlier, "Building Religious Communities with Books: The Quaker and Anglican Transatlantic Libraries, 1650–1710," in *Before the Public Library: Reading, Community, and Identity in the Atlantic World, 1650–1850*, ed. Mark Towsey and Kyle B. Roberts (Leiden: Brill, 2018), 34–51; J. William Frost, "Quaker Books in Colonial Pennsylvania," *Quaker History* 80, no. 1 (Spring 1991): 1–23; Wolf, *Book Culture* and *Library of James Logan*.

58. Francis Daniel Pastorius, "Copies of Letters [Letterbook]," 63–64, MS 8631, Pastorius Papers and Digital Library, HSP.

59. Lloyd Zachary (1701–1756), a nephew of Richard and Hannah Hill, later studied medicine at St. Thomas's Hospital in London under Dr. William Cheselden, established a successful medical practice in Philadelphia, and became one of the original trustees of the Philadelphia Academy. See Tolles, *Meeting House*, 226–27.

60. Pastorius, "Copies of Letters [Letterbook]," 113. In saying, "I deal plainly, being by Birth a Franconian," Pastorius is probably punning on the English adjective "frank," which sounds like the "Franc" in "Franconian." The German phrase "frank und frei" means "frankly" or "straight out." The effect of this pun clearly derives from Pastorius's interest in correspondences between the English and German languages. He most likely did not mean to imply that all people of the German region of Franconia were plain dealers.

61. Pastorius, "Bee-Hive," 2, 4.

62. Christoph Schweitzer has remarked that "the concept of originality was unimportant to authors of Pastorius's time. He followed pre-established patterns by finding suitable phrases for his thoughts in the classics, in Christian writings, especially the Bible, and in the rich emblematic literature." Schweitzer, introduction to *Deliciæ Hortenses or Garden-Recreations* and *Voluptates Apianæ* by Francis Daniel Pastorius, ed., Christoph E. Schweitzer, Studies in German Literature, Linguistics, and Culture 2 (Columbia, S.C.: Camden House, 1982), 5. For other literary treatments of Pastorius's work, see Arthur F. Engelbert, "Francis Daniel Pastorius in his Literary Activities" (Ph.D. diss., University of Pittsburgh, 1935); Patrick M. Erben, *A Harmony of the Spirits: Translation and the Language of Community in Early Pennsylvania.* (Chapel Hill: University of North Carolina Press for the Omohundro Institute of Early American History and Culture, 2012), esp. chaps. 2, 3, and 4; Erben, "'Honey-Combs' and 'Paper-Hives': Positioning Francis Daniel Pastorius's Manuscript Writings in Early Pennsylvania," *Early American Literature* 37, no. 2 (2002): 157–94; Erben, "Promoting Pennsylvania: Penn, Pastorius, and the Creation of a Transnational Community," *Resources for American Literary Study* 29 (2003–4): 25–65; Erben, "Writing and Reading a 'New English World': Literacy, Multilingualism, and the Formation of Community in Early America" (Ph.D. diss., Emory University, 2003); Hans Galinsky, "Three Literary Perspectives on the German in America: Immigrant, Homeland, and American Views," in *Eagle In the New World: German Immigration to Texas and America*, ed. Theodore Gish and Richard Spuler (College Station: Texas A&M University Press, 1986), 102–31; Harold Jantz, "German-American Literature: Some Further Perspectives," in *America and the Germans: An Assessment of a Three-Hundred-Year History*, ed. Frank Trommler and Joseph McVeigh (Philadelphia: University of Pennsylvania Press, 1985), 283–93; Jantz, "Pastorius, Intangible Values," *American-German Review* 25, no. 1 (1958): 4–7; Marion Dexter Learned, "From Pastorius's Bee-Hive or Bee-Stock," *Americana Germanica* 1, no. 4 (1897): 67–73; Harrison T. Meserole, "Francis Daniel Pastorius," in *American Poetry of the Seventeenth Century* (University Park: Pennsylvania State University Press, 1985), 293–94; Rosamund Rosenmeier, "Francis Daniel Pastorius," in *American Colonial Writers, 1606–1709*, ed. Emory Elliott, *Dictionary of Literary Biography*, vol. 24 (Detroit: Gale, 1984), 245–47; Oliver Scheiding, "The Poetry of British America: Francis Daniel Pastorius, 'Epibaterium, Or a hearty Congratulation to William Penn' (1699) and Richard Lewis, 'Food for Criticks' (1731)," in *A Handbook of American Poetry: Contexts—Developments—Readings*, ed. Scheiding. WVT Handbücher zum Literturwissenschaftlichen Studium 15 (Trier: Wissenschaftlicher Verlag Trier, 2014), 23–36; Christoph E. Schweitzer, "Excursus: German Baroque Literature in Colonial America," in *German Baroque Literature, The European Perspective*, ed. Gerhart Hoffmeister (New York: Ungar, 1983), 178–93; Schweitzer, "Francis Daniel Pastorius, the German-American Poet," *Yearbook of German-American Studies* 18 (1983): 21–28;

and DeElla Victoria Toms, "The Intellectual and Literary Background of Francis Daniel Pastorius" (Ph.D. diss., Northwestern University, 1953).

63. Pastorius, "Bee-Hive," 68.

64. On promotional literature, see Stephen Greenblatt, *Marvelous Possessions: The Wonder of the New World* (Chicago: University of Chicago Press, 1991); Myra Jehlen, *American Incarnation: The Individual, the Nation, and the Continent* (Cambridge, Mass.: Harvard University Press, 1986); Howard Mumford Jones, "The Colonial Impulse: An Analysis of the 'Promotion' Literature of Colonization," *Proceedings of the American Philosophical Society* 90, no. 2 (1946): 131–61; Paul J. Lindholdt, "The Significance of the Colonial Promotion Tract," in *Early American Literature and Culture: Essays Honoring Harrison T. Meserole*, ed. Kathryn Zabelle Derounian-Stodola (Newark: University of Delaware Press, 1992), 57–72; and Karen Schramm, "Promotion Literature," in *The Oxford Handbook of Early American Literature*, ed. Kevin J. Hayes (Oxford: Oxford University Press, 2008), 69–91.

65. William Penn's promotional texts on his newly acquired colony of Pennsylvania include: *A brief account of the province of Pennsylvania, lately granted by the king, under the great seal of England, to William Penn and his heirs and assigns* (London: Benjamin Clark, 1681); *A Further Account of the Province of Pennsylvania* [London, 1685]; *Information and Direction to Such Persons as are Inclined to America, More Especially Those Related to the Province of Pensilvania* ([London?]: reprinted 1686); *A letter from William Penn proprietary and governour of Pennsylvania in America: to the committee of the Free Society of Traders of that Province, residing in London . . . To which is added, an account of the city of Philadelphia* ([London]: Andrew Sowle, 1683); and *Some Account of the Province of Pennsilvania in America; Lately Granted under the Great Seal of England to William Penn, &c. Together with Priviledges and Powers necessary to the well-governing thereof. Made publick for the Information of such as are or may be disposed to Transport themselves or Servants into those Parts* (London: Benjamin Clark, 1681). Translations into German of Penn's accounts include: *Beschreibung der in America neu-erfundenen Provinz Pensylvanien* ([Hamburg]: Henrich Heuss, 1684); and *Eine Nachricht wegen der Landschaft Pennsilvania in America* (Amsterdam: Christoff Cunraden, 1681; 2nd ed., Frankfurt, 1683).

66. Because the *Deliciæ Hortenses* collection of poetry has been edited and published in a modern edition by Christoph Schweitzer—thus calling attention to Pastorius's greater oeuvre—poetry from the collection is not included in this reader. See Pastorius, *Deliciæ Hortenses*.

67. Scheiding, "Poetry of British America," 23–36.

68. On German Baroque poetry, a major literary influence on Pastorius, see Robert M. Browning, *German Baroque Poetry, 1618–1723* (University Park: Pennsylvania State University Press, 1971); A. G. de Capua, *German Baroque Poetry: Interpretive Readings* (Albany: State University of New York Press, 1973); Gerald Gillespie, *German Baroque Poetry* (New York: Twayne, 1971); Gerhart Hoffmeister, ed., *German Baroque Literature: The European Perspective* (New York: Ungar, 1983); Volker Meid, *Barocklyrik* (Stuttgart: Metzler, 1986); and Jeffrey L. Sammons, *Angelus Silesius* (New York: Twayne, 1967). For the application of the "Baroque" as a literary and historical period and aesthetic sensibility to colonial America, see Hans Galinsky, *Amerika und Europa: Sprachliche und sprachkünstlerische Wechselbeziehungen in amerikanischer Sicht* (Berlin: Langenscheidt, 1968), 137–80; Schweitzer, "Excursus."

69. On Opitz, see Barbara Becker-Cantarino, "Martin Opitz," in *German-Baroque Writers, 1580–1660, Dictionary of Literary Biography*, vol. 164, ed. James Hardin (Detroit: Gale, 1996), 256–68.

70. According to the *Oxford English Dictionary*, an "omer" was a dry measure in ancient Israel, equal to a tenth of an ephah (about 2.3 liters, or about 4.3 U.S. dry pints); it is also a pot or vessel holding such a measure.

71. Pastorius, "Ship-Mate-Ship," 8.

72. Ibid, 10.

73. Ibid, 10–35.

Part 1

PRINTED
TEXTS

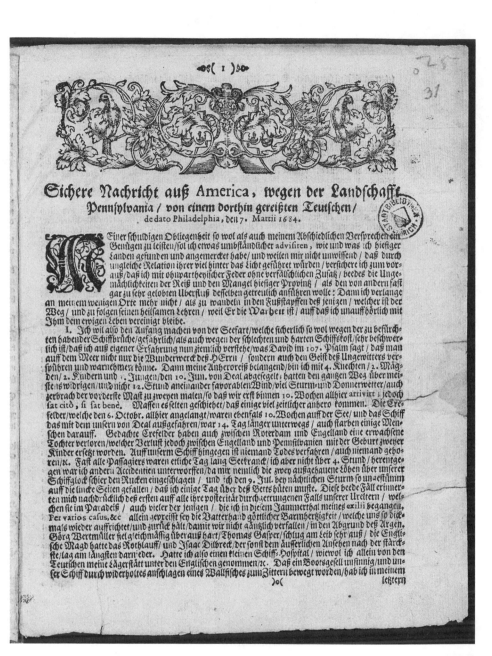

Sichere Nachricht auß America, wegen der Landschafft Pennsylvania / von einem dorthin gereißten Teutschen /

de dato Philadelphia, den 7. Martii 1684.

Einer schuldigen Obliegenheit so wol als auch meinem Abschiedlichen Versprechen ein Genügen zu leisten/sol ich etwas umbständlicher advisiren, wie und was ich hiesiger Landen gefunden und angemercket habe/ und weilen mir nicht unwissend / daß durch ungleiche Relation ihrer viel hinter das Licht geführet würden / versichere ich zum vorauß/daß ich mit ohnpartheyischer Feder ohne verfälschlichen Zusatz / beedes die Ungemächlichkeiten der Reiß und den Mangel hiesiger Provintz / als den von andern fast gar zu sehr gelobten Uberfluß desselben getreulich anführen wolle : Dann ich verlange an meinem wenigen Orte mehr nicht / als zu wandeln in den Fußstapffen deß jenigen / welcher ist der Weg / und zu folgen seinen heilsamen Lehren / weil Er die Warheit ist/ auff daß ich unauffhörlich mit Ihm dem ewigen Leben vereinigt bleibe.

I. Ich wil also den Anfang machen von der Seefart/welche sicherlich so wol wegen der zu befürchten habender Schiffbrüche/gefährlich/als auch wegen der schlechten und harten Schiffskost/sehr beschwerlich ist/daß ich auß eigener Erfahrung nun ziemlich verstehe/was David im 107. Psalm sagt / daß man auff dem Meer nicht nur die Wunderwercke deß HErrn / sondern auch den Geist deß Ungewitters verspühren und warnehmen könne. Dann meine Anheroreiß belangend/bin ich mit 4. Knechten / 2. Mägden / 2. Kindern und 1. Jungen/den 10. Jun. von Deal abgesegelt: hatten den gantzen Weg über meistens widrigen/und nicht 12.Stund aneinander favorablen Wind/viel Sturm/und Donnerwetter/auch zerbrach der vorderste Mast zu zweyen malen/so daß wir erst binnen 10. Wochen allhier arrivirt; jedoch sat cito, si sat bene. Massen es selten geschiehet/daß einige viel zeitlicher anhero kommen. Die Crefelder/welche den 6. Octobr. allhier angelangt/waren ebenfals 10.Wochen auff der See/ und das Schiff das mit dem unsern von Deal außgefahren/war 14. Tag länger unterwegs / auch starben einige Menschen darauff. Gedachte Crefelder haben auch zwischen Roterdam und Engelland eine erwachsene Tochter verloren/welcher Verlust jedoch zwischen Engelland und Pennsylvanien mit der Geburt zweyer Kinder ersetzt worden. Auff unserm Schiff hingegen ist niemand Todes verfahren / auch niemand geboren/ꝛc. Fast alle Passagiers waren etliche Tag lang Seekranck/ ich aber nicht über 4. Stund/ herentgegen war ich andern Accidentien unterworffen/da mir neimlich die zwey außgehauene Löben über unserer Schifflock schier den Rucken eingeschlagen / und ich den 9. Jul. bey nächtlichen Sturm so unaestümm auff die lincke Seiten gefallen/ daß ich einige Tag über deß Betts hüten muste. Diese beede Fäll erinnerten mich nachdrücklich deß ersten auff alle ihre posterität durchzerrungenen Falls unserer Ureltern / welchen sie im Paradeiß / auch vieler der jenigen / die ich in diesem Jammerthal meines exilii begangen. Per varios casus, ꝛc allein gepreißt sey die Vatterhand göttlicher Barmhertzigkeit /welche uns so dickmals wieder auffrichtet/und zurück hält/damit wir nicht gäntzlich verfallen / in den Abgrund deß Argen. Görg Wertmüller fiel gleichmässig überauß hart/Thomas Gasper/schlug am Leib sehr auß/ die Englische Magd hatte das Rothlauff/ und Isaac Dilbreck/der sonst dem äusserlichen Ansehen nach der stärckste/lag am längsten darnieder. Hatte ich also einen kleinen Schiff-Hospital / wiewol ich allein von den Teutschen meine Lägerstätt unter den Englischen genommen/ꝛc. Daß ein Bootsgesell unsinnig/und unser Schiff durch widerholtes anschlagen eines Wallfisches zum Zittern bewegt worden/hab ich in meinem

)◦(

letztern

Writings on the Founding of Germantown and Descriptions of Early Pennsylvania

Certain News from America, Concerning the Country of Pennsylvania
(*Sichere Nachricht auß America, wegen der Landschafft Pennsylvania*; 1684)

INTRODUCTION TO THE TEXT

In a never before published translation and new annotation by Patrick M. Erben, Francis Daniel Pastorius, *Sichere Nachricht auß America, wegen der Landschafft Pennsylvania, von einem dorthin gereißten Teutschen, de dato Philadelphia, den 7. Martii 1684*, Pastorius's first and most immediate account from Pennsylvania, is included here as the most representative of his descriptive and promotional writings. The only known original is located at the Zentralbibliothek Zürich in Switzerland; the present translation is based on a photographic reproduction of the Zürich original by Marion Dexter Learned and published in his *Life of Francis Daniel Pastorius* (Philadelphia: Campbell, 1908).

Pastorius authored this text as a manuscript report to the Pietist members of the German Society (later Frankfurt Land Company), who had appointed him as agent for their land purchases. Recognizing its potential appeal as a promotional tract for immigrants from other German-speaking states, especially religious dissidents such as Quakers, Anabaptists, and other Pietists, they had *Sichere Nachricht* printed as a small pamphlet (with no imprint and with neither printer nor publication place or date shown). Their effort to print and distribute Pastorius's report already bespeaks their apparent goal—to promote immigration to Pennsylvania and to sell land to German-speaking settlers rather than to move there themselves.

It is unclear how many copies of *Sichere Nachricht* were printed and distributed, but the extreme rarity of the text today does not necessarily imply a small print run. Thus almanacs were among the most numerous and widely distributed print publications in early America, yet many issues are extremely rare today because of their ephemeral nature: when the year covered by an almanac was over, the paper they were printed on would be used for other purposes. Similarly, small promotional tracts would most likely also be repurposed either by the immigrants who had carried them to America or by readers remaining in Europe who ultimately decided against immigration.

Pastorius's account was disseminated not only in print but also in manuscript copies through a network of Pietist and Quaker sympathizers throughout the German-speaking states. For example, a handwritten transcription appears in a collection of German and Dutch reports from Pennsylvania gathered by the Lübeck pastor Jaspar Könneken.[1] The strong interest in accounts from Pennsylvania, especially those by Pastorius, sent as reports and letters to his Pietist sponsors and to his father, Melchior Adam Pastorius, becomes evident when surveying their successive publications. The elder Pastorius was clearly in contact with the Frankfurt Pietists and took great interest in publicizing his son's work and achievements in America: a broadside print of a letter by Pastorius to his father and stepmother was published alongside *Sichere Nachricht*, though it is much shorter and far less detailed.[2] Melchior Adam's promotion of his son's writings from Pennsylvania continued with the publication of Francis Daniel's *Kurtze geographische Beschreibung der letztmahls erfundenen Americanischen landschafft Pensylvania*, which combined details already related in *Sichere Nachricht* with information from letters written to his father and family, and which the elder Pastorius included as an appendix to his own *Kurtze Beschreibung der Reichs-Stadt Windsheim* (Nuremberg, 1692). It must have given Melchior Adam great pleasure to publish side-by-side reports of the two towns—one in Germany and one in America—where he and his son were mayors.

In the late nineteenth and early twentieth centuries, German American historians, literary scholars, genealogists, and even public figures such as Oswald Seidensticker, Marion Dexter Learned, and Samuel W. Pennypacker would engage with various elements of Pastorius's work, including translations of his promotional writings. Pennypacker published a translation of *Sichere Nachricht* (translator unnamed) in his *Settlement of Germantown, Pennsylvania, and the Beginning of German Emigration to*

1. Jaspar Könneken [Caspar Köhn], MS fol. 356–72, "Geistliches Ministerium" [1683–84], Archiv der Hansestadt Lübeck, Germany. For an English-language edition of this collection, see Könneken, *Letters relating to the Settlement of Germantown in Pennsylvania, 1683–4: From the Könneken Manuscript in the Ministerial-Archive of Lübeck,* trans. and ed. Julius Friedrich Sachse (Lübeck and Philadelphia, 1903).
2. Francis Daniel Pastorius, "Copia, eines von einem Sohn an seine Eltern auss America abgelassenen Brieffes sub dato Philadelphia, den 7. Martii 1684." Photographic reproduction of original at the Zentralbibliothek Zürich (Zurich Central Library) in Marion Dexter Learned, *The Life of Francis Daniel Pastorius* (Philadelphia: Campbell, 1908), unnumbered page following 124.

North America (1899), and a new translation of both *Sichere Nachricht* and *Beschreibung* by Gertrude Selwyn Kimball appeared in *Narratives of Early Pennsylvania, West New Jersey and Delaware*, edited by Albert Cook Myers (1912). Kimball's translation, in turn, has been excerpted in several late twentieth-century anthologies of American literature emphasizing multilingual beginnings (e.g., in Carla Mulford's *Early American Writings*, 2001).

Although Kimball's translation and the annotations by Myers are generally strong, they are more than a century old, and their publication, diction, and editorial treatment remain enmeshed in the late nineteenth- and early twentieth-century ethos of discovering and appraising specific *national* origins. As demonstrated in our introduction to this reader, Pastorius's work unfolded primarily against the background of radical Protestant—especially Quaker and Pietist—reform and transatlantic migration. Our new translation and edition take into account research on Pietist communication networks and the circulation of Pietist writings in both manuscript and print. For example, the original German text of *Sichere Nachricht* obscures the identity of the Pietists of the German Society in Frankfurt, who had purchased land in Pennsylvania and appointed Pastorius as their attorney, by simply printing "N. N." or "Nomen Nescio" (I do not know the name). The insertion of "Germans" by Kimball or Myers perhaps squares with the attempt of the original publisher to broaden the appeal of the text beyond the narrow concerns of a group of Protestant dissidents by withholding their names. And, by using "Frankfurters" instead, the transcription of *Sichere Nachricht* in the Könneken manuscript only indirectly refers to Pastorius's Frankfurt Pietist sponsors. Nevertheless, the Kimball translation and Myers annotations are still highly usable and available online via Google Books.

Pastorius's enthusiasm for participating in William Penn's "holy experiment" is still highly visible in *Sichere Nachricht*: as he senses and tries to deal with the Pietists' reluctance to follow him to America, Pastorius builds—with both subtlety and pathos—a dual narrative of exile and new beginnings, of promises fulfilled (William Penn's granting of the land) and promises broken (the Pietists' anticipated reneging on theirs). Unlike the later *Beschreibung*, *Sichere Nachricht* is not yet overdetermined by various publication and promotion schemes but provides a perspective in which almost everything is in a state of flux: the legal status of the settlement, the composition and the inhabitants of the presumed *German* town, the natural and economic opportunities, and the degree of spiritual and personal rejuvenation and transformation that induced Pastorius to take the decisive step to leave everything behind. Though translated and republished before, *Sichere Nachricht* forms the indispensable beginning of both Pastorius's journey to America and the unfolding of his writings and thought about his life there.

Certain News from America, Concerning the Country of Pennsylvania,
by a German who traveled there, dated Philadelphia, March 7, 1684.

To fulfill my dutiful obligation as well as my parting promise, I will report in some more detail how I have found and what I have observed in these lands here; and because I am not unaware that through uneven accounts many have been deceived, I assure you in advance that I will, with impartial pen and without any falsifying additions, state faithfully both the inconveniences of the journey and the shortcoming of this province, as well as the almost too greatly praised abundance of the same: for in my lowly place I desire nothing more than to walk in the footsteps of Him who is the way and to follow His saving teachings, because He is the truth, so that I will forever more remain joined with Him in eternal life.

I. Thus I will begin with the sea voyage, which is certainly dangerous because of the shipwrecks that are to be feared and very arduous because of the poor and hard fare on board. I therefore now understand very closely what David says in Psalm 107,[3] that at sea one may feel and perceive not only the wonderful works of the Lord but also the spirit of the storm. Concerning my passage hither: I departed from Deal[4] with four male servants, two female servants, two children, and one youth[5] on June 10 and had the whole way mostly adverse and not even twelve hours at a time favorable wind, as well as many tempests and thunderstorms. Also, the foremast broke twice, so that we arrived here only after ten weeks; however, *sat citò, si sat benè*,[6] because it rarely happens that anyone comes here much quicker. The Crefelders,[7] who arrived here on October 6, were also at sea for ten weeks, and the ship that left with us from Deal was on its way 14 days longer, and several people died on it. Said Crefelders also lost an adult

3. Psalm 107:23–24: "Others went out on the sea in ships; / they were merchants on the mighty waters. / They saw the works of the LORD, / his wonderful deeds in the deep."

4. A historic port town in Kent, England, a few miles northeast of Dover, Deal was the last place in Europe that Pastorius saw before his departure for America in 1683.

5. In his genealogical sketch in the "Bee-Hive," Pastorius identifies the individuals in his party as Jacob Shoemaker (Schumacher), Georg Wertmüller, Isaac Dilbeck, his wife, Marieke, their two boys, Abraham and Jacob, Thomas Gasper, Cunrad Backer (Conrad Rutter) and an "English maid, called Frances Simson" (223). The servants in Pastorius's group were paid by the Frankfurt Land Company (originally, the "German Society") to establish the settlement in Pennsylvania and presumably prepare, along with Pastorius, for the arrival of the Frankfurt Pietists; thus they were not Pastorius's personal servants but rather employees he was meant to supervise. Nevertheless, his references to them reveal his own social elitism and upper-class family background.

6. "'Soon enough, if but well enough.'" Attributed to Saint Jerome.

7. On his way to Pennsylvania, Pastorius had visited the Quaker meeting at Krefeld (modern spelling) on the lower Rhine, a community with connections to English Quakers as well as the Pietist community in Frankfurt that had chosen Pastorius as their representative. The Krefeld Quakers had also purchased land in Pennsylvania and agreed to let Pastorius work as their agent upon arriving in Pennsylvania. Thirteen Quaker families from Krefeld arrived in Philadelphia in October 1683 and settled in the newly surveyed Germantown.

daughter between Rotterdam and England, a loss that was nevertheless made up by the birth of two children between England and Pennsylvania. On our ship, however, no one died and no one was born, etc. Almost all passengers were seasick for several days but myself only four hours. Yet I was subject to several other accidents, as two carved lions over the ship's bell fell down and almost broke my back; also, during a nightly storm on July 9, I fell so hard on my left side that I was confined to bed for several days. These two incidents shall remind me emphatically of the first fall of our forebears in paradise, which they passed down to all their posterity, but also of the many others I committed in this vale of misery of my exile.[8] *Per varios casus, etc.*[9] Praise be alone to the fatherly hand of divine mercy, which lifts us up so often and holds us back so that we do not utterly fall into the abyss of evil. Georg Wertmüller also fell extremely hard, Thomas Gasper had a bad rash on his torso, the English maidservant had an erysipelas, and Isaac Dilbeck, who otherwise seemed the strongest from his outward appearance, was ill for the longest time. Thus I had a small ship hospital, though I alone among the Germans took my berth among the English, etc. That a sailor went insane and that our ship was shaken by a whale repeatedly slamming against it, I already reported in my previous letter. The diet on board was rather poor, and we lived *medicè ac modice*.[10] Every ten people received weekly three pounds of butter, daily four jugs of beer and two jugs of water, everyone for lunch two bowls of peas, four lunches per week meat, and three lunches of fish, which we had to prepare with our own butter; and we had to save enough of each lunch so we could have food left for supper. The worst part of it all was that both the meat and the fish were salted and stank to such a degree that we could barely enjoy half of it. And had I not, upon the advice of good friends in England, provisioned myself with various refreshments, it probably would have gone very badly. Thus, it has to be observed by all who are willing to travel hither that they should either, if there are many of them, cover their own food or negotiate with the captain concerning the quantity and quality, i.e., how much and of what kind of food they should receive daily. And in order to bind him more closely to it, one has to hold back some of the money for the passage to be paid over here. Also, if possible, one should

8. Although Pastorius often referred to his earthly life as a form of exile (from God), he also considered his immigration to Pennsylvania to be an exile from his former life in Europe.

9. "'Through various hazards and events.'" Pastorius is quoting from Virgil's *Aeneid*, book 1, lines 204–5: "Per varios casus, per tot discrimina rerum / tendimus in Latium" (Through various hazards and events / we make our way into Latium). He thus links his journey to Pennsylvania to two formative epics in Western culture— Genesis, with Adam and Eve's expulsion from paradise, and the *Aeneid*, with Aeneas's exile from Troy and subsequent founding of Rome.

10. "Medically and moderately." Pastorius is punning on the fact that he and his shipmates were both sick and poorly fed.

arrange for a ship that departs for the city of Philadelphia, because with the others that stop in Upland, one is subjected to all kinds of inconveniences.[11]

My company consisted of many sorts of people. There was doctor of medicine with his wife and eight children,[12] a French captain, a Dutch cake baker, a pharmacist, glass blower, stone mason, blacksmith, cartwright, cabinet maker, cooper, hat maker, cobbler, tailor, gardener, farmer, seamstresses, etc.,[13] in all some 80 persons besides the crew. They were not only different regarding their age (the oldest woman was 60 years old, the youngest child only twelve weeks old) and their abovementioned trades, but also of such different religions and conduct that the ship, which carried them hither, could not unfittingly be compared to Noah's Ark, provided that not more unclean than clean (rational) animals are found in it.[14] Among my servants some belong to the Roman Catholic, the Lutheran, the Calvinist, the Anabaptist, and the Anglican Church but only one Quaker. On August 11, we cast the lead[15] for the first time and realized that we were close to the great sandbank and thus had to backtrack in order to sail around it, running more than 100 miles off course.

On the 16th of the same month we joyfully came within sight of America and, on the morning of the 18th, arrived in Delaware Bay, which is 30 English miles long, 15 wide, and also of such uneven depths that our ship, drawing 13 feet of water, repeatedly got stuck upon the sand.

11. The small town of Upland is located about fifteen miles downriver from Philadelphia. The inconveniences Pastorius mentions were probably related to overland travel to Philadelphia through marshy areas along the Delaware River.

12. One of the most important friends Pastorius found on his passage to America was the Welsh physician and prominent Quaker Thomas Lloyd (1640–1694), a close confidant of William Penn, who chose Lloyd to be president of the Provincial Council and lieutenant governor from 1690 to 1693. During the Keithian controversy, Lloyd sided with the orthodox Quakers against George Keith and his followers. After Lloyd's early death, Pastorius remained in close contact with his children, especially Lloyd's daughters Hannah Hill, Rachel Preston, and Mary Norris. Pastorius wrote a cycle of anniversary poems, entitled "Ship-Mate-Ship," dedicated to Lloyd and his family on the anniversaries of their joint passage on the ship *America* and their landing in Philadelphia. These poems are published for the first time in chapter 5 of this reader.

13. Pastorius did not record the identity of these other individuals in his letters or other accounts of his journey, his point here being to report the great diversity among his fellow travelers, who represented many nations, religions, and walks of life.

14. Pastorius here compares the human passengers on his ship, the *America*, to the animals on board Noah's Ark in the Book of Genesis. According to Old Testament law, animals were separated into ritually clean (animals that are allowed as food or sacrifice, such as cattle, sheep, and goats) and unclean (all other animals). By tying "rational" as a definition to "clean," Pastorius may be distinguishing the mental faculties of the passengers. Given the spiritual objective of his journey, however, a distinction between believers and unbelievers (converted and unconverted) individuals may be more likely. Either way, Pastorius purposefully seems to leave open which passengers belong to which group.

15. Sounded the depth of the ocean.

On the 20th we passed New Castle,[16] Upland, and Dunicum[17] and happily arrived, praise be to God, at dusk in Philadelphia. There I delivered on the following day the letters I had with me to W[illiam] Penn and was received by him with affectionate friendliness. Of this very worthy man and famed ruler, I should properly

II. write many things, but my quill (though it is from an eagle[18] that recently a so-called savage brought to my house) is far too weak to express the high virtues of this Christian, for this he is indeed. He frequently asks me to dine with him and also to walk or ride in his always edifying company. And because I was recently gone from here for eight days in order to fetch provisions from New Castle, he did not see me for that length of time and came to my little house himself and desired I should be his guest several times a week, etc. He heartily loves the [Frankfurters],[19] and he once said publicly in my presence to his councilors and attendants: I love the [Frankfurters], and I want that you should love them too, even though I have otherwise never heard a similar command from him. These words pleased me so much more because they fully agree with God's command (see 1 John 3:23).[20] I can at the moment say no more than that Will[iam] Penn is a man who honors God and is honored by Him in return: who loves what is good and is justifiably loved by all good people, etc. I do not doubt that many will come here themselves and experience in deed that my pen has in this matter not written enough.

III. Of the quality of the land I can report anything certain only after one or more years of experience; the Swedes and Dutch,[21] who have cultivated the land for 20 years

16. New Castle, Delaware, is located on the mouth of the Delaware River at the northern end of Delaware Bay. Though originally settled by the Dutch West India Company, it became part of Pennsylvania with Charles II's charter to William Penn in 1681 and then the colonial capital of Delaware after its split from Pennsylvania in 1704.

17. Pastorius is referring to Tinicum, a township and island southwest of Philadelphia; it is the site of the first recorded European settlement in what is today Pennsylvania by Swedish colonists in 1643.

18. In Europe, quill pens were most commonly made from goose feathers, and it would have seemed curious to European readers that Pastorius was using a quill made from an eagle feather. Pastorius frequently sets up contrasts between the material conditions of writing in Europe and America, including comparisons of the finer and coarser paper available on either side of the Atlantic.

19. Here "N. N." (*Nomen nescio*, i.e., "I do not know the name") was inserted in the printed text, probably to conceal the original recipients of Pastorius's letter and make the text more applicable to a wider readership in German-speaking territories. Handwritten copies of Pastorius's letter (such as the version in the Könneken manuscripts located in the Archiv der Hansestadt Lübeck, Germany) include the word "Frankfurters," reflecting Penn's high regard for the Frankfurt Pietists (also known as "Saalhof Pietists," after the place where they met) whom he had visited on a missionary journey with other Quakers in 1677. In 1683, Penn would welcome Pastorius as their representative to Pennsylvania.

20. 1 John 3:23: "And this is his command: to believe in the name of his Son, Jesus Christ, and to love one another as he commanded us."

21. The colony of New Sweden was established on the lower Delaware River from 1638 to 1655, when it was conquered by Dutch colonial forces in the Second Northern War. Henry Hudson began exploring and claiming land along the east coast of North America for the Dutch East India Company in 1609, with the United Netherlands giving a patent to the New Netherland Company in 1614, which surveyed and claimed the Delaware River valley. After several Anglo-Dutch wars, the Netherlands ceded New Netherland to the English in 1674.

or longer, are in this as well as in most other matters double-tongued,[22] *laudatur ab his, culpatur ab illis.*[23] It is certain that the soil does not lack in fertility, and it would reward, just as in Europe, the labor of our hands, if one were to work and manure it properly, which are the two things it lacks the most. For the abovementioned old inhabitants are poor agriculturists, for some of them have neither barns nor stables, leave their grain harvest lying in the open air for several years without threshing it, and let their cattle, horses, milk cows, and pigs, etc. run summer and winter in the woods, which is why they reap little benefit from them. Certainly, the penance with which God has punished Adam's disobedience so that he must eat his bread by the sweat of his brow also applies to his descendants in these lands, and thus those who hope to spare their hands may stay where they are; *Hic opus, hic labor est.*[24] And it is not enough to bring money over here without the inclination to work, for it runs through your fingers, and I may say with Solomon: it has wings.[25] Inasmuch as in the past year many people from both England and Ireland, as well as Barbados and other American islands, arrived here and this province does not yet produce sufficient food-stuffs for such a multitude, all victuals are rather expensive and most of the money leaves the country for it. However, we hope to gain with time a surplus in both, because W. Penn will coin money and agriculture will be improved, etc. Workers and farmers are first most needed here, and I rather wish for a dozen strong Tyrolese to cut down the thick oak trees, for wherever one turns, one may say: *Itur in antiquam sylvam.*[26] Everything is but a forest and very few open places are to be found, in which, as in several other things, my preconceived hope has been betrayed, as for example that in this kind of wild orchard neither apples nor pears are to be found and also that during this very cold winter neither deer nor turkey etc. were to be found. The wild grapes are rather small and more suited to make vinegar than wine; the walnuts have very thick shells and only so few thick kernels in them that the difficulty of cracking them is barely worth it. The chestnuts and hazelnuts, however, are a bit tastier, as are the peaches, apples, and pears, and no fault is to be found with them, only that there are not as many as some people desire, etc. However, we have more rattlesnakes (whose bite is deadly) in this country than we would like. I

Nevertheless, in the 1680s, the Delaware River valley was still home to several thriving Dutch and Swedish settlements. The Swedish Lutheran church of Gloria Dei was established in 1700, for example, and served as the site of the ordination of the German Pietist theologian Justus Falckner in 1703.

22. They are deceitful or duplicitous.

23. "'He is praised by some, condemned by others.'" Horace, *Satires*, book 1, satire 2, line 11.

24. "'This is the hard work, this is the toil,'" Virgil, *Aeneid*, book 6, line 190.

25. Pastorius is alluding to Proverbs 23:5: "Cast but a glance at riches, and they are gone, for they will surely sprout wings and fly off to the sky like an eagle."

26. "'They [Aeneas and Achates] are gone into the ancient forest,'" Virgil, *Aeneid*, book 6, line 179. The full line reads: "Itur in antiquam silvam, stabula alta ferarum" (They are gone into the ancient forest, the deep coverts of wild beasts).

further have to add *tanquam testis oculatus*[27] that on October 16 I found pretty (March) violets in the woods. *Item*, after I laid out the city of Germantown on October 24, and returned with seven others on the 25th, we came across a wild grapevine that had run up a tree and carried about 400 grapes, for which we cut the tree down and all eight of us got our fill and each could even take home a hat full of grapes. Also, when I was eating with William Penn on August 25, after the meal a single root of barley was brought in, which had grown in a garden here and had 50 stalks on it. However, not all seeds produce this much and it is as we say: one swallow does not make a summer. Yet I do not doubt that we will soon come upon more such examples of fruitfulness, when we seriously put the plow to the land. I lament the vines that I brought with me, for they were moistened with seawater when we were already in Delaware Bay, and all but two were ruined. The frequently mentioned W. Penn has planted a vineyard of French grapevines, and its growth may be viewed with pleasure and reminded me, when I saw them, of the 15th chapter of John[28] and lead me to a contemplative state of mind.

IV. Philadelphia daily increases more and more in houses and inhabitants, and now a jailhouse is being built so that those, who do not want to live in a Philadelphian manner, may be disciplined, because there are many here to whom fittingly applies what the dear friend [Jacob van de Walle][29] notes in his letter that we have more trouble with the spoiled Christians than with the Indians. Moreover, towns are being laid out here and there; specifically, the [German] Society has begun to build a town named Frankfurt about 1.5 miles from here, where they have erected a mill and glassmaker's shop. Not far from there lies our Germantown, where already 42 people live in 12 households; they are mostly linen weavers and not too skilled for agriculture. These upright people have used all their fortune on the journey so that, if they had not received an advance on provisions from William Penn, they by necessity would have to serve others. They have already bravely paved the way to the said Germantown by frequently going back and forth, and I cannot say more about that town than that it is situated on fruitful black soil and half surrounded like a natural fortification by charming springs. The main street herein is 60 and the cross street is 40 feet wide; each family has a farmstead of three acres, etc.

V. Concerning the inhabitants, I cannot classify them better than into the natural and transplanted ones, for if I called the former wild and the latter Christians, I would do many among both a great injustice. Of the latter I already mentioned above that the

27. "As an eyewitness."

28. Here Pastorius returns once again to the theme of fruitfulness—both physical and spiritual. John 15:5: "I am the vine: you are the branches. If a man remains in me and I in him, he will bear much fruit; apart from me you can do nothing."

29. Jacob or Jacobus van der Walle was a member of Pastorius's Pietist circle in Frankfurt and an investor in the Frankfurt Land Company, which appointed Pastorius as their agent and purchased 15,000 acres of land in Pennsylvania.

ship coming over here cannot be compared to Noah's Ark.[30] The Lutheran preacher, who is supposed to show the Swedes, as a *statua Mercurialis*,[31] the way to heaven, is, to put it in one word, a drunkard.[32] Similarly, there are many false coins[33] and other wicked persons here, whom, in good time, the wind of divine retribution will hopefully blow away like the chaff; on the other hand, there is also no lack of god-fearing people, and I may say in all honesty that in Europe one would nowhere see posted as it is in our Philadelphia, for example, that someone has found this or that and the person who lost it may get in touch with him, but also the reverse: this and that has been lost and who returns it will receive a reward, etc.

Of these recently transplanted foreigners I will now not say any more other than that among them several Germans can be found, who have already lived in this land 20 years and have thus become naturalized, such as people from Silesia, Brandenburg, Holstein, Switzerland, etc. and even someone from Nuremberg, named Jan Jaquet; but of the *per errorem*[34] so-called savages I briefly want to give my account. The first whom I saw were two of them who at Upland approached our ship in a canoe. I presented them a swig of brandy, for which they wanted to pay me with a sixpence, and because I refused such payment, they gave me the hand and said, "Thanks, brother!" They have strong limbs, a swarthy body and paint their face red, blue, etc. in all various manners. In summer they go completely naked, except that they cover their private parts with a cloth, and in winter hang thick woolen cloth on themselves. They have coal-black hair, even though the Swedish children who are born here have snow-white hair, etc. I once ate with W. Penn, when one of their kings sat with us at the table, and W. Penn (who can speak their language rather well) told him that I was a German, etc. He also came to my house on October 3, and another king and queen on December 12. Also, many common people come running to me frequently, but I almost always show them my love with a piece of bread and a drink of beer, through which a mutual love is awakened in them, and they consistently call me "Teutschmann,"[35] also "Carissimo" (that is, brother). NB: their language is manly and in my estimation seems hardly inferior to the Italian in

30. Although earlier in the text Pastorius *does* compare the passengers on his ship to the passengers on Noah's Ark, he qualifies them here as not sufficiently similar because he felt that many of the Christians on their way to Pennsylvania did not deserve that title and would thus be counted among the "unclean" animals on the Ark.

31. "Statue of Mercury," Mercury being not only the god of travelers and merchants but also of thieves and tricksters.

32. Most likely, Pastorius is referring to Jacob or Jacobus Fabritius, a Dutch-speaking Lutheran minister who was said to be either German or Polish by birth. Fabritius had been accused of drunkenness and unruly behavior at his first employment in New York City (as noted in the *Documentary History of the State of New-York*), from where he moved to Wicaco in New Sweden (Pennsylvania) to become the pastor of the Swedish Lutheran church of Gloria Dei.

33. By metaphorically calling the Swedish settlers "false coins," Pastorius means they are deceitful or fraudulent people.

34. "Erroneously."

35. "German man" or "German."

gravity, etc. Concerning their manner and nature, one has to further distinguish them, so to speak, in those who have conversed with the Christians for a while and those who have just begun coming out of their hovels. For the former are sly and crafty, for which they have to thank the abovementioned Mouth-Christians:[36] *semper enim aliquid haret.*[37] One of those recently pawned his carrying strap as a pledge that he would bring me a turkey, but he instead brought me an eagle and tried to tell me it was turkey, etc. But when I let him know that I had seen other eagles, he confessed to a Swede (who happened to be there) that he did it as a fraud, assuming I would not know such birds yet, because we had just arrived in this land. Another tasted the brandy at my fireplace in this manner: he stuck his finger in it and then into the fire in order to see whether water was mixed into it, etc. etc. The latter ones, however, have an honest disposition, offend nobody, and we do not need to fear them at all. One thing lately touched my heart, when I was considering the sincere admonition of our savior that we, his disciples, should not worry about the next day, as the pagans do.[38] Ah, I thought to myself, how often everything is now the reverse! When we Christians are not provisioned for one or more years, how fainthearted we get? But these pagans leave their care to GOD with a wonderful resignation: I once saw four of them eating together; the ground was both their table and bench; a pumpkin boiled in plain water without butter or seasoning boiled was their sole meal; their spoons were shells, which they used to scoop up the warm water, and their plates were oak leaves, which they neither had to wash after their meal nor have much trouble finding when needed again. Ah, dear friends, let us learn from these people not to resist contentment, so that in the future they do not put us to shame in front of the judgment seat of Jesus Christ, etc. etc.[39]

Of the people who came over here with me, a half dozen has already passed away, but my servants and I have been in good health and appetite the entire time, except that Isaac Dilbeck was a bit unwell for eight days and Jacob Schumacher hit himself in the foot with an axe on October 1st and was unable to work for a week, etc. Of the Crefelders, no one has died yet, except Herman op den Graeff's[40] late mother, who, tired of these worldly vanities, departed soon after her arrival here to enjoy the joys

36. Those who call themselves "Christians" but do not follow their profession of faith in their actions.

37. Probably quoting from Francis Bacon, *De Augmentis Scientiarum* (1623), here Pastorius means to say, "'Audacter calumniare, semper aliquid haeret'" (Slander boldly, something always sticks). Pastorius was an avid reader of Bacon.

38. See Matthew 6:25, 32: "Therefore I tell you, do not worry about your life, what you will eat or drink: or about your body, what you will wear. . . . For the pagans run after all these things, and your heavenly Father knows that you need them."

39. Pastorius is referring to 2 Corinthians 5:10: "For we must all appear before the judgment seat of Christ, that each one may receive what is due him for the things done while in the body, whether good or bad."

40. Herman op den Graeff was one of the leaders of the thirteen Krefeld Quakers who settled Germantown.

of heaven. The wife of Abraham Tunesen,[41] our farm tenant, has now been lying in my little house in a very weak condition for more than two months, was completely insensible for a while but is recovering from day to day.

Concerning the purchased land: it is divided into three types, namely, first the 15,000 acres together in one piece and on a navigable water. Second, 300 acres in the city's liberties, which is the stretch of land between the Delaware and the Schuylkill. Third, three lots in the city to build houses. When, after my arrival, I asked W. Penn for the warrants to survey the said three different parts and bring them into possession, his answer was at first that concerning

I. That the three lots in the city, and the 300 acres in its liberties not legally belong to the [Frankfurt Company] because they had been purchased after He, William Penn, had already departed from England and the books had been closed, &c. After I represented to him, however, that you are the vanguard of all Germans and thus to be taken into special consideration, etc., he had three lots next to one another surveyed from the portion of his youngest son.[42]

&c.   12.   11.   10.   9.   8.   7.   6.   5.   4.   3.   2.   1.

The double line represents the Delaware River, on which the city[43] is situated, but the numbers show the location of the following houses and farmsteads: 1. A Swede named Swan. 2. The Lutheran Church. 3. The pastor's house. 4. An English man. 5. A Swede named Andres. 6. William Penn's youngest son. 7. The [Frankfurt Company]. 8. Fort Philip. 9. The Society[44] and its trading house. 10. The Blue Anchor Inn.[45] 11. James Claypoole[46] 12. etc. There are other houses, which are unnecessary to be named here. Thus, first lies the Delaware, then there is a broad street, after which follows our first lot, 100 feet wide and 400 long, at whose end comes an alley, then our second lot, of the same width and length, then another alley, and finally our third lot. On each lot can be built two houses in the front and two in the back next to each other. In sum, twelve houses with their proper farmsteads[47] may be built suitably, all facing the street, etc. If

41. Abraham Tunesen was also one of the original Krefeld settlers; his surname is variously spelled "Tunesen," "Tunis," or "Tünies."

42. William Penn's youngest son at the time was William Penn Jr. (1679–1720).

43. Philadelphia.

44. The Free Society of Traders, a joint-stock company founded by several prominent Quakers in 1681 to promote the settlement and economic development of Pennsylvania, was dissolved in 1723.

45. A wooden structure built in 1681, the Blue Anchor Inn served as a famous tavern in Philadelphia for two hundred years.

46. A Quaker merchant and founding member of the Free Society of Traders, James Claypoole (1634–1687) purchased 5,000 acres of land in Pennsylvania and settled there in 1683.

47. Though Pastorius is discussing the city lots in Philadelphia, he probably expected even settlers living in the city to have at least some access to agricultural land and income. This idea also agrees with William Penn's plan for the city, which incorporated ample greenspace for gardening and farming.

we do not want to lose these lots, however, we necessarily have to build three houses, i.e. one house on each lot, within two years. With our servant, I have already built a small house on the front lot, half below and half above the ground. Although it is only 30 feet long and 15 wide, it could accommodate 20 people when the Crefelders were staying with me. On the oilpaper window above the door, I wrote: *Parva domus, sed amica bonis, procul este prophani.*[48] W. Penn recently saw it and was pleased. Moreover, I dug a seven foot deep, twelve foot wide, and 20 foot long cellar on the Delaware River and am now occupied with building a stable. Having cleared all three lots of trees, I will soon fence them in and plant Indian corn. NB: Fencing in all the land is exceedingly difficult and expensive, but we cannot do without it because of the horses, cows, and pigs running free. Also, one cannot sow any rye or wheat in such new land in the first year, but only Indian (or, as it is called among you, Turkish) corn, which however neither tastes nor satisfies as well.

II. Concerning the three hundred acres in the city's liberties, I appealed several times to W. Penn and especially urged that B. Furly[49] had promised those as part of the sale, etc. Yet he did not want to agree to it for a long time, for the reason that only as much had been reserved for the city's liberties as purchasers of 5000 acres had been found while he was still in England, among which the [Frankfurters] had not been included. After I submitted another petition, he finally gave me the good news a few days ago that he, out of an especially favorable disposition toward you, would still grant me the said 300 acres, but no other people who had purchased after the books had been closed, no matter who they are. I thus intend to make a beginning by planting Indian corn soon on these 300 acres (which are located no more than half an hour from this city), so we are better able to raise cows and pigs, increase our fruitfulness, and thus help those who come over later.[50]

III. Concerning the 15,000 acres, two main difficulties occurred, namely that W. Penn did not want to assign all in one piece so that no large areas in the land

48. "'A small house, but a friend to the good; stay away, ye profane!'" Virgil, *Aeneid*, book 6, line 258. In this section of the Roman epic, Aeneas visits the temple of Apollo at Cumae, where the Sibyl (Apollo's priestess) helps him find the opening to the underworld by performing animal sacrifices. When the ground shakes and opens a gaping chasm, the Sibyl wards off dark creatures of the underworld by crying out: "Stay away, O stay away, ye profane!"

49. An English Quaker who permanently settled in the Dutch port city of Rotterdam, where he was successful as a shipping merchant, Benjamin Furly (1636–1714) had widespread connections to dissident Protestants across Europe, including the Frankfurt Pietists. He thus became William Penn's chief agent on the Continent for the sale of Pennsylvania land and served as a clearinghouse for information about Penn's colony. Though Furly's wide-ranging reading, eclectic learning, and unorthodox spiritual ideas sometimes put him at odds with more mainstream Quakers, they also attracted a range of notable early Enlightenment thinkers as well as religious radicals, such as John Locke and Franciscus Mercurius van Helmont, who were known to stay at his home. A catalog of Furly's library was printed in 1714 (*Bibliotheca Furliana*) and provides an insight into Furly's comprehensive intellectual interests.

50. Here Pastorius again hints at the promise of his Frankfurt friends to join him in Pennsylvania; his having put all affairs in good order, they presumably had few excuses not to do so.

would be unsettled or empty, also not on the Delaware River, where everything had already been taken up by others anyway. Nevertheless, after I repeatedly put forth orally and in writing that it would be prejudicial toward us and our descendants to be stuck completely among the English, especially since B. Furly had sent the [Frankfurters] Penn's letter, in which He had promised our nation something different, etc., He finally gave me a warrant to have our land together in one piece, provided that we could settle within a year 30 families on the 15,000 acres, in three townships, with ten households each, counting the three that are already here (lacking the 30 families, however, he does not want to be held to the agreement to give the land all in one piece). I, for my small part, certainly wish that we could receive a small separate province and thus prevent all the more any kind of oppression. If one of you could become free in yourself to come over here and bring that many families, all of your best interest would be advanced incomparably, especially as He, William Penn, just told me the day before yesterday, he would in that case prefer you to all the English who made their purchase earlier but are not here yet and assign certain privileges to our New Franconia (as he called our designated land). But if it would be too difficult for you to transport that many families in such a short time, in my humble opinion it would be good, if the friends of [the Frankfurters] could take on a few thousand acres from you and help, out of the abundance with which they have been blessed, several households to come over here, so that the 15,000 acres may be assigned to us without division and English neighbors interspersed between us, especially as He wants to give us the land not too far from this city, specifically at the Schuylkill, above the falls, where He himself intends to build a house and establish a small manor.[51] The land close to the river is quite hilly and not unsuitable for planting vineyards; further in, it is more level and fertile; the worst part is that one cannot take a boat across the falls and cliffs (except when it has rained a lot and not without danger), etc. Since I did not know what you intended to do in this matter, which nevertheless is very important, and also because I did not have the money in hands to pay for having the oft-mentioned 15,000 acres surveyed (costing £28 sterling, at five shillings per 100 acres local currency), I have to wait until receiving your resolution, in order not to overstep the limitations of a faithful agent. In order to be able to assign the three arrived families to their 600 acres, I have taken up 6,000 acres for a township along with the Crefelders (who, although they are already here, could not get the 18,000 acres they bought in one piece), of which they have 3,000 and we have 3,000 acres. I laid out this town on October 24th and named it Germantown; it is situated only two hours walking distance from here, on fertile soil and on pretty brooks,

51. William Penn began the construction of "Pennsbury Manor" shortly after his arrival in Pennsylvania in 1682. He envisioned a country estate similar to those owned by the English nobility, but he would rarely live there since much of his time in Pennsylvania was spent in political affairs in Philadelphia. A re-creation of Penn's estate was constructed and opened to the public in the 1930s.

which I already reported above. I had to do this, because W. Penn does not want to give any group their portion separately, but all must live together in townships and towns. He did not do this without weighty reasons, the foremost being that in this manner children can be kept in schools and be instructed in all that's good, that neighbors assist each other kindly and helpfully, and that all together lift up their voices to praise and extol God's grace in public gatherings. Thus, you may assign the families you will bring over in the future only one-hundred acres and take in about the same amount of rent.[52]

Concerning my household, I would like to set it up in good High-German manner, for which Jacob Schumacher and the old Swiss man are very helpful, yet the Dutch servants I have with me are not suitable for this purpose, especially the maid, who cannot get along with the English woman, so that, in order to keep the peace, I have to release the latter from service, because I cannot so easily get rid of or find other employment for the former one with her two children. I very much hope to get as soon as possible a High-German maid, whom I could trust more, as I can now, alas, not do. If you want that your hopes are not disappointed, only send Germans, for the Dutch, as my unfortunate experience teaches me, are not so amenable, which is certainly a highly necessary quality in these new lands, etc. I have among my servants no carpenter and thus need several to be sent here for the construction of houses. I can inform you that in writing up contracts with them you should take note that now their daily wages are much diminished, and they do not receive, beyond their board, more than [two?][53] shillings, for which reason most of them do not work and rather want to leave our province. NB: All craftsmen have a fixed wage and one can only make half the profit with merchant goods, and even in three or four years, little profit is to be made with those, as the Society[54] will sufficiently learn. The reasons are that 1. each new arrival brings along so many clothes and utensils that he does not need anything for several years. 2. There is very little money here, although for many the desire for it is that much greater. On November 16 was the annual fair in our Philadelphia, but I barely made a few pound sterling.[55] 3. One cannot yet send from this country any return goods to England, etc. As W. Penn primarily intends to establish weaving and viticulture, send us therefore at the next best opportunity good grapevines, because there can be no doubt about

52. Pastorius thus suggests a system in which the Frankfurt investors could function as absentee landlords, renting out their Pennsylvania farms in a kind of hereditary tenant system, with the tenants passing on the right to live on and work the farms, while paying rent (in money or goods) to the owners of the land. Although still trying to please the "German Society" (later renamed "Frankfurt Land Company") at this point, he would increasingly try to divest himself of the obligations to the investors during next two decades.

53. Original number unclear.

54. Free Society of Traders.

55. Pastorius may have sold some cloth brought over from Europe at the fair (where, as he mentions later, textiles could be sold for profit). But it is unclear what Pastorius and the other employees of the German Society would have had to sell in November 1683 since neither manufacturing nor agricultural production could have been established in Germantown by then.

their progress.[56] Also send us seeds for field and garden, especially lentils and millet, etc., also NB several large iron cook pots and nesting kettles, an iron stove, because the winter here is usually as cold as it is with you and the rough northern winds are much more tempestuous; also, several bedspreads or mattresses, for I did not bring more with me than necessary and already have one more servant. If you wanted to send several pieces of fustian[57] and Osnaburg linen cloth,[58] it could be sold to great advantage, etc.

A tanner could start his trade here to great advantage, since we can here and in the neighboring provinces get plenty of skins, specifically two raw ones for one prepared one, and the best kinds for a pair of shoes, etc., only one would need to invest a certain capital for it, but such seed of money could in short time bring a rich harvest, which I want to pose for your full consideration. The two most necessary things are, 1. To build comfortable houses on the lots in this city, which could be rented out at a high price and annually make twelve on each hundred invested. 2. To build a brick kiln, for which W. Penn has promised to give us a suitable space, for as long as we are not burning any bricks, our architecture can only be wooden. Other craftsmen may remain at home for several more years, before coming over here. etc. etc.

I give this succinct reply to your four questions:[59] 1. W. Penn has laid the foundation for a just government and published from time to time useful laws. 2. He keeps neighborly friendship with the governors of all bordering provinces and also hopes that the still pending dispute with Lord Baltimore will very soon be settled and removed by royal decree.[60] 3. Said W. Penn is much beloved and praised by the people, insomuch that even the old, dissolute inhabitants have to recognize that they have never seen such a wise governor. Ah, what emphatic and penetrating sighs did this dear man on the first day of the new year send to heaven and to the throne of our EmmanueEl, because the true "Philadelphia" and brother-love is not yet so abundantly found as He wishes and for which he, as a faithful father of the country, is in constant care. 4. The Indians (of

56. Although both William Penn and Pastorius hoped to establish a thriving viticulture in Pennsylvania, in his manuscript of horticultural and agricultural knowledge, "The Monthly Monitor" (see selections in chapter 7 of this reader), Pastorius chronicles his largely unsuccessful attempts to plant and cultivate grapevines. Since his birthplace of Sommerhausen on the Main was (and still is) a center of wine making, he hoped to reproduce an important element of his home culture.

57. A thick durable, twilled cloth.

58. A coarse type of plain fabric made from flax, "Osnaburg" being the old English name for the German city of Osnabrück, where it probably originated.

59. The letter or set of instructions including these four questions has not been preserved.

60. A lengthy legal dispute between William Penn and his heirs, on the one hand, and Charles Calvert, Lord Baltimore, on the other, arose because of conflicting and overlapping royal charters. Penn and Calvert met in 1683 in New Castle to resolve their dispute over the boundary line between Pennsylvania and Maryland (eventually Pennsylvania's Lower Counties would become Delaware), yet the dispute persisted among their heirs until the boundary line surveyed by Mason and Dixon was approved by King George III in 1769.

whose nature I reported earlier on) diminish in number daily, move several 100 miles further into the country, etc.[61]

Now you might perhaps like to ask, whether I would advise with a clear conscience one or another among you to transport themselves over here? I answer with good deliberation that I desire your physical presence with all my heart; however, if you 1. do not find the liberty to do so in your own conscience, and if you cannot resolve yourselves to face 2. the difficulties and dangers of the lengthy journey, and 3. the lack of most conveniences, such as stone houses, delicate food and drink, etc. for one or two years, then follow my advice and remain for a while where you are; if these points, however, do not weigh on you too heavily, then go forth the sooner the better from the European Sodom, while thinking of Lot's wife, who left with her feet but stayed home with her heart and inclination. Ah, my dearest friends, I very much wish that I could express with this eagle's quill the love to be carried over to you and prove indeed that it is not mere lip-love but an affection that desires more for you than for myself. As my heart is bound to yours through the bonds of love, let us now grow together like trees which the right hand of God has planted by streams of water so that we may bring forth not only leaves but fruit in good season: fruits of repentance, fruits of peace, fruits of righteousness. For what profits such a useless tree, though the gardener spares it yet for some years, digs around it with all diligence and cultivates it, yet finally, no improvement following, cuts it down and casts it into the oven?[62] Forgive me this parable, dear friends; here we daily deal with such unfruitful trees, cut them down, and use them for firewood. It is at least a good-hearted warning that can do no harm. I commend you all to the divine influence, without which our fruitfulness is incomplete. The Lord, who has given us our will, may also give us fulfillment! Amen.

61. According to the oral tradition memorialized in Benjamin West's painting "Penn's Treaty with the Indians" (1771–72), William Penn met with the Lenape in 1682 under the famous "treaty elm" at Shackamaxon to agree on a peaceful cession of land. Though Penn and the Lenape leader Tamenend appear to have agreed on several land deeds, the Shackamaxon treaty cannot be verified. In any case, Penn and subsequent settlers in Pennsylvania—both English and German—steadfastly held to the claim that the indigenous people of Pennsylvania had been treated fairly and that their retreat inland had been based on peaceful land cessions.

62. A collage of biblical references playing on the themes of fruitfulness and fruitlessness, which Pastorius applies to the Frankfurt Pietists wavering in their resolve to join him in Pennsylvania. See Psalm 1:3: "He is like a tree planted by streams of water, which yields fruit in season and whose leaf does not wither"; Luke 3:8: "Produce fruit in keeping with repentance"; Galatians 5:22: "But the fruit of the Spirit is love, joy, peace, patience, kindness, goodness, faithfulness, gentleness and self-control"; Philippians 1:9–11: "And this is my prayer: that your love may abound more and more in knowledge and depth of insight, so that you may be . . . filled with the fruit of righteousness that comes through Jesus Christ—to the glory and praise of God"; Luke 13:6–9: "Then he told this parable: 'A man had a fig tree, planted in his vineyard, and he went to look for fruit on it, but did not find any. So he said to the man who took care of the vineyard, 'For three years now I've been coming to look for fruit on this fig tree and haven't found any. Cut it down! Why should it use up the soil?' 'Sir, the man replied, 'leave it alone for one more year, and I'll dig around it and fertilize it. If it bears fruit next year, fine! If not, then cut it down'"; and Matthew 6:30: "But if God so clothes the grass of the field, which today exists, and tomorrow is thrown into the oven, won't he much more clothe you, you of little faith?"

Enclosed, I send you an example of the Indian coins customary here, with six of the white ones and three of the black ones making one English farthing, and the said Indians no longer want to buy anything for silver money but only and exclusively pay with their coins, for they mostly want to leave this land and move several hundred miles further into the woods: for they have a superstition that as many Indians have to die each year, as Europeans come over here, etc.

I have given you this information to be found faithful to the duty incumbent upon me, for which I entertain the greatest care, and for which W. Penn, other upright people, as well as my own conscience (which I value as the equal of thousands of others) can give me an irreproachable testimony. That it would be difficult for me to care for so many servants and householders in such a valuable—but also impoverished—land, you can easily judge. Only my trust in the heavenly Father surmounts all. My heartfelt greetings to all other friends,

I remain always your faithful and most devoted

N. N.[63]

Preface (Vorrede) to *Circumstantial Geographical Description of Pennsylvania* (*Umständige Geographische Beschreibung Der zu allerletzt erfundenen Provintz Pensylvaniæ*; 1700)

INTRODUCTION TO THE TEXT

Also in a never before published translation and new annotation by Patrick M. Erben, the "Vorrede" (Preface) to Francis Daniel Pastorius, *Umständige Geographische Beschreibung Der zu allerletzt erfundenen Provintz Pensylvaniæ, In denen End-Gräntzen Americæ In der West-Welt gelegen* (Frankfurt and Leipzig: Andreas Otto, 1700) is included here because it stands in marked contrast to the main tract's own promotional and rather utilitarian purpose of attracting further immigration to and economic development of Pennsylvania.[64] The text used for this translation is the reliable typographic reproduction of the 1700 edition published by Friedrich Kapp in Krefeld in 1884.

---

63. Like the obscured reference to the Frankfurt investors in the manuscript text above, "N. N." here in the printed text also keeps Pastorius's identity veiled. Most likely, the publishers hoped to increase the appeal of the description across German-speaking lands by taking out specific references to Pastorius and the Frankfurt group. A direct identification would have marked Pastorius's account as a specifically radical Pietist scheme rather than an account of immigration to America appealing to potential settlers of various religious stripes.

64. The full text of Pastorius's *Umständige Beschreibung* would go well beyond the spatial limitations of this reader but is available in the original German and in English translation online on Google Books.

The collaboration between Melchior Adam Pastorius and the Frankfurt Pietists in publishing and promoting Francis Daniel's reports in print culminated in 1700 with the publication by Andreas Otto in Germany's premier publishing centers, Frankfurt and Leipzig, of Pastorius's *Umständige Geographische Beschreibung,* which included a new preface by Pastorius, another expansion of *Sichere Nachricht* with a variety of chapters on the history, settlement, location, natural resources, inhabitants, religious groups, and economic opportunities in Pennsylvania as well as a series of letters by Pastorius to his father and to his Pietist sponsors, and a brief notice by William Penn to Melchior Adam, confirming that Francis Daniel was still living and thriving in Pennsylvania. In addition, the text included edited and translated versions of William Penn's letter to the Free Society of Traders and of Thomas Paskell's *An Abstract of a Letter,* both published in 1683. It is unclear how much Pastorius himself was actually involved in the compilation and framing of this publication. His preface takes pains to establish his loftier reasons for immigrating to Pennsylvania in an apparent attempt to refute any assumptions of personal enrichment and vainglory.

As the longest publication by Pastorius distributed in Europe, *Umständige Geographische Beschreibung* also received the most attention and enjoyed the widest circulation. Book digests and review publications such as *Monatlicher Auszug aus allerhand neu-herausgegebenen nützlichen und artigen Büchern* (1700–1702) published reviews of the text, and other periodicals even garnered additional letters by Pastorius; the popular monthly *Tentzel's Monatliche Unterredungen* published a letter by Pastorius to his German friend Georg Leonard Model and another to his father, Melchior Adam. This high public profile led to a second edition of *Beschreibung* in 1704, when it was, ironically, bound with the account published by Daniel Falckner, titled *Curieuse Nachricht von Pensylvania* (Frankfurt and Leipzig: Andreas Otto, 1702). Falckner and Pastorius had become inveterate enemies, fighting over the fate of the Frankfurt Land Company in Pennsylvania. That the same printer, Andreas Otto, published both accounts first separately and then bound them together demonstrates that the Frankfurt Pietists (who had first retained Pastorius and then Falckner as their agents) were now primarily interested in promoting the sale of lands in the colony.

Although subsequent waves of German immigration gave rise to many new descriptions of Pennsylvania and other destinations in America, leaving Pastorius's tracts more or less neglected, in the nineteenth century, antiquarian excitement over rediscovering accounts of the founding of the British colonies and a search for the origins of the United States would combine with a surge of nationalist excitement in Germany to spur the emergence of Pastorius scholarship. In 1850, however, a selective and unfortunately skewed edition and translation by Lewis H. Weiss of Pastorius's 1700 *Beschreibung,* titled *Particular Geographical Description of the Lately Discovered Province of Pennsylvania, Situated on the Frontiers of this Western World, America* (Memoirs of the Historical

Society of Pennsylvania 4) especially misrepresented the purpose of Pastorius's journey and descriptions by eliminating many of the passages emphasizing his spiritual motivations and utopian aspirations. And, in 1884, in introducing a typographic reproduction of the 1700 edition of *Beschreibung* (which again made this tract widely available), the German scholar Friedrich Kapp tinged Pastorius's work in a nationalist glow and praised him for establishing the very foundation of a German ethnic and cultural presence in America that scholars in the Western Hemisphere were all too glad to pick up on.

By 1700, Pastorius had been relieved of his duties as agent and attorney of the Frankfurt Land Company and been replaced by Daniel Falckner. Thus *Beschreibung's* structuring as a more typical promotional account belies Pastorius's withdrawal from the business affairs of the Frankfurt Pietists. His preface, however, hammers home Pastorius's emphasis on his spiritual purpose in immigrating to and settling in Pennsylvania; it is also an example of Pastorius's antiacademic raillery, which condemned the pride and sophistic disputations of theologians and academics as well as the puffery of young German noblemen at European courts, although such sentiments by no means represented a rejection of academic knowledge and intellectualism on his part. Indeed, Pastorius was proud of his European education and even flaunted it among the Quaker elites of Pennsylvania. Nevertheless, his preface avows a strict search for a higher moral and spiritual purpose. Pastorius clearly felt that he needed to reframe his earlier experience in light of a spiritual goal that was getting lost in the political, economic, and geographical development of the Pennsylvania colony (or "province," as it was formerly called). The publisher's address to the "Well-Inclined Reader," when compared to Pastorius's own preface, exemplifies this dichotomy between spiritual purpose and material opportunities.

THE TEXT

To the Well-Inclined Reader[65]

I here introduce you to the Province of Pennsylvania, lately discovered in America by expeditions sent out by the English King Charles Stuart I, and its inhabitants, among whom are Christians and natural, wild people,[66] as well as each of their laws, forms of government, habits and customs, as also the towns and commerce already established

65. Written by the publisher or editor of the tract and not by Pastorius, this address focuses on establishing the credibility and authority of the text to follow and on increasing the appeal of Pennsylvania as a destination for immigrants from German-speaking lands. In contrast, Pastorius's preface describes his experiences in Pennsylvania and his perceptions of the young colony from the perspective of a spiritual quest.

66. The German original uses the phrase "natürliche wilde Leute" (natural wild people), which Gertrude Selwyn Kimball's 1912 translation in Myers, *Narratives of Early Pennsylvania* casts as "native savages," thus displaying a more strongly biased rhetoric than the seventeenth-century text.

there, all described most reliably by the province's governor William Penn himself as well as the authorized representatives of the English and High-German societies there.[67]

And it should be noted that, in 1684, this province already had 4000 Christian souls in it; therefore, after 16 whole years have now passed, it follows that, through annually arriving ships as well as the Christians' own increase, the province has become much more populous and has been raised to greater heights in agriculture, houses, and commerce—especially through the laudable vigilance, good conduct, and wise decisions of the above-said governor, William Penn, whom the English King Charles Stuart II has granted these lands forever as an English feudal realm, for the annual tribute of two beaver skins. All of this will be learned in more detail in its proper order.

Fare thee well, dear reader, whom I am further obliged to serve upon the arrival of other reports.

NB: The publisher received this[68] from the hand of Melchior Adam Pastorius J.V.D.,[69] councilor and historian of His Excellency, the Prince of Brandenburg, and whose son is indeed still a resident of Pennsylvania.

Preface[70]

It is sufficiently known to all of my family and friends in what manner, from infancy onward and after casting childish things aside, I have regulated the path of my temporal state toward a happy eternity and striven in all my actions to recognize the solely benevolent will of God, to fear his omnipotent power, and to learn to love, laud, and honor from my heart his unfathomable grace and mercy. And although I have begun and completed, next to a general curriculum of liberal arts, the study of law, I additionally made myself sufficiently acquainted with the Italian and French languages and then went on the so-called Grand Tour in good company through several countries. Yet in all places and at all times, I have applied my greatest diligence and effort for nothing else but to discover where and among which people and nations a true devotion, love, knowledge,

---

67. The original 1700 Andreas Otto imprint of Francis Daniel Pastorius's *Umständige Geographische Beschreibung* included a reprint of the 1684 publication *Beschreibung der in America neu-erfundenen Provinz Pensylvanien*, which was a German translation of William Penn's 1683 *A letter... to the Committee of the Free Society of Traders*; it also included a German translation of Thomas Paskell's *An Abstract of a Letter from Thomas Paskell of Pennsylvania* (1683). The English Quaker Thomas Paskell or Paschall (1634–1718) was one of the first immigrants to purchase land in Pennsylvania. He came to Pennsylvania in 1681 or 1682 and was a member of the Free Society of Traders, which promoted land sales and the settlement of the colony. Pastorius himself was the representative of the German Society (later the Frankfurt Land Company).

68. "This" refers to the complete following text; the publisher hopes to confirm the authenticity of the account by naming its source: Pastorius's father, Melchior Adam, was both the closest relation to Francis Daniel and a legal authority in his own right.

69. "J.V.D" stands for "Juris Utriusque Doctor," doctor of both civil and canon law, canon law comprising the laws of a church or religious community, especially of the Roman Catholic Church, although Melchior Adam Pastorius was Lutheran.

70. This marks the start of Pastorius's preface (Vorrede) proper.

and fear of God may be found and learned. I met at universities and academies more learned people than one can count, but there were as many individuals as there were religions and sects, high-flying ideas and pointed questions; in sum, there was much talk and prating of the vain, worldly wisdom of which the apostle says: *Scientia inflat.*[71]

But I cannot write with a clear conscience that I have met at any place in the Netherlands or France with a professor who with the whole-heartedness of a youth and the soul of a disciple directed in all seriousness his students to a pure love of Jesus or to the understanding of the Holy Trinity.

Certainly, there is no lack of Christians in speech and name only, who go around with their worldly wit and love the lust of the flesh, the lust of the eye, and their vainglorious manners (the devil's trifolium[72]). But, of those who strive to obtain with fear and trembling their salvation, live without deceit, and delve with all the power of their inward being into their core to find God, the highest good, there was *rara avis in terris.*[73]

I finally found at the University of Cambridge[74] and in the city of Ghent[75] a few devoted men who, remaining in secrecy, were with their whole being resigned to our dear Lord and who, when they sensed my earnest inquiry, taught me many good lessons, encouraged me in my resolve, and generally aided my quest. Thus, I was eventually shown the birth chamber (only 4 ells[76] long and 4 ells wide) of the most glorious Emperor Charles V at the princely court at Ghent, with the reminder that this newborn prince was given by one of his godparents a costly bound Bible with a golden inscription: *Scrutamini scripturas,*[77] which he indeed read diligently and learned from it that he would have to die with nothing but the only true merit of JESUS Christ.

I further saw during my Tour in Orleans, Paris, Avignon, Marseille, Lyon, and Geneva many thousands of young people from Germany, who are in the habit of emulating only the vanities of clothing, languages, foreign customs and ceremonies, and make unbelievable expenses in learning horse jumping, riding, dancing, fencing, and swinging pikes and flags. Thus, a great part of their German patrimony is wasted on the useless vanities of the world, whereas not one thought is spent on the love of God and on the God-pleasing wisdom of the discipleship of Christ. Indeed, anyone who would like to say something of the holy Augustine, Tauler, Arndt,[78] and other devout men's writings

---

71. "'Knowledge puffs up,'" from Paul's 1 Corinthians 8:1.

72. Although literally a three-leaf clover, metaphorically a "trifolium" is any tripartite union or concept, whether positive or negative.

73. "'A rare bird on this Earth,'" from the Roman satirist Juvenal.

74. The University of Cambridge was established in 1209.

75. A city in the Flanders region of Belgium, Ghent was the birthplace of the Holy Roman Emperor Charles V in 1500.

76. An ell is a former English unit of length, equivalent to about 45 inches.

77. "'Let us search the scriptures,'" from John 5:39.

78. The three Christian theologians most revered by seventeenth-century Pietists were Saint Augustine of Hippo (354–430), Church Father and author of *Confessions* (ca. 400) and *City of God* (426); the German mystic

and *Soliloquiis cum Deo*[79] has to be decried as a pietist, sectarian, or heretic. And no one who is drunk with the Aristotelian worldly wisdom[80] wants to listen to any reasoning or be disciplined by the spirit of God.

Thus, after the conclusion of my Tour, I sat in my cabinet for a brief retreat and recalled in my memory everything that the theater of the world had so far brought to my view and could find no permanent happiness in anything. I also despaired that in my fatherland[81] and all of Germany a place could be found where, in the future, one could abandon the old habit of mere *Operis operati* [dead works], enter into the pure love to God with all of one's heart, mind, and might, and also love one's neighbor as oneself.

I hence thought to myself if it would not be better if I were to present the knowledge and education given to me by the grace of the highest giver and father of light to the newly discovered American peoples in Pennsylvania and thereby make them partakers in the true understanding of the Holy Trinity and true Christianity.[82]

[..]83

---

and theologian Johannes Tauler (ca. 1300–1361); and Johann Arndt (1555 1621), author of *Wahres Christentum* (1605–10; *True Christianity*)—a perennial favorite of radical German Protestants—and one of the most important forerunners of German Pietism.

79. "Soliloquies with God."

80. For Pastorius and other Pietists, Lutheran theology relied too heavily on an Aristotelian model of understanding, according to which faith derives from the intellect rather than from a complete transformation of the soul by God. Pastorius also rejected the preponderance of Aristotelianism in early modern universities because, in perpetuating a professoriate expounding Aristotelian ideas, it created a closed and elite system that did not allow outside views.

81. By "fatherland," Pastorius probably meant Franconia, where he was born and grew up and where both Sommerhausen and Windsheim are located. Although what would become a united German state in the late nineteenth century was a multitude of independent kingdoms and principalities, most belonging to the Holy Roman Empire, during the seventeenth century, a common language and culture nevertheless created a protonational identity among those who resided there. Pastorius and many of his emigrant contemporaries referred to the larger community of German-speaking states as "Germany" (Teutschland).

82. Pastorius frequently praises the inborn morality he believed the Native peoples possessed, but there is very little evidence that he attempted to convert them to Christianity. Nevertheless, the conversion of the Native peoples was a common and much-repeated justification for Europeans in their immigration to and colonization of America.

83. The here-omitted remainder of the preface (Vorrede) consists of a brief geographical positioning of Pennsylvania.

Writings on Religious Controversy

Henry Bernhard Koster, William Davis, Thomas Rutter & Thomas Bowyer, four Boasting Disputers Of this World briefly REBUKED (1697)

INTRODUCTION TO THE TEXT

What follows is a transcription and annotation of a photographic facsimile of Francis Daniel Pastorius, *Henry Bernhard Koster, William Davis, Thomas Rutter & Thomas Bowyer, four Boasting Disputers Of this World briefly REBUKED. And Answered according to their Folly, which they themselves have manifested in a late Pamphlet, entituled, Advice for all Professors and Writers* (New York: William Bradford, 1697), held at the Historical Society of Pennsylvania and made from the only reported original, held at the Bevan-Naish Library in Birmingham, England. Pastorius's *Four Boasting Disputers* has never been reprinted since its original publication—neither in a contemporary nor in a more recent edition. The pamphlet *Advice for all Professors and Writers* mentioned in its title and from which Pastorius quotes at length appears to be lost. Believing that it had been published in both German and English and thus was circulating among readers in Germany, England, and America made Pastorius fear the lasting damage it could do to the transatlantic reputation of the Quakers and compelled him to write and publish *Four Boasting Disputers* as a rebuttal. Even in the absence of the work to which it responds, however, *Four Boasting Disputers* provides a potent impression of Pastorius's uncharacteristically irate involvement in the events of the Keithian controversy; it constitutes his most vocal and public defense of mainstream (or orthodox) Quakerism and the character of prominent Friends, especially William Penn. Despite its verbose style and many obscure references, *Four Boasting Disputers* deserves attention and inclusion in this reader because it reveals how deeply Pastorius felt the Keithians' attack on the Quakers—made even worse by the four named individuals—to be an attack on his fervent hopes for peace, piety, and religious renewal in his new homeland. For Pastorius and other Germantown Quakers, the Keithian controversy unfolded in two stages: first, the charges leveled and pursued against mainstream Pennsylvania Quakers by George Keith and his followers during the late 1680s and early 1690s; and, second, the leveling of those same charges by radical Pietist mystics who arrived from Germany in 1694, in particular, Heinrich Bernhard Köster (Henry Bernhard Koster). In order to understand its events and Pastorius's vehement response to them, a brief review of the controversy itself is necessary: valuing a personalized faith over a set of doctrines establishing church discipline, Quakers traditionally regarded any inspired religious testimony as a valid expression of the Inner Light or indwelling spirit of God. The university-trained theologian George Keith, shortly after arriving in Pennsylvania in 1688, began lambasting fellow Quakers for their supposed ignorance of both Scripture and the basic tenets of Christianity. He called for a set of doctrines to which current and prospective members of the Society of Friends would have to consent in a public statement of faith. And he asserted that the Quakers' emphasis on the Inner Light served to diminish Christ's physical nature and even to deny his bodily return on the Day of Judgment. Shocked by the apparent "literal-mindedness" of what Keith proposed, "orthodox" Quakers initially refused to comment on the doctrinal issues he had raised. When, however, several Quaker ministers accused Keith of heresy for denying the sufficiency of the Inner Light and for preaching two different Christs—one within and one without—he increased the pitch of his attacks, personally denouncing the most prominent Pennsylvania Quakers and public office holders, including Deputy Governor Thomas Lloyd and the minister Samuel Jennings.

Ostensibly disagreeing over the changed location of a Quaker Meeting in the spring of 1692, Keith and his followers established a separate meeting and dubbed themselves "Christian Quakers." The Quaker establishment rejected the new meeting and disowned Keith. With the support of William Bradford, the only printer in Pennsylvania at the time, Keith moved the debate from the oral culture of the Quaker Meetings into the public sphere of print. In order to curb Keith's public denunciations, the Quakers brought a libel suit against both Keith and Braford. The climax of the controversy occurred in 1693, when Keith and his followers disrupted an "orthodox" meeting and demolished a gallery for ministers. In early 1694, Keith left Pennsylvania for London to present his grievances at the London Yearly Meeting, the highest authority in early Quakerism. He eventually leveled similar charges at the London Friends, who concluded that "George Keith is Gone from the blessed unity of the peaceable spirit of our Lord

[. . .] and hath separated himself from the holy fellowship of the Church of Christ."[1] Keith became an Anglican minister in 1700 and returned to Pennsylvania for a two-year visit in 1702.

As Quaker Meeting records demonstrate, a number of Germantown residents joined the Keithians early on, including the Krefeld settlers Herman and Abraham op den Graeff as well as Isaac Jacobs van Bebber.[2] Though in his manuscript writings Pastorius reacted to the spread of the controversy among the Germantown settlers, he recorded his unwillingness, as justice of the peace, to take a stand on it.[3] With the arrival of Johannes Kelpius's Pietist group in 1694, however, the German immigrant community became thoroughly embroiled in the dispute. Kelpius and his followers championed a mystical union of the individual believer with Christ. The mystics' physical, even erotic concept of Christ sharply clashed with the Quakers' Inner Light theology. Although Kelpius and most of his followers avoided open doctrinal disputes, Heinrich Bernhard Köster, a more quarrelsome member of the group, tried to direct German and English Pennsylvania Quakers back to orthodox Protestantism and to reinstate the rites of baptism and communion shunned by mainstream Quakers. Köster joined with English Keithians such as William Davis, Thomas Rutter, and Thomas Boyer to form an independent religious community, whose doctrinal positions were close to the Baptists'.[4] In 1696, the group violently disrupted the Quaker Yearly Meeting at Burlington. Having witnessed the incident, Pastorius broke his public silence on the issue by printing—with the Quakers' approval—the anti-Keithian pamphlet *Four Boasting Disputers Of this World Briefly REBUKED*, a vehement attack on Köster (Koster), Davis, Rutter, and Boyer.

Pastorius's line of attack against Köster and his followers is fourfold: a condemnation of their unfriendly treatment of the Quakers in general and of the specific misrepresentations of Quakerism in their writings; a passage-by-passage deconstruction of Köster's *Advice for all Professors and Writers*; a rejection of their behavior at the 1696 Quaker Meeting (their "boasting"); and, finally, a complete ridicule of their separate religious community and its practices. Charging the Köster group with restaging the calamity of Babel with its confusion of languages and scattering of peoples across the Earth, Pastorius takes aim not merely at members of the group but at the entire religious

1. London Friends, as quoted in Butler, "Power, Authority," 39.
2. See Frost, *Keithian Controversy*, 371–75, for a list of Keithian Quakers, including those from Germantown.
3. See entry 38 of "Silvula Rhytmorum Germanopolitanorum," Pastorius's poetic miscellany in the "Bee-Hive" in chapter 5 of this reader for his poem on the Keithian controversy, titled "Zur Zeit der Anno 1692 in Pennsilvanien entstandenen Trennung."
4. The records of the Pennepek Baptist Church in Bustleton (now a Philadelphia neighborhood) state that "William Davis, with one Henry Bernard Koster a Germane, and some more made up a kinde of Society, did Break bread, Lay on hands, washed one anothers feet, and were about having a Community of Goods. But in a little time they disagreed, and broke to pieces." As quoted in Butler, "Into Pennsylvania's Spiritual Abyss," 160.

and spiritual confusion wrought upon Pennsylvania by the Keithians. But his rebuttal, meant to denounce Köster and to destroy his credibility in America and across the Atlantic, abounds in self-important linguistic and learned punning, and it is hard to follow all its religious, historical, and scriptural references and allusions. Published in 1697, *Four Boasting Disputers* marks the nadir of Pastorius's efforts to cling to and defend the utopian hopes he had pinned to the community-building projects of the Pietists and Quakers. He must have realized that he had himself fallen prey to self-righteous vitriol and decided to pull back: from the time he first started work on his "Bee-Hive" manuscript in 1696, Pastorius dedicated most of his reading and writing to the more private or small-circle efforts of his manuscript writing and circulating.

THE TEXT

Henry Bernhard Koster,[5] *William Davis,*[6] *Thomas Rutter*[7] *& Thomas Bowyer,*[8] *four Boasting Disputers Of this World briefly REBUKED.* And answered according to their Folly which they themselves have manifested in a late Pamphlet, entitled, *Advice for all Professors and Writers.*

Though this their said Pamphlet[9] doth not establish the place where it was printed, yet mentioning so many things of *Babylon,*[10] for example, *The Counsils, Clergie, and Universities of Babylon*, page 2. *The Babylonian Churches*, page 4. *The Babylonian Beasts,*

5. German Pietist Heinrich Bernhard Köster immigrated to Pennsylvania in 1694, where he joined Johannes Kelpius's group of mystics. A self-appointed Lutheran minister in Germantown and Philadelphia, he became best known as a Keithian and the leading anti-Quaker voice in the area. Köster broke with Kelpius to form his own society called "Irenia," or the "True Church of the Brotherly Love." After wrangling with the Pennsylvania Quakers, Köster returned to Germany in 1699, where he would remain until his death in 1749.

6. Welshman William Davis, who arrived in Pennsylvania shortly after Penn, joined the Keithians in the early 1690s and attempted to build with Köster the communitarian experiment Pastorius criticized in *Four Boasting Disputers*. In 1700, Davis published the tract *Jesus the Crucified Man, the Eternal Son of God*, which expresses his criticism of the Pennsylvania Quakers and his overall religious views.

7. English Quaker Thomas Rutter followed William Penn to Pennsylvania, where he joined Keith's faction in the 1690s. With Köster, he tried to form a religious community associated with the Seventh Day Baptists. He was also active in the governing body of Germantown. A blacksmith by trade, Rutter pioneered iron manufacturing in colonial Pennsylvania.

8. Apart from his involvement with Köster, Davis, and Rutter, nothing is known about Thomas Bowyer.

9. *Advice for all Professors and Writers* (no longer extant).

10. In radical Protestant rhetoric (both among Pietists and Quakers), the use of both "Babel" and "Babylon" conflated the pride of the construction of the Tower of Babel and the ensuing confusion of languages with the moral and spiritual corruption associated with the city of Babylon in the Old Testament and the New Testament Book of Revelation. Although Protestants, narrowly speaking, identified the Catholic Church as the modern Babylon, radical Pietists and Quakers extended their use of "Babylon" to include mainstream Protestant Churches they considered corrupt, such as the Anglican and Lutheran Churches. In the broadest sense, "Babel" and "Babylon" applied to any corrupt and confused religious group or institution.

page 7. *The four chief Quarters of Babylon*, page 8.[11] And being it self thoroughly full of Bable,[12] or Confusion, it thereby plainly disposeth, that it was hatched in the very Center of that great City, whose wise and learned men, most able (in their own Conceit) to advise others, can not write but this sinisterly,[13] even with their right hands. At present not intending to touch all the fo[u]nd and unfound expressions, occurring almost in every Paragraph of the said Pamphlet, leaving it to such as by the *poor dark Devil without a Body*, page 1&c. are or may be concerned,[14] to make their own Apology, [I] shall only take a little Notice,

    I. Of some swelling words of these vain Braggards;
   II. Of the Unreasonableness of their Challenge;
  III. Of their abusing and traducing W. P.[15] in particular.
  IV. Of their slandering and misrepresenting the People called *Quakers* in general; &
   V. Of their self guiltiness of what they charge us withal

§. 1

Page 2. They stile themselves, *The Brethren in America*; page 7, *The true Church of Philadelphia or Brotherly Love*, &c.

This sounds mightily afar off, and some silly Women in *Germany*, who may happen to see their Pamphlet, which probably for that end and purpose was Printed in the high Dutch tongue,[16] (besides the English) will be ready to think this Church or Brotherhood something real and considerable. But to undeceive those, who prefer Truth before Fiction and Falshood, I herewith must inform them that all these specious Names and Epithets in the pages above quoted, and more others, are meer *Kosterian* Chimera, an idle fancy. He the said H.B. *Koster* arriving here in *Pensilvania*, his heart and head filled with Whimsical and boisterous Imaginations, but his Hands and Purse emptied of the Money, which our Friends beyond Sea imparted unto him, and some in this Company,[17] was as cunning as to intice and induce four or five to a Commonalty of goods, and so ferried a Plantation near *German Town*, upon a track of Land given

11. In this text, quotations from or references to Köster's pamphlet *Advice for all Professors and Writers* are set in italics.

12. Babble or Babel.

13. A pun on the two senses of the word "sinister," which comes from the Latin *sinister* meaning "on the left" or "inauspicious," whence its other current sense of "threatening, causing, or intending evil or harm." Thus Pastorius means to say that Köster and his friends are sinister even when they pretend to be the opposite.

14. In other words, only people possessed by Satan would actually care to discover every false expression or accusation found in Köster's pamphlet.

15. William Penn.

16. High German.

17. On their journey to America, Johannes Kelpius and his group of mystics—which included Köster—were supported in London by the Quakers' Meeting for Sufferings, which raised funds for their living expenses and Atlantic passage. Pastorius is thus trying to expose the ingratitude of Köster and his followers for now reproaching the mainstream Quakers.

unto them, calling the same IRENIA,[18] that is to say, The Home of Peace, which not long after became ERINNIA,[19] The House of raging Contention, and now returned to the Donour,[20] the Brethren in *America* being gone and dispersed, and the Church of *Philadelphia* (falsly so called) proving momentary, and of no moment, *Mark* 3:25.[21]

Page 3. They tell, how *they entered the 22th day of* September, 1696, *into our yearly Meeting at Burlington, and there lifted up their Voices like Trumpets, and broke our Friends voices in the air,* &c.

That at such a time and place (we being assembled not to quarrel with any Brawlers, but to worship the living God in Spirit and in Truth, waiting for the enjoyment of his Comfortable presence,[22] H.B. *Koster*, with some not much unlike unto himself, came into our Meeting-House, and there as Trumpets of an uncertain sound, were blown by the Prince of the Power of the Air,[23] who ruleth and operateth in the Children of Unbelief, we do not deny. Neither is the Impudency of these our adversaries a New thing unto us; For several others before them, acted likewise by him, who made bold to appear in the midst of the Sons of God when they came to present themselves before the Lord, *Job* 1:6,[24] entered into Friends Meeting houses, and by their ill behaviour and disorderly Interruptions, attempted to disturb the People religiously therein gathered. With these troublesome men of Belial,[25] H.B.K. W.D. T.R. T.B. and the rest of their Fraternity,[26] in whose behalf they have signed their Pamphlet, may fome out their own shame as they will. We, measurably quickened with Christ, are set down in a safe and heavenly hiding place, *viz.* his powerfull Name, having that satisfactory assurance, that there the Enemy and his wicked Instruments cannot approach nor hurt us, Praises to the Lord of God for ever.

18. "Irenia"—from the Greek word for and goddess of peace, Eirene—was the name of Köster's own religious community, which he formed after breaking with Johannes Kelpius in 1697.

19. "Erinnia" may simply be Pastorius's coinage from merging the word "error" with the community's name, "Irenia," thus making it a place of error or, as Pastorius says, "raging Contention." Perhaps it is also a pun on the Erinyes (known in English as the Furies), goddesses of vengeance in Greek mythology, who, according to the *Iliad*, took vengeance on people who had sworn false oaths, something Pastorius may have surmised the Köster group had done.

20. It is unclear who donated the land for Köster and his followers to create their short-lived communitarian experiment.

21. Mark 3:25: "And if a house be divided against itself, that house cannot stand."

22. Quakers commonly worshiped in silence until the Holy Spirit moved one of those present to speak.

23. In Ephesians 2:2, Satan is called "prince of the power of the air."

24. Continuing to compare Köster and his group to Satan and his followers, Pastorius invokes Job 1:6: "Now there was a day when the sons of God came to present themselves before the Lord, and Satan came also among them."

25. Belial appears in both the Hebrew Bible and the Old Testament in "sons of Belial" or "children of Belial," referring to worthless or lawless people and also as a synonym for Satan.

26. It is unknown who else belonged to Köster's group.

§. II.

Page 4. *They challenge every opposing Writer or Professor*, but with this Proviso, *That none who will not be accounted by them as a vagabond Egyptian*,[27] *and his answer as a railing Pamphlet, must write again, unless he have first appeared upon the publick Theater and Stage of the Church and of the world unto a dispute, at Philadelphia, &c. or in the Houses of the four Subscribers as are mentioned, and of others.*[28]

The Church of these disputers and the World are very close one by the other, and *if the ignorant Babes, Pietists and* [. . .] will take the Counsel given them by these advisers, p. 8, *and seek this Church*, they need not to travel farther than towards this Theater of the World, where they may be sure to find her. But ours being in God, and the members thereof chosen out of the world, and redeemed from the Contentiousness & other vain Customs of the same, will never engage in such a stage play or Theatrical Jangling and Wrangling with these Bablers and Mountebanks[29] of Babylon; In whose four chief Quarters we are not so well acquainted as to find out their respective houses and lodgings, where they like Milstones having no grist to grind, set themselves on fire; on fire of hell, *James* 3:6[30] and So as *Egyptians* against *Egyptians, Isa.* 19:2,[31] with divided Tongues[32] work and promote their own Destruction, *Psalm* 55:9,[33] what reason they had to huff and hector in their Cartel, p.1 and 2 with a *Let it be known to all the World, and Let it be known unto all the Nations*, &c. And yet to suppress and smother this their monstrous Product, after it came from the Press, communicating only a few Copies to those who went out from us, because they were not of us, as also some to a *Maryland* Doctor,[34] delivering more to the Parties challenged, nor to any of the People called *Quakers* who they therein most foully disperse and defame, the Ingenous and Impartial Reader may judge.[35] If they have written and printed, in haste, and now repent in leasure, as the Proverb saith, they will confess and forsake; which is the worst [ill?]

27. In Acts 21:38, Paul is at first mistaken for the Egyptian and false prophet of the Jewish faith who led an uprising of thirty thousand men that was crushed by Marcus Antonius Felix, the Roman procurator of Judea. The incident was described by the Jewish historian Josephus.

28. If Pastorius is quoting it correctly, Köster's pamphlet demanded a written or oral declaration of allegiance to the faith by any Quaker responding to the publication. This demand would have reflected the Keithians' overall advocacy for formal and mandatory declarations of faith from all members of the Society of Friends or Quakers.

29. Mountebanks would sell quack medicines from a platform, hence, by extension, the term refers to any boastful, unscrupulous pretenders.

30. James 3:6: "And the tongue is a fire, a world of iniquity: so is the tongue among our members, that it defileth the whole body, and setteth on fire the course of nature; and it is set on fire of hell."

31. Isaiah 19:2: "And I will set the Egyptians against the Egyptians: and they shall fight, every one against his brother, and every one against his neighbour; city against city, and kingdom against kingdom."

32. Another reference to the confusion of languages at the Tower of Babel (Gen. 11:1–9).

33. Psalm 55:9: "Destroy, O Lord, and divide their tongues: for I have seen violence and strife in the city."

34. Unclear to whom Pastorius is referring here.

35. If Köster and his group withheld the printed pamphlet from his opponents or even suppressed it, as Pastorius alleges, this may explain why no copies exist.

with them, and unto all Gain-sayers of Truth, as at the contrary hand I heartily should pitty their Condition, in case they or any of them here-after should go on in their Wrath, Lyes and Clamorous barking against God[']s everlasting Truth, and the Possessors, as well as the Professors thereof, which the Lord as certainly hath determined to exalt in this the day of his great Power, as the unbelieving, the abominable and all Lyars shall be cast down in the lake and bottomless Pit.

§. III.

The railing and scandalous Reproaches, wherewith they endeavour to render *W.P.*[36] odious in the ears of all Nations of the world [. . .] thereunto they direct their advice, as beforesaid, are a base and detestable perverting and misconstruction of his words, fully answered by our Friend *Thomas Ellwood*, in his Book, called, *Truth defended*,[37] from page 113 to page 123. If these detractors, especially *W.P*'s old *servant Tho. Rutter (cujus nunc spirant mendacia folles)*[38] be able to reply to something thereat, let them forge as opprobrious weapons as ever they can, and Truth will be further defended by it self, against all their peevish and malicious objections. I at this time aim not to enlarge about a passage so amply and solidly refuted. This only I would put *Tho. Rutter* in mind, that Ingratitude is one of the blackest Crimes among honest men, and an hard matter to have his words wrested, and to be required with Slanders for kindness, or to feel a Sting, wherein good reason, Honey might be expected.[39] Concerning *Solomon Eccles's*[40] expression, I here (loathing needless repetitions, or *actum agere*[41]) additionally refer our doting Opposers likewise to the 112th page of the above cited Treatise, and proceed to

§. IV.

Page 2. They say, *That the root of Anti-christianity, that is to say, the Denyal of Jesus in the flesh, is to be found among the* Quakers. And at the bottom of the same p.2. *That*

---

36. William Penn.

37. Thomas Ellwood, *Truth defended and the friends thereof cleared from the false charges, foul reproaches, and envious cavils, cast upon it and them by George Keith* (London, 1695). In his bibliography of Quaker writings included in the "Bee-Hive" (see chapter 4 of this reader), Pastorius cites this and a number of other anti-Keithian tracts by Ellwood. A prominent Quaker writer, Thomas Ellwood (1639–1714) is also well known for reading Latin to the blind John Milton.

38. "Whose [puffed up] lungs now breathe out lies." Pastorius is loosely quoting a phrase from Juvenal's *Satires,* satire 7, line 111.

39. Pastorius interprets Penn's employment of Rutter as a servant upon his arrival in Pennsylvania as a form of patronage, for which Rutter should be grateful. Thus he considers Rutter's criticism of the theological precepts of the Quakers in general and of Penn in particular to be a form of severe ingratitude. In Dante's *Inferno*, traitors to their benefactors, such as Brutus and Judas, are placed in the fourth ring of the ninth—the lowest—circle of hell.

40. Solomon Eccles, also known as "Solomon Eagle," was an English composer of church music who became Quaker. Pastorius cited his book *A Musick Lector, or the Art of Musick* (London, 1667) in his bibliography of Quaker authors (see chapter 4 of this reader).

41. "To act the act," which, as a needless repetition, is thus supposed to be a self-conscious pun.

the Quakers *deny Jesus to be properly the Son of God,* Item, page 4. *That the* Quakers *say, Christ hath offered that which is not himself, but only a Garment,* &c. And in the said 4th page, *That the* Quakers *deny God in his most high Spirit*[']*s and Godhead*[']*s Power to be the Father of Christ's Body, and Mary the Mother.*

All this I declare to be down right Calumnies and an absolute untruth in the whole and every part of it, as to all unprejudiced persons, who but cursorily (for he that runs may read here)[42] will view or inspect the several solemn Confessions published from time to time by the said People concerning their Faith, and what they believe of Jesus Christ our Lord and Saviour, both as he is true God and Perfect Man, must needs most conspicuously appear. For this despised People (by those Scorners called *Quakerian Spirits*, page 7) always sincerely believed in their hearts, and contested with their Mouths, that Christ Jesus is the OWN AND ONLY BEGOTTEN Son of God, the express Image (or Character) of his Substance; He in the Father, and the Father in him; He and the Father ONE, in essence, goodness, will and works; EQUAL in Power, Glory and Majesty; the same individed and indivisible Jehovah; that *therefore the Evangelical Prophet Isa.* 7:14[43] & [. . .]:6 did right well say, His Name should be IMMANUEL (God with us) the Mighty God, the everlasting Father, &c.

And as the *Quakers* constantly owned and correctly contended for Christ[']s Divinity or Godhead, as part of the precious Faith delivered to them. So they in the manner upon all occasions professed and still do profess, that Christ Jesus, the Word of God, when the fullness of time was come, (whereof *Jacob* prophecied many ages before, *Gen.* 49:10)[44] *viz*, under *Cesar Augustus*, in the days of *Herod* was made flesh,[45] took upon him the Nature of Man, the form of a Servant, partaking of Flesh and Blood, as Children do, made of a Woman, born of the blessed Virgin *Mary*, in *Bethlehem* of *Judea*, after he was conceived in her by the overshadowing of the holy Ghost, &c. So that they in uprightness of their hearts acknowledge God Almighty to be most properly the Father of Jesus Christ, both in respect of his eternal Generation, and also of this his Conception in the appointed Time But *Mary* to be his Mother only in relation to the last, and not to the former.

For inasmuch as Christ Jesus is the true unchangeable God, having neither beginning of days nor end of Life, he was before *Mary, Abraham*, or any thing that was made,

---

42. A pun on the Latin root of "cursorily," *cursor*, which means "runner."

43. Isaiah 7:14: "Therefore the Lord himself shall give you a sign; Behold, a virgin shall conceive, and bear a son, and shall call his name Immanuel."

44. In Genesis 49:1, Jacob calls together his sons to tell them what "shall befall [them] in the last days." Genesis 49:10: "The sceptre shall not depart from Judah, nor a lawgiver from between his feet, until Shiloh come; and unto him shall the gathering of the people be."

45. According to Luke 2:1, Jesus was born during the reign of Roman emperor Caesar Augustus. And Matthew 2:2 mentions Herod as king at the time of Jesus's birth.

visible and invisible, *John* 1:15 and 8:58, *Col.* 1:16.[46] He was before *John* his fore runner, although he came after him, *John* 1:[30?].[47] He was the Lord of David, as well as of the fruit of his Loyns, *Matt.* 22:45, *Acts* 2:30.[48] Both the Root and of God according to the Spirit of holiness, *Rom.* 1:4.[49] He was before any of the Fathers were, the first-born of every Creature, *Col.* 1:15,[50] but concerning the flesh *Rom.* 9:5.[51] He came of the Fathers of the seed of *Abraham*, and of the stock of *David*; He himself being *David* our Prince, the Prince of our Peace, blessed forever. *Ezek.* 37:24, 25.[52]

Moreover it is the unanimous Faith and Confession of those called *Quakers*, That Christ Jesus, as God, or according to his Godhead, is IMMORTAL, and never was nor can be killed; and that by reason he through death might destroy him, that had the power of death, i.e. the Devil, he took part of Flesh and Blood *Heb.* 2:14.[53] He the glorious Messenger of the Covenant (fulfilling the Prophecy of *Malachi* 3:1)[54] came to his Temple, the prepared Body, which the *Jews* did destroy, but could never destroy him, who by his own Omnipotency was able to raise it up again in three days, *John* 2:19.[55] He suffered for us in the flesh, and was put to death in the flesh, 1 *Peter* 3:18, 4:1.[56] Consecrating thereby, as through the VAIL to as a new and living way, freely to enter in to the holiest, *Heb.* 10:19.[57] All which (if we hearken to the Sophistry of these deluding

46. John 1:15: "John bare witness of him, and cried, saying, This was he of whom I spake, He that cometh after me is preferred before me: for he was before me." John 8:58: "Jesus said unto them, Verily, verily, I say unto you, Before Abraham was, I am." Colossians 1:16: "For by him were all things created, that are in heaven, and that are in earth, visible and invisible, whether they be thrones, or dominions, or principalities, or powers: all things were created by him, and for him."

47. Numbering illegible, but probably John 1:30: "This is he of whom I said, After me cometh a man which is preferred before me: for he was before me."

48. Matthew 22:45: "If David then call him Lord, how is he his son?" Acts 2:30: "Therefore being a prophet, and knowing God had sworn with an oath to him, that of the fruit of his loins, according to the flesh, he would raise up Christ to sit on his throne."

49. Romans 1:4: "And declared to be the Son of God with power, according to the spirit of holiness, by the resurrection from the dead."

50. Colossians 1:15: "Who is the image of the invisible God, the firstborn of every creature."

51. Romans 9:5: "Whose are the fathers, and of whom as concerning the flesh Christ came, who is over all, God blessed for ever. Amen."

52. Ezekiel 37:24, 25: "And David my servant shall be king over them; and they all shall have one shepherd: they shall also walk in my judgments, and observe my statutes, and do them. And they shall dwell in the land that I have given unto Jacob my servant, wherein your fathers have dwelt; and they shall dwell therein, even they, and their children, and their children's children for ever: and my servant David shall be their prince for ever."

53. Hebrews 2:14: "Forasmuch then as the children are partakers of flesh and blood, he also himself likewise took part of the same; that through death he might destroy him that had the power of death, that is, the devil."

54. Malachi 3:1: "Behold, I will send my messenger, and he shall prepare the way before me: and the Lord, whom ye seek, shall suddenly come to his temple, even the messenger of the covenant, whom ye delight in: behold, he shall come, saith the Lord of hosts."

55. John 2:19: "Jesus answered and said unto them, Destroy this temple, and in three days I will raise it up."

56. 1 Peter 3:18: "For Christ also hath once suffered for sins, the just for the unjust, that he might bring us to God, being put to death in the flesh, but quickened by the Spirit." 1 Peter 4:1: "Forasmuch then as Christ hath suffered for us in the flesh, arm yourselves likewise with the same mind: for he that hath suffered in the flesh hath ceased from sin."

57. Hebrews 10:19: "Having therefore, brethren, boldness to enter into the holiest by the blood of Jesus."

Seducers, page 3) would be a direct Opposition to the words, *Heb.* 9:16.[58] *Having offered himself, or by the Sacrifice of himself.* But we know, their inference to be naught, and by far not so tolerable, as if one should conclude that because *H.B.K*'s Body was newly baptized or plung'd in water, therefore he himself was not.[59] The Apostle *Peter* was quite ignorant of such an inconsiderate Consequence, saying in his first Epistle chap. 2:24.[60] *That Christ his own self have our sins in his Body on the Tree.* This the *Quakers* believe, and is (I am certain) sound Doctrine, parallel with that of *Heb.* 9:26.[61]

Page 5. They say, *That many of the* Quakers *in Preachings and writings revile the Baptism and Supper of Christ, &c. desiring us, to shew them, by what second Decree and Message of Christ and his Apostles the Union of the Spirit with outward Creature, as Water, Bread, Wine, and the like, hath been abrogated.*

I wonder, that men so forward to dispute upon the publick Theater of Church and World should be so unskilled in disputing, as to require us to prove the abolishing of an Union, we all along denied. They holding the affirmative, ought first to evince, that Christ Jesus united himself, the Quickening Spirit with Water, *Bread, Wine*, and the like outward Creatures. John the *Baptist* who was sent to prepare the way before Christ, told his hearers in the Wilderness, *I indeed have baptized you with Water, BUT He* (Christ Jesus) *shall baptize* you with the *holy Ghost*, Mark 1:9,[62] by which [. . .] he did not intimate an Union of the Spirit with the outward Water, but rather thereby contra-distinguish them both from each other. Christ in the days of his flesh made the same difference, *Acts* 11:16,[63] and *Peter* well remembering the words of his Lord and Master, excludeth that corruptible Element of Water, and the outward Washing, from Christ[']s Baptism, 1 *Peter* 1:23 & 3:21.[64] *Paul* knowing only one Baptism of the one Lord, *Eph.* 4:5,[65] saith, *It is made by the one Spirit,* 1 *Cor.* 12:13.[66] Not by the one Spirit

---

58. Hebrews 9:16: "For where a testament is, there must also of necessity be the death of the testator."

59. Heinrich Bernhard Köster (Henry Bernhard Koster; H.B.K.) and his followers, in breaking away from mainstream Quakers, rejected the Quakers' refusal to practice baptism; their religious community practiced baptism as a sign of rebirth.

60. 1 Peter 2:24: "Who his own self bare our sins in his own body on the tree, that we, being dead to sins, should live unto righteousness: by whose stripes ye were healed."

61. Hebrews 9:26: "For then must he often have suffered since the foundation of the world: but now once in the end of the world hath he appeared to put away sin by the sacrifice of himself."

62. Mark 1:9: "And it came to pass in those days, that Jesus came from Nazareth of Galilee, and was baptized of John in Jordan."

63. Acts 11:16: "Then remembered I the word of the Lord, how that he said, John indeed baptized with water; but ye shall be baptized with the Holy Ghost."

64. 1 Peter 1:23: "Being born again, not of corruptible seed, but of incorruptible, by the word of God, which liveth and abideth for ever." 1 Peter 3:21: "The like figure whereunto even baptism doth also now save us (not the putting away of the filth of the flesh, but the answer of a good conscience toward God,) by the resurrection of Jesus Christ."

65. Ephesians 4:5: "One Lord, one faith, one baptism."

66. 1 Corinthians 12:13: "For by one Spirit are we all baptized into one body, whether we be Jews or Gentiles, whether we be bond or free; and have been all made to drink into one Spirit."

united with the outward Creature. And *Heb.* 9:10.[67] That the Rites or Ordinances imposed on those under the Law, consisting in Meats, Drinks and divers Baptisms, were only until the time of Reformation, pursuing *vers.* 11.[68] But Christ being come, &c. That the People called *Quakers* proclaim, and say, *Christ, the desire of all Nations is come; The Refiner and Purifier of the Sons of* Levi[69] *is come: The Repairer of the Breach, and Restorer of Paths to dwelling, is come: Christ, the* SUBSTANCE *is come.* The Day of the Lord[']s Redemption is dawned; all Figures, Types and Shadows are vanisht away; and it is not them that vilifie the Baptism and Supper of our Lord Jesus, who sensibly can witness their sins thereby washed off, and their inward Man nourished by the living Bread which comes down from Heaven; but it is those *Anabaptists*[70] themselves, who (like *Simon Magus*)[71] rather defile the Waters, than that the Waters should cleanse their Souls; and who (though dipped over head and ears, yet as filthy Dreamers, *Jude* v. 8[72]) do dream as if they did eat, but when they awake, are empty. They fain would perswade others, that the bread which they break, is the Communion of the Body of Christ, and nevertheless are so infatuated as to assert, pag. 8. *That the body of Christ is absent from the Saints on Earth*; and so they must eat, (or rather fancy to eat) what they have not.[73]

67. Hebrews 9:10: "Which stood only in meats and drinks, and divers washings, and carnal ordinances, imposed on them until the time of reformation."

68. Hebrews 9:11: "But Christ being come an high priest of good things to come, by a greater and more perfect tabernacle, not made with hands, that is to say, not of this building."

69. In the Old Testament, Levi is the third son of Jacob. Levi's sons were Gershon, Kehat, and Merari (Num. 3:17). The descendants of Levi were chosen as priests and thus held no actual territory in Israel. The sons of Levi were specifically charged with the care of the Tabernacle, which contained the Ark of the Covenant. Here, "Sons of Levi" more broadly designates a group of people specially chosen to serve God.

70. It is remarkable that Pastorius is arguing vehemently against adult baptism since he is living in a community, Germantown, that by the mid-1690s included several Mennonite families (such as the family of the famous paper maker William Rittenhouse) who, as Anabaptists, believed in adult baptism. Thus he sacrifices a larger belief in religious tolerance to his allegiance to and defense of his newly adopted denomination—Quakerism.

71. Simon Magus or Simon the Sorcerer is mentioned in Acts 8:9–24. A Samaritan religious figure at the time of the Apostles, Simon is converted to Christianity by Philip the Evangelist. Simon clashed with the Apostle Peter over the difference between water baptism and baptism with the power of the Holy Ghost. When Simon offers Peter money for conferring upon him the power to baptize with the Holy Ghost, Peter condemns him as wicked. Thus Pastorius here tries to distinguish between a lower order of baptism—by water—practiced by Köster's sect and the baptism conferred by the power of the Holy Ghost or Holy Spirit, which was claimed by the Quakers.

72. Jude verse 8: "Likewise also these filthy dreamers defile the flesh, despise dominion, and speak evil of dignities." The Epistle of Jude in the New Testament lists false teachers and heretics in the early church without specifically identifying them. For Pastorius, the terminology of "filthy dreamers" and the charge of speaking "evil of dignities" (church authorities) helped him turn Köster's (and earlier, George Keith's) charges against the Quakers against the critics themselves. Whereas Köster charged the Quakers with antinomianism (the breaking of church law) for disregarding the sacraments of baptism and communion, for example, Pastorius here identifies Köster and his followers as the "filthy dreamers" for defying the "dominion" or authority of the Quaker leadership. In the religious climate of early Pennsylvania, heresy and orthodoxy were very much in the eye of the beholder.

73. Pastorius thus alleges an inconsistency in the sacrament of communion (or, in Protestantism, the Lord's Supper) as practiced by Köster and his group but not practiced by the Quakers.

§. V.

That these our false Accusers are themselves guilty of what they blame the People called *Quakers* withal, (I hope) by the foregoing is partly evident, to such whose Eyes are not blinded by Partiality. Yet seeing they stigmatize us with *Spiritual Babylon & Anti-christianity*, pag. 2. I here, in short (though not obscure) Arguments shall demonstrate, that these our Assaulters themselves are both *Babylonians and Anti-Christs.*

Babylonians, 1. Because of the *Babylonian Nature* they are in; grievous Revolters, Slanderers, Corrupters, *Jer.* 6:28.[74]

2. Because of the confusedness of their Language, some not understanding the Speech of the others, who cryed for Water to be plunged in, so that they were scattered before they [finish't?] the Tower of their imaginary Church.

Anti-christs, Because they set themselves against the Lord's anointed, under a fair pretence to be for him. Christ in the greek signifieth *Anointed,* and the Preposition *Ant,* as well for as against (see *Matt.* 17:27, *Luke* 2:34[75]). The very *Papists* make a great shew of Christ[']s coming in the flesh, dishonouring all their Temples, Cloisters and Chappels, yea, and many of their Streets and High-ways with the Images of a Woman holding a Child in her Arms, which they call *Jesus* and *Maria* his Mother: Before these statuary or painted Deities they bow their Knees, and commit Idolatry.[76] *Anti-christs* in a high degree, in a gross and most Palpable manner.

But our present Adversaries *H.B.K. W.D. T.R. & T.B.* are more subtil; they impudently charge us with the *Denyal of Christ[']s coming in the flesh,* and would have the World have that good Opinion of them, as if they did confess him so to be come, alledging 1 *John* 4:3[77] when in the mean time they combine and take part with our old Adversaries,[78] owning, in their carnal Mind, Christ no otherwise but after the flesh, decaying Christ, as Christ, to have had any existence before that Body, which was born of the *Virgin* Mary, arguing thus for that Body of flesh, to call it strictly and simply Christ Jesus. Now if this their Position be true, then Christ had his beginning and original about 1697 years ago, and his goings forth were not from the days of Eternity,

74. Jeremiah 6:28: "They are all grievous revolters, walking with slanders: they are brass and iron; they are all corrupters."

75. Matthew 17:27: "Notwithstanding, lest we should offend them, go thou to the sea, and cast an hook, and take up the fish that first cometh up; and when thou hast opened his mouth, thou shalt find a piece of money: that take, and give unto them for me and thee." Luke 2:34: "And Simeon blessed them, and said unto Mary his mother, Behold, this child is set for the fall and rising again of many in Israel; and for a sign which shall be spoken against."

76. As most Protestants did, Pastorius rejected the intense Catholic veneration of Mary as the mother of Jesus and thus the mother of God (in German, "Mutter Gottes"), especially expressed in many statues and images depicting her holding the Christ child.

77. 1 John 4:3: "And every spirit that confesseth not that Jesus Christ is come in the flesh is not of God: and this is that spirit of antichrist, whereof ye have heard that it should come; and even now already is it in the world."

78. Thus Pastorius accuses Köster and his followers of betraying the Protestant cause and essentially reverting back to Catholicism.

contrary to *Micah* 5:2.[79] Then these *American Brethren* (when one day or another they should be willing to put forth a Confession of their Faith and Principles, which the World is still wanting) can only say, Christ the flesh is come, but not Christ is come in the flesh, which to deny, is according to 1 *John* 4:3[80] to be that *ANTI-CHRIST*. The People called *Quakers* can and do truly say, That he who is come in the flesh is Christ; and that he who was manifest in the flesh, & purchased us with his own Blood, is God above all, praised and Magnified forever and forever, *Amen*.

Francis Daniel Pastorius

THE END

Printed and Sold by *William Bradford* at the Bible in *New York*, 1697.

🪺

A Missive of Sincere Affection to the so-called Pietists in Germany (Ein Send-Brieff Offenhertziger Liebsbezeugung an die so genannte Pietisten in Hoch-Teutschland; 1697)

INTRODUCTION TO THE TEXT

The following is an annotated translation by Patrick M. Erben of the copy of an original of Francis Daniel Pastorius, *Ein Send-Brieff Offenhertziger Liebsbezeugung an die so genannte Pietisten in Hoch-Teutschland* (Amsterdam: Jacob Claus, 1697), located at the Library Company of Philadelphia. Pastorius's *Send-Brieff* is a German-language complement to his English-language *Four Boasting Disputers* published in New York by William Bradford in the same year. It was never republished and appears here for the first time translated into English.

Whereas *Four Boasting Disputers* defended Quakers in America (and perhaps England), Pastorius's *Send-Brieff* tried to defend them among Pietist readers in Germany. Although cast as a letter to his Pietist sponsors in Frankfurt, it was meant to be published and to dispel any negative opinions about the Quakers spread by Heinrich Bernhard Köster's pamphlet *Advice for all Professors and Writers* (no longer extant), which Pastorius believed had been published in both English and German. It was also a response to a letter sent to Germany by a recent radical Pietist immigrant follower of Johannes

---

79. Micah 5:2: "But thou, Bethlehem Ephratah, though thou be little among the thousands of Judah, yet out of thee shall he come forth unto me that is to be ruler in Israel; whose goings forth have been from of old, from everlasting."
80. See note 77.

Kelpius, published in 1695 as *Copia Eines Send-Schreibens auß der neuen Welt* (Copy of a Missive from the New World).[81] The follower claimed that Pennsylvania Quakerism was in shambles, Quaker meetings had fallen apart, and the colony presented a fertile mission field for the newly arrived Pietist immigrants.[82]

Against this background of anti-Quaker rhetoric published in America and Europe, Pastorius used his *Send-Brieff* to plead with his German-speaking former compatriots in Europe not to judge the Quakers based on the prejudices spread about by others but to search for common spiritual principles and to judge the Quakers by their own words and writings, such as those found in Robert Barclay's *Apology for the True Christian Divinity* (1678). After first flattering the German Pietists for their part in a larger European movement toward renovation of the Christian Church, Pastorius devoted the body of his *Send-Brieff* to presenting his view of the Keithian controversy and his opposition to Köster's attacks on the Quaker establishment and beliefs. Pastorius thus continued the pamphleteering of the Keithian controversy for an overseas audience, specifically Pietists and other religious dissidents who could potentially be sympathetic toward the Quakers but who were, he believed, misled by Köster.

By writing and publishing his *Send-Brieff*, Pastorius took one of the most significant steps of his life, squarely and publicly aligning himself with Thomas Lloyd, William Penn, and the orthodox Quakers. For his German-speaking readers in Pennsylvania, this step would not have come as a surprise: Pastorius's personal and political affiliation with the orthodox Quakers was already well known there. In this letter written in German to his *former* Pietist friends, however, Pastorius's wholehearted defense of the orthodox Quakers revealed his public embrace of the Society of Friends and his formal identification as a Quaker. Although its ostensible purpose was to declare his "Sincere Affection to the so-called Pietists in Germany" (as its translated title makes clear), the primary and actual purpose of Pastorius's *Send-Brieff* was to declare his affection for the so-called Quakers in America; thus it functions both as a mirror for the German Pietists and as a lesson in religious tolerance. "Quaker" was originally an insult directed at members of the Society of Friends by their detractors; when Quakers themselves used

---

81. *Copia Eines Send-Schreibens auß der neuen Welt. . . . Germandon in Pennsylvania Americæ d. 7. Aug. 1694* has been attributed to Johann Gotfried Seelig but also to Daniel Falckner, both members of the Kelpius group, and is thought to have been published in Halle in 1695. For an English translation, see [Johann Gotfried Seelig], "Copy of a Report from the New World, being an Account of the dangerous Voyage and happy Arrival of some Christian Fellow-travelers, who undertook their Pilgrimage to the end of spreading the Belief in Jesus Christ. Job xxi 8. Printed in the year 1695," trans. Oswald Seidensticker, *Pennsylvania Magazine of History and Biography* 11 (1887): 427–41.

82. [Seelig], *Copia Eines Send-Schreibens*: "[The Quakers] have separated publicly and have thereby caused such a confusion amongst themselves that pieces of their established meetings lie scattered all over[. . . .] A door to a great harvest thus has been opened here, which the LORD opens more and more for us[. . . .] Every week, three gatherings take place in [Jacob Isaac's] house, where Küster speaks publicly for the great edification of many. He also holds a meeting once a week in Philadelphia, where he speaks in English" (translated from the original German by Patrick M. Erben).

the term, they usually paired it with the modifier "so-called" to emphasize its origin in religious intolerance. In addressing the Frankfurt Pietists as "so-called Pietists [*so genannte Pietisten*]," Pastorius reminded them that, like the Quakers, they had suffered from religious intolerance and shared a history of persecution. The sign of "affection" Pastorius sent the Pietists, therefore, was also a warning: if you believe the lies about the Quakers spread by Köster and others, you will join the ranks of religious bigots and become little more than hypocrites.

THE TEXT

A Missive of Sincere Affection to the so-called Pietists in Germany

Friends!

A few years ago a rumor reached us here that in Italy a number of people had perceived the manifest errors and coarse, superstitious practices of the papist churches, left them, and turned to a state of quietness, wherefore they received the derisive nickname "Quietists."[83] We also heard that in this, our earthly fatherland of the German nation, another group of people have risen, who, in order to punish the all too vexing fashionable vice and malice among themselves and others, strive to lead a God-pleasing life and are therefore called Pietists.[84] This rumor has caused no small joy among those who felt the Lord's precious and commendable work and effect in their own souls and still feel strongly from day to day, sensing in their reassured hope that now the time has arrived when the Almighty will humble those who have elevated themselves through their vain human laws and Godless character, and destroy their crown and give it to him who is chosen to have it and whose right it is to reign a thousand years, yeah, in all eternity. I, in my small place, have rejoiced in the said rumor more thoroughly than in any newspaper that has reached me from Europe during my 13 years here.[85] Since I was not insensible to the fact that such common talk usually does not contain the complete

83. Quietism was a reform movement within the Catholic Church that gained prominence in the 1670s and 1680s, especially as a result of the work and thought of the Spanish mystic Miguel de Molinos. Often viewed by Roman Catholic Christians as a complementary movement to Pietism, Quietism advocated an inner passivity that would ideally lead to a perfect union with God. It was, however, declared a heresy by Pope Innocent XI in 1687.

84. Though the works of important precursors of Pietism include the early seventeenth-century writings of the mystic Jacob Boehme and those of Johann Arndt (e.g., *Wahres Christentum* [1605–10; *True Christianity*]), the beginning of Pietism is often thought to be marked by the publication of Philipp Jakob Spener's *Pia Desideria* (1675). Pietists strove for a practical reformation of Protestant Christianity through leading a more godly life and having a personal, inward relationship to Jesus Christ the Redeemer (for a more detailed discussion of Pietism, see the introduction to this reader).

85. Pastorius arrived in Pennsylvania in 1683.

truth, I then said to myself "Quietists, Pietists, are but names. True Christians strive with fear and trembling, to live quietly and piously. Phil. 2:12, 1 Tim. 2:2."[86] Thus, I immediately asked for more certain news what your own and actual principles are that distinguish you from various sects of Christendom, and what might be your outward conduct and condition in this vile world; also, whether you, like others who want to live in Christ a God-like life, have to suffer under persecution in a country where through a secular peace treaty[87] the door is still kept closed to the spiritual-apostolic religion, yet apostates are being tolerated.

Thereafter it happened that several men as well as women, learned and unlearned (who were also named Pietists on the other side of the ocean), arrived here in Pennsylvania, pursuing a deceitful illusion of universal love and particular piety.[88] Yet they soon revealed openly (and still continue to reveal) through their own discord, quarrelsomeness, and other fruits of the flesh what kind of trees they are and that the bare leaves of the hypocritical testimony of the mouth do not matter.[89] I do not say this because I did not expect something better among many of you (even though many of those who have arrived here indeed do not seem to be of a simple and sincere heart). Rather, I wish to encourage all those who, next to myself, have heard the heavenly call and voice of our savior to a greater faithfulness to seek steadfastly, with due diligence and serious zeal, the desired goal and treasure. In addition, I humbly ask for the liberty among one or the other amongst you, to communicate, for the sake of a hopeful quickening in the Lord among the members of Christ over here, how and in what manner the merciful and graceful hand of God has taken possession of you, has lead you, and still leads you, and in how far his kingdom has entered and spread in your souls? I also request you to enclose in your correspondence some of your published writings. In return, I am glad to do the same if requested, all in untainted love and for the advancement of God's glory and eternal truth, which after the long night of the announced apostasy now dawns

86. This epigram is also contained in the "Silvula Rhytmorum Germanopolitanorum," the poetic section of the "Bee-Hive" (see chapter 5 of this reader). Philippians 2:12: "Wherefore, my beloved, as ye have always obeyed, not as in my presence only, but now much more in my absence, work out your own salvation with fear and trembling." 1 Timothy 2:2: "For kings, and for all that are in authority; that we may lead a quiet and peaceable life in all godliness and honesty."

87. Pastorius refers to the Peace of Augsburg or the Augsburg Settlement of 1555, which was to set an end to the struggles between Catholics and Lutherans in the Holy Roman Empire. It established the principle of *Cuius regio, eius religio* (literally, "Whose realm, his religion"), which allowed each prince to determine the state religion in his realm. Besides Catholicism, Lutheranism, and Reformed Protestantism, no other Christian religious denominations were tolerated, thus resulting in the frequent persecution of Pietists and other Protestant dissidents. Pastorius's critique of the Augsburg Settlement echoes similar sentiments among radical Protestants across Europe and was thus meant to build common ground between Pietists and Quakers.

88. Pastorius specifically means the followers of the mystic Johannes Kelpius who arrived in Pennsylvania in 1694, including Heinrich Bernhard Köster and Daniel Falckner.

89. Kelpius's followers were supposed to await in quiet devotion and celibacy the second coming of Christ in the Pennsylvanian wilderness. But several members of his group refused to adopt Kelpius's eremitic and abstemious lifestyle.

with heavenly brightness. Praise, thanks, and glory be to the God of heaven and earth for this and other unspeakable blessings![90]

I could probably receive such a relation easily from some corresponding acquaintances and relatives in high as well as low Germany, but either do not know the same sufficiently, or they may report, with a partial pen, things differently than they truly are.[91] Thus, I turn directly to you, knowing full well how harmful it is not only to spread wicked lies but also to accept and believe them at the disadvantage for their neighbor. One of the abovementioned new arrivals has already produced his masterpiece in this regard by pouring out his derisive, even hostile mind in a letter sent from here to Germany, which (as I heard reliably from Amsterdam) has already been printed and published. Besides other falsehoods, it mentions **"that George Keith has begun to reveal the pride and severe ignorance of God's word among the so-called Quakers, and has thereby caused such a confusion among them that here and there pieces of their meeting structure lie scattered about and that they now complain about the vanity and foolishness of their teachers, many of whom had already come as far as devaluing Christ's righteousness, blood, and death, and such other grave absurdities, which have arisen amongst them due to their ignorance of the Scriptures, etc."**[92] This has compelled me, in order to save the truth and represent the innocence of these unfairly defamed, faithful witnesses and servants of Jesus Christ, whose books I have read for the most part and whose oral testimonies and sermons I have frequently heard for more than 13 years, to deny and refute most solemnly with these present lines the fictitious accusations of this reckless defamer.

What the abovementioned new arrivals said about three years ago regarding the so-called Quakers and their teachings, when they were in England and needed money for their passage, can be gleaned from their written statement to John Field:[93] **"that they considered the so-called Quakers citizens of Jerusalem; that they had grown from a fertile and lasting root, at first having to take hold through many struggles in a hard rock, and that no storms could remove the kingdom of God as their goal, and, finally that they were a bastion and free city against those collected from the**

---

90. Up to this point in the letter, Pastorius seems intent on renewing his friendship with the Frankfurt Pietists by suggesting a rekindled communication and exchange of ideas, experiences, and publications.

91. Emphasizing the need to judge the Pietists' faith and conduct firsthand by their actual words, Pastorius slyly argues that the Pietists should grant the same courtesy to the Quakers.

92. Pastorius is directly quoting from *Copia Eines Send-Schreibens auß der neuen Welt*, attributed to Johann Gotfried Seelig (or Daniel Falckner) and published in Germany in 1695. In German print publications of the time, quotations were indicated by boldface rather than italic type.

93. Pastorius is trying to establish that Kelpius's Pietist followers were self-serving hypocrites who took advantage of Quaker generosity during their layover in London on the way to America but who then slandered the Quakers once they arrived in Pennsylvania. London Quakers had collected funds to sustain Kelpius and his followers during their travels and to pay for their passage to America. The London Quaker John Field (ca. 1647–1724) was a teacher, preacher, and writer; Pastorius lists numerous works by Field in his bibliography of Quaker writings, including several anti-Keithian tracts (see chapter 4 of this reader).

jaws of hell in Babylon." These formerly flattering hypocrites—now ungrateful guests—continue in their letter to John Field: **"It is not yet apparent what you will be in the future, but it is our abundant joy that we not only see your zeal and your order in the service of God, but also so many signs of a permanent ancient spirit amongst you that the gates of hell will wear themselves out against you. Your grey hair and your sorrows adorn your community like gemstones, etc."** When I now consider more closely these people's art of biding their time, which has now broken forth into an embittered, unfounded accusation, I would like to say with Isaac, the voice is Jacob's, but the hands are Esau's hands, or rather Joab's, who embraces with one and stabs with the other![94] How have our citizens of Jerusalem—rooted in a solid rock through their hard battles and wearing out the gates of hell—turned so quickly into proud, ignorant, vain fools? But the so-called Quakers pay very little attention to such personal abuse; they can console themselves knowing that their language of Christian humility and divine wisdom refutes and discredits their opponents among all who have eyes to see. Yet they always recognize their duty and obligation to answer any real accusation that slanders the truth in which they stand with solemn meekness, whenever God gives them leave to do so.

Thus you must know that George Keith, after he had left too much room to the evil inspirations of the adversary and had fallen into haughtiness, hate, and envy toward his brothers and other such damnable works of darkness, was rightly expelled, along with all his followers, by the so-called Quakers from their society as an unfit, rotten fish and was disowned by virtue of the power that Christ gave to his church. But that therefore pieces of their meeting structure lay scattered here and there, is, to give the child its proper name, a wanton falsehood. There is no more truth to this than if one agreed that because during the time of the apostles many of them left who were not a part of them (1 John 2:19);[95] several used to leave their meetings (Heb. 10:25);[96] Demas came to love the world again (2 Tim. 4:10);[97] and Hymeneus and Alexander were delivered to Satan for their shipwrecked faith and blasphemy;[98] and thus pieces of the first apostolic church's meeting structure lay scattered here and there.

94. According to Genesis 27, Jacob tricked his older brother, Esau, out of his birthright by disguising himself as his much hairier brother and eliciting the blessing he desired from his blind father, Isaac. And Joab was the nephew of King David and the commander of his army, whom David later accused of various betrayals and then had killed. Pastorius thus accuses the Kelpius group, especially Köster, for betraying their former benefactors.

95. 1 John 2:19: "They went out from us, but they were not of us; for if they had been of us, they would no doubt have continued with us: but they went out, that they might be made manifest that they were not all of us."

96. Hebrews 10:25: "Not forsaking the assembling of ourselves together, as the manner of some is; but exhorting one another: and so much the more, as ye see the day approaching."

97. 2 Timothy 4:10: "For Demas hath forsaken me, having loved this present world, and is departed unto Thessalonica; Crescens to Galatia, Titus unto Dalmatia."

98. Members of the early church at Ephesus, Hymenaeus and Alexander allegedly erred in their faith, described as a "shipwreck with regard to the faith" and were thus "handed over to Satan" (1 Tim. 1:19–20).

No, not at all! The Christians of that time often came together in unity, of one mind and one heart, as spiritual members of one body, through the bonds of peace tied to one another, etc. And thus act the so-called Quakers today: they are peaceful citizens of the heavenly Jerusalem, the glorious city of God, into whose always open gates nothing mean, pernicious, or deceiving can enter. For outside of it are the barking dogs and all those who love lies; they are allowed to write impudently into the open field, without consideration to natural fairness and a sense of shame, that the teachers of the so-called Quakers denigrate Christ with his justice, blood, and death. Yet they [the Quakers] confess firmly and unanimously that Christ Jesus is the eternal, only begotten Son of God, who was made by his heavenly father for both salvation and righteousness, so that in the fullness of time he came into the flesh, moved about in the body prepared for him by God, healed all those who had been taken over by the devil, whose work to destroy has been the primary cause and goal of his coming into the flesh, in which he suffered the sins of the whole world, the righteous one for the unrighteous. But, N.B.,[99] not just so we should through faith alone and imputation (through merely visionary attribution) enjoy and become part of this, but to follow his footsteps through his light, power, and glory (1 Peter 2:21),[100] i.e. to walk as he walked (1 John 2:6);[101] not in vanity like the heathen, etc. (Eph. 4:17),[102] but cautiously like the wise (Eph. 5:15);[103] uprightly, in the love and fear of the Lord, virtuous, righteous, and pious (Tim. 2:12[104] etc.); making our members into weapons and service of righteousness (Rom. 6:13, 19, etc. etc.).[105]

This the so-called Quakers believe. Their teachers, sent not by or through human beings but by Jesus Christ and God the father, testify and preach unanimously that the blood of the immaculate Lamb of God, which was killed from the beginning of the world, cleanses all sins, sanctifies and justifies before God all those who believe in the light and walk in the light in child-like obedience. They also claim, moreover, with irrefutable reasons, that our righteousness has to be better than of the Pharisees

99. "Nota bene" (Note well): observe carefully or take special notice.

100. 1 Peter 2:21: "For even hereunto were ye called: because Christ also suffered for us, leaving us an example, that ye should follow his steps."

101. 1 John 2:6: "He that saith he abideth in him ought himself also so to walk, even as he walked."

102. Ephesians 4:17: "This I say therefore, and testify in the Lord, that ye henceforth walk not as other Gentiles walk, in the vanity of their mind."

103. Ephesians 5:15: "See then that ye walk circumspectly, not as fools, but as wise."

104. Pastorius mistakenly cites Timothy (Tim.) here, but the passage he is actually referring to is from Titus 2:12: "Teaching us that, denying ungodliness and worldly lusts, we should live soberly, righteously, and godly, in this present world."

105. Romans 6:13: "Neither yield ye your members as instruments of unrighteousness unto sin: but yield yourselves unto God, as those that are alive from the dead, and your members as instruments of righteousness unto God." Romans 6:19: "I speak after the manner of men because of the infirmity of your flesh: for as ye have yielded your members servants to uncleanness and to iniquity unto iniquity; even so now yield your members servants to righteousness unto holiness."

and Scribes, who only say but don't do as they say. From the true witness of the Holy Spirit, among the prophets, evangelists, and apostles and no less in their own hearts and consciences, they [the Quakers] are assured that who does right, is righteous, and takes part in Christ's righteousness. Just as, on the opposite, the unrepentant and disobedient mock Christ's obedience, which he rendered his heavenly father until the most wretched death on the cross. Thus they cannot be heirs of the kingdom of God (1 Cor. 6:9),[106] but will receive the wages of their unrighteousness (2 Peter 2:13)[107] and will reap (oh, what a pitiful, terrible harvest!) what they have sowed (Gal. 6:7),[108] namely, the eternal damnation of the flesh (Gal. 6:8),[109] disgrace, wrath, misery and fear, etc. (Rom. 2:8; Prov. 22:8; Job 4:8, 9, etc.).[110] What do the manifold friendly invitations, serious admonitions, patient lamentations, and sharp threats of God left to us in the entire Holy Scriptures aim at other than to move use to love Him, fear him, keep his commandments, and live saintly and righteously?

Although many Lutherans (the religion in which I was born and raised) consider this impossible, the so-called Quakers know, however, that without this it is not possible to be an upright disciple of Christ.[111] Those who truly feel that Christ (whom the father gave all power in heaven and earth) rules within their souls can through him—or, rather, he through them—do anything. Those who do not believe this and grant the devil more power than the incarnate Son of God will easily be overcome by the former, rather than to resist him and to put him to flight, which they consider impossible. For now, I will spare you the apparent untruth and vile accusation (arguing *ad hominem*) against the poor Quakers which that the writer[112] uses to preoccupy [his readers]. Instead, pray for God's mercy that the same may see his hateful and therefore lying heart revealed in the light of Christ and have it cleansed in His holy blood through true remorse and penance, so that his ultimate reward may not be to go with other liars to the pit of the fire-burning wrath of God.

106. 1 Corinthians 6:9: "Know ye not that the unrighteous shall not inherit the kingdom of God? Be not deceived: neither fornicators, nor idolaters, nor adulterers, nor effeminate, nor abusers of themselves with mankind."

107. 2 Peter 2:13: "And shall receive the reward of unrighteousness, as they that count it pleasure to riot in the day time. Spots they are and blemishes, sporting themselves with their own deceivings while they feast with you."

108. Galatians 6:7: "Be not deceived; God is not mocked: for whatsoever a man soweth, that shall he also reap."

109. Galatians 6:8: "For he that soweth to his flesh shall of the flesh reap corruption; but he that soweth to the Spirit shall of the Spirit reap life everlasting."

110. Romans 2:8: "But unto them that are contentious, and do not obey the truth, but obey unrighteousness, indignation and wrath." Proverbs 22:8: "He that soweth iniquity shall reap vanity: and the rod of his anger shall fail." Job 4:8, 9: "Even as I have seen, they that plow iniquity, and sow wickedness, reap the same. By the blast of God they perish, and by the breath of his nostrils are they consumed."

111. In contrasting Lutherans and Quakers here, Pastorius claims that Lutherans reject the idea of an earthly sanctification of human beings, whereas Quakers believe humanity can and should strive for perfection.

112. It is unclear whether Pastorius is here referring to Köster or the writer of the *Copia Eines Send-Schreibens auß der neuen Welt* (Johann Gotfried Seelig or Daniel Falckner); either way, he continues to refute what he believed were lies about Quakerism spread among German readers.

In the half-century since the Lord has awakened them, the so-called Quakers have become so well known in England as well as here in America through their innumerable writings, Christ-like life, and patient suffering that they can rebut all tongues that oppose them and all slanderous pens that are deceiving [people] even abroad. And I wish with all my heart that you and all my beloved country-people who are concerned about their salvation should own and read their books in our mother tongue. There are large volumes in print by George Fox, Edward Burrough, William Smith, Samuel Fisher, Isaac Pennington, Robert Barclay and others, all in folio.[113] Since the same are in English and (as far as I know) only a few tracts are translated into German, I direct you, to begin with, to Robert Barclay's *Catechism* and so-called *Apology*;[114] primarily, however, I direct you to the in-dwelling Word of God, from which come forth and arise all good words and salutary teachings, as well as sufficient power to save our souls. If people would one day properly listen to and follow the word hovering in their heart and mouth, all academic quarreling, war of words, and blasphemy would soon find an end. I remember very well that in my youth I heard thousands and thousands of times the name Quaker and Enthusiasts called out (by those pompous and boastful roosters who are allowed to crow on their dunghill—the pulpit—the loudest). Since I am convinced, however, that many of the same know the actual meaning of neither the one nor the other name, I deplore the blindness of which they themselves are ignorant and that they will perish, in their corrupt nature, through their wicked defamation of something they know nothing about. On the other hand, I lament even more those who increase the measure of the blows to be expected hereafter; even though they understand the outward meaning of what they oppose and inwardly in their consciences know better as well, they nevertheless refuse to walk in Christ's narrow path of the cross. This reminds me of a conversation I had with a not quite so dumb, so-called canon,[115] who wanted to convert me from my erstwhile Lutheran faith with the following argument: **If the letter of the Scriptures alone were to be taken as the ground rule,** he said, **then it necessarily follows (and daily experience confirms) that as many sects will appear as sophistical heads come upon it who can and want to make themselves a following through their eloquence and other contributing coincidences, which Luther, Calvin, Menno,[116] and many**

---

113. George Fox, Edward Burrough, William Smith, Samuel Fisher, Isaac Pennington, and Robert Barclay were prominent Quaker writers, all of whom Pastorius cites in his bibliography of Quaker writings included in the "Bee-Hive" (see chapter 4 of this reader).

114. Robert Barclay (1648–1690) is often called the "apologist" for Quakerism: his *An Apology for the true Christian Divinity* (1676) was considered the most eloquent and powerful justification of Quaker beliefs. His *A Catechism and Confession of Faith* (1673) concisely formulated Quaker beliefs and doctrines.

115. A type of cleric in the Catholic Church.

116. Martin Luther, John Calvin, and Menno Simons were three of the most prominent figures of the Protestant Reformation.

others before and after them have done. **If one says, however, that the Scriptures are not the only foundation of our faith,** he continued, we consequently have to acknowledge, for that purpose, the traditions of the Roman Catholic Church, which have been propagated from hand to hand, and from generation to generation; or, however, we must recognize a higher principle, namely, the same Spirit that inspired and moved the first writers [of the Bible], which a certain people in England[117] have been said to be doing. **And if,** this canon concluded, **the rumor of this kind of people is true and if they truly teach and live according to this book,** pointing with his finger to a duodecimo,[118] which, besides a French map, lay under a gilded crucifix standing on a table, into which, however, I did not ask to look, **I have to confess, that they have a better foundation than we Catholics, and I would like, if I was still younger and fresher,** since he was quite old and had then broken a leg from falling down a staircase, **do anything to visit these people and to converse with them, etc.** Judging the significance of this argument I leave to those who can distinguish good from evil without affected and preconceived, inculcated delusions. It was far too weak to turn me toward the Papist church, which has been built on the sand of vain and opportunistic people's statutes. On the contrary, it weakened to no small degree the great illusion of the religion I inherited from my father,[119] so that I sometimes began to think what the reason might be that in the first, apostolic community no one was considered a true member of the same or considered a righteous Christian who did not possess the spirit of Christ and did not act according to its directions, and why today this spirit (for which one cries and sings at the top of one's voice, in Papist as well as Protestant temples, Veni Sancte Spiritus, reple Corda,[120] etc.) no longer leads and rules Christianity? Eventually, I was freed more and more from my unbelief and the godlessness that had been deeply inculcated in me at the universities. According to the talent given to me, I can now testify, for the glorification of God and as a well-meaning reminder to you all, that our heavenly father now wants to give his holy, good, and certain spirit to all those who pray for it in child-like faith and with a steady resolution to obey its salutary instruction and impulse.

Thus I entreat for you all at the throne of divine mercy (with which He also revealed and announced that the sum of all teachings is to fear God and keep his commandments) to busy yourselves next to me, and I next to you, to follow honorably

---

117. A reference to the Quakers, who believed in the indwelling of the Holy Spirit in every human being.

118. A "duodecimo" is a book using a size of paper created by folding and cutting a single sheet from a printing press into twelve leaves.

119. Francis Daniel's father, Melchior Adam Pastorius, had converted to Lutheranism. In this passage, therefore, Pastorius claims that his own commitment to Lutheranism was already wavering in Germany before he immigrated to Pennsylvania and became part of the Quaker community there.

120. "'Come, Holy Spirit, fill [my] heart,'" which refers to a prayer sequence in the Roman Catholic liturgy known as the "Golden Sequence."

our high and heavenly calling, and not only to know and profess the voice of Jesus Christ in our hearts, but also to follow obediently and patiently the saints who have come before us. This is the door where he stands and knocks; blessed are all those who answer him, for to them he enters, etc. Oh, the sweet presence of Jesus! Everything else is excrement and pride; all an outward shadow play; all subtle scholasticism and rationalism is in vain and futile in comprehending divine things. Non Disputatio Deum comprehendit, sed Sanctitas.[121] Sanctification and purity of heart is the way to see God, who is invisible—yea, completely unknown and will be in all eternity—to all those who are wise in worldly things and learned in the flesh. Therefore, let us trust in the so clearly dawning truth that is in Christ Jesus, or rather is Christ Jesus himself, and which alone can make us truly free and finish the good work that has been begun to His due honor and glory.

Amen.

From Your loving Friend,
Francis Daniel
Pastorius.

Germantown in Pennsylvania
The last day of December
1696.

P.S.

Concerning this country here, I wrote many years ago to my friends in spirit and in blood, whom I had left behind,[122] a circumstantial account[123] (which they had printed without my knowledge) which should still be sufficient for now. God, who is a god of peace as well as war, gave William Penn (who is also derisively called a Quaker and now in his absence is being railed at and reviled with various kinds of epithets by some of the abovementioned new arrivals) this province to govern as his property, which he received from the King of Great Britain[124] almost 17 years ago. God has preserved us, a defenseless people, amidst all the war and calls of war in distant as well as in *neighboring* countries until this present time in a state of happy retirement and has thereby strengthened our faith all the more, because he alone can avert our outward and inward enemies from us and give us physical and

---

121. "'It is not the disputant but the saint who understands God.'" Pastorius is quoting from the medieval Christian mystic Saint Bernhard of Clairvaux, *De Consideratione* (ca. 1150; *On Consideration*).

122. His friends among the Frankfurt Pietists and the members of his family.

123. Presumably, Pastorius is referring to his *Sichere Nachricht* (1684; *Certain News*; see chapter 1 of this reader for an original English translation). Although he might possibly be referring to his *Kurtze geographische Beschreibung der letztmahls erfundenen Americanischen landschafft Pensylvania*, which was bound with Melchior Adam Pastorius, *Kurtze Beschreibung der Reichs-stadt Windsheim*, published in Nuremberg, 1692, it is unlikely he would have referred to this text as published "many years ago" when he was writing the *Send-Brieff* in late 1696.

124. King Charles II.

spiritual peace, as long as we trust only in Him as our mighty protector. I further recommend us all to his all-encompassing protection. To Him alone are due, and are thus given by me in the most humble gratitude, laud, praise, honor, and majesty, now and in all eternity.

Amen.

Writings on Education

A New Primmer or Methodical Directions To attain the True Spelling,
Reading & Writing of ENGLISH (1698)

INTRODUCTION TO THE TEXT

The following text is a transcription and annotation of a copy of Francis Daniel Pastorius, *A New Primmer or Methodical Directions To attain the True Spelling, Reading & Writing of ENGLISH. Whereunto are added, some things Necessary & Useful both for the Youth of this Province, and likewise for those, who from forreign Countries and Nations come to settle amongst us* (New York: William Bradford, 1698), held at the Historical Society of Pennsylvania and made from an original on deposit in Friends' House, London, April 1939. According to Quaker historian J. William Frost, Pastorius's primer was "the only textbook written by an American Friend before 1774."[1] Though its actual circulation and use as a schoolbook remain to be determined, Pastorius clearly used the *Primmer* in his own schoolrooms.[2] It has never been republished or edited,

---

1. Frost, *Quaker Family in Colonial America*, 100.
2. For example, the students in Pastorius's Philadelphia Quaker school (who included his own sons) must have studied the *Primmer* and then produced a manuscript book titled "Genetliacum or an hearty Congratulation," which Pastorius incorporated and enlarged upon in his "A few Onomastical Considerations, enlarged From the Number of Sixty Six to that of One Hundred; and Presented or rather Re-presented to William Penn, . . . lately also the Father of John Penn, an innocent & hopeful Babe, by whose Nativity & Names sake they were first contrived." This manuscript contained investigations of and epigrammatic writings into the significance and history of a given name, such as William Penn's American-born son John. These exercises share with Pastorius's *Primmer* the effort to discover deeper moral and spiritual meanings below the surface denotation of words and names.

appearing here for the first time in a scholarly edition as a unique window into the history of literacy and language instruction in early America.[3]

A New Primmer was the first book of English language instruction printed in America specifically for non-English-speaking immigrants. Pastorius's work was modeled in part on Quaker founder George Fox's own primer, *Instructions for right-spelling, and plain directions for reading and writing true English* (1683). Historian of literacy Jennifer Monaghan calls both primers "doctrinal works . . . steeped in Christian devotional material."[4] And, as approved by the Quaker Yearly Meeting, *A New Primmer* does indeed mix religious and language instruction. Thus it combines a long list of religious and moral precepts with specific scriptural references, and a section on the names of months and days of the week instructs readers to refer to these with numbers instead of their pagan names, thus displaying the primer's underlying Quaker sensibilities.

The exclusive use of English in his primer as well as his other schoolbooks (unpublished and no longer extant) demonstrates that Pastorius regarded English as the lingua franca of the Pennsylvania colony. In dedicating the "Bee-Hive" commonplace manuscript book (begun around the same time that Pastorius wrote his *New Primmer*) to his sons, he even called English their mother tongue. Besides teaching spelling, reading, and writing, the primer acquaints English-speaking children as well as non-English-speaking immigrants with the peculiarities of the English language. One list guides learners through the pronunciation of vowel and consonant combinations, though it is doubtful such a list could have truly acquainted German or Dutch youths with the considerable differences in pronunciation between English and their respective mother tongues. Another helps learners differentiate the meaning of homophones—"Words, which almost are the same in Sound, yet differ in Sense and Orthography."[5] But, beyond its language instruction, *A New Primmer* reflects Pastorius's desire to create spiritual and linguistic harmony among Pennsylvania's diverse ethnic, religious, and language communities.[6] And he saw English as a means to achieve that Philadelphian harmony, threatened as it was by the doctrinal and political strife wracking the colony in the 1690s.

Much more than a guide to language and doctrine, the *New Primmer* projects Pastorius's vision of a Christian utopian community, and especially of a Christian utopian family. Toward achieving that vision, it teaches its students a key premise of Quaker reform: that human society could not become godly without a fundamental change in human language. Pastorius hoped to create a language portal through which

3. Since few readers today will likely use Pastorius's primer to practice spelling, the editors took the liberty of shortening certain sections, such as the word lists. All omissions are indicated with ellipses and annotations identifying the omitted content.

4. Monaghan, *Learning to Read and Write*, 93, 94.

5. Pastorius, *New Primmer*, 50.

6. On Pastorius's efforts to use teaching and language instruction to bridge differences, see Erben, *Harmony of the Spirits*, 159–93.

a new generation could be led to a more harmonious and purer society. Against the background of the Keithian controversy, its wealth of biblical references made perfect sense. Responding to the Keith and Köster factions' attacks on mainstream Quakers for their alleged lack of Bible knowledge and deviance from Christian doctrine, Pastorius made every effort to advance and give guidance toward a Quaker civic and linguistic code firmly rooted in Scripture.[7]

THE TEXT

A

New Primmer

OR

Methodical Directions

To attain the True Spelling, Reading & Writing of

ENGLISH.

Whereunto are added, some things Necessary & Useful both for the
Youth of this Province, and likewise for those, who from foreign Countries
and Nations come to settle amongst us.

By F.D.P.

All Blessings Come Down Even From God; His Infinite Kindness Love & Mercy,
Now, of Old & Perpetually, Quickeneth Refresheth and Strengtheneth
True Upright Willing Xtians & Young Zealots.
Examples prevail above Precepts.

Printed by William Bradford in New York, and Sold by the Author in Pennsilvania.
[..]⁸

Vowels,   a. e. i. o. u. y.

Consonants,   b p c k q d t f v g h j r s s z l m n x.

---

7. Although *A New Primmer* was his only published schoolbook, Pastorius also compiled a number of no longer extant manuscript manuals for a wide variety of subjects, from "Lingua Latina or Grammatical Rudiments" and "A Breviary of Arithmetick" to "Vademecum or the Christian Scholar's Pocket Book" in English to "Anleitung zur Englischen Sprach" (Directions for the Use of the English Language) in German. His several translations of Quaker classics, such as William Penn's *A Key, Opening the Way to Every Capacity* (1693; "Wᵐ Penns Schlüssel von mir übersetzt") and Penn's *Some Fruits of Solitude* (1682; "Wᵐ Penns Früchte der Einsamkeit, von mir verteutscht") into German specifically served a German-speaking student body. Unfortunately, all of these manuscript books seem to have been lost. See Pastorius, "Res Propriæ," and Learned, *Life of Francis Daniel,* 275–76.

8. *A New Primmer* begins with listing the alphabet in various types, omitted here to save space.

Diphthongs and Double Letters, aa, ai, ay, aw, av, ea, ee, eo, eu, ew, ey, ie, oa, oe, oi, oo, ow oy, ue, ui, uo, uy, w, &c.

ch, cc, ff, fl, gh, gu, kn, ll, ph, pr, pl, qu, ss, sh, sl, st, th, wh, &c.

Now when you know this Page right well,
Dear Children, then begin to Spell.
[. . . . .]⁹

Words of Two Syllables.

Ab-hor, bar-ren, con-stant, de-test, ex-cept, flat-ter, glo-ry, hus-band, in-ward, king-dom, lo-ving, mis-tress, no-thing, ob-ject, post-script, quick-set, rem-nant, sloath-ful, traf-fick, vul-gar, wick-ed, xer-xes, yrk-som, ze-no.
[. . . . .]¹⁰

Words of Four Syllables.

A-me-ri-can, be-ne-fac-tor, con-tent-ed-ness, dis-a-gree-ment, ex-pe-ri-ment, fi-de-li-ty, gra-ti-fi-ed, he-te-ro-dox, ir-re-gu-lar, la-bo-ri-ous, me-tro-po-lis, na-tu-ra-list, o-be-di-ent, per-se-ve-rant, qua-li-fi-ed, re-mis-si-on, sub-stan-ti-al, tem-po-ri-zer, un-du-ti-ful, won-der-ful-ly, xe-no-cra-tes, ze-no-bi-a.
[. . . . .]¹¹

Examples for the different Pronunciations of the Vowels,
Consonants, Diphthongs and Double Letters.

A. §. And, art, ask, ale, dame, grace, father. §. All, call, small, tall, a, [. . .], ant, am, as, at, that, what, apt, dark, substance, particular, affection, application. §. Metal.

E. §. Embark, enter, vertue, jest, there. §. Chest, here, evening, be, he, she, me, we. §. Care, have, vice, voice, likeness, rarely. §. Vices, voices. §. Needles [*needless.*] Leanes [*leanness*] ravel, rivel, drivel, shrivel, shovel, [*hovel.*]¹²

I. §. Bit, quit, will, win, live, children, give, sin, visible. §. Bite, quite, wile, wine, life, child, strive, blind, grind, fight. §. Carriage, marriage, parliament, cousin, medicine, (*medicinal*) evil, devil, venison, (*swingil*) §. Bird, third, first, with. §. Sirrah!
[. . . . .]¹³

---

9. Here follow several more double letter pairs and then a list of two-syllable words.
10. List of two-syllable words continues, followed by lists of three-syllable, then four-syllable words.
11. The list of four-syllable words continues, followed by lists of five-, six-, and seven-syllable words.
12. Words in square brackets here and in section X are inserted by Pastorius.
13. Text continues in the same vein for O, U, and Y.

AA. Aaron, Baal, Isaac.

Æ. §. Nathanael, Israelite. §. Cæsar.

AI. Air, pair, stair, affair, faith, gain, daily,

[. . . .]14

FLE. Trifle, riffle, baffle, muffle.

GLE. Reagle, struggle, angle, entangle, single, intermingle, gurgle.

KLE, Sickle, tickle, wrinkle, sparkle.

PLE, Maple, steeple, triple, principle, simple, example, apple, pimple.

SLE, Pulse.

TLE, Title, kittle, rattle, wrestle, epistle, apostle.

XLE. Axle   ZLE. Dazle.15

CRE. Acre, massacre, lucre.

CHRE. Sepulchre.   OURE. Soure

TRE. Mitre, nitre, salpetre.

> *Thus, CHILDREN, you can Spell and Read*
> *unjoyned Words,*
> *Go on, peruse what next this little Book affords.*

I.

A few OBSERVATIONS *for the very Novices, Readers & Writers.*

1. A Vowel maketh a Syllable, with or without any other Letter, as, *I am a Man.* *Ophel*16 *is not Urim.*17

2. The like doth a Diphthong (or two Vowels, which have no Consonant between them) as, *aw, ay, easy, either, ours or yours.*

3. But a Consonant cannot make a Syllable it self alone, it must needs have a Vowel before or behind, save the Interjection *St!* whereby we bid men to be silent.

4. A Syllable is a perfect Sound, made like as the former Observations do declare.

5. According to other Primmers, no Syllable contains (in the English Tongue) above eight Letters, as, *Thoughts, shouldst, strength*, but I am constrained to except the *Streights* of Calice.18

6. A word consisteth of one or more Syllables, never above eleven; see pag. 7.

---

14. Text now presents examples for other vowel combinations, followed by vowel and consonant combinations (of which the last page is excerpted below).

15. Dazzle.

16. Hebrew word *ophel* appears in the Hebrew Bible and the Old Testament as the name for an elevated part of a settlement, such as in Jerusalem or Samaria.

17. In the Hebrew Bible and the Old Testament, the Urim and Thummim are elements of the breastplate worn by the High Priest. The phrase "Urim and Thummim" means "Light and Truth."

18. By which Pastorius means the Pas de Calais (the strait between the English Channel and the North Sea), which is the shortest distance between England and France and is also called the Strait of Dover.

7. A word hath as many Syllables as there are Vowels in it, as, *Pennsilvania in America*
   Except 1. Double Vowels and Diphthongs, *may be esteemed a good peaceable Country*,
   Exc. 2. If it end in *e* or *es*, *because God multiplies there [. . .] Mercies more and more*,
   Exec. 3. The *u* after *g* and *q*, *And some by the guidance of a meek and quiet Spirit are
   come out of all Quarrelings.*

8. The Consonant of the following Syllable ought to be pronounced with the fore-going
   Vowel SPELL, *Colour, Modest, Calamity*, but PRONOUNCE *Col-lour, Mod-dest,
   Cal-lamity.*

9. Every Diphthong and double Letter maketh his Syllable long, as in *good, redeem,
   teacher,*
   [. . .], [. . .].[19]

   Except 1. *our* and *ous* at the words end, as in *labour, saviour, vertuous, dangerous.* 2.
   Ain, in *bargain, certain, fountain, villain.* 3. *Ue*, in *ague.* 4. *Ui* in *build, buy.*

10. For facilities sake, we say, *wusted* for worsted, *vitles* for victuals, [. . .] for hand-ker-
    chief, *dander* for dandruff, [. . .] for [. . .],[20] *'ent* for is not.

11. All Sentences and proper Names begin with Capital Letters, as, *By faith Abel, Enoch,
    Noah, Abraham, Sarah, Isaac, Jacob, Joseph, Moses, Rahab, Gedeon, Barak, Sampson,
    Jephtae, David, Samuel, and others, pleased God*, Heb. 11.[21]

12. The threefold Accent, *viz.* the *Circumflex* (~) which insisteth long upon a Syllable:
    The *Acute* (´) which insisteth not with so full a sound as the former: The *Grave* (`) which
    insisteth on very little, are obvious enough in the Pronunciation, but the Characters
    thereof not yet seen by me in English Writings.

II.
The most common ABBREVIATIONS.

&, *and*; &c. *and so forth*; h. *holy*; viz. *to wit*; i.e. *that is to say*; qtd. *as if he should say*;
wth, *with*; wch, *which*; mt, *ment*; ye, *the*; yt, *that*; yu, *thou*; yr, *your*; ym, *them*, wn,
when; o're, *over*; tho', *though*; I'm, *I am*; I've, *I have*; I'll, *I will*; he'll, *he will*; we'll, *we
will*; don't, *I do not*; 'tis, *it is*; there's, *there is*; wou'd, *would*; I heard 'em say, *them*; han't,
has not; shan't, *shall not*; his man's run away, *has*; God b'w'e, *God be with you*; men o'th
Country, *of the Country*.

III.
POINTS *of* DISTINCTION *To be observed in
Reading and Writing, for keeping the Sense.*

19. Text illegible.
20. Text illegible.
21. The biblical verses referred to by Pastorius are not quoted or paraphrased in our notes where they are
self-explanatory (such as the names here) or where their meaning is encapsulated in his text.

A _Comma_ (,) is a little stop or breathing.
A _Semi-colon_ (;) is a stop some-what longer.
(:) A _Colon_ is half a Period, commonly put in the middle of a sentence, like as
(.) A _Period_, or full stop, at the end thereof. As for Example,

Little Children, it is the last Time: And as ye have heard, that Anti-christ shall come, even now are there many Anti-christs; wherefore we knew, that it is the last Time. 1 John 2:18.

(?) An _Interrogation_ is put after a query, Can men gather Grapes of Thorns, or Figs of Thistles? _Matt._ 7:16

(!) An _Admiration_ or Exclamation O the depth of the Riches both of the Wisdom and Knowledge of God! how unsearchable are his Judgments, and the Ways past finding out! _Rom._ 11:33.

[ ] A _Parenthesis_ or _Crotchers._

( ) A _Parenthesis_ is an insert of some words within two hooks, which may be left out, and yet the sentence entire and perfect: _I often Times purposed to come unto you, (but was let hitherto) that I might have some fruit among you also, even as among other Gentiles._ Rom. 1:13 add 1 Tim. 3:2.

(-) An _Hyphen_ is a Note of Union between two Syllables or words; _High-minded, Self-willed, Judgment-Seat, Pen-knife-sheath, Fresh-Water-Fish._

(") Is a _NB._ or ☞ for extraordinary Passages.

(') An _Apostrophe_ is a mark of Elision, _It's true, 'tis true, advanc'd._

(‖) A Parallel.

(Î) An Oblisque.

(^) An Afterism.

(§) A Section.

(¶) A Paragraph.

IV.

The Names and Order of the BOOKS _current in the_ BIBLE,
_which (being a Greek word) signifieth Book; and is indeed the best of Books
that ever were Written or Printed by Mans hand._

The _Hebrews_ usually named their Books from some of the first words thereof, e.g.
The first Book of _Moses_ they called _Bereshith_, i.e. _In the beginning._
The second, _Ve-le-she-meth_, i.e. _Now these are the Names._
The third, _Va-ji-kra_, i.e. _And called_ (for so it begins in the Hebrew)
The fourth, _Bam mid-var_, i.e. _In the Wilderness._
The fifth, _El-le-ha-dab-ba-rim_, i.e. _These the words, &c._

But the Greek Interpreters, and others from them, called the first *Genesis*, because it declareth the Creation and Generation of the World and of Men.

The second, *Exodus*, because the passing out of the Children of *Israel* out of *Ægypt*, is therein related.

The third, *Leviticus*, because it treats of the Laws and Orders of the *Levites*.

The fourth, *Numbers*, because it tells in the beginning, the sum of the Children of *Israel*.

The fifth, *Deutronomy*, which is the second Law, or the Law repeated the second time.

Some of the rest are denominated from the Declaration of Matters and Things therein contained: Some from the Names either of the Writers, or of them to whom they were written, as *Joshua, Judges, Ruth*, first and second of *Samuell*, first and second of *Kings*, first and second of *Chronicles, Ezra, Nehemiah, Esther, Job, Psalms, Proverbs, Ecclesiastes*, (which signifies Preacher) *Solomons Song, Isaiah, Jeremiah, Lamentations, Ezekiel, Daniel, Hosea, Joel, Amos, Obadiah, Jonah, Micah, Nahum, Habakkuk, Zephaniah, Haggai, Zechariah, Malachi*.

Books of the New-Testament.

Matthew, Mark, Luke, John, The Acts, (viz. of the *Apostles*) the Epistle to the *Romans*, first and second to the *Corinthians, Galatians, Ephesians, Philippians, Colossians*, first & second to the *Thessalonians*, first & second to *Timothy, Titus, Philemon*, To the *Hebrews*, the Epistle of *James*, first and second of *Peter*, first, second & third of *John, Jude, Revelations*.

Books called Apocrypha.

The first & second of *Esdras, Tobit, Judith*, the rest of *Esther, Wisdom, Ecclesiasticus, Baruch*, with the Epistle of *Jeremiah, The Song of the three Children, The Story of Susannah, The Idol Bell & the Dragon, The Prayer of Manasseh*, The first and second of *Maccabees*.

Besides these aforementioned, many other good Books were written by the holy Men of God, which, through the Injury of Times, were lost, e.g. *Enoch's Prophecy*, quoted *Jude* v. 14. *The Books of the Wars of the Lord*, Num. 21:14. *The Book of Jasher*, Jof. [Josh.] 10:13. 2 Sam. 1:18. *The Book of Nathan*, 2 Chron. 9:29. *The Book of Shemaials*, chap. 12. 15. *The Book of Jehu*, 1 King. 16. *The Epistle of Paul to the Laodiccans*, Col. 4:16. And many things were never written at all, *John* 21:25. But whatsoever things were written afore time, were written for our Learning, &c. *Rom.* 15:1, 2 *Tim.* 3:16. Therefore, Young People, give attendance to Reading, 1 *Tim.* 4:13. Remember CHRIST[']S, *How readest thou? Luke* 10:26. and *Philips, Understandest thou what thou readest? Acts* 8:30. And if any of you lack Wisdom, let him ask of God, *James* 1:5. A man may read the figure on the Dial, but he cannot tell how the Day goes, unless the Sun shine. Oh, the sweet and pleasant *Sun of Righteousness!*

V.

General and Particular
DUTIES of True CHRISTIANS
Agreeing to wholsom Words, and to the Doctrine
which is according to Godliness, 1 *Tim.* 6:3.

Being by Nature Children of Wrath, even as others, *Eph.* 2:3. Children of Disobedience, *Col.* 3:6. all under sin, and gone out of the way, *Rom.* 3:9, 12. but convinced or reproved thereof by Gods holy Spirit, *John* 6:8. they harden not their hearts, *Heb.* 3:8, 13. sorrowing to repentance, 2 *Cor.* 7:9. they are troubled, because of their Transgressions, *Psal.* 31:9. ashamed, *Rom.* 6:21, mourning, *Matt.* 5:4, and weeping bitterly, *cap.* 26:75, they confess their faults, *James* 5:16, 1 *John* 1:9, *Dan.* 9:5, smite upon their breast (that Nursery of all evil, *Matt.* 15:19) and beseech Gods Mercy, *Luke* 18:13, repent, & are converted, *Acts* 3:19, turn themselves to the Lord, *Joel* 2:12, from Darkness to Light, and from the Power of Satan to God, *Acts* 26:18, forsake their Wickedness, *Isa.* 55:1, depart from Iniquity, 2 *Tim.* 2:19, abhor that which is evil, and cleave to that which is good, *Rom.* 12:9.

[...]²²

If Husbands,

They have Wives, as though they had none, 1 *Cor.* 7:29, dwell with them, according to knowledge, giving Honour unto them, as unto the weaker Vessel, 1 *Peter* 3:7, love them, *Eph.* 5:28, are not bitter to them, *Col.* 3:19.

If Wives,

They are in subjection to their Husbands, 1 *Peter* 3:5, learn of them, 1 *Cor.* 14:35, are sober, chaste, discreet, grave, shamefaced, not slanderers, keeping at home, guiding the House, &c. *Titus* 2:4, 1 *Tim.* 3:11, and 2:9, & 5:14.

If Parents,

They bring and train up their Children in the way they should go, *Prov.* 22:6, in the nurture and admonition of the Lord, not provoking them unto Wrath, Eph. 6:4, nor Anger, lest they be discouraged, *Col.* 3:21, love them, by chastening them betimes, *Prov.* 13:24, not with-holding Correction from them, but beating them with the Rod, *chap.* 23:13. *Heb.* 12:9. instruct them in the Truth, *Isa.* 38:19. *Deut.* 6. 6. *Joel* 1:3. and give them good gifts, *Matt.* 7:11.

---

22. Similar examples and biblical references continue for several pages, providing a scriptural guidebook and phraseology for Christian living. In the sections immediately following, Pastorius continues the same approach while focusing on specific groups of people in society.

If Children,

They honour and reverence their Father and Mother, *Heb.* 12:9. are subject unto them, *Luke* 2:51. obey them, *Eph.* 6:1. in all things, *Col.* 3:20. do not mock, despise, nor curse them, but honour and assist them, when old and poor, *Matt.* 15. 5. *Gen* 45:9, 10, 11.

If Masters,

They deal justly with their Servants, *Col.* 3:24. forbearing Threatenings, *Eph.* 6:9, knowing that they also have a Master, in Heaven, *Col.* 4:1, despise not their Cause when contending with them, *Job* 31:13. let them go free, after appointed time, *Jer.* 34:9, 14, &c.

If Servants,

They are obedient to their Masters, in singleness of heart, not with Eye-service, as men-pleasers, but with good will, doing service, as to the Lord, and not to men, *Eph.* 6:5, *Col.* 3:22, with all fear, not only to the good and gentle, but also to the forward, 1 *Peter* 2:18, not gain-saying, not purloining, &c. *Titus* 2:9.

[..]²³

Thus as God hath distributed to every man, and called every one, so they walk, 1 *Cor.* 7:17, and live to his Will, 1 *Peter* 4:2 (which they desire to be done in Earth, as it is in Heaven, *Matt.* 6:10) soberly, righteously and godly in this present World, *Titus* 2:12.

[..]²⁴

IV.

PROVERBS are so far from being inconsistent with *Truth*, that they are rather *delightful words of Truth*, as goads and nails fastened by the Masters of Assemblies, to admonish the Sons and Daughters of men, *Eccles.* 12:10. more precious Monuments & Reliques of ancient Times, than all the Statues and Moth-eaten Rags worshipped by Popish Idolaters. *Proverbs* are wrinkled and gray hair'd Sayings of our most experienced and judicious Ancestors, often containing a whole and wholesome Sermon in seven words: *Golden Money,* (so called from *admonishing*) of an old Coin, yet nevertheless current still in our Age, and harmlessly coveted after, even by such who hate Covetousness. *Solomon,* that wise and famous King of *Israel,* set many thereof in order, *Eccles.* 12:9. and spake himself three Thousand, 1 *Kings* 4:32. *Paul,* that eminent Apostle of Christ, and other divine Pen-men, used Proverbs, yea, of prophane Writers and Poets, *Acts* 17:28, 1 *Cor.* 15:33. *Titus* 1:12, 2 *Peter* 2:22. Not many years ago, the most Noble and tryed man of our Day and Generation that ever mine Eyes did see, bestowed some hours of his solitude and retirement, in digesting a little Book full, well deserving the Re-impression in this part of the world, and to be translated into other Languages, as

---

23. Text continues with similar biblical references for the following groups: stewards, subjects, elders, youngers, widows, virgins (and unmarried), willing to marry, and married.

24. Text continues for several more pages with general precepts of Christian conduct—a type of roadmap for building a Philadelphian community of brotherly love.

it is already in the *German Tongue*. I being provided with a good store of all sorts of the like sharp and witty *Apothegms* or short Sentences, (which under Thousand Heads I collected when yet a Lad and Scholar) was willing to insert any thereof in this place; but seeing the next preceeding Chapter did enlarge beyond expectation, and I not finding liberty within myself to diminish the same: (rather to add these following few words, *viz.*

That Peace and Mercy will be upon all who walk according to that Rule, converting holy Words in holy Works, shewing thereby their Faith. For though the just do live by Faith, *Rom.* 1:17, yet that Faith must be coupled with Charity, or it profiteth nothing, 1 *Cor.* 13:2, 2 *Peter* 1:5. It must have Works, or it is dead by it self, *James* 2:17. Love and good Works, the certain Mark of Discipleship, and unavoidable Effects of Regeneration. Works not of the Law, but of the Gospel, which Christ worketh in his Saints by his holy Spirit. Whosoever hath not that Spirit, is no *Christian, Rom.* 8:9. and all these, who are past feeling, Reprobates, 2 *Cor.* 13:5, *Eph.* 4:19.) I therefore at present omit PROVERBS, reserving them for another more reasonable Opportunity, in case these my first Fruits prove not fruitless, and meet with a kind and candid Reception, which I submissively hope for.

VII.

An Alphabetical *Collection of Words, which almost are the same in Sound,*
yet differ in Sense and Orthography.

A
Accidence, *accidents*
Acts, *ax, ask.*
Adapt, *adopt.*
[. . . .]25

VIII.

An Explanation of some difficult Words.
Absolve, To acquit.
Acerbity, Sowerness.
Adopt, to take for his Child.
[. . . .]26

    A. *Hard words to thee are light to me.*
    B. *Bright words to me are hard to thee.*

---

25. Text continues through a full alphabetical listing of difficult words for several pages.
26. Text continues these examples for several more pages.

IX.

Some PROPER NAMES *out of the holy Writ, Alphabetically placed,*
with their signification in English.

Aron, a Teacher.
Abigail, the Fathers joy.
Abram, a high Father.
[...]²⁷
Some Proper Names of a later [. . .] *and Original.*

A

Albert, Algernon, Anthony, Arthur, Archebald.

B

Bennet, Baldwin, Bryan.

C

Charles, Christopher.
[...]

Names of Women
Arabella, Agnes, Alice, Amy, Annis.
Bertha, Beatrice, Bona, Bridget.
Christian, Cicely, Constance.
[...]²⁸

X.

Serviceable Remarks concerning Numbers, Time, Weights, Measures & Money.

NUMBERS are charactered either by ten Figures, as 1, 2, 3, 4, 5, 6, 7, 8, 9, 0 or by seven Numeral Letters, I, V, X, L, C, D, M.

1, 2, 3, 4, 5, 6, 7, 8, 9, 10, 11, 12, 13, 14, 15, 16, 17, 18, 19, 20, 21, 22, 30, 33, 40, 44, 50, 55, 60, 66, 70, 77, 80, 88, 90, 99, 100, 101, 105, 110, 115, 234, 1000, 1200, 1340, 5678, 9999, 10000, 23000, 100000, 345000, 1000000, or one Million, 10000000, or ten Millions, 100000000, or an hundred of Millions.

In Writing and Pronouncing these Figures we proceed from the left hand to the Right, but in *Distinguishing* the same, contrary wise from the Right to the Left.

Millions,	*Thousands,*	*Units,*
1 2 3,	4 5 6,	7 8 9.
9 9 9,	9 9 9,	9 9 9.

---

27. Text continues this list of biblical names for several pages.
28. Text continues with modern names beginning D through Z.

I, II, III, IV, V, VI VII, VIII, IX, X, XI, XII, XIII, XIV, XV, XIX, XX, XXVI.
XXXVII, XL, XLIX, L, LI, LXII, LXXIII, LXXXIV, XCIX, C, CX, CXL, CCL,
CCCLX, CD, D, DC, M, MDCLXVI.

Besides these two sorts of Characters, there are also Counters usual in reckoning together, &c.

     I. *Head-Numbers*: one, two, three, four.

     II. *Ordinal Numbers*: The first, second, third.

     III. *Implicit Numbers*: a pair, or a couple, a dozen, a score.

     IV. *Abstractive* or *formal*: 1, 2, 3, 4.

     V. *Material*: 5 yards and 3 quarters.

     VI. *Divisive* or *equal*; *equally equal*, 4, 8, *or inequally equal* 2, 6.

     VII. *Inequal*, 3, 5, 7, 9.

     VIII. *Perfect*, 6. made up by all his Particles, 1, 2, 3.

     IX. *Imperfect, diminished*, 8. *Superabounding*, 12.

     X. *Compounded*, 12. which can be divided by 3 times 4, or by 4 times 3.

     XI. *Uncompounded*, 3, 5, 7.

     XII. *Digitus*, [less than ten] 1, 2, 3, 4, 5, 6, 7, 8, 9.

     XIII. *Articulum*[29] [having a 0 annexed] 10, 20, 30.[30]

     XIV. *Compacted*, 11, 12, 13, 14, &c.

     XV. *Homogeneous*, whole, 2, 3, 4, or *broken*, called fraction, ½, ⅔.

     XVI. *Heterogeneous*, or *mixed*, 2¾.

The parts or parcels of a Number; the *whole* being 60, the *half* thereof is 30, the *third* part 20, the *fourth* or a *quarter*, 15, the *fifth*, 12, the *sixth*, 10, the *tenth*, 6, the *twelfth*, 5, the *twentieth*, 3, the *sixtieth*, 1.

     To know what ones Daily Expenses come to in a whole Year.

Six Pence[31] a day makes in the year six Pounds, six half pounds, six Groats,[32] and six Pence.

Again, Seven Pence a day comes in the year to seven Pounds, seven half Pounds, seven Groats and seven Pence. The like reckon of any other Sum, &c.

---

29. "Articulum" is an antiquated reference to the unit of ten; the "articulum" joins the unit of ten to the (single-digit) unit (the "digitus or "digitum"). For other antiquated numbering systems or terms, see David A. King, *The Ciphers of the Monks: A Forgotten Number-Notation of the Middle Ages* (Stuttgart: Franz Steiner, 2001).

30. Words in square brackets in sections XII and XIII are inserted by Pastorius.

31. Plural of a penny in British currency.

32. English silver coins issued from 1351 to 1662, in value equal to four pennies. Later also, fourpenny pieces.

How to SET DOWN the value of any Sum:
[Put over Pounds *L.* over Shillings *s.*[33] over Pence *d.* and over Farthings *q.*][34]
Take this following Table for an Example.

	L.	s.	d.	q.
For three farthings, write	000	00	00	3
For a Penny,	000	00	01	0
For a Groat,	000	00	04	0
For six pence half Penny,	000	00	06	2
For a Shilling,	000	01	00	0
For 15 Pence Farthing,	000	01	01	1
For twenty Shillings	001	00	00	0
For sixty four Pounds, 9 shillings, seven Pence,	064	09	07	0
For five hundred fifty eight Pounds Two shillings, 3 farthings,	558	02	00	3
L.	623	14	09	1

[. . . .][35]

Measures, Weights and Coyns mentioned in the holy Scripture, reduced into English
VALUATION.[36]

1. *Measures of* APPLICATION.

A (*Common*) *Cubit*, from the Elbow to the fingers end, is a foot and a half.
A holy Cubit contained two of the common Cubits, or a full yard.
The Kings Cubit, a foot and nine inches.
A Geometrical Cubit, 3 yards, or 9 foot.
A Reed, six Cubits and an hands breadth.
A Mile, as much as a man could go in half a day, between Meal and Meal.
A Sabbath day journey, 600 paces.

2. *Of* CAPACITY; *Of dry Things.*
A *Kab*, one quart.
An *Omer*, one quart and half.
A *Seah*, a gallon and half.

33. Monetary unit and coin of the old British currency before decimalization, the shilling was equal to 12 old pence (5 new pence) or one-twentieth of a pound.
34. Words in square brackets are inserted by Pastorius. A farthing was a quarter of an old penny; a British coin of this value; figuratively, a farthing is the least possible amount.
35. Here follows a multiplication table.
36. In Pastorius's definitions in this section, only outdated terms, those not commonly known in the United States, or ancient Hebrew measures for which Pastorius has not provided the English equivalents commonly used in his time are annotated.

An *Epha*, half a Bushel[37] and one Pottle.[38]

A *Lethec*, seven bushels and one quart.

An *Homer* or *Cor*, 14 bushels and 1 pottle.

Of Liquids.

A *Log*, half a pint.

A *pot* or *Soxuary*, a pint and half.

A *Chornix* or *measure*, one quart.

A *Firkin*, four gallons and a half.

A *Bath*, 9 gallons and three quarts.

WEIGHTS *of Appension or Counterpoise.*

A (*common*) *Shekel* weighed a quarter of an Ounce.

A *Shekel of the Sanctuary*, half an ounce.

The *Kings Shekel*, 3 Drachms.[39]

A *Pound*, 12 Ounces.

A (*common*) *Talent*, 3000 quarter of an Ounce.

A *Talent of the Sanctuary*, 3000 half Ounce.

The *Kings Talent*, 9000 Drachms.

A *Mules Burthen*, two hundred weight.

MONEY.

A *Mite*,[40] three parts of one C. it weighed half a Barley Corn.

A *Quadrant* or *Farthing*, two Mites.

An *Assary*, half Penny Farthing.

A *Keshita*, one penny half penny.

A *Drachm* or *Penny*, 7 Pence half penny.

A *Gerak*, twelve pence.

A *Didrachm*, or (*common*) *Shekel*, 1 shilling 3 pence.

The *Kings Shekel*, 1 shilling 10 pence half penny.

A *Shekel of the Sanctuary*, *Stater* or *Silvering*, 2 shill. 6 pence.

A (*common*) *Shekel of Gold, Piece*, [. . .], *Darius*, or *Drachm of Gold*, 15 shillings.

A *Pound of Gold*, 75 Pounds.

A *Talent of Gold*, 2250 Pounds.

A *Talent of Gold of the Sanctuary*, 4500 Pounds.

---

37. Unit of dry and liquid measure, the British bushel is equal to 8 gallons or 32 quarts (about 36.4 liters), whereas the U.S. bushel is equal to 4 pecks or 32 U.S. quarts (about 35.2 liters).

38. Former unit of capacity for corn, fruit, and so on, the pottle was equal to 2 quarts or half a gallon (about 2.3 liters).

39. Principal silver coin of ancient Greece, the drachma was equal to a quarter of an ancient Jewish shekel.

40. In Great Britain, a mite was equal to half a farthing; generally, a person's modest contribution to a cause or charity.

Thus much of sacred Scriptures Money.

[*Auri sacra fames offecit omnibus & vis*][41]

[..][42]

A Table of *TIME*.

Sixty Minuits make 1 Hour. 24 Hours, 1 Day. 7 Days, 1 Week. 28 (some years 29) 30 or 31 Days, 1 Month. 12 Months, 1 Year. A Year contains 8760 Hours, or 365 Days, or 52 Weeks, 1 Day, and near 6 hours (which 6 hours every 4th year making a day, [. . .], then the 12th or last Month to have 29 days and that year vulgarly called a leap year.

The Heathens called the Days of the Week, and some Months after the Names of their Idols,[43] *Sunday, Moonday, Tuesday, Wednesday, Thursday, Friday, Saturday, March, April, May, June July, August, September, October, November, December, January, February.*[44] But those who hold fast the form of sound words, call them as they are called in holy Scripture, *viz.* the *first, second, &c.* day of the Week; and the *first, second, &c.* Month of the Year; see Exod. 12:2, chap. 16:1, John 2[:1].[45] willing to be circumspect in all things that the Lord hath commanded, making no mention of the Names of other Gods, neither letting them be heard out of their Mouths, Exod. 23:13.[46] but walking every moment in the fear and dread of the Almighty true and living God, who by his everlasting Word and Wisdom in six days created the World, i.e. the Heavens and all the Host of them, the Earth, and the Sea, and all things that are therein, &c. yea, who so loved the (in wickedness lying) world, that he give his only begotten son, that whosoever believeth in him should not perish, but live through him; Unto whom be Honour, Majesty, Glory and Dominion, forever and ever. *Amen.*

---

41. "The cursed lust for gold is the obstacle and force in everything." Latin insertion by Pastorius.

42. Here continue several more pages on international currencies and exchange rates in the seventeenth century.

43. Before the British Empire began to fully use the Gregorian calendar in 1752, it started the calendar year with the month of March rather than January (hence, February was called the last month). In any Quaker writing of Pastorius's time, therefore, the first month is March, the second month is April, and so forth. Nevertheless, one may find Quakers using Roman names of the months from September to December since they are simply derived from Roman ordinal numbers (September meaning "seventh month," and so forth). This section, therefore, is an important reflection of Quaker language reform and concludes, like a prayer, with the word "Amen" ("So be it").

44. Quakers in particular objected to days of the week and months being named after Norse gods (such as Wednesday for "day of Woden or Odin") or Roman gods or emperors (such as January for Janus and August for Augustus).

45. Exodus 12:2: "This month shall be unto you the beginning of months: it shall be the first month of the year to you." Exodus 16:1: "And they took their journey from Elim, and all the congregation of the children of Israel came unto the wilderness of Sin, which is between Elim and Sinai, on the fifteenth day of the second month after their departing out of the land of Egypt." John 2:[1]: "And the third day there was a marriage in Cana of Galilee."

46. Exodus 23:13: "And in all things that I have said unto you be circumspect: and make no mention of the name of other gods, neither let it be heard out of thy mouth."

Now Children, you know how to Spell
And how to read this Primmer *well.*
Hence search the Books of holy Men,
And then returning, take the Pen,
Because it is worth but a Mite,
If ye can Read, and not Write.

    Reading makes a full Man, *Writing* an exact Man, saith *Francis Bacon;*[47] and *Francis D. P.* doing the Will of God, Happy Men and Women.

An Additional Hymn of the Beloved of my Soul.[48]

*T*he Angel of the Covenant
              is to his Temple come,
The holy One *in Israel,*
              the King of Salem, *whom*
A long while we have longed for;
              therefore our hearts rejoyce,
And filled with the holy Ghost,
              cannot be void of Voice.
If we do not, the stones will speak,
              the speechless Babes will cry.
The Sucklings of Jerusalem,
              the dumb Mouths which did aye.
Again, when Christ *had open'd them,*
              out of their Graves will praise,
The goodness of our Saviour,
              If we that live do cease
But no, my Pen hath utterance,
              and goes now to declare
The Objects of my Faith and Hope,
              Joy, Worship, Love and Care,
The Anchor of my Victory and Crown,
              for which I strive,

47. Francis Bacon wrote in his essay "Of Studies" (*The Essayes or Counsels, Civill and Morall*; 1625): "Reading maketh a full man; conference a ready man; and writing an exact man." Note that, after beginning to quote Bacon's motto, but before expanding on it, Pastorius emphasizes the first name they have in common.

48. Pastorius first wrote "An Additional Hymn of the Beloved of My Soul" as entry 39 in the "Silvula Rhytmorum Germanopolitanorum," the poetic miscellany of his "Bee-Hive" manuscript (see chapter 5 of this reader). We have included both versions since they represent one of the few examples of Pastorius's poetry appearing in both manuscript and print during his lifetime.

My Rest and Consolation,
                        mine everlasting Life,
My spiritual Meat and Drink indeed,
                        the living Bread and Water,
Which I of Old was told to take,
                        when I yet was an hater
And Enemy of his Reproofs;
                        but at this present time,
Through Judgment feelingly redeemed,
                        exalt him in my Rhime,
And glorifie his pow'rful Name,
                        Hosanna! *Oh* Hosanna!
To him who comes from Heaven down,
                        the Angels food and Manna,
The Horn of my Salvation,
                        the Ark and Throne of Grace,
My Wisdom, Way, Truth, Righteousness,
                        my blessings Strength and Peace,
My Fortress, 'Rock, & steadfast Ground,
                        the precious Corner stone,
The Word, the good and perfect Gift,
                        the true Light alone,
Sufficient and marvelous, who doth
                        in all that blossom
Discern the very hidden Thoughts
                        and intents of their Bosom,
The King, Prince, Lord and Governour,
                        the Prophet, Head & Preacher,
The godly Shepherd of his Church,
                        Guide, Counsellor and Teacher,
My high Priest truly merciful,
                        harmless and undefiled,
Melchisedek, *by whom I am*
                        through Bloodshed reconciled,
The Lamb of God, and Passover,
                        for my sins sacrificed,
A full Propitiation and Ransom
                        greatly priced,
My Mediator, Advocate

and Intercessor there,
Where I, with Zion's Children,
          once expect to have a share,
Yea, with the well-beloved Son,
          and Image of the Father,
The brightness of his Majesty,
          the their all or rather
Jehovah *and* Immanuel,
          God self forever blessed,
Professed by the Hypocrites,
          by Upright Ones possessed.
Thus much of the Messiah now,
          whom in good Confidence,
(Who cleanseth, and who purifieth
          my Soul and Conscience)
I call my dear and choicest Friend,
          my Bridegroom and my Brother
My first and last, mine all in all,
          JESUS, and not another.
               F. D. P.
               FINIS

Part 2

MANUSCRIPT
TEXTS

Fig. 2 | Francis Daniel Pastorius, title page from "Alvearialia." MS 8845, Francis Daniel Pastorius Papers, Historical Society of Pennsylvania.

4 🐝

Commonplace, Encyclopedic, and Bibliographic Writings

"Alvearialia, Or such Phrases and Sentences which in haste were Booked down here, before I had Time to Carry them to their respective proper Places in my English-Folio-Bee-hive"

INTRODUCTION TO THE TEXT

The following selections are annotated transcriptions from Francis Daniel Pastorius, "Alvearialia, Or such Phrases and Sentences which in haste were Booked down here, before I had Time to Carry them to their respective proper Places in my English-Folio-Bee-hive," MS 8845, Pastorius Papers and Digital Library, Historical Society of Pennsylvania. Because the "Alvearialia" manuscript was an important element in Pastorius's system of collecting, excerpting, ordering, and evaluating ideas and concepts, the present selections have been made to highlight this process, especially the manuscript's function as a temporary holding place for quotations and citations he would eventually transcribe into more permanent form in his larger "Bee-Hive" manuscript.

Meaning "things relating to beehives" (*alvearium* is Latin for "beehive"), "Alvearialia" was a precursor to Pastorius's larger commonplace book and encyclopedia, the "Bee-Hive." As described on one of its title pages, "Alvearialia" was not a formal commonplace book but a loosely bound collection of papers of various sizes including informally collected excerpts from Pastorius's readings. He did not record the date he bound these papers together and gave them two proper title pages as well as a bibliography of the authors he consulted; the entries in the manuscript begin in the early 1690s and range over a number of years. The selections provided here represent a small slice of Pastorius's method of taking notes from books he read, especially those he only borrowed and would not have further access to later on; these notes constitute an undigested culling of important ideas and concepts from each source that would allow him later on to have access to the most important phrases, in writing his encyclopedia entries in the "Bee-Hive," for example.

The second title page of "Alvearialia" reflects on the process of screening and filtering the results of his studies by binding the worthy elements in a "book" and giving them a formal beginning. Mirroring Pastorius's mental activity, which went hand in hand with his material selection process, "Alvearialia" physically manifests his initial attempts to select ideas and concepts from other writers that were worthy of being written down, bound together, and introduced formally. Instead of discarding these preliminary steps, Pastorius deemed them necessary for his readers' contemplation. The Latin title "Tantum Quæntum lac Infantum" (Something like Milk for an Infant) perfectly expresses the dual significance of these first stages. Although milk is the first nourishment for an infant, and more substantial fare will follow, it is also the essential food for a developing human being. Pastorius regards the excerpts gathered in this manuscript book as evidence of his initial and possibly "immature" readings and selections, yet they were also essential for the development of his subsequent, more refined work in the "Bee-Hive": their value depended on their function within his larger project. Though, by themselves, the excerpts he collected might be immature or preliminary, in the larger context of Pastorius's reading and writing, they served to emphasize the need for constant critical evaluation and revision.

THE TEXT

Looking over of late my Rejectanea or Waste papers, among a great heap of others I met also with these here partly Inclosed, & partly Stich'd together which making (as you see) a pretty Little Book, deserve (me thinks,) a Frontispiece or Title page, And forasmuch as all what's Cancell'd is Inserted in mine English Bee-Hive in folio, I thought Convenient to call them

Tantum Quæntum lac Infantum,[1] Or

Talia Qualia Alvearialia,[2]

What others did Contrive, I carry to my Hive.

1. "Something like Milk for an Infant."
2. "Such Things as Relate to Beehives."

Desiring those, to whose hands they may Come, that perhaps shall never have the Opportunity to behold mine abovesaid Alphabetical Hive to make good use of these hasty Puddings or Schediasms,[3] minding always the h: Apostles wholsom Admonition:

1 Thess. 5:2[1]

Omnia Explorantes, Bonum tenete.[4]

The Ear trieth words, &c Job 34:3

Read, Reader, Read Judiciously

Shun Implicit Credulity:

Prove first and then Approve what's Good;

Judge not of things not understood.

These foregoing few lines are in lieu of a Preface and if any would have me dedicate it to some Body, I herewith Complementally consecrate the same <u>To himself</u> of what quality Soever

provided nevertheless he be One of the Excellent Spirited in this New English World, &c.

Or a true English Soul, as the Athenian Oracles phrase is.[5]

NB. <u>Post haste</u>[6] did write these Sheets: So Zoilus,[7] the Nibbler, says well, he can't read all, & therefore calls me Scribbler; <u>But</u> if he can not, another can, whom I dare call a Better man.

[. . . .]

The Authors, whereout I (after the manner of Bees) have gather'd the little Honey & Wax which you find in the following Sheets,[8] are

1. the first Volume of the Athenian Oracle, page 1.
2. Reginald Scot[']s discovery of Witchcraft,[9] p. 35.

---

3. Extemporized works, jottings.

4. "'Test everything. Hold on to the good.'" Pastorius is again quoting 1 Thessalonians 5:21.

5. The *Athenian Oracle*, published in 1703, was a series of questions and answers collected from *The Athenian Mercury*, a periodical written by the Athenian Society in London between 1690 and 1697, edited by John Dunton.

6. This reference to the speed with which Pastorius prepared the excerpts in this collection reveals an important aspect of the "Alvearialia": whenever someone would lend him a book, as quickly as possible, he would excerpt the most important ideas in unprocessed, raw form. More careful consideration and deliberate placement would take place later, on the pages of the "Bee-Hive."

7. The Greek critic and grammarian Zoilus (ca. 400–320 B.C.) was famous for his severe criticism of Homer; by extension, any censorious, malicious, or envious critic.

8. Wherever possible, the notes to the following list use entries from Pastorius's bibliographies of Quaker and non-Quaker writings assembled in his "Bee-Hive" (see below in this chapter). Pastorius added this list of sources later, when he produced the title pages and bound the previously loose sheets of papers in a volume, naming it "Alvearialia." The numbers after the titles refer to pages in "Alvearialia" where Pastorius used each source rather than to page numbers in the source texts themselves.

9. Reginald Scot, *The discovery of witchcraft, with a discourse upon devils and spirits* (London, 1665).

3. The Rights of the Christian Church asserted againstt all priests who Claim an Independent Power over it; anonymous;[10] p. 41.

4. E.W. the husbandman's Manual,[11] p. 53.

——R. B. Nine Worthies[12]——

5. Wm Temples two Volumes of Letters, and his Observations on the United Provinces of Netherland,[13] p. 57

6. Edward Cocker's Arithmetick,[14] p. 72

7. Poor Robin's Almanack, 1686,[15] p. 73

8. Francis Quarles Emblems & Hieroglyphicks,[16] p. 77.

9. The True born Englishman, D. Foe,[17] p. 85

10. Henry Sacheverell's Sermon,[18] p. 91

11. Ainsworth's Annotations upon the 5 books of Moses, Psalms,[19] p. 93

12. Mamut or the Turkish Spy's[20] first Volume, p. 103

    Eiusdem[21] Seventh & eighth Volumes, p. 125

13.   p. 113[22]

14. *William Penn's divers Treatises,[23] p. 147

15. Don Diego Saavedra's two Volumes of 100 Emblems,[24] p. 157

10. Despite his "anonymous," Pastorius is referring to Matthew Tindal, *The Rights of the Christian church asserted, against the Romish, and all other priests who claim an independent power over it. With a preface concerning the government of the church of England, as by law establish'd. Part 1.*, 3rd corr. ed. (London, 1707).

11. Edward Welchman, *The husbandman's manual: directing him how to improve the several actions of his calling, and the most usual occurrences of his life, to the glory of God, and the Benefit of His Soul* (London, 1706).

12. Robert Burton [Nathaniel Crouch], *The History of the Nine Worthies of the World* (London, 1687).

13. Sir William Temple, *Letters written by Sir W Temple Bart and other ministers of State, both at home and abroad, containing an account of the most important transactions that passed in Christendom from 1665 to 1672, in two volumes* (London, 1700); Temple, *Observations upon the united provinces of the Netherlands* (London, 1693).

14. Edward Cocker, *Cocker's arithmetick: being a plain and familiar method* (London, 1694).

15. William Winstanley (Poor Robin), *Poor Robin, 1686 an almanack of the old and new fashion* (London 1686).

16. Francis Quarles, *Emblemes* (London, 1709).

17. Daniel Defoe, *A True Collection of the Writings of the Author of the True-Born Englishman, corrected by himself* (London, 1703).

18. Henry Sacheverell, *Sermon the Peril of false Brethren, both in Church and State* (London, 1710).

19. Henry Ainsworth, *Annotations upon the five bookes of Moses, and the booke of the Psalmes, and the Song of Songs or Canticles* (London, 1627).

20. Giovanni Marana, *Letters writ by a Turkish spy, who lived five and forty years undiscovered at Paris: giving an impartial account to the Divan at Constantinople, . . . and now published with a large historical preface and index to illustrate the whole* (London, 1687).

21. "The same" (the preceding title).

22. Title reference left blank in the original.

23. It is unclear which of William Penn's many works or which compilation of his works Pastorius is referring to here. The bibliography of Quaker writings Pastorius assembled most likely includes all the works by Penn that Pastorius consulted.

24. Diego de Saavedra Fajardo, *The Royal Politician represented in one hundred Emblems, written in Spanish by Van Diego Sa* [, . . .] *done into English by Sir Ja. Astry* (London, 1700).

16. Still Ainsworth's Annotations upon the Song of Songs,[25] p. 169

17. Theophrasti Paracelsi Opera in folio, two volumes,[26] p. 170

18. Francesco de Don Quavedo of Visions,[27] p. 181

19. Pietas Hallensis, Concerning the Orphan-house at Glaucha,[28] p. 198

20. Ashhurst's Remarks on Nath. Heywood's Life,[29] p. 201

21. Henry Coley's Almanack, 1698,[30] p. 205

22. Geo. Parker's Almanack, 1699, against John Partridge,[31] p. 206

23. John Partridge's Almanack, 1699,[32] p. 211

24. Jane Lead's Message to the Philadelphia Society &c, Bundle of Revelations untied &c,[33] p. 212

25. Jacobi Viverÿ Werelt's Beschrÿvinghe,[34] p. 213

26. N.H. the husband forced to be Jealous,[35] p. 216

27. Culpepper's Physician's library or the London Dispensatory,[36] p. 221

28. Le Febure's compleat Body of Chymistry,[37] p. 224

29. Edward Phillip's Theatrum Poetarium,[38] p. 230

25. Henry Ainsworth, *Solomon's Song of songs. In English metre: with annotations and references to other scriptures, for the easier understanding of it* ([Amsterdam?], 1623). Pastorius did not record the edition he used.

26. Though Pastorius does not specify the edition, it is perhaps Paracelsus, *Aureoli Philippi Theophrasti Bombasts von Hohenheim Paracelsi* [...] *Opera Bücher und Schrifften* [...] (Strassburg, 1616).

27. Francisco de Quevedo, *The Visions of Don Francisco de Quevedo Villegas, knight of the Order of St. James* (London, 1667).

28. August Hermann Francke, *Pietas Hallensis: or a publick demonstration of the foot-steps of a divine being yet in the world: in an historical narration of the orphan-house* (London, 1705)

29. Henry Ashurst, *Some remarks upon the life of that painful servant of God Mr. Nathanael Heywood* [...] *by Sir H. Ashurst, Bart* (London, 1695).

30. Henry Coley, *Merlinus Anglicus junior, or, The starry messenger for the year of our redemption 1698* [...] (London, 1698).

31. George Parker, *An ephemeris of the coelestial motions, heliocentrick and geocentrick, the year of our Lord, 1699* (London, 1699); John Partridge, *Merlinus liberatus being an almanack for the year of our blessed Saviour's incarnation, 1699* (London, 1699).

32. See note 31.

33. Jane Lead, *The messenger of an universal peace: or a third message to the Philadelphian Society* (London, 1698); *A Fountain of Gardens* [...] (London, 1696). Lead's *Fountain of Gardens* begins with "A Bundle of Revelations Untied, And to be Dispersed to such as are Impartial Seekers, and Unwearied Searchers into the Deep things of GOD [...]," which Pastorius noted as the main title.

34. Jacobus Viverius, *Hand-boeck; of cort begrijp der caerten ende beschrijvinghen van alle landen des werelds* (Amsterdam, 1609).

35. Anon., *Five romances in one volume. Viz. Zayde, a Spanish history. Zingis, a tartarian history. The amours of Charles Duke of Mantua, and the Countess of Rovera. The husband forct to be jealous; or, the good fortune of those women that have jealous husbands. The cimerian matron, a notable example of the power of love and wit* (London, 1696).

36. Nicholas Culpcpcr, *Pharmacopocia Londinensis: or, The London dispensatory* (London, 1661).

37. Nicaise Le Fèvre, *A compleat body of chymistry wherein is contained whatsoever is necessary for the attaining to the curious knowledge of this art* [...] (London, 1664).

38. Edward Phillips, *Theatrum poetarum, or, A compleat collection of the poets especially the most eminent, of all ages, the antients distinguish't from the moderns in their several alphabets* [...] (London, 1675).

*however, from p. 235 to 242 much is taken out of the Life of Ambrosius Merlin, written by Thomas Heywood in 4°;[46] quem merito Valem dixeris atque Magum,[47] a prophetical poet.

39. Bartholomaeus Ziegenbalg and Heinrich Plütscho, *Propagation of the Gospel in the East: being an account of the success of two Danish missionaries, lately sent to the East-Indies, for the conversion of the heathens in Malabar* […] (London, 1709).

40. John Tomkins, *Piety Promoted, In a Collection of the Dying Sayings of Many of the People Call'd Quakers* (London, 1701).

41. See note 33.

42. See note 26.

43. Although it is not clear which text Pastorius is referencing, the Test Acts were a series of English penal laws that subjected those seeking public office to a religious test and imposed various civil restrictions on Roman Catholics and nonconformists, such as the Quakers. These laws were not repealed until the nineteenth century.

44. John Beaumont, *An historical, physiological and theological treatise of spirits, apparitions, witchcrafts, and other magical practices* (London, 1705).

45. See note 40.

46. Thomas Heywood, *The life of Merlin, sirnamed Ambrosius. His prophesies, and predictions interpreted; and their truth made good by our English annals* (London, 1641).

47. "Who is said to be a great poet and magician."

48. Thomas Lynford, *Some dialogues between Mr. G. and others with reflections upon a book called Pax vobis* (London, 1687). The book referred to in the title is [Evan Griffith], *Pax vobis, or, Gospel and liberty: against ancient and modern papists. By E. G. preacher of the Word* ([London?], 1687).

49. Alessandro Giraffi, *The second part of Massaniello, his body taken out of the town-ditch, and solemnly buried, with epitaphs upon him* [. . . .] *The end of the commotions. By J. H. Esquire* (London, 1652).

50. Michel Rousseau de la Valette, *The Life of Count Ulfeld, great master of Denmark, and of the Countess Eleonora his wife done out of French; with a supplement thereunto, and to the account of Denmark formerly published* (London, 1695).

51. John Hepburn, *The American defence of the Christian golden rule, or An essay to prove the unlawfulness of making slaves of men* (New York, 1715).

52. Arthur Dent, *The pain-mans* [sic] *path-way to heaven* (London, 1654).

53. Most likely a version of Eustache Le Noble de Tennelière, *The cabinet open'd, or The secret history of the amours of Madam De Maintenon with the French King. Translated from the French copy* (London, 1690).

42. Tho. Creed's The Life of Alexander the Great,[54] p. 278

43. Will. Chandler's brief apology,[55] p. 312

44. Culpeper's Astrological Judgment of Diseases,[56] p. 312

45. Free-holder begun the 23th day of December 1715,[57] p. 333

46. A Dream at Woodstock,[58] p. 297

–Gazettes or News-Letters, Ibid.,[59] p. 330

47. Joseph Glanvil's Saducismus Triumphatus,[60] p. 335

48. Robert Boyle's Medicinal Experiments, 3 parts,[61] p. 316

49. John Tomkin's Piety promoted, third part,[62] p. 300

50. Reflections upon the book Pax Vobis,[63] p. 75

51. The Loyal Americans Almanack 1715,[64] p. 76

52. R. Hawkin's the Life of Gilbert Latey,[65] p. 303

53. Anth. Willh. Böhm's the faithful Steward,[66] p. 316.

54. Reliquiæ Ludolfianæ, (+Hen. Will. Ludolf),[67] p. 318

55. William Penn's & George Whiteheads Serious Apology,[68] p. 154

56. Frances Shaftoe's Narrative,[69] p. 345

57. Ralph Winterton's Considerations upon Eternity,[70] p. eadem[71]

54. Textual reference not found.

55. William Chandler, A. Pyot, J. Hodges, *A Brief Apology in Behalf of the People Called Quakers* (London, 1694).

56. Nicholas Culpeper, *Culpeper's semeiotica uranica: or, An astrological judgment of diseases* (London, 1671).

57. Joseph Addison, *The Free-holder* [magazine/journal], nos. 1–55, 23 Dec. 1715–29 June 1716.

58. Anon., *A dream at Woodstock: occasion'd by a late journey thither* (London, 1714).

59. No reference to the specific title of a newspaper or gazette.

60. Joseph Glanvill, *Saducismus triumphatus: or, Full and plain evidence concerning witches and apparitions. In two parts. The first treating of their possibility; the second of their real existence* (London, 1689).

61. Robert Boyle, *Medicinal experiments: or, A collection of choice and safe remedies, for the most part simple, and easily prepared: useful in families, and very serviceable to country people* (London, 1693).

62. See note 40.

63. See note 48.

64. Unclear reference.

65. Richard Hawkins, *A Brief Narrative of the Life and Death of that Antient Servant of the Lord and his People, Gilbert Lately* (London, 1707).

66. Anton Wilhelm Böhm, *The faithful steward: Set forth in a sermon preach'd at St. James's, being the fourth, Sunday after Epiphany, 1712* (London, 1712).

67. *Reliquiæ Ludolfianæ: the pious remains of Mr. Hen. Will. Ludolf; consisting of I. Meditations upon retirement from the world.... VI. A homily of Macarius* (London, 1712).

68. William Penn and George Whitehead, *A Serious Apology for the principles and practices of the people call'd Quakers* (London, 1671).

69. Frances Shaftoe, *Mrs. Frances Shaftoe's Narrative, concerning the many [...] things the [hears] in Sir Theophilus Oglesthorpe's family and among others that the pretended prince of Wales was the so Theophilus' Son* (London, 1707).

70. Jeremias Drexel, *The considerations of Drexelius vpon eternitie. Translated by Ralph VVinterton Fellow of Kings Colledge in Cambridge* (London, 1632).

71. "The same page" (as the previous reference, p. 345).

58. London Yearly Meeting's Epistle 1718, p. 303[72]

59. Dr. Stoughton's Elixir Magnum, p. Ibid[73]

60. George Withers Abuses Stript & Whipt, p. 304[74]

61. The Spectator, Vol. 1, p. 156. 5th Vol. 2nd p. 156; Vol. 3rd p. 156. 10th; Vol. 4th,[75] p. 355.

62. Abraham Cowley's Works, in fol. 1668,[76] p. 292

63. William Hughes Flower Garden & Compleat Vineyard,[77] p. 319

64. Julian the Apostate, in 8°, 1682,[78] p. 320

65. Francis Bacon's Resuscitatio in fol, 1647,[79] p. 321

66. The Life & death of Lazarillo de Tormes[80] in which book was a defect from p. 5 to 21, and from p. 74 to 95, and from 100 to 117, p. 156

67. John Nichol's Hourglass of Indian News,[81] p. 353

68. Francis Fairweather's pleasant prognosticon,[82] p. 326

69. Richard Peeke's Three to one: an English-Spanish Combat,[83] p. 327

70. The pleasant history of Jack of Newberie,[84] p. 353

71. W. Kempe's the Education of Children in Learning,[85] p. 327

72. The Secret History of Q. Elizabeth & the E. of Essex,[86] p. 354

73. Sir David Lindsay's Works in 12° 1714 at Belfast,[87] p. 357

72. The epistles of the London Yearly Meeting, the highest authority of the Society of Friends, held great importance for Quakers around the world. Quaker epistles were modeled on the New Testament advisory or admonitory epistles sent to groups of the faithful. Yearly Meetings sent them to other Yearly Meetings to maintain cohesion among separate groups of Quakers.

73. Richard Stoughton, *Stoughton's elixir magnum stomachicum: or, The great cordial elixir for the stomach: so often mentioned in the Gazette* ([London?], n.d.).

74. George Wither, *Abuses stript, and whipt. Or Satirical essayes* (London, 1613).

75. *The Spectator*, published by Joseph Addison and Richard Steele in London, 1711–12.

76. Abraham Cowley, *The works of Mr Abraham Cowley* (London, 1668).

77. William Hughes, *The flower garden and compleat vineyard* (London, 1683).

78. [Samuel Johnson], *The account of the life of Julian the Apostate* ([London?], 1682).

79. Francis Bacon, *Resuscitatio, or, Bringing into publick light severall pieces, of the works, civil, historical, philosophical, & theological, hitherto sleeping; of the Right Honourable Francis Bacon* (London, 1657).

80. Diego Hurtado de Mendoza, *The pleasant adventures of the witty Spaniard, Lazarillo de Tormes: of his birth and education, of his arch tricks* [. . .]: *being all the true remains of that so much admired author: to which is added The life and death of young Lazarillo* ([1688]).

81. John Nicholl, *An Houre Glasse of Indian Newes, or a true and tragicall discourse, shewing the most lamentable miseries* (London, 1607).

82. Unclear reference.

83. Richard Peeke, *Three to one being, an English-Spanish combat, performed by a westerne gentleman, of Tauystoke in Deuon shire with an English quarter-staffe, against three Spanish rapiers and poniards, at Sherries in Spaine, the fifteene day of Nouember* (London, 1626).

84. Thomas Deloney, *The pleasant history of John Winchcomb: in his younger years called Jack of Newbery, the famous and worthy clothier of England* [. . .] (London, [1680]).

85. William Kempe, *The education of children in learning: declared by the dignitie, utilitie, and method thereof* (London, 1588).

86. [Person of Quality], *The secret history of the most renowned Queen Elizabeth and the E. of Essex* (London, 1689).

87. David Lindsay, *The works of the famous and worthy knight, Sir David Lindsay of the Mount: alias, Lyon, King of Arms. Newly corrected and vindicated from the former errors wherewith they were corrupted: and augmented*

74. The history of Genesis in 8°, 1708,[88] p. 358

75. A new Academy of Complements in 12°, 1717,[89] p. 296

[. . . .]

Though mine English Bee-Hive in Folio contains

1. Variety of words, phrases and Anglicisms

2. Verity of Common Sayings, Sentences & Proverbs,

3. Rarity of More Important Matters, &c.

Yet in this present Rhapsody[90] or Confused Mish-mash of mine you'll find mostly ingredients for a Phraseology,[91] the chief things themselves having been carried into said Hive Immediately out of the above mentioned Authors, which are but a very few of those I have perused, &, as it were, pick-pursed; however ye must not call me a Plagiary[92] neither; for it was done by their leave, consent & permission. Qui vis enim dixit, Si libet, ecce! licet.[93]

Ask each man by himself, and doubtless he will say

If ye be pleas'd to pick, ev'n ten times more, you may.

[. . . .]

Inferenda in Alvearium[94]

<u>The Athenian Oracle vol. 1 in 8°, 1704</u>; Interlita sunt Illata.[95]

Mean and trifling, a true English Soul, to the end of time, albeit with all possible dispatch. In his vegete and perfect man-hood. A moisture on the glass of a Telescope hinders the eye, tho' of the most exquisite sight from distinguishing distant Objects, p. 2. Scparate Souls retain their Individuation, & are neither divisible nor unible, p. 2. The Earth shall not be annihilated, but burnt up & refined, p. 3. Every individual person in heaven & hell shall see and hear all that passes in either State, p. 4. Souls are not pre-existent, but only Contemporary with their Embrio's, p. 4. Every man has as particular good Angel, Matt. 18:16 & 19:14, which presides over 'em tho' never a

---

with sundry works, &c. (Belfast, 1714).

88.   Richard Herne, *The history of Genesis. Being an account of the Holy lives and actions of the Patriarchs; explained with pious and edifying explications, and illustrated with near forty figures* (London, 1708).

89.   Anon., *A new academy of complements; or the lover's secratary* [*sic*]. *Being wit and mirth improv'd, by the most elegant expressions us'd in the art of courtship* (London, 1715).

90.   Literary work consisting of miscellaneous or disconnected pieces; a written composition having no fixed form or plan.

91.   Collection or handbook of the phrases or idioms of a language; a phrasebook.

92.   Plagiarist.

93.   "Which is to say, if it pleases you—look!—it is allowed." In other words, Pastorius encourages his readers to go and check—look up—his sources for their authenticity.

94.   "Entries incorporated into the 'Bee-Hive.'" The following sections are therefore crossed out, indicating that their content or most relevant phrases have been transferred.

95.   "What is stricken out is brought in." The material deleted here was transferred—to the "Bee-Hive."

vitious,[96] Luke 19:10.[97] Kingdoms have their Tutelary Guardians, Bodinus[98] his relation of his friend's Celestial Monitor, p. 5. The Soul of a fool is no less excellent than that of Solomon except in accidental affections, p. 6. Better to cheat an other than ones self, p. 6. Some will say they had rather spend five hours than be cheated of five shillings. Those men are the poorest in the World, who think they want more, not those that possess less, p. 6. Creatures may live without air. Fishes do not breathe, having no lungs, the organs of breathing, p. 7. History therein leaves us in the dark. Polygamy was customary among the Jews, to prevent worse Consequences disagreeable to, but is against the Law of Nature drawing the most fatal Inconveniencies with it as we may see in the Seraglios of the Eastern World. Love divided into various Channels or Beds is like a River sen'd at the same rate, always lessen'd, sometimes lost, p. 8. My Lord Bacon[99] thus observed, that a man is the most tickled where the skin is thinnest, & the place not accustomed of touching, p. 9. Miracles how far ceased, p. 10. After so hard a tug, *nachdem er so lang gestrebt*;[100] In the Law of God we find not the least foot step of any set Ceremonial nuptials, p. 11. Glass, vitreal bodies. Against Judicial Astrology. p. 15. 'Tis an easie matter to stumble in the dark. Of the Inhabitants of the Moon consult Domingo Gonzales or Bergerac's true history of those regions, p. 16.[101] Many will complement you very handsomely who at the same time, if they had a handsome opportunity, would cut your throat, p. 17. All things subject to change (not by the flux of Time, for Time destroys nothing, but by motion & antipathies in Nature, p. 18. Against transmigration of Souls, p. 19. Where the Paradise was, p. 19. Dead Swallow and flies may be brought to life again by the heat of the Sun, or the application of warm ashes, p. 20.

[. . . . .]

<u>The Rights of the Christian Church asserted Against the Romish, & all other Priests, who claim an Independent Power over it. Part I. The Third Edition in 8° London 1707.</u>

Preface. English men are bound to no laws, they never consented to, by themselves or Representatives, pag. 10. Penalty is the Sanction of the Law, p. 15. The Love of power, natural to Churchmen, p. 25. Nothing more inconsistent with the Laws which relate to the Church than an Empire within an Empire, p. 36. The king's spiritual supremacy

---

96. Vicious.

97. Luke 15:10: "Likewise, I say unto you, there is joy in the presence of the angels of God over one sinner that repenteth." In other words, angels are *not* watching over vicious or unrepentant people.

98. Jean Bodin (1530–1596) was a French jurist and political philosopher.

99. The English philosopher, statesman, scientist, jurist, orator, and author Francis Bacon (1561–1626) is often called the "father of empiricism and the scientific method."

100. "After he strove for so long."

101. Domingo Gonzales [Francis Goodwin], *De man in de maen Eeen verhael vnen reyse derwaerts* (Amsterdam, 1651); Cyrano de Bergerac, *The comical history of the states and empires of the worlds of the moon and sun* (London, 1687).

the Characteristick of the Church of England against popery and Fanaticism, p. 40. A book finely gilt. Justus quam extra formosior.[102] p. 63. One would be apt to think that high Church woman like, was pleas'd best with those who flatter most, 71. Churches–places to fiddle in, p. 72. The notion of an Independent Power in the Ecclesiastick now prevails, p. 80. Since the Laity must lose what the clergy gain, it can't be an unnecessary Caution to 'em, to be upon their guard, p. 82. The Principle on which the Reformation is built is the Right every one has of judging for himself and of acting according to his judgment in all those things which relate only to God and his own conscience, 89. These natural rights of mankind can't be made over to Prince or Priest, Ibid. Church in the Scriptural Sense always signifies the Christian people, sometimes with, & sometimes without, their ministers, whereas divines industriously labour'd to have it signify the Clergy, exclusively to the People, to give designing men a pretext to insult & domineer over the Church, p. 87. Errant Priestcraft & as ridiculous, as of the drummers and trumpeters, should call themselves the army exclusive of all others, p. 88. According to the usual Cant, I submit all to Mother Church, p. [. . . ?].

Now the Book itself

Man can't grant more than they have to bestow, pag. 3. Men being naturally by a state of freedom and Equality, can't lose the same without their own consent, in form-ing themselves into bodies Politick by a majority, p. 6. Governments owe their being to Consort, not Conquest, p. 9. God implanted in man that inseperable principle of feelings his own happiness, p. 10. A necessary duty of worshipping God according to Conscience, p. 15. Persecution is the most comprehensive of all Crimes, in destroying the end & the design of all Religion, the honour of God, and the good of mankind, future as well as present, p. 18. The doctrine of Persecution makes men play the devil for God's sake, p. 19. The good of the Country is the Supreme Law, & we are oblig'd to fight for its safety against men of our own religion, p. 20. The highest Injustice to force man to profess such speculative opinions as they can't believe, p. 22. Man's religion descends, not (like his lands, from father to son, but every one when capable, is to chuse his own Church, p. 23. The clergy claim a Legislative & Executive Power, belonging to them by a divine unalterable Right, p. 30. These pretended divino Jure Governours[103] command not only about indifferent matters, but determine what people shall believe & profess, excommunicate their Spiritual subjects for whatever they judge to be contempt, contumacy[104] & disobedience, p. 31. Anno 1581 at Edinburgh the Independent Kirk commanded a Fast on the same day when the king would have the Citizens to treat the

102. "Just how beautiful the outside." Pastorius is suggesting that the Roman Catholic Church is like a finely gilded book that is beautiful on the outside *only.*
103. "Rulers by divine right."
104. Perverse and obstinate resistance to or disobedience of authority; rebellious stubbornness.

French Embassador at a splendid dinner, p. 34. One would rather be kill'd outright than that none should have any commerce & converse with him i.e. to be excommunicated, p. 42, p. 43. The thunder of the Pope's Excommunications made people adore him out of fear as the Indians do the devil, ibid the Ecclesiasticks do not pretend to all at once; their way is to get one thing first, then another, next a third. For Rome was not built in a day, p. 53. The clergy have no Legislative power, but only a Right to advise, p. 63. The hearts of men are in the hands of the Lord, to wind & turn as he pleases. Unlawful not only to pray with (an Excommunicated) him, but for him, p. 72. The Clergy excuses their unjust Judgments, that the sentence was pronounc'd *clave errante*[105] p. 73. The Priest of Apollo cry'd: Iam furor humanos nostro de pectore Sensus expulit, & totu spirant praecordia Phoebum.[106] The Clergymen no more than the people can send an Embassador from God, who alone chuses his own Embassadors, p. 78. What Credential or what Mission can these pretend to who at the best are only Commentators, Note-makers or sermon-makers on those Doctrines which the Embassadors of God once delivered to the Saints? Ibid. They do not scruple to call their pulpit-speeches the word of God. They have the key of Heaven & Hell at their girdle. No room for the Independent power of any set of priests, p. 81. A Minister of Satan endeavours to put into his clutches as many as he can; so do not the ministers of Christ, p. 85.

*Excommun: Priests shut the doors of Churches, to prevent the worship of God in 'em, and open the same as a sanctuary to all sorts of rogues & villains, p. 94.

The clergy took upon 'em to be the sole Judges of Religion, that they might, without controul, impose what selfish doctrines they pleas'd, p. 99. These Christians and those heathen druids sacrifice men by burning 'em alive, p. 100. As God made the world by his word, so Priests would make him by theirs, [. . . ?], p. 103. Their own Creature–God. Christ instituted no new Rites but only superadded the remembrance of his sufferings to the Eucharist or hymn of thanksgiving, p. 105. Wickliff[107] saith that Excommunication & such like measures are not founded in the Law of Christians but cunningly invented by anti-Christians, p. 107. All Christians, Priests, & the only sacrifices of our Religion are Prayers, Praises & Thanksgivings, 108. Priests or Sacrificers Orthodoxy, which every Sect confine to themselves, p. 113. God commands men, on pain of Eternal punishment, to follow the dictates of their consequences, but the Priest commands the contrary, & so disputes the dominion with the Almighty, p. 116. Christians are haloo'd on by their Priests to worry & devour one another, p. 118. In defiance of the Scriptures. Acts do as

105. "By an erring judge." Excommunications, Pastorius suggests, can be undone if the judge making the decision did so in error.
106. "'Now has divine madness driven all mortal thoughts from my breast, and my heart is filled with Phoebus' inspiration.'" Pastorius is quoting from Claudius Claudianus, *De Raptu Proserpinae* (The Rape of Proserpina), book 1, translated by Maurice Platnauer.
107. English Bible translator, reformer, and theologian John Wycliffe (1320s–1384) was an important dissident among Roman Catholic priests in the fourteenth century.

fully express the mind as words, p. 123. Clothes of Beasts/kids are of no divine obligation tho' God himself so clothed our first parents, p. 124. A whole army of Lay-preachers, Acts 5:14, Phil. 1:14, [p.] 133. Some say, that the laity have power to preach Charitatively but not authoritatively, p. 135. The clergy owne that the baptism of boys tho' done in sport & jest to be good, p. 137. And the Papists allowed the Baptizing by women to be valid ibid.[108] Men must not do evil that good may come of it. The Ethiopian Eunuch was a good Christian,[109] tho' no Church man, he returning to his own Country where there was no Church, p. 139. The Charitable principle of Occasional Communion, p. 140. Safer to go to Pesthouses than to such Churches, where Charity, moderation and other Christian virtues are preached against Ibid. Priests let themselves in the place of God, p. 141, and so manage the simplicity of the poor laity as to make 'em fight their battels, & ruin and destroy one another, p. 143. Their lives might serve for a very good Rule, if men could act quick contrary to them, p. 145. Swearing and nonswearing Jacobites,[110] p. 147. The brazen Serpent proving the Occasion of superstition was stamp'd to powder, ibid. Directions received from inspired persons laid aside, ex. gr.[111] saluting with a holy kiss, the whole order of deaconnesses, p. 152. Anointing the sick with oil, abstaining from blood and things strangled, the washing of one anothers feet, p. 153, John 13:8. Presbyter and Bishop in the N.T. are always used synonymously, p. 152. Tho' Antichrist in the Prophetick Stile is described as a single person, yet his Name is Legion, since all are more or less concern'd who claim an Independent power, and by virtue of it exalt the Clergy above the Laity, p. 160, 2 Thess. 2:3, 4.

[. . . . .]

Out of William Penn's divers Writings, voluminous apologies.[112]

William Penn's great case.[113]

The Infelicity of governments to see and hear by the eyes and ears of other men, which is equally unhappy for the people. Patience outwearies persecution. A knotting Whip cord to lash their own posterity. Turn their own Executioners, and without any other warrant than their own guilt hang themselves. An Anti-Protestant and truly

---

108. On the same page (p. 137).

109. In Acts 8:27, Philip the Evangelist went from Jerusalem to Gaza, where he met the Ethiopian eunuch, who had been to Jerusalem to worship and was returning home.

110. The Jacobites were members of a political movement in Great Britain and Ireland that sought to restore the Roman Catholic Stuart King James II of England and his heirs to the throne.

111. For example.

112. Here "apologies" means "defenses" (of the Quakers). It is unclear why Pastorius abandoned his earlier practice of noting the page numbers for each excerpt.

113. William Penn, *The Great Case of Liberty of Conscience Once more Briefly Debated and Defended by the Authority of Reason, Scripture, and Antiquity* (London, 1670). Written while Penn was in prison, *The Greatest Case* is one of his foremost pleas for religious freedom.

anti-Christian path, [...?] Let him reflect upon his own morality, & not forget his breath is in his nostrils. A decimating Clergy, whose best arguments are fines and imprisonments. Where they can not give faith, they will use force. Ancient and modern traditions the Christian religion intreats all, but compells none. Martyrs enacted their religion with their own blood, & not with the blood of their Opposers. Fear of men slavish. Sense corporal and intellectual, to discern things and their differences. They impose an uncertain faith (not pretending to be infallible, themselves,) upon certain penalties. Take away our reason and faith, and like Nebuchadnezar[114] let us graze with the beasts of the field. It's Cruelty in the abstract. They deign not so much to convince the soul as to destroy the body. Force may make an hypocrite. Faith grounded upon knowledge and consent makes a Christian. A good-natured person. Corporal punishment for a meer mental Error, & that not voluntary too is inadequate. Faults purely Intellectual is intolerable hard to measure. Our ancestors retreat reform. Our back-march, <u>apostacy</u>. Money the prop of men. He carries his own penalty (prison) with him. <u>Conscience</u>. The effect and superstructure is ever less noble than the cause and foundation. Must we not see because our eyes are not like theirs. A Surmise is no certainty, neither is a maybe or conjecture any proof. If accusations must stand for proofs, we must grant to be criminals. It is a Jesuitical moral to suspect a man of an evil design and then kill him to prevent it. Their lazy life and intolerable avarice. The Noachical[115] principles tending to the acknowledgment of one God and a just life. The Romans had thirty thousand Gods. Curiosity never mist of proselites. Tertullian[116] that learned and judicious apologist tells us that it is not the property of religion to compell to religion. Bonner revived.[117]

Our first reformers were great Champions for liberty of Conscience. Grotius[118] says, that not a rigid, but easy government suits best with the northern people. To be deprived of liberty of Conscience is a slavery in the midst of the greatest liberty. Religion

114. Nebuchadnezzar (ca. 634–ca. 562 B.C.) was the king of Babylon during the Neo-Babylonian Empire. In the Old Testament, Daniel interprets Nebuchadnezzar's dream, predicting that his "dwelling shall be with the beasts of the field, and they shall make thee to eat grass as oxen" (Dan. 4:25). Later, he suffers from an apparent bout of madness, as he "was driven from men, and did eat grass as oxen" (Dan. 4:33).

115. Noachian; ancient or antiquated.

116. Tertullian (ca. 155–ca. 240) was an early Christian writer from Carthage, part of the Roman Empire in North Africa. Because, in his most famous defense of Christianity, the *Apologeticus* (197), he emphasized the principle of freedom of religion as a fundamental human right, Tertullian inhabits an important place in Penn's own defenses of and writings on religious liberty.

117. Bishop of London Edmund Bonner (ca. 1500–1596) initially helped Henry VIII in his split from the Roman Catholic Church but eventually reconciled with Catholicism. He became infamous as "Bloody Bonner" for persecuting heretics during the reign of the Catholic Queen Mary I (r. 1553–58). Thus "Bonner Revived" would be a reference to a persecutor, whether church or government figure, of religious dissidents like the Quakers.

118. The Dutch jurist and theologian Hugo Grotius (1583–1645) laid the foundations for international law, contributing to the idea that relations between countries should be governed by mutually agreed upon laws, rather than by force or warfare. As a follower of Arminianism, a religious school of thought declared heretical by Dutch Calvinists, Grotius had to flee the Netherlands and live in exile in France; he became an outspoken critic of religious intolerance.

by blood and torments is not defended, but polluted. Kings of bodies, not of souls. Ceremonies but the shirts & suburbs of religion. Nothing worse than legal tyranny. [. . . ?] a distemper scandalous and immoral. Such as came to visit the imprisoned have been imprisoned themselves for their charity. Oppressors: widows, poor & fatherless are all fish for their net. Words are but so many intelligible marks and characters employed to inform us of each others conceptions. To heal animosities. What we call a whale today, we must not call a sprat tomorrow. A peaceable assembly circumstatiated with all tokens of Christian devotion, no rout or riot. We are not surprized or scar'd of their ugly phrases. Losers have leave to speak.

Title Pages from the "Bee-Hive"

INTRODUCTION TO THE TEXT

The following are annotated transcriptions of all five title pages from Francis Daniel Pastorius, "His Hive, Melliotrophium Alvear or, Rusca Apium, Begun Anno Domini or, in the year of Christian Account, 1696," UPenn MS Codex 726, Rare Book and Manuscript Library, University of Pennsylvania, his largest manuscript book, commonly referred to as the "Bee-Hive." Pastorius added new title pages as he added new sections and expanded the scope of the work. The title pages of the "Bee-Hive" constitute its statement of purpose; they delineate Pastorius's methods of commonplace writing, his ideas for the transfer of knowledge from Europe to America, and the role of the intellectual in a nascent society such as that of colonial Pennsylvania. Even though these title pages do not appear sequentially in the "Bee-Hive," they are presented together here as an introduction to Pastorius's magnum opus.

The "Bee-Hive" is an immense conglomeration of ideas, sayings, excerpts, and original poetic compositions, which Pastorius began in 1696 and continued for the rest of his life. At its core, the "Bee-Hive" fulfills the classic purpose of a commonplace book as a memory device—a storage system for the knowledge collected to help readers and writers retrieve, as Pastorius tells us on the first title page, "remarkable words, Phrases, Sentences or Matters of moment." Ultimately, the "Bee-Hive" became not only a vehicle for collecting different kinds of knowledge but also a meditation on the process of collecting knowledge and even a definition of knowledge itself. To those ends, Pastorius assembled various title pages, placing the more recent ones ahead of the original title pages. Thus the first (original first) title page, to which Pastorius refers several times, is now on page 55 of the folio manuscript of the "Bee-Hive." Rather than merely providing title and author as the title pages to modern books do, Pastorius's title pages include mottos, descriptions, meditations, and other prefatory material meant to express the purpose and larger ethos of the collector's activity. As such, they are ideally suited to provide modern-day readers a glimpse of Pastorius's goals and ideals in assembling the "Bee-Hive" before they delve into the larger work.

Its multiple title pages, reflecting the various stages of the "Bee-Hive," reveal the compiler's ever-evolving process of knowledge collection. Although Pastorius ideally conceived of the "Bee-Hive" as the final stage of preliminary manuscripts and common-place books (including the "Alvearialia"), such finality eluded him as he searched for ways to make the "Bee-Hive" both all-inclusive (containing the largest amount of knowledge possible) and accessible (able to direct its readers or users easily and quickly to the knowledge they needed). Following the central metaphor of the "Bee-Hive," Pastorius hoped to carry the product of others' writings (the nectar found in flowers) into a central location (the hive), where it would be stored (in honeycombs) and refined into wisdom (honey) through various techniques of refinement and commentary. The "Bee-Hive" thus also eludes definitions of originality—Pastorius himself repeatedly says that everything and nothing in this collection is his. More akin to the postmodern deconstruction of the largely Romantic notion of the "author" as a self-contained genius, Pastorius already recognized the impossibility of definitively distinguishing his or any author's own ideas and forms of expression from those of others, yet he still attempted to attribute as completely as possible the sources of his excerpts while highlighting his own commentary and thoughts.

Although the "Bee-Hive" contains, as Pastorius characteristically puns, many nooks and crannies, it is helpful to delineate the main elements of the manuscript book for a general orientation or roadmap:

1. The title pages.
2. The bibliographies, listing Pastorius's sources from which he excerpted as well as the works of his broader reading.
3. The "Emblematical Recreations," pithy observations that derive insights from the contemplation of material objects.
4. The "Onomastical Considerations," observations on the meaning of a person's name or on a person's namesake in history (such as a series of observations on the name John, dedicated to William Penn's only son born in America).
5. The "Silvula Rhytmorum Germanopolitanorum," a poetic miscellany, consisting of Pastorius's original meditations on moral and religious subjects as well as occasional poetry reflecting on important people in his life, events, and books he read.
6. The "Alphabetical Hive," the encyclopedic section of the "Bee-Hive," where Pastorius condensed information from his far-flung reading on a variety of self-selected keywords, practical and mundane as well as philosophical and

abstract. Pastorius eventually moved from an alphabetical to a numbered-entry system, which he used to supplement and continue the original compilation.

In our selected texts from the "Bee-Hive," we chose to include the title pages and, in the sections to follow, the bibliographies, poems from the "Silvula Rhytmorum," and entries from the "Alphabetical Hive."

THE TEXT

For as much as our Memory is not Capable to retain all remarkable words, Phrases, Sentences or Matters of moment, which we do hear and read, It becomes every good Scholar to have a *Common-Place-Book*, & therein to Treasure up whatever deserves his Notice, &c. And to the end that he may readily know, both whither to dispose and Insert each particular, as also where upon Occasion to find the same again, &c. he ought to make himself an Alphabetical Index, like that of this *Bee-Hive*,[119] beginning infra page 10.[120]

And Seeing it is the largest of my Manuscripts, which I in my riper years did gather out of excellent English Authors, whose Names ye may see pag. 56, &c. My *Desire, Last Will and Testament is*, that my Two Sons John Samuel and Henry Pastorius shall have & hold the same with the Rest of my Writings, mentioned infra page 386 to themselves & their heirs for ever, and not to part with them for any thing in this World; but rather to add thereunto some of their own, &c. Because the price of Wisdom is above Rubies and cannot be Valued with the precious Onyx or Sapphire: And to get Understanding is rather to be chosen than Silver and Gold, &c.

Prov. 16:16. Job 28:16, 18.   Francis Daniel Pastorius.

In this Volume I only collected the Best out of English (or Englished)[121] Books, as you may see from fol[io] 55 to 64. Excepted never the less some few lines out of the *Dutch*[122] *Writings*

---

119. First mention of "Bee-Hive" as the title to this, Pastorius's largest manuscript book and a title that has been commonly adopted by scholars and nonscholars alike, even though it differs from the manuscript's formal title ("His Hive . . .") and from other, variant titles Pastorius uses on his subsequent title pages.

120. "Below" [on] page 10. To improve accessibility and highlight connections between subjects, Pastorius included frequent cross-references to other parts of the "Bee-Hive" manuscript. These page references are retained here to underscore his practice, even when, for constraints of space, the referenced sections are not represented in this reader.

121. Translated into English.

122. Pastorius here adopts the American English usage of "Dutch" to mean "German."

1. of *Sebastian Franck*,[123] an honest & notable man in his Time, Vid. Fol.[124] 59, num. 114, 115, 118.

2. Item[125] out of Georgy *Horny* Arca Mosis; Ejusdemq. Orbe Imperante & Politico, vid. fol. 60, num. 138.[126]

3. Item out of Henrici Cornelÿ Agrippae libello de Vanitate Scientiarum, vid. fol. 59, num. 31.[127]

4. Item out of Johannis Valentini *Andreae* Menippo sive Dialogis Satyricis, vid. fol. 59, num. 32.[128]

5. Item out of the high-German Medicinal & Chirurgical Works of *Theophrastus Paracelsus*, fol. 60, num. 219;[129] whereof these are printed in the same year, viz. 1603, both in folio at Strassburg & in 4° at Frankfort, I quote them only Parac. Fol. & Parac. 4° where in their very Compleat Indexes or Tables you may look for the pages, as also in mine Alvearialibus (a small Manuscript in 8°) from page 170 to 274.

    Of these writings I further carried a deal into my Collectanea Theologica,[130] and into my Talia Qualia Medicinalia,[131] &c.

6. Item out of Nehemiae *Grew's* Tractatu de Sale Cathartico Ebeshamensi,[132] vide fol. 59, num. 125.

7. Item Petri *de Vege* Medici Gratianopolitani Tractatus duo, I. Pestis praecavendae & curandae Methodus certissima, II. Per Dogmaticorum cum Spagiricis.[133] in 12°. 1628. Petrus de Vege sive[134] Vegaeus.[135]

---

123. Sebastian Franck, *Chronica, Zeÿtbuch vnd geschÿcht bibel von anbegyn biss inn diss gegenwertig M.D.xxxi. jar* (Strasbourg, 1531); Franck, *Paradoxa ducenta octoginta, das ist CCLXXX Wunderred vnd gleischsam Räterschafft* (1534).

124. "See folio."

125. "Also."

126. Georg Horn, *Arca Mosis; sive, Historia mundi. Quae complectitur primordia rerum naturalium omniumque artium ac scientiarum* (Rotterdam: Lugd. Bat. & Roterod., Ex Officina Hackiana, 1668); Horn, *Orbis politicus: imperiorum, regnorum, principatuum, rerum publicarum: cum Memorabilium Historicis & Geographia veteri ac recenti* (1668).

127. Heinrich Cornelius Agrippa von Nettesheim, *De incertitudine et vanitate omnium scientiarum et artium* (Leiden, 1643).

128. Johann Valentin Andreae, *Menippus, sive, Dialogorum satyricorum centuria, inanitatum nostratium speculum, cui accessit index titulorum* . . . "Coloniae Brandenburgicae Völcker" (Berlin, 1673).

129. Pastorius seems to be referring to a comprehensive collection of writings by Paracelsus, such as *Aureoli Philippi Theophrasti Bombasts von Hohenheim Paracelsi* [. . .] *Opera Bücher und Schrifften* [. . .] (Strasbourg, 1616).

130. Pastorius's manuscript book "Collectanea Theologica" seems to be no longer extant or has not yet been found.

131. See excerpts from "Talia Qualia Medicinalia" in chapter 7 of this reader.

132. Nehemiah Grew, *Tractatus de salis cathartici amari in aquis Ebeshamensibus et hujusmodi aliis contenti natura & usu* (London, 1695).

133. "Spagyrist": one who produces herbal medicine through alchemical procedures.

134. "Or."

135. Petrus de Vege, *Petri De Vege Gratianopolitani medici Tractatus duo. 1. Pestis praecauendae & curandae methodus certissima. 2. Pax dogmaticorum cum spagyricis* (Tournes, 1628).

8. Item Cornelÿ *Drebelÿ* Belgae Tractatus duo, I. de Natura Elementorum, II. quinta Essentia in 12°. 1628.[136]

9. Item Ian *Zoets* Wintersche Avonden. gedruckt tot Utrecht, in 12°. 1650.[137]

10. Item Guldene Annotatien van Franciscus *Heerman*; den vÿfthiende Druck, t'Amsterdam, in 12°. 1676.[138]

[. . . . .]   The covetous [. . .] will bind;[139]
But Boaz hand-fuls leaves[140]   For honest Ruth to find:
Here joyfully she gleans   Whole Ephahs[141] without pains.

Quod licuit quondam licit et nunc;[142] atq. modestis Virginibus fas est sollicitare Viros,
To Court.

Amlÿt affinam sic suavis Rutha Boazum   Invectis precibus, spicilegaq. manu.
Et. Virtute sua.[143]adde infra pag. 1.[2d],

§ 3.

{Doctus; Fortis; Sospes, Castus, Pinquis}

2. Omnis homo non est Dives, {Pauper; Servus; Liber; Turpis; Sanctus} qui Dive habetur.

{Segnis; Gnavus; Prosper[us]; Stultus}[144]

Some are for Learning {Riches; Wisdom; Beauty}in Esteem; But oftentimes not what they seem.

Some are for Strength{Health; Wealth; Wit}in great Esteem; But oftentimes not what they seem.

Mancher scheinet Reich {Klug; Starck} zu seÿn; Ist aber nichts als bloser Schein.

---

136. Cornelis Drebbel, *Cornelii Drebbel . . . Tractaus de natura elementorum* [. . .] (Frankfurt, 1628).

137. Jacobus Viverius and Jan Zoet, *Wintersche Avonden* [. . .] (Utrecht, 1650).

138. Franciscus Heerman, *Guldene* [. . .] (Amsterdam, 1699). Pastorius notes: "In this Hive there are also alledged a few notable Sentences of the primitive Fathers, viz. Ignatius, Polycarpus, Dionysius, Justinus Martyr, Irenaeus, Tertullianus, Clemens Alexandrinus, Origenes, Gregorius Thacem [?], Cyprianus, Arnobius, Lactantius, Eusebius Caesariensis, Athanasius, Hilarius, Cyrillus, Ephraem Syrus, Basilius Magnus, Gregorius Nazianzenus, Epiphanius, Ambrosius, Gregorius Nyssenus, Theotoretus, Hieronymus, Chrysostomus, Augustinus, Petrus Chrysologus, Prosper, Fulgentius, Gregorius Magnus, Isidorus, Beda, Johannes Damascenus, Nicephorus, Theophylactus, Anselmus, Rupertus, Bernardus, Petrus Lombardus, Alexander Hales, Bonaventura, Thomas Aquinas. N. B. Those of Thomas à Kempis you'll find in my Collect. Theolog. in 4°."

139. The top of this manuscript page suffers from severe damage, making these passages illegible.

140. In the Old Testament Book of Ruth, Boaz notices Ruth gleaning grain in the fields. After learning of her poverty, he invites her to eat with him, and he deliberately leaves grain for her to claim while keeping a protective eye on her. They later marry and have a son, Obed, the father of Jesse and grandfather of David.

141. An ancient Hebrew unit of dry measure, the ephah was equal to a tenth of a homer or about one bushel.

142. "Which was allowed once and is allowed now; and the divine law is."

143. "Thus sweet Ruth has won over Boaz as her husband with outspoken prayers, a grain-collecting hand, and her virtue."

144. Here, as well as in the English and German variations of the same sentiment below, Pastorius breaks up each epigram by inserting—in brace brackets {}—brief lists of words that could substitute for the words immediately preceding; for example, "Doctus" instead of "Dives," "Riches" instead of "Learning," or "Klug" instead of "Reich," and so on. Latin: "Every man is not Rich, {Learned; Strong; Safe, Virtuous, Fat / Lazy; Vigorous; Prosperus; Stupid} who has riches, etc."

Fett ist gleichwohl nur geschwulst.[145]

Frequenter Opinio fallit.[146]

3. Men of Learning, Sense and Reason   Have *to ev'ry thing a Season.*
    As the Summer serves the Mason,   And the Winter-time the Thrasher:
    Market-days the Haberdasher,   Sun-shine Hay-harv'st & the Washer.
      Omnia Tempus habent;   Tempore quaeq. suo.[147]
      Alles hat seine Zeit,   Lachen und Traurigkeit.[148]

4. An *Encyclopady* of all that can be known,
    Those very *well* may make by Common placing d[. . . ?]
    The *better* sort of things, out of the *best* of Books,
    Who happily their Spears beat into Pruning hooks.

5. I acknowledge with Macrobius,[149] that in this Book all is mine, & nothing is mine; Omne meum nihil meum[150] and though Synesius[151] says, It's a more unpardonable theft, to steal the labours of dead men, than their garments, magis impium mortuorum lucubrationes quam Vestes furari, yet the wisest of men concludes, there's no new thing under the Sun, Nihil novi sub sole, and an other, that nothing can be said, but what has been said already, Nihil dicitur, quod non dictum prius.[152] Seneca writes to Lucilius[153] that there was not a day in which he did not either write somethings or read & epitomize some good author. Vide omnino Spectator num. 316.[154]

    Here many Books Quint-essensed you see, give thanks to God, who thus enabled me.

155

---

145. "Many people seem to be rich {wise, strong}, yet it is only an illusion / just as fat is only a type of swelling."
146. "Opinion often deceives."
147. "All things have their time / At the time of its own."
148. "Everything has its time / Laughing and Sadness."
149. Abrosius Theodosius Macrobius (fl. ca. 400) was a Latin scholar, grammarian, and philosopher.
150. "Everything is mine and nothing is mine." Each Latin phrase in this section exactly repeats the point just made in English, thus reinforcing with some irony the point that there is nothing new under the sun.
151. Synesius (ca. 373–414 B.C.) was a Greek bishop in North Africa.
152. The Latin precepts in this section match exactly the English versions given by Pastorius.
153. Seneca (Lucius Annaeus Seneca; 4 B.C.–A.D. 65) was a Roman Stoic philosopher, statesman, dramatist, and satirist; Gaius Lucilius (ca. 180–103 B.C.) was the earliest Roman satirist.
154. "See everything in the *Spectator* number 316." *The Spectator* was a short-lived daily publication dedicated to the intellectual improvement of a broad readership and published by Joseph Addison and Richard Steele in London from 1711 to 1712. Pastorius's reference thus dates this part of the "Bee-Hive" to around 1712 or later.
155. The horizontal lines in this section indicate the beginnings of new title pages.

Fig. 3 | Francis Daniel Pastorius, detail from title page in seven languages, "Bee-Hive." UPenn MS Codex 726, Rare Book and Manuscript Library, University of Pennsylvania.

Η τ.ύ Φρανζισχύ Δανιήλις Πασ[τ]ορίώ   *Κυψέλη Μελιττών*[156]
FRANCISCUS DANIEL PASTORIUS *Alvear* ISTUD
JURE SIBI PROPRIO VNDICAT ATQ. SUIS.[157]
FRANCIS DANIEL PASTORIUS'S PAPER-*Hive*,
WHOSE BEGINNING ONCE WAS IN PAGE FIFTY-FIVE[158]
FRANZ DANIEL PASTORIUS SŸN *Bie-Stock*.
FRANTZ DANIEL PASTORIUS SEIN *Immen-korb*.
L'Avia (ALBIO Ò CUPILE) DI FRANCESCO DANIELE PASTORIO.
La Ruche (AUGE, PANIER OU CATOIRE) DE FRANÇOIS DANIEL
PASTORIUS.

In these seven Languages I this my Book do own, vide infra p. 7 num. I
Friend, if thou find it, Send the same to Germantown:
Thy Recompense shall be the half of half a Crown:
But, tho' it be no more than half the half of this,
Pray! Be Content therewith, & think it not amiss.
Yea and if, when thou com'st, my Cash perhaps is gone,
(For Money is thus scarce, that often I have none)
A Cup of Drink may do: or else, alas! thou must
Trust unto me a while, As I to others Trust,
Who failing make me fail: A thing extreme unjust!
To which I have no lust; But must per Force, poor Dust.

      Freund, *Was du findest, wiedergieb,*
      Sonst hält man dich vor einen Dieb

---

156. "Of Francis Daniel Pastorius, the Bee-Hive." Pastorius writes his name and title of the manuscript on this title page in seven languages: Greek, Latin, English, Dutch, German, Italian, and French.
157. "Franciscus Daniel Pastorius claims this hive to himself by proper right and to his own."
158. "ADDE PAG. 54, 51, 49, 9, 8, & 7." in the right margin.

In diesem; und in jenem Leben
Folgt anders nichts als Höllen-pein.
Gott Selbst hat diß Gesetz gegeben
Zu thun, wie man Gethan will seÿn.[159]
Quod Tibi vis fieri, hoc facias Alÿs.[160]

2. *My Brains I may not longer break, When now the Hive itself does speak.*

Come Friend! Be't Gentleman or Groom,
Peruse me in my Master's Room;
But never talk of Borrowing,
He mightily dislikes the Thing &c.
I once was lent, and almost lost;
Henceforth I'll keep at home,

And to my two Sons It saith:
Part not with me! I'm excellently good,
If rightly us'd & rightly understood.
You full well know your father never would
Have sold this Hive for 7 lbs. of Gold.
Or 462 sh. Currt. Silver Money of Penn
Silvania.

And thus attending on my Post,
Fear nothing that may come.
    F.D.P.
Freitus Dei Praesentiâ,
Fatigabo Difficultates Patientiâ,
Frustraborq. Dolos Prudentiâ.
Fortunante Deo Pietas Fert Denique Palmam, vide infra pag. 55 & 67.[161]

    Ρόδον Μελίσας μέν γλυχή σάξει Μέλι,
    Ενθεν δ Αράχνες άιανόν ίον πίει.[162]   Adde infra pag. 54, § 3.

    Rosa quidem Apibus Mel dulce stillat,
Sed inde Aranea grave efficit Venenum.[163]
From that Rose, whence the Bees their sweetest *honey* pluck,
The Spiders, Trantules, the worst of Venom suck.
Besser bringt man Honigseim
Immengleich von fernen heim,
Als dass man nach art der Spinnen

159. "Friend, What thou findest, return / Otherwise you will be considered a thief / In this and in the next life / nothing follows but the pains of hell. / God Himself has given this command / to do unto others as you would have them do onto you."
160. "Whatever you should wish would be done to you, do this unto others."
161. "Delighted by the presence of God, / I shall pass known difficulties, / And I shall frustrate deceit with prudence. / Prosperous by God, Piety supports the hand, see below pages 55 & 67."
162. "A rose indeed by the bees a sweet honey distills, / But thence a spider a burdensome venom produces."
163. "The rose provides sweet honey for the bees, / but from the same place it also pours horrid poison for the spiders."

Selbst was giftigs solt ersinnen.[164]

Αγαπά Μέλι Αρχτος.[165] Mel diligit *Ursus*.

Ursus Ego: laetor liquidi dilcedine Mellis,

Inq. meis Nectar dispono dapsile Cellis.[166]

Μή νεμέσα Βαιόισι, Χάρις Βαιόισιν όπηδεί.[167]

Ne parviducas *Parva*, est sua gratia Parvis.[168]

I with Demochares,[169] *small Things* to scorn forbid:

Oft in a little Place great Treasures may be hid.

    A Nightingale is better than a kite. Lev. 11:14.

    No Alms, nor Gift above the Widows Mite. Mark 12:42.

A small Diamond is of more worth than the largest Brick.

In Kleinen Säcken ist das best Gewürtz.[170]

1.*Pastor-Apes* dulci distendit Nectare	Cellas
Ut Coqua quaeq. Queat coquitare Jocanter	Ofellas.
Quas Mel laetificat vetulas (turpes) vernale	Puellas,
Has Aloë reddit moerentes fellea	Bellas.[171]

    Flattery . . . Honey   glad

                       makes people

    Veracity . . . Aloes   sad.

2. Franciscus Daniel *Pastorius*, Alvear istud

    Condidit, Ergo Suae Posteritatis erit.

Posteritatis erit Pastori, siqua superstes;

    Sin Orbus post hac, Orbis habeto Favos?

Est prius in Votis, ast haec Suprema Voluntas.

    Vota, Voluntatem subdo, Jehova, Tibi.

Velle Tuum, non Velle meum, fiat Sanctissime Jesu,

    Nostrum Velle sit harmonicum.

---

164. "It is better to bring honey / home like the honeybee / than one should like the spider / devise something poisonous."

165. "The Bear loves honey."

166. "A bear loves honey. / The Bear [is] I: [I am] rejoiced by the sweetness of flowing honey, / And in my cellar, I arrange my bountiful nectar."

167. "Do not despise the little things, grace has regard for the little things."

168. "Small, the young duke is not, his grace is small."

169. Demochares (ca. 355–275 B.C.) was an Athenian orator and statesman.

170. "The best spices come in the smallest bags."

171. "*The Queen Bee* fills the honeycomb with sweet nectar / So that some cook could cook morsels happily. / And Whichever girls aging in the spring, the honey delights, / The nectar renders the ugly ones beautiful as they're wasting away from bitterness."

Fac tamen, ut quod vis, id simul ipse velim.[172]

    Gottes fügen Mein Vergnügen:

    Gottes Schickung Mein Erquickung.

    Alles Gott Ergeben Ist das beste Leben.

    Was   mehr

       Gott will, und nicht

    Wann   eh'r.

    Alles was Er thut, Ist uns nütz und gut.

    Seine Lieb und Treü Ist alle morgen neü, etc.

    Zeitliches Leiden Bringt Ewige Freüden.

Alles Creütz und Hertzenleidt Dienet uns zur Seeligkeit;

Denn Welchen der Herr lieb hat, den Züchtiget Er. Heb. 12:6.[173]

    Μὲ Χρισ(τ)ε χυβέρνα[174] Te Duce Salvus ero.[175]

    Alle tritt und schritt Geh Herr Jesu mit.[176]

3. Ad nasutos Vitilitigatores, quos *Zoilos,*[177] *Momos,* Homeromastiges et Aristarchos appellamus.

172. Franciscus Daniel Pastorius, this beehive
    He formed, therefore it will be his offspring.
    It will be the offspring of Pastorius, if at all surviving;
    But if destitute after this, will it have honeycomb rings?
    It is first in pledge, but this Highest Will.
    The pledges, I subdue free will, Jehovah, for you.
    Sacred Jesus, do your will, not my will,
    Let Our Will be harmonious.
    Suppose nevertheless, that what you wish, I might at the very same time wish.
173. God's decree is my pleasure:
    God's providence is my refreshment.
    All that God provides is the best life.
    What God wants and not more / When God wants, and not before.
    Everything he does is for us meet and good.
    His Love and Faithfulness is every morning new, etc.
    Temporal suffering brings eternal happiness.
    All cross and heartache serves our blessing;
    For whom the Lord loves, he chastens. Heb. 12:6.
174. "Christ, direct me."
175. "With your guidance I shall be safe."
176. "In all your steps, walk with the Lord Jesus."
177. "To the large-nosed Brawlers, whom we address [as] Zoilos." This section is a preemptive jibe at potential critics of Pastorius's writings and endeavors in the "Bee-Hive." The Greek grammarian, Cynic philosopher, and literary critic Zoilus (ca. 400–320 B.C.), is known as one the first literary critics of the epic Greek poet Homer; thus, in subsequent generations, "Zoilus" became synonymous with "slanderer of poets." Momus was the Greek god or personified spirit of mockery and harsh criticism. "Homeromastiges" is the plural of "homeromastix," a nickname for Zoilus, meaning "Homer whipper" or "scourge of Homer." Aristarchus of Samos was an early Greek astronomer and the first to present a heliocentric model of the known universe (later credited as such by Copernicus). His inclusion in this list of archcritics was based on the common misconception that

Dum Sugillatis, dico, Sic Sutor Apellem!

Ne crepites ultra, Cerdo, tuam Crepidam.

Sed non nullus ait, Facies Cornicula risum,

Quando suas Plumas Grex Avium repetet.

Non moror hoc, Veniant omnes omnino Canorae,

Galbula[178] Frater erit; Quid Philomela? Soror.

Noctua,[179] Striae, Bubo, Scops, Nycticoraxq. facessant;

A quibus accept nil, nihil hae referent.[180]

Censure this Book, most freely, Friends, and spare not;

Like or Dislike, Praise or Dispraise, I care not.

Cry: Foolish *Jack-daw*,[181] when the tender-feather'd Flock

Once re-demand their Plumes, Thou art our Laughing-stock.

However, if my Pains be rightly understood,

I doubt not but you will/some will say: The greatest part is good.

I am a Bee, (no Drone)[182] tho' without Sting,

Here you may see, what Honey-Combs I bring.

Sufficient to supply Your want & Satisfy

The Readers Appetite, etc.

To painful *Bees* Some do prefer (I spie,)

Aristarchus's contemporaries considered the heliocentric view as sacrilegious and extended that rejection to Aristarchus himself.

178. To ward off the voices of some presumably harsh critics, Pastorius next invokes several songbirds and their melodious voices. Galbula, a member of the jacamar family, lives in the tropical Americas and is known to have a piping song. Philomela, according to Greek mythology, was a princess of Athens who was raped and mutilated by her sister's husband, Tereus, but upon exacting her revenge, she was transformed into a nightingale, whose song was henceforth thought to be a sorrowful yet beautiful lament.

179. This line lists birds that stand for useless critics or commentators on an author's writings, birds with presumably haunting or croaking calls. Noctua are all nocturnal birds; Striae are birds with linear markings; Bubo are owls in general; Scops, a particular species of owl; and Nycticorax, a species of night heron with a croaking, crow-like call.

180. To the large-nosed Brawlers, whom we address [as] Zoilos, Momos,
Homeromastiges and Aristarchos.
While you beat someone, I say, thus I shall call [you] shoemaker!
Do not beat any further your sandal, O cobbler!
But someone says, you would make little horns for a laugh,
Whenever the flock should seek back its bird feathers.
I do not delay over this, let all sweet singing birds come from everywhere.
The brother will be Galbula; What will be the nightingale? Sister.
Noctua, Striae, Owl, Scops, Nycticoraxq. Let them all depart;
From whom one receives nothing, and they bring back nothing.

181. The jackdaw is a small, gray-headed crow known for taking bright objects back to its nest. Pastorius uses jackdaws as a metaphor for the readers who steal other people's work.

182. A drone is a male bee, which, unlike the female worker bee, does not have a stinger and does not gather nectar and pollen. Gender notwithstanding, Pastorius sees himself as a worker bee (though one "without Sting") and his collecting knowledge as a gathering of nectar and pollen for the hive, in this case, the "Bee-Hive."

The idle *Drone*, the Wasp & Butterflie;
Alas! To these they give more leave to thrive,
Than Honey-Birds, who labour for the Hive!
And when perhaps once gotten into grace,
By *Gnats*[183] again are beaten out of Place. Vide Peach. Emb. 50.
        So Men of good Desert
        Must often stand apart.
And as Fr. Quarles says in his Emblems:[184]
    The Plougman's Whistle & the Trivial Flute
    Find more Acceptance than Apollo's Lute.[185]
        Item: Men prefer unskilled Tongues
            Ev'n to Seraphick[186] Songs.

Nullum est hic Dictum, quod non dictum sit prius. Terentius.[187]

1. *Apes,* ut ajunt, imitari debemus, quae vagantur, & Flores ad Mel faciendum idoneos.
    Deinde, quicquid attulere disponunt, ac per Favos digerunt. Seneca Epist. 84.
        Floriferis ut Apes in Saltibus omnia libant,
        Omnia nos itidem Depascimur aurea dicta,
        Aurea, Perpetua Semper dignissima Vita. Lucretius,[188]
    Legere et non Seligere est Negligere.[189]
    Lire, et ne point Noter, c'est Radoter.[190]
    Vergeefs is dan uw Werck gedaen,
    Wanneer ghy Leest, en merckt niets aen.[191]
        Reading is null & quite of none effect

183. Pastorius's note: "In the Latin called Gnathenes, & in the English Pick-thanks, Clam-backs, Sneezing Companions, etc."
184. Francis Quarles (1592–1644) was the author of *Emblems* (1635), one of the most popular books of poetry in seventeenth-century England.
185. Apollo was considered the Greek god of music and poetry, among many other things.
186. Seraphic; angelic.
187. "'Nothing has been said here that has not been said before.' Terence." The Roman playwright Publius Terentius Afer (ca. 195–ca. 159 B.C.) was likely born in North Africa and brought to Rome as a slave, where he was educated and eventually freed.
188. Lucretius (Titus Lucretius Carus; ca. 99–ca. 55 B.C.) was a Roman poet and philosopher whose only known work is *De Rerum Natura* (*On the Nature of Things*).
189. Bees, so that they affirm, we owe to imitate, which wander, & Making suitable flowers to honey.
    Then, whoever arranges and distributes to bring through the honeycomb, Seneca Epist. 84.
    Flowery so that Bees in a forest extract all,
    We consume all the said gold in like manner,
    The Gold, Always Constant most suitable for life. Lucretius,
    To gather and not to select is to neglect.
    To read, and not note down, is to ramble.
190. French: "To read, and not note down, it is to ramble."
191. Dutch: "A work is done in vain, / If one reads, and does not take any notes."

Unless we cull & for ourselves select.

The Chief & Choicest which we see,

Ev'n in Superlative Degree.

Dum Legis atq. Nihil proprios Excerpis in Usus,

Te fallis, Tempusq. Tuum; Vaga Lectio Lusus.[192]

All ye that Read, & nothing Note

Are mad caps, (say the French) and dote.

Or work in vain, (the Low-Dutch quote),

And lose your Time as I do vote.

But again, Non Chartae t'm, sed Cordi plurima fige,

Sunt Similes Bijugi Liber atq. Memoria [. . . ?][193]

The rarest things and Cases,

The fairest Words and Phrases,

Put in thy Common-Places;

Yet still not there alone,

For Tables ev'n of Stone,

May break, be lost and gone.

Then write the letters of both in heart & mind,

Where thou art sure to find

The rarest Cases and fairest Phrases Quicker than in Common-Places.

2.   Ad *Lectorem Benevolum* qui Nomine dignus Amici.

Haec Ego collegi quae Tu *Lectissima*, Lector, Jure vocare potes; Nam legis & relegis.

Si nihil hic discas, temet culpaveris ipsum, Hoc *Sententiolas* mille Volumen habet.

Multa tibi Veterum Liber hic, nec pauca Novorum

Scriptorum Canones doctaq. Dicta refert:

His, licet ambiguis, nihil ominus utere mecum;

Quae bona sunt lauda, Falsaq. linque malis.[194]   adde pag. 7, num. 3.

Diß Buch ist gleich der Welt: Die Zeilen wie die Leut,

192. "When you read and do not properly excerpt anything in the practice, / You waste your time; rambling reading is just play."

193. "Fix most things in the heart, not on paper. / A book and memory are like two brothers."

194. To *the benevolent reader* who is by name worthy of friendship.
     Here I assemble what you the most excellent, reader, by duty can invoke; for you to collect and recollect.
     If here you learn nothing, you will have condemned yourself, this volume has a thousand sentences.
     It tells you much of old books, and having been informed little of new writers, it bears the canon.
     Words matter:
     These, although ambiguous, nevertheless I use.
     Whereby good things are praised, and forsake things that are false by mischief.

Wer lauter gute sucht, Verlieret Müh und Zeit.[195]

Excusa Maculas, quas aut Incuria Scribae

Fecit, vel Calamus praecipitanter arans;

Nam veniam pro Laude peto, laudatus abunde,

Non fastiditus si tibi, Lector ero.[196]

    Adde infra pag. 7, § 3, and pag. 1, § 1, 3 &4, and pag. 54 § 5.

Read Reader, read this Book; but make a difference

'Twixt what was done in haste & what with Diligence.

Ne sis nimium, nimiumq. Severus;

Nam quandoq. bonus dormitat Homerus.[197]

    That find'st ill-hammer'd Rimes, Homerus sleeps sometimes.

Blockt in de Boeken vry, Nocktans met dit Besluyt dat ghy,

Gelÿck een Bye, Wilt Honigh suygen [...][198]

    Vale piu una Pecchia che mille Mosche.[199]

3.   *Ad Lectorem Stomachosum*: qui est Inimicus et hostis.

Lis mihi Corrector, resecando superflua Lector, Veraq. Digneris, q. desunt, jungere Veri.[200]

    Read not to Contradict, nor to Believe; But to weigh & Consider. Fr. Bacon.

Omnia explicates Bonum tenete, 1 Thess. 5:2[1].

Sunt Bona, sunt quaedam Mediocria; sunt Mala plura.

Quae legis hic, sic fit, Lector inique, Liber.[201]

Hier ist was guts, hier ist was schlechts;

Hier ist was krumms, hier ist was rechts;

Hier ist was Mittelmässigs auch,

Nach aller solcher Bücher brauch.

Quod tibi displiceant haec Collectanea nostra,

---

195. "This book is like the world, the lines like people, / Who seeks to find only good ones, wastes effort and time."

196. "Forgive the stains, which, I proclaim, the negligent hand of scribe, / or the pen plowing headlong at least produced; / For I seek forgiveness instead of praise, having been praised abundantly, / If you are not fastidious, reader, I will be."

197. "Do not be too, too much severe, / For [even] good Homer falls asleep sometimes."

198. "Freely study in those Books / With the Decision that you, / Like a Bee, / want to suck Honey [...?]"

199. "A single bee is worth more than a thousand flies."

200. "*To the angry reader*: who is unfriendly and hostile. / Be my corrector, O reader, by cutting out superfluous things, judging what's true, and what is lacking, and joining the truth.
'Test everything. Hold on to the good.' 1 Thess. 5:2[1]."

201. "There are good things, there some things that are mediocre; there are many bad things. / Whichever things you bring here, unjust reader, may the book be just."

Nil moror, aut miror; Mel sine Felle cupis.[202]

Wers besser kann dann ich,

Der freue Sich in Sich,

Und schone dieser Mühen.

Wers aber nicht Versteht,

Urtheile nicht, es geht

Ihm sonst wie jenem Schuster.

Auch hinter diesem Tuch Schützt ein Apell diß Buch.[203]

Malo, meus Codex Tineas ut pascat inertes, Quam te, mellilegus,[204]

Morne caso stomache.[205]

melancholice.[206]

He, who reads to grow but Bitter, And not Better, is more fitter

For to be a Stockins-Knitter, Or to drive a Cart or Litter,

Than to play the Cushion-Sitter, Ready to make Authors titter.

Censor iniquus eorum, quae sapienter a vittam herilem

Ad gnavi saepe Cleanthis Sunt lucubrata Luce.[207]

Adde infra pag. 8 § 3 & 5, and pag. 1 § 3 & 4, and pag. 54, § 4.

This English Manuscript in folio of mine

Is better, Zoilus,[208] than any one of thine:

Thou findest fault with this, And art thyself amiss.

When thou art dead and gone It will survive thy —-s.

When Cobblers[209] judge, then say,

Calceolarÿ[210] stay!

You never will be what I am,

Therefore ne ultra, Crepidam![211]

---

202. German: "Here is something good, Here is something bad / Here is something crooked, Here is something straight / Here is even something mediocre / Following the common usage of all books." Latin: "That this collection displeases you / I neither care nor worry; you desire honey without bitterness."

203. "He who can do this better than I, / may find joy in himself / and spare these efforts. / But he who does not understand it / judge not / or it will happen to him as a certain cobbler / and behind this cloth an appeal protects this book."

204. "I, like you, prefer gathering honey so that my book might feed the unskilled bookworm."

205. "Dreary stomachache."

206. "Dreary melancholy."

207. "'The unjust censor of those things which wisely from the life of the master / to the life of the student,' Cleanthes often [says] to the industrious, 'are carried industriously by lamplight.'" The Greek Stoic philosopher Cleanthes (330–230 B.C.) was successor to Zeno as head of the Stoic school in Athens.

208. See note 177.

209. Here and often in his writing, Pastorius uses "cobbler" in the negative or critical sense of clumsy workman or mere botcher.

210. A genus of flowering plants found in Central and South America, *Calceolaria* is also known as "lady's purse," "slipper flower," "pocketbook flower," and "slipperwort."

211. "Not above the sandal!" (Cobbler, stick to your last!)

Oh, impudent & shameless sham!
Θεοί χυψέλης ὀυροί ἐισιν ἀργιθαλὸς χαί Ανθρύνη.[212]
Acuti Alvearis Inspectores Parus & Crabro.[213]

4.   The Ear trieth words as the Mouth tasteth Meat, Job 34:3.
Therefore according to the Apostle Admonition, 1 Thess. 5:2[1].
Prove all things: hold fast that which is good, vide infra pag. 78.
     Let not anything which I have written be accepted without Trial,
or further than it agreeth with the Truth, saith Henry Ainsworth
in an appendix to his Annotations upon the 5 books of Moses.[214]
And so say I, Come Reader; try, What Words & things ensue:
hold fast that which is true.

FRANCIS DANIEL PASTORIUS
HIS
HIVE, BEE-STOCK,
MELLIOTROPHIUM.
ALVEAR, OR,
RUSCA APUM &C (*Vide Num.* 1015)
See page 1, 54 & 55
BEGUN ANNO DOMINI, OR IN THE YEAR OF CHRISTIAN ACCOUNT
CICICCXCVI. MDCLXXXXVI 1696 &c. &c.
WHICH PLAINLY SHEWS, THAT WE MAY WORD ANYTHING MANY
WAYS TO THE SAME INTENT.
ADD THE TITLE-PAGE OF MY BREVIARY OF ARITHMETICK IN 4°.

2.   Franciscus Daniel Pastorius *Osor honoris*,
Osor Luxuriae, Corditus Osor *opum*
De hac Idololatrica Trinitate Impiorum (Pride, Luxury & Avarice)Vide infra p.
81 § 24.[215]
Honour, Pleasure, Earthly Treasure;
Or what else Worlds-Fools do prize, Is disdained by the Wise, 1 John 2:15.
By The Lovers of true Wisdom, viz. the Wisdom of God, Christ Jesus, 1 Cor.
16:22, & 1:24.

212. "The guardian gods of the beehive will be the white clay and the hornet [wasp]."
213. "The keen inspectors of the beehive are the titmouse and the wasp."
214. Henry Ainsworth, *Annotations upon the five bookes of Moses, and the booke of the Psalmes, and the Song of Songs or Canticles* (London, 1627).
215. "Francis Daniel Pastorius, hater of honor, / hater of luxury, and prudent hater of work. / Of this idolatrous trinity of impious things (pride, luxury, and avarice), see below p. 81 § 24."

Whom to love is real *Philo-sophy*, &c. &c.

Vivendi & Moriendi Scientia. *Seneca.*[216]

3. He that hath my Commandments (Saith our Saviour, John 14:21)
    and keepeth them, he it is that loveth me: (add d. c. x 15 &
    15 & 10) And he that loveth me, shall be loved of my FATHER,
    and I will love him, & will manifest myself to him.

    And to whom *CHRIST manifests or reveals himself*, he it is that
    knoweth him; which knowledge is Life Eternal, John 17:3;
    1 John 5:20, & in regard thereof all things are to be counted
    but Loss & Dung. Phil. 3:8.

    To him all the Prophets give Witness, Acts 10:43, & the Scriptures
    testifie of him, John 5:39, for that end & purpose that we
    should Come to him, p. 40.

    Learn of him, and so find Rest for our never dying Souls, Matt.
    11:29; and have Life more abundantly, John 10:10 & 20:31,
    viz. that we should know him greater in us, than he that is in
    the World, ch. 4, [p.] 4.

    Binding the strong man, and spoiling his good, Matt. 12:29.

    Saving us to the uttermost, Heb. 7:25, and to be al in all, Col. 3:11.

4. Faecunda Alvus,[217] a Rich Stock.

    Alveu, Alvear, Alveare, Alvearium, Mellarium, Mellitrophium.[218]
    Apes dant Opes. *Honey brings Money.* Varro quotannis
    Alvearia sua locata habebat quinis millibus pondo mellis, 5000
    lbs.[219] See p. 85 & 53.

5. For as much now as it is *profitable to be Industrous*, and that the
    hand of the diligent makes Rich, Prov. 10, 14, etc. Let us
    spend more of our Time in Study than in Idleness; and slip
    not one hour, wherein we should neglect or lose any Oppor-
    tunity to lay up some thing in Store for the future. Want,
    Use or Delight both of our own Selves & of our Fellow-Mortals.

---

216. "'Knowledge of living and of dying,' Seneca."
217. "An eloquent beehive."
218. All words that mean "beehive."
219. "Bees deliver aid. *Honey brings Money.* Varro had his own beehives producing 5,000 pounds of honey annually."

Omnia Conando docilis Solertia vincit;[220] Ergo Nulla dies Sine
    Nulla dies abeat, quin   [línea] ducta Supersit.[221]
    Count that day spent in vain, whose Setting Sun
    Views from thy hand no *Line*, nor nothing, run.
Studium & Constantia, Labor & Tolerantia Colligent ab Infantia
    Docta & Elegantia Lectorem delectantia.[222]

6.   The Bee is little among such as flie, but her fruit is the Chief of
        Sweet things. *Ecclesiasticus* 11:3. *Honey's* good, Prov. 24:13.
        What's sweeter than honey, *Judges* 14:18. Answer: The
        Judgments of the Lord, Psal. 19:9, add Psal. 119, 102, 103 for
        therewith Zion shall be redeemed, Isa. 1:27, &c.
    John's meat was Locusts & wild honey, Matt. 3:4. But butter &
        honey shall Imanuel, Christ Jesus eat, Isa. 7:15, and everyone
        that is left in the land, Ibid v. 22. Add Job 20:17, Cant. 5:1.
    The Contents of this Manuscript see folio post Indicem, ante p. 1.[2d]
    F. D. P. Favos Diligentia Parat[223] add p. 55.

---

220. "'By application a docile shrewdness surmounts every difficulty.'" Pastorius is quoting the Roman poet and astrologer Marcus Manilius (fl. A.D. 1st century).

221. "'No day without—No day should be suffered to pass, without—[this line] leaving a memorial of itself.'" From the Roman historian Pliny the Elder (A.D. 23–79), who attributed this notion to the Greek painter Apelles. It is unclear why Pastorius inserts the long dashes and omits the word "linea" (line)—perhaps to pretend that his commonplacing was a constant effort of remembering.

222. "Zeal & perseverance, work & endurance gather from infancy / learnedness & elegance delighting the reader."

223. "Diligence prepares the honeycomb." Pastorius frequently uses three-word phrases that have his initials, FDP, as the first letters of each word (here "Favos Diligentia Parat"); he calls them "onomastical devices"— associations of a person's name or initials with a witty or wise saying, moral, or insight.

FRANCIS DANIEL PASTORIUS
HIS BOOK 1696.

[I was in Nuce. Or rather nothing but Nuces][224]

1. NOCTURNA ME VOLVE MANU, ME VOLVE DIURNA; STILLA CAVAT LAPIDEM, QUID NON SOLERTIA VINCAT.[225]

Saepe legendo.[226] *Multum non multa.*[227]

Studium et Constantia[228]   A Bee may gather honey,

Labor & Tolerantia[229]   and a Spider poison

Colligunt ab Infantia[230]   from the same Flower.

Docta et Elegantia[231]   *Duo cum faciunt idem, non est idem.*[232]

Lectorem delectantia[233]

There is nothing that can be said now, which has not been said before.

2.   And of all things, which have been said before in the English tongue, Thou wilst find in this Manuscript Some little hint, Pattern, Model, Platform, President,[234] Instance, Ensample[235] or Example, &c.

No Thought can form with Reason what's not here;

And Since Things in their Native Garb appear,

Thou needst not take this Saying upon Trust,

Peruse the Book, and thou wilst find me Just.   F. D. P.

Or according to a Sentence of S. Augustin:[236]

Ubi amatur, non laboratur, Et si laboratur, labor amatur.[237]

---

224. This line is both hard to read and obscure. According to the *OED*, "nuce" is a seventeenth-century variant of "noose." Pastorius may have been referring to the difficult position he was in during the 1690s because of the Frankfurt Land Company affair, the Keithian controversy, and, in particular, the disputes with Heinrich Bernhard Köster and his associates.

225. "At night and day, I move the hand / The drop hollows the stone, which is not won by skills."

226. "'But many books.'" The complete quotation from Giordano Bruno, *Il Candelaio* (1582; The Torchbearer), is "Gutta cavat lapidem non bis, sed saepe cadendo; sic homo fit sapiens non bis, sed saepe legendo" (A drop hollows out the stone by falling not twice, but many times; so, too, is a person made wise by reading not two, but many books).

227. "'Not many things, but much.'" Pliny the Younger, *Epistles* book 7, epistle 9, line 15.

228. "Study and determination."

229. "Toil & endurance."

230. "Collecting from infancy."

231. "Training and elegance."

232. "Two things produced from the same are not the same."

233. "Entertaining the reader."

234. Precedent.

235. Illustrative instance.

236. Saint Augustine or Augustine of Hippo (354–430), Church Father and writer of many theological works.

237. "'Where love is, there is no labor, and if there is labor, the labor is loved.'" Augustine.

3. Where Love is, there's no Labour; and if there be Labour, the Labour is loved.

   A *Banquier*[238] of other men's Imaginations.

   One Line is fine, the Other Course, and why?

   The Pen now sharp, then dull, the Inkhorn dry.

Hic Labor, hoc Opus est;[239] Noveris si rectius istis, Candidus imperti: Si non, his utere mecum.[240]

4. This Book Seem's tall and Small,
   Of no Esteem at all;
   Yet I would very fain,   —Deo—[241]
   That any *who doth find*   }   Redde cuiq. Suum.[242]
   The same, would be so kind }   Mihi Meum, Tibi Tuum.[243]
   To Send it me again.   }   Vide supra,[244] p. 1.

5. Omne tulit punctum, qui miscuit utile dulci. *Horat.*[245]

   Ergo Scripsit Franciscus Daniel Pastorius horis

   Haec succisivis sua *Miscellanea*, quae si

   Forsan ei rapies, rapient tua Viscera Corvi.[246]

   Hic liber est meus, Abstine manus! Ulciscitur Deus Pastorianus;

   Deus Abrahami, Isaaci & Jacobi. Deus Danielis. &c. Deus omnium Fidelium.[247]

The Contents of this portable volume of Importation.[248]

1. which, having several times been fenced in by Stitching more Sheets thereunto, got quite an other Form or Face than Its first was, even in the eyes of the Compiler himself.

238. Banker.
239. "'This is the hard work, that is the toil,'" from Virgil, *Aeneid*, book 6, line 129. Pastorius's quotation is a variant of original line: "Hic opus, hoc labor est."
240. "'If you can better these principles, tell me; if not, join me in following them.'" Here Pastorius is somewhat loosely quoting from Horace, *Epistles*, book 1, epistle 6, lines 67–68, the original of which runs: "Si quid novisti rectius istis, candidus imperti; si nil, his utere mecum."
241. "By God."
242. "Return to each his own."
243. "Mine to me and yours to you."
244. "See above."
245. "'He wins every hand who mingles profit with pleasure.' Horace." Pastorius is quoting from Horace's *Ars Poetica, or the Epistle to the Pisones*.
246. "Thus wrote Francis Daniel Pastorius for hours in his miscellany following here, which perhaps if you should seize it, ravens will seize your organs."
247. "This book is mine, hands off! The God of Pastorius [literally, the God of shepherds] will take vengeance; the God of Abraham, of Isaac & Jacob. The God of Daniel etc. The God of all the faithful."
248. Although this table of contents also became outdated with subsequent additions and changes to the "Bee-Hive," it provides a useful portrait of the complexity and copiousness of Pastorius's largest manuscript book.

The Alvearium[249] itself, being the chief Bulk of this manuscript, begins p. 231.

The Title-Page thereof, see pag. 1. 54 & 55.

Some thing by way of a Preface to the Peruser. Ÿsdem pag.

The Index or Inventory was once on pag. 56. But a more handsom & Compleater Table thou wilst find just before these seven leaves.[250]

The Authors, out of which It is collected. Pag. 56, 57, 58, 60, 61.[251]

Some Inscriptions transcribed out of my Itinerary. Pag. 2, 3, 4, 5, 6, 7, 8, 9, 10.

Some Epitaphs out of my Te moneant Lector tot in uno funera Libro,

Tempore quod certo   Tu quoquam funus eris. Pag. 11 &c.

Emblematical Recreations from pag. 25 to pag. 54.

Symbola Onomastica F.D.P. pag. 55 1st.

Onomastical Considerations pag. 88 and [. . .] to page 260.

Poëtical Raptures pag. 71 to page 140.

A Short Caveat to I.S.P. & H. P.[252] concerning Poëtry. pag. 77.

Some other good Admonitions unto the same. pag. 77, 381.

Catalogus variorum librorum.[253] pag. 377 &c.

Genealogia Pastoriana. p. 220 2nd.

A Catalogue of mine other Manuscripts. Pag. 386, which are neither for the most learned, nor the most unlearned, and where unto I desire but a Friendly & Impartial Reader. A Bee & not a Spider.

2.   At the first undertaking of this Book my mean Scope was, for the future Imitation of my two Sons, onely to collect *Common Proverbs,* witty Sentences, wise and godly Sayings, with the like substantial Marrow of other Men's Writings, &c. See pag. 55.

But afterwards considering the *Copiousness* of *Words, Phrases* & Expressions in the English (my said two Sons Country-language; For seeing I and my wife are both Germans, I dare not well call it their Mother)-Tongue, which they, if possible, should perfectly learn To Read & Write, and to Indite, I took as much pains & patience as to Import into this Alphabetical Alvearium all & Singular Terms, Idioms, manners of Stile & Speech used in the same. Now Inasmuch the former is to supply the place of

---

249. The alphabetically ordered, encyclopedic section of the "Bee-Hive."

250. Not included in this selected text, the index Pastorius refers to was eventually outpaced by the sheer volume of his commonplace collecting and encyclopedic entries, thus necessitating the creation of an external index.

251. Pastorius's bibliographies of his sources is included later in this chapter.

252. "I.S.P. & H.P.": With "Iohann," an alternate spelling of "Johann" in mind, Pastorius is addressing his sons, Johann (John) Samuel and Heinrich (Henry).

253. "A catalog of various books."

honey, so these latter I would have to be accounted if not for wax, yet for hive-dross, &c. See pag. seq.[254]

The language nowadays spoken in England & Colonies thereunto belonging is not the ancient Britan-Tongue, No not the least Offspring thereof; But a Mingle-mangle of Latin, Dutch & French; Relicks or Remains of the Roman, Saxon & Norman Conquests. Most Mono Syllables are of a Dutch Origin, ax, ox, fox, Cow, Corn, horn, hard drink, spin &c. Words of many syllables are either brought in by the Romans, Multitude, audacious, implicate, prudently. Or by the Normans, buckler, strange, dangerous, delay, advance, maintain, &c. And besides those there are also Hebrew, Arabick, Greek, Italian, Spanish, Danish and Welsh words in the said English Tongue. See my miscellany Remarks Concerning it pag. 151.

Hence it is that when other Europeans cannot deliver their minds but by expressing one thing by one word the English may do it commonly by two; Oftentimes by three or four: —ex. gr.[255] Spirit, Ghost. grateful, thankful. alterable, mutable, changeable. breadth, latitude. Sepulchre, tomb, grave. a Count, Earl, Grave. Promote, advance, further. Remission, Pardon, Forgiveness. bad, ill, naught. Impediment, obstruction, lett, hindrance, stop. acquit, exonerate, discharge, free. Congregation, Meeting, Gathering, assembling, Coming together, &c. More Examples the hive itself furnisheth almost in every Cranny! Therefore ye I.S.P. and H.P. for whose sake it is made, Read the Same Over & Over & Over, But not Overly: mind What and How you are reading.

Venturaeque hyemis memores aestate Laborem   Ne fugite![256] Et

Quod Natura negat Vobis Industria praestet.[257]   F. D. P.

FRANCIS DANIEL PASTORIUS
HIS ALPHABETICAL HIVE   } or Bee-Stock:
OF MORE THAN TWO THOUSAND HONEY-COMBS,   Rusca Apum.
BEGUN IN THE YEAR 1696.

1.   When he took this in hand, he did not think To shew to any man his Paper and his Ink; his only Purpose was in black and white With his two little ones (departing) to abide. Nevertheless this may live when he is dead; And thus he leaves it to the perusing of his Readers; not Caring a doit, whether they will like or dislike it.

254. See the "following" page.
255. For example.
256. "'Mindful of winter, do not flee toil in summer.'" Pastorius is loosely quoting from Virgil, *Georgics*, book 4, line 156.
257. "And whatever nature denies you, your industriousness will provide."

He knows, that it will not please all, and doubts not, but it will please Some. Quod tibi displiceant quaedam Proverbia Lector Nil moror, aut mirror; Mel Sine Felle cupis.—Mel nulli sine Felle datur.[258] There is hive-dross on all the Crannies of any hive.

Ubi mel, ibi fel, war Keÿser Lortharÿ I Symbolum.[259]

Wo Honig ist, da sind auch Bitterkeiten; Wo freüden sind, da folget auch das Leiden.[260]

But as Bees do not extract the Venom of herbs, So do not ye wring out the dregs, &c. Rather,—Behold, how *Virgil* could In days of old discover gold.[261] Among the mud, dirt, excrements & mould of Ennius' dung-hill[262] more than ordinary foul'd. And so in Emptying this my hive, I would all Bee-masters or honey-men have to take their Choice. Every man what he pleaseth. &c.

Herbalists

Some make use of Books as *Botanicks* of Plants, Commending those above the rest which are most effectual in Physick; Others *Gentle Women*-like delight chiefly in those which smell and please their fancy best; I in Reading will look out for both, viz.: wholsom Precepts & quaint Expressions. *vide page 54.*

Whereas many prefer meer *Kick-shaws* beyond *Solid Meats*, I had rather choose to Set before them the dainties of other men, than the course food of mine own.

According to the free Law of hospitality, they may either

Eat heartily, or pick a Bone: Read in this Book, or Let alone.

Nemo per me cogitur plus sapere quam velit, inqt. Erasmus Rot. In Epist. ad Marcum Laurium.[263]

My dishes are drest not as at a feast but as at an Ordinary, nor placed in so methodical an Order as they might have been;

I taking things at an adventure, so as they happened to come into hands. &c.

258. "Certain proverbs that might be unsatisfactory to you, reader, I keep none, or I admire none; you desire the honey without the bitterness—no honey is delivered without bitterness."

259. "'Where there is honey, there is bile' was the motto of [Holy Roman] Emperor Lothair I."

260. "Where there is honey, there are also bitter things; where there are joys, there also follow sorrows."

261. In Virgil's epic poem, the central hero, Aeneas, travels into the underworld to see his father, Anchises. The sibyl Deiphobe tells him to take the bough of gold he will find growing near her cave and present it to Proserpine, wife of Pluto, ruler of the underworld. Beyond this direct literary allusion, Pastorius is perhaps also expressing a common Renaissance and humanist impulse to attain artistic greatness through veneration and emulation of the writers of classical antiquity.

262. According to legend, Virgil was once seen reading a volume of the earlier Roman poet Quintus Ennius. When asked what he was doing, he replied: "Plucking pearls from Ennius's dunghill" (as quoted in Anne Fadiman, *Ex Libris: Confessions of a Common Reader* [New York: Farrar, Straus and Giroux, 1998], 106). Though the "dunghill" could simply be read as "refuse" or "garbage," it could also mean the fertile remains of a former genius. Pastorius leaves it up to his readers what they might consider his present work.

263. "'No-one is forced on my account to taste more than he wants,' says Erasmus of Rotterdam in his epistle to Marcus Laurius."

2. As soon as the Weather grows more warm, I am in hopes my Bees will swarm,
   And Tripartited then will be, And this their Hive no less than Three.
   Whereof, me thinks, Each shall contain The things I here in Prose explain.
   The First: Variety of Words, Phrases and Anglicisms. Phraseology.
   The Second: Verity of Common Sayings & Proverbs.
   The Third: Rarity of more Important Matters.
These things, I say, they may Contain, Truth-loving Reader in the mean
   Make use of this So as it is; (For I am troubled when I miss)
   Of good, of better and of best—Thou hast thy Choice, Excuse the Rest. So be it.
Amen.

   Then the 2000 and odd Titles Comprized in this Book will be written in a Black
Character or Old English Letters.

3. If in this Folio Some Lines be found, Which seem not right, not orthodox nor
sound;
Pray! be so kind, so Courteous and so fair To *pass them by*, till things appear more Clear.
Sis mihi Corrector, resecando superflua, Lector; Veraq. digneris quae desunt jungere
Veris. | Multum enim adhuc restat opera, multumq. restabit; Neq. ulli nato post mille
Secula [after 100,000 years] praecludetur Occasio aliquid adjiciendi! Seneca Epist.
64.[264]
Adjice Tu nostris igitur, superadjice nostris; sic qui vix Liber est, grande Volumen erit.
Nulla dies abeat, quin Linea scripta supersit, Et sic Codiculus fiet Amice Liber.[265]

Go Sluggard! go, learn of the *Ant*, To gather food for time of Want; *Prov.* 6:6.
Of *Bees* returning to their hive Learn in Collecting how to thrive.
Ass, Ox and horse with greater Sort Teach thee the knowledge of thy Lord.   *Isa.* 1:3.
Without the which thou wilt be worse, Than Ant & Bee, Ass, Ox, and horse.
   even as a *Mule*, whose mouth must be held in with bit and bridle.   *Psal.* 32:9.
Cur nihil addis iners his nostris cur nihil infers? Odit ut expertes Liber hic, Sic odit
inertes.

264. "'Be my corrector, reader, by cutting out superfluous things; may you be judged worthy to join those things
that are absent from the truth. Certainly, much work remains and much more there will remain; and to know
no-one born after 100,000 years will be denied the opportunity of adding something!' Seneca, Epistle 64."
265. "Therefore, you add to our labors, and continue to add to our labors above and beyond; thus, whatever is
currently scarcely a book, will become a great volume. May no day go away without a written line being added,
and thus from this little notebook a friendly book will be made."

Adde parum parvo; Parvo super adde pusillum, Tempore non longo Librum comple-
bimus illum.[266]
Not so Completely, no; but still (for thus I mean,) Poor Ruth finds liberty in Boaz's
fields to glean.
The Moral of the Industrious Bee, viz. Cull what we find best, Athen. Oracle p. 43.
Posito Livore, Candido Animo ad haec legenda accedas.[267]

Bibliographies of Quaker and Non-Quaker Writings from the "Bee-Hive"

INTRODUCTION TO THE TEXT

The following bibliographies are taken in their entirety from Pastorius's "Bee-Hive"
manuscript book: Francis Daniel Pastorius, "His Hive, Melliotrophium Alvear or, Rusca
Apium, Begun Anno Domini or, in the year of Christian Account, 1696," UPenn MS
Codex 726, Rare Book and Manuscript Library, University of Pennsylvania.

Examining the breadth of readings that Pastorius undertook and the ideas he
extracted from those readings, whose sources he listed in three major bibliographies, can
help us reconstruct the content of his mind. Two of those bibliographies are located in
the "Bee-Hive" and list the books by Quaker and non-Quaker authors that he consulted.
Where Pastorius extracted something from a book for inclusion in the "Bee-Hive,"
he would mark that book's listing with an asterisk, allowing us to trace through these
bibliographies the book culture that Pastorius inhabited during the time he lived in
Pennsylvania.

And because he often extracted thoughts from books he borrowed and then put
those thoughts into the "honeycombs" of the "Bee-Hive," by matching the honeycomb
entries to the books Pastorius was reading, we can see what he selected and what he left
out of his bibliographies. For such purposes, it is useful to know what books Pastorius
had access to. His bibliographies also permit us to set a lower boundary on the books
that were available in early Pennsylvania. Their listing of several hundred volumes of
Quaker and an even larger number of non-Quaker books testifies to a vibrant book
culture and to the wide range of topics discussed by Pastorius and his contemporaries
in early Pennsylvania. Although religious tracts, particularly those defending Quaker

266. "Why are you inactive, adding nothing to these our things? And why do you introduce nothing to us?
Just like this book hates those who reject it, so it hates those who are inactive. Add a little bit to a little book;
and then add a little more to the little book. In no time we will complete it."
267. "With envy being set aside, may you approach to read these things with a shining, bright spirit."

thought and practices, predominate, numerous works of natural science, history, anthropology, and literature are also listed.

In the short maxims preceding the bibliographies, Pastorius urges his readers to pay less attention to the identity (specifically the denomination or religion) of the authors and more to the substance of what they have written. Nevertheless, his division of writings into Quaker and non-Quaker clearly proved that, for Pastorius, the arc of truth tilted toward his newfound co-religionists, the Society of Friends. His belief that membership in this group held special significance—both on an intellectual and particularly on a spiritual level—is also proven by his inclusion of works by special non-Quakers in the bibliography of Quaker writings. For example, a work by one of the Frankfurt Pietists he revered most, Maria Juliana Baur von Eyseneck, is listed among the Quaker works, as is Francis Bacon's *Sylva Sylvarum*, although other works by Bacon are listed in the non-Quaker bibliography.

The Quaker bibliography appears in two places in the "Bee-Hive" (pages 55–58 and 61–65),[268] alongside the bibliography of non-Quaker works. Pastorius later added an appendix (pages 375–76), which lists some of the Quaker books for a second time. This reader presents the modern citations of the works that Pastorius references and provides their page counts when these are known. In cases where there are multiple editions, the first edition is listed unless there is reason to think that Pastorius used a later edition. The books in the appendix are listed with those in the primary bibliography. Any works that Pastorius listed a second time there are listed only once. Although original spellings have been retained, punctuation has been modernized. The entries have been placed in alphabetical order of the author's last name and numbered sequentially, except for a few entries with incomplete citations, which are listed in "Sources with Bibliographic Ambiguities." As in the original manuscript, an asterisk denotes a work that Pastorius used in preparing an entry in the "Bee-Hive."[269]

Pastorius's third major bibliography is his list of books that he owned, which appears in his "Res Propriæ" manuscript and was published in Marion Dexter Learned's biography of Pastorius.[270] "Res Propriæ" lists a number of Pastorius's own manuscripts as well as the printed books he owned. Readers may compare this list of books owned by Pastorius with the books listed in his Quaker and non-Quaker bibliographies in

268. The numbering refers to the original page numbers assigned by Pastorius.
269. The Quaker bibliography printed below updates and expands an earlier version assembled in Alfred L. Brophy, "The Quaker Bibliographic World of Francis Daniel Pastorius," *Pennsylvania Magazine of History and Biography* 122, no. 3 (July 1998): 241–91. On Pastorius's breadth of reading and bibliographies, see also Brophy, "The Intellectual World of a Seventeenth-Century Jurist: Francis Daniel Pastorius and the Reconstruction of Pietist Thought," in *German? American? Literature?: New Directions in German-American Studies*, ed. Winfried Fluck and Werner Sollors (New York: Peter Lang, 2002), 43–63; and Lyman W. Riley, "Books from the 'Beehive' Manuscript of Francis Daniel Pastorius," *Quaker History* 83 (1994): 116–29.
270. Learned, *Life of Francis Daniel*, 274–84.

order to understand the significant role played by the circulation and borrowing of books—and the excerpting of passages from them—in the dissemination of knowledge in early America. Each book listed below is followed by an abbreviated reference to a modern bibliographic work in which it may be found and by a unique serial number or letter and number combination—or, in the case of Smith, by part and page numbers.

Abbreviations:

BLC	*The British Library Catalogue of Printed Books to 1975* (London: C. Bingley, 1979–87)
Bristol	Roger Pattrell Bristol, *Evans' American Bibliography Supplement* (Charlottesville: Bibliographical Society of the University of Virginia, 1962)
ESTC	*English Short Title Catalogue,* 3rd ed. on CD-ROM (London: British Library, 2003)
Evans	Charles Evans, *Bibliography of Books Printed in America, 1641–1800* (New York: Smith, 1901–20)
NUC	*The National Union Catalogue, Pre-1956 Imprints* (Washington, D.C.: Library of Congress, 1968–81)
Smith	Joseph Smith, *Descriptive Catalogue of Friends' Books* (London: Smith, 1859)
OCLC	Online Computer Library Center–WorldCat online, https://www.worldcat.org.
STC	Alfred W. Pollard and Gilbert R. Redgrave, *A Short-Title Catalogue of Books Printed in England, Scotland, and Ireland, and of English Books Printed Abroad, 1475–1640* (London: Bibliographical Society, 1956)
STC (2nd ed.)	Alfred W. Pollard and Gilbert R. Redgrave, *A Short-Title Catalogue of Books Printed in England, Scotland, and Ireland, and of English Books Printed Abroad, 1475–1640,* 2nd ed. (London: Bibliographical Society, 1976)
Wing	Donald G. Wing, *Short-Title Catalogue of Books Printed in England, Scotland, Ireland, Wales, and British America, and of English Books Printed in Other Countries, 1641–1700* (New York: Modern Language Association of America, 1972–88)
Wing (2nd ed.)	Donald G. Wing, *Short-Title Catalogue of Books Printed in England, Scotland, Ireland, Wales, and British America, and of English Books Printed in Other Countries, 1641–1700,* 2nd ed., newly rev. and enl. (New York: Modern Language Association, 1994)

Wing (CD-ROM 1996)   Donald G. Wing, *Short-Title Catalogue of Books Printed in England, Scotland, Ireland, Wales, and British America, and of English Books Printed in Other Countries, 1641–1700*, 2nd ed., newly rev. and enl. on CD-ROM (Alexandria, Va.: Chadwyck-Healey, 1996)

THE TEXT: BIBLIOGRAPHY OF QUAKER WRITINGS FROM THE "BEE-HIVE"

Forasmuch as the Old Index, beginning formerly at this side, was not only too Compact, being pressed together in the narrow Bounds of three Pages, but also defective & without true Alphabetical Order, &c. I at the latter Renewal or Renovation of this Manuscript (whereof it is never like to have any more, having had enough already,) thought it most convenient & suitable to those hands that will accomplish this Alvearium, to Remove the said unhandsom and vitious Table,[271] by tearing the same, and prefix a better & compleater at the very Entrance or Threshold of this Book, to which I refer the inquisitive Reader for his more satisfactory Content. And whereas (as Plinius saith) Ingenuum est Fateri per Quos profeceris,[272] I shall set down the several Authors, out of which this present Hive is collected.

And ye (John Samuel & Henry Pastorius,) dear & well beloved Children!
    At Leasure hours and Candle-light
    Where others play, or lose their Sight;
    Read ye these Books, I here have set,
    Or other goods ones, you can get; See pag. 375, 376, 377, 378, 379, 380.
    But where you meet an Asterisk, *
    Think that your Father, being brisk,
    Perused them, and like a Bee,
    From thence did gather, what you see.
In hoc Alveario, Favis multifario.
    Non sibi, Sed vobis, Mellificavit Apis.
        <u>Sive potius</u> Apicula Germanopolitana,[273] FDP.

271. The old or former index.
272. "'It is honorable to acknowledge the sources through which you have derived assistance.'" Pastorius took this motto from Pliny the Elder, whose thirty-seven-volume collection of knowledge *Natural History* (*Naturalis Historia*) may have served as a model of sorts for his own writings. For further details on Pastorius's principles of using and acknowledging his sources, see Grafton, "Republic of Letters," 1–39.
273. "In this hive are many honeycombs. / Not for himself, but for you, the bee makes honey. / Or rather, a little bee of Germantown."

Of making of Books, there's never an End[274]
And many good hours in reading we spend;
The Purpose whereof for ever should be,
For Writers to teach: for Readers to see
    How to fear the LORD,
    And to Keep His WORD.   Eccles. 12:12, 13.
Non juvat innumeros legere & legisse Libellos,
Si facienda fugire si fugienda facis.[275]

Read all the Books thou canst, thy Labour is in vain;
As long as't Heart's unchang'd, they're turning but the Brain.

Alles Lesen ist Vergebens,
Ohne Besserung des Lebens.[276]

           Non Quis, Sed Quid.[277]
In this Volume, as ye find, Friends & No-friends speak their Mind.
    But Reader, of these Two, Care more for WHAT, than WHO.
        Non tam quis dicat, quam quid dicatur odora.[278]

As we are not to look at the Vessel or Instrument by or through whom it may please
God to Convey something for our edification, so as to overvalue its gifts, parts &
Endowments, though never so excellent. At the other hand we ought to take care, not
to disregard, slight or despise any thing mediately handed forth from God, because of
the meanness of the Instrument, Seeing it's <u>he</u> alone that works all in All.
[. . . .]

Out of the writings of those true Christians whom the World in scorn calls Quakers,
which harmless name this harmless people cannot but own.

274. The sections from here to the beginning of the bibliographies appear on page 63 of the "Bee-Hive," where
Pastorius inserted them as a running commentary on making, reading, and collecting books. We inserted these
passages here to avoid interrupting the following bibliographies.
275. "It does not help to read without end and read innumerable books / if you avoid doing what must be done,
and if you do things you should avoid."
276. "All reading is in vain, / without changing one's life."
277. "Not who, but what." Although Pastorius is saying that the substance of the books matters, not who wrote
them, he nevertheless felt compelled to divide the works in his bibliographies into those by Quaker authors and
those by non-Quaker authors.
278. "Not so much who speaks but rather what is being said smells like."

1. Robert Allan, *The Cry of Innocent Blood, Sounding to the Ear of Each Member in Parliament being a short relation of the Barbarous Cruelties Inflicted Lately Upon the Peaceable People of God called Quakers* (London, 1670). 8 pp. Wing A1045-B.

2. William Ames, *Een getuygenis van den Wegh des levens: tot die gene, die daar na hongeren* (Amsterdam, 1677). 36 pp. OCLC 30549865.

3. William Ames, *Good Counsel and Advice to all the Friends of Truth* (London, 1661). 14 pp. Wing A300.

4. John Anderdon, *Against Babylon and Her Merchants in England* (London, 1660). 15 pp. Wing A3078.

5. William Ames, *Een getuygenis van den Wegh des levens: tot die gene, die daar na hongeren* (Amsterdam, 1677). 36 pp. OCLC 30549865.

6. Anon., *To All Friends and People in the Whole Christendome (So Called) That they May See What was the Government of the Church of the Jewes, the Government of the Church of Christ in the Primitive Times* (London, 1658). 29 pp. Wing A1321.

7. Anon., *The Ancient Testimony of the Primitive Christians and Marters yof Jesus Christ, Revived Agt. Tythes: Or, a Relation of the Sufferings of William Dobson* (London, 1680). 13 pp. Wing A3074.

8. *Anon., *An Answer to a Scandalous Paper . . . Subscribed Edward Breck* (London, 1656). 7 pp. Wing B4339.

9. Anon., *A Declaration of the Marks and Fruits of the False Prophets* (n.p., 1655). 15 pp. Wing D711.

10. Anon., *Female Grievances debated in six dialogues between two young ladies concerning love and marriage* (London, 1707). 164 pp. ESTC T191348.

11. Anon., *Innocency defended: containing an answer to some injurious charges and unjust reflections of the Lord Cornbury, governour of the province of New-Jersey &c., against the people call'd Quakers . . .* (Philadelphia, 1707). OCLC 81108317.

12. Anon., *The Pleasures of Matrimony, intermix'd with variety of merry and delightful stories* (London, 1688). 228 pp. Wing P2565.

13. Anon., *The Religious Assemblies of the People Called Quakers Vindicated: Whereunto is Added a More General Declaration in the Case* (London, 1683). 8 pp. Wing R907.

14. Anon., *Some Queries to be Answered in Writing or Print by the Masters* (London, 1654). 16 pp. Wing S4564.

15. Anon., *A Test and Protest Against Popery from the Conscientious Christian Protestants Called Quakers* (London, 1680). 18 pp. Wing T793.

16. Anon., *Wits Cabinet or, A companion for young men and ladies* (London, 1698). 188 pp. Wing W3215F.

17. *Benjamin Antrobus, *Buds and Blossoms of Piety, with some fruit of the spirit of love* (London, 1691). 128 pp. Wing A3522.

18. John Axford, *Hidden Things Brought to Light for the Increase of Knowledge in Reading the Bible: Being an Explanation of the Coins, Money-weights, Measures Mentioned in the Bible* (London, 1697). 33 pp. Wing A4280A.

19. R.B., *Admirable Curiosities, Rarities, and Wonders in England, Scotland, and Ireland, or, An account of many remarkable persons and places* (London, 1684). 232 pp. Wing C7307.

20. R.B., *England's Monarchs, or, A compendious relation of the most remarkable transactions, and observable passages, ecclesiastical, civil, and military which have hapned during the reigns of the kings and queens of England* (London, 1691). 236 pp. Wing C7316.

21. R.B., *Extraordinary adventurers and discoveries of several famous men* (London, 1683). 233 pp. Wing C7323.

22. R.B., *The General History of Earthquakes* (London, 1694). 176 pp. Wing C7328.

23. R.B., *Historical Remarks of the ancient and present state of London and Westminster* (London, 1703). 156 pp. ESTC T71208.

24. R.B., *The History of the Kingdom of Scotland* (London, 1696). 178 pp. Wing C7335A.

25. R.B., *The History of the two late Kings Charles II and James II, being an impartial account of the most remarkable transactions, and observable passages, during their reigns* (London, 1693). 176 pp. Wing C7340.

26. R.B., *The Kingdom of Darkness: or, The history of demons, spectres, witches, apparitions, and possessions, disturbances, and other supernatural delusions* (London, 1688). 169 pp. Wing C7342.

27. R.B., *Martyrs in flames, or Popery (in its true colours) displayed* (London, 1693). 180 pp. Wing C7344A.

28. R.B., *The surprizing Miracles of Nature and Art* (London, 1683). 222 pp. Wing C7349.

29. R.B., *The unfortunate court-favorites of England: exemplified in the fatal fall of divers Great men* (London, 1695). 181 pp. Wing C7351.

30. R.B., *Unparallel'd Varieties: or, The matchless Actions and Passions of Mankind, displayed in near four hundred notable instances* (London, 1699). 159 pp. Wing C7354.

31. R.B., *A view of the English acquisitions in Guineas and the East Indies* (London, 1686). 182 pp. Wing C7356.

32. R.B., *The wars in England, Scotland and Ireland: Containing an account of all the battles, sieges, revolutions, accidents, and other remarkable transactions in Church and State during the reign of King Charles I* (London, 1737). 192 pp. ESTC T110495.

33. R.B., *Winter-evenings entertainments: in two parts* (London, 1705). 170 pp. ESTC T219033.

34. R.B., *Wonderful Prodigies of Judgment and mercy: discovered in near three hundred memorable histories* (London, 1699). 178 pp. Wing C7362.

35. Francis Bacon, *Sylva Sylvarum, or Natural History: in ten centuries* (London, 1664). 64 pp. Wing B330.

36. Daniel Baker [attributed to Thomas Hart by Pastorius], *The Prophet Approved, by the Words of His Prophesie Coming to Passe* (London, 1659). 4 pp. Wing B484.

37. Daniel Baker, *A Single and General Voice: Lifted Up Like a Trumpet Sounding Forth the Lords controversie, Concerning London, with Her Governors, Priests, and Citizens* (London, 1659). 18 pp. Wing B485.

38. *Richard Baker, *A Testimony to the Power of God, Being Greater than the Power of Satan: Contrary to all those who hold no Perfection Here, No Freedom from Sin on this Side of the Grave* (London, 1699). 32 pp. Wing B5414d.

39. John Bank, *An Epistle to Friends, Showing the Great Difference Between a Convinced Estate and a Converted Estate and Between the Profession of the Truth, and the Possession Thereof* (London, 1692). 20 pp. Wing B652.

40. Giacomo Baratti, *The Late Travels of S. Giacomo Baratti, an Italian Gentleman, into the Remote Countries of the the Abissins, or of Ethiopia Interior: wherein you shall find an exact account of the laws, government, religion, discipline, customs, &c. of the Christian people that do inhabit there* 230 pp. Wing B677.

41. Robert Barclay, *An Apology for the true Christian Divinity, as the same is held forth, and preached, by the People in Scorn, Quakers . . . translated into High Dutch, Low Dutch, and French, for the Information of Strangers* (London, 1703). 34 pp. ESTC T85687.

42. Robert Barclay, *Baptism and the Lord's Supper Substantially Asserted* (London, 1696). 125 pp. Wing B724A.

43. Robert Barclay, *The Possibility and Necessity of the inward Immediate Revelation of the Spirit of God: towards the foundation and ground of true faith* (London, 1686). 28 pp. Wing B732.

44. Robert Barclay, *Truth cleared of Calumnies: wherein a dialogue betwixt a Quaker and a stable Christian is examined* (Aberdeen, 1670). 72 pp. Wing B738.

45. *Robert Barclay, *Truth Triumphant through Spiritual Warfare, Christian Labors and Writings of that Able and Faithful Servant of Jesus Christ* (London, 1692). 908 pp. Wing B740.

46. Willem Bartjens, *De vernieuwde cyfferinge* (Amsterdam, 1708). 184 pp. OCLC 29936601.

47. Elizabeth Bathhurst, *Truth's Vindication: or a Gentle Stroke to Wipe Off the Foul Aspersions and False Accusations and Misrepresentations, Cast Upon the People of God Called Quakers, Both With Respect to Their Principle and their Way of Proselytizing People Over to Them* (London, 1679). 104 pp. Wing B1137.

48. William Bayly, *An Arrow Shot Against Babylon out of Josephs Bow* (London, 1663). 26 pp. Wing B1518.

49. William Bayly, *A Collection of the Several Writings of that true Prophet, . . . William Bayly* (London, 1676). 774 pp. Wing B1517.

50. William Bayly, *General Epistle to All Friends* (London, 1662). 4 pp. Wing B1527.

51. William Bayly, *For the King and Parliament and this Councel and Teachers* (1664). 10 pp. Wing B1526.

52. *William Bayly, *Pure encouragements from the Spirit of the Lord: as a joyful Salutation with full Assurance of Victory, unto the noble army of the Lamb against whom the Gates of hell shall never prevail* (London, 1664). 8 pp. Wing B1534.

53. William Bayly and John Crook, *Rebellion rebuked: in an answer to a scandalous pamphlet entitled The Quaker converted to Christianity* (London, 1673). 56 pp. Wing C7212. *William Bayly, *A Testimony of Truth against all the Sowers of Dissention, Strife, and Discord amongst the people of God, by what practice, or under what pretence soever* (London, 1667). 8 pp. Wing B1540.

54. William Bayly, *The true Christ Owned: In a Few Plain words of Truth, by way of reply to all Such Professors or Profane who Lay to the Charge the Elect People of God called Quakers* (London, 1667). 23 pp. Wing B1542.

55. William Bayly, *A Warning from the Spirit of Truth, unto All Persecutors, and Enemies of the dear Children of God* (London, 1658). 42 pp. Wing B1544.

56. John Beaumont, *An historical, physiological, and theological Treatise of Spirits, Apparitions, Witchcrafts and other Magical Practices* (London, 1705). 400 pp. ESTC 111486.

57. John Beevan, *A Loving Salutation to all People Who have any Desires after the Living God* (London, 1660). 8 pp. Wing B1696.

58. William Bennit, *A Collection of Certain Epistles and Testimonies of Devine Consolation, Experience and Doctrine* (London, 1685). 216 pp. Wing B1891.

59. *Gervase Benson, *A second testimony concerning oaths and swearing* (London, 1675). 23 pp. Wing B1901.

60. [Robert Berd], *To the Parliament of . . . England: A Representation of the Outrages and Cruellties Acted Upon the Servants of Christ, At Two Meetings at Sabridgworth in Hartford-shire* (London, 1659). 6 pp. Wing B1958.

61. *Edward Billing, *Words in the Word: To Be Read by Friends in the Simplicity, Feltin the Power, and Received in the Love* (London, 1661). 7 pp. Wing B2904.

62. E.B. [Edward Billing or Edward Burrough?], *An Alarm to all Flesh: With an Invitation to the True Seekers: An Arrow Shot Against Babylon Out of Joseph's Bow Warning (once more) from God, unto all such Rulers, Teachers, and People in England who are, or may be, Persecutors about Religion and Worship* (London, 1660). 10 pp. Wing B598.

63. William Bingley [attributed to Moses West by Pastorius], *A Grievous Lamentation over Thee O England: Or, the Greatest Part of thy Inhabitants, who have withstood the day of their visitation* (London, 1683). 8 pp. Wing B2921.

64. *George Bishop, *The Dominion of the seed of God throughout all generations* (London, 1667). 8 pp. Wing B2991.

65. George Bishop, *A Few Words in Season; or, A Warnings from the Lord to the Friends of Truth* (London, 1660). 3 pp. Wing B2993.

66. *George Bishop, *Mene Tekel: Or, The Council of Officers of the Army, Against the Declarations* (London, 1659). 50 pp. Wing B3000.

67. George Bishop, *New England Judged Not by Man's But by the Spirit of the Lord* (London, 1661). 198 pp. Wing B3003.

68. George Bishop, *A Vindication of the Principles and Practices of the People Called Quakers* (London, 1665). 75 pp. Wing B3014.

69. George Bishop, *The Warnings of the Lord to this Generation* (London, 1660). 44 pp. Wing B3016.

70. George Bishop, *The Warnings of the Lord to the King of England and his Parliament* (London, 1667). 19 pp. Wing B3015.

71. *George Bishop, *Yet one Warning more, Or the Tender of the Lord's Love to the lawyers, judges, rulers of these Nations* (London, 1661). 6 pp. Wing B3019.

72. Sarah Blackborow, *The Just and Equall Balance Discovered: With a True Measure whereby the Inhabitants of Sion Doth Fathom and Compass all False Worshipps and Their Ground* (London, 1660). 14 pp. Wing B3064.

73. John Bockett, *A diurnal speculum* (London, 1696). 288 pp. Wing B3387.

74. John Bockett, *The Poor Mechanick's Plea Against the Rich Clergy's Oppression* (London, 1700). 48 pp. Wing B3389.

75. John Bockett, *Pride expos'd and oppos'd: or, the root, branches, and fruit thereof briefly discover'd* (London, 1710). 100 pp. ESTC T66957.

76. James Bolton, *Judas His Thirty Pieces Not Received, But Sent Back to Him, For his Own Bag . . . Being Something by way of an answer to a Letter that was sent . . . from Robert Rich in Barbadoes, which was for the distribution of a certain sume of money to seven churches . . . wherein it is manifested . . . Quakers cannot partake of his gift* (n.p., ca. 1660). 15 pp. Wing B3506.

77. Edward Bourne, *A Looking-Glass Discovering to all People What Image they Bear* (London, 1671). 27 pp. Wing B3847.

78. Edward Bourne, *A Warning from the Lord God Out of Zion* (London, 1660). 18 pp. Wing B3849.

79. John Braithwait, *To all Those that Observe Days, Months, Times and Years* (London, 1660). broadside Wing B4208.

80. Robert Bridgman, *Some reasons why Robert Bridgman, and his wife, and some others in Hvntington-shire, have left the society of the people called Quakers* (London, 1700). 21 pp. Wing B4494.

81. William Britten, *Silent Meeting A Wonder to the World: Yet Practised by the Apostles and Owned by the People of God . . . called Quakers* (London, 1671). 16 pp. Wing B4826.

82. John Burnyeat, *The Truth Exalted in the Writings of that Eminent and Faithful Servant of Christ, John Burnyeat* (London, 1691). 264 pp. Wing B5968.

83. John Burnyeat, see also George Fox, *A New England Fire-Brand*.

84. Edward Burrough, *A Declaration to all the World of Our Faith and What We Believe who are Called Quakers* (London, 1661). 8 pp. Wing B5997.

85. Edward Burrough, *A declaration of the sad and great Persecution and Martyrdom of the people of God called Quakers in New-England for the worshipping of God* (London, 1660). 32 pp. Wing B5994.

86. Edward Burrough, *A Description of the State and Condition of All Mankinde Upon the Face of the Whole Earth* (London, 1657). 14 pp. Wing B5999.

87. Edward Burrough, *A Faithful Testimony Concerning the True Worship of God* (London, 1659). 14 pp. Wing B6002.

88. *Edward Burrough, *A general Epistle to all the Saints: being a visitation of the Father's love unto the whole flock of God* (London, 1660). 16 pp. Wing B6005.

89. Edward Burrough, *A Measure of the Times* (London, 1657). 39 pp. Wing B6012.

90. Edward Burrough, *A Standard Lifted Up and Ensigne Held Forth to all Nations* (London, 1658). 32 pp. Wing B6030.

91. Edward Burrough, *Persecution Impeached, as a Traytor Against God, his laws and government: Being a Brief Answer to a Book, Called Semper Iidem* (London, 1661). 38 pp. Wing B6016.

92. Edward Burrough, *Truth (the Strongest of All) Witnessed Fully in the Spirit of Truth, Against All Deceit* (London, 1657). 63 pp. Wing B6051.

93. Edward Burrough, *A Visitation and Preservation of Love unto the King and Those Call'd Royalists* (London, 1660). 39 pp. Wing B6054.

94. Edward Burrough, *The Wofull Cry of Unjust Persecutions and Grievous Oppressions of the People of God in England* (London, 1657). 35 pp. Wing B6058.

95. John Camm, *The Memory of the Righteous Revived: Being a Brief Collection of the Books and Written Epistles of John Camm and John Audland* (London, 1689). 332 pp. Smith, part 1, pp. 367–77.

96. William Caton, *A Journal of the Life of that Faithful Servant and Minister . . . William Caton* (London, 1689). 83 pp. Wing C1514.

97. Thomas Chalkley, *A Loving Invitation to Young and Old, in Holland, and Elsewhere: to Seek and Love Almighty God, and to Prepare in Time for their Eternal Welfare* (London, 1710). 18 pp. NUC C0278931.

98. Hugh Chamberlen, *A few Queries relating to the Practice of Physick* (London, 1694). 122 pp. Wing C1873.

99. *William Chandler, A. Pyot, J. Hodges, *A Brief Apology in Behalf of the People Called Quakers* (London, 1694). 86 pp. Wing C1934A.

100. Josiah Child, *A new Discourse of Trade: wherein is recommended several weighty points relating to companies of merchants* (London, 1693). 234 pp. Wing C3860.

101. Christopher Cheesman, *An Epistle to Charles the II King of England and to Every Individual Member of His Council* (Reading, 1661). 8 pp. Wing C3773.

102. Christian Chemnitz and Melchior Kromayer, *Disquisitio anti-Sociniana circa mysteria de SS. trinitate, et Christo* (Sengenwald, 1653). 40 pp. OCLC 165340602.

103. Richard Claridge, *Lux Evangelica attestata: or, A Further Testimony to Sufficiency of the Light Within. Being a Reply to George Keith's Censure in his book, intitled, An Account of Quaker Politics* (London, 1701). 98 pp. Smith, part 1, p. 411.

104. Richard Claridge, *Mercy Covering the Judgment Seat and Life and Light Triumphing Over Death and Darkness* (London, 1700). 39 pp. Wing C4434.

105. Henry Clarke, *Here is True Magistracy Described and the Way to Rule and Judge the People Set Forth* (London, 1660). 8 pp. Wing C4455.

106. Johann Claus, *Der Entdecker entdeckt oder kurze Antwort auf das Schreiben Heinr. Cassels* (Amsterdam, 1678). OCLC 311427463.

107. *William Cleevelye, *The deceitful spirit discovered in its secret and mysterious working; and in the power of God is judged and condemned by one that was once ensnared thereby* (London, 1667). 4 pp. Wing C4625A.

108. Joseph Coale, *Some Account of the Life, Service, and Suffering of an early Servant and Minister of Christ, Joseph Cooale* (London, 1706). 263 pp. ESTC T73588.

109. Josiah Coale, *The books and Divers Epistles of the Faithful Servant of the Lord, Josiah Coale (contains a Vindication of the Light Within, Against Darkness, Error and Blasphemy of John Newman)* (London, 1671). 228 pp. Wing C4751.

110. Josiah Coale, *An Invitation of Love to the Hungry and Thirsty* (London, 1660). 7 pp. Wing C4754. Josiah Coale, *The Last Testimony of that Faithful Servant of the Lord, Richard Farnworth* (London, 1667). 12 pp. Wing F488.

111. Josiah Coale, *A Testimony of the Fathers Love unto all that Desire after Him* (London, 1661). 22 pp. Wing C4749.

112. Josiah Coale, *A Vindication of the Light Within* (London, 1699). 8 pp. Wing W698. Josiah Coale, see also Ambrose Rigge, *A Visitation of Tender Love* (Quaker bibliography entry 454 below).

113. John D. Collens, *A Touch-Stone, whereby Protestant Religion as it Stands at this Day in England May be Tryed* (London, 1660). 18 pp. Wing C5234.

114. John D. Collens, *A Word in Season to All in Authority* (London, 1660). 26 pp. Wing C5235.

115. *Edward Cooke, *For each Parliament man now sitting at Dublin in Ireland* (London, 1661). 8 pp. NUC C0668914.

116. Benjamin Coole, *His Honesty the truest policy: shewing the sophistry, envy, falsehood, and perversion of George Keith* (London, 1700). 166 pp. Wing C6046.

117. D.V. Coornhert, *Wortel der Nederlantsche oorloghen, met aenwysinghe tot inlantsche eendracht* (1590). 60 pp. OCLC 747629284.

118. Samuel Cradock, *The harmony of the four evangelists* (London, 1668). 223 pp. Wing C6748.

119. *Richard Crane, *A Fore-Warning and a Word of Expostulation unto the Rulers, Magistrates and Priests of England* (London, 1660). 8 pp. Wing C6811.

120. Richard Crane, *A Short but Strict Account Taken of Babylons Merchants* (London, 1660). 22 pp. Wing C6815.

121. *Stephen Crisp, *The Copie of a Letter from Germany* 3 pp., postscript to George Keith, *The Benefit, Advantage and Glory of Silent Meetings* (London, 1670). 18 pp. Wing K144.

122. Stephen Crisp, *A Description of the Church of Scotland* (London, 1660). 15 pp. Wing C6928.

123. *Stephen Crisp, *An Epistle to Friends Concerning the Present and Succeding Times Being a Faithful Exhortation and Warning to All Friends* (London, 1666). 19 pp. Wing C6931.

124. *Stephen Crisp, *A Faithful Warning and Exhortation to Beware of Seducing Spirits* (London, 1684). 20 pp. Wing C6936.

125. Stephen Crisp, *Een Geklanck des allarms, geblaesen binnen de landtpaelen van 't Geestelijck Egypten; t'welck gehoort sal worden in Babylon, etc.* (Amsterdam, 1671). 32 pp. OCLC 557872429.

126. Stephen Crisp, *De Gronden en oorsaecken, van de ellende der Nederlanden ontdeckt, als mede de middelen van derselver herstellinge aengewezen, etc.* (Amsterdam, 1672). 15 pp. OCLC 17751549.

127. Stephen Crisp, *Een klaren wegh, geopent, voor de eenvoudighe van harten . . . Den tweeden druk* (Haerlem, 1670). 15 pp. OCLC 771066545.

128. Stephen Crisp, *A Memorable Account of the Christian Experiences, Gospel Labours, Travels and Sufferings of that Ancient Servant of Christ Stephen Crisp* (London, 1694). 543 pp. Wing C6920.

129. Stephen Crisp, *Scripture Truths Demonstrated in Thirty Two Sermons, or Declarations* (London, 1707). 607 pp. NUC C079259.

130. Stephen Crisp, *Several Sermons: or, Declarations of Stephen Crisp* (London, 1693). 175 pp. Wing C6941.

131. John Crook, *The case of swearing, at all, discussed: with several objections answered* (London, 1660). 29 pp. Wing C7197.

132. John Crook, *The Design of Christianity, Testified in the Books of John Crook* (London, 1701). 421 pp. NUC C0802327.

133. *John Crook, *An Epistle of Love to All that Are in Present Sufferings* (London, 1660). 21 pp. Wing C7204.

134. John Crook, *An Epistle to all that Profess the Light of Jesus Christ within to be Guide* (London, 1678). 10 pp. Wing C7206.

135. John Crook, Samuel Fisher, Francis Howgill and Richard Hubberthorne, *Liberty of Conscience Asserted and Several Reasons Rendered Why No Outward Force Nor Imposition Ought to be Used in Matters of Faith and Religion* (London, 1661). 8 pp. Wing L1960.

136. *John Crook, *Sixteen Reasons drawn from the Law of God, the Law of England, and Right Reason to shew why divers true Christians called Quakers refuse to Swear at all* (London, 1661). 8 pp. Wing C7213.

137. John Crook, *Truth's Principles, or those Things About Doctrine and Worship which are Most Surely Believed and Received Among the People of God Called Quakers* (London, 1663). 23 pp. Wing C7219.

138. *John Crook, *Truth's Progress, or, a Short Relation of its First Appearance and Publication after the Apostacy* (London, 1667). 20 pp. Wing C7222.

139. Samuel Crossman, *The Young Man's Calling, Or the whole Duty of Youth* (London, 1678). 425 pp. Wing C7272.

140. William Crouch, *The Enormous Sin of Covetousness Detected with its Branches, Fraud, Oppression, Lying, Ingratitude* (London, 1708). 350 pp. Smith, part 1, p. 495.

141. William Crouch, *Posthuma Christiana: or, . . . A Brief Historical Account . . . of His Convincement of, and Early Sufferings for the Truth* (London, 1712). 224 pp. Smith, part 1, p. 495.

142. Nicholas Culpeper, *The English Physician, or, An astrologo-physical discourse of the vulgar herbs of this nation* (London, 1652). 266 pp. Wing C7500.

143. Richard Davies, *An Account of the Convincement, Exercises, Services, and Travels of Richard Davies, with some Relation of ancient friends and the Spreading of Truth in North Wales* (London, 1710). 260 pp. ESTC T134682.

144. William Dewsbury, *The Faithful Testimony of that Antient Servant of the Lord, and Minister of the Everlasting Gospel William Dewsberry: His Books, Epistles, and Writings* (London, 1689). 405 pp. Wing D1267.

145. William Dewsbury, *To All the Faithful Brethren Born of the Immortal Seed of the Father of Life* (London, 1661). 8 pp. Wing D1276.

146. *William Dewsbury, *The Word of the Lord to all the Inhabitants in England* (London, 1666). 8 pp. Wing D1282.

147. William Dewsbury, *The Word of the Lord to his Beloved City, New Jerusalem* (London, 1663). 7 pp. Wing D1283.

148. *Jonathan Dickinson, *God's Protecting Providence, Man's Surest Help and Defense in Times of the Greatest Difficulty . . . Evidenced in the Remarkable Deliverance of Robert Barrow . . . from the Cruel Devouring Jaws of the Inhumane Canibals of Florida* (London, 1700). 85 pp. Wing D1390A.

149. John Dunton, *The Athenian Spy: discovering the secret letters which were sent to the Athenian society by several ingenious ladies, relating to the management of their affections* (London, 1709). 22 pp. ESTC T128332.

150. Jeremiah Dyke, *De wurdige Tisch-genoss: an der heyligen Gnaden-Tafel unsers Herrn und Heylands Jesu Christi* (Hanau, 1670). 559 pp. OCLC 43551611.

151. *Solomon Eccles, *A Musick Lector, or the Art of Musick* (London, 1667). 28 pp. Wing E129.

152. Laurence Echard, *The history of England: from the first entrance of Julius Caesar and the Romans, to the end of the reign of King James the first* (London, 1707). 980 pp. ESTC T145502.

153. Paul Egard, *Geistlich-königliches Priesterthum Christi nach der heiligen Schrift* (Frankfurt, 1682). OCLC 634736469.

154. Francis Ellington, *A Few Words to All who Professe Themselves to be of the Protestant Religion* (London, 1665). 17 pp. Wing E542.

155. Thomas Ellwood, *An Answer to George Keith's Narrative of His Proceedings at Turners Hall . . . wherein his Charges Against Divers of the People Called Quakers . . . are Fairly Considered, Examined, and Refuted* (London, 1696). 232 pp. Wing E612.

156. Thomas Ellwood, *A Caution to Constables and other Inferiour Officers concerned with Execution of the Conventicle-Act* (London, 1683). 18 pp. Wing E616.

157. *Thomas Ellwood, *Davideis: The Life of David King of Israel: a sacred poem in five books* (London, 1712). 310 pp. ESTC T84827.

158. Thomas Ellwood, *A Further Discovery of that Spirit or Contention and Division which Appeared of Late in George Keith* (London, 1694). 128 pp. Wing E623.

159. Thomas Ellwood, *The glorious Brightness of the Gospel-day: dispelling the shadows of the legal dispensation: and whatsoever else of human invention has been super-added thereunto* (London, 1707). 91 pp. OCLC 11982707.

160. Thomas Ellwood, *The history of the life of Thomas Ellwood, or an Account of his birth, education, etc. with divers Observations on his Life and Manners when a Youth* (London, 1714). ESTC T84832.

161. Thomas Ellwood, *Sacred History: Or, the Historical Part of the Holy Scriptures of the Old Testament* (London, 1705). 576 pp. Smith, part 1, p. 567.

162. Thomas Ellwood, *Sacred History: Or, the Historical Part of the Holy Scriptures of the New Testament* (London, 1709). 423 pp. ESTC N021295.

163. Thomas Ellwood, *Truth defended and the friends thereof cleared from the false charges, foul reproaches, and envious cavils, cast upon it and them by George Keith* (London, 1695). 171 pp. Wing E629.

164. Edmund Elys, *A vindication of the doctrine concerning the light within, against the objections of George Keith, in his book, entituled, The deism of W. Penn* (London, 1699). 8 pp. Wing E698.

165. Maria Juliana Baur von Eyseneck, *Lebenslauff und Abschieds-Reden einer recht christlichen Witwe* (London, 1689). 47 pp. OCLC 798971967.

166. *Richard Farnworth, *Antichrist's Man of War Apprehended: and encountrd withal, by A Soldier of the Armie of the Lamb; otherwise, An Answer to a Book set Forth by . . . Edmund Skipp* (London, 1655). 68 pp. Wing F470.

167. *Richard Farnworth, *The brazen Serpent lifted up on high, or, A discourse concerning election and predestination* (London, 1658). 33 pp. Wing F472.

168. *R.F. [Richard Farnworth], *Christian Religious Meetings Allowed by Liturgie Are No Seditious Conventicles, Nor Punishable by the Late act, Or, What Persons and Meetings Are Owned and Allowed by the Liturgie of the Church of England* (1664). 30 pp. Wing F476.

169. Richard Farnworth, *A Confession and Profession of Faith in God: by his people who are in scorn called Quakers* (London, 1658). 16 pp. Wing F478.

170. *Richard Farnworth, "An Epistle to the Reader," in James Naylor, *Several Petitions Answered* (London, 1653). 64 pp. Wing N316A.

171. *Richard Farnworth, *The Pure Language of the Spirit of Truth . . . Or Thee and Thou* (London, 1656). 8 pp. Wing F496.

172. *Richard Farnworth, *The Quakers plea with the Bishops at their Ecclesiastical Courts* (London, 1663). 21 pp. Wing F500.

173. Jane Fearon, *Absolute Predestination not Scriptural: or, Some Questions upon a Doctrine which I heard Preache'd, 1704, to a People called Independents* (London, 1705). 40 pp. NUC 0058425.

174. Jane Fearon, *A Reply to John Atkinsons Pretended Answer to Absolute Predestination Not Scriptural* (London, 1709). 104 pp. Smith, part 1, p. 594.

175. Issacus Fegyverneki et al., *Enchiridion Locorum communium Theologicorum, rerum, exemplorum, atque phraseon sacrarum* (London, 1588). 381 pp. OCLC 55558980.

176. Jeremias Felbinger, *Een Christelik Bericht, hoc de aerdsche Politien der Rechtgeloovigen behooren wolbestelt te gymn* (Amsterdam, 1660). OCLC 249044602.

177. Jeremias Felbinger, *Das Newe Testament Treulich aus dem Grichischen ins Deutsche übersetzt* (Amsterdam, 1660). 14 pp. OCLC 557751766.

178. Henry Fell and John Stubbs, *For Presbyter John and All His Subordinate Kings and Princes* (London, 1660). Wing H604.

179. Lydia Fell, *A Testimony and Warning given forth in the Love of Truth: and is for the governor, magistrates and people . . . of Barbados* (London, 1676). 20 pp. Wing F625.

180. Margaret Fell, *A brief Collection of remarkable Passages and Occurrences relating to the Birth, Education, Life, Conversion, Travels, Services, and deep Sufferings of that ancient, eminent, and faithful servant of the Lord Margaret Fell* (London, 1710). 7 pp. OCLC 83271752.

181. Margaret Fell, *The Standard of the Lord revealed: by which he hath led and guided and preserved his people since Adam to this day* (London, 1667). 132 pp. Wing F635.

182. John Field, *An answer to A catechism against Quakerism by N.N. Shewing his abuse of the people called Quakers* (London, 1693). 36 pp. Wing F860A.

183. John Field, *Friendly Advice in the Spirit of Love unto Believing Parents, and their Tender Off-Spring in Relation to their Christian Education* (London, 1688). 17 pp. Wing F864.

184. John Field, *The Christianity of the People called Quakers asserted, by George Keith* (London, 1700). 1 pp. Wing F861B.

185. John Field, *The Creed Forgers Detected in Reply to a pamphlet false called the Quakers creed* (London, 1700). 16 pp. Wing F862.

186. John Field, *An Humble Application to the Queen and Her Great Council the Parliament of England, to Suppress Play-Houses and Bear-Baitings* (London, 1703). 15 pp. Smith, part 1, p. 607.

187. John Field, *Light and Truth Discovering Sophistry and Deceit: or, a reply to a book called a Plain Discovery of Many Gross Falsehoods . . . by George Keith* (London, 1701). 44 pp. Smith, part 1, pp. 606–7.

188. John Field, *Some Observations on the Remarks upon the Quakers, or, the busie priest's envy detected and folly manifested* (London, 1700). 18 pp. Wing F865.

189. John Elliott, *The saving grace of God owned and scripturally asserted.* (London, 1693). 59 pp. Wing E548B.

190. John Field, *The Weakness of George Keith's reasons for renouncing Quakerism* (London, 1700). 22 pp. Wing F868.

191. *Samuel Fisher, *The Testimony of Truth Exalted By the Collected Labours of . . . Samuel Fisher who Died A Prisoner for the Testimony of Jesus and Word of God* (London, 1679). 856 pp. Wing F1058.
See also Richard Hubberthorn and Samuel Fisher, *Supplementum Sublatum.*

192. Mary Forster, *These Several Papers was sent to the Parliament* (London, 1659). 72 pp. Wing F1605.

193. George Fox, *That All Might See who they were that had a Command: and Did Pay Tythes; and who they were that had a Law to Receive them* (London, 1657). 22 pp. Wing F1931.

194. George Fox, *To All that Would Know the Way of the Kingdom, Whether they be in Forms, Without Forms, or Got Above All Forms* (London, 1660). 14 pp. Wing F1945.

195. *George Fox, *The Arraignment of Popery Being a Short Collection . . . of the State of the Church in Primitive Times* (London, 1667). 111 pp. Wing F1750A.

196. George Fox, *An Answer to a Paper Which Came from the Papists Lately Out of Holland who Goeth About to Vindicate the Pope, Jesuits, and Papists* (London, 1658). 68 pp. Wing F1742.

197. George Fox, *Answer to Thomas Tillam's Book Called the Seventh Day Sabbath* (London, 1659). 32 pp. Wing F1747.

198. George Fox, *Collection of Many Select and Christian Epistles* (London, 1698). 557 pp. Wing F1764.

199. *George Fox, *Concerning Marriage: how God made them male and female in the beginning* (London, 1661). 8 pp. Wing F1767.

200. George Fox, *The Copies of Several Letters which were Delivered to the King: Being written by Sundry Friends in the Truth . . . George Fox, Alexander Parker, James Naylor, Henry Fell, John Sowter, William Smith, William Caton, and G[eorge] W[hitehead]* (London, 1660). 54 pp. Wing F1778.

201. George Fox, *To the Council of Officers of the Armie and the Heads of the Nation* (London?, 1659?). 8 pp. Wing F1955.

202. George Fox, *A Cry for Repentance unto the Inhabitants of London Chieflie: And Unto All the World* (London, 1656). 6 pp. Wing F1779.

203. George Fox, *A Declaration from the Harmless and Innocent People of God Called Quakers Against All Sedition Plotters and Fighters in the World: For Removing of the Ground of Jealousie and Suspition from Both Magistrates and People in the Kingdoms, Concerning Wars and Fighting* (London, 1660). 8 pp. Wing F1787.

204. George Fox, *An Epistle to all People On the Earth . . . shewing to all the People Upon Earth, that they may Come to an Understanding of Themselves* (London, 1657). 20 pp. Wing F1805.

205. *George Fox, *An epistle to be read in all the assemblies of the righteous* (London, 1666). 9 pp. Wing F1807.

206. George Fox, *An Epistle to Friends* (London, 1678). 11 pp. Wing F1810.

207. George Fox, *For the King and Both Houses of Parliament Sitting at Westminster, Subscribed by G. Fox, J. Stubbs, F. Howgill, R. Hubberthorn, R. Scostrope* (London, 1661). 22 pp. Wing F1821.

208. *George Fox, John Stubbs, and Henry Fell, *For the King and His Council* (London, 1660). 7 pp. Wing F1822.

209. *George Fox, *Gospel family-order: being a short discourse concerning the ordering of families, both of Whites, Blacks, and Indians* (London, 1676). 22 pp. Wing F1829.

210. George Fox, *Gospel Truth Demonstrated* (London, 1706). 1,090 pp. NUC F0273853.

211. George Fox, *The Ground of High Places: and the End of High Places and a Rest for the People of God, above all the High Places of Earth* (London, 1657). 25 pp. Wing F1834.

212. *George Fox, *Journal* (London, 1694). 728 pp. Wing P1260A.

213. George Fox, *An Instruction to Judges and Lawyers* (London, 1658). 40 pp. Wing F1848.

214. George Fox, *The Line of Rightousness and Justice Streched Forth Over All Merchants . . . an Exhortation unto all Friends and People Whatsoever . . . that Ye All Do that Which is Just* (London, 1661). 8 pp. Wing F1857.

215. George Fox, *The Line of Righteousness and Justice stretched fourth over all merchants, etc.* (London, 1661). 8 pp. Wing F1857.

216. George Fox and John Burnyeat, *A New England Fire-Brand Quenched being Something in Answer unto a Lying, Slanderous Book, Entitled George Fox Dissected out of his Burrows* (London, 1679). 2 vol. in 1, 233 pp., 255 pp. Wing F1865.

217. *George Fox, *A Paper Sent Forth into the World from Them that are Scornfully Called Quakers Declaring the Ground and Reasons why they Deny the Teachers of the World, who Profess themselves to be Ministers, and dissent from them* (London, 1654). 8 pp. Wing F1872.

218. George Fox, *The Papists Strength, Principles, and Doctrines . . . Answered and Confuted* (London, 1658). 99 pp. Wing F1877.

219. George Fox, *To The Parliament of the Comon-wealth* (London, 1659). 23 pp. Wing F1958.

220. George Fox, *The Pearl Found in England, This is for the Poor Distressed . . . from the Royal Seed of God* (London, 1658). 20 pp. Wing F1879.

221. George Fox, *The Priests and Professors Catechism: For them to Try Their Spirits* (London, 1657). 36 pp. Wing F1882.

222. George Fox, *Priests Fruit Made Manifest and the Vanity of the World Discovered* (London, 1657). 6 pp. Wing F1883A.

223. George Fox, *The Serious Peoples Reasoning With the Worlds Teachers and Professors* (London, 1659). 8 pp. Wing F1900.

224. George Fox, *Several Papers Given Forth* (London, 1660). 54 pp. Wing F1902.

225. George Fox, *Something in Answer to Lodowick Muggletons Book* (London, 1667). 36 pp. Wing F1914.

226. George Fox, *Something in Answer to that book called The Church-faith, set forth by Independents and the other* (London, 1660). 24 pp. Wing F1915.

227. George Fox and Richard Hubberthorne, *Truth's Defense Not the Refined Subtlty of the Serpent held forth in Divers Answers to Severall Queries made by Men (Called Ministers) in the North* (York, 1653). 107 pp. Wing F1970.

228. George Fox, *A Visitation to the Jewes, from them whom the Lord hath Visited from on High* (London, 1656). 36 pp. Wing F1978.

229. George Fox, *A Warning to All Merchants of London, and such as buy and sell with an Advertisement to them to lay aside their superfluity and with it to Norrish the Poor* (London, 1658). 6 pp. Wing F1985.

230. George Fox, *A Warning to All Teachers of Children which are called School-Masters and School-Mistresses* (London, 1657). 6 pp. Wing F1984.

231. George Fox (Younger), *England's Sad Estate and Condition Lamented in this Just Complaint Taken Up Against the Greatest Part of Her Inhabitants* (London, 1661). 13 pp. Wing F2000.

232. *George Fox (Younger), *A Noble Salutation and Faithful Greeting unto Thee, Charles Stuart* (London, 1660). 24 pp. Wing F2008.

233. Margaret Askew Fell Fox, *A Call to the Universal Seed of God, Throughout the Whole World* (London, 1665). 17 pp. Wing F625A.

234. Margaret Askew Fell Fox, *The Standard of the Lord Revealed* (London, 1667). 130 pp. Wing F635.

235. John Freame, *Scripture-Instruction: Digested into Several Sections, By Way of Question and Answer* (London, 1713). 179 pp. Smith, part 1, p. 706.

236. Abraham Fuller, *The Testimony of Abraham Fuller: Concerning the Death of his Son Joseph* (n.p., 1687). 12 pp. Wing F2381A.

237. John Furly, *A Testimony to the True Light: Which is the Way of Life and Righteousness* (London, 1670). 32 pp. Wing F2541A.

238. Robert Gell, *An essay towards the amendment of the last English translation of the Bible* (London, 1659). 805 pp. Wing G470.

239. William Gibson, *Eine christliche An-sprache, an die Obrigkeit in Dantzig und Schiedlitz: Wegen etlicher alldar verfoltgen Christen* (Amsterdam, 1679). 12 pp. OCLC 753406049.

240. William Gibson, *Election and Reprobation Spiritually Experimentally Witnessed* (London, 1678). 111 pp. Wing G681.

241. William Gibson, *Life of God* (London, 1677). 152 pp. Wing C686.

242. Thomas Goodwin, *Moses and Aaron* (London, 1625). 332 pp. STC 11951.

243. *Daniel Gould, *A Brief Narration of the sufferings of the people called Quakers; who were put to Death at Boston in New England* (New York, 1700). 38 pp. Evans 911.

244. Baltasar Gracian, *The Art of Prudence, or a Companion for Men of Sense* (London, 1705). 280 pp. ESTC T109264.

245. John Gratton, *The Clergy-Man's Pretence of Divine Right to Tithe, Examined and Refuted* (London, 1703). 79 pp. NUC G393150.

246. John Gratton, *A Treatise Concerning Baptism and the Lord's Supper* (London, 1695). 99 pp. Wing G1586.

247. Theophilius Green, *A Narrative of Some Passages of the Life of Theophilius Green* (London, 1702). 31 pp. Smith, part 1, p. 863.

248. Thomas Greene, *A Lamentation Taken Up for London* (London, 1665). 8 pp. Wing G1844.

249. C.H., *De bisschop voor Groningen; op de maniere van tragi-comedie* (Groningen, 1672). 32 pp. OCLC 837723443.

250. Thomas Hart, *The Prophet Approved by the Words* (London, 1658). 14 pp. Wing B484.

251. Charles Harris, *A Scriptural Chronicle of Satan's Incendiaries: viz, Hard-Hearted Persecutors and Malicious Informers with their Work, Wages, and Ends* (London, 1670). 19 pp. Wing H919.

252. *Charles Harris, *The Wolf Under Sheep's-Clothing Discovered, or the Spirit of Cain, Appearing in the Bishop of Liechfield* (London, 1669). 23 pp. Wing H920.

253. Jeremiah Haward, *Here Followeth A True Relation of Some Sufferings Inflicted upon the Servants of God . . . called Quakers* (London?, 1654). 8 pp. Wing H1547.

254. *Richard Hawkins, *A Brief Narrative of the Life and Death of that Antient Servant of the Lord and his People, Gilbert Lately* (London, 1707). 156 pp. Smith, part 1, p. 925.

255. Roger Haydock, *A Collection of the Christian Writings, Labours, Travels and Suffering* (London, 1700). 35 pp. Smith, part 1, p. 927.

256. *Roger Haydock, *The Skirmisher Confounded* (London, 1676). 15 pp. Wing H1206.

257. Jeremiah Haward, *Here Followeth A True Relation or Some of the Sufferings Inflicted Upon the Servants of the Lord, who are Called Quakers by this Generation of Evil-Doers* (London, 1654). 8 pp. Wing H1547.

258. Richard Head, *The Life and Death of Mother Shipton* (London, 1684). 54 pp. Wing H1258.

259. Roger Hebden, *A Plain Account of certain Christian Experiences, Labours, Services, and Sufferings of that ancient Servant and Minister of Christ Roger Hebden* (London, 1700). 136 pp. Wing H1346A.

260. G. Hegentijii, *Itinerarium Frisio-Hollandicum* (1630). 177 pp. OCLC 257246642.

261. Joseph Helling, *A Salutation from the Breathings of the Life to the Faithful in the Kingdome and Patience of Jesus Christ* (London, 1661). 8 pp. Wing H1383.

262. Pieter Hendricks, *Antwoord op eenige beschuldigingen die Gerrit Roosen* (Rotterdam, 1683). 16 pp. OCLC 30550004.

263. John Higgins, *Christian Salutation to all the People of God (Often in Scorn Called Quakers)* (London, 1663). 8 pp. Wing H1952.

264. Hannah Hill, *A Legacy for Children: being some of the Last Expressions and Dying Sayings of Hannah Hill, Jr.* (Philadelphia, 1717). 22 pp. Smith, part 1, p. 950.

265. Richard Hodden, *The One Good Way of God: Contrary to the Many Different Ways of Men's Making. With Loving Warnings, Exhortations and Cautions, to All Sorts of Men, Concerning their Souls* (London, 1661). 54 pp. Wing H2283.

266. Wolfgang Helmhard von Hohberg, *Georgica curiosa aucta, das ist, Umständlicher Bericht und Klarer Unterricht von dem adelichen Land- und Feld-Leben auf alle in Teutschland übliche Land- und Haus-Wirthschafften gerichtet* (Nuremburg, 1701). 870 pp. OCLC 18275211.

267. Johann Heinrich Horb, *Gottes gnädige Heimsuchung der Reichsstadt Windsheim* (Frankfurt, 1685). 275 pp. OCLC 257976630.

268. Georg Horn, *Orbis politicus: imperiorum, regnorum, principatuum, rerum publicarum: cum Memorabilium Historicis & Geographia veteri ac recenti* (1668). 158 pp. OCLC 13363113.

269. Luke Howard, *A Few Plain Words of Instruction* (London, 1658). 20 pp. Wing H2985.

270. Edward Burrough and Francis Howgill, *To the Camp of the Lord in England* (n.p., 1656). 24 pp. Wing H3184.

271. Francis Howgill, *The Great Case of Tithes and Forced Maintenance Once More Revived* (London, 1665). 73 pp. Wing H3165.

272. Francis Howgill, *An Information and also Advice to the Armie . . . and Also to All People who Seeks Peace and Righteousness* (London, 1659). 11 pp. Wing H3167.

273. Francis Howgill, *The Inheritance of Jacob Discovered, After His Return Out of AEgypt* (London, 1656). 38 pp. Wing H3168.

274. Francis Howgill, *A Lamentation for the Scattered Tribes Who are Exciled Into Captivity and Are Now Mingled Among the Heathen* (London, 1656). 35 pp. Wing H3170.

275. Francis Howgill, *The Measuring Rod of the Lord Stretched Forth Over all Nations and the Line of True Judgment laid to the Rulers Thereof* (London, 1658). 32 pp. Wing H3171.

276. Francis Howgill, *Mistery Babylon The Mother of Harlots Discovered . . . In Answer to a Book Titled The Directory for the Publick Worship of God through England, Scotland, and Ireland* (London, 1659). 32 pp. Wing H3173.

277. Francis Howgill, *Oaths No Gospel Ordinance but Prohibited by Christ* (London, 1666). 84 pp. Wing H3174.

278. Francis Howgill, *The Popish Inquisition Newly Erected in New England, whereby their Church is Manifested to be a Daughter of Mysterie Bablyon . . .* (London, 1659). 120 pp. Wing H3177.

279. Francis Howgill and Edward Burrough, *The Visitation of the Rebellious Nation of Ireland* (London, 1656). 38 pp. Wing H3188.

280. Richard Hodden, *The One Good Way of God Contrary to the Many Different Ways of Mens Making. With Loving Warnings, Exhortations and Cautions, to All Sorts of Men Concerning their Souls* (London, 1661). 54 pp. Wing H2283.

281. Robert Howlett, *Anglers Sure Guide: Or Angling Improved, and methodically digested* (London, 1706). 296 pp. ESTC T72892.

282. *Richard Hubberthorn, *Truth cleared, and the deceit made manifest or, An answer to . . . Powel, who is one of the chief priests of Wales* (London, 1654). 17 pp. Wing H3241.

283. *Richard Hubberthorn, *The Horn of the He-Goat Broken: Or, An Answer to a Lying Book Called, the Chasing the Young Quaking Harlot Out of the Citie* (London, 1656). 12 pp. Wing H3234.

284. *Richard Hubberthorn, *The Innocency of the Righteous Seed of God Cleared from all Slanderous Tounges and False Accusers* (London, 1655). 15 pp. Wing H3226.

285. Richard Hubberthorn, *Something that Lately Passed in Discourse Between the King and Richard Hubberthorne* (London, 1660). 6 pp. Wing H3234.

286. *Richard Hubberthorn and Samuel Fisher, *Supplementum Sublatum: John Tombes His Supplement Or, Second Book About Sweating, Disproved, and Made Void* (London, 1661). 6 pp. Wing H3236.

Richard Hubberthorn, *Truths Defense*, see George Fox and Richard Hubberthorn (Quaker bibliography entry 227 above).

287. Samuel Hunt, *Instructions for Children and others, by way of Question and Answer* (London, 1703). 60 pp. ESTC T228439.

288. Thomas Hurste, *The Descent of Authoritie, or The magistrates patent from heaven* (London, 1637). 33 pp. STC 14007.

289. *Thomas Hutchinson, *Forced Uniformity Neither Christian Nor Prudent: Presented to those in Authority Whom it May Concern* (London, 1675). 8 pp. Wing H3836.

290. James Jackson, *The Friendly Enquirer's Doubts and Objections Answered: Concerning the Light Within* (London, 1698). 106 pp. Wing J73.

291. Samuel Jennings, *The State of the Case Between Friends in Pennsylvania and George Keith* (London, 1694). 80 pp. Wing J670.

292. *Bartholomew Keckermann, Systema Logicae* (Hannover, 1610). OCLC 639719062.

293. George Keith, *The Benefit, Advantage and Glory of Silent Meetings* (London, 1670). 18 pp. Wing K144.

294. George Keith, *The Christianity of the People Called Quakers Asserted, by George Keith: in Answer to a Sheet Called, A Serious Call to the Quakers* (London, 1700). 16 pp. Wing C861.

295. George Keith, *Gross Error and hypocrisie detected in George Whitehead and some of his brethren* (London, 1695). 23 pp. Wing K172.

296.*George Keith, *The Pretended Antidote Proved Poyson: Or, The True Principle of the Christian and Protestant Religion Defended and the Four Counterfeit Defenders thereof Detected and Discovered . . . James Allen, Joshua Moodey, Samuel Willard and Cotton Mather* (Philadelphia, 1690). 224 pp. Evans 515.

297.*George Keith, *Refutation of Three Opposers of Truth, By Plain Evidence of Holy Scripture* (Philadelphia, 1690). 73 pp. Evans 516.

298. George Keith, *A Serious Appeal to All the More Sober, Impartial and Judicious People in New England* (Philadelphia, 1692). 67 pp. Wing K205.

299.*George Keith, *The True Christ Owned as He Is* (n.p., 1679). 107 pp. Wing K219.

300. George Keith, *Truths Defense of the Pretended Examination by John Alexander of Lieth of the Principles of those Called Quakers* (London, 1682). 254 pp. Wing K255.

301. *George Keith, *The Universal Free Grace of the Gospel Asserted* (London, 1671). 136 pp. Wing K288.

302. Thomas Kent, *The Fall of Man Declared and the Way Declared in Plainness and According unto Truth* (London, 1661). 30 pp. Wing K318.

303. Athanasius Kircher, *The Vulcanors, or burning and fire-vomiting mountains, in the world, with their remarkables* (London, 1669). 68 pp. Wing K624.

304.*Nicholas Knight, *A Comparison Between the True and False Ministers in their Calling, Lives and Doctrine* (London, 1675). 22 pp. Wing K691.

305. Wilhelm Christoph Kriegsmann, *Symphonesis Christianorum, oder Tractat von den einzelnen und Privat-Zusammenkünfften der Christen* (Frankfurt, 1678). 60 pp. OCLC 258209138.

306. Jean de Labadie, *Justum Judicium de Justa Bonorum a malis, quod ad unionem communionem ecclesiasticam attinet* (Amsterdam, 1675). OCLC 69064383.

307. Thomas Lawson, *An Appeal to the Parliament Concerning the Poor: That there may not be a beggar in England* (London, 1660). 4 pp. Wing L722.

308. Thomas Lawson, *Baptismalogia, or, A Treatise Concerning Baptisms whereto is Added: A Discourse Concerning the Supper* (London, 1677/78). 168 pp. Wing L723.

309. Thomas Lawson, *Dagon's Fall Before the Ark; or, The Smoke of the Bottomless Pit Scoured Away . . . written, primarily as a Testimony Agst the Old Serpant His Wisdom . . . His Arts, Inventions, Comedies or Interludes . . . taught in Christian Schools* (London, 1679). 94 pp. Wing L724.

310. Thomas Lawson, *A Mite into the Treasure: Being a Word to Artists, Especially the Heptatechrists, the Professors of the Seven Liberal Arts . . . Showing what we Own Herein Being According to God . . . and What we Deny* (London, 1680). 52 pp. Wing L726A.

311. Thomas Lawson, *A Treatise Relating to the Call, Work and Wages of the Ministers of Christ* (London, 1680). 118 pp. Wing L728.

312. Thomas Leader, *The wounded-heart, or the Jury-Man's offences declared and ingenuously acknowledged for the satisfaction of those who were thereby troubled* (London, 1665). 11 pp. Wing L793.

313. Levinus Lemnius, *A Discourse touching Generation: collected out of Levinus Lemnius, a most learned physitian* (London, 1664). 382 pp. Wing L1043A.

314. Benjamin Lindley, *The Necessity of Immediate Revelations, Towards the Foundation and Ground of True Faith, Proved; . . . Answer to the Dark Attempts of Thomas Bennett Against Them; in his Nine First Chapters, of his Pretended Confutation of Quakerism* (London, 1710). 124 pp. Smith, part 2, p. 125.

315. Benjamin Lindley, *The Shiboleth of Priesthood* (London, 1678). 18 pp. Wing L2311.

316. Patrick Livingstone, *Plain and Downright Dealing with Them That Are With Us* (London, 1667). 24 pp. Wing L2605.

317. London Yearly Meeting, *To George, King of Great Britain, &c. The Humble Address of the People Commonly Called Quakers* (London, 1714). 1 pp. NUC T0239830.

318. Benjamin Loveling, *The Plain-Dealing of the Quakers* (London, 1704). 6 pp. NUC L0517639.

319. *Nicholas Lucas, *A True and Impartial Narration of the Remarkable Providences of the Living God of Heaven and Earth: Appearing for Us His Oppressed Servants Called Quakers . . . who most Unrighteously were at Hertford Sentenced to be Transported Beyond the Seas* (London, 1664). 14 pp. Wing T2496.

320. Thomas Lurting, *The Fighting Sailor Turned Peaceable Christian: Manifested in the Convincement and Conversion of Thomas Lurting* (London, 1710). 46 pp. Smith, part 2, p. 137.

321. E.M., *A Brief Answer unto the Cambridge Moddel: which is to go to the two universities to be read by all the Doctors and Students* (London, 1658). 14 pp. Wing M15.

322. Thomas Markham, *An Account of the Life and Death of Thomas Markham* (London, 1695). 24 pp. BLC 4152 f. 23.

323. Charles Marshal, *An Epistle to the Flock of Christ Jesus* (London, 1672). 20 pp. Wing M740.

324. Charles Marshal, *Sion's Travellers comforted and the Disobedient warned: In a Collection of Books and Epistles of that faithful Minister of Christ Jesus Charles Marshal* (London, 1704). OCLC 642750900.

325. Henry Mason, *The Cure of Cares, Or a Short Discourse declaring the condition of Worldly Cares* (London, 1627). 51 pp. STC 17605.

326. Henry Mason, *Hearing and doing: the ready way to blessednesse* (London, 1656). 776 pp. Wing M915.

327. *Martin Mason, *The Boasting Baptist Dismounted, and the Beast Disarmed and Sorely Wounded Without Any Carnel Weapon* (London, 1656). 12 pp. Smith, part 2, p. 153.

328. *Martin Mason, *A Faithful Warning, with Good Advice from Israel's God to England's King and His Council* (London, 1661?). 13 pp. Wing M928.

329. *Martin Mason, *The Proud Pharisee Reproved* (London, 1655). 55 pp. Wing M933.

330. Thomas Maule, see Philalethes

331. John Matern, *A Testimony of that dear and faithful man, John Matern* (London, 1680). 32 pp. Wing P683.

332. Johann Matthiae, *Ramus olivae septentrionalis primus baccas nonnullus Religiosae paci suaviter redolentes et concordiae Ecclesiasticae Sacras, inter Christianos diffundens, praemittitur Apographum literarum ejusdem Argumenti* (1657). 119 pp. OCLC 248393984.

333. John Maynard, *A Memento to Young and Old* (London, 1669). 191 pp. Wing M1451.

334. Matthew Meade, *En oligo Christianos: The Almost Christian Discovered; or, The false professor tryed & cast* (London, 1660). 3 pp. Wing M1547A.

335. Joseph Mede, *The apostasy of the latter times* (London, 1641). 152 pp. Wing M1590.

336. Joseph Mede, *Clavis Apocalyptica: ex innatis et insitis visionum characteribus eruta et demonstrata* (Cantabrigiae, 1627). 27 pp. STC 17766.

337. Johann Michaelis, *Apostolischer Glaubens-Grund/ Welchen Durch den Druck aller Welt darzulegen* (1695). OCLC 248826988.

338. Henry Mollineux, *Antichrist Unvailed by the Finger of God's Power* (London, 1695). 276 pp. Wing M2393.

339. Mary Southworth Mollineux, *Fruits of Retirement; or, Miscellaneous Poems Moral and Divine Written on a Variety of Subjects* (London, 1702). 174 pp. NUC M0692041.

340. John Moon, *A Real Demonstration of the True Order in the Spirit of God* (London, 1663). 10 pp. Wing R456A.

341. *Paul Moon, "Some Passages and Proceedings in Court," appended to George Fox, *An Instruction to Judges and Lawyers* (London, 1659). 40 pp. Wing F1848.

342. Thomas Morford, *The Baptist and Independent Churches (So Called) Set on Fire By a Bright Shining Light Revealed From Heaven* (London, 1660). 43 pp. Wing M2727.

343. Sylvanus Morgan, *Horlogiographia Optica, Dialling universal and particular: speculative and practical* (London, 1652). 144 pp. Wing M2741.

344. *James Naylor, *An Answer to a Book Called the Quakers catechism: put Out by Richard Baxter* (London, 1655). 51 pp. Wing N259.

345. *James Naylor, *Answer to Twenty Eight Queries Sent Out by Francis Harris to Those People he Calls Quakers* (London, 1655). 26 pp. NUC N0083118.

346. *James Naylor, *Antichrist In Man, Christ's Enemy . . . An Answer to a Book titled, Antichrist in Man the Quakers' Idol* (London, 1656). 17 pp. Wing N263.

347. James Naylor, *A collection of sundry books, epistles, and papers written by James Nayler, some of which were never before printed. With an impartial relation of the*

most remarkable transactions relating to his life (London, 1716). 770 pp. ESTC T102522.

348. *James Naylor, *Deceit Brought to Day-Light in a General Answer to Thomas Collier* (London, 1656). 28 pp. Wing N269.

349. *James Naylor, *Discovery of the Beast Got Into the Seat of the False Prophet . . . Or, An Answer to a Paper Set out by T. Winterton, wherein he would Prove Something Against the Quakers if he Could* (London, 1655). 19 pp. Wing N271.

350. *James Naylor, *A Foole Answered According to His Folly* (London, 1655). 26 pp. Wing N280.

351. *James Naylor, *Liefde tot de verloorene: ende een handt uyt-gestreckt tot de hulpe-loose, om uyt het duyster te leyden* (Amsterdam, 1669). 62 pp. OCLC 80911612 (An English translation/citation of this work is James Naylor, *Love to the Lost and a Hand Held Forth to the Helpless, To Lead Out of the Dark* [London, 1665]. 80 pp. Wing N278).

352. *James Naylor, *Milk for Babes and Meat for Strong Men . . . being the Breathings of the Spirit Through His Servant James Naylor* (London, 1661). 28 pp. Wing N299.

353. *James Naylor, *A Publike Discovery of the Open Blindness of Babel's Builders: in answer to a book intitled A Publike Discovery of a Secret Deceit* (London, 1655). 48 pp. Wing N305.

354. *James Naylor, *A Second Answer to Thomas Moore, to that which he calls his Defense Against Popism* (London, 1655). 35 pp. Wing N314.

355. James Naylor, *Several Petitions Answered, that were put by the Priests of Westmoreland* (London, 1653). 64 pp. Wing N316A.

356. James Naylor, *A Vindication of Truth as Held Forth in a Book Entitled, Love to the Lost* (London, 1656). 57 pp. Wing N326.

357. *James Naylor, *Weakness Above Wickedness and Truth Subtilty . . . An Answer to a Book Called Quakers Quaking Devised by Jermey Ive's* (London, 1656). 30 pp. Wing N327.

358. James Naylor, *Wickedness Weighed: in an Answer to a Book Called The Quakers' Quaking Principle . . . Set Forth by Ellis Bradshaw* (London, 1656). 28 pp. Wing N331.

359. *James Parke, *To the Flock of God Everywhere Gathered* (n.p., 1666). 8 pp. NUC P0096680.

360. James Parke, *The Hour of God's Judgments Come and Coming Upon the Wicked World* (London, 1690). 24 pp. Wing P373.

361. Alexander Parker, *A manifestation of divine love, or, Some spirituall breathings consisting of two generall epistles, directed in manuscript to the flock of God in the west of England* (London, 1660). 21 pp. Wing S475.

362. *James Parnell, *Goliahs Head Cut Off with His Own Sword, in a combat betwixt little David . . . and Great Goliah . . : In a reply to a book, . . . Propounded by James Parnell* (London, 1655). 91 pp. Wing P531.

363. *James Parnell, *A Shield to the Truth, Or the Truth of God Cleared from Scandalls and Reproaches Cast Upon It by Scandalous and Reproachful Tongues* (London, 1655). 44 pp. Wing P537.

364. Franciscus Daniel Pastorius, *Disputatio inauguralis de rasura documentorum* (Altdorf, 1676). 24 pp. OCLC 831257982.

365. Melchior Adam Pastorius, *Contemplatio terrestrium vanitatum* (S.I., 1674). OCLC 165823321.

366. Melchior Adam Pastorius, *Institutio Christiana Hominis Interni* (Frankfurt, 1682). OCLC 800613006.

367. Anthony Pearson, *Great Case of Tythes Truly Stated* (London, 1657). 37 pp. Wing P889.

368. *William Penn, *An Account of W. Penn's Travails in Holland and Germany* (London, 1694). 270 pp. Wing P1245.

369. *William Penn, *An Address to Protestants of All Persuasions More Especially the Magistracy and the Clergy, for the Promotion of Virtue and Charity* (London, 1692). 256 pp. Wing P1249.

370. *William Penn, *A Brief Answer to a False and Foolish Libel Called the Quakers Opinions* (London, 1678). 26 pp. Wing P1259.

371. William Penn, *A Brief Guide Mistaken and Temporizing Rebuked, or, A Reply to Jonathan Clapham's Book intitled, A Guide to True Religion* (London, 1670). 55 pp. Wing P1299.

372. William Penn, *A Brief Account of the Rise and Progress of the People Called Quakers* (London, 1694). 131 pp. Wing P1257.

373. *William Penn, *A Call to Christendom, in an Earnest Expostulation with Her to Prepare for the Great and Notable Day of the Lord* (London, 1695). 46 pp. Wing P1261.

374. *William Penn, *Christian Liberty as it was Soberly Desired in a Letter to Certain Foreign States, upon Occasion of their Late Severity to Several of Their Inhabitants* (London, 1674). 8 pp. Wing P1265.

375. *William Penn, *The Christian Quaker and His Divine Testimony Stated and Vindicated from Scripture, Reason and Authority* (London, 1699). 254 pp. Wing P1267.

376. *William Penn, *Continued Cry of the Oppressed for Justice, being a Farther Account of the Late Unjust and Cruel Proceedings of Unreasonable Men Against the Persons and Estates of Many of the People call'd Quakers* (London, 1675). 34 pp. Wing P1270.

377. *William Penn, *A Defence of a Paper Entitled, Gospel-Truths, Against the exceptions of Bishop of Cork's Testimony* (London, 1698). 119 pp. Wing P1273.

378. *William Penn, *England's Present Interest Discovered* (London, 1676). 62 pp. Wing P1280.

379. *William Penn, *An Epistle Containing a Salutation to all Faithful Friends, A Reproof to the Unfaithful, and a Visitation to the Enquiring in a Solemn Farewell to them all in the Land of My Nativity* (London, 1682). 7 pp. Wing P1283.

380. *William Penn, *The Great Case of Liberty of Conscience Once more Briefly Debated and Defended by the Authority of Reason, Scripture, and Antiquity* (London, 1670). 55 pp. Wing P1299.

381. *William Penn, *The Guide Mistaken and Temporizing Rebuked* (London, 1668). 63 pp. Wing P1301.

382. William Penn, *The Harmony of Divine and Heavenly Doctrines: Demonstrated in Sundry Declarations on Variety of Subjects Preached at the Quakers Meetings in London* (London, 1696). 236 pp. NUC P0201515.

383. *William Penn, *Judas and the Jews Combined Against Christ and His Followers: being a Re-Joynder to the Late Nameless Reply, called, Tyranny and Hypocrisie Detected made against . . . The Spirit of Alexander* (London, 1673). 130 pp. Wing P1307.

384. William Penn, *Just Censure of Francis Buggs Address* (London, 1699). 43 pp. Wing P1308.

385. *William Penn, *A Just Rebuke to One and Twenty Learned and Reverend Divines (So Called): being an Answer to an Abusive Epistle Against the People Call'd Quakers* (London, 1674). 32 pp. Wing P1311.

386. William Penn, *A Key to Open Every Way to Every Common Understanding: How to Discern the Difference Betwixt the Religion Professed by the People Called Quakers and their Adversaries* (London, 1694). 44 pp. Wing P1313.

387. William Penn, *William Penn's Last Farewell to England: being an epistle containing a salutation to all faithful friends* (London, 1682). 6 pp. Wing P1317.

388. *William Penn, *More Fruits of Solitude* (London, 1702). 111 pp. Smith, part 2, p. 309.388. *William Penn, *No Cross, No Crown* (London, 1682). 600 pp. Wing P1328.

389. *William Penn, *One Project for the Good of England, that is, Our Civil Union is Our Civil Safety* (n.p., 1679). 11 pp. Wing P1334.

390. *[William Penn], *The Peoples Ancient Liberties Asserted in the Trial of William Mead and William Penn* (London, 1670). 62 pp. Wing P1335.

391. William Penn, *Primitive Christianity Revived in the Faith and Practice of the People Called Quakers* (London, 1696). 122 pp. Wing P1342.

392. William Penn, *A Reply to a Pretended Answer, By A Nameless Author, to W.P.'s Key* (London, 1695). 156 pp. Wing P1354.

393. William Penn, *Sandy Foundation Shaken* (London, 1668). 36 pp. Wing P1356.

394. *William Penn, *Saul Smitten to the Ground: being a brief but faithful narrative of the dying remorse of a late living enemy . . . Matthew Hide* (London, 1675). 16 pp. Wing P1358.

395. *William Penn, *A Seasonable Caveat against Popery, Or a Pamphlet Entitled An Explanation of the Roman Catholick Belief, briefly examined* (London, 1670). 38 pp. Wing P1359.

396. *William Penn and George Whitehead, *A Serious Apology for the principles and practices of the people call'd Quakers* (London, 1671). 190 pp. Wing W1957.

397. *William Penn, *The Skirmisher Defeated and Truth Defended: being an Answer to a Pamphlet, Entituled, A Skirmisher Made Upon Quakerism* (London, 1676). 41 pp. Wing P1364.

398. *William Penn, *Some Fruits of Solitude in Reflection and Maxims Relating to Conduct of Human Life* (London, 1693). 134 pp. Wing P1369.

399. *William Penn, *The Spirit of Alexander the Copper-Smith Lately Revived, Now Justly Rebuked, or, An Answer to a late Pamphlet intituled, The Spirit of the hat, or the government of the Quakers* (London, 1673). 28 pp. Wing P1374.

400. *William Penn, *The Spirit of Truth Vindicated: Against that of Error and Envy . . . in a Late Malicious Libel, Intituled, The Spirit of the Quakers Tryed* (London, 1672). 138 pp. Wing P1375.

401. William Penn, *Tender Counsel and Advice: by way of Epistle to all Those Who are Sensible of Their Day of Visitation* (London, 1696). 47 pp. Wing P1378.

402. William Penn, *A Testimony to the Truth of God, As Held by the People Called Quakers* (London, 1699). 56 pp. Wing P1380.

403. *William Penn, *To the Churches of Jesus throughout the World* (London, 1677). 13 pp. Wing P1387A.

404. *William Penn, *A Treatise of Oaths, Containing Several Weighty Reasons why the People Call'd Quakers Refuse to Swear: And those Confirmed by Numerous Testimonies Out of Gentiles, Jews, and Christians* (London, 1675). 160 pp. Wing R1400, P1388.

405. *William Penn, *Truth Exalted in a Short but Sure Testimony Against All Those Religions, Faiths, and Worships that have been Formed in the Darkness of Apostacy* (London, 1671). 20 pp. Wing P1390.

406. *William Penn, *Truth Rescued from Imposture, or, A Brief Reply to a Meer Rhapsodie of Lies, Folly and Slander* (London, 1670). 71 pp. Wing P1392.

407. *William Penn, *Urim and Thummi: or, The Apostolical Doctrines of Light and Perfection Maintained* (London, 1674). 32 pp. Wing P1393.

408. [William Penn,] *A Just Censure of Francis Bugg's Address to the Parliament Against the Quakers* (London, 1699). 42 pp. Wing P1308.

409. Edward Penington, *Some brief Observations upon G. Keith's earnest Expostulation* (London, 1696). 24 pp. Wing P1146.

410. Edward Penington, *A modest detection of George Keith's (miscalled) Just vindication of his earnest expostulation* (London, 1696). 56 pp. Wing P1144.

411. Edward Penington, *Rabshakeh rebuked, and his railing accusations refuted* (London, 1695). 96 pp. Wing P1145.

412. Isaac Penington, *An Answer to that Common Objection Against the Quakers, That they Condemn All But Themselves* (London, 1660). 8 pp. Wing P1151.

413. Isaac Penington, *The Axe Laid To the Root of the Old Corrupt-Tree And the Spirit of Deceit Struck at in Its Nature* (London, 1659). 42 pp. Wing P1152.

414. Isaac Penington, *Babylon the Great Described: The City of Confusion Whereof In Every Part whereof antichrist Reigns, which Knoweth Not the Order and Unity of the Spirit, But Striveth to Set Up an Order and Uniformity According to the Wisdom of the Flesh* (London, 1659). 56 pp. Wing P1153.

415. Isaac Penington, *An Examination of the Grounds or Causes to which are said to Induce the Court of Boston in New-England to Make that Order or Law of Banishment Upon Pain of Death Against Quakers* (London, 1660). 99 pp. Wing P1166.

416. Isaac Penington, *The Jew Outward: Being a Glass for the Professors of this Age* (London, 1659). 28 pp. Wing P1174.

417. Isaac Penington, *Some Queries concerning the Work of God in the world which is to be expected in the latter Ages thereof* (London, 1660). 8 pp. Wing P1200.

418. *Isaac Penington, *A question to the professors of Christianity, whether they have the true, living, powerful, saving Knowledge of Christ or no?* (London, 1667). 54 pp. Wing P1184.

419. Isaac Penington, *The Scattered Sheep Sought After* (London, 1659). 28 pp. Wing P1187.

420. Isaac Penington, *Some things relating to Religion proposed to the Consideration of the Royal Society (so termed)* (London, 1668). 24 pp. Wing P1205.

421. Isaac Pennington, *Den wegh des levens ende doots, openbaer gemaeckt ende voor e menschen geset* (1661). OCLC 69066265 (English translation/citation: Isaac Penington, *The Way of Life and Death Made Manifest and Set Before Men* [London, 1658]. 100 pp. Wing P1219).

422. Isaac Penington, *The Works of the Long-Mournful and Soberly Distressed Isaac Penington . . . In Two Parts* (London, 1681). 496 pp. Wing P1149.

423. John Penington, *Fig Leaf Covering discovered, or Geo. Keith's explications and retractions of divers passages out of his former books proved insincere, defective, and evasive* (London, 1697). 139 pp. Wing P1227.

424. John Penington, *Keith against Keith, or, some more of George Keith's Contradictions and Absurdities* (London, 1696). 152 pp. Wing 28.

425. John Penington, *The people called Quakers cleared by Geo. Keith from the false doctrines charged upon them by G. Keith* (London, 1696). 54 pp. Wing P1229–P1230.

426. J.P. [John Perrot], *To the upright in heart, and faithful people of God: being an epistle written in Barbado's the 3 of the 9ᵗʰ month* (London, 1662). 10 pp. Wing P1635.

427. John Peters, *A brief Narration of the Life, Services, and Sufferings of John Peters* (London, 1709). 144 pp. OCLC 19327638.

428. Michael Pexenfelder, *Apparatus eruditionis tam rerum quam verborum per omnes artes et scientias, instructus opera et studio.* (Nürnberg, 1670). 14 pp. OCLC 12180206.

429. *Philalethes, [Thomas Maule], *For the Service of the Truth* (Philadelphia, 1703). 8 pp. Evans 1135.

430. Daniel Phillips, *A Dissertation of the Small Pox* (London, 1702). 119 pp. NUC P0325387.

431. Daniel Phillips, *Proteus Redivivius, or the Turner of Turner's Hall truly represented* (London, 1700). 30 pp. Wing P2063.

432. Daniel Phillips, *Vindiciae Veritatis: or, An Occasional Defence of the Principles and Practices of the People Called Quakers in Answer to John Stilling* (London, 1702). 260 pp. NUC P0325393.

433. Henry Pickworth, *A Narrative of a Charge Against Francis Bugg, and His Evasions and Shufflings at Sleeford in Lincolnshire* (London, 1701). 32 pp. Smith, part 2, p. 415.

434. Henry Pickworth, *A Reply to Francis Bugg's Pretended Answer to a Narrative of a Charge Against Him* (London, 1701). 15 pp. Smith, part 2, p. 416.

435. Joseph Pike, *Treatise Concerning Baptism and the Supper* (London, 1710). 242 pp. Smith, part 2, p. 422.

436. Richard Pinder, *Bowels of Compassion Towards the Scattered Lord* (1659). 11 pp. Wing P2261.

437. Richard Pinder, *A Loving Invitation (to Repentance and Amendment of Life) Unto All the Inhabitants of the Island of Barbados* (London, 1660). 16 pp. Wing P2263.

438. Richard Pinder, *The Spirit of Error Discovered in the Accounted Pastors and Teachers of the Island Bermuda, In the West Indies* (London, 1660). 24 pp. Wing P2264.

439. William Poppel, *A Letter to Mr. Penn with his Answer* (London, 1688). 8 pp. Wing P2964.

440. Peter Price, *The Unequal Unyoked, and the Equal Yoked* (London, 1683). 20 pp. Wing P3397.

441. Samuel Puffendorf, *An introduction to the History of the principal kingdoms and states of Europe* (London, 1700). 515 pp. Wing P4179.

442. Caleb Pusey, *The Bomb Searched and Found Stuffed With False Ingredients* (Philadelphia, 1705). 76 pp. Evans 1230.

443. Caleb Pusey, *Daniel Leeds, justly rebuked for abusing William Penn* (Philadelphia, 1702). 28 pp. OCLC 152428751.

444. Caleb Pusey, *A Modest Account From Pennsylvania of the Principal Difference in Point of Doctrine Between George Keith and those of the People Called Quakers from whom he Separated* (London, 1696). 68 pp. Wing P4248.

445. *Caleb Pusey, *Proteus Ecclesiasticus, Or George Keith Varied in Fundamentals and Proved An Apostate With Remarks of Daniel Leed's Almanac for the Year 1703 by Way of Post-Script* (Philadelphia, 1703). 60 pp. Evans 1144.

446. Caleb Pusey, *Satan's Harbinger Encountered . . . Being Something in the way of an Answer to Daniel Leeds' His Book, Entitled, News of a Trumpet* (Philadelphia, 1700). 144 pp. Evans 948.

447. Caleb Pusey, *Some Remarks Upon a Late Pamphlet Signed Part by John Talbot, and Part by Daniel Leeds, Called the Great Mystery of Fox-Craft* (Philadelphia, 1705). 40 pp. Evans 1231.

448. William Rawlinson, *Robert Bridgman's Reasons for leaving the Quakers (upon examination) proved unreasonable* (London, 1700). 48 pp. Wing R370.

449. William Rawlinson, *The Universality of the love of god asserted in a Testimony to his free grace in Jesus Christ* (London, 1700). 72 pp. Wing R371.

450. Andreas Reyher, *Manuductio Poetica* (Gothae Schall, 1654). 40 pp. OCLC 246109668.

451. John Reynolds, *The Triumph of God's Revenge Against the crying and execrable Sin of wilful and premeditated murder* (London, 1679). 182 pp. ESTC T147138.

452. Ambrose Rigge, *To All Who Imprison and Persecute the Saints and Servants of God for Meeting Together in His Name, and Fear, To Worship Him as He Requireth* (London, 1659). 8 pp. Wing R1495.

453. Ambrose Rigge, *A Scripture-Catechism for Children* (London, 1672). 110 pp. Wing R1489.

454. Ambrose Rigge, *To the Whole Flock of God Everywhere* (London, 1660). 8 pp. Wing R1497.

455. Ambrose Rigge, *A Visitation of Tender Love (Once More) From the Lord Unto Charles II* (London, 1662). 8 pp. Wing R1500. [Pastorius attributed to Josiah Coale]

456. John Rous, *A Warning to the Inhabitants of Barbados: Who Live in Pride, Drunkennesse, Covetousness, Oppression and Deceitful Dealings* (n.p., 1656). 8 pp. Wing R2045.

457. *Thomas Rudyard, *The Anabaptists Lying Wonder, &c, Returned upon Themselves* (London, 1672). 11 pp. Wing R2174.

458. *Thomas Rudyard, *The Barbican Cheat Detected, Or, Injustice Arraigned: Being a Brief and Sober Disquisition of the Procedure of the Anabaptists* (London, 1674). 36 pp. Wing R2177.

459. Thomas Rudyard, *The Case of Protestant Dissenters . . . for Information of . . . justices of the peace, grand jurors, petty juries* (London, 1680). 8 pp. Wing R2180.

460. *Thomas Rudyard, *The Case of Protestant Dissenters Prosecuted on Old Statutes, Against Papists* (London, 1682). 6 pp. Wing R2178.

461. Thomas Rudyard, *The Cause of the Widows and Fatherless Pleaded With the Judges and Magistrates of England* (London, 1665). 16 pp. Wing R2181.

462. Guilielmus Saldenus, *Christelijke Kinder-School onderwisende de jonge jeugd in de eerste beginselen* (Utrecht, 1668). 196 pp. OCLC 46851566.

463. Thomas Salthouse, *A Candle Lighted at a Coal from the Alter* (London, 1660). 24 pp. Wing S471.

464. Thomas Salthouse, *A Manifestation of Divine Love, Or, Some Spiritual Breathings Consisting of Two General Epistles* (London, 1660). 21 pp. Wing S475, P382.

465. Edward Sammon, *A Discovery of the Education of the Scholars of Cambridge* (London, 1659). 14 pp. Wing S537.

466. Johann Jacob Schütz et al., *Compendium juris brevissimis verbis* (Frankfurt, 1697). 745 pp. OCLC 311858984.

467. Henry Scougal, *The Life of God in the Soul of Man, or, the Nature and Excellency of the Christian Religion* (London, 1677). 128 pp. Wing S2101.

468. *William Shewen, *A Brief Testimony Against Tale-bearers, Whisperers and Back-Biters* (n.p., 1686). 24 pp. Wing S3418.

469. William Shewen, *Counsel to the Christian Traveler* (London, 1683). 224 pp. NUC S0504409.

470. William Shewen, *A Few Words Concerning Conscience* (London, 1675). 46 pp. Wing S3421.

471. *William Shewen, *True Christians Faith and Experience Briefly Declared Concerning God* (London, 1675). 242 pp. Wing S3424.

472. *William Sixmith, *Some Fruits Brought Forth Through a Tender Branch in the Heavenly Vine Christ Jesus* (London, 1679). 27 pp. Wing S3925.

473. Humphrey Smith, *A Collection of the Several Writings and Faithful Testimonies of that Suffering Servant of God* (London, 1683). 340 pp. Wing S4051.

474. *Humphrey Smith, *Hidden Things Made Manifest by the Light* (London, 1658). 20 pp. Wing 4062.

475. *Humphrey Smith, *Something in reply to Edmund Skipp's Book Called the Quaker's Blazing Star* (London, 1655). 22 pp. Wing S4073.

476. *William Smith, *Balm from Gilead: A Collection of the Living Testimonies* (London, 1675). 595 pp. Wing S4287.

477. William Smith, *A general Summons from the authority of Truth, unto all ecclesiastical Courts and officers* (London, 1668). 27 pp. Wing S4304.

478. William Smith, *Innocency and Conscientiousness of the Quakers asserted and cleared from the evil surmises, false aspersions, and unrighteous suggestions of Judge Keeling expressed in his speech made the seventh of the seventh month at the sessions-house in the Old-Baily* (London, 1664). 16 pp. Wing; S4308.

479. William Smith, *The Morning-Watch: or, a Spiritual Glass Opened, wherein a Clear Discovery is Made of that which Lies in Darknesse, from whence wars, contentions, and destructions do arise concerning a professed religion* (London, 1660). 60 pp. Wing S4317.

480. William Smith, *A new Catechism* (London, 1665). 112 pp. Wing S4318.

481. William Smith, *A Real Demonstration of the True Order in the Spirit of God, and of the Ground of all Formality and Idolatry with a Few Words Unto Such as are Concerned in it* (London, 1663). 10 pp. Wing R456A.

482. William Smith, *Some queries propounded to this professing generation the people called Baptists, or any professors upon the earth for them to answer, and heedfully weigh and consider* (London, 1659). 10 pp. Wing S4331.

483. *William Smith, *Sweet oyle poured forth through the horn of salvation, and is freely sent abroad to search the wounded spirits, and to relieve the weak and feeble travellers* (London, 1660). 8 pp. Wing S4335.

484. *William Smith, *A Tender Visitation of the Father's Love, To All the Elect-Children, or, An Epistle unto the Righteous Congregations who in Light are Gathered* (London, 1660). 16 pp. Wing S4336.

485. William Smith, *The True Light Shining in England, To Give Unto All Her Inhabitants the Knowledge of Their Ways Wherein They May Behold Things Past, and Things that Are, and Thereby Come to Repentence* (London, 1660). 23 pp. Wing S4339.

486. *William Smith, *Wisdom of the Earthly Wise Confounded* (London, 1679). 15 pp. Wing S4345.

487. Philipp Jakob Spener, *Das geistliche Priesterthum auß göttlichem Wort* (Frankfurt, 1687). 166 pp. OCLC 165800071.

488. Rowland Stedman, *Sober Singularity, or, An antidote against infection by the example of a multitude* (London, 1660). 16 pp. Wing S5376.

489. Amos Stodart, *Something Written in a Lying, Scandalous Book printed for E.B. in Pauls Churchyard . . . the Author of it is said to be Called Powel* (London, 1655). 8 pp. Wing S5707.

490. Henry Stubbe, *A light shining out of darkness, or, Occasional queries* (London, 1699). 230 pp. Wing S6058.

491. John Taylor, *An Account of the Some of the . . . Travels and Perils by Sea of John Taylor* 612d.

492. Thomas Taylor, *Gods Controversie with England declared* . . . (London, 1661). pp. Wing T575.

493. Thomas Taylor, *Kennzeichen eines wahren Christen* (Helmstadt, 1682). OCLC 311913515.

494. Thomas Tryon, *Some memoirs of the life of Mr. Thomas Tryon, late of London, merchant* (London, 1705). 128 pp. ESTC N23690.

495. Thomas Taylor, *A Testimony for the Lord, the Good Shepherd Against All the False Shepherds and Hirelings of the World* (London, 1675). 15 pp. Wing T586.

496. Thomas Taylor, *Truth's Innocency and Simplicity Shining Through the Conversion* (London, 1697). 151 pp. Wing T591.

497. *Jacob Telner, "A Treatise Showing the Many Gross Absurdities and Pernicious Errours that Naturally Follow from the False Glosses Upon the . . . Chapter to the Romans by a Member of the Religious Society of Universal Love" (unpublished manuscript).[279]

498. William Temple, *Miscellanea: I. A Survey of the Constitutions and Interests of the Empire, Sueden, Denmark, Spain, Holland, France, and Flanders; with their Relation to England in the Year 1671* (London, 1680). 238 pp. Wing T646A.

499. William Thompson, *The Care of Parents, is a Happiness to Children: or, The Duty of Parents to their Children* (London, 1710). 24 pp. Smith, part 2, p. 740.

500. William Thompson, *Religion Epitomized: Or, a Short Discourse of the Nature of True Religion* (London, 1710). 25 pp. Smith, part 2, p. 740.

501. Raphael Thorius, *Tobacco: a poem in two books* (London, 1716). 40 pp. ESTC N13439.

502. John Tomkins, *A Brief Testimony to the Great Duty of Prayer, Shewing the Nature and Benefit Thereof* (London, 1695). 132 pp. Wing T1831.

503. John Tomkins, *A Brief Concordance of the Names and Attributes within Sundry Texts Relating Unto Our Blessed Lord and Saviour* (London, 1697). 206 pp. Wing T183.

504. John Tomkins, *The Harmony of the Old and New Testaments and the Fulfilling of the Prophets Concerning Our Blessed Lord and Saviour Jesus Christ* (London, 1697). 146 pp. Wing T1833.

505. *John Tomkins, *Piety Promoted, In a Collection of the Dying Sayings of Many of the People Call'd Quakers* (London, 1701). 3 vols. NUC P0360010.

506. *John Tomkins, *A Trumpet Sounded: Or, A Warning to the Unfaithful, To Prize the Day of Their Visitation, Before It Be Over* (London, 1703). 96 pp. Smith, part 2, p. 748.

---

279. According to Hull, *William Penn and the Dutch Quaker Migration*, 249, Telner wrote this "Treatise" in opposition to the Keithian Quakers but never published it.

507. *William Tomlinson, *A Short Work But of the Greatest Concern* (London, 1696). 72 pp. Wing T1852.

508. William Tomlinson, *A Word of Information to Them That Need It Briefly Opening Some Most Weighty Passages of Gods Dispensations Among the Sons of Men, from the Beginning* (London, 1660). 47 pp. Wing T1854.

509. Thomas Upsher, *To Friends in Ireland and Elsewhere: A Mournful Word to the Merry-Hearted in Zion* (Philadelphia, 1700). 22 pp. Evans 956.

510. Thomas Upsher, *An Answer to a pamphlet, intitled, An Account of an Occasional Conference between George Keith and Thomas Upsher* (London, 1701). 32 pp. NUC U0209793.

511. Ralph Venning, *Sin, the plague of plagues, or, Sinful sin the worst of evils* (London, 1669). 352 pp. Wing V226.

512. Richard Vickris, *A Few Things of Great Weight Offered to the Consideration of All Sober People, and to Friends of Truth More Particularly Concerning their Children* (London, 1697). 44 pp. Wing V338.

513. Richard Vivers, *The Vicar of Banbury Corrected: or, An Answer to Benjamin Loveling* (London, 1703). 16 pp. NUC V0205573.

514. Jacobus Viverius and Jan Zoet, *De Wintersche Avonden, of Nederlandsche Vertell-inghen* (Utrecht, 1650). OCLC 68858644.

515. Claas Jansz Vooght, *Quadrans Astronomicus and Geometricus* (Amsterdam, 1681). 24 pp. OCLC 65024038.

516. *Richard Waite, *The Widdow's Mite Cast into the Treasury of the Lord God, and given forth to the Upright-hearted* (London, 1663). 8 pp. Wing W225.

517. Robert Wastfield, *A True Testimony of Faithfull Witnesses Recorded . . . wherein the Wicked Designs and Cruel Practices of Several of the Rulers, Priests and People of the County of Sommerset Against the Innocent are Plainly Discovered* (London, 1657). 98 pp. Wing W1036.

518. Morgan Watkins, *The Day Manifesting the Night, and the Deeds of Darkness Reproved by the Light* (London, 1660). 14 pp. Wing W1065.

519. *Morgan Watkins, *The Marks of the True Church, The Virgin and Spouse of Christ that Brings Forth by a Holy Seed the Birth that Pleaseth God, and the Marks of the False Church, or Whore, that Brings Forth the Evil Seed* (London, 1675). 27 pp. Wing W1067.

520. Morgan Watkins, *Swearing denyed in the New Covenant and its Pretended Foundations Rased* (London, 1660). 15 pp. Wing W1069.

521. Morgan Watkins, *The Things that Are Caesars Rendered Unto Caesar and the Things that are Gods Rendered Unto God* (London, 1666). 30 pp. Wing W1070.

522. *Morgan Watkins, *A Lamentation Over England* (London, 1664). 48 pp. Wing W1066.

523. Samuel Watson, *A Mirrour to Distinguish the True Ministers of the Gospel From the False and Apostate Ministers* (London, 1683). 44 pp. Wing W1098.

524. Thomas Watson, *The Godly Man's Picture drawn with a Scripture Pensil* (London, 1666). 11 pp. Wing W1124.

525. Thomas Watson, *A Plea for Almes, delivered in a Sermon at the Spital* (London, 1658). 68 pp. Wing W 1137.

526. Thomas Watson, *Heaven taken by Storm, or, The holy violence a Christian is to put forth in the pursuit after glory* (London, 1669). 216 pp. Wing W1127.

527. John Webster, *Saints Perfect Freedom: or, Liberty in Christ Asserted, in Opposition to All Yokes of Bondage* (London, 1654). 87 pp. Wing W1213.

528. *Moses West, *A Treatise Concerning Marriage Wherein the Unlawfulness of Mixt-Marriage is Laid Open From the Scriptures of Truth . . . Recommended More Particularly to the Youth of Either Sex Amongst the People Called Quakers* (London, 1707). 39 pp. Smith, part 2, p. 873.

529. Nathaniel Weston, *A Warning from the Mouth of the Lord Through His Servant to the People of England* (London, 1660). 7 pp. Wing W1480.

530. Dorothy White, *A Lamentation Unto this Nation and Also a Warning to all People of this Present Age and Generation with the Voice of Thunder Sounded Forth from the House of the Lord God* (London, 1660). 8 pp. Wing W1751.

531. Dorothy White, *A Visitation of Heavenly Love Unto the Seed of Jacob Yet in Captivity* (London, 1660). 9 pp. Wing W1795.

532. Thomas White, *A Little Book for Little Children* (Boston, 1702). 94 pp. OCLC 55830491.

533. Thomas White, *A method and instructions for the divine art of meditation* (London, 1655). 16 pp. Wing W1847B.

534. *George Whitehead, *Cain's Generation Discovered: In Answer to an Epistle [in] A Short and Full Vindication of that Great and Comfortable Ordinance, of Singing Psalms . . . Also Several Queries to them that Profess the Scriptures to be their Rule to Walk By* (London, 1655). 14 pp. Wing W1898.

535. *George Whitehead, *The Case of the Quakers Concerning Oathes* (London, 1674). 51 pp. Wing W1899. [Pastorius attributed this work to Gervase Benson.]

536. *George Whitehead, *The Case of the Suffering People of God* (London, 1664). 11 pp. Wing W1901.

537. George Whitehead, *The Christian Doctrine* (n.p., 1693). 20 pp. Wing W1095.

538. George Whitehead, *The Due Order of Law and Justice Pleaded Against Irregular and Arbitrary Proceedings in the Case and Late Imprisonment of George Whitehead and Thomas Burr* (London, 1680). 103 pp. NUC W0259683.

539. George Whitehead, *The Path of the Just Cleared and Cruelty and Tyranny Laid Open, or, A Few Words to You Priests and Magistrates of this Nation . . . Wherein your Oppresion and Tyranny is Laid Open* (London, 1655). 26 pp. Wing W1944.

540. George Whitehead, *Quakers No Deceivers: Management of an Unjust Charge Against them Confuted* (London, 1660). 33 pp. Wing W1948.

541. George Whitehead, *A Rambling Pilgrim or Profane Apostate Exposed, Being an Answer to Two Persecuting Books . . . The Pilgrim's Progress From Quakerism to Christianity* (London, 1700). 47 pp. Wing W1901.

542. George Whitehead, *The Rector Examined, About His Book Scandalously Stiled, An Antidote Against the Demon of Quakerism by John Meriton* (London, 1699). 47 pp. Wing W1953.

543. George Whitehead, *A Seasonable Account of Christian Testimony and Dying-Words of Some Young-men* (Philadelphia, 1700). 19 pp. Evans 950.

544. George Whitehead, *A Sober Expostulation with Some of the Clergy: Against their Pretended Convert Francis Bugg and his Repeated Gross Abuses of the People called Quakers* (London, 1697). 144 pp. Wing W1959.

545. *George Whitehead, *Truth and Innocency Vindicated and the People Called Quakers Defended in Principle and Practice Against Invididious Attempts and Calumnies* (London, 1699). 72 pp. Wing W1969.

546. George Whitehead, *Truth Prevalent; and the Quakers Discharged from the Norfolk Rectors' Furious Charge In a Sober Answer to Their Book, Falsely Stiled, The Principles of the Quakers Further Shewen to be Blasphemous and Seditious* (London, 1701). 187 pp. Smith, part 2, p. 904.

547. George Whitehead, *A Word of Tender Admonition to King Charles II and to this Present Parliament* (London, 1660), in *Copies of Several Letters which were Delivered to the King* (London, 1660). 54 pp. Wing F1778.

548. John Whitehead, *A Manifestation of Truth Concerning the Scriptures . . .* (London, 1662). 16 pp. Wing W1979.

549. John Whitehead, *A Small Treatise wherein is Briefly Declared Some of Those Things I Have Heard and Seen and Learnt of the Father* (London, 1665). 24 pp. Wing W1982.

550. John Whitehead, *This to the King and His Councel Subscribed by John Whitehead and Many More: Something in Answer to an Order Made by the House of Lords* (London, 1660). 8 pp. Wing W1983.

551. John Whiting, *Judas and the Chief Priest, Conspiring to Betray Christ and His Followers; Or An Apostate Convicted and Truth Defended, in Answer to George Keith's Fourth (False) Narrative* (London, 1701). 259 pp. Smith, part 2, p. 917.

552. John Whiting, *Truth and Innocency Defended: Against Falsehood and Envy: and the Martyrs of Jesus, and Sufferers for his Sake, Vindicated* (London, 1702). 212 pp. NUC W0263174.

553. Robert Wilkinson, *The Saint's Travel to Spiritual Canaan: Wherein is Discovered Several False Rests Short of the True Spiritual Coming of the Christ in His People* (London, 1648). 142 pp. NUC W0311695.

554. *Humphrey Wollrich, *This is Written in Plainess of Heart and Bowels of Love to any Persecutors* (London, 1661). Wing W3299.

555. *Humphrey Wollrich, *A Visitation to the Captive-Seed of Israel* (London, 1661). 15 pp. Wing W3305.

556. Joseph Wyeth, *Anguis Flagellatus: Or, A Switch for the Snake Being an Answer to the Third and Last Edition of A Snake in the Grass* (London, 1699). 548 pp. Wing W3757.

557. Joseph Wyeth, *Primitive Christianity Contained in the Faith and Practice of the People Called Quakers, Being in Answer to a Pamphlet Entitled, Primitive Heresie &c.* (London, 1698). 58 pp. Wing W3761.

558. Joseph Wyeth, *Remarks on Dr. Bray's Memorial* (London, 1701). 51 pp. ESTC T61204.

559. Joseph Wyeth, *A Vindication of William Penn Against Thomas Budd* (London, 1697). Wing W3763.

560. Thomas Wynne, *An Antichristian Conspiracy Detected and Satan's Champion Defeated* (London, 1679). 54 pp. Wing W3781.

Pastorius included two works for which complete citations have not been located:

William Smith, Real Christianity [remainder of title illegible];

*William Southbey, Christian [...] on Negro and Indian Slaves, 1714?. Evans identified two anti-slavery works by Southeby that were printed in 1715 and 1717, although no extant copies of either have been located. Southeby, William, An Anti-Slavery Tract, Philadelphia, Printed by Andrew Bradford, 1715, Evans 1781; Southeby, William, An Anti-Slavery Tract, Philadelphia: Printed by Andrew Bradford, 1717, Evans 1929. 582d Perhaps those refer to this broadside.

Pastorius also referred to Thomas Budd but did not identify which of Budd's works he was citing.

A

1. *Henry Ainsworth, *Annotations upon the five bookes of Moses, and the booke of the Psalmes* (London, 1627). 276 pp. STC (2nd ed.) 211.

2. *Heinrich Cornelius Agrippa von Nettesheim, *De incertitudine et vanitate omnium scientiarum et artium* (Leyden, 1643). OCLC: 26859865.

3. Joseph Alleine, *Alarm to Unconverted Sinners* (London, 1703). 180 pp. ESTC 006357301.[280]

4. Richard Allestree, *The government of the thoughts: a prefatory discourse to The government of the tongue, by the author of The whole duty of man* (London, 1700). Wing (2nd ed. 1994) A1132A.

5. *Johann Valentin Andreae, *Menippus, sive, Dialogorum satyricorum centuria, inanitatum nostratium speculum, cui accessit index titulorum.* "Coloniae Brandenburgicae Völcker" (Berlin, 1673). 8 pp. OCLC 23628556.

6. *Anon., *An Account of the illegal prosecution and tryal of Coll. Nicholas Bayard, in the province of New-York, for supposed high-treason, in the year 1701/2* (New York, 1702). Evans 1038.

7. *Anon., *The Elements of Principles of Geometrie* (London, 1684). Wing (CD-ROM, 1996) E495aA.

8. *Anon., *The eloquent master of languages, that is a short but fundamental direction to the four principal languages* (Hamburg, 1693). 32 pp. Wing (CD-ROM 1996) E635A.

9. *Anon., *The husband forc'd to be jealous, or The good fortune of those women that have jealous husbands. A translation by N.H.* (London, 1668). Wing (CD-ROM 1996) D1188A.

10. Anon., *Memorable accidents, and unheard of transactions, containing an account of several strange events. . .* (London, 1693). Wing (2nd ed.) L1100A.

11. *Anon., *A new academy of complements; or the lover's secratary [sic]. Being wit and mirth improv'd, by the most elegant expressions us'd in the art of courtship* (London, 1715). ESTC T86876.

12. Anon., *The writing scholar's companion: or, Infallible rules for writing true English with ease and certainty* (London, 1695). 192 pp. Wing (2nd ed.) B1829.

13. Wilhelm Erasmus Arends, *Early piety recommended in the life and death of Christlieb Leberecht von Exter. son of Dr. Von-Exter, Physician to His Prussian Majesty* (London, 1708). ESTC T142888.[281]

---

280. Pastorius lists this 1703 work by Alleine as *Alarm to the Unconverted*, whereas its full title is *Alarm to the Unconverted Sinners*.

281. Pastorius has listed the 1708 English translation of Arends's work, whose original German text is lost.

14. *Henry Ashurst, *Some remarks upon the life of that painful servant of God Mr. Nathanael Heywood, . . . by Sir H. Ashurst, Bart.* (London, 1695). ESTC R35289.

15. Marius d'Assigny, *The art of memory. A treatise useful for all, especially such as are to speak in publick* (London, 1697). 110 pp. Wing (2nd ed. 1994) D281A.

16. Marius d'Assigny, *Rhetorica Anglorum, vel Exercitationes oratoriæ in rhetoricam sacram & communem* (London, 1699). Wing (2nd cd.) D285.[282]

17. *Member of the Athenian Society, *The athenian oracle: being an entire collection of all the valuable questions and answers in the old Athenian mercuries. . . By a member of the Athenian Society. Vol. I.*[283] (London, 1704). ESTC T64233.

B

18. *Francis Bacon, *The essaies, and, Religious meditations of Sir Francis Bacon* (Philadelphia, 1688). 86 pp. Wing (CD-ROM 1996) L915.

19. Francis Bacon, *Resuscitatio, or, Bringing into publick light severall pieces, of the works, civil, historical, philosophical, & theological, hitherto sleeping; of the Right Honourable Francis Bacon* (London, 1657). Wing (CD-ROM 1996) B319.

20. *Thomas Barlow, *Looking-glass displaying the sweet face of popery* (London: Benjamin Harris, 1683). ESTC R478715.[284]

21. *Richard Baxter, *The parent's pious gift: or, a choise present for children* (Edinburgh, 1701). ESTC N471551.

22. *John Beaumont, *An historical, physiological, and theological treatise of spirits, apparitions, witchcrafts, and other magical practices. Containing an account of the genii or Familiar spirits* (London, 1705). 400 pp. ESTC T111486.

23. Francis Beaumont, *The works of Mr. Francis Beaumont, and Mr. John Fletcher; in seven volumes. Adorn'd with cuts. Revis'd and corrected: with some account of the life and writings of the authors* (London, 1711). ESTC T138981.

24. John Bellers, *Proposals for raising a colledge of industry of all useful trades and husbandry, with profit for the rich. A plentiful living for the poor, and a good education for youth. Which will be advantage to the government, by the increase of the people, and their riches* (London, 1695). 10 pp. Wing (CD-Rom 1996) B1829.

25. John Bellers, *Essays about the poor, manufactures, trade, plantations, & immorality, and of the excellency and divinity of inward light demonstrated from the attributes of God, and the nature of mans soul, as well as from the testimony of the Holy Scriptures.* (London, 1699). Wing (CD-ROM 1996) B1828.

282. Pastorius lists this 1697 d'Assigny work as "Rhetorica Anglorum: a Latin Rhetorick, adapted to the genius of the English nation."
283. In his entry for *The Athenian Oracle*, after "Vol. I," Pastorius has written: "the 2nd Edition in 8°[octavo] 1704. [space] Vol. II. [space] Vol. III."
284. Pastorius has recorded the publisher's name—Benjamin Harris—as the author instead of Thomas Barlow.

26. *Anton Wilhelm Böhm, *The glorious epiphany: a sermon preach'd at St. James's in the Chappel of his late royal highness Prince George of Denmark* (London, 1710). 32 pp. ESTC T101961.[285]

27. *Anton Wilhelm Böhm, *The life of a Christian: a sermon on the occasion of the death of His Royal Highness Prince George of Denmark* (London, 1709). ESTC T169204.

28. Anton Wilhelm Böhm, *The faithful steward: Set forth in a sermon preach'd at St. James's, being the fourth,* Sunday *after Epiphany, 1712* (London, 1712). ESTC 186180.

29. Giovanni Bona, *A guide to eternity: extracted out of the writings of the Holy Fathers, and ancient philosophers. Written originally in Latine, by John Bona: and now done into English, by Roger L'Estrange Esq.* (London, 1676). Wing (CD-ROM 1996) B3544B.

30. Sir John Borough, *The soveraignty of the British seas* (London, 1651). Wing (2nd ed. 1994) B6129.

31. *Peter Boyer, *The history of the Vaudois. Wherein is shewn their original; . . . Dedicated to the King of England, and newly translated out of French by a person of quality* (London, 1692). 168 pp. Wing (CD-ROM 1996) B3919.

32. Thomas Budd, *Good order established in Pennsilvania & New-Jersey in America, being a true account of the country; with its produce and commodities there made* (Philadelphia, 1685). Wing (2nd ed.) B5358.

33. *John Bunyan, *Grace abounding to the chief of sinners in a faithful account of the life and death of John Bunyan* (London, 1692). 192 pp. Wing (2nd ed.) B5528.[286]

34. *John Bunyan, *The pilgrim's progress from this vvorld to that which is to come: . . . and safe arrival at the desired countrey.* (Boston, 1681). Wing (CD-ROM 1996) B5566.[287]

35. *Nicholas Byfield, *The spirituall touch-stone, or, The signes of a godly man. . . . By Nicolas Byfield, late preacher of Gods Word at Isleworth in Middlesex* (London, 1637). 130 pp. STC (2nd ed.) 4237.

C

36. *John Casimir, [*Catalogus medicamentorum chymicorum*] or *The treasury of chymical medicaments*[288] (London, 1682). Wing (CD-ROM 1996) C1212A.

37. Miguel de Cervantes, *The history of the renowned Don Quixote de la Mancha* (London, 1703). ESTC N33121.

38. Miguel de Cervantes, *Novelas ejemplares* (London, 1640). STC (2nd ed.) 4914.

285. Pastorius informally refers to this 1710 work by Böhm as "his Sermon upon the epiphany of Christ."
286. Pastorius notes: "NB: in this book §124 he [Bunyan] accuseth the Quakers of 8 errors."
287. Pastorius notes: "NB: this John Bunyan wrote in all 60 books. Edw. Burrough calls him one of Gog's army."
288. Variant titles of Casimir's 1682 work: *Treasury of chemical medicaments*; *To all ingenious well-wishers to the practick-part of physick*; *Treasury of chymical medicaments*.

39. Hugh Chamberlen, *A few queries relating to the practice of physick* (London, 1694). Wing (CD-ROM 1996) C1873.

40. Sir Josiah Child, *A discourse concerning trade, and that in particular of the East-Indies* (London, 1689). Wing (CD-ROM 1996) D1590.[289]

41. Marcus Tullius Cicero, *Tully's offices, in three books. Turned out of Latin and into English. By Sr. Ro. L'Estrange* (London, 1688). Wing (2nd ed. 1994) C4312.

42. *Richard Claridge, *A Letter from a clergy-man in the country, to a clergy-man in the city, containing free thoughts about the controversie, between some ministers of the Church of England, and the Quakers: with seasonable advice to his brethren, to study peace and moderation* (Philadelphia, 1702). 12 pp. Evans W017897.

43. *Edward Clark, *The Protestant school-master. Containing, plain and easie directions for spelling and reading English, with all necessary rules for the true reading of the English tongue. Together with a brief and true account of the bloody persecutions, massacres, plots, treasons, and most inhumane tortures committed by the papists upon Protestants* (London, 1680). Wing (2nd ed.) C4437.

44. *Edward Cocker, *Cocker's arithmetick: being a plain and familiar method* (London, 1694). ESTC R224062.

45. *Edward Cocker, *England's pen-man: or, Cocker's new copy-book* (London, 1678). Wing (2nd ed. 1994) C4825.

46. Jan Amos Comenius, *The gate of languages unlocked: or, A seed-plot of all arts and tongues; containing a ready way to learn the Latine and English tongue . . . afterwards much corrected and amended by Joh. Robotham* (London, 1673). 417 pp. Wing (CD-ROM 1996) C5517A.

47. Jan Amos Comenius, *Janua linguarum reserata: or a seed-plot of all languages and sciences* (London, 1638). 338 pp. STC (2nd ed.) 15077.5.

48. James Cooke, *Mellificium chirurgiæ. Or The marrow of many good authours* (London, 1648). ESTC R12520, Wing (2nd ed. 1994) C6012.

49. William Congreve, *The works of Mr. William Congreve; in three volumes. Containing his plays and poems* (London, 1717). ESTC 52951.

50. *Edmund Coote, *The English school-master; teaching all his scholars, of what age soever, the most easy, short, and perfect order of distinct reading, and true writing our English tongue, that hath ever yet been known, or published by any* (Dublin, 1684). Wing (CD-ROM 1996) C6076.

51. *Elisha Coles, *A dictionary, English-Latin, and Latin-English* (London, 1679). 1,024 pp. Wing (2nd ed. 1994) C5069B.

52. Abraham Cowley, *The works of Mr Abraham Cowley* (London, 1668). 148 pp. ESTC R471113.

289. Pastorius may have had in mind Child's 1693 treatise *A new discourse of trade* (London, 1693), ETSC R5732.

53. Robert Craghead, *Advice for assurance of salvation* (Belfast, 1702). 184 pp. ESTC T230205.

54. Nathaniel Crouch., *Delights for the ingenious, in above fifty select and choice emblems, divine and moral, ancient and modern* (London, 1684). ESTC R479314.

55. Nathaniel Crouch, *The English heroe: or, Sir Francis Drake revived* (London, 1687). Wing (CD-ROM, 1996) C7321A.

56. Nathaniel Crouch, *Female excellency, or The ladies glory. Illustrated in the worthy lives and memorable actions of nine famous women, who have been renowned either for virtue or valour in several ages of the world* (London, 1688). Wing (2nd ed. 1994) C7326.

57. Nathaniel Crouch, *The History of the Nine Worthies of the World (1695)* (London, 1687). Wing (2nd ed.) C7337.

58. Nathaniel Crouch (R.B.), *A journey to Jerusalem: or, a relation of the travels of fourteen English-men, in the year, 1669. . . . In a letter from T.B. in Aleppo, to his friend* (London, 1672). Wing (2nd ed. 1994) C7341.

59. Nathanial Crouch, *The vanity of the life of man. Represented in the seven several stages thereof, from his birth to his death. With pictures and poems exposing the follies of every age* (London, 1688). 92 pp. Wing (CD-ROM 1996) C7355.

60. *Nicholas Culpeper, *The English physician enlarged* (London, 1698). Wing (CD-ROM 1996) C7514A.

61. Nicholas Culpeper,[290] *Pharmacopoia Londinensis; or, The London dispensatory further adorned by the studies and collections of the fellows now living* (London, 1675). Wing (CD-ROM 1996) C7534.

62. Nicholas Culpeper, *Culpeper's last legacy: left and bequeathed to his dearest wife* (London, 1655). Wing (2nd ed. 1994) C7518.

63. *Nicholas Culpeper, *Culpeper's semeiotica uranica: or, An astrological judgment of diseases* (London, 1671). Wing (CD-ROM 1996) C7548A.

64. Nicholas Culpeper, *Culpeper's school of physick. Or The experimental practice of the whole art* (London, 1659). Wing (2nd ed. 1994) C7544.

D

65. John Davenport, *Knowledge of Christ indispensably required of all men that would be saved; or Demonstrative proofs from Scripture, that crucified Jesus is the Christ* (London, 1653). Wing (CD-ROM 1996) D361.

66. John Darrell, *True narration of the strange and grevous vexation by the Devil, of 7 persons in Lancashire, and William Somers of Nottingham* (England, 1600). STC (2nd ed.) 6288.

---

290. "Culp.Ph.Libr." (Culpeper's Pharmaceutical Library) in left margin.

67. William Davis, *Jesus the crucifyed man, the eternal Son of God, or, An answer to an anathema or paper of excommunication* (Philadelphia, 1700). 34 pp. Wing (2nd ed.) D438A.

68. *William Dell, *The tryal of spirits both in teachers & hearers* (London, 1653). Wing (CD-ROM 1996) D931/D924.

69. William Dell, *Christ's spirit, a Christians strength* (London, 1651). 38 pp. Wing (2nd ed.) D919.

70. William Dell, *Baptismōn didaché: or, The doctrine of baptisms* (London, 1648). Wing (2nd ed.) D914.

71. *Thomas Deloney, *The pleasant history of John Winchomb in his younger years called Jack of Newbery, the famous and worthy clothier of England* (London, 1700). Wing (CD-ROM 1996) D965.

72. John Denham, *Poems and translations, with The Sophy* (London, 1668). Wing (CD-ROM 1996) D1005.

73. Arthur Dent, *The pain-mans [sic] path-way to heaven* (London, 1654). Wing (CD-ROM 1996) D1054.

74. Daniel Duncan, *Wholesome advice against the abuse of hot liquors, particularly coffee, chocolate, tea, Brandy, and Strong-Waters* (London, 1706). ESTC T116372.

75. William Dyer, *Christ's famous titles, and a believer's golden chain* (London, 1666). 254 pp. Wing (2nd ed.) D2936.

76. *Jeremiah Dyke, *Good conscience: or A treatise shewing the nature, meanes, markes, benefit, and necessitie thereof* (London, 1629). 326 pp. STC (2nd ed.) 7416.5.

E

77. *John Earle, *Micro-cosmographie. Or, A peece of the world discovered; in essayes and characters* (London, 1629). 300 pp. STC 7442.

78. Laurence Echard, *A general ecclesiastical history* (London, 1702). ESTC T137774.

79. Thomas Elyot, *The bankette of sapience, compyled by syr Thomas Eliot knyghte, and newely augmented with dyverse tytles and sentences* (London, 1539). STC (2nd ed.) 7630.

80. Desiderius Erasmus, *Twenty select colloquies. Made English by Ro. L'Estrange* (London, 1680). 264 pp. Wing (CD-ROM 1996) E3210.

81. Roger L'Estrange, *A Discourse of the Fishery* (London, 1674). Wing (2nd ed.) L1236.

82. Robert L'Estrange, *Fables of Aesop and other eminent mythologists: with morals and reflexions. By Sir Roger L'Estrange, Kt.* (London, 1692). Wing (CD-ROM 1996) A706.

83. George Etherege, *The works of Sir George Etherege: containing his plays and poems* (London, 1704). ESTC T138423.

F

84. *Owen Felltham, *Resolves: divine, morall, politicall* (London, 1631). STC (2nd ed.) 10759.

85. *Nicaise Le Fèvre, *A Compleat Body of Chymistry* (London, 1664). Wing (CD-ROM 1996) L925.

86. John Flavel, *A saint indeed: or The great work of a Christian* (London, 1668). Wing (CD-ROM 1996) F1187A.

87. August Hermann Francke, *Faith in Christ, inconsistent with a sollicitous concern about the things of this world* (London, 1709). 24 pp. ESTC T90995.

88. *August Hermann Francke, *Pietas Hallensis: or a publick demonstration of the footsteps of a divine being yet in the world: in an historical narration of the orphan-house* (London, 1705). 240 pp. ESTC T145067.

89. *Sebastian Franck, *Chronica, Zeÿtbuch vnd geschÿcht bibel von anbegyn biß inn dißgegenwertig M.D.xxxi. jar* (Strasbourg, 1531). OCLC 19494930.

90. *Sebastian Franck, *Paradoxa ducenta octoginta, das ist CCLXXX Wunderred vnd gleischsam Räterschafft* (Ulm, 1534). OCLC 23907466.

91. Stephen Ford, *The evil tongue tryed, and found guilty; or, The hainousness and exceeding sinfulness of defaming and back-biting, opened and declared* (London, 1672). 360 pp. Wing (CD-ROM 1996) F1509.

92. Emanuel Ford, *The most famous, delectable, and pleasant history of Parismus, the most renowned prince of Bohemia* (London, 1704–05). ESTC T129137, Microfilm.

93. John Fox, *Time and the end of time: or, Two discourses; the first about redemption of time, the second about consideration of our latter end* (London, 1670). 250 pp. Wing (CD-ROM 1996) F2024.

G

94. John Gadbury, *De cometis: or, a discourse of the natures and effects of comets* (London, 1665). Wing (CD-ROM 1996) G81.

95. John Gadbury, *Genethlialogia. Or, The doctrine of nativities & horary questions* (London, 1661). Wing (CD-ROM 1996) G84A.

96. *Alessandro Giraffi, *The second part of Massaniello, his body taken out of the town-ditch, and solemnly buried, with epitaphs upon him. . . . The end of the commotions. By J.H. Esquire* (London, 1652).[291] Wing (2nd ed.) H3113

97. Joseph Glanvill, *Saducismus triumphatus: or, Full and plain evidence concerning witches and apparitions. In two parts. The first treating of their possibility; the second of their real existence* (London, 1689). Wing (CD-ROM 1996) G824B.

---

291. Pastorius's note in the "Bee-Hive" on this 1652 Giraffi work: "Truth never look'd so like a Lie as in Aniello's historia."

98. George Granville (Baron Landsowne,) *Poems upon several occasions* (London, 1712). ESTC T55586.

99. William Greenhill, *The sound-hearted Christian* (London, 1670). Wing (CD-ROM 1996) G1859.

100. Nehemiah Grew, *Tractatus de salis cathartici amari in aquis Ebeshamensibus et hujusmodi aliis contenti natura & usu* (London, 1695). Wing (2nd ed.) G1959.

101. *Robert Grosseteste, *The last testament of the twelve patriarchs the sons of Jacob translated out of Greek by Robert Grosthead . . . of Cambridge* (New York, 1695). Wing (CD-ROM 1996) L507AB.

102. William Guthrie, *The Christian's great interest* (Boston, 1701). 234 pp. Evans 977.

H

103. Richard Herne, *The history of Genesis. Being an account of the Holy lives and actions of the Patriarchs; explained with pious and edifying explications, and illustrated with near forty figures. . .* (London, 1708). ESTC T122767.

104. *John Hepburn, *The American defence of the Christian golden rule, or An essay to prove the unlawfulness of making slaves of men. By him who loves the freedom of the souls and bodies of all men, John Hepburn* (New York, 1715). ESTC W37213.[292]

105. *Oliver Heywood, *Closet-prayer a Christian duty: or, A treatise upon Mat. VI, VI. tending to prove that the worship of God in secret, is the indispensible duty of all Christians,* (London, 1671). Wing (CD-ROM 1996) H1762.

106. *Oliver Heywood, *Heavenly converse: or, A discourse concerning the communion between the saints on earth, and the spirits of just men made perfect in Heaven* (London, 1697). Wing (CD-ROM 1996) H1767A.

107. *Thomas Heywood, *The life of Merlin, sirnamed Ambrosius. His prophesies, and predictions interpreted; and their truth made good by our English annals* (London, 1641). Wing (CD-ROM 1996) H1786.

108. *John Hill, *The young secretary's guide: or, A speedy help to learning* (London, 1687). Wing (CD-ROM 1996) H1991B.

109. *George Horn, *Arca Mosis; sive, Historia mundi. Quae complectitur primordia rerum naturalium omniumque artium ac scientiarum* (Lugd. Bat. & Roterod., Ex Officina Hackiana, 1668). Worldcat OCLC 14300153.

110. George Horn, *Orbis Politicus* (London, 1668). OCLC 464911844.

292. Pastorius has listed John Hepburn's 1715 response to Thomas Lowry as "Thomas Lowry his answer to Predestination / Children & Idiots Salvation / Water Baptism in 8° 1715." The ESTC W37213 record for the John Hepburn work has these general notes: "'A short answer to that part of predestination . . , By Thomas Lowry'—p. [2], 45–62, with separate title page." & "'Good news to all parents of such children. . .'—p. 63–74, signed: Thomas Lawry [sic]." & "'Salvation without outward baptism . . . By Thomas Lowry'—p. [75]–89; with separate title page."

111. John Hepburn, *The American defence of the Christian golden rule, or An essay to prove the unlawfulness of making slaves of men* (New York, 1715). Evans 1678.

112. *Nicolas Hunt, *New-borne Christian: or, A lively patterne, and perfect representation of the saint-militant child of God* (London, 1631). STC (2nd ed.) 13990.

113. *Robert Hunter, *Answer to what has been offer'd as argument against the validity and force of an act of Assembly* (New York, 1716). 8 pp. ESTC W18252, Evans 1796.

J

114. King James I of England, *Basilicon Doron* (Cambridge, 1603). 88 pp. OCLC 560880664.

115. *Kaspar Janthesius, *Itinerarium Caspari Janthesii . . . ab authore ipso revisum et . . . auctum* (1637). OCLC 668691570.[293]

116. David Jones, *A compleat history of Europe: or, A view of the affairs thereof, civil and military* (London, 1699). ESTC R13275.

117. Juvenal, *Satires of Juvenal, and Persius* (London, 1693). Wing (CD-ROM 1996) J1288.

K

118. Benjamin Keach, *War with the devil, or, The young man's conflict with the powers of darkness* (New York, 1707). Evans 1207.

119. *Elias Keach, *A discourse of the nature and excellency of the grace of patience: delivered in two sermons* (London, 1699). Wing (CD-ROM 1996) K108B.

120. *William Kempe, *The education of children in learning: declared by the dignitie, utilitie, and method thereof* (London, 1588). STC (2nd ed.) 14926.

121. Thomas à Kempis, *Following of Christ* (London, 1575). ESTC S104617, STC (2nd ed.) 23967.

122. Thomas à Kempis, *Rules to live above the world while we are in it* (London, 1716). 440 pp. ESTC T199767.

L

123. *Jane Lead, *The heavenly cloud now breaking: or, the Lord Christ's ascension-ladder, sent down* (London, 1701). 64 pp. ESTC T139838.

124. *Jane Lead, *A message to the Philadelphian Society*, 108 pp. (London, 1696). Wing (CD-ROM 1996) L787.

---

293. Pastorius spells Janthesius's name differently for this 1637 work, and he includes the Latin word "Scriptum" in the title.

125. *Jane Lead, *The revelation of revelations: an essay towards the unsealing, opening and discovering the seven seals, the seven thunders, and the New-Jerusalem state* (London, 1701). ESTC N13224.

126. Daniel Leeds, *An almanack for the year of Christian account 1687* (Philadelphia, 1686). ESTC W34528.

127. Daniel Leeds, *News of a trumpet sounding in the wilderness, Or, The Quakers antient testimony revived* (New York, 1697). Wing (CD-ROM 1996) L914.

128. *Titan Leeds, *The American almanack for the year of Christian account, 1714* (New York, 1713). Evans 1612.

129. *Titan Leeds, *The American almanack for the year of Christian account, 1715* (New York, 1715). Evans 1747.

130. *Titan Leeds, *The American almanack for the year of Christian account, 1716* (Philadelphia, 1715). Evans 1748.

131. *Titan Leeds, *The American almanack for the year of Christian account, 1718* (Philadelphia, 1717). Evans 1889.

132. *Titan Leeds, *The American almanack for the year of Christian account, 1719* (New York, 1718). Bristol B567.

133. *Titan Leeds, *The American almanack for the year of Christian account, 1720* (Philadelphia, 1719). Evans 2028.

134. *Edward Leigh and Henricus a Middoch, *Critica Sacra* (Amsterdam, 1679). OCLC 643398893,

135. Robert Leighton, *Three posthumous tracts* (London, 1708). ESTC T70891.

136. John Locke, *A common-place book to the Holy Bible: or, the Scriptures sufficiency practically demonstrated. . . . and explained by others more plain* (London, 1697). Wing (CD-ROM 1996) L2737.

137. John Locke, *Essay Concerning Human Understanding* (London, 1710). ESTC T63941.

138. *Jeremiah Love, *Clavis medicinæ: or, The practice of physic* (London, 1674). Wing (CD-ROM 1996), L3187A.

139. Robert Loveday, *Letters domestick and foreign, to several persons, occasionally distributed in subjects philosophical, historical, and moral* (London, 1676). Wing (CD-ROM 1996) L3229A.

140. Reliquiæ Ludolfianæ, *The pious remains of Mr. Hen. Will. Ludolf; consisting of I. Meditations upon retirement from the world. . . . VI. A homily of Macarius* (London, 1712). ESTC T165835.

141. *Thomas Lupton, *A thousand notable things of sundry sorts, enlarged. Whereof some are Wonderfull, some strange, some pleasant divers necessary, a great sort profitable, and many very precious* (London, 1675). Wing (2nd ed.) L3500.

142. *Giovanni Marana, *Letters writ by a Turkish spy, who lived five and forty years undiscovered at Paris: giving an impartial account to the Divan at Constantinople . . . and now published with a large historical preface and index to illustrate the whole* (London, 1687). Wing (CD-ROM 1996) M565B.

143. Gervase Markham, *Markham's master-piece revived; containing all knowledge belonging to the smith, farrier, or horse-leach, touching the curing all diseases in horses* (London, 1694). Wing (2nd ed.) M665A.[294]

144. *Andrew Marvell, *Directions to a painter for describing our naval business: in imitation of Mr. Waller* (London, 1667). ESTC R13880.[295]

145. William Massey, *Musa parænetica; or, a tractate of Christian epistles, on sundry occasions, in verse* (London, 1717). 66 pp. ESTC T99288.

146. Josiah Martin, *A Vindication of Women's Preaching: As Well from Holy Scripture and Antient Writings, as from the Paraphrase and Notes of the Judicious John Locke* (London, 1717). 128 pp. ESTC T93891.

147. *Cotton Mather, *The wonders of the invisible world. Observations as well historical as theological, upon the nature, the number, and the operations of the devils* (Boston, 1693). Wing (CD-ROM 1996) M1172.

148. William Mather, *The Young Man's Companion* (London, 1695). Wing (CD-ROM 1996).

149. Matthew Mead, *The good of early obedience, or the advantage of bearing the yoke of Christ betimes* (London, 1683). 456 pp. Wing (CD-ROM 1996) M1555.

150. Matthew Mead, *En oligo Christianos: The almost Christian discover'd or, The false professor tryed and cast* (London, 1664). Wing (2nd ed.) M1547.

151. Matthew Mead, *The Two Sticks Made One* or *the Excellency of Unity* (London, 1691). 32 pp. Wing (2nd ed.) M1562.

152. Joseph Mede, *Diatribæ pars IV. Discourses on sundry texts of Scripture* (London, 1652). Wing (2nd ed.) M1598.

153. John Milton, *The poetical works of Mr. John Milton. In two volumes* (London, 1707). ESTC T134605.[296]

154. Miguel de Molinos, *The spiritual guide, which disintangles the soul; and brings it by the inward way* (London, 1699). 180 pp. Wing (CD-ROM 1996) M2388.

155. Joseph Moxon, *Mathematicks made easie: or, a mathematical dictionary, explaining the terms of art, and difficult phrases used in arithmetick, geometry, astronomy,*

---

294. Of the multiple known editions of this Markham book, this 1694 edition is the most recent one with this title.

295. Pastorius credits Sir John Denham as author of this 1667 work, whereas ESTC R13880 credits Andrew Marvell.

296. There are two possible editions of this Milton collection that Pastorius might have consulted, a 1705 edition (ESTC T134227) and the 1707 edition listed in the text.

astrology, and other mathematical sciences (London, 1692). Wing (CD-ROM 1996) M3007.

N

156. *M.N. [William Camden], *Remaines, concerning Britaine: but especially England, and the inhabitants thereof* (London, 1614). STC (2nd ed.) 4522.

157. *Cornelius Nepos, *The lives of illustrious men* (London, 1713). ESTC T83004.

158. *Francis de Neville, *The Christian and Catholike veritie; or, The reasons and manner of the conversion of Francis de Neville* (London, 1642). Wing (2nd ed.) N502.

159. *John Nicholl, *An Houre Glasse of Indian Newes, or a true and tragicall discourse, shewing the most lamentable miseries* (London, 1607). STC (2nd ed.) 18532.

P

160. *J.W.P., *A letter to some divines concerning the question, whether god since Christ's ascension, doth any more reveal himself to mankind by the means of divine apparitions?* (London, 1695). Wing (2nd ed.) P72.

161. Seth Partridge, *The description and use of an instrument, called the double scale of proportion* (London, 1685). Wing (2nd ed.) P632.

162. *Henry Peacham, *Minerva Britanna or A Garden of Heroical Deuises* (London, 1612). ESTC S114357.

163. Edward Pearse, *Serious warning to a timely and thorough prepreation for death* (London, 1673). ESTC R219398.

164. *Richard Peeke, *Three to one being, an English-Spanish combat, performed by a westerne gentleman, of Tauystoke in Deuon shire with an English quarter-staffe, against three Spanish rapiers and poniards, at Sherries in Spaine, the fifteene day of Nouember* (London, 1626). STC (2nd ed.) 19529.[297]

165. William Petty, *A treatise of taxes & contributions shewing the nature and measures of crown-lands. . .* (London, 1667). Wing P1938.[298]

166. *Edward Phillips, *Theatrum Poetarum; or, a compleat Collection of the Poets, especially the most eminent of all ages, 2 parts in 1 vol.* (London, 1675). Wing (CD-ROM 1996) P2074A.

167. Katherine Philips, *Poems by the most deservedly admired Mrs Katherine Philips, the matchless Orinda* (London, 1678). Wing (CD-ROM 1996) P2035.

168. B.R. Phy [William Loddington], *the Christian a Quaker; the Quaker a Christian, demonstrated in a letter to a most worthy person in this city, giving answer to this*

---

297. This 1626 work by Peeke (spelled "Pike" by Pastorius) was published in the same year by a different publisher (ESTC S94649).

298. This 1667 Petty work was cited in Pastorius's Quaker bibliography, but because the author was not a Quaker, the editors have relocated it here.

little book, entituled A Dialogue between a Christian and a Quaker (London, 1674). Wing L2802.

169. John Piggott, *His sermon preached the 7ᵗʰ of Sept 1704, being the solemn thanksgiving-day for the late glorious victory obtain'd over the French and Bavarians at Blenheim near Hochstet* (London, 1704). ESTC T14068.

170. Pliny the Younger, *Pliny's panegyrick upon the Emperor Trajan, dedicated to the Princess Sophia of Hanover*, translated by George Smith (London, 1702). 176 pp. ESTC N12177.

171. *William Popple, *A rational catechism: or, An instructive conference between a father and a son* (London, 1687). 163 pp. Wing (CD-ROM 1996) P2966.

172. William Popple, *A rational catechism: or, An instructive conference between a father and a son* (London, 1687). ESTC R25590.

173. Matthew Prior, *Poems on several occasions* (London, 1707). ESTC T75635.

Q

174. Francis Quarles, *Emblemes* (London, 1709). ESTC T94279.

R

175. *Walter Raleigh, *The history of the world, in five books* (London, 1687). Wing (2ⁿᵈ ed.) R168A.

176. *John Rawlet, *The Christian monitor, containing an earnest exhortation to an holy life, with some directions in order thereto* (London, 1687). 60 pp. Wing (2ⁿᵈ ed.) R347D.

177. William Rawley, *Resuscitatio or, brinigng into publick light several pieces of the works civil, historical, philosophical, and theological, hitherto sleeping of the right honourable Francis Bacon* (London, 1671). Wing (CD-ROM 1996) B321 and B317.

178. Carew Reynell, *The true English interest, or an account of the chief national improvements by Carew Reynell* (London, 1674). Wing (CD-ROM 1996) R1215.

179. John Reynolds, *The Triumphs of God's Revenge against the crying and execrable sin of willful and pre meditated murder, with his [. . .] punishment there of, in 37 [. . .] histories* (London, 1629). STC (2ⁿᵈ ed.) 20943

180. *Ralph Robinson, *Christ all in all* (London, 1656). Wing (CD-ROM 1996) R1706.

181. Francis Rouse, *Academia coelestis: the heavenly university: or, the highest school, Where alone is that Highest Teaching, The Teaching of the Heart* (London, 1702). ESTC T107246.

S

182. Diego de Saavedra Fajardo, *The Royal Politician represented in one hundred Emblems, written in Spanish by Van Diego Saavedra, done into English by Sir Ja. Astry, two volumes* (London, 1700). Wing (CD-ROM 1996) S211.

183. *Henry Sacheverell, *The Peril of false Brethren, both in Church and State* (London, 1710). ESTC T200567.

184. *William Salmon, *Polygraphice: or The arts of drawing, engraving, etching, limning, painting, washing, varnishing, gilding, colouring, dying, beautifying and perfuming* (London, 1685). Wing (CD-ROM 1996) S448.

185. *Richard Sault, *My Second Spiera: being a fearful example of an atheist who died in despair at West-minster by R.S. a minister of the church of England. Reprinted at* [...]. (London, 1693). Wing (CD-ROM 1996) S733B.[299]

186. *Reginald Scot, *The discovery of witchcraft, with a discourse upon devils and spirits* (London, 1665). Wing (CD-ROM 1996) S945.

187. Lucius Annaeus Seneca, *Seneca's morals by way of abstract. Of benefits, Part I. The sixth edition. To which is added, a discourse, under the title of An After-thought. By Sir R. L'Estrange, Kt.*[300] (London, 1696). Wing (CD-ROM 1996) S2520.

188. *Frances Shaftoe, *Mrs. Frances Shaftoe's Narrative, concerning the many* [...] *things the* [hears] *in Sir Theophilus Oglesthorpe's family and among others that the pretended prince of Wales was Sir Theophilus' Son* (London, 1707). ESTC T41596.

189. *J.S. [John Shirley], *The accomplished ladies rich closet of rarities, or the ingenious gentlewoman and servant-maids delightfull companion* (London, 1687). 238 pp. Wing (CD-ROM 1996) S3498A.

190. Marshall Smith, *The vision, or a prospect of death, heaven and hell, with a description of the resurrection and day of judgment. A sacred poem* (London, 1702). ESTC T76530, Foxon S525.

191. William Smith, *The history of the holy Jesus. . . . To which is added, the lives and deaths of the holy evangelists and apostles* (Boston, 1716). ESTC W4668.

192. *Franceso Spira, *Spira respirans: or, The way to the kingdom of heaven by the gates of hell; in an extraordinary example* (London, 1695). 70 pp. Wing (2nd ed.) S4986.

193. M. Stennet, *The curious traveller. Account of the Spanish cruelties in the West-indies, with cuts* (London, 1742). ESTC T12931.[301]

194. *James Stewart, *Answer to a letter writ by a Mihn Heer Fagel, the states of Holland and west Friesland, concerning the repeal of the penal laws and* [...] (Edinburgh, 1688). Wing (CD-ROM 1996) S5534.

195. Arthur Stringer, *The experienc'd huntsman* (Belfast, 1714). ESTC N48125.

---

299. Pastorius cites the author of this 1693 work by Richard Sault as "J.S."

300. Of Seneca's *Morals,* Pastorius notes: "This book being lent to me but for a short time, I digested only the preface, post script and after-thought however every line of the whole is worth any man's while of common placing (or just the summries & marginals) as I myself afterwards have extracted the most notable expressions into this alveatium" (see entry 170 on p. 113 of "Bee-Hive").

301. Unable to locate an edition of Stennet's *The curious traveller* published in Pastorius's lifetime.

196. Henry Stubbe, *A light shining out of darkness: or Occasional queries submitted to the judgment of such as would enquire into the true state of things in our times . . . and augmented with sundry material discourses concerning the ministry* (London, 1659).

197. John Suckling, *The works of Sir John Suckling. Containing all his poems, letters and plays* (London, 1709). ESTC T99823.

T

198. *W. T., *The new testament epitomized, or the contents of all the chapters done into verse by W.T.* (London, 1708). 56 pp. ESTC T182285.

199. *Jacob Taylor, *The Eclipses of the sun and moon calculated for twenty years, from 1698 to 1717, and his Almanacks for the years 1702–1705 . . . 1712, 1713 . . . 1719* (New York, 1698). 76 pp. ESTC W5356.

200. *Sir William Temple, *Letters written by sir W Temple Bart and other ministers of State, both at home and abroad, containing an account of the most important transactions that passed in Christendom from 1665 to 1672, in two volumes* (London, 1700). Wing (CD-ROM 1996) T641.

201. Sir William Temple, *Observations upon the united provinces of the Netherlands* (London, 1693). Wing (CD-ROM 1996) T662.

202. *Gabriel Thomas, *an historical and geographical account of the province and country of Pensilvania, and of West-New Jersey* (London, 1698). Wing (CD-ROM 1996) T964.

203. George Thompson, *Aimatiasis: or, the true way of preserving the bloud in its integrity, and rectifying it* (London, 1670). Wing (CD-ROM 1996).[302]

204. John Tribbechov, *The Christian traveller: A farewel-sermon preach'd in the Church of St. Catharine . . . To the Palatines*, in 1710. ESTC T165550.

205. John Tribbechov, *A funeral sermon on the death of His Royal Highness Prince George of Denmark* (London, 1709). 40 pp. ESTC T110470.

206. Thomas Tryon, *The Countryman's Companion* (London, 1684). Wing T3176A.

207. Thomas Tryon, *Dreams and Visions* (London, 1689). Wing (CD-ROM 1996) T3197B.

208. Thomas Tryon, *The good-housewife made a doctor, or health's choice and sure friend* (London, 1692). Wing (2nd ed.) T3181A.

209. Thomas Tryon, *Miscellania* (London, 1696). Wing (2nd ed.) T3185.

210. Thomas Tryon, *The Way to health, long life and happiness, or a discourse of Temperance* (London, 1697). Wing (CD-ROM 1996).

302. Of Thompson's *Aimatiasis*, Pastorius notes: "A vindication of the Lord Bacon and the author from the indolent garrulity of Henry [Stubbs?]."

211. *Thomas Tusser, *Five hundred points of good husbandry* (London, 1672). Wing (CD-ROM 1996) T3369.

V

212. *Ralph Venning, *Orthodox paradoxes, theological and experimental* (London, 1677). Wing (2nd ed.) V222A.

W

213. William Wake, *The genuine epistles of the apostolical fathers, St Barnabas, St Ignatius, St Clement, St Polycarp* (London, 1710). ESTC T97402.

214. Edmund Waller, *Poems written upon several occasions* (London, 1664). Wing (CD-ROM 1996) W514.

215. *Samuel Ward, *Woe to Drunkards* (London, 1622). STC (2nd ed.) 25055.5.

216. *Thomas Watson, *Art of Divine Contentment* (London, 1655). Wing (2nd ed.) W1102A.

217. John Webster, *Displaying of supposed witchcraft* (London, 1677). Wing (CD-ROM 1996) W1230A.

218. *Edward Welchman, *The husbandman's manual: directing him how to improve the several actions of his calling, and the most usual occurrences of his life, to the glory of God, and the Benefit of His Soul* (London, 1706). 60 pp. ESTC T192356.

219. Robert Wild, *Iter boreale . . . with other poems* (London, 1660). 24 pp. ESTC N747107.

220. John Wilmot, Earl of Rochester, *Poems on several occasions* (London, 1691). ESTC R1390.

221. *John Winchcomb. *The pleasant history of Iohn Winchcomb*, By Thomas Deloney (London, 1630). 92 pp. ESTC S116614.

222. William Winstanley (Poor Robin), *Poor Robin, 1686 an almanack of the old and new fashion.* (London, 1686). ESTC 28254.

223. *Ralph Winterton (translator), Jeremias Drexel, *The considerations of Drexelius vpon eternitie. Translated by Ralph Winterton Fellow of Kings Colledge in Cambridge* (London, 1632). ESTC S115741.

224. *George Wither, *Abuses stript, and whipt. Or Satirical essayes* (London, 1614). STC (2nd ed.) 25895.

225. George Wither, *Hymns of the Old Testament* (London, 1621). 72 pp. STC (2nd ed.) 25923.

226. *George Wither, *A satyre, dedicated to His most excellent Maiestie* (London, 1614). 96 pp. ESTC S120257, STC (2nd ed.) 25916.

227. *George Wither, *The shepherd's Hunting, being certain in eclogues* (London, 1615). 128 pp. STC (2nd ed.) 25922.

228. *Charles Wolseley, *The unreasonablenesse of atheism made manifest* (London, 1669). Wing (CD-ROM 1996) W3314.

229. John Worlidge, *Systema Horticulturae or the art of gardening in three books* (London, 1683). Wing (CD-ROM 1996) W3605.[303]

230. Hannah Woolley, *The ladies delight, or a rich closet of choice experiments and curiosities* (London, 1672). Wing (CD-ROM 1996) W3279.

231. *Josiah Woodward, *An account of the progress of the reformation of manners, in England, Scotland, and Ireland . . .* (London, 1703). ESTC N16133.

232. Josiah Woodward, *A kind caution to prophane swearers. By a minister of the Church of England.* (London, 1701). ESTC T193334.

Y

233. *William Y. Worth, *A new treatise of artificial wines, or a Bacchean magazine* (London, 1690). Wing (CD-ROM 1996) Y220.

SOURCES WITH BIBLIOGRAPHIC AMBIGUITIES

1. (13) *Anon., *The New-England primer enlarged. For the more easy attaining the true reading of English. To which is added, Milk for babes* (Boston, 1701). This version was not located.

2. (14) *Anon., *The Christian's daily devotion; with directions how to walk with God all the day long: being a continuation of the Pastoral-letter, from a minister to his parishioners. By the author of the Pastoral-letter* (London, 1707). 22 pp. ESTC N52118. Pastorius cites a 1700 edition, which has not been located.

3. (24) *Anon., *The ancient and honourable way and truth of God's sacred rest of the seventh-day Sabbath. Plainly discovered . . . to its strict and intire observation,* (London, 1724). ESTC T191819. Pastorius cited an unlocated 1689 version.

4. (103) *Sebastian Franck, *Warhafftige beschreibunge aller theil der welt* (Frankfurt, 1567). OCLC 42898976. Uncertain if this is the correct citation.

5. (122) *T.H., *A guide for the childe and youth, in two parts* (London, 1667). ESTC R177789. Pastorius cites an unlocated 1700 version.

6. *Aureoli Philippi, *Theophrasti Paracelsi*. No citation located.

7. (226) Francis Quarles, *Argalus and Parthenia* (London, 1629) ESTC S112006.[304]

---

303. Of the eight known editions of Worlidge's *Systema Horticulturae*, it looks like Pastorius may have had in mind not the 1683 edition but either the 1701 edition (ESTC T118695) or the 1708 edition (ESTC T94225).
304. Pastorius may be referencing another, equally likely edition for Quarles's *Argalus and Parthenia*: the 1688 edition (ESTC R33685).

8. *Thomas Rogers, *Another pious person's prefaces to Thomas of Kempis* (1629). No citation located.

9. Ejusd. *Discourse of Advancement of Learning*.[305]

☙

"Alphabetical Hive," the Encyclopedic Section of the "Bee-Hive"

INTRODUCTION TO THE TEXT

The following encyclopedic entries are transcribed and annotated in their entirety from Pastorius's "Bee-Hive" manuscript book: Francis Daniel Pastorius, "His Hive, Melliotrophium Alvear or, Rusca Apium, Begun Anno Domini or, in the year of Christian Account, 1696," UPenn MS Codex 726, Rare Book and Manuscript Library, University of Pennsylvania.

Unlike modern encyclopedias, the "Alphabetical Hive" does not contain consistently formatted entries, each digesting the broad knowledge on a subject into a single, seemingly authoritative entry. Rather, Pastorius gathered the essence of several authors' writings on a given subject, thus providing a cross-section of contemporary and historical opinions or perspectives. Pastorius eventually abandoned the original alphabetical ordering system for a system of numbered entries corresponding to a separate alphabetical index, which allowed him to enter cross-references into the alphabetical section of the "Alphabetical Hive" and thus to expand on the original entries when his reading and collecting yielded further knowledge or ideas on a subject. He took extreme care to make these entries neat and legible, thus demonstrating his desire to provide a reference tool for future generations in his family and community, which also makes the "Alphabetical Hive" the most accessible and readable section of the "Bee-Hive" for modern readers trying to explore the original manuscript available online through the University of Pennsylvania Libraries. We therefore provide only a few sample entries to illustrate Pastorius's technique and encourage readers to search the digital facsimile for specific subjects in their respective fields of interest. The subject entries selected here represent topics that were of particular interest to Pastorius, such as language, slavery, and education.

---

305. This might be a reference to Francis Bacon, *Of the advancement and proficience of learning* (Oxford, 1640), STC (2nd ed.) 1167.5.

Language, add Speech, Tongue, Original Tongue, English Tongue:[306] linguæ differentes (expressa Babylonis vestigial) numerantur ab audoribus septuaginta due, non connumerando diveras adjustu jury dialectos,[307] true Canting. A linguist rather than a realist. Strange gibberish. State English, Court English, Secretary English, Plain English; the last the best. Whatsoever tongue will gain the race of perfection must run on these four wheels, Significancy, Easiness, Copiousness & Sweetness, so that we may express the meaning of our minds aptly, readily, fully & handsomly. [...]. The language of Canaan for purity and verity. [...] Hebrew, Greek and Latin makes no minister of God. <u>G. F. Journal</u>.[308] The languages began at Babel; & the beast & whore have power over them. &c. Ad. P. 281, a linguist: In heaven all speak the L[anguage] of Canaan (which some think is the Hebrew tongue) if indeed they make any articulate sound. [...] We first learn to read our Native tongues, which [we] speak without teaching. [...] Latin, Greek & Hebrew, which last is the easiest of them all Wm. Dell Tr. of Spir.[309] p. 186. We can speak none but our Mother tongue. The knowledge of tongues is laudable: Barcl[ay].[310] p. 421. [...] He had the Command of near twenty languages. [...]

The dead & living <u>Languages</u>. Hebrew the ancientest, Greek the most Copious, & Latin the finest. Hebrew & Greek S. Augustine[311] calls the precedent or Original Tongues. [...]. L[anguage] by attention & use may be learned, all the L[anguages] of the world signify nothing to us, unless we learn also, God's language, thereby to converse with him, Ludolf, p. 51.[312] 'tis the Speech of the heart only, which is acceptable to God, bare words are too outward, and the strength of the Spirit often loses by the great Care of fine language, Id. P. 9d. [...].

306. "Alphabetical Hive," entry 456.

307. "The different languages (expressions of the vestiges of Babel) are numbered by the authors as seventy-two, not counting any adjustments for many others judged to be dialects."

308. George Fox, *Journal* (London, 1694).

309. William Dell, *The tryal of spirits both in teachers & hearers* (London, 1653).

310. Since Pastorius did not indicate which of Robert Barclay's works he meant, it is most likely Barclay's most famous work, *An Apology for the true Christian Divinity, as the same is held forth, and preached, by the People in Scorn, Quakers . . . translated into High Dutch, Low Dutch, and French, for the Information of Strangers* (London, 1703).

311. Although Pastorius does not say which work by Augustine (the early Christian Church Father and bishop of Hippo) he cited, it was probably *De Trinitate*, which was the work most occupied with language and language philosophy.

312. Pastorius probably means the German jurist and linguist Hiob Ludolf, who dedicated the latter part of his life to the study of African languages. Ludolf moved to Frankfurt am Main in 1678, where Pastorius could have met him or at least heard of his work. See Jürgen Tubach, "Hiob Ludolf," in *Biographisch-Bibliographisches Kirchenlexikon*, vol. 5 (Herberg: Bautz, 1993), cols. 317–25.

Nominal Christians.[313] Where is that Spotless church, Eph. 5:27? There are Spots or pride, envy, malice &c. in all those called Churches of the world, Baker *Power*[314] p. 30. They call Christ Lord, & crucify him afresh at the same time by a vain conversation. Carnal, outside Christians. Babylon calls herself Lamb, bride, & is a harlot committing fornication throughout all Nations & Sects, Penn's Call[315] p. 22. Take the name of Christ into their mouths & depart not from Iniquity, p. 23. Think with themselves, they have Xst[316] to their Saviours, p. 25. Follow other Lovers than Jesus, whose spouse they profess to be, p. 38. Cry Hosanna, but in works crucify him. Heathenism Christian'd, p. 39. Christians not having the Spirit of Xst. Ludolf p. 111. Watk. Marks[317] p. 25. The nice sort of our modish Christians do Lord's work too slothfully, & seek their own too eagerly.

Pietism.[318] When some students at Lipsick[319] began to lead a serious and sober life, they were by the others 1688 in derision called Pietists. Boehm piet.,[320] p. 18 & charged with abundance of heretical opinions, fanatick & enthusiastick notions: the pulpits rang with this new-coin'd Name, & P[ietism] was now the common subject of discourse up and down Germany. Idem[321] Mr. AH Franck[322] & other (so-called) Pietist—divines at Hall.

Schools.[323] The reformation of S[chools] is highly necessary at this time, Fr. Orph. Altr.[324] p. 40. There are now many Charity-schools erected in England for teaching poor children, by way of Subscriptions to be paid yearly (during pleasure) towards the Charge, methods, Rules, & Orders whereof may be seen, in a little book, printed in 12° 1716,

---

313. "Alphabetical Hive," entry 2401. Pastorius wrote a great deal about the "nominal Christians" he found upon settling in Pennsylvania.

314. Richard Baker, *A Testimony to the Power of God, Being Greater than the Power of Satan: Contrary to all those who hold no Perfection Here, No Freedom from Sin on this Side of the Grave* (London, 1699).

315. William Penn, *A Call to Christendom, in an Earnest Expostulation with Her to Prepare for the Great and Notable Day of the Lord* (London, 1695). The consecutive page references are also to this work.

316. Christ.

317. Morgan Watkins, *The Marks of the True Church, The Virgin and Spouse of Christ that Brings Forth by a Holy Seed the Birth that Pleaseth God, and the Marks of the False Church, or Whore, that Brings Forth the Evil Seed* (London, 1675).

318. "Alphabetical Hive," entry 2356.

319. Leipzig.

320. A. W. Boehm [Böhm], *A Short Account Of Some Persons who have been instrumental in promoting the most Substancial Points of Religion in some Parts of Germany. Whose Proceedings some have endeavoured of late to render Odious by the new-invented Name Of Pietism* (London, n.d.). Not listed in Pastorius's "Bee-Hive" bibliographies.

321. "Also."

322. August Hermann Francke, *Pietas Hallensis: or a publick demonstration of the foot-steps of a divine being yet in the world: in an historical narration of the orphan-house* (London, 1705).

323. "Alphabetical Hive," entry 839.

324. Theologian and clergyman August Hermann Francke (1663–1727), a leader of the Pietist movement in Germany, founded the world-famous orphanage and Francke Foundations (Franckesche Stiftungen) in Halle in 1695.

the Grey-Coat School.[325] Such as are employed in the Instruction of Children must be of a meek Temper, & humble behavior, and have a good government of themselves & their passions, &c. Char. Schools, p. 14.[326] The Childrens Names to be called over every morning & afternoon: and if any be missing, to be put down with Notes for Tardy or Absent; and great faults, as lying, Swearing, Stealing, Truanting, &c. likewise to be noted down in Monthly or weekly Bills to be laid before the Masters. Id. p. 19. Children shall come to School clean wash'd & comb'd. Concerning the tyranny of Schoolmasters, Id. num. 157. The Ignorance & undiscerning of the generality of Schoolmasters Ibid. They send young Children to School, to keep them out of harms way, Id. By taking Rods & Feruths from Schools, they almost fill'd the land with knaves and Fools. *With half a man's age in School's confound'd*, Id. Eye his brain is a little perfum'd. Publick S[chools] preferable to private. [. . .] add. Education, nm. 4669. *Corripe nunc verbis duris, nunc utere Virga*, Id.[327] *pueris dant crustula blandi Doctores, elementa velint ut discere prima*, Horat.[328] Or Scholars Cakes the Master does bestow, that in their learning they should not be slow! Charity S[chools]. for a liberal & religious education of poor Children encouraged by Spect. nm. 294.[329] Whether the Education at a publick School, or under a private Tutor is to be preferred. vid. Id. num. 303.[330] Some Children are barbarously used for not performing Impossibilities. Ibid. At School we very often contract such friendships as are a service to us all the following parts of our lives, Ibid. Charity S[chools]: a great Instance of a publick Spirit, Spect. vol. 4. p. 163. School-masters licensed Tyrants,[331] Id. vol. 2. p. 306.

325. Also known as "Grey Coat Hospital," the Grey Coat School was a secondary school established through donations by the Church of England as a boarding school that, starting in 1701, allowed both boys and girls to attend.

326. A reference to the orphanages and charity schools of August Hermann Francke.

327. "'Correct now with harsh words and now use the rod.'" Pastorius is quoting from Palingènio Stellato Marcello, *Zodiacus Vitae* (Venice, 1536), a didactic poem divided into twelve books, one for each sign of the zodiac.

328. "'Even as teachers sometimes give cookies to children to coax them into learning their ABC.' Horace." The larger quotation from Horace, *Satires*, book 1, satire 1, lines 24–26, reads: "Quamquam ridentem dicere verum quid vetat? Ut pueris olim dant crustula blandi doctores, elementa velint ut discere prima" (What is to prevent one from telling truth as he laughs, even as teachers sometimes give cookies to children to coax them into learning their ABC?).

329. *The Spectator* was published by Joseph Addison and Richard Steele in London, 1711–12.

330. "See the same [*The Spectator*], number 303."

331. There is distinct irony in this reference. The Philadelphia School Board scrutinized Pastorius's actions after he beat a student of his school, one Israel Pemberton, son of a noted Philadelphia figure, Phineas Pemberton. Israel wrote a letter describing the incident to Thomas Makin, the other schoolmaster of the Philadelphia school (Israel Pemberton letter to Thomas Makin, July 22, 1698, Pemberton Papers, HSP). He received a letter noting "master Pastorus unkindness" a little while later afterward from another friend, commiserating with Israel (Letter of Richard Johns to Israel Pemberton, September 5, 1698, Pemberton Papers, HSP). Makin offered to remove Israel from Pastorius's realm, and there is no extant response from Pastorius himself about the matter.

Slavery.[332] Consider seriously with yourselves, if you were in the same slavish Condition, as the blacks are, (and indeed you do not know, what Condition you or your Children, or your Children's Children may be brought into, before you or they shall dye,) you would think it hard measure; yea, and very great bondage and Cruelty, Id.[333] p. 18, Luke 6:36. Keep your fortnights meetings among your blacks, & train them up in the fear of the Lord, Id. p. 31. Let them have 2 or 3 hours of day once in the week to meet together, to wait upon the Lord, p. 22. Send me over a black boy of your Instructing, that I may see some of your fruits, and as I shall see, I shall make him a free man, or send him to you again, Ibid. Slaves at wheels of his Chariots, Leeds 1718.[334] Slaves to the power of darkness, to be a perpetual galley Slave is worse than death itself. That part of mankind whose portion it is to live in servitude. Spect.[335] I scorn to be their Slave, whose Equal I am born, *With* the thralldom Cowley's love verses[336] pg. 5. Their worse than Egyptian S[lavery], he used him after so servile and base a manner. S. Prosper, when of a Reader of the h. Scriptures he became a devout practitioner, set all his servants free, both men and maids, yielding them a competency to live on.

Universities.[337] When your drossy doctors have done the utmost to you, you are but plain Naturalists, & teach for money, when as you had been better to have kept flocks & herds, and turned husbandmen, that would bring more honour to God, E.M. Mod. p. 12.[338] You see the people are prophane & you do them no good, but even begin to be a shame to the nation. Ibid. And yet you have been learning 7 or 8 years at Oxford & Cambridge, and one that never was there, shall confound 20 of you in the things of God, &c. Id. p. 13. the Number of the Students of the New University of Hall in Saxony amounts to above 3000 anno 1705. […] Academia, a wood near Athens, wherein the Philosophers used to study, Peacham p. 185.[339] Return not thence unletter'd with disgrace, But rather leave thy life in that brave place, Id. […] Signal places for idleness, looseness, prodigality, &c. Tr. exalted.[340]

332. "Alphabetical Hive," entry 2425.
333. There is no referenced text listed.
334. Possibly a reference to Titan Leeds, *The American almanack for the year of Christian account, 1718* (New York, 1717).
335. *The Spectator*, but no issue is referenced.
336. Abraham Cowley, *The works of Mr Abraham Cowley* (London, 1668).
337. "Alphabetical Hive," entry 1270.
338. E. M., *A Brief Answer unto the Cambridge Moddel: which is to go to the two universities to be read by all the Doctors and Students* (London, 1658).
339. Henry Peacham, *Minerva Britanna or A Garden of Heroical Devises* (London, 1612).
340. William Penn, *Truth Exalted in a Short but Sure Testimony Against All Those Religions, Faiths, and Worships that have been Formed in the Darkness of Apostacy* (London, 1671).

Poetry

"Silvula Rhytmorum Germanopolitanorum," Poetic Miscellany in the "Bee-Hive"

INTRODUCTION TO THE TEXT

The following selections of poetry are transcribed and annotated from the "Silvula Rhytmorum Germanopolitanorum," the poetic miscellany in Pastorius's "Bee-Hive" manuscript book: Francis Daniel Pastorius, "His Hive, Melliotrophium Alvear or, Rusca Apium, Begun Anno Domini or, in the year of Christian Account, 1696," UPenn MS Codex 726, Rare Book and Manuscript Library, University of Pennsylvania. The selections were made to reflect the variety and range of Pastorius's poetic endeavors and the many individuals in early Pennsylvania with whom he exchanged books and poetry; they are numbered as Pastorius originally numbered them in the "Bee-Hive."

In keeping with early modern conventions, Pastorius prefaced his miscellany of original poetry with a humility topos disavowing any pretensions to poetic greatness or skill: "Whereas now in the few next ensuing Leaves the Reader will find a Miscellany of my sorry Rimes, I would not have him think, that I made them with a purpose to be accounted a Poet, No, by no means, Non tanto sum dignus honore [I am not worthy of such honor]; but only to try whether Versifying and Turning of the Spooling-wheel were things compatible at the same Times." To take him at his word, Pastorius had no pretensions to being a professional poet but championed the typical Quaker focus on a "useful" occupation, such as weaving, which he pursued along with his poetic compositions. The purpose of these poems, besides personal reflection and diversion, was the edification of his friends.

Consisting of 495 entries of varying lengths, and moving from mostly German to mostly English while also using Latin, French, and Dutch, the "Silvula Rhytmorum Germanipolitorum" (A Little Forest of Rhymes from Germantown) contains—as a forest contains a variety of trees—a variety of poems from different genres and modes, on different subjects, and for different occasions and audiences. We find brief epigrams musing on the spiritual significance of an object (such as a clock), witty or wise sayings and mottoes, versified thoughts about his reading subjects (which were sometimes copies of inscriptions Pastorius made into books before he returned them to the friends who had lent them to him), poems of praise dedicated to his closest friends (such as the "Epibaterium" celebrating Penn's third visit to Pennsylvania in 1699), poems of instruction to his sons, and reflections on and sometimes critiques of both the events of his day and significant moments or themes in history. Overall, the poems range from the very personal and emotional to the philosophical, religious, and political.

Despite his disavowal of poetic skill, the poems collected in the "Silvula" demonstrate Pastorius's knowledge of and experimentation with a variety of poetic genres, meters, and styles. And his instructions to the young Quaker woman Jane Fenn (entry 475), then an indentured servant of David Lloyd, regarding her poetic attempts, which she had sent him for his commentary, reveal his self-conscious embrace of poetry as an avocation. (Pastorius would place Fenn [later Hoskens or Hoskins] on a par with famous female poets such as Anne Bradstreet and Mary Herbert.) The "Silvula" thus encapsulates Pastorius's cultivation of his role as intellectual and poetic advisor to a range of friends, from the socially elite and to the disadvantaged. For literary studies, this collection of poetry constitutes a virtual laboratory of styles and influences that vastly expands our understanding of the poetic range and interests of early American writers, especially those with a primarily religious orientation. Pastorius's focus on the aesthetic qualities of his poetry belies the common misconception that Quaker poets rejected creativity for the sake of piety and humility. Historians of early Pennsylvania and students of the history of ideas will find this collection to be an invaluable repository of names, historical references, books, and events, weaving a rich tapestry of a specific place in time and one individual's special way of thinking.

SILVULA RHYTMORUM GERMANOPOLITANORUM.[1] F. D. P.

Stat animi Sententia hunc Librum tripartiri; & Carmina sequential Amicis elar-
giri, Ut possint illa legere Germ: Angli & Latini; Silentem Vitam degere Est moris
pecorini, &c.[2]

I.

Den leüten dieser Welt Verglcich ich meine Schrift,
Beÿ welchen man Viel Wort, u. wenig Witz antrift.[3]

2.

Verachtestu diß buch, Eÿ doch Verwirfs nicht gar;
Ich schrieb es meistentheils wann ich noch schläfrig war.[4]

3.

Dass Hanns Milan hier war, Verspührt man den baümen
Die er zum theil gefällt, zum theil gepflantzet hat,
Damit die Nach-Welt nun an solcher Arbeit stat
Von mir auch was empfang, so fang ich an zu Reimen;
Und schreibe solche Ding die dem Gemüth gesund;
Dann Hannsens Baum-gewächs sind eintzig vor den mund.[5]

[. . . . .]

5.

Ad Lectorem propitium:

Carmina quando vocas mea mi lectissima Lector,
Creditur; In lecto plurima composui.[6]

6.

Obtrectatori:

Judice non opus est nostris nec Vindice rhytmis.
Judex & Vindex, si sapis, esto Tibi.[7]

---

1. "A Little Forest of Rhymes from Germantown."
2. "The judgment of the mind stands over this book to divide it into three parts;
   And To expand the following poems for friends, so that they could read them in German,
   English, and Latin; to lead a quiet life is something worthy of a mortal sin, &c."
3. "I compare my writings to the people of this world. / Among whom one may find many words but little wit."
4. "If you despise this book, do not dismiss it altogether / I mostly wrote it when I was still sleepy."
5. "That Hans Milan was here one can tell from the trees / He cut down some of them and planted others, / So that posterity may now receive instead of such work / Something from me as well, I begin to versify; / And write things that are healthy for the mind; / For the fruits of Hans's trees are only for the mouth."
6. "*To the inclined reader:* / Whenever you, O reader, call my poems the most readable, / it is believable, in reading I composed most of them."
7. "*To my detractor:* / There is no need of a judge or an avenger for our rhymes. / If you are wise, let there be a judge and avenger for you."

7.

Die gern mit disputiren ihr theüre Zeit verlieren, sind Narren. Prov. 20:3.
Weise leüt Vermeiden allen Streit. 1 Cor. 11:16.[8]

8.

A Christian helps ev'ry man as much as he can.

9.

How happy could men be in all their Course of life,
If they did strive to *love*, as they do love to *strive*.
Wie klüglich könnten wir, Ja glücklich allhier leben,
Wann Lieben uns so lieb wolt seÿn als Widerstreben![9]

10.

Quod Salva sis Britannia,   Dein Wohlfart Groß Britannien
Quòd crescas Pennsilvania,   Dein Wachsthum Pennsilvanien,
Quòd Superes Albania,   Dein Schutz u. Schirm Albanien,
À Domo est Urania,   Kommt sammtlich von Uranien.
Regit et Tegit omnia Coelum.
Hoc etiam si quid Veri mens augurat, inter hos motus
Orbis nos reget atqu. teget.[10]

11.

Cuncta sunt horaria, mutaqu, nefaria, quae sunt in hoc mundo;
Ista qui non despicit, nec aeterna respicit par est furibundo.[11]
Wir, sammt allem was wir thun, nehmen doch behend ein End,
Wohl uns! Wenn der Höchste Gott solches gut zu seÿn Verlehnt.[12]
Ergo Quicquid agis (breve Tempus!) respice Finem.[13]

---

8. "Those who like to waste their precious time disputing, are fools. Prov. 20:3. / Wise people avoid all wrangling. 1 Cor. 11:16."

9. The first two lines of this poem translate into English the German of its last two lines, and vice versa. As in much of Pastorius's multilingual poetry, the English and German versions here reflect the same meaning but place a language-specific nuance into the poetic language.

10. That you might be safe, Britannia,
   That you might grow, Pennsylvania,
   That you might survive Albania,
   All comes from Urania [heaven]
   From heaven he reigns and he covers all of heaven.
   If the mind foretells, anything of truth, this thing also among these motions
   of the world he rules and covers.
   The Latin and German lines reflect the same idea.

11. "All things are hourly changeable [and] wicked which are in this world; / whoever does not look down on these things, he does not look on eternal things and is equal to the one who is insane."

12. "We, with everything we do, quickly come to an end, / Happy are we, if the almighty God looks favorably upon it [our endeavors]."

13. "Therefore, whatever you do (the time is short) look to the end."

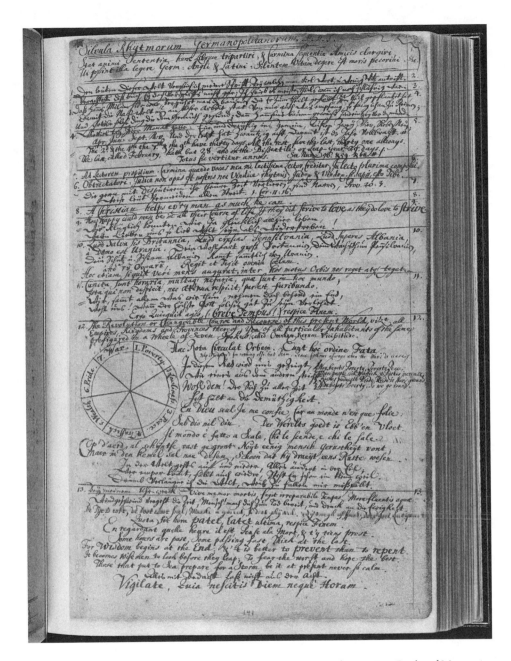

Fig. 4 | Francis Daniel Pastorius, detail from "Bee-Hive." UPenn MS Codex 726, Rare Book and Manuscript Library, University of Pennsylvania.

The Revolution or Changeable Course and Recourse of this present World,[14] vizt all
Empires, Kingdoms and Provinces thereof; Yea of all particular Inhabitants of the
same, prefigured in a Wheele of Seven Spokes, called Omnium Rerum Vicissitudo.[15]
Haec Rota, Circulat Orbem. Eunt hoc ordine Fata.[16]
War is ordain'd for nothing else but Peace,
Peace follows always when the wars do cease.

    In diesem Rad wird uns gezeigt,
    Wie eines aus dem andern steigt.
    Wohl dem! Der Sich Zu aller Zeit
    Fest halt an die Demüthigkeit.[17]

War begets Poverty, Poverty Peace
Then people will traffick & Riches increase
Riches produceth Pride, Pride is War's ground
War begets Poverty, So we go round.

    En Diue seul je me confie,
    Car au monde n'est que folie.[18]

Sub dio nil diu.[19]   Der Werelts goedt is 'en Vloet.[20]
Il mondo é fatto a Scale, Chi le scende, e chi le sale.[21]

    Op d'aerd, al schijntse vast, gegront
    Noijt eenig mensch gerustheijt vont;
    Maer in den hemel sal nae desen,
    Schoon dat hÿ draeijt, eens Ruste wesen.[22]

In der Welt gehts auf und nieder
Alles ändert in der Eil;
Wer empor kommt, fällt auch wieder,
Steht Er schon ein kleine weil.
Drumb Verlaügne ich die Welt,
Weil zu fallen mir mißfällt.[23]

14. See figure 4 for Pastorius's drawing.
15. "The changing nature of all things."
16. "This wheel encircles the world. All fates go by this order."
17. "This wheel shows us / how one arises from the other. / Happy is he who at all times / holds on to humility."
18. "I trust in God alone, / because the world is nothing but folly."
19. "Under God, nothing is for a long time."
20. "The world's weal is ebb and flow."
21. "The world is made of stairs, those who descend them, and those who climb them."
22. "On the Earth, though she seems to be rooted firmly / there has never been any human certainty / But in heaven after this one / although it turns, there shall be Rest."
23. "In the world, it goes up and down / everything changes in a flash; / He who rises also falls, / once he's been standing for a little while. / Thus I renounce the world, / For I do not like to fall."

Beÿ meinem Uhr-werck:[24]

    Vive menor mortis, fugit irreparabile Tempus more fluentis aquae.[25]

Windgeschwind vergeht die Zeit,

Mensch! mach dich zum Tod bereit,

und denck an die Ewigkeit.[26]

        De Tijt is cort; de Doot comt snel;

        Maekt u gereet, so doet ghij wel

          't Zij vroegh of spaet, Doet goet Laet quaet.[27]

    Quota sit hora patet, latet ultima, respice Finem.

    En regardant quelle heure il est,[28]

Some hours are past, Some passing fast, Think at the last.

For Wisdom begins at the End; & t'is better to prevent than to repent.

It becomes wise men to look before they leap; To fear the worst and hope the best.

Those that put to Sea, prepare for a Storm, be it at present never so calm.

    Alles mit Bedacht Laß nicht aus der Acht.[29]

    Vigilante, Quia nescitis Diem neque Horam.[30]

Ferner an gedachtem Uhrwerck:[31]

    Motibus arcanis. Chieto fuori, Commoto dentro.[32]

Ein Christ gleicht einer Uhr; Sein Zeiger kann nicht gehen,

    Wann Gotts bewegungen in Ihme stille stehen.[33]

    Redimentes Tempus, quoniam dies mali.[34]

    Auch böse Zeiten sind dem guten Menschen gut,

    Weil niemals böses Er: und böses ihm nichts thut.

    Er führt durch beedes Glück all Zeit nur einen Muth.[35]

14.

    Diewiel die Welt aus nichts gemacht,

---

24. "*At my clockwork.*"

25. "Live mindful of death, time flees unrecoverable like flowing water."

26. "Time flies like the wind. / Man! Prepare for death, / and think of eternity!"

27. "The Time is short; Death comes quick / Be ready, and you will do well / Be it early or late, Do good [&] Leave evil."

28. "Which hour lies open, the final one is hidden, look to the end. / Regarding what time it is."

29. "Everything with care; do not cease to be mindful."

30. "'Be watchful because you do not know the day, nor the hour.'" Pastorius is quoting from Matthew 25:13, but see also Mark 13:33.

31. "*Furthermore, on an imagined clockwork.*"

32. "A hidden movement, calm on the outside, commotion, within."

33. "A Christian is like a clock; his hand cannot move, / if God's movements in him are standing still."

34. "'Redeeming the time, for the days are evil.'" Pastorius is quoting from Ephesians 5:16.

35. "Even evil times are good for a good person / Because he never does any evil and evil does nothing to him. / He maintains the same spirit through both kinds of fortune."

so nennt man sie auch nichtig;
Der Mann aus Erden fortgebracht
heißt Irdisch Sofern richtig.
Das Weib formirt aus einem bein,
muß darumb auch ja beinern (peinend) seÿn.[36]

15.

Schau diesen Cirkel an, das bild der Ewigkeit,[37]
Da Anfang, Mitt und End ist sonder Unterscheid;
Auch merck zu deiner Lehr hier kürtzlich angedeüt
Zweÿ Wörtgen: Meid und Leid! Wodurch insonderheit
Du den bestimmten Streit, mit Teüfel, Welt u. Fleisch;
Und was dein Heÿl bereidt
Kannst kämpfen Ritterlich: und wann nach dieser Zeit
Der Herr austheilt die Beüt
Seÿn fähig und bereit
Sammt allen Siegenden auf Seiner Rechten Seit
Zu tragen Palm und Cron in Ew'ger Himmels-Freüd.[38]
Praestant AEterna Caducis.[39]
Non hic expecto, sed imposterum, Thomas de Kempis.[40]

36. "Because the world is made of nothing / therefore one calls it insignificant [or vain]; / As man is made from earth / he is thus correctly called earthly. / The woman was formed from bone / therefore has to be bony (tormenting)." Pastorius is here making a double pun. One pun alludes to the account in Genesis describing the first human, Adam, being created from earth; the name Adam itself may be a play on the Hebrew word *adamah* meaning "earth." The other pun works only in German: since Genesis describes how the first woman, Eve, was made from a rib taken from Adam's body, Pastorius calls woman "beinern (peinern)," with *beinern* meaning "made from bone" and *peinern* meaning "to torment" (the connection relies on the archaic word *Gebein* for bones). Although the second pun is only one in a series of sardonic allusions to wives that most likely came from Pastorius's frosty relationship with his own wife, he speaks with admiration of many other women—married and unmarried—in his poetry.

37. The manuscript includes a circle surrounding the words "Symbolum Aeternitatis" (Symbol of Eternity).

38. Look at this circle, an image of eternity,
    There is no difference between beginning, middle, and end;
    Also note for your instruction what is briefly mentioned—
    Two words: avoid and misery! Through which you can especially
    Fight valiantly the battle against devil, world, and flesh;
    And against whatever begrudges your salvation.
    And when, at the end of this time,
    The Lord dispenses the reward
    Be able and prepared
    With all who are victorious on his right side
    To carry palm and crown in eternal celestial joy.

39. "They prefer the eternal to the temporal."

40. "'Hope not in the now but in the future,' Thomas à Kempis." Pastorius is quoting from Thomas's devotional classic *The Imitation of Christ* (ca. 1418–27).

Sint Temporalia in usu AEterna in desiderio.[41] Idem.

Mein' Lohn will ich im Himmelreich, nicht auf der Erd empfangen;

Brauch ich das Zeitlich, so ist doch das Ewig mein Verlangen.[42]

Non est Mortale quod opto.

Elige Vixisse Semel, Perÿsse semel AEternum est.—Augustin.[43]

Wie der Rauch vergeht diß Leben,

Mensch! Setz deine rechnung eben;

Und stirb, eh'es kommt zum Sterben.

Dass du freÿ seÿ'st vom Verderben.[44]

    Verte sex folia, & lege Sub dio nil diu.[45] &c.

16.

Resurgam, totus mutatus ab illo. Mea Spes post Fata superstes.[46]

    Wiewohl der Tod in stücker bricht,

    Diß sterblich Haus der Erden;

    So stirbt doch meine Hoffnung nicht

    Daß mir einst werde werden

    Auffs neüe Eines zugericht befreÿet von beschwerden.

       Hoc spero, Huc adspiro.[47]

17.

F.D.P. Epitaphium.[48]

Christ came & suffered for me, to Save

Mine In- and Outward man; to be no Slave

To Sin, nor in the world a wretched knave.

But that I should by him here & hereafter have

The Liberty which he to his Redeemed gave

From first to last to All. Therefore o brave!

That is in Rest with him; this in the grave.

---

41. "'They are temporal in practice and eternal in desire [hope].'" And quoting from the same work here as well.

42. "I want to receive my reward in heaven and not on Earth; / though I need what is temporal, I desire what is eternal."

43. "'I seek nothing that is mortal. / Choose to have lived once, to have died once, it is an eternal thing.'—Augustine." Pastorius misattributes this quotation from Ovid to Augustine.

44. "This life passes like smoke, / Man! Set right your reckoning; / And die, before death comes. / So that you are free from doom and damnation."

45. "Turn six pages, and read under God, nothing is for a long time."

46. "*I will rise*, wholly changed by him. My hope, you survive after death."

47. German: "Though death breaks into pieces / this mortal house on Earth / my hope shall never die / that I will once receive / a new one [life] without ailments." Latin: "This thing I hope for, to this thing I aspire."

48. "*FDP Epitaph*." By extension, an epitaph is a brief composition characterizing a deceased person, expressed as though intended to be inscribed on that person's tombstone. In the seventeenth and eighteenth centuries, poets commonly composed their own epitaphs before their own deaths, thus imagining how future generations might remember them. Pastorius later crossed out the entire section except "Here let the Body . . . Rising of the Just."

Here let the Body sleep in undisturbed Dust,
whose Soul above expects the Rising of the Just.

18.

Qualis Vita, Finis ita.[49]

Sehr beschwerlich fällt das Sterben einem welcher leicht gelebt;
Leicht hingegen dem der schwerlich in der † Schul hat gestrebt.
So daß uns nun Tod und Leben leicht und nicht beschwerlich seÿ,
Halten wir uns all Zeit fertig und bereit zu beederleÿ.[50]
Ad utrumqu. Parati.[51]

19.

Hic alimenta mihi maxima praebet Amor.[52]

Wer Christi Creütz von hertzen liebt,
Und durch gedult darin sich übt.
Dem wirds zuletzt als täglich brod;
Wornach er trachtet nacht und tag,
Ohn welchs er gantz nicht leben mag.
Ja achtets vor die größte Noth.
Wann solches etwan außen bleibt,
Und ihn im Lauf nicht Vorwarts treibt,
Er seüffzend als lebendig todt.[53]

[. . . . .]

24.

Impiorum idololatrica Trinitas:

Concupiscentia Carnis, Oculorum & Superbia Vitae. 1 John 2:5.[54]

The triple League of hell.

Much idolized Trinity, World's honour, gold and Luxury,
Tho' thousands are who for you call, yet unto me is Jesus all.

49. "Whatever life is, this is the end."
50. "Dying is hard for someone who has lived loosely; / Easy, however, for the one who strove hard in the school of the Cross. / So that death and life shall be light and not troublesome, / We stay ready and prepared for both at all times."
51. "For both be prepared."
52. "Love provides me the greatest nourishment."
53. He who loves Christ's Cross with all his heart
And applies himself patiently in it
Will at last consider it his daily bread;
Which he desires day and night.
Without which he entirely does not want to live
Yea, he considers it his greatest necessity.
If it does not affect him inwardly,
And does not drive him forward on his course of life,
Will moan like the living dead.
54. "*The wicked, idolatrous trinity:* / The desire of the flesh, of the eyes & the pride of life. 1 John 2:5."

Pure gold, true honour, meer delight, that never vanish out of Sight.

But you fade without stop or stay; the Thief steals earthly gold away,

Vain honour onorates the mind, and Luxury of every kind,

Is full of peril, and doth hurt both Soul and body. So in short

Let honour Alexander spur, and Luxury an Epicur, and gold a Midas;

Yet I shall Say still To me is Jesus all. See Num. 64.

Franciscus Daniel Pastorius osor honoris, osor luxuriate, Corditus osor opum[55]

I loved Luxury & gold and honour once,

But loving now the LORD I hate them for the nonce.

    Ich sage zu dem Gold, zur Wollust u. zur Ehr,

     Hab ich eüch schon geliebt, ich lieb eüch nun nicht mehr.[56]

Ick scheyd van Pracht en Eer, en van de snoode Lust;

Hoe wijder die van mijn, hoe naerder ick ter ruft.[57]

25.

The Fear of GOD keeps from Sin.

The Fear of Man makes to Sin.

O, Gottes-furcht, du bist sehr hoch zu preisen!

Und magst mit recht der Weißheit Anfang heißen

Die welche sich umb dich mit Ernst befleißen

In ihrem Sinn ein änderung verspühren:

Du pflegest sie vom bösen abzuführen,

Daß selbige kein sünd noch schand anrühren.

Nun Menschenfurcht, von dir auch was zu melden,

So muß ich dich mit scharfen Worten schelten,

Vergallter Feind der sieghaft Christen-helden!

Die welche dir beÿ sich ein Eingang geben,

Und mehr vor dem Geschöpf, als ihrem Schöpfer beben,

Die treibest du zu allen Laster-leben.[58]

---

55. "Francis Daniel Pastorius: hater of honor, hater of luxury, hearty hater of works."

56. "I say to gold, to lust, and to honor: / Though I loved you once, I no longer love you now."

57. "I part from Splendor and Honor, and from wicked Lust / The further they are from me, the closer I am to rest."

58. O fear of God, you are to be praised most highly!
    And may justifiably be called the source of all wisdom
    Those who seriously strive for you
    Feel a change in their mind:
    You continually turn them away from evil,
    That they touch neither sin nor disgrace.
    Now, fear of man, to say something about you,
    I have to scold you with sharp words,
    Bitter enemy of victorious Christian heroes!
    Who give you an opening to themselves,

26.

Proximus sum Egomet mihi.[59]

Tho' thou deservest it, Yet I will have the best;

So partial is Self, So unjust Interest.

27.

Cibi modicus, Sibi medicus.[60]

Wer mäßig und nicht müßig, Hat alles überflüßig,

Wird keines Dings Verdrüßig.

    Vice versa: Wer müßig u. nicht mäßig,

      Versoffen u. gefräßig, ist Jederman Verhäßig.

Mäßig und nicht müßig Leben Hat dem Artzt kein Geld zu geben;

Müßig und nicht mäßig seÿn bringt dem Artzt sein Nahrung ein:

Füllet ihm den Säckel fein.[61]

Medico equidem benè est, Si malè sit alÿs.[62]

[..]

35.

    Delight in Books from Evening Till

    Mid-night when the Cocks do sing;

    Till Morning when the day doth spring:

    Till Sun-set when the Bell doth ring.

    Delight in Books, for Books do bring

    Poor men to learn most every thing;

    The Art of true *Levelling*:[63]

    Yea even how to please the king.

    Delight in Books, they're carrying

    Us so far, that we know how to fling,

    On waspish men (who taking wing

    Surround us) that they cannot sting.

    And tremble more for the creature than the creator,
      You drive them into lives of vice.

59. "I am closest to myself."

60. "He who is moderate in food is doctor to himself."

61. "Those who are moderate and not idle, have everything in abundance, / and will not get tired of anything. / Vice versa: Those who are idle and not moderate, / drunks and gluttons, are odious to everyone. / If you live moderately and not idly, you do not need to pay the doctor anything; / Living idly and not moderately gives the doctor his sustenance: / nicely fills his purse."

62. "It goes well for the doctor indeed, if it goes poorly for others."

63. The Levellers were a political movement during the English Civil War that emphasized popular sovereignty, extended suffrage, equality before the law, and religious tolerance, all of which were expressed in the manifesto "Agreement of the People."

ut ungant potius quam pungant.[64]

Das sey aller Bücher Summ,

<u>Glaub</u> an Christum, u. Leb frumm.[65] Ex Fide Vita.[66]

36.

Quietisten, Pietisten,

Sind nur Nahmen, wahre Christen,

Müssen doch mit Furcht u. beben, Phil. 2:12,

streben Still und fromm zu leben, 1 Tim. 2:2.[67]

37.

Unweiser Mensch was soll der äußerliche schein?

Wann du aus hertzens-grund kein kirchenglied willst seyn.[68]

38.

Zur Zeit der Anno 1692 in Pennsilvanien entstandenen Trennung.[69]

Jedes schonet seiner Art,

Tÿger, Wolf u. Leopard

Eÿ wie kommts dann daß ein Christ

Wider seines Gleichen ist?

Da ihm doch sein Herr gebeüt

Liebe, Fried u. Einigkeit. Joh. 13:34.

Econtrà, Omnis Apostata est Persecutor sui ordinis.

Die fehler meiner brüder

sind mir zwar gantz zu wider: 1 Tim. 5:22.

Doch wegen eines Worts Iac, 3:2, 2 Tim. 2:14.

Ihr Zeügniß zu vernichten, u. freventlich sie richten, Röm. 14:13.

1 Cor. 4:5, befind ich meines Orts

Zu seÿn ein luft-streich kämpfen, 1 Cor. 9:26.

Ein Gottlos Geistes Dämpfen, 1 Thess. 5:19.

Ein art des bruder-Mords, 1 Joh. 3:15.

Drumb wann nun andre fechten,

64. "That unguent is better than pungent."

65. "That shall be the sum of all books. / Believe in Christ and live piously."

66. "From faith comes life."

67. "Quietists, Pietists / Are but names, for true Christians / must in fear and trembling, Phil. 2:12, / strive to live quietly and piously, 1 Tim. 2:2."

68. "Unwise person—why the outward pretense? / when from the bottom of your heart you do not want to be a member of the church."

69. *"At the time of the schism that occurred in Pennsylvania in 1692."* This poem reveals Pastorius's deep spiritual and psychological turmoil over the split among Pennsylvania Quakers in the Keithian controversy of the early 1690s. See the volume introduction for an account of the events of the controversy and Pastorius's response to it. Though the German and English poems below are very similar in spirit, each version has notable differences; thus the German is given here in a literal translation, whereas Pastorius's English version better translates the true sense of the German poem.

Umb Schrift u. buchstab rechten,

Will ich (ohn heüchelchein)

Biß mich der Herr ruft, schweigen, 1 Peter 3:10.

Friedfertig mich erzeigen, Röm. 12:18.

Und umpartheÿisch seÿn, Iac. 3:17.

Das Gute treülich üben, 2 Thess. 3:13.

Mein Freünd u. Feinde lieben, Matt. 5:44.

Dann das bringt keine Schmertzen,

Kein unruh in dem hertzen;

Kein Zwiespalt, sondern Freüd, Röm. 2:7.

Ja Himmlisches Vergnügen

Wann wir uns endlich fügen

Zur Wieder-Einigkeit,

Die uns als Christen ziemet,

und Paulus höchlich rühmet, Phil. 2:1; Col. 3:12.

Abmahnt von Zanck und streit, 1 Cor. 11:16; Eph. 4:31.

Die gern mit disputiren

Ihr theüre Zeit verlieren

sind Narren, Prov. 20:3; Zum beschluß

Wünsch ich, daß Gottes Wille

erfüllt werd in der Stille; 1 Thess. 4:11; 1 Tim. 2:2.

Daß Jedermann Verdruß

an After-reden habe, 1 Peter 2:1; Iac. 4:11.

Und Vielmehr seine gabe

bestätt in stäter Buß, Matt. 3:2, 8 & 4:17.[70]

70. Each spares his own kind,
    Tiger, wolf, and leopard
    So how is it that a Christian
    Is against its own kind?
    Even though his Lord commands
    Love, Peace, and Unity? John 13:34.
    Conversely, every apostate persecutes his own kind.
    Even though the errors of my brothers
    Are completely odious to me: 1 Tim. 5:22.
    But to judge them for the sake of a word, James 3:2, 2 Tim. 2:14.
    And to erase their testimony and judge them wantonly, Rom. 14:13,
    1 Cor. 4:5. For my part I consider
    A kind of beating the air, 1 Cor. 9:26.
    A godless suppression of the spirit, 1 Thess. 5:19.
    A kind of fratricide, 1 John 3:15.
    Thus, while others are fighting now,
    Debating scripture and letters,
    I will (without hypocrisy)
    Keep silence until called by the Lord, 1 Peter 3:10.

Derohalben lasset uns, die in der Heiligung des Geistes u. im Glauben der Wahrheit—zum Frieden und zur Seligkeit berufen sind, (nach des H. Apostels Vermahnung,
Eph. 4.) Wandeln, wie sichs gebührt, mit aller Demuth sanftmuth u. gedult, einer
den andern In der Lieb Vertragende, und weichende Von denen die Zertrennung u.
äergerniß anrichten, außer der Lehre die wir gelernt haben. Röm. 16:17. Dann obwohl
ärgerniß kommen u. Rotten unter uns seÿn müssen, Matt. 18:6; 1 Cor. 11:19. So ist doch
das Wehe über dem Menschen, durch welchen solche kommen; Matt. d. 1. Und werden
durch sothaner Sectirer süße Wort u. prächtige reden auch die unschuldigen hertzen
verführt, Röm. 16:18; daß sie ihrem eigenen Verderben nachfolgen, 2 Peter 2:2.[71]

Darumb Grund-gütig großer Gott!
Erbarme dich der Noth,
Worin manch Menschenkind
Verfället durch die Sünd;
Die selbigs von dir scheidt, Jes. 59:2
O lieb! O Einigkeit! 1 Joh. 4:16 & 5:8.
Und brings durch Jesum Christ

Conduct myself peacefully, Rom. 12:18.
And be impartial, James 3:17.
Faithfully endeavor to do good, 2 Thess. 3:13.
Love my friend and foe, Matt. 5:44.
For that produces no pain,
No unrest in my heart;
No discord, but gladness, Rom. 2:7.
Yea, heavenly joy
When we finally submit
To reunification,
As it is right and proper for us Christians,
And that Paul praises most highly, Phil. 2:1; Col. 3:12.
Warns against quarreling and fighting, 1 Cor. 11:16; Eph. 4:31.
Those who like to dispute
Lose their precious time
Are fools, Prov. 20:3; To finish
I wished that God's will
Will be fulfilled in quietude; 1 Thess. 4:11; 1 Tim. 2:2.
So that everyone loathes
backbiting and gossip, 1 Peter 2:1; James 4:11.
And rather uses his talent
in constant repentance, Matt. 3:2, 8 & 4:17.

71. "Therefore let us—who are called through the sanctification of the Spirit and in the knowledge of truth
are called to peace and blessedness (following the exhortation of the Holy Apostle, Eph. 4.)—conduct ourselves
properly, with all humility, meekness, and patience, one reconciling with the other in love and parting from those
who cause division and vexation, except for the lesson we have learned, Rom 16:17. For although vexation will
come and parties will be amongst us, Matt. 18:6; 1 Cor. 11:19, woe shall be upon him who causes such; Matt. d.
l ["der letzte," i.e., "the last," here referring to the last verse cited from Matthew] And through such sectarians
and their sweet words and magnificent speeches the innocent hearts are being seduced, Rom. 16:18; so that they
go into their own demise, 2 Peter 2:2."

Worvons gewichen ist. Amen.[72]

None deals with his own hard; Tyger, Bear, Wolf, Lion, Pard.

What provok's so harshly than Christian against Christian?

When Christ command's constantly Love & Peace & Unity. John 13:34, etc.

(Therefore) With each that is in Love,

And harmless as a Dove

I have good fellowship.

But who hate and surmise, altho' like Serpent wise,

To them I give the slip.

Sound Doctrine I approve

As much as men behoove;

Yet talking is but foul,

And meerly idle Noise,

If I to Wisdom's Voice Not hearken in my soul.

Pray! what can me availe high knowledge?

When I deale most spitefully with most,

And by my learned Pride Committing fratricide,

Do quench the holy Ghost.

You who at present rattle, with outward matters meddle

& shamelessly do brawl;

Be sure you are in danger, vid Matt. 5:22.

And take this from a Stranger:

You do not well at all.

What foolishness to quarrel

About an empty Barrel?

When we can have the taste

Of holy kingdom's Wine;

When we can richly dine

With Christ, as at a feast.

First called unto Peace, I runn still thus the Race of Christianity;

In bearing and forbearing,

Also in dearly Chearing,

Both Friend and Enemy.

Not willing for to render

Backbiting, wrong or Slander;

(Which is to beat the air.)

72. "Therefore, kind and holy God! / have mercy upon us in our troubles, / into which many of your human children fall through sin / that separates them from you, Isa. 59:2 / O Love! O Unity! 1 John 4:16 & 5:8. / And bring it back through Jesus Christ / from whom it has departed. Amen."

But rather for to strive, that I may mend my life,
& make mine Inward fair.
This will do harm to none, rejoycing everyone
Who wishes and expects,
That such, as are defiled,
May soon be reconciled
To God and His Elects.
So Brethren! I conclude, remaining gladly mute,
As I was all along,
Till God again inspireth,
& from my mouth requireth
A more delightsom Song.

39.

CANTICUM,[73] OR AN HYMN OF THE BELOVED OF MY SOUL.

The Angel of the Covenant is to his Temple come,
The holy One in Israel, the King of Salem, whome
A long while we have longed for; therefore our hearts rejoyce,
And filled with the Holy Ghost cannot be void of Voice.
If we do not the stones will speak, the speechless Babes will cry
The Sucklings of Jerusalem, the dumb mouths which did dy
Again when Christ had open'd them, out ouf their graves will praise
The goodness of our Saviour, if we that live do cease.
But no; my lips have utterance, my Pen goes to declare
The object of my Faith & hope, Joy, Worship, Love & Care.
The author of my Victory and Crown, for which I strive,
My Rest and Consolation, mine everlasting Life.
My spiritual Meat & Drink in deed, the living bread & water,
Which I of old was told to take, when I yet was an hater
And Enemy of his reproofs; But at this present time
Through Judgment feelingly redeem'd exalt him in my Rime;
And glorify his pow'rful Name, Hosanna! oh Hosanna!
To him who comes from heaven down, the Angels food and manna,
The horn of my Salvation, the Ark and Throne of Grace,
My Wisdom, way, Truth, righteousness, my Blessing, Strength & Peace.
My Fortress, rock & Stedfast ground, the pretious Cornerstone,
The word, the good & perfect Gift, the true Light alone
Sufficient and marvellous, which does in all that blossom

73. Part of an ancient Roman drama, the *canticum* was chanted or sung and accompanied by music.

Discern the very hidden Thoughts and Intents of their bosom.
The Lord, the Prince, the Governor, the Prophet, head & Preacher,
My high-Priest truely merciful, harmless & undefiled,
Melchisedec,[74] by whom I am through bloodshed reconciled.
The Lamb of God & Passover for my sins sacrificed,
A full Propitiation and Ransom greatly priced;
My Mediatour, Advocate and Intercessor there,
Where I with Zions Children once expect to have a Share.
Yea with the well beloved Son & Image of the Father,
The brightness of his Majesty, the heir of all, or rather
JEHOVAH and Emmanuel, God self for ever blessed,
Professed by the hypocrites, by Upright-ones possessed.
Thus much of the Messias now, whom in good Confidence
(Who cleanses & who purifies my Soul and Conscience,)
I call my dear and choicest Friend, my Bridegroom & my Brother,
My First and Last, mine All in All, Jesus and not another. Deus meus et Omnia![75]

40.

In fine Calendarÿ mei Oeconomici:[76]
Welcher glücklich denkt zu Enden,
Gürte klüglich seine Lenden,
Wercke fleissig mit den Händen;
Lass auch stets sein Hertz sich wenden
Zu dem obersten Regenten
All und jeder Elementen;
So wird er ihm Segen senden,
Und Vermehren dessen Renten.
O, dass wir diß recht erkennten![77]

[...]

42.

Before Rob. Barclay's Apology:[78]
Vain Writers, what have ye? bare clay.

---

74. Melchizedek, whose name means "king of righteousness," was not only a king but also a priest, who blessed Abraham in Genesis 14.

75. "God of mine and all!"

76. "*At the end of my household calendar.*"

77. "He who gladly thinks of the end, / gird up one's loins, / work busily with his hands; / and always turn his heart / to the highest ruler / of all and every element; / thus he will send him blessings, / and multiply his income. / O, that we were to understand this fully!"

78. Robert Barclay, *An Apology for the true Christian Divinity . . . translated into High Dutch, Low Dutch, and French, for the Information of Strangers* (London, 1703).

But Barclay has a Vein of gold,
And his Apology I could
Compare to pure Pearls, Nay!
To Rubys and to Diamonds;
Against the gates of hell who stands
A Witness for the Mystery
Of Godliness and Piety.
[of Christian Divinity] adde num. 342.

43.

Before Jer. Dyke's Treatise of good Conscience[79]
In these like Books I found much strife;
But this I may commend to all,
Both Friends and Fiands, & who shall
Be earnest on Eternal Life.
Tho' Dyke in some things should mistake
(which, if not, were a Rarity)
Yet I in Christian Charity
Would have his ashes none to rake.
Our duty is to reverence
The Gifts of God in every man,
Endeavouring as much as we can
To get and keep good Conscience.
Gotts-vergeßne sind beflissen
Zu betriegen und zu liegen,
Darauf sind sie abgericht;
Aber leüte von gewissen
Nicht zu heucheln,
Noch zu Schmeigeln,
Sich u. keinem andern nicht.[80]

[...]

48.

Before the compleat Justice, whereinto I inserted the Explanation of some Law Terms:[81]
By adding few lines I do expect

---

79. Jeremiah Dyke, *Good Conscience, or, A Treatise Shewing the Nature, Meanes, Markes, Benefit, and Necessitie thereof* (London: Milbourne, 1635).

80. "Those who disregard God are keen / to cheat and lie, / that's what they are bent on; / But people with a conscience / are solicitous not to dissemble / nor to flatter, / neither themselves nor anybody else."

81. Richard Chamberlain, *The complete justice, being a compendious and exact collection out of all such statutes and authors as may any ways concern the office of a justice of peace. Very much enlarged. . . . Together with a proper charge to be given at the Quarter sessions* (London: Atkins, 1681).

No Briths by birth to teach, but to direct
My loving Countrymans (the Dutch's)[82] defect,
    Who English'd does himself to them connect.

[. . . .]

50.

Wahn and Gewohnheit, Zweÿ Tÿrannen,
Fast alle Menschen übermannen;
Und machen, daß mans Guth veracht
Hingegen nach dem bösen tracht.[83]

51.

Ein Jung der die Schaaf hüten soll, und selbst die hund daran hetzt. Malus Pastor; Prediger.
    Betrachte diesen knaben recht,
    Und sag mir dann; Ist es nicht schlecht,
    Daß man so einem losen knecht
    Ein solch hoch-wichtigs Amt aufträgt.[84]

[. . . .]

53.

Five thousand lbˢ of honey
Had Varro of his hives.[85]
Yearly and every year, (*vide supr.* p. 55)
Five hundred £ˢ of money
Some men get with their wives;
Besides the gold they wear:
If I had annual money
£ˢ fifty of my Wife,
What she doth earn or sell;
And fifteen lbˢ of honey
By this my paper hive,
All things me thinks were well.
But seeing both is less,
When ever in a stress,
I bless Contentedness;

---

82. Pastorius here adopts the common American English rendering of "Deutsch" (German) as "Dutch," which gave rise to the common usage "Pennsylvania Dutch" for the German immigrants of Pennsylvania.

83. "Delusion and habit, two tyrants, / that surmount almost all people; / And lead to them despising good / and instead striving after evil."

84. "*A Boy Who is Supposed to Herd Sheep but Puts the Dog to It. Bad Shepherd; Preacher* / Look at this boy closely, / And tell me then; isn't it bad; / That such a loose servant / receives such a highly important office."

85. In 36 B.C., the Roman soldier, scholar, and writer Marcus Terentius Varro proposed "The Honeybee Conjecture," which used mathematics to explain the hexagonal shape of honeycomb cells.

Abhorring all Excess.

[..]

55.

Before J. S. P.'s book of Arithmetic.

None can do business, nor to Preferm't mount

That did not learn to Read, to Write & to account.

Ergo, Learn well to Read & write, to Cypher and Indite, At last a little Latin;

For Latin is the thing, which often times does bring From leathern Cloths to Sattin.

But then beware of Satan, the chief Instigator to all Pride and highmindedness;

Be thou humble! and fear always God, & thou wilst not need to fear men.

The Fear of the LORD keeps us from Sin, but the Fear of men leads us thereinto.

Serve God with fear and trembling, that by degrees thou mayst come to serve him without fear,

Yea even with gladness of ♥.

[..]

58.

Many Children have been lost,

Because their Parents spare the Cost;

Allowing them money to buy hooks

Denying the same, when to be laid out for books.

Giving them rather 20p for koeckskens,[86]

Than 10p for boeckskens.[87]

No wonder, if this their Offspring doth afterwards delight more in Brimmers[88] than Primmers, (in patinis[89] than paginis[90]) In that to which they were brought up, than where they are Strangers to at all. And if they must sit in koeckskens, when others vide Psal. 113:8. Prov. 22:29.

59.

Een en dertigh allentwegen,

Buyten, Twee, Vier, Seven, Negen,

En de laetst heeft Twintigh acht,

Daermee is het Jaer volbracht.

Op een ander Melodye.

De Erst, Derd, Vÿfst en Sest, de Achst en Elfste dragen

Door al het Iaer de Last van Een en dertigh dagen,

---

86. "Cakes." Four lines below, "sit in koeckskens" (sit in cakes—i.e., give oneself over to gluttony) stands in ironic opposition to "set him with princes" in Psalm 113:8.

87. "Books."

88. A "brimmer" was a full cup or glass.

89. Probably derived from French *patin* (plate), "patinis" were plates of food.

90. Derived from Latin *pagina* (page), "paginis" meant "pages."

De Tweede ende Vierdt, de Sevendt ende Negenst,
Die seggen Dertigh zyn genoegh, en ons't gelegenst;
De laetste weygert oock dit Pack te ondergaen,
En neemt maer twintigh acht, of twintigh negen aen.[91]

60.

Pallida *Luna* plait, Rubicunda flat, Alba serenat.[92]
If the moon be pale, 'twill rain, snow or hail;
If red, then let us mind, that we must have some wind;
If she be white & clear, the Weather shall be fair.

61.

When the *Sun* does go to bed,
& his Covering then is red,
He rises Prince-like fair;
The weather everywhere,
throughout our hemisphere,
Is that day very clear.
the evening red, and morning grey,
is the presage of a fair day.
But rising from the bed
his Covering being red,
he will not be so kind;
The best we with him find
that day, is Rain and Wind.

62.

Many go to hell, for not doing well. *Matt.* 25:42; *Luke* 12:47.
More go to the Devil, that are doing evil. 1 *Cor.* 6:9; *Matt.* 7:23.
But few go to heaven. *Matt.* 7:14. The rest resists the Leaven,

---

91. Thirty-one for them all
Outside, Two, Four, Seven, Nine
And the last has Twenty-eight
Therewith the Year is completed.
On another Melody.
The First, Third, Fifth and Sixth, the Eighth and Eleventh carry
Through all the Year the Burden of Thirty-one days,
The Second and the Fourth, the Seventh and the Ninth,
They say Thirty is enough, and suit us best;
The last refuses to suffer this Load, too
And takes only twenty-eight, or twenty-nine.
Pastorius's numbering of the months of the year is based on the old-style (or Julian) calendar in use in the British colonies until 1752; accordingly, the legal year began on March 25, which made March the first and February the last month of the year.
92. "With a pallid moon, it rains; with a red moon, it is windy; with a white moon, it will be calm."

Which would work in these noddies their Spirits, Souls & bodies.

63.

N.B.—Mind, Children, mind it well,
There is a twofold *Leaven,*
The one works towards heaven, *Matt.* 13:33.
the other towards hell; *Matt.* 16:6, 1 *Cor.* 5:6.
Of *this,* pray! do beware:
And take of THAT great Care. *Luke* 13:24.

64.

Honour, Pleasure, Wealth & Treasure;
Or what else the <u>World</u> does prize,
Is disdained by the Wise.
Pleasures prove commonly Serpents with Stings,
Honours are Burthens, & Riches have wings:
Virtue's wise Offspring affect not these things.
From things impertinent, Superfluous and vain
Wisdom commands her Children to abstain.
He that condemns Wealth, Pleasure and Renown,
Shall in Contentment's Kingdom wear the Crown.

65.

Time flees away without delay.
So day by day
All flesh, tho' gay,
To Death must pay
Its Tribute; Nay
Poor Mortals pray!
Mind what I say:
The strongest may
As soon decay,
As Sun's hot ray
Makes grass to hay.
In this World's-play
You must not stay.
Away! away!
Sumus Peripatetici,
quicquid resistant Medici;
His enim praestant Ethici
Quorum thema, homo schema
Oritur et Moritur. Attamen

Lethum non omnia finit. Sunt immortales animae; Post funera vivunt.

Our souls are eternal à parte post. &c.[93]   See Soul, Eternity, Immortality.

66.

To Caleb Pusey's book Intit'led *Daniel Leeds Justly Rebuked for abusing Wm. Penn,* etc.[94]

D.L. Daniel Leeds—Devilish Lier. W.P.[95] Veritas Vincit, Praevalet.[96]

Daniel Leeds; anagram—The END of his scribbling is a DEAL of LIES.

Since Daniel Leeds delights to DEAL in LIES,

That Counterbanded uglie Merchandize;

Caleb Pusy's business I commend

In putting this Lier's work to an END.

To whom I wish sincerely to repent. Amen. F.D.P.

67.

These five words[97] *Time flees away without delay* I would, if possible, retract; But Seeing *Littera Scripta manet,*[98] I kindly entreat the Reader, to take this my Palinody[99] for them.

Mine error, fault, mistake or Crime

of what I said above of Time,

I here recant in Prose and Rime.

Being hitherto of that vulgar opinion, as if time were the most *unstablest thing* in the world even like a ship adrift, that nowhere anchors; I last night changed my thoughts or mind & am now fully perswaded of the Contrary. Men that are under sail may fancy and tell us, the Shore moves urbes, silvaeq. recedunt;[100] but I can believe that no more. They themselves are subject to motion & mutation passing away as water, Gen. 49:4 or Clouds driven with every wind, Jude [v.] 10, 12 &c &c &c.

Time is, Time was, and Time shall be,

the *stablest thing* men's eyes do see.

93. "We are Wanderers, / Whatever the doctors might resist; / To them, certainly, the ethical thinkers are superior / Whose theme follows this plan: a man / is born and dies. But yet / Death does not finish all things; the souls are immortal. They live after death. / Our souls are eternal apart from the body. &c."

94. Caleb Pusey, *Daniel Leeds, justly rebuked for abusing William Penn* (Philadelphia, 1702). Quaker early settler of Pennsylvania and business partner and supporter of William Penn, Caleb Pusey (1650–1727) became one of the most vocal supporters of the orthodox Quakers during the Keithian controversy; he wrote several pamphlets attacking the Keithians, especially the Quaker Daniel Leeds (1651–1720), who settled in New Jersey and published an almanac printed by William Bradford in Philadelphia. Criticized by the Quaker establishment for supposed falsehoods in his almanac, Leeds joined the Keithian faction and became one of the most ardent critics of the Pennsylvania and New Jersey Quakers.

95. William Penn, whose side Pastorius took as usual when Penn was attacked by the Keithians.

96. "The truth conquers, it prevails."

97. Pastorius drew a diagonal line from "Time flees away without delay" at the beginning of entry 65 in the "Silvula" to the beginning of entry 67.

98. "The written word remains."

99. Obsolete form of "palinode": an ode or song recanting or retracting something in an earlier poem.

100. "Cities and the forests recede."

For to believe that Time *flees away*, is certainly one of the most bruttish popular Notions.
that invaded not only the Brittish, but universally all other Nations
be they of what Religion they will, or use any sort of the many adorations;
Whereas they should rather conceive Time to be a fixed *Pole* that measures all kind
of Motions.

When then flees Time away? I answer Now & Never. How long will Time remain?
I say for ever & ever. If but one minute of It were gone or lost, there would be an hole,
made into Eternity, when Time cannot be denied to be the smallest, yet inherent and
inseparable part or particle. Time is nothing else but a Moment during from generation
to generation; Past, present & future are only grammatical Inkhorn Terms: the Divine
Penmen of holy Scripture have used those Times or Tenses promiscually one for an
other, knowing the real Indifferency thereof. See Pauli Tossani Loc. Comman. Theolog.
p. 673.[101] and this every dull-pated man may easily comprehend if he come to whet
his brain a little upon this Consideration, that As Yesterday neither is, nor can be, so
tomorrow does us no good. The Instant time is all in all, and the present still the best
for the present. A living Dog better than a dead Lion, &c.

Time once elaps'd can't be recovered, and that to follow hereafter is not in thy
power, make therefore of *this* which is at hand

Pray do not *this* most pretious thing mispend
Which brings insensibly thee nearer to thy End!

Here I willingly would enlarge, & give more satisfactory Proofs of what I now assert;
But Time itself (without which we can do nothing) calls me to some other business.
And to make amends for my former base & fond Imagination concerning the same,
I go to obey it, and to employ the twinkling of an eye to the best of my capacity. And
being thus upon the Spur, I abruptly add
The Sun runs round the world, forsooth, Let no man doubt;
The rest of Planets too—(each Lake flows in and out;
All Sublunaries have their Over-throw or Rout;
But Time stands always fast, It faces but about.
Nevertheless do not thou o transitory Pilgrim of this variable world, hencefrom
Conclude, Time to be like a Weather-Cock. Otherwise I shall look upon thee as Such
an One, who in thy whimsical giddiness doest mean that the steeple under thy feet is
a turning, when thou thyself continually changest & alterest forward & backward, as
it happens to those that are putting off from the banks of a River, to whom the Shore
seems to move backwards, and do not perceive that it is they that go from them &
move forwards.

101. In 1628, the Reformed Protestant theologian Paul Tossanus (1572–1634) published a revised edition of
Izsák L. Fegyverneki's theological handbook *Enchiridii locorum communium Theologicorum, rerum, exemplorum
atque phrasium sacrarum*, a first published in Basel in 1586.

69.

Hanns has his hands & tongue at his command,
He keeps most fast what he did promise, and
Verspricht, und lieferts nicht, das ist ein Schand.[102]

70.

Over mijn eerste Bie-Corf, dewelcke ick Koopte voor 10ˢʰ.
    den 2ᵉⁿ der 4ᵉⁿ Maent 1705.
     swermde den 6ᵉⁿ der 3en maent 1706

Ghy garderet BY EEN de Sap van Soete Bloemen
En daerom Kan Ick u my goede BYEN noemen.
Van all wat Vleugels hoeft zijt ghy het beste Beest,
Terwijl wat soet en goedt ghy allenthenen leest.
Alwaer een Edel Veldt gewoont is Reuck te geven,
Daer pleght ghy Neerstigk Dier op Kruydekens te sweven:
Waer oyt een Roos ontluyckt, Of waer een Lely gaept,
Daer is het dat ghy ought, En was en honigk raept.
Maer soo in eenig Bloem misschien yet mochte schuylen,
Dat met een gifting Vocht het Lichaem kan vervuylen
Daer schey ghy veerding af; daer kruypt ghy nimmer in,
Maer laet het voor een Pad; of voor een grijs'lyck Spin.
Ick slacht de BYEN, en Ick tracht een Bij te wezen,
Niet traegh; maer dragende in't Boeck by't Boecken lesen.
Ick swerm met mijn Gemoedt door alderhande kruyt,
En treckter anders niet als was en Honigk uyt.
Dies is dit Boeck een Korf van duysent honigk-raten,
Ja, noch een duysent meer; die alle Menschen baten.
Doch merckt hier dit verschil, de Bij spijst maer het Lijf;
Te voeden Ziel en Geest is mijner Penn bedrijf.[103]

102. "He makes promises but does not deliver; that is a shame."
103. About my first Beehive, which I bought for 10 shillings.
    The second [day] of the fourth month [June] of 1705.
    Swarmed the sixth [day] of the third month [May] of 1706.
    You gather the Juice of Sweet Flowers
    And that is why I Can call you my good BEES.
    Of all that has wings you are the best beast,
    When you make what is sweet and good.
    Whereas a Noble Field usually smells
    you, Busy Animal, tend to glide on the herbs:
    wherever a Rose buds, or where a Lily yawns,
    There you harvest, and collect wax and honey.
    But if in any Flower there is hidden away,

Magnis tamen excido coeptis.[104] Vide supra Pag. 54.

> Dit Rymdicht (seggt ghy) is seer wel aeneen Gevoeght
>
> Geen wonder want het is met Catsens Calf geploeght.
>
> De Bye is kleyn onderde vliegende Gedierten,
>
> Maer hare vrucht is het voornaemste der soetigheden. Jesu Sirach 11:3.[105]

71.

At the forehead of a little Book of mine Intituled, The Widows Double Mite to Cypher & to Write.[106]

> Go slender Product of my Pen,
>
> Be visiting the Sons of men;
>
> And if some slander scoff & mock,
>
> Think, those are but of Ishmaels stock, &c.
>
> But if perhaps an Israelite,
>
> who loves to cypher and to write,
>
> Is willing to commune with thee,
>
> Deny him not thy Company.
>
> To him I give thee leave to sell
>
> Thine own Self, Pray serve him well,
>
> And do for him all what thou canst,
>
> He finding such things as thou wantst,
>
> Will at the Year of Jubilee
>
> From all thy Drudg'ry set thee free.

That which can pollute the Body with poisonous liquid,
That you do not touch; there you never crawl into,
But leave it for a Toad; or for a grisly Spider.
I fight [with] the BEES, and I try to be a Bee,
Not slow; but by carrying a book while reading it.
I swarm with my mind through all sorts of herbs
And extract nothing but wax and Honey.
So this Book is a Hive of a thousand honeycombs,
Yes, and another thousand; that benefit all People.
But note the difference, the Bee feeds but the body;
Feeding Soul and Spirit is my pen's occupation.

104. "'Yet I failed greatly in these undertakings.'" Pastorius is referring to the inscription on Phaethon's tomb in Ovid's *Metamorphoses*, book 2, lines 327–28: "hic : sitvs : est : phaethon : cvrrvs : avriga : paterni / tqvem : si : non : tenvit : magnis : tamen : excidit : avsis" (Here Phaethon lies who the Sun's journey made / dared all though he by weakness was betrayed). In shortening and modifying the inscription, Pastorius puts a humble turn upon the earlier claims about his work written in Dutch.

105. "This Rhyme (you say) is very well joint / No wonder because it is plowed by Catsen's calf. / The Bee is small among the flying Animals, / But her fruit is the chief of sweets. Jesu Sirach [Ecclesiasticus] 11:3." The phrase "plowed by Catsen's calf" is self-deprecatory wordplay, meaning that this "well joint" (aptly versified) rhyme was rather crudely executed in the manner of a calf plowing a field.

106. Pastorius's manuscript book "The Widows Double Mite to Cypher & to Write" is no longer extant.

72.

Before Sir Roger L'Estrange his Seneca's Morals by way of Abstract, in 8°.[107]

> Annaeus Seneca, dead sixteen hundred years,
> By Sir L'Estranges skill, o strange! again appears
> In this sad vale of Tears;
> he leav's his Gown behind, & now a jacket wears
> Of English stuff and sounds his Morals in our Ears
> Against both Hopes & Fears.
> Whoever through him the Voice of Wisdom hears
> Does well when heavenwards he all desires rears,
> But here bears and forbears.

    In which two words is compromized or epitomized all the Philosophy of Epictetus,[108] vide infra num. 1054.

[. . . .]

74.

To my Collection of the Young Country Clerks[109] Solemn Forms.

> Ungefehr vor zwantzig Jahren[110]
> hatt ich einen Ueberfluß
> an dergleichen Formularen.
> Die ich nun fast mit Verdruß
> (Weil ich Jene nicht wollt spahren)
> hin u. wieder samblen muß;
> Kinder, was mir widerfahren,
> schreib ich als ein Abschieds-kuß,
> Daß ihr diese mögt bewahren
> Euch und Euren zum Genuß.[111]

75.

Anno 1706. The sixth day of the Third,[112] the weather being warm,

---

107. Lucius Annaeus Seneca, *Seneca's morals by way of abstract. Of benefits, Part I. The sixth edition. To which is added, a discourse, under the title of An After-thought* (London, 1696) in his bibliography of non-Quaker writings. The Stoic philosopher Seneca (ca. 4 B.C.–A.D. 65) was forced to commit suicide for his alleged complicity in the Pisonian conspiracy to assassinate Emperor Nero. Sir Roger L'Estrange (1616–1704) was an English writer and royalist who translated Seneca's *Morals*.

108. The Greek Stoic philosopher Epictetus (A.D. 55–135) believed that all external events were determined by fate and should be accepted, but that individuals were responsible for their own actions.

109. See the excerpts from Pastorius's collection of legal forms, "The Young Country Clerk's Collection," in chapter 8 of this reader.

110. Pastorius's note: "Viz. Anno 1678" (namely, in the year 1678).

111. "About twenty years ago / I had a surplus of forms / which I now have to collect with some displeasure / (because I did not want to keep them) / children, what happened to me / I write as a good-bye kiss, / so that you might preserve them / for the pleasure of you and yours."

112. May 6th.

I heard the trumpets sound about our country-farm;
As if some Soldiers were come to do us harm:
Their noise methinks was thus: Alar'm, Alar'm, Alar'm!
But after I look'd down upon a Corinths-arm,[113]
Behold a King[114] of bees surrounded by his *Swarm:*
Which I took up & now sometimes refresh with barm.
He is praiseworthy, whom their diligence doth charm.
This for I S P[115] my first-born Son.

76.

1706. The same month, called May,
 the twenty second day,
 the Weather cool & dull,
 My hive again too full
 Sent forth his second Bee
 upon an Apple-tree;
 His second Swarm I say,
 who first would fly away
And yet at last did stay[116]
Kept back by A.P.'s[117] ting-tong.
  For H.P. my youngest Son.[118]

77.

1706. Den Ein und Zwantzigsten des Monats Junius,
Gab I. S. P. sein Stock den ersten Willkomms gruß;
Er schwärmte unversehns, u. wir erfuhrens kaum,
Doch endlich hieng er dar an einem Pfersich-baum:
Die Sonn schien mächtig heiß, und wir unzeitig froh;
Dieweil wir keinen Korb von Glaß, stein, holtz noch stroh
In unserm Haus, Was raths? Der best vor diese Sorg
Ist Nachbar Arets hülf, Lauf Jung geschwind u. borg!
Nun dieß gieng trefflich an, Der Schwarm wurd eingefaßt

---

113. "Corinths-arm" is probably a wordplay allusion to Pastorius's newborn son Johann Samuel holding his protected arm up for his father's bees to swarm on as if he were an ancient Greek (Corinthian) soldier in armor.

114. It was not until the sixteenth or seventeenth century that the sex of the ruling bee of a hive was definitively found to be female. Pastorius, perhaps in following Virgil's tract on bees in his *Georgics*, seems to hold on to the older notion that the ruler of the hive was male, a king, thus allowing him to apply that title to his son.

115. Johann Samuel Pastorius. (With "I S P" here, as with "I. S. P." elsewhere, Pastorius has alternate German spelling of his son's first name in mind: "Ioann.")

116. Pastorius's note: "Den 16. Tag nach dem Ersten schwärmen" (The 16th day after the first swarming).

117. Anna Pastorius, Francis Daniel's wife.

118. Henry or Heinrich Pastorius, their second son.

und an die Mutter selbst vom Sohne Zugepaßt. *Nembl: an A.P. meine Ehefrau.*[119]

78.

Gleich wie ein Kind, das einst vom Feüer ist versehrt,

Das Feüer allzeit fürcht; Sind wir hierbeÿ gelehrt,

Was früher in dem Holtz umb hohle Baüm zu sehen,

damit es uns nicht mehr wie dißmahl möchte gehen.

Wir hohlten alsobald ein alten Stamm nach Haus,

Und machten nach und nach Vier brafe Körb daraus.

Den Zweyten Julius kam I S P's schon wieder,

Recht auf den eilften Tag[120] freüt Eüch ihr Honig-Sieder,

Dann die Colonien von diesem Stock allein

die bringen Jahr zu Jahr wohl hundert Gulden ein;

Und eüer meiste müh ist, Ja nicht zu versaümen,

daß Ihr die Schwärme faßt, bißher von Pfersich baümen.[121]

79.

Bisher ging alles wohl! Nun kehret sich das blat,

Dieweil des Vatters Stock sein Kön'g verschwörmet hat;

Flucks kommt ein Company von frembden beÿ u. raubt,

die Meinen wehren sich, doch sonder Ober-haubt:

119. Here Pastorius is creating a humorous scene of what happened when his son Johann Samuel received his
first hive of bees:
1706. On the twenty-first of the month of June
I. S. P. [J. S. P.] gave his stock of bees the first welcome greeting;
It swarmed immediately, and we could barely tell where it went,
When finally it hung on a peach tree:
The sun was shining mighty hot, and we were all happy prematurely;
Meanwhile, we did not have a hive of glass, stone, wood or straw
In our house, so what to do? The best relief for such a problem
Was neighbor Arets—run quick, my son, and borrow!
Now that worked excellently; the swarm was captured
And given by the son to the mother herself
      That is, to A. P., my wife.
120. Pastorius's note after "Recht auf den elften Tag" (Right on the eleventh day) in poem 78: "Nach dem ersten
Schwärmen" (after the first swarming).
121. Just as a child who once was harmed by fire,
Fears fire at all times; this [the incident in poem 77] instructed us,
What used to be seen in the wood around hollow trees,
So that it would not go as before.
We thus soon fetched home an old [tree] trunk,
And made, one after another, four handsome hives out of it.
The second of July I. S. P. came back again,
Right on the eleventh day, rejoice you honey cookers,
For the colonies of this bee stock alone
Bring in from year to year one-hundred guilders;
And your biggest trouble is not to miss,
That you capture the swarms from the peach trees.

Drumb fiels auch übel aus, Ach leider! was dann mehr?
Der allererste Korb wird auch am ersten leer.
Ist diß, o treüe Thier, auch so beÿ Eüch der lauff[?]
So geb ich gantz betrübt das Bienen-Reimen auf.[122]

Rege incolumi mens omnibus una est, Amisso rupere fidem, *Virg.*[123] Adde infra Num. 127.

80.

Temple, L'Estrange and *Turkish Spy,*[124]
The Rhetoricians Ternary;[125]
Our English Tongue thus amplifly (beautify)
That Great & Small may learn thereby,
Who read their Books attentively,
Redundant in Variety
Exuberant   Adde infra Num. 1411.

81.

Zu meines Johann Samuels Weberstul
Extremitäten soll man meiden,
Mein Schifflein flieget zwischen beÿden.[126]
Job 7, 6. Ut radius, sic Vita fugit.[127]
My shuttle through the middle flies,
Let all men shun Extremities
Een jegh'lÿck mag syn Ambacht loven,
De Weverÿ gaet allen boven.[128]

---

122. Everything went well 'til now! But now the tide is turning,
While the father's [Francis Daniel's] bee stock has swarmed away from the king,
Soon a company of strangers moves in and robs them,
Mine are fighting back, but without their leader:
Thus it ended badly. Oh alas! And what then?
The first hive is the first one to be empty.
Is it, Oh faithful animals, the same course for you?
So I give up quite saddened the rhyming about bees.

123. "'If he is well, then all is well. But if he perishes, they break their faith,' Virgil." From Virgil's *Georgics*, book 4 (here lines 212–13), which is dedicated to beekeeping: Virgil assumed that the ruler of a beehive was a king (thus "he"), with whom the fate of the hive rose or fell.

124. William Temple (1628–1699) was an English statesman and essayist; Roger L'Estrange (1616–1704) was a British pamphleteer and journalist; and *Letters Writ by a Turkish Spy* was a collection of fictional letters, supposedly written by a fictitious spy named "Mahmut"; the collection was at least in part written by Giovanni Paolo Marana (1642–1693).

125. A "ternary" is something composed of three elements. Here Pastorius likely has in mind Aristotle's three principles of rhetoric (logos, pathos, and ethos).

126. "*On My Johann Samuel's Loom*
One should avoid extremes, / My little shuttle flies between both."

127. "Like a ray of sunlight, thus life flies."

128. "Although each may praise his profession, / Weaving transcends them all."

I love to weave both night & day,
    But not like old Penelope,
The constant and faithful wife of Ulysses, who to deceive her Suitors, desired respite till that piece of work she had in hand were ended but would all along undo by night whatsoever she did by day;[129] For this is to labour in vain.
    1707/8 Ist dieser Weberstul in seinen gang gebracht,
    Und in dem Neüen Jahr das erste Stück gemacht.
    Spinnt nun, ihr Weiber, spinnt, damit Er tag u. nacht
    Fortwebe; Dann ich bin auf Eüern Dienst bedacht:
    Doch nehmet diese Lehr vor allem wohl in acht,
    Daß Eüer garn sey fein eben, rein und sacht,
    So kriegt ihr solches Tuch, daß Eüch das Hertze lacht.[130]
    Maer denckt dat ick alsdoon oock mynen Loon verwacht.[131]
    Twixt high and Low The Weaver's Shuttles fly,
    Friends, mind the golden Means of Mediocrity.
    Manibus Pedibusq'u laboro. Nocteque, Dieque.[132]

82.

My Lot being cast among the English *Nation*,
The Wise men's Stone born in the first *Taxation*[133]
Of all the World procures me *Sustenation;*
Mean while I keep a school for *Occupation*[134]
And make their choicest books my *Recreation:*
Besides in this my Hive such *Preparation*
As to retain of each some *Observation*
Or other, finding here mine *Approbation*
Which beating back from me false *Accusation*

---

129. In Homer's *Odyssey*, the faithful wife of Odysseus, Penelope, devises various stratagems to put off having to marry any of her suitors when her long-absent husband is thought to have died. In the best-known stratagem, alluded to by Pastorius, insisting she must first finish weaving a burial shroud for her elderly father-in-law, each night Penelope secretly unweaves what she has woven that day. At last, after many years, she is reunited with her husband, Odysseus.

130. 1707/8 This loom is brought into motion
    And the first piece of the New Year has been woven.
    Spin now, you women, spin, so that day and night it can keep weaving;
    For I am dedicated to your service:
    But take this lesson to heart among all others,
    That your yarn shall be nicely smooth, pure and soft,
    Then you will get such cloth that your heart rejoices.

131. "But remember that I also expect my pay."

132. "I work with hands and feet. By night and by day."

133. Jesus Christ, who, according to the New Testament, was born at the time that Emperor Augustus had ordered a census to be conducted for the purpose of taxation.

134. Pastorius's Germantown school.

Of Laziness & of Wine's *Inflammation,*
Can tend not to the Least's least *Derogation,*
But is to better Skills a *Provocation*
(That want not, as I do Nat'ralization,
To Joyn their Wills & hands in *Emulation.*

83.

Before the Common-place Book to the Holy Bible, in 4° printed at London by
Edw. Jones anno 1697.[135]
 The primitive Belief & godly Practice was
 Such as this Book contains; But Christendom since has
 Apostasiz'd from Faith, & from the Form of words
 Sound, good & Scriptual: Such as this Book affords.
 In stead hereof a heap of Crabbed Terms remains,
 By Councils, Popes, Divines (Oh! Interfering Brains)
 Hatch'd, patch'd & Idoliz'd, Set up for Sacred Creeds,
 On which their Offspring now, as dainty victuals, feeds.
 Whoever likes it not, and for the former breaths,
 Is called a Heretick worth hundred thousand Deaths.
 What then should I here wish? what better things desire,
 Than all that would retire, out of this dirty Mire,
 And live a holy life & love what's true and plain,
 And herein persevere: Not fall away again,
 Like one of late has done, But see now where he is,
 Among the Chemarims[136] and broad Phylacteries;[137]
First Theudas-like a Guide into the Wilderness. add [Acts] 5:36 & 2:38.
[. . . . .]

87.

At the End of my Ampelogy[138] *& Vineyard Observations.*
 Great God, Preserver of all things.
 Most Gracious King of Kings!
 Thou bountiful good husbandman,

---

135. John Locke, *A common-place book to the Holy Bible: or, the Scriptures sufficiency practically demonstrated
. . . and explained by others more plain* (London, 1697).
136. In the Hebrew Bible and Old Testament, the *chemarim* were idolatrous priests.
137. Small leather boxes containing slips with passages from Scripture, secured by leather straps to the forehead
and left arm. The men of Israel were commanded to wear phylacteries as a reminder of their obligation to keep
the Law of Moses; thus any outward religious object or sign that is valued more than the spiritual belief it is
supposed represent or refer to. Pastorius most likely jibes at George Keith in this poem because Keith had, after
his return to England from Pennsylvania, converted to Anglicanism and become an Anglican priest.
138. Viticulture or the cultivation of grapes for wine.

Canst do what no man can.
And whereas I, O Lord with thine
Am grafted in the Vine
CHRIST JESUS our Redeemer dear
By him some Fruits to bear,
Spare not, spare not the Pruning knife,
To Keep my Soul alive;
The Judgments of thy righteous hand
In this wild woody land
As well as elsewhere are the way,
Therefore for these I pray.
Withhold them not householder wise,
When Sprigs & Twigs do rise,
That full of leaves do springs & spring
& yet no Clusters bring.
Make me my God, a fruitful Branch
Below here, till I launch
To Thee, into Eternity,
Where we shall Instantly
In Praising & Adoring spend
That Time which has no End!   Adde infra Num. 212.
Hallelu Jah! Hallelu Jah! Soli Deo Gloria, In sempiterna Secula. Amen.[139]

88.

Upon the Friendly Advice to the Inhabitants of Pennsylvania—printed Anno 1710.[140]
A.B.C. All honest patriots prudent & wise
    Take this Advice;
But those that wish the Government destroy'd
Chuse David Lloyd,[141]
Choice is the thing, whereby we stand or fall,
This day Ends all. viz. the 1st of October.

---

139. "Hallelujah! Hallelujah! Glory to God alone, forever and ever, Amen."
140. Isaac Norris, *Friendly advice to the inhabitants of Pensilvania* (Philadelphia: Andrew Bradford, [1710?]).
141. David Lloyd (1656–1731) was an American lawyer and politician from colonial Chester, Pennsylvania. When he first arrived, Lloyd was William Penn's personal lawyer. He also became attorney general of Pennsylvania and a member of the Popular or Quaker Party, serving in the Pennsylvania General Assembly. Pastorius personally reviled Lloyd for colluding with the German land speculator Johann Heinrich Sprögel to defraud him and other Germantown residents of land they had purchased from the Frankfurt Land Company.

89.

To Wm. Russel's No Seventh Day Sabbath Commanded by Jesus Christ in the New Testa-
ment in 4° 1663.[142]

> In Spirit & in Truth God's worshipped, Ergo
> The Shadows once before, are now à Tergo.[143]
> Old Testamental Types that Roe fulfills,
> Which upon Mountains leaps, skipps upon Hills.

Cant. 2:8. Gen. 22:13.

[. . . . .]

92.

> Willstu *Geld u. Gut ausleihen*
> Must der Freundschaft dich Verzeihen;
> Dann der tag zum Wiedergeben
> Pflegt die Freundschaft aufzuheben.[144]

> Fare well Friendship, when I lend,
> For the day
> To Repay
> To all Friendship puts an End.

> Alas & Wo! to them that borrow,
> For the day
> To Repay
> Brings a deal of Grief and Sorrow.

93.

Zu meinem Anhang zu[145] *Timothei von Roll seinem Neüen Blumen-Büchlein in 12°.*[146]

> Wer keinen Garten baut,
> Und nichts von Blumen weiß;
> Niemals zurücke schaut
> Ins Irrdisch Paradeiß:
> Ist nur ein Sclav und Knecht
> Zum Pflug u. Fluch bestimmt, Gen. 3:17.

---

142. William Russel, *No seventh-day-sabbath commanded by Jesus Christ in the New-Testament* (London, 1663).
143. "From behind" or "from the rear."
144. "If you want to lend money and goods / you have to give them up for the sake of friendship; / for the day of return / usually puts an end to friendship."
145. "On my appendix to."
146. Thimotheus von Roll, *Der Schweitzerische Botanicus, Auß des seligen P. Thimothei a Roll, Cappuc. Hinder-lassenen Garten-Künsten, Uber den Kraut- und Blumen-Garten, Auch die Spalier, Nach der Natur und Kunst eingerichtet Durch Einen Liebhaber der Garten-Recreation* (Zug, Switzerland, 1687).

Und ihm geschiehet recht

Daß er sich selbst benimmt

All die Ergötzlichkeit,

Die aus dem Garten fließt

Und man in dieser Zeit—

Auch wohl hiernach genießt, &c.[147]

Vide Gen. 2:15 & 3, 23, Isa. 51:3, Ezek. 36:35, Rev. 2:7, Cant. 4:12, Jer. 31:12, Joel 2:3, Amos 9:14, Psal. 72:7 & 92:12, Prov. 1:28 & 14:11, Isa. 66:14, Cant. 5:13, 1 Peter 1:24.

Lukas 12:27 befiehlt uns Christus ausdrücklich der Lilien wahrzunehmen, &c. und Cant. 2:1 nennt Er sich selbst Ein Blume Zu Saron, ein Rose in thal; oder nach der Nieder-Teütschen übersetzung.[148]

Een Roose van Saron, Een Lelie der Dalen;

Diens Schoonheyt de Oogen des Hertens bestralen,

Diens reucke de Voeten bevreyden van dwalen:

diens deugden de Lieden ontlasten van Qualen.[149]

vide infra Num. 213.

94.

Weinstöck die viel Trauben tragen,

Baüme, derer Frücht behagen.

Und *Gesträuche* voll von beeren,

Alle Gott den Herren ehren,

Kraut u. Blumen mancher Art,

Hoch und nieder, rauh und zart,

Bringen Artzeney u. Speiß,

Alle gar zu Gottes Preiß.

Darumb laßet uns auch loben

Unsern Schöpfer hocherhoben

147. *On my appendix to Timothei von Roll's new Flower Book in 12°* [duodecimo format].
He who does not make a garden,
And knows nothing of flowers;
Never looks back
Into the earthly paradise:
Is only a slave and a servant
Destined to the plow and to the curse, Gen. 3:17
And it serves him right
That he takes away from himself
All the pleasure
That flows from a garden
And which one may enjoy in this time and the next, &c.

148. "In Luke 1:27, Christ explicitly commands us to heed the lilies, &c. and in Cant. [Song of Solomon] 2:1 he calls himself the Flower of Sharon, a rose in a valley; or, according to the low-German [i.e., Dutch] translation."

149. "A Rose of Sharon, A Lily of the Valley / Whose Beauty lights the Eyes of the Heart, / Whose fragrance frees our Feet from wandering: / whose virtues release Folks from Disease."

Auff von ihm bestimmte Weiß. Jes. 62:9; Joh. 4:24.[150]

ade infra Num. 140.

95.

Blumen A B C.

    Augentrost gar wohl bekannt;
    Braune Mägdlein, so genannt,
    Hirne-stärckend Camomill,
    Hertz-erfrischend Daffodil,
    Licht-voll blauer Ehrepreiß,
    Fritillaria schwarz und weiß,
    Granadilla bald verschwindt,
    Auserlesner Hyacinth,
    Ihr Ionquilles bey dem Thron
    Der durchleücht' gen Königs-kron,
    Dich Lavendulam ich kan
    Setzen zu den Majoran;
    Nelcken aller Blumen Ruhm,
    Milch-farb Ornithogalum,
    Liebliches Perpetuel,
    Quendel köstlich, hell u. schnell,
    Garten-Zierrath rothe Ros'n,
    Buntgeschmückte Schweitzerhos'n,
    Wunder-schöne Tulipan,
    Und wohl-Edler Valdrian,
    Wetter-röslein rein und fein,
    Ysop, Zotter nägelein,
    Sind mein's A B C's beschluß;
    Wer mehr haben will, der muß
    Hand anlegen ohn Verdruß;

150. Vines that yield many grapes,
Trees that have pleasing fruits,
And shrubs full of berries,
All honor God the Lord,
Plants and flowers of all kind,
High and low, rough and tender,
Bring medicine and food,
All together for God's praise.
Thus let us also praise
Our Creator in the highest
According to his preordained way. Isa. 62:9; John 4:24.

So thut man mit Adam buß. *Gen.* 3:19.[151]

96.

Time's running: Running Time Gallops in every Clime, &c. Läßt sich an keinen Pfahl binden.[152]

Veritas Filia Temporis.[153]

Time the Mother of what's True,

Doth distinguish White from Blue.

Black, saith She, is no good hue.

Mother-Time as well as Rue

Gives dimm-sighted Fools their Due

That they may observe what's True. But,

If they refuse it,

And will not use it,

Patience par Force.

For, what men would not cure,

They justly must endure.

151. *Flower ABC*
   Augentrost [Eyebright] well known to all;
   Braune Mägdlein [Pheasant's eye] are thus called,
   Brain-strengthening *Camomill* [Chamomile],
   Heart-refreshing *Daffodil,*
   Blue *Ehrepreiß* [Veronica], full of light,
   Fritillaria black and white,
   Granadilla soon is gone,
   Exquisite *Hyacinth,*
   You *Inquilles* [Jonquils] by the throne
   Königs-kron [Kaiser's crown], flooded with light,
   You, *Lavendulam* [Lavender] I can plant,
   Next to the *Majoran* [Marjoram];
   Nelcken [Carnations], the glory of all flowers
   Milk-colored *Ornithogalum,*
   Lovely *Perpetuel* [Perpetuelle],
   Quendel [Broad-leaved Thyme] delicious, bright and quick,
   Garden-ornaments red *Ros'n* [Roses],
   Colorfully decked out *Schweitzerhos'n* [Marvel of Peru],
   Beautiful *Tulipan* [Tulips],
   And noble *Valdrian* [Valerian]
   Wetterröslein [Flower-of-an-hour] pure and fine,
   Ysop [Hyssop], *Zotter nägelein* [Bog bean],
   Are my ABC's completion;
   Who wants to have more
   Has to put his hands to it without complaint;
   Thus one does penitence with Adam. Gen. 3:19.
   To preserve the poem's role as an ABC, Pastorius's German flower names and his Latin flower genus names have been retained, with closest English flower names given in square brackets when the German and English names do not coincide exactly.
152. "Cannot be tied to any post."
153. "Truth is the daughter of time."

Harm hatch, Harm catch.

Nemo laeditur nisi a Se ipso.[154] add num. 201.

97.

Some murmure at poor *Time* and say, We want it;

And then of *Patience*, Oh! That God would grant it!

But let me tell those ff's[155] that they should plant it:

So God might grant it, & they never want it.

For the old Saying is, Ora ET Labora.[156]

Wishes are no Horses, nor no horse-Rhadish neither.

98.

Liebe Gott den Allerhöchsten,

Über alles, und den Nechsten

Als dich Selbst; Diß ist die Summ

Von dem gantzen Christenthum.

Hoc facias, et Salvus eris.

So nun Jemand zu mir spricht

Höchst u. Nechst das reimt sich nicht:

Denen geb ich zu verstehen,

Auf die Sachen mehr zu sehen,

Dann der Sylben Thon zu drehen.[157]

99.

F.D.P. his Epitaph.

Christ came and suffered for me, To save

Mine In-and Outward man, To be no Slave

To Sin, Nor in the world a wretched knave:

But that I should by him here & hereafter have

The Liberty, which he to his Redeemed gave

From first to last To All. Therefore o brave!

---

154. "No one is hurt but by himself."

155. Here the scribal abbreviation "ff" could stand for the plural Latin word "fratres," meaning "brothers" or for the plural English word "friends," thus more specifically referring to the Quakers or Society of Friends. Clearly, Pastorius always enjoyed punning on multiple meanings.

156. "Pray AND Work."

157. *Love God the most high,*
Above everything, and your neighbor
As yourself; That is the sum
Of all of Christianity.
This do, and thou shalt be saved.
So if now someone tells me "Höchst" [highest] and "Nechst" [next, neighbor] do not rhyme:
I give them to understand,
To pay more attention to the [meaning of the] things,
Than to twist the syllables' sound.

That (the inward man) is in Rest with God, This (the outward) in the Grave.
So let the Body sleep in undisturbed dust,
Whose Soul above expects the Rising of the Just.

100.

F.D.P., gebohren den 26 September 1651, schrieb diß folgende anno 1711:

> Komm lang Verlangte Todes-Stund,
> Du Endschaft meiner Leiden!
> Es ist doch Ja der alte Bund,
> Daß Seel und Leib muß scheiden.
> Der Leib kehrt wiederum zur Erd
> Worvon Er war genommen;
> Damit die Seel Erhöhet werd
> Zu Gott und allen Frommen.
> Ich hab in dieser Welt gelebt
> Voll dreÿmahl zwantzig Jahre,
> In manchen Ländern umbgeschwebt,
> Durch Vielerleÿ Gefahre:
> Nun Geh ich in die Ewigkeit,
> Wo Gott selbst ist die Sonne;
> Wo Er mir längst hat zubereit
> Ein Wohn-stätt voller Wonne.
> Da will ich Ihn Zu aller Frist
> Verherrlichen und loben;
> Dann was hier unten Stückwerk ist,
> Wird Völlig seyn dort-oben.
> Gehabt Eüch wohl mein Weib u. Söhn,
> Beharrt im wahren Glauben;
> Verachtet böser leüt Gehöhn,
> Und achtet nicht ihr Schnauben.
> Mein Gott u. Heyland, welcher hat
> Mich biß anher erhalten,
> Wird hoffentlich mit Seiner Gnad
> Auch ob den meinen walten.
> In Sein Händ befehl ich nun
> Mein Geist, beseit Eüch allen,
> Ihr werdet, so ihr recht werdt thun,

Ihm Ewiglich gefallen. *Acts* 10:34; *Gen.* 4:7 &c.[158]

My Faith doth reach beyond Mortality,

For though my body dies, It is not I

Nam a nobiliori fir denominatis.[159]

[. . . . .]

104.

Ad Lectorem qui Sensu audiendi destituitur—An den Tauben Leser.[160]

Weil nun dieses Buch zu kauf,

Kaufs und thue dein Augen auf,

TAUBER MENSCH! So kanstu hören

Hunderttausend gut Lehren.[161]

158. "F.D.P., born September 26, 1651, wrote the following in 1711":
Come thou long desired hour of death,
You, end to all my suffering!
It is indeed the old covenant
That soul and body have to separate,
The body returns again to the earth
From where it came;
So that the soul can rise up
To God and all the pious.
I have lived in this world three times twenty years,
Drifted around many countries,
Through many kinds of danger:
Now I go into eternity,
Where God himself is the sun;
Where he has already prepared for me
A dwelling full of joy.
There I want at all times
Glorify and praise him;
For what are mere fragments down here,
Will be complete up there.
Be well, my wife and sons,
Persevere in true faith;
Despise the scorn of evil people,
And do not mind their huffing.
My God and Savior, who has
so far preserved me,
Will hopefully with his grace
Watch over my family as well.
In his hands I now commend
My spirit, beside you all.
You will, if you do right,
Please him forever more. Acts 10:34; Gen. 4:7 &c.
159. "Because from 'nobly' is it made and named."
160. "To the Reader Who Is Deprived of the Sense of Hearing—To the Deaf Reader."
161. "Because you are about to buy this book / buy it and open your eyes, / DEAF PERSON! Thus you can hear / one hundred thousand good lessons."

105.

Ad Auditorium qui caret usu oculorum—An den Blinden Zuhörer.[162]

> Weil nun dieses Buch zu kauf,
>
> Kaufs und thue dein Ohren auf,
>
> Wann en dir wird vorgelesen,
>
> BLINDER MENSCH! Du bist genesen.[163]

106.

Ad Illum, qui Surdus est et Caecus—An den der weder Siht noch höhrt.[164]

> Weil du beydes *Taub und Blind,*
>
> Alle Wort vergebens sind;
>
> Dennoch kannstu Sehn und Hören,
>
> Was dich Gottes Geist will lehren.[165] Turn in

107.

> As often as thou dost *awake*
>
> Then Heavenwards thy Thoughts betake;
>
> Sigh, Sigh to God, & meditate
>
> Of him, his Law, and thine Estate.

vizt how things stand between the Lord and thy poor Immortal Soul.

108.

> When in the Morning thou dost *rise,*   Lift up to God thy hand and Eyes,
>
> And praise his Name, who has all night   Preserv'd thee till the dawning Light;
>
> Then afterwards begin to pray   That he may keep thee all the day,
>
> From those great dangers, which befall   Both young and Old, both great & small.

Haec aliunde recepi.[166] (These 4 lines are an other man's Composition.)

109.

> Before thou shut'st thine Eyes to *sleep,*
>
> Look up to God and cry, Lord keep
>
> My Soul and Body, and all mine,
>
> I give 'em Thee, preserve what's Thine.

110.

> When thou sit'st down to *Eat and Drink,*
>
> Then on the Want of Others think,
>
> And pray to God thy Lord that He

---

162. "*To the Listener Who Is Deprived of the Use of the Eyes*—To the Blind Listener."

163. "Because you are about to buy this book / buy it and open your ears, / when it is being read to you / BLIND PERSON! You are healed."

164. "*To Him, Who Is Deaf and Blind*—To Him, Who Can Neither See nor Hear."

165. "Because you are both *deaf and blind,* / All Words are in vain; / Nevertheless you can see and hear, / What God's Spirit wants to teach you."

166. "This I received from another." Source of these lines not found.

May feed the poor as well as thee;
Not only so, But with them share
Most lib'rally, what thou canst spare.

111.

Good God, most full of Grace, whose Mercy has no End,
Receiving Sinners still, which do repent and mend;
Grant, that I so my knees may penitently bend,
As never Thee o Lord, henceforward to offend.

112.

Jehovah God of Gods, Jehovah Lord of Lords!
Forever Sanctify mine *Actions, Thoughts & Words,*
My Spirit, Soul and Body conserva et custodi[167]

113.

Epitaphium eines blindgebohrnen:

Hier ligt mein blinder Freünd zuletzt im Tod entschlafen,
All dessen Lebenszeit als eine duster Nacht,
Voll eitler Träume war; Wie wird er umb sich gaffen,
Wann er an jenem Tag klar sehend auferwacht![168]

114.

The Law is *Good*, if rightly pleas'd/us'd,
Lawyer L. extremely *bad,*
He has the same well in his head;
But I could wish he had
It likewise in his hand!
Amen saith all the Land.

115.

Upon my Money-Scale-Box:[169]

The Lord requireth perfect Wights, Impartial & right,
A wicked Ballance he abhors; Good Scales are his delight.
He weighs our Actions, Paths & hearts; Men white and yellow dust,
Therefore pray! Never Over-reach your Brethren, But be Just!
Do, as ye would be done unto; Shun Falsehood & deceit;
So God shall recompense you there, As he here was obey'd.
Nec Falli, nec Fallere Mens est.[170]

---

167. "My Spirit, Soul and Body preserve and guard."
168. "*Epitaph of Someone Born Blind*: / Here lies my blind friend lately passed in death, / All the time of his life like a dark night, / Was full of vain dreams; how he will gawk around, / When he awakes on that day with a clear vision!"
169. Money-scale boxes were used not only to contain money, but to weigh it as well.
170. "Neither be deceived, nor is the mind deceived."

Betriege Niemand nicht!
Du must, umb recht zu wägen,
All Zeit zusammen legen
Gewissen und Gewicht.[171]
God ponders all our Goings,
Our thoughts, Our Words, our Doings;
The Outside of the Platter
Is not the *weightier* matter,
Which should not be omitted. Matt. 23:23.
But N.B.—Judgment, Mercy and Faith,
As Christ Our Saviour saith.
Even the Scales before you Poise,
And let your Party have the Choice.
Eligat Ipse Bilancem. Or Trutina pensetis utraque.[172]   adde supra num. 33.

116.

Early to Bed & Early to Rise,   Makes a man healthy, wealthy and Wise.
Früh auß dem Bett, und früh darein,   Macht weiß, Gesund und Reich zu seÿn.[173]
[. . . .]

120.

John Samuel and Henry Pastorius.

Concerning the next foregoing Leaves, which contain some of my
rhytmical Fancies I would not have you spend any time in the
Imitating thereof. For as to Poesie I give you the same Council,
Ovidius Naso[174] had given to him by his Father:
Saepe Pater dixit—Studium quid inutile tentas?
Moeonides nullas ipse reliquit Opes.[175]
From Poëtry Poverty in all ages arose,
Therefore my Children content you with Prose,
Or at least, Let Meeter-making not be your Profession, but Recreation,
Not only because Poëts seldom die rich, but also because that he is
twice an Ass that is a Riming one; and that I never knew
none, who was not a Lover of strong Liquor.
Poëtae Potum, amant & sua Pocla Camoenae, Faecundi Calices quem

---

171. "Do not cheat anyone! / In order to weigh fairly, you have to / always join conscience and weight."
172. "He himself chooses the two-pan balance." Or "He should think about balancing its pans."
173. The German is an exact translation of the English, with some words rearranged to provide the end rhymes.
174. The poetry of Ovid (Publius Ovidius Naso; 43 B.C.–A.D. 17) was much imitated during the Middle Ages and greatly influenced Western art and literature.
175. "Father often said—what useless studies [i.e., poetry] do you follow? / Even Moeonides [nickname for Homer] did not leave behind any wealth."

non fecere disertum? *Horat. &c.*

Evacuare Scyphos nostri potuere Parentes, Possumus & nostros
    evacuare Scyphos.¹⁷⁶ &c &c.

And if these Sheets should happen to fall into any other mans hand,
    I say no more but
        Read Reader, read judiciously,
        Shun implicit Credulity;
        Prove first and then approve the good,
        Judge not of things not understood.*¹⁷⁷

Job 34:3; 1 Thess. 5:2[1].

[. . . . .]

123.

Anno 1712 I made the aforesaid Dan. Leed's American Almanack¹⁷⁸ speak thus:
    My name for the present Sev'n teen hundr'd and 12,
    My dwelling-place upon the uppermost shelf;
    My Father Nick. D-L that Philomat Lier,
    Of changes of Weather a special Espier, &c.
    Who, when he has told you all what he can tell,
    Both he and his Bastard must mince it to Hell. Isa. 47:14.
    For by such like Prophets as now they have been,
    The Inside of Heaven shall never be seen.
    Here blessed Truth reigneth, and has its abode,
    But random Predictions are shutted abroad.
    So Fables & Stories and Fictions forsake,—
    Ye Almanack-makers remember the Lake. Rev. 21:8.
    Where Fibbers and Vipers forever shall burn,
    Therefore, oh! therefore poor Wretches return. Isa. 45:1.

[. . . . .]

125.

Before the *Young Masons Arithmatical Companion:*¹⁷⁹

---

176. "Poets love drinking & the muses their goblets, for whom have the flowing goblets / not made eloquent? Horace &c. / Our parents have not been able to empty out the drinking goblets for us. We can empty out our own / drinking goblets."

177. Pastorius's note: "For it is altogether Impossible, that a Merchant should be a Competent Judge about the games, Sports & pleasures of an Hunter, Or this (huntsman) about the great delight an industrious Scholar takes in the perusing of good books & manuscripts, because The first hunts but for money, the second for a Conny, This last (like Bees) for honey. Every one following his Natural Instinct, & the mighty Byas of Education."

178. See note 94 above. Pastorius is most likely referring to Daniel Leeds, *The American Almanack for the Year of Christian Account 1713* (Philadelphia: William Bradford, 1712).

179. No book with the title *Young Masons Arithmatical Companion* could be found. Either Pastorius is referring to a manuscript volume written by an Arthur Jones, or he meant another book that he listed in his bibliography

Arthur Jones doth Claim this Book,
Into which he thinks to look,
And therein to take his Pleasure
Some times, when he is at leasure;
Some times, when he wants to know
How much People him does owe.
Some times also, how to Measure;
For, Masonry lays up Treasure
By her Perches, Feet and Inches,
To a Fist, that rightly clinches, &c.
Mason-work affords me Treasure,
Trow'l & Plumb-Rule yield much Pleasure,
And the Winter Ev'nings Leasure,
To sit down, and Learn to Measure.

[..]

134.

If any be pleased to walk into my poor Garden, I heartily bid him or her welcom, thus:

Friend, Coming in a friendly wise,	From East, West, North or South,
Take here the Owners own Advice:	Put nothing in thy mouth,
But freely Fill thy Nose and Eyes	With all my Gardens Growth.
For, if thou imitate the Apes,	And Clandestinely steal my Grapes,
One wishes thee the Belly-Gripes,	An other hundred Scaffold-Stripes, &c.
Therefore, Pray, Curb thine Appetite,	And mind what I hereunder write:
Do not covet,	Though thou love it;
But without any Bluster	Go Buy a lusty Cluster.

Now, On those Terms, I give Thee leave to Enter, And Penetrate from both Ends to the Center:

But do not Break, nor Take Stalks, Fruits or Seed, For We hereby are Otherwise Agreed. Such-like Contracts bind without Seal & hand, A good Mans Word exceeds a bad Ones Bond.

[..]

138.

When Anno 1711 Christopher Witt[180] removed his Flower-Beds close to my Fence:

of non-Quaker writings, William Mather, *The Young Man's Companion* (London, 1695).
180. Born in England in 1675, Christopher Witt (De Witt or deWitt) was Pastorius's neighbor in German-town and one of the most notable individuals in colonial Pennsylvania. He came to Pennsylvania in 1704 and joined the hermit followers of Johannes Kelpius at the Wissahickon. Trained as a physician in England, Witt practiced medicine in Pennsylvania when Kelpius's followers disbanded after his death in 1708. He gained fame in Pennsylvania and beyond as a physician, clockmaker, organ builder, as a cultivator of and trader in medicinal herbs and plants, and as a botanist.

Floribus in propriis habet et sua gaudia Pauper, Atque in Vicinis gaudia Pauper habet.[181]

Ein Armer Mann, schon hat Er wenig, Ist gleichwol in sein Eigen König;

Auch darff Er auf seins Nachbarn Auen, Die Blumen übern Zaun anschauen.[182]

My Neighbour's herbs & Flowers I freely may behold;

And so mayst thou some hours, With mine still make more bold:

Those which are thine go chuse, To use or to abuse. For

This Maxim is for ever known All men are Kings upon their Own,

And there may act as they think fit, Or as supported by their wit.

       & Aliquid Boni propter Vicinum Bonum.[183]

[. . . . .]

141.

<u>People are diversly Opinioned</u>, And a Wise man laughs at that which makes the Lady weep, viz. the unlooked for Decay of one of her most excellent Tulips, even the Fools-Coat, &c. Mens Judgments differ as the distant Poles, what one approves, the Other now Controll's [*sic*].

Some Gentle Woman like delight chiefly in those Flowers, that are as beautiful as they themselves; Others bring Grocers-Noses along with them, & search for such as are of a sweet & lasting Smell. Others again, to wit Herbalists will commend none, but what's effectual in Physick, &c.

    For my Part, I ere thought, that Ladies-Smocks

        Would Scurvy cure like Holie-hocks;

But Doctors say, This side the Moon, None like to that call'd from the Spoon.

      Cochlearia, Löffelkraut,[184] Spoon-wort or Scurvy-grass.

142.

He certainly is in the Right Who <u>mingles Profit with Delight</u>.

    Hic Consitor horti Omne tulit punctum, qui miscuit Utile Dulci.[185]

Füglich und klüglich hats jener bedacht, Und alles nach unserer Meinung gemacht,

Der Seinen Lustgarten dermassen auffputzte, daß solcher Ergetzte, und ebenfalls Nutzte.

Weißt du, wie ich diesen heiß? Ein wohl ge-ordnets Paradeiß,

das gantz von keinen Schlangen weiß;

      Ein Platz recht Zierlich, Und Profitierlich,

        Welcher deme der ihn bauet, Oft beschauet und behauet.

---

181. "The poor man has joy in his own flowers and also in his neighbor's."

182. "A poor man, even though he has little, is nevertheless king of his own [realm] / he may also view the flowers growing across the fence in his neighbor's meadows."

183. "Something good for the sake of a good neighbor."

184. "Spoonwort," scurvy grass. See note 56 to chapter 7.

185. "That gardener abided by all the [crucial] points who mixed utility with pleasure."

Durch das was er genießt, Sein' sauer, Schweiß u. Fleiß Verzuckert und Versüßt.[186]

Et prodesse volunt, & delectare Coloni.[187]

[. . . . .]

204.

Before a little book, Intitled The Negro Christianized, printed at Boston in 1706 in 12°[188]

Those who're Christianiz'd in deed, Their Negroes Christianize

And teaching them th' Apostles Creed. vide p. 44 in dicto libellulo[189]

Them further do Baptize [p 46.]

Into the Name & Pow'r of God, which washes Souls from Sin;

For outward water is but odd, where Cleansing wants within.

The pure in heart shall see the Lord, Of whatsoever Race,

We're well assured by his Word, That he regards no Face (p. 25. dicti libelluli]

Be't white on black, It matters not, God looks unto the Mind,

The sin: and not Sun: burn'd spot Does no Acceptance find.

Some Negroes are in heav'n glad, Their Masters sad in hell,

The which if they no slaves had had, Might be for ever well,

But, having shewed no Mercy (to their poor Drudges here) shall have Judgment (here-after) without Mercy. James 2:13.

There is threefold Servitude, 1st Some with Joshua (Josh. 24:15) do serve the Lord which is perfect Liberty, and their exceeding great Reward is God, & with God, Gen 15:1, Prov. 23:18. **2.** Many serve the Devil and their sinful Lusts Pride, Covetousness &c. But God will recompense their Iniquities, and they shall have their part of everlasting Punishment in the Lake which burns with fire and Brimstone, Rev. 21:8. **3.** Not a few must Serve Men, and be perpetually imploy'd upon other People's business; work, sleep, eat and drink when it pleases their Masters, walk their Masters pace, and which is worst love and hate as their Masters do, and go to Church, where their Masters will have 'em go, &c.

---

186. "Justly and prudently he has considered, and done everything according to our opinion, / Who has arranged his pleasure garden to delight and become useful. / Do you know what I call that? A well-ordered paradise, / that knows nothing of any serpents; / A Place quite nice and profitable, / Which, he who cultivates it, often inspects [but also: contemplates] and trims. / By enjoying it, he will have sugared and sweetened his bitterness, sweat, and labors."

187. "And the colonist will receive profit and delight."

188. Cotton Mather, *The Negro Christianized; An Essay to Excite and Assist the Good Work, the Instruction of Negro-Servants in Christianity* (Boston: B. Green, 1706). Though Mather exhorted Christian slaveholders to convert their slaves to Christianity and treat them well, he did not ask those same Christian slaveholders to free their slaves. Mather thus stands out as one of the chief apologists for a type of "Christian slavery" in early America.

189. "See p. 44 in the said little book."

A thing most unjust and abominable; therefore Alterius non sit, qui Suus esse potest.[190] And as we ought to preserve our own Liberty, so we should not Invade that of an other.

Quod tibi vis fieri, hoc facias alÿs.[191]

The dutys of Masters toward their Servants See in the Commonplace Book to the h. Bible in 4° 1697.[192] Some use their Servants worse than Beasts, as if they were not made of the same Elements, whenas there is a Tenderness due to them, they not only being men, but a kind of humble Friend, and Fortune having no more Power over them than over their Masters & saith Seneca.[193] And William Penn in his Reflexions and Maxims,[194] Remember, that he whom those callest Slave, is thy Fellow-Creature and that God's goodness, not the Merit, has made the Difference betwixt thee and him. Therefore, Mix kindness with authority, and Rule more by Discretion than Rigour, Item, Reward a good Servant well and rather quit than disquiet thyself with an ill one, &c. Diogenes[195] being told where his Run-away Servant Manes[196] was, would not do so much as to fetch him, but said, If Manes can live without Diogenes, why should it seem hard to Diogenes, to live without Manes? Another Cynick, Servant to Zeniades,[197] being askt, how he could bear that Servitude? made answer, A lion does not Serve his keeper, but the keeper his Lion. And things thus rightly Considered, there are abundance of Servi Servorum[198] in Pennsylvania.

What Pudder of unrimed Stuff!	Some here perhaps will cry;
To whom I say, 'Tis well enough	Truth is good Poësy.
And tho' loose Prose to them seems rough,	Yet this plain Verity
Most ev'ry Ass & ev'ry Buff	With ease may versify.

[...]

190. "'Let no man be another's who can be his own.'" This is the final sentence from the fable "The Frogs Who Desired a King" ascribed to Aesop. But the saying is also attributed to Cicero as well as to Paracelsus.

191. "Do onto others as you would have them do unto you." One of the many iterations of the Golden Rule in Pastorius's "Bee-Hive."

192. John Locke, *A common-place book to the Holy Bible: or, the Scriptures sufficiency practically demonstrated . . . and explained by others more plain* (London, 1697).

193. Although the Roman Stoic philosopher, statesman, and dramatist Seneca (Lucius Annaeus Seneca; 4 B.C.–A.D. 65) was once a tutor and then an advisor to Emperor Nero, he was later forced to commit suicide for his alleged complicity in the Pisonian conspiracy to assassinate the emperor.

194. William Penn, *Some Fruits of Solitude in Reflection and Maxims Relating to Conduct of Human Life* (London, 1693).

195. The Greek philosopher and best-known Cynic Diogenes (400–325 B.C.) emphasized self-sufficiency and the need for natural, uninhibited behavior, regardless of social conventions.

196. When his slave Manes ran away from him, Diogenes is said to have dismissed the supposed loss with characteristic humor.

197. The Corinthian Zeniades (also spelled "Xeniades"), who lived ca. 350 B.C., is reported to have bought Diogenes the Cynic when he was captured by pirates and sold as a slave.

198. "Servi Servorum," which literally means "servants of the servants," is also a pun on one of the titles of the pope, "Servus Servorum Dei" (Servant of the Servants of God).

1713. Ultimo Septembris;[199] when Isaac Norris[200] did lend me Peacham's Emblems[201] & some other Books: Grata mutuò datorum Librorum Recordatio.[202] The Borrower is Servant to the Lender. Prov. 22:7. Cou'd I make Images, like Peacham's dextrous hand, Then here the word of God & Sharon's Rose shoul'd stand, with such high-flying Rimes, I underneath wou'd Scribble, that Zoilus[203] himself thereat might hardly nibble; But since I dare not paint, a. I shew but that I am Oblig'd by lended Books, in this short anagramm: Isaac Norris__ Sic Rosa Nari. So welcome can no Rose to human Nostrils be, As is thy Word o! Lord thy holy Word to me, b. And my poor thankfulness, most Gracious God, to thee.

a. Deut. 4:15 &c. b. Cant. 4:10 &c., Psal. 119, 162, Hosea 14:6.Adds. infra Num. 333.

[. . . . .]

330.

These to my Esteemed Friend James Logan at Philadelphia quæ de Fraterno Nomen Amore trahit.[204]

Jacobus Loganus.[205] anagramma: Usus bona Logica.[206]

Est Logos æterni locuples Sapientia Patris, Hac Usus Logica, discis ubique Bona.
Imprimis Christi Jesu memorabile dictum, Quod tibi vis fieri, Tu facias aliis.
Posthinc Sactorum toties hortantia Verba, Virtutem sequitor: Ne Vitiis pateas. &c.[207]
Non ceu doctorus, sed gratitudinis ergo.
Hoc Anathema dicat docte Logane Tibi F.D. P.
osor honoris, osor Luxuriæ, corditus Osor opum.[208]

Germanopoli, die XI[I] mensis, qui vel a Febri, vel a Februa derivatque.[209]

If we did reason right & perfect Logick chop,

199. The last day of September 1713.
200. Isaac Norris (1671–1735) was a Quaker merchant and important political figure in early colonial Pennsylvania. He married Mary Lloyd, the daughter of Pastorius's close friend Thomas Lloyd, and became Pastorius's close friend as well.
201. Henry Peacham, *Minerva Britanna or A Garden of Heroical Devices* (London, 1612).`
202. "I gratefully return the books and acknowledge the lender."
203. The Greek grammarian, Cynic philosopher, and literary critic Zoilus (400–320 B.C.) is noted for his severe criticisms of Homer's poems.
204. "Which derives from the name for brotherly love."
205. It was common in seventeenth-century elite European circles to Latinize personal names. "Jacobus Loganus" is Pastorius's Latin version of James Logan.
206. "Use good Logic."
207. "The eternal Word [Jesus Christ] is the precious knowledge of the Father. This use of logic is good to learn anywhere. Especially, Christ Jesus gave this memorable command, 'Do unto others as you would have them do unto you.' Next, the saints [prophets] often exhort [us with] the maxim, from which virtue follows: Do not be deceived by vice, &c."
208. "It is not just doctors [who heal], but also gratitude. / This anathema [in original sense of offering] was given the learned Logan by F. D. P. / who despises honor, luxury, and all things [worldly objects]."
209. "Germantown, the XI[I]. Month [February], which is derived from fevers or purification." Pastorius is alluding to two possible etymologies of the Latin name "Februarius."

Endeav'ring day & night To get to Wisdom's Top,

We should in stead of glass Meet with the precious Gemm,

To do to Others as We would be done by them.

This was Christ's doctrine and, if fully understood,

Is the Eternal Band of Peace, the noblest Good.

With this runns parallel what holy Prophets taught,

To shun the Sin as hell: Be Vertuous, not naught.

Old Pagan Epictet on two Words (as I hear)

did all, his Groundwork set, to wit, Bear and Forbear.

But now a days the chief and usual Business

Is to be large, not brief; An hours Task, seldom less.

And after we compare the Writings, Surely't looks,

that neotericks/new-ones Volumes are, the ancient Little Books.

In these, which have been first, we richly find, whereby

To Satisfy our Thirst; [the latter leave us dry] the last themselves are dry. paucis exceptis.[210]

Fides Doctrinaque Prisca Forti Deliciosa Palato Fere[211]

[. . . . .]

341.

Ad Ja. Loganum, cum ipsi restituerem <u>Saavedrae</u>[212] <u>Emblemata Politica</u>.[213]

Magna Saavedrae Picturas reddo loquentes, Qui simul et Vitæ Segregis author erat.*[214]

Me gratum linquunt, quoscunque remitto, Libelli: Si quis amat Grates, Commodet ille nihi.[215]

These Emblems I perus'd now thirty five years past In the Italian Tongue, here Anglifi'd at last.

As long as Babel stands, men will Translations want,

Out of their Tacitus & Aristotle cant; &c.

But at its dreadful Fall Christ's Divine Light shall rise,

And make all Emperours, all Kings & Princes wise,

---

210. "With a few exceptions."

211. "Faith and the doctrine of love are about equally delicious to the palate."

212. Diego de Saavedra Fajardo (1584–1648), a Spanish diplomat and man of letters during the Thirty Years' War, published the anti-Machiavellian work *Epresas Politicas. Idea de Un Príncipe Político Cristiano* (1640), short essays about the ideal of a Christian prince. The Italian translation Pastorius later mentions was published in Venice in 1648. The English translation is *The Royal Politician represented in one hundred Emblems, written in Spanish by Van Diego Saavedra, done into English by Sir James Astry, two volumes* (London, 1700). In communicating with the learned James Logan, Pastorius clearly emphasizes his own multilingual past (a German reading a Spanish book in Italian translation) and present (a German reading a Spanish book in English translation).

213. "To Jacob Logan, to whom I returned Saavedra's *Emblematica Politica*."

214. "The great Saavedra's pictures [emblems] speak in defense of what he also wrote in the *Secluded Life*."

215. "They [the emblems] leave me freely, and I return the book: if someone loves thanks, he should not lend anything."

Nay, wiser than once was the wisest, (Solomon,)

Pray! loyal Subjects pray, that this be hast'ned on

By GOD; For humane hands & Brains are too weak

Her Bullworks, Trenches, Walls & Bastions so to break

Down to the ground, that they there in their Rubbish lie,

An Ensign of HIS wrath, to all Eternity.   Faciat Divina Potestas![216]

* He besides his One hundred Emblems and other political Tracts wrote also a pretty little Book in Commendation of a private plantation Life, which I formerly have read, done into the high German-Language. Hoc bene qui latuit, bene vincit, in Orbe scabroso-doloso-lutoso.[217] Ich beginn aber Zu Zweifeln, ob nicht Anthonius de Guevara[218] das Lob des Landlebens gemacht habe.[219]

[...]

351.

Anno 1714 Titan Leeds[220] (a Lad not yet 16 years of age, Son to Daniel Leeds, that Diabolical Lier,) published his first Diary. ABC.

> A new Titan does now rise,
>
> Brings us Yearly Almanack-lies,
>
> Comes before his Father dies. &c.

Tom says, Oh! that my Wife were like Leeds's Almanack,

Within, three Months I might be rid of such a Pack:

No, no! replies his Dame, The priest said otherwise,

> We are & must be Joyn'd, till either of us dies;
>
> Death's hand alone can write our General Release,
>
> And change our daily Broils with Everlasting Peace,
>
> Hence, and from none besides, expect Quietus es[t].[221]

M.M. Memento Mori![222] Mors Meta Malorum Matrimoniorum.[223]

---

216. "May the Divine Power make it so!"

217. Pastorius would seem to be purposefully rearranging and expanding on a motto from Ovid's *Tristia* (a collection of letters written in elegiac couplets during his exile from Rome), namely, "Bene vixit, bene qui latuit" (To live well is to live concealed). Pastorius writes instead: "Hoc bene qui latuit, bene vincit, in Orbe scabroso-doloso-lutoso" (To live concealed is to win [at living] well in this harsh, painful, and dirty world).

218. The Spanish chronicler and moralist Antonio de Guevara (1481–1545) attempted to invent a model for rulers in his didactic text *Reloj de Príncipes* (Valladolid, 1529; *The Dial of Princes*), which became one of the most influential books sixteenth- century Europe.

219. "However, I am beginning to suspect it was Antonio de Guevara who made praise of country life."

220. Pastorius reviled Titan's father, Daniel Leeds, because he had taken a harsh stance against the orthodox Quakers during the Keithian controversy. Pastorius was also suspicious of almanacs because of their predictions of the weather and the genre's general reputation for fabrication. Titan Leeds is better known as the target of a literary joke by Benjamin Franklin, who predicted Leeds's death in the first edition of his *Poor Richard's Almanack* (1732).

221. "Quietus est" means "He is finished" or "at rest" (dead).

222. "A reminder of death!"

223. "Death is the result of bad marriages."

Dearly Esteemed Friend Griffith Owen.[224] Germantown the 16th of the 3rd month 1714[225]

My last Chimacterick[226] (Nine multiplied by Sev'n),[227]

Maybe will bring me home, to'r long home, even Heav'n;

where God our Father dwells in everlasting Bliss,

where we his Children then shall see Him as He is,

And where the holy Ghost our Spirits shall inflame

Eternally to praise and Celebrate His Name.

However by Neglect we must not kill ourselves,

Therefore pray, Doctor look for me, upon thy Shelves

A gentle Purge which can (as I do think) expell

my Fever's burning heat: So no more now, Fare well. F.D.P.

  Thy Spaw-water's Salt did me much good these two years agoe.

   Sal Catharticum sive Mirabile, Epson Salt.[228] Vide infra num. 379.

[. . . .]

Epibaterium,[229] *Or a hearty Congratulation to William Penn, Chief Proprietary of the*
  Province of Pennsilvania &c. Upon his third Arrival into the same,

For which good Patriots these sev'ral years did long,

And which Occasions this his German's English Song.

Who'f old could talk with him but in the Gallic Tongue.

  Ter Fortunatus, Felix, et Faustus ad Indos Tertius Adventus sit, Guiliellme, tuus!

Let Heroic Poets Tote of War and warlike Men,

My Reed (shrill Oaten-Straw!) does Welcome Wm. Penn,

A man of Love & Peace, abominating Strife,

To him its Welcome sounds, and to his dearest Wife,

And to his hopeful Son, his Daughter and all His,

With Cordial Wishes of God's everlasting Bliss.

The third time welcome Penn! Of good things (as we see

---

224. The Pennsylvania Quaker physician, colonist, and statesman Griffith Owen (1657–1717) was Pastorius's personal physician and one of his most valued friends.

225. May 16, 1714.

226. A "chimacteric" was a type of physical convulsion; Pastorius was never specific in his writings about his physical ailments.

227. Pastorius was sixty-three years old when he wrote this.

228. "Cathartic salt or wonderful [salt], Epsom salt."

229. An *epibaterion* was a poetic composition used in classical Greek literature. In ancient Greece, a person who had gone abroad would usually call together friends upon returning home and recite a number of verses in thanks to the gods for his or her safe return. Here Pastorius adapts the convention to become himself the singer reciting verses for his friend's (Penn's) return to Pennsylvania, his true home.

In Sacred History,) there have been often three.[230]
Thrice Balaam's Ass would turn, & thrice the Prophet smites,[231]
And three times blesses he the blessed Israelites.[232]
Thrice every year the Jews must keep their Solemn Feasts,[233]
And Solomon the Wise thrice sacrifices Beasts.[234]
His Father David thrice (an exercised man,[235]
According to God's heart,) bows down to Jonathan.[236]
Elijah stretches him upon the Widow's Boy
No less than thrice, & thus death's Power does destroy.[237]
Thrice to his windows goes my Name Sake op'ning them
And ev'ry day prays thrice toward Jerusalem.[238]
Three times a Voice was heard, Rise Peter, kill & eat,[239]
Wild Beasts & creeping things make lawful Gospell-Meat.[240]
Paul's suff'rings threefold were, on this & th'other wise,[241]
For Satan's Buffeting he sighs to Heaven thrice.[242]
Thrice therefore Welcome Penn! (is my repeated cry,)
The third time to the land of thy Propriety!
Thy Province, into which these thirty one years past
My Lot, by Providence, most happily was cast.
Here in its Infancy thy Face I first did see
The one and twenti'th of the Sixth Month [August], Eighty three. 1683.
When the Metropolis (which Brother-Love they call,)[243]

230. Note by Pastorius: "I wittingly omit to speak of the holy & transcendent Three, who bear Record in Heaven & Earth, 1 John 5, 7, 8 as also of the three Angels, whom Abraham entertained in the plains of Mamre, Gen. 18:2. Heb. 12:2. Neither do I quote, that three men of each Tribe were to describe the promised land, Josh. 18:4 nor that all the Males were three times in the year to appear before the Lord God, Exod. 23:17 nor that divers goodly persons, having many Sons, had but three Daughters, 1 Chron. 25:5, Job 1:2. Item what I concerning this mystical Number might have allegorized out of Deut. 14:28, 29; Ezek. 15:14; Dan. 3:24 and 10:2; Matt. 13:33; Mark 9:5; Luke 10:36, &c. and from Natural Philosophy, how all Elementary things consist of three, viz. Sal, Sulphur and Mercurius. But only add the ancient Latin Proverb, in no more than three words, Omne Trinum Perfectum; i.e., Of all Good things there must be Three."
231. Note by Pastorius: "Num. 22:28, 32, 33."
232. Note by Pastorius: "Num. 24:10."
233. Note by Pastorius: "Deut. 16:16."
234. Note by Pastorius: "1 Kings 9:25."
235. Note by Pastorius: "1 Sam. 24:5, 1 Kings 11:4, Acts 13:22."
236. Note by Pastorius: "1 Sam. 20:41."
237. Note by Pastorius: "1 Kings 17:21."
238. Note by Pastorius: "Dan. 6:10, 13; Add Psal. 55:17."
239. Note by Pastorius: "Acts 10:13, 16, and 11:17, 10."
240. Note by Pastorius: "1 Cor. 10:25, Titus 1:15, Matt. 15:11."
241. Note by Pastorius: "2 Cor. 11:25, Acts ch. 14 & 16 & 27."
242. Note by Pastorius: "2 Cor. 12:8."
243. Note by Pastorius: "In Greek Philadelphia, Rom. 12:10, by reason of the Brotherly Affection & Kindness, which therein should abound, and not Philagyria, or Love of Money, as it is English'd, 1 Tim. 6:10 and Juxta

Three houses, & no more, could number up in all.
No Fulness then of Bread, no Idleness, no Pride,
Where into Belial since did many-ones misguide.[244]
There in thy Company I with my Soul's delight
At Intervals might sit till mid-time of the night.
Then (as the Chearing Sun) though visitedst poor Caves,[245]
Pray! let us not forget those Emblems of our Graves.
But ever mindful of the Mercies of the Lord,
Thank Him for what He did so graciously afford,
In our first Meeting-Tent of Pine and Chest-nut boord.[246]
How be't thy Presence was withdrawing from us, ere
We understood what things in Pensilvania were
Of good or evil use, to follow, or t' avoid,
The wisest of us all was honest Thomas Lloid.[247]
Some lent their itching Ears to Kuster, Keith & Budd,
And miserably fell into the Ditch of Mud,
Where they may stick & stink; For as a sightless whelp,
So stark-blind Apostates do grin at profer'd help:
They spend their Mouths, & fain with vain words would ensnare,
Or if this will not do, scold, back-bite, bug-bear, scare;
Hereof, brave William Penn, me thinks thou hadst thy share.
And yet the second time cam'st Safe to this thy Land,

Ovidium: crescit Amor Nummi. &c. Qu. Argenti Studium vestra dum regnat in Urbe, Cur à Fraterno Nomen Amore trahit? Resp. Romulus, Abimeleck, Esau, Cain atq: Jehoram Fratres Frater habet; Gratia rara tamen" (according to Ovid: the love of money increases &c. Question: Why does the study of silver [money] rule in your city, which draws its name from brotherly love? Response: Romulus, Abimeleck, Esau, Cain, etc.: Jehoram [Old Testament king] has [many] brothers; gratitude, however, is rare).

244. Note by Pastorius: "Ezek. 16:49. The Pit without a Bottom / Brought forth these Sins of Sodom; / Ye, who Commit the same, / Are guilty of its Flame."

245. Note by Pastorius: "The caves of that time were only holes digged in the Ground, Covered with Earth, a matter of 5 or 6 feet deep, 10 or 12 wide and about 20 long; whereof neither the Sides nor the Floors have been plank'd. Herein we lived more Contentedly than many nowadays in their painted & wainscoted Palaces, as I without the least hyperbole may call them in Comparison of the aforesaid Subterraneous Catatumbs or Dens. Vide Heb. 11:38. I myself purchased one of the old Tho. Miller for 5 £ then Curr[en]t Silver Money of Pennsylvania in the midst of the Front-street at Philad[elphi]a, whenas the Servants, I had along with me, could have made a far better in less than two days, had they but known how to handle the spade."

246. Note by Pastorius: "Our first Meeting-house in the s[ai]d City was nothing else than a Lodge or Cottage, nailed together of Pine-boards, Imported from New-York, and sold a hundred foot at 10 Shill[ings]. And never the less the LORD appeared most powerfully in that Tabernacle of Shittim wood, (See mine Onomastical Observations, Num. 1606). Glory be to His Name for ever and ever."

247. Note by Pastorius: "This my well beloved Ship-mate has been no less Conspicuous for his Integrity & irreprovable Life, than for his singular Learning, Prudence & great Knowledge in things Physical, Civil & divine, whereby (tho' Deputy Govern[o]r of this Province,) he was not puffed up at all, but of an affable, mild & truly Christian Temper, Yet Zealous for the Truth, and undaunted in its defense, his Charity still being greater than his Intellect, and his Love towards GOD the greatest of all three."

Dogs, who at distance bark, bite not when near at hand.
Now I thought all was well, the Country full of Folks,
The City stately built, some houses's tall as Oaks,
The Markets stall'd with Beef, whereof we nothing knew,
When (as aforesaid,) Hutts & Wigg-wams were so few.
However, feeble things we are below the Moon!
Change upon change, alas! befalls us very soon,
Till She with other Stars & Planets (which now meet
Above our heads,) wil be the Pavement for our Feet.
Mean while away again, home to Great Britain thou
Downward th' Atlantic Sea must sail, ascend'st the Prow
Of that unlucky Ship; unlucky, why? Because
In her a harmless Lamb is carried to the Claws
Of Tygers, Bears and Wolves, who since they can't devour,
Shut him up in the Fleet, as form'rly in the Towr,
Old Baily's Bale-dock, and such Dungeons, apt to scour, &c.
Ay, sorry Turky quill! stop, stop, & say no more,
Make not afresh to bleed a newly healed Sore.
This World, thou knowst, has been most troublesom to the Best,
And so will always be: In Christ they find their Rest,[248]
The which suffices them. Job's Motto (If God would
Ev'n slay, I'ld trust in Him,) remains their strongest Hold.[249]
They can Forget, Forgive & render good for Bad,[250]
Bless & Intreat when wrong'd; both sorrowful & glad.[251]
Rejoicing in the LORD, continually rejoice,[252]
Laugh at their Enemies, and at the cackling noise
Of their Persecutors, whom (scornful Brats!) God scorns,[253]
And in His fiery Wrath at last cuts off their horns.
For after he has try'd the Patience, Faith & Hope
Of His Espoused-Ones, and they do not Elope,
But firmly Cleave to Him, he Crowns & Comforts them

248. Note by Pastorius: "John 16:33, Heb. 11:36 &c."
249. Note by Pastorius: "Job 13:15."
250. Note by Pastorius: "1 Peter 1:9. F. D. P. acer Eremi Penniaci Cultor, Te Colo Penne bene / God Almighty
pleas to Bless / Penn, and Penn's brave Wilderness."
251. Note by Pastorius: "1 Cor. 4:13, 2 Cor. 6:10."
252. Note by Pastorius: "Phil. 4:4."
253. Note by Pastorius: "Psal. 2:4."

With Kisses of his Mouth: No Cross, No Diadem.[254]

God proves first, then approves; first wounds, then heals; first kills,

Then quickens by His WORD: first empties, and then fills,

With Pleasures, which none dare Compare to any thing:

Prais'd & extolled be the Name of Zion's King!

But why do I rehearse these Truths to thee dear Friend,

Who hast experience'd them beyond what I intend

To mention in my Rime except that thread-bare Lie

(Penn in America a Jesuite did Die?)

No sure! the self-same Man, whom Gazetteers have slain

So many Years agoe, lives still, or lives again:

Loves JESUS, and abhors the Insects of the Sect,

Wherewith black Loyol did this latter Age infect.

I say thou liv'st, dear Penn, Thanks be to GOD on high,

That to the Prince of Life thou art yet very nigh;

Yea nearer, I believe, than thou hast ever been,

Before this Province was by thee the third time seen.

The third time and the last, I question not, He will

Grant our Petition, and abundantly fulfill

Thy Body once aside, It undisturbed may

Sleep fast at Pennsberry; thy Soul Return & stay

With Him, from whom she came, as those do who are gone

Already, and their Task here faithfully have done,

Tho' younger than we both. In French now Je conclus,

    Ici, et au Ciel Penn est le Bien-Venu!

    Pour en avoir de Tout, il faut aussi un peu d'Allemand.[255]

Whereas, Loving and dearly Esteemed Friend, in thy Travails in Holland and Germany thou hast heard & learned somewhat of my Mother-tongue; I hereby make bold to subjoin a few lines in the same, as followeth:

    Penn heißt auf Welsch ein Haubt, auf Nieder Teutsch ein Feder,

    Die man zum schreiben braucht; das Haubt ersinn't entweder

    Gut oder Bös, womit die Königin paar Geldt,

    Durch Hülff der Feder Zwingt, die Gross und kleine Welt.

    Nein, wanns hier Wünschens gält, so wolt ich, daß mein Feder

254. Note by Pastorius: "Psal. 75:8, 10; Cant. 1:2; Heb. 12:5 &c. W. P. Veritas Vincit, Prævalet. D. L. Diabolus Latrat. / All Devilish Lyars delight in Lurking-holes. / Vult Vertus Patere: Dolus Latere. / Whenas Plaindealing Truth Will shine to both the Poles. / Wahrheit: Wie der Palm-baum steht, / Wann Dir Lügen untergeht" (Truth: As the palm tree stands / When your lies come down).

255. "In French now I conclude, / Here, and in heaven Penn is welcome! / And to have it all [to conclude] / it also takes a little German."

Ein solchen Nach-druck hätt, damit sich Ja Ein jeder
Als ein gehorsam Glied ergäbe Jesu Christ,
Der da das Eintzig Haubt der wahren Kirchen ist;
So wäre weder Heid, noch Jud; auch kein Papist.[256]

[...]

397.

Upon Wm. Penn's Defence of a paper, Entitled Gospel-Truths, agt. the Exceptions of the Bishop of Corks Testimony.[257]

The chiefest Gospel-Truths are nobly here Defended
Against the Bishops Slant who nothing else Intended
Than by his Fopperies to dimm and darken them;
but Wm. Penn detects the Bishop's Strategem:
So Truth for ever stands,
And free'd of Falshood's Bands,
Does penetrate more Lands.
The Bishop's Vessel strands.

[...]

422.

On John Locke's an Essay Concerning Humane Understanding. London in 8°. 1710.

John Locke has had good Luck he of late did get
The Golden (long-lock'd) key to Plato's Cabinet,
Where this Philosopher Lock'd his Ideas fast, Most for Men's benefit by Locke unlock'd at last.
These Inward Mental forms, if Formed, as they ought,
Inform our Reason, and Inforce Work, Word & Thought
With Truthful Arguments; But being out of Shape,
Men Falsehood, Errors, Lies by no means can escape,
And so mis-taking take
Boke-berries[258] for a Grape.

---

256. "Penn" means in Welsh a head, in low-German [Dutch] a quill,
    Which one uses for writing; the head devises either
    Good or evil, and with it the Queen
    Forces both rich and poor to pay her money
    No, if I had one wish, I would have it that my quill/pen
    Had such an impact that everyone would become
    A submissive part of Jesus Christ,
    Who is the only head of the true Church.
    Then, there would be no heathen, no Jew, and no Papist.
257. William Penn, *A Defence of a Paper Entitled, Gospel-Truths, against the exceptions of Bishop of Cork's Testimony* (London, 1698).
258. The purple fruit of the pokeweed, pokeberries grow in clusters that resemble small grapes but may cause gastrointestinal problems if ingested.

[. . . . .]

432.

When anno 1716. William Armstrong gave a pretty little Book, Intitled <u>A brief Apol-</u>
<u>ogy</u> &c.[259] unto Griffith Jones, who brought it to me for perusal, I scribbled this in it:

Griffith Jones does ow this Book,	(He never yet Paid for it,)
As a Gift the same he took	And is not to Restore it. &c.

But the Question is, whether the Apostle <u>Paul oweth his Girdle</u> upon such or another
account? Acts 21:11.

Answ. No; because the Greek Text saith expressly, Τὸν ἄνδρα οὗ ἐστιν ἡ ζώνη αὕτη, the
man, whose this Girdle is (qui est cette ceinture).[260] And still the Translator make him
to ow it, whenas, (no doubt, according to his own wholsom Exhortation Rom. 13:8.)
he Oweth no man any thing but LOVE. Besides, I may own (or ow, if it be all one) a
thing which is not mine, and not own an other which is really mine.

<u>Love is a Debt</u>, which tho' we Pay, We still do Ow, and Ow alway.

<u>Love is a Debt</u>, which tho' a Christian pays, He still does ow & ows the same always.

[. . . . .]

451.

When, after the general or Yearly Meeting at Philadelphia (17th of the 1st month)[261]
was ended, my beloved Physician <u>Gr. Owen prepared for his Journey towards New</u>
<u>England</u>,[262] the Adversary of Mens Eternal happiness would Impudently Suggest some
distrustful Thoughts, the, which never the less by the immediate Inspiration of our
heavenly Comforter, I answered by way of Paradox, as well the better to Confound
the Wicked One, as also the more firmly to fin and fasten the Anchor of my hope on
Jehovah, the Rock of Ages, who alone is able to Save the utmost , & to restore to a
State of former health (if it be his good Will & Pleasure,) even with a Word. Matt. 8:8.

Advers[ary].	Thy Doctor goes his ways,	To Check New England's Ills.
Answ[er].	No, no! he ever stays,	My Soul with good things fills.
Advers.	He surely thither goes,	And there will teach and preach.
Answ.	No, no! his hands & Toes	Are always within Reach.
Advers.	Behold, Asides he Starts,	And Just now takes his horse.
Answ.	What then? tho' he departs	It is not for the worse,
	God some times hides his Face,	And still is very near:
	His wholsom Saving Grace	Soon does again appear.
Advers.	What strange thing now is this,	At once to go and stay?

259. William Chandler, A. Pyot, J. Hodges, *A Brief Apology in Behalf of the People Called Quakers* (London,
1694).
260. "(which is this belt)."
261. March 17.
262. Pastorius's close friend Griffith Owen went on several missionary journeys to New England for the Quakers.

Answ.	Did not the Son of his	Among the Prophets play?
Advers.	I mean that Mortal Man,	Who Med'cine to thee gives.
Answ.	And I th' Physician,	By whom each Creature lives.
Advers.	Say! art thou not afraid,	That One goes whilst thou'rt ill?
Answ.	No, no! For, as I said,	My Soul has yet her Fill,
	By him, who is All Love,	And present ev'ry where:
	Where Will does move above	My low and trembling Sphere.

[. . . . .]

458.

The 4th of the 3d month 1717,[263] Elisabeth Hill sent me the little Book, Intitled A Legacy for Children, being some of the last Expressions & Dying Sayings of Hannah Hill Junr. Into which I wrote what followeth, & so restored it To my well-beloved Friend Elizabeth Hill.[264]

[left-hand column]
Elisabeth! this Book of mine
Let henceforth (as a gift) be thine;
      vide pag. 9.
I read it over thrice a day,
Since in my hands the same did stay,
And now return it unto thee,
But twice from first to last to see
Each week, how Mother's Name Sake dear,
Thy loving Sister, in God's Fear
Has laid her tender Body down, page 21.

Hereafter wearing that bright Crown,
In Heaven for all faithful ones
Laid up; whenas both Wasps & Drones
Lake-ward are going, when they die;
Fear therefore God, Truth magnify,
Due Respect to thy Parents give,

263. May 4th, 1717.

264. Elizabeth (or Elisabeth) Hill was the daughter of Richard and Hannah Hill (Hannah Sr. being the daughter of Pastorius's good friend Thomas Lloyd). Elizabeth's older sister, Hannah Jr., had died on August 2, 1714, of a "violent Fever and Flux," and her conversations with and testimonies to her family and other Quakers were recorded and subsequently circulated in manuscript form, published in 1717 by her father: Hannah Hill [Jr.], *A Legacy for Children, Being some of the last expressions, and dying sayings of Hannah Hill, Junr. Of the City of Philadelphia, in the Province of Pensilvania, in America, aged eleven years and near three months* (Philadelphia: Andrew Bradford, [1717]). Evidently, Elizabeth gave Pastorius the book shortly after it was published.

Plainness embrace, and thou shalt <u>live</u>.

Live for evermore with those named
<u>page 10 & 34</u> as also with her, that gave
thee this wholsom Advice, <u>page 19</u>
in the glorious & over-Joyful presence of God, & our Lord Jesus Christ. So be it, Amen.

[right-hand column]
This Book here, coming back, two other such demands,
For else't had never gone out of P . . .'s hands,
Who with the like brave Stuff his Library adorns,
And in regard thereof both Gold and Silver Scorns;
Because by <u>that </u>we reap great Profit to our Minds,
But <u>this</u> (lov'd too too much,) Men's Understanding blinds.
Dear Betty! then succeed in Sister Hannah's stead,
The holy Scriptures oft, with other good Books, read,
Delight in Needle-work, Delight likewise to write,
And Letters full of Sense (as She did,) do Indite,   <u>vide page 32.</u>
So thou wilt truly be, (as I may truly say,)   <u>F.D.P.</u>
The most Accomplish'd Maid in Philadelphia.

                            Germantown the 6th day of the 3d month, 1717.[265]

[..]

463.

Allermassen ungebührlich	ist der Handel dieser Zeit,
Dass ein Mensch so unnatürlich	and're drückt mit Dienstbarkeit.
Ich möcht einen solchen fragen,	Ob er wohl ein Sclav wolt seÿn?
Sonder Zweiffel wird Er sagen,	ach bewahr mich Gott! Nein, Nein.
Warum müssen dann den Rücken	Mann mit Weib und Kindern bücken
Unters Joch der Sclavereÿ,	ohne Einst zu werden freÿ?
Antwort: Wer kan dieses ändern?	In Americanischen Ländern
Nimmet man es nicht so scharff	weil man Knecht u. Mägd bedarff.
Aber, sind sie wahre Christen,	die da nur zu allen Fristen
Suchen ihren Eigen-Nutz?	Eÿ das glaub der Höllen butz![266]

[..]

265. May 6, 1717.
266. Beyond all measure improper   are practices of this age,
     that a man so unnaturally   others presses with servitude.
     I want to ask such a man,   if he himself wants to become a slave?

466.

The Memory of the Just is blessed, and their Seed and name shall remain for Ever. Prov. 10:7, Isa. 66:22.

<u>Griffith Owen departed</u> out of this troublesom World the 18th of the 6th month [August], 1717.

Great LORD at thy Command, (when Thou doest say,	Job 4:9.
Return ye Sons of Men!) This house of Clay	Psal. 90:3.
Is soon dissolved, and the Souls then goe	Job 34:20.
From Sinful Breasts to Misery and Woe:	Isa. 3:9, 11.
From Sanctified Hearts they do ascend	Luke 16:22.
Into that glorious Rest, which has no End.	2 Tim. 2:10.
Thrice happy are all these, whom GOD does call	Matt. 25:24.
Hence thither to Himself, their all in All.	1 Cor. 15:28.
Our Griffith Owen reigns with CHRIST's blest Poor,	Luke 6:20.
Why mourn we than in Atad's Threshing-Floor?	Gen. 50:10.
Ere long we shall be there, where he now is,	Job 14:1.
(No more to part,) in Ever-lasting Bliss.	1 Thess. 4:17.
Friends, Deep fetch'd Sighs Press down,	
what's more than this.	John 11:35, Luke 8:52.

[right-hand side]
    Epitaph
What here of Griffith Owen lies;
Is only what of all men dies:
His Soul and Spirit live above
With God in pure & perfect Love.
His Name & Fame beneath Survive
With us, who are as yet alive.
His Exhortations left behind
let all and ev'ry one so mind
We will endeavour so to mind,
That they like he, by God's good Grace,
In Faithfulness may End this Race.

Without doubt will he say,
Then why have to bend their backs
under the yoke of slavery,
Answer: Who can change this?
people don't take it so seriously
But, are they true Christians
Seek to fulfill their self-interest?

"O God help me!" No, no of course.
man with wife and children
without ever becoming free?
In the American lands
because they need their servants.
who at all times
Ha! May the devil believe that!

[. . . . .]

471.

If in <u>Christ's Doctrine</u> we abide, Then God is surely on our Side;
But if we Christ's Precepts transgress, Negroes by <u>Slavery</u> oppress,
And White Ones grieve by <u>Usury</u>, (Two evils, which to Heaven cry:)
We've neither God, nor Christ his son, But straight aways travel Hell-wards on.

472.

Though some in their Descanting
Say, <u>knowledge is not wanting</u>;
Yet they to Ignorance ow
More than themselves do know:
True knowledge can't but save
From all the Sins, men have.

[. . . . .]

474.

Among Christ's Followers   Are no Extortioners,
No biting <u>Usurers</u>   Nor <u>Negro</u>-(worryers) buffeters.
All these are Satan's Tools,   Abominable Fools,
Not worthy of Christ's Name,   To which they bring but Shame.

475.

<u>Jane Fenn</u> sent me the 5th of the 11th month 1717/8[267] a Sheet full of Rimes of her own
Make; Upon which I answered her the next ensuing day &c.

Loving Friend.
Thy Rimes I read, & like them pretty well;
For they do run, but run not parallel:
One wants some Feet, the other does abound,
which matters not, the Matter being Sound.
Go thou but on! thou wilst <u>most of</u> thy Sex surpass,
And be a Poëtress, as <u>famous</u> Sappho was.

Mind, that each of these my two last Verses having two feet more than the former, are
of a different race or species; But leave out the underlined words, and they'll be of due
length.

Now forasmuch as thou hast a virtuous Inclination to Poëtry, I shall briefly observe
to thee, that several books in the holy Scriptures of Truth (viz. Job, the Psalms, Solomon's Song, the Lamentations of Jeremiah, the 3rd Chapter of Habakhuk, &c.) are

267. January 5, 1718.

Divine Poëms.[268] Item, that Debra[269] (once supreme governess in Israel,) was endowed with a Poëtick—no less than Prophetick Spirit, witness her Triumphal hymn upon the Over-throw of Jabin, King of the Cananites. Item, that Hannah[270] (wife of Elkanah,) could make Psalms of Thanksgiving. And that Mary (the blessed Virgin, Mother of our Lord & Saviour C. J.[271]) has Out-done all the Rest in her most celebrated Magnificat,[272] being the Song of Songs, on the highest of Subjects; to which Elizabeth's Well-Come (Luke 1:42) is if it were an Antiphona,[273] or (as we call it now a days,) an Intrada.[274]

Finally I here shall set down the Names of some English and Scotch women, who well skill'd in Versifying left us divers[e] good works behind, to wit 1. Jane Gray,[275] 2. Anne Askew,[276] 3. Mary Wroth,[277] 4. Catherine Philips,[278] 5. Margaret, Duchess of New-Castle,[279] 6. Mary, Countess of Pembroke,[280] 7. Elizabeth Carew,[281] 8. Mary Morpeth,[282] 9. Mary Molineux,[283] To these Nine Muses of Great Britain I shall add the Tenth, sprung up in New-England, viz. Anne Broadstreet [*sic*],[284] &c. So having inserted supra Num. 82. & p. 7 num. 2. & hoc pag. Num. 467 & 466, I concluded thus[:] So

---

268. Pastorius lists parts of the Old Testament written as poetry.

269. Deborah was an Old Testament prophet and the only female judge mentioned in the Bible. In the Book of Judges, Deborah led a successful counterattack against the forces of Jabin, King of Canaan, and his military commander Sisera.

270. In the Book of Samuel, Hannah is the wife of Elkanah and mother of Samuel.

271. Christ Jesus.

272. The Song of Mary appears in Luke 1:46–55. When Mary's cousin Elizabeth praises Mary's faith, in response, Mary sings what is now known as the "Magnificat."

273. In Christian music, an "antiphon" is a song performed by one voice or choir section answering another.

274. An "intrada" is now understood to be a musical prelude or introductory piece.

275. De facto monarch of England for nine days in 1553, Lady Jane Grey (1536–1554) was falsely convicted of treason and executed. A humanist and Protestant, she was posthumously regarded as not only a political victim but also a martyr.

276. The English poet Anne Askew (1520–1546), a Protestant who was condemned as a heretic, is the only woman on record known to have been both tortured in the Tower of London and burned at the stake.

277. The English Renaissance poet Lady Mary Wroth (1587–1651) was one of the first British women writers to have achieved an enduring reputation.

278. The Anglo-Welsh poet, translato, and woman of letters Catherine (or Katherine) Philips (1632–1664) achieved renown as translator of Pierre Corneille's *La Mort de Pompée* (1643; *The Death of Pompey*) and *Horace* (1640), and for her editions of poetry.

279. An English aristocrat, prolific writer, and scientist, Margaret Cavendish, Duchess of Newcastle-upon-Tyne (1661–1717), published under her own name at a time when most women writers published anonymously.

280. Mary Herbert (née Sidney), Countess of Pembroke (1561–1621), was one of the first English women to achieve a major reputation for her poetry, poetic translations, and literary patronage.

281. Lady Elizabeth Carew (1500–1546) was an English courtier and reputed mistress of King Henry VIII. Her husband and close friend to the king, Sir Nicholas Carew, was executed for his alleged involvement in the Exeter conspiracy.

282. Although Mary Morpeth or Mary Oxlie of Morpet is said to have been an early seventeenth-century Scottish poet, nothing is known of her actual life.

283. Mary Mollineux (née Southworth; 1651–1696) was an English Quaker poet, whose collection of manuscript poetry was published posthumously as *The Fruits of Retirement: Or, Miscellaneous Poems, Moral and Divine* (1702).

284. Anne Bradstreet (1612–1672) was the first British American to publish a volume of poetry, entitled *The Tenth Muse Lately Sprung Up in America* (London, 1650).

now Jane Fenn, my lovely Poëtess, Hear, how I did in by-past days express My Mind to those, whom I my Sons do call, who are at age, and only two in all, vide supra num. 128. The same I here to thee would likewise tell, Take't not a miss, and Fare at present well!
[. . . . .]

479.

Anno 1717/18 the 25th day of the XIth month,[285] I gave to Ann Marle,[286] who was our Nurse 4 weeks one of my Primmers, where into I wrote a good deal of English Rimes, & at the beginning thereof, that I gave her the Book, Because She Nurs'd my Daughter very well, My Grand Child too, the crying Daniel, Who when he lives this & an other Year, May for himself his Thankfulness declare: Mean while his Parents are oblig'd to her, And say that She deserves this Character:

A noble Nurse in deed!

Not ignorant to feed

New-born Babes that cry:

Moreover to apply

All useful things to those

Rest-wanting women close.

Love her, who to do right,

Endeavours day & night.

[. . . . .]

485.

Thomas Lurting & others on board with him, though Quakers, were the hardiest men to fight, yet would take none of the plunder, Th. Lurt. p. 18.[287] In which book I scribbled what followeth:

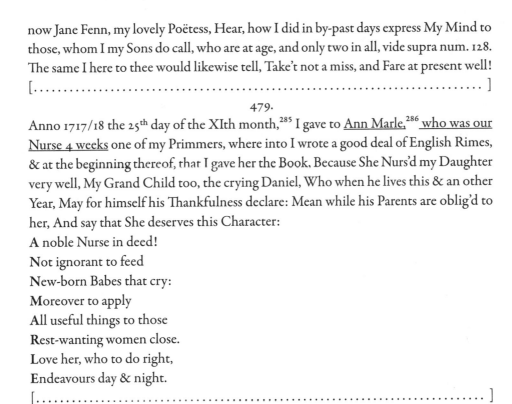

God's works are gradual:* Here Quakers fight, p. 18.   *2 Peter 3:18, 1 John 2:13.
According to the Measure of their Sight. p. 19.   Mark 8:23, 24, 25.
The Day first dawns, and Twilight thrusts out Night,   2 Peter 1:19.
Before the rising Sun does shine more bright.   Prov. 4:18.
The Lord of Hosts, (who changes not at all)   Isa. 1:24, James 1:17.
Whom now a days the God of Peace we call,   Rom. 15:33 & 16:20.
His Armies still demands, as General   Rev. 17:14, Heb. 2:10.
(In Heaven & on Earth,) both great & small.   Matt. 26:53, Luke 4:36, & 8:25.
Christ's Souldiers to His Voice always attend,   John 10:3, 27.

285. January 25, 1718.
286. Ann Marle was born in Whitemarsh Township, Philadelphia County, in 1696, married Richard Dilworth in 1721, and had two children. She passed away in 1749 in Philadelphia.
287. Thomas Lurting, *The Fighting Sailor Turned Peaceable Christian: Manifested in the Convincement and Conversion of Thomas Lurting* (London, 1710).

And from His Will and Pleasure do depend,   Rev. 14:4.
For none obtain the Crown but those that spend   2 Tim. 2:5.
Their Lives in hard-fought Fields, unto the End.   Matt. 10:22 & 24:13. 2 Tim.
                                                             4:7, 8.

486.

The 25th of the 6th month 1718[288] (when within 4 days, [taking the Nights with it,] I
Copied 44. Quart-Leaves on 43. Pages of *Lydia Norton's Journals*[289] to & in Barbados,
which she on her departure out of our Province took along,) I in great haste prefixed
these few lines, thereunto:

> Friend Lydia Norton,
> Go and Set forth on
> Thy Journey, and the Lord
> Be pleased to afford
> His Presence so to be
> for Ever-more with thee,
> As he has to this day
> Been thy sure Staff & Stay
> That many may Believe,
> On him, & never grieve
> That holy Spirit who
> Will teach him what to Do
> And what to leave undone,
> So that when dead & gone,
> They may out of the Dust
> Arise among the Just,
> & Praise our God on high
> To all Eternity.
> Amen. F.D.P.

Repent & Relent, saith dear Lydia Norton.

Thus they will be brought to the whole Duty of Man, which is to Believe in God & be
Careful to maintain good Works, Titus 3:8. to Believe in the Light, & walk in the Light,
John 12:35, 36. to Fear God, which is true Believing, and keep his Commandments.
Eccles. 12:13, 1 Cor. 7:19. &c.

288. August 25, 1718.

289. Lydia Norton was an itinerant Quaker preacher from Salem, Massachusetts, and a member of the Monthly
Meeting there. She went on several missionary journeys along the Eastern Seaboard and the Caribbean Islands,
including a trip south in 1717. She probably met Pastorius during that journey. See Pastorius's August 24, 1718,
letter to Norton in chapter 6 of this reader.

"Ship-Mate-Ship"—Poems Dedicated to Thomas Lloyd and Daughters on the Anniversaries of Their Landing in Philadelphia

INTRODUCTION TO THE TEXT

The following text is the first modern transcription and annotation of Francis Daniel Pastorius, "Ship-Mate-Ship, An Omer full of Manna, For Mary, Rachel, Hannah, The Daughters of brave Lloyd, By brave Men now enjoy'd [Composition Book]," MS 8846, Pastorius Papers and Digital Library, Historical Society of Pennsylvania. This manuscript collection encompasses Pastorius's most accomplished and sustained poetic endeavors and is represented here with minimal omissions.[290]

Entitled "Ship-Mate-Ship" on the cover and "An Omer full of Manna" on the title page, the manuscript book includes anniversary poems commemorating Pastorius's arrival in Philadelphia on August 20, 1683, on the ship *America*. He dedicated these poems about his "ship-mates" (hence the title "Ship-Mate-Ship," reflections on the condition of being in the same ship or community), to three daughters of his now deceased dear friend, the Welsh Quaker Thomas Lloyd. Pastorius wrote the first poem, with a prose preface, in 1714, sending an annual installment to Lloyd's daughters in honor of their father and their continuing friendship. Pastorius additionally copied the poems into the "Silvula Rhytmorum," the poetic miscellany of the "Bee-Hive," demonstrating that he highly valued these particular poetic compositions. Stemming from the personal subject matter and its intimate intended audience, the "Ship-Mate-Ship" poems give lucid emotional insight into Pastorius's life and circle of friends and family. They also provide a fascinating window into the lives of prominent Quaker families in the first three decades after the establishment of Pennsylvania in 1681.

---

290. We have, however, omitted Pastorius's thirteen-page verse meditation on the life of Jesus Christ not only to conserve space but also, and more important, because it is less in keeping with the personal nature of the other poems of "Ship-Mate-Ship."

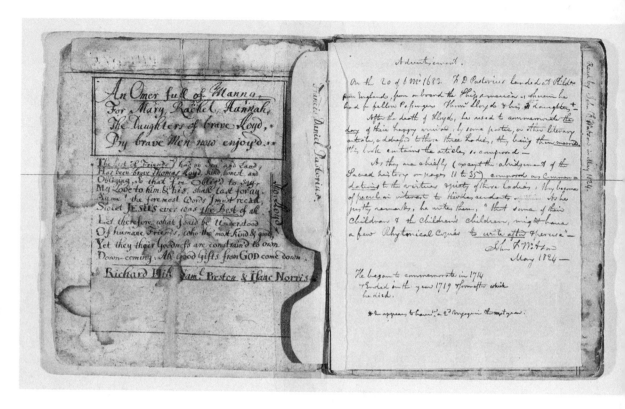

Fig. 5 | Francis Daniel Pastorius, title page from "Ship-Mate-Ship. An Omer full of Manna." MS 8846. Francis Daniel Pastorius Papers, Historical Society of Pennsylvania.

An	Omer	full	of	Manna,
For	Mary,	Rachel,	Hannah,[291]	
The	Daughters	of	brave	Lloyd,*
by	brave	Men	now	enjoy'd.**

*The best of Friends, I had on Sea and Land, as been brave Thomas Lloyd, kind, honest, and Obliging, So that I'm Oblig'd to say, My Love to him & his, shall last for ay. Ay me! the foremost Words I must recall Sweet JESUS ever was the Best of all. Let therefore what I said be Understood Of humane Friends, who tho' most kind & good, Yet they their Goodness are constrain'd to own Down-coming: All good Gifts from GOD come down.

Tho: Lloyd

**Richard Hill, Samuel Preston & Isaac Norris

291. In the original, Pastorius labeled Mary with "3," Rachel with "2," and Hannah with "1," supposedly because he could never remember who was the eldest, middle, and youngest daughter. Perhaps he also wrote them in this order to make a rhythmically better line and create a rhyme with "Manna."

An Old Proverb
Bona cum Bonis Navigatio[292]
Good Company on Sea, as I have had,
Occasions Passengers, Oft to be glad,
And makes their Journey short; tho. bad & sad.
F.D.P.

Scripta Sunt
per
Franciscum Danielem Pastorium
Germanopoli
Pennsylvaniæ[293]
1714
Born in Germany at Limpurg[294]
October 4th
Anno Domini
1651.
Pater illi Natus Erfurti[295] 21st Septb. 1624.

---

292. "The good sailing with the good."
293. "Written by Francis Daniel Pastorius of Germantown, Pennsylvania."
294. Pastorius was born in Sommerhausen, Franconia, which was at the time ruled by the Count of Limpurg.
295. "Whose father was born in Erfurt." Pastorius's father was Melchior Adam Pastorius.

Dearly Esteemed Friends, Rachel Preston, Hannah Hill & Mary Norris.[297]

The abovesaid 20th day of the 6th month called August, (from the Emperour Augustus in whose Reign, these One thousand Seven hundred, fourteen years agoe, the Word, which in the Beginning was with God, & was God, has been made Flesh,) is the Anniversary Feast of our happy Arrival at Phil-Adelphia, or the City of Brother- & Sister-Love, (the Greek Name signifying the one as well as the other,) which seems to be almost totally Eclipsed in many Microcosms thereof by that termed in the holy Scriptures of Truth Love of the World and the things therein, 1 John 2:15. but more especially love of Money, 1 Tim. 6:10. For this latter ([. . .] in between the Lord & our Souls,) always & unavoidably darkens & obscures the former. Therefore it is matter of Joy and gladness to see you & your dear Husbands still to love the Brotherhood, (1 Peter 2:17) and to dwell in Unity together: (Psalm 133) In this Phil-Adelphia I would have you to remain and solidly to ponder these few Texts, Gen. 13:8, Acts 7:26, Heb. 13:1, Rom. 12:10, 1 Peter 1:22 & 1 John 3:16. If you continue here, it will make for your Everlasting Welfare hereafter, 1 John 3:14. And besides, a threefold Cord is not easily broken, Eccles. 4:12, So now, on this Festival of ours, thinking back, and thanking the Almighty for His innumerable Mercies, (which to them that fear Him endure forever, Psalm 136 and) which have not been a wanting unto me poor Worm, ever from the day of my Birth, both in the land of my Nativity, & in sundry forreign Countries, but above all from that Instant wherein I resolved to exile my Self into Penn Silvania. He the Great Jehovah not only preserving me in this my last Journey, but also by his singular good Providence allotting me your ever beloved Father (Thomas Lloyd,) to by my Ship-mate: a Blessing & Favour of Heaven, which I acknowledge myself uncapable sufficiently to acknowledge, and as it would be in me the blackest Ingratitude (worse than that of the most unthankful Negro's,)[298] if I should not heartily Love you & every one of yours for his sake, who was so extreme kind & obliging towards me, (an unknown Stranger,) whenas some others have Reason to love (and no question do love) him ever for your sake, because ye are his own (Father-like) Daughters, Filiæ Patrÿsantes, as I might stile you to him, if he still were with us, &c. I herewith make bold to declare mine unfeigned Affection & Respect to Both, giving you the Trouble of perusing a whole sheet of paper, which I intend to fill up with Prose & Rime, though but a Stammerer of the English Tongue; However I hope, and beg of you, that ye will be pleased to receive it with that Sincerity of ♥, as it was written in. Dear and Loving Friends, Let us on this solemn Occasion reflect a little further upon the unfathomed Goodness of

296. August 20, 1714.
297. As noted above, Pastorius placed numbers over the names of the Lloyd daughters to remind himself of the order of their birth, with Hannah (1) being the eldest, Rachel (2) the middle, and Mary (3) the youngest.
298. Despite his antislavery activism, Pastorius most likely harbored the common racial prejudices of the time.

the Lord God of Israel, who with the same Arm of Power, whereby He led his people of old through the red Sea, has Carried us over the tempestuous Atlantick Ocean, and in the hollow of his hand did hide us from the cruel enslaving Turks, once supposed to be at our heels: giving us a Captain (Joseph Wasey)[299] civil & courteous enough, against whom nevertheless some of the rudest Sort of our Company murmured, in so much that they were almost ready to use Violence, as the malcontent Jews likewise have done against Moses. &c. Let us, I beseech you, thankfully consider how bountiful God has been to us after we set our feet on fast ground again in this then wilderness land, this long space of One & thirty years; (parallel with the good Reign of the righteous king Josiah, to whom the Prophetess Huldah said in the name of the Lord, Because thy heart was tender, &c. thou shalt be gathered into thy Grave in peace and thine eyes shall not see all the Evil, which I will bring upon this place, 2 Kings 22:19 &c. Now if we hitherto had, and hereafter shall have him for a Pattern in our Lives, our Ends will be the same with his, Amen). For, has not he the Lord, during the Continuance of this said Term given us Life, Breath and Being, Food and Raiment? And does he not as yet even, show'r down upon us all the Comfortable things which we enjoy? Is it not he that enlightens our Understandings, quickens our Sense, & makes us willing to run the Race of his Commandments? Pray, who supplies our Wants? who helps us in our distresses? Who inclin'd at our Entrance into this Province the very Bowels of the Proprietary, (William Penn,) So as to submit himself to each New-Comer's weak State & humerous Condition, taking all possible Care for 'em, as a compassionate Father for his unskilful Children? Has it not been the Lord? Yes surely, He at that time made us look on this uncultivated Colony as on a pleasant Field; and such (I dare affirm,) it was in deed, forasmuch as Charity abounded exceedingly among those that had any share in the Blessed Truth, Christ Jesus, whose powerful presence was frequently felt in our small Meetings, & Praised & magnified be his glorious Name for evermore! He it is that kept us unarmed creatures all along in Ease and Peace, making as it were the Indians our Charissimos or Brethren, when in other neighbouring Provinces, they killed & destroy'd many of the Inhabitants. He prospered our Endeavours, filled our Barns with Plenty, & his loving kindness did never fail us, not with standing elsewhere the young Lions were lacking & fainting for hunger and thirst, &c.

Are we not then highly engaged, beyond what others can be, to a humble & bowed-down Thankfulness unto the Only Potentate of Heaven and Earth for these manifold Blessings & Priviledges, Temporal & Spiritual, and to the utmost Diligence and Constancy in His Service, so as to wait on Him day & night, and to put all our Trust and Confidence in Him, who to try our Faith, Love, Hope and Patience, exercised

299. Joseph Wasey (or Vasey) was the captain of the ship *America* on which both Thomas Lloyd and Francis Daniel Pastorius arrived in Pennsylvania in 1683.

us with some unruly, revolting & troublesom Spirits, and afterwards by the Removal of your dear Father to his long & everlasting Home of Bliss and Happiness, made you altogether Orphans, and one of the three a sorrowful widow, causing you moreover to mourn for divers of yours, whom he the wise Gardener in their Infancy and Prime of their Youth, as beautiful Flowers transplanted from among thorns & ugly weeds into his Paradise, where they now blow and flourish for ever & ever: And one of them but lately,[300] to wit in this selfsame Sixth month, at whose Burial I was greatly refreshed both in the Meeting-house & Grave-yard; but much more, when (before we came thither, and after we went thence,) I in the Face and Countenance of the deceased young Maidens loving Parents very legibly and Intelligibly could read the Resignation of their own Selves into the unalterable good Will of our God, who gives & takes, & can give again, and is only and alone worthy of all honour, Glory, Renown & Thanksgiving, To whom be it Eternally render'd from us all.

Francis Daniel Pastorius.

A Token of Love & Gratitude

Just one and thirty years, or (says one, you know who,)
Eleven thousand, and Three hundred Twenty two
Whole Days & Nights are past, since we arrived here,
At Phil-a-del-phi-a, where ye, three Sisters dear,
In Love together link'd, still arm in arm do hold,
Each other, as they paint the Charities of old.
Should mine Arithmetick proceed, and multiply,
(Like God His Blessings does,) it would (Be pleas'd to try,
And pardon, when ye find an Overly Mis-take,), Of Minuts, Seconds call'd, most thou-
sand Millions make.

Thus long ye have been here! and ev'ry moment He
(Or if this Web of Time in smaller Thrums can be
Divided) has bestow'd some Benefits on you,
Brave husbands, Store of goods, & hopeful Children too. &c.
Oh! That my slender Quill could further set in ranks
His Graces to our Souls before your Eyes, that Thanks
Might as of one heart rise to Him the Holy-One,
And like pure Incense yield sweet Savour at His Throne:
Where with the Cherubims, and Spirits of Just men,
Your Parents worship Him, and that not now & then,

---

300. Pastorius refers to the death and burial of Hannah Hill Jr., the daughter of Hannah and Richard Hill. Hannah Jr. had died on August 2, 1714, of a "violent Fever and Flux," and her conversations with and testimonies to her family and other "Friends" were recorded in manuscript form, later published by her father. See note 264.

As we poor Mortals do, Confin'd below the Sky
To Faint & Weakness; but always, Incessantly.
John Delaval[301] with them his Strength about this bends,
And all Eternity in Halle lu-Jahs, spends.
Your Brother Mordecai[302] (I speak what I believe,)
And those your tender Babes, who left this Vale of Grief,
Of sorrows & of Tears, to Heaven's Majesty
He his Te Deum sings; they their Hosanna cry.
There they expect that ye and your Relations may
Depart, in due time, out of these Tents of Clay,
Into the Mansions, which the Lord prepar'd above,
For all his Followers, that live and die in Love,
Like Thomas Lloyd has done; whom God there does regard,
And in his Offspring here his Faithfulness reward.
Now, not with standing he for you (his Daughters,) longs,
To mix your Melodies with his Celestial Songs;
Yet I say, Tarry ye! Let me the first fall sick,
Ascend and meet him in my last Climacterick.[303]
       or L.X.IIIth <u>Year of Age, I am in, and almost out.</u>
I'm far from Flattering! and hope, ye read my Mind,
Who can't, nor dare forget a Ship-mate true & kind,
As he your Father was to me, (an Alien,)
My Lot being newly cast among such English men,
Whose Speech I thought was Welsh,[304] their words a Canting[305] Tune,
Alone with him I could in Latin then commune:
Which Tongue he did pronounce right in our German way,[306]
Hence presently we knew, what he or I would say.
Moreover to the best of my Remembrance,
We never disagreed, or were at Variance;

---

301. John Delaval was the first husband of Hannah Lloyd (later Hill); he died in 1693.
302. Mordecai Lloyd (1669–1694) was a son of Thomas Lloyd and a brother of Hannah, Rachel, and Mary.
303. As an adjective, "climacteric" refers to the effect of a critical event or point in time, critical, decisive, epochal; as a noun, it refers to a critical period or moment in history or in a person's life or career.
304. At the time of his passage to Pennsylvania in 1683, Pastorius spoke little or no English; he felt like an alien among his predominantly English-speaking shipmates. Although correctly applied to members of the Lloyd family—who were from Wales—the term "Welsh" was linked in Pastorius's mind to the German word *Kauderwelsch*, an umbrella term for a confused manner of speaking, an unintelligible foreign language or mixture of languages, which is how the Lloyds' speech must have sounded to him.
305. With "Canting," Pastorius is alluding both to the peculiar phraseology of a religious sect or class, such as the Quakers, on the one hand, and to a diabolical inspiration, on the other.
306. Using continental rather than English vowels to pronounce Latin words.

Because God's sacred Truth, (whereat we both did aim,)
To her indeared Friends is every where the same.[307]
Therefore't was he that made my Passage short on Sea,
'Twas he and William Penn, that caused me to stay
In this then uncouth land and howling Wilderness,
Wherein I saw that I but little should possess,
And if I would return home to my Father's house,
Perhaps great Riches and Preferments might espouse. &c.
How be't naught in the World could mine Affection quench
Towards Dear Penn, with whom I did converse in French.
The Vertues of these Two, (and three or four beside,)
Have been the chiefest Charms, which forc'd me to abide.
And though these Persons, whom I mention with Respect,
(Whom God, as Instruments, did graciously elect
To be His Witnesses unto this faithless Age,)
Are at a distance now from our American Stage,[308]
On which as Actors, or Spectators we appear,
Their Memory Survives: To me they're very near.
I often wish, I might their Patience so express
As I the Want thereof ingenuously confess.
Good Lord! What Injuries bore your said Genitor
Of Villains, whilst he was Lieutenant Governour?
It seem'd to me, he would his Master equalize,
And suffer wretched fools his Station to despise,
Especially George Keith, well nigh devour'd by Lice
But honest Thomas Lloyd has laid his body down
In Rest & Peace with God & now does wear the Crown
Of Immortality, of Glory, and of Life,
Laid up also for us, if lawfully we strive.

F.D.P.

Fortunants Deo, Pictus Fert Deniquam Palmam.[309]

---

307. An allusion to friends as well as Friends (Quakers).
308. Thomas Lloyd had been dead and William Penn had returned to England for some years when Pastorius composed this poem in 1714.
309. "God's favor at last bears a painted sign [banner]." This acrostic bears the initials "F. D. P." twice.

<u>Germantown the 20th day of the VIth month [August] 1715</u>[310]
Dedicated by the Papists to their St. Bernard, but
Being to us the Anniversary Feast of Thanksgiving for
our happy Arrival at the Metropolis in this Province.

Rachel Preston, Hannah Hill and Mary Norris.

Your kindness, wherewithal my last years Meeters met,
Does this new Monument of Ship-mate-ship beget,
Which, if received with the same Benevolence,
May rise as high again, & shew Twelve month hence
Some Matters as I hope, of greater Consequence,
Unless mine Ink dry up, my Memory and Sense,
My Moisture radical,[311] or my small diligence.

Dear Friends, An other year, besides the Thirty one,
(Whereof my former Sheet,) is now elaps'd and gone,
Sith we landed here on Phil-Adelphia's shore,
Our Duty then requires to praise the Lord once more,
For all His Goodness in the Plurality,
Which Ev'ry one of you enjoy'd as well as I:
This Second Paper shall enumerate but some,
In Grammar's threefold Tense, Past, Present & to Come.
I. God's Mercies over us have been before we were
Produced on the stage of this Terrestrial Sphere;
He pour'd us out as Milk within our Mother's Womb,   <u>Job 10:10.</u>[312]
And least we always should be sulking in this Tomb,   <u>Jonah 2:2.</u>
Did curdle us like Chees, and when yet raw & fresh,
Fill up the tender skin with Sinews, Bones & Flesh.
Our Bodies thus prepar'd, He graciously would give
A never-dying Soul, thereby to move and live
To move and live to Him, in whom we live & move,
Oh! That we therefore might Obedient Children prove!
Dread, love & worship God, the Only Father, which
Beyond all Fathers is most bountiful and rich.
'Tis He & He alone, that made us what we are,
And of His handywork did ever since take care,

---

310. August 20, 1715.

311. A popular medical notion in classical antiquity and the Middle Ages for explaining aging and the occurrence of fevers, "radical moisture" (*humidum radicale*) was more broadly linked to the life force that one could not replenish through food or medicine.

312. All marginal references, including all Bible references, are by Pastorius.

By Angels, Parents, Friends; Nay oft by wretched Foes,
Who aiming at the Head, could scarcely hit our Toes.
So having been (poor Things!) a Ninemonth closed in
A dark and narrow Vault (Concluded under Sin,
Old Adam's Progeny,) were usher'd, that we should
As well our Genitors, as other Men behold;
But presently we Wept, quite over-whelm'd with Fears,
Forecasting that we came into a Vale of Tears.
How be't, they kiss'd, they buss'd, & dandled us so long,
Till with their Cogging, and melodious Mid-wife's Song
They dun'd our Juicy Ears, that in our Nurse's Lap,
Outweari'd by these Tunes, we took a gentle Nap;
Soon wak'ned of our Trance, they laid us to the Breast,
The which of all the Sports (me thinks,) has been the best.
For when we grew some years, discerning Sad from Glad,
They sent us to the School, where we learn'd good & bad,
More of the last than first – Had not our Parents Skill
Surpass'd our Master's Wit, how ill alas! how ill
Would things still be with us? Had God withheld His light?
We were as blind as Moles; But Thanks to Him! Our Sight
Increased with our Age; wherefore I humbly bless
The Fountain of this Gift, the Sun of Righteousness!
Whose comfortable Beams, improved as they ought,
Will warm our fainting hearts, & grant us what we sought,
When I from Franckenland*[313] and you from Wales*** set forth,   *Francia Orientalis.[314]

       ***Cambria Septentrionalis.[315]

The one out of the East, the others of the North,

In order to Exile Ourselves towards the West,
And there to serve the Lord in stillness, Peace & Rest.
He gave us our Desires; For one that rightly seeks
Does never miss to find: A matter of eight weeks
Restrained in a Ship, America by name,

---

313. Franconia, where Pastorius was born, is today located in northern Bavaria.

314. "Eastern France." Pastorius is playing on the fact that his native Franconia is located *east* of France and that both are, at least in part, ethnically and linguistically descended from the Franks, a prominent confederation of Germanic tribes during the early Middle Ages. This also indicates that Pastorius is seeking a broader European rather than a specifically German identity.

315. "Northern Wales." "Cambria" is the Latin name for Wales.

Into America, (Am o/a rica*)[316] we came.   *Bitter-Sweet
A Countrey Bitter-sweet, and pray! how can't be less?
Consid'ring All the world does lie in wickedness.
And though (I know,) some thought that Pennsylvania's scheme
Predicted better, and would of Utopia dream,
(An extramundane Place, By Thomas Morus[317] found,
Now with old Groenland lost,)[318] where all are safe and sound;
Yet is it parcel of the Earth and cursed ground,
In which Thorns, Thistles, Tares & noisom Weeds abound,   Gen. 3:17, 18.
As largely as in that, from whence we Sail did strike,
The world, (the Wicked World,) is ev'rywhere alike.
But not withstanding He, who Conquer'd it, will keep
His Babes, that trait in Him; For else th' Atlantick Deep
Had been my Grave, whereof I might abundance tell,
And instance unto you, that when the Lion fell
Upon my Back, and when next in a frightful Storm
Once I myself did fall, there crawling as a worm,
Brave honest Thomas Lloyd has been the Only man,
That heal'd me by God's help, Our Great Physician,
Our Maker, Saviour and our Prophet, Priest & King,
Good Shepherd, Teacher, Guide; our All and Ev'ry thing.
To Him, the Holy-One we His Redeemed bow
And Glory, Majesty, Renown and Praises owe,
For what He upon us did hitherto bestow
In two parts of this Globe, especially here,
II. Where we at present breathe, which Tense tho ne're so near,
I hardly comprehend: It suddenly posts by,
Ev'n in an Instant, and the Twinkling of an Eye.
'Tis nothing but a Now, a Now, that can not last,
Pronounce it with all haste & with all haste it's past.
A Weaver's shuttle is not half so swift or fleet,
This momentary Jot has rather Wings than Feet:
It vanishes like smoke, like dust before the wind,
And leaves, (as sounding Brass,) an Echoing Voice behind,

316. Wordplay combining the Latin "amo" (I love) with the Spanish "rico" (rich). In other words, Pastorius is equating the quest for America with a quest for wealth.
317. The term "utopia," which literally means "no place," was coined by Sir Thomas More for his 1516 book *Utopia*.
318. Probably a reference to the Norse settlements in Greenland, which were abandoned in the fifteenth century.

Which minds us, that it should be carefully imploy'd,
So as the same has been by honest Thomas Loyd,
My quondam[319] real Friend, whom with this Epithet
I worthily respect, and never shall forget
His many courtesies to my Departing-hour
Altho' my years should reach to other Sixty four.
     For almost thirty two I did in Europe spoil,   **I.**
     And thirty two this day on Penn Silvania's Soil   **II.**
     Accomplish; what remains? to read, write, toil & moil.   **III.**
If you, his Daughters and Your Families, and I
With mine do follow him, we may be sure to die
In Favour with the Lord, and Unity with Friends,
By three things he excell'd, Faith, Love & Patience;
And this (to wit the last,) adorned thus his life,
That I may truly say, It/she was his second wife.
Concerning CHARITY, (the Center of my Trine,)
It did as clearly as his other Virtues shine.
He kindly deal'd with all, to ev'ry one did good,
Endearing chiefly God, and then the Brotherhood.
His Christian BELIEF was grounded on the Rock,
And so could easily endure the hardest Shock.
Sound he has been at heart, profound & Orthodox,
Opposed by George Keith's dull Lowing of an Ox,   Vox Bovis, non Hominis[320]

A bull of Bashan, who went willfully astray;
But honest Thomas Lloyd continued in the Way
Christ Jesus, with straight Steps: If we walk on in them,
We shall undoubtedly get to Jerusalem,
The City of the Saints Solemnity above,
Built of the purest gold, wall'd, pav'd & ciel'd with Love.
III. I say, we shall arrive (and that is yet to come,)
Ere long in Paradise, our long & lasting Home;
For when what we call Time, (a thing at best but short,
And to be us'd as Paul the Brethren does exhort,)   1 Cor. 7:29.
Will once be swallow'd up with Death in Victory,
Those Tenses needs must cease to all Eternity.

319. Onetime, former.
320. "The voice of an ox, not of a human."

ETERNITY, a word, whereof I fain would speak,
Because I feel, it does a deep Impression make
Upon my Spirit; But as Augustin was out
In such like Mysteries, and proved too too stout,
Reproved by a Child, that tried to transfuse
The Waters of the Sea into his little Sluce:[321]
So, if by Millions, yea by thousand Millions more
In stead of Units, I shall nine & ninety Score
Fine Bales Genoa[322] all over multiply,
'Twill but a Hair-breadth be as be as to ETERNITY.
The Stars & Jacob's Seed,[323] are without number, and
He is a Shatter-pate, that counts Grass, Drops & Sand:
A perfect Bedlam, ay! Who with Simonides
Presumes to chalk out God and Everlastingness.[324]
Let us be therefore wise, and thus retract our Days,   I.
Which from our Cradle up in Idleness and Plays,
Or infinitely worse have frequently been spent,
That for transacted Sins we seriously repent:
And take what heed we can, that in this running Time   II.
We nothing may mis-do, mis-think, mis-speak, mis-rime;
But so prepare ourselves, to have when going hence,
With us for Company a pure good Conscience.
As to FUTURITY, None of us all can say,   III.
That either you, or I, shall see another day.
And whether we survive in this our Mortal State,
One or more Almanacks, they'll all grow out of Date.
For this good Reason we commit that unto Him,
Who rides, above all Times, upon the Cherubim.   2. Sam 22:11 & Psal. 18:10
He sees the Pristine, and what henceforth must ensue,
Like present evermore: Gives ev'ry one his Due.

---

321. Sluice. According to legend, Augustine of Hippo (354–430) was walking along the seashore contemplating the mystery of the Trinity when he encountered a child who said he was trying to pour all the water contained in the sea into a small hole he had made in the sand. When Augustine pointed out that this was a futile endeavor, the child supposedly replied, no more futile than your attempt to explain the mystery of the Trinity. Pastorius has chosen this story to illustrate his inability to comprehend or put in words the abstract concept of eternity.
322. Pastorius is referring to a type of fine cloth made in Genoa, Italy.
323. Genesis 28:14. "And thy seed shall be as the dust of the earth, and though shalt spread abroad to the west, and to the east, and to the north, and to the south: and in thee and in thy seed shall all the families of the earth be blessed."
324. The Greek poet Simonides of Ceos (566–468 B.C.) is credited with certain skeptical sayings regarding the gods and eternity, which Pastorius seemed to interpret as denials of both God and eternity.

And those, who faithfully their Talents here imploy,
Shall be rewarded there with Crowns & Countless Joy.
   Thus I am finishing my homely lines, and crave
   Dear Ship-mates your Excuse, if they perhaps should have
   Been Bolder than Welcome. Fare well, remembring me
   Each to her Hus- (band, or her House – and Bed –) Allie,
  Who am your loving and affectionate **F.D.P.**
NB. Though I knew the aforenamed three Sisters above 32 years,
Yet I never knew that Hannah was the Eldest, till the 15th of the 6th month [August] 1715.
   A grievous sore Mis-take, which yet escap'd the Hatchel;
   I'm pardon'd that I gave the Precedence to <u>Rachel:</u>
   The same I now shall give to <u>Hannah,</u> whilst we live.

Hannah Hill,   <u>Germantown the 20th of the VIth month (here antidated)</u>[325] <u>1716</u>
Rachel Preston,   Whereon we happily cast Anchor before Philada.
  and   these <u>three and thirty</u> years agoe,
Mary Norris   Which those of us, who then all be alive,
ought most Thankfully to remember,
Besides what our Lord and Saviour <u>the same</u>
<u>Space of Time</u>, whilst He was in the Flesh,
upon Earth, has done and suffered, &c.
Whereof some-thing more in the subsequent Leaves.
Dear Shipmates, Loving Friends, I promis'd you last year
Somewhat of Consequence, wherewith I now appear
Six months before the Term; But read ye't then, and say:
Our <u>Shipmate</u> F.D.P. was honest in his Pay.
As for the rest, Excuse the Rimer's stutt'ring Tongue,
And courteously receive this Fare-wells Swan-like song:[326]
A short Abridgement of the Sacred History,
Which treats of Him, that is King of Eternity.   <u>Jer. 10:10.</u>
God's and the Virgin's Son, (whose years are without End,   <u>Psal. 102:27.</u>

---

325. Although Pastorius's notation would seem to mean that he had written or sent this anniversary poem *later* than the date given, the next anniversary poem (for the year 1717) reveals that he had confused "antedate" with "postdate." In the 1717 poem, Pastorius referred to his "last Anniversary Paper, the Antidating of which yields me great Satisfaction," since it thus served as "a Farewell Swanlike Song" for Rachel Preston, who died on August 14, 1716. Therefore, Rachel could only have received the 1716 anniversary poem as a "Farewell" song if Pastorius had written and sent it *earlier* than August 14 and *post*dated, rather than antedated, it with the personally and historically significant date of their landing in Philadelphia, August 20. If Pastorius had actually known about Rachel's death, he most likely would have addressed the 1716 poem only to Hannah and Mary.
326. Swan song; final gesture, effort, or performance given just before death or retirement.

Whereof He <u>thirty three</u> to all men's good, did spend
In this mischievous World,) shall be my present Theme,
Shame be to those that dare think evil of the sheme.

      Or, Hony soit, qui mal y pense!
      Au Nom de JESUS il commence,
      Et en Luy Seul il me confie
      Le Monde est ple in de Tromperie.[327]

[...][328]

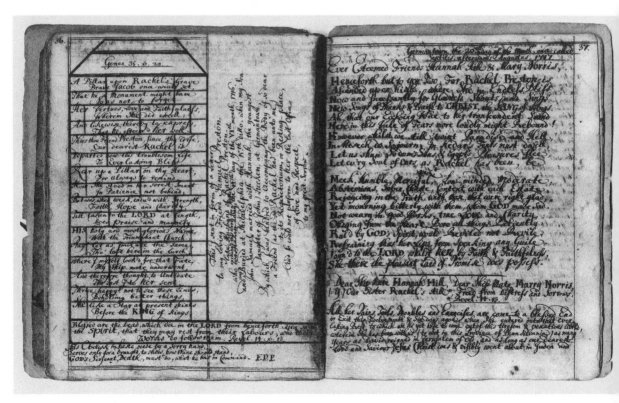

Fig. 6 | Francis Daniel Pastorius, commemorative poem for Rachel Preston from "Ship-Mate-Ship. An Omer full of Manna." MS 8846. Francis Daniel Pastorius Papers, Historical Society of Pennsylvania.

327. "Cast shame onto whoever thinks ill! / In the name of JESUS it [FDP's poem] begins, / And in him alone it tells me: / The World is full of deception."
328. Omitted here for the reasons given in note 290 is Pastorius's thirteen-page verse meditation on Jesus's birth, life, and death, annotated by Pastorius himself with biblical cross-references and other sources.

Gen. 35:20.

A Pillar upon Rachel's Grave

Brave Jacob once would set,
That he a Monument might have
So as not to forget
Her Vertues, Love and Faithfulness,
Wherin She did excell;
And likewise therby to express,
That he esteem'd her well.
Thus thou Friend Preston, Since thy Wife,
Our dearest Rachel is
Departed now this troublesom Life
To Everlasting Bliss,
Rear up a Pillar on thy Heart,
For always to remind,
How She stood in her sorest Smart
In Patience not behind;
But was, when weak, endu'd with Strength,
Faith, Hope and Charity,
Till taken to the LORD at length,
Does praise and magnify
HIS holy and most glorious Name,
with the Triumphant Church.
Pray let us Imitate the same,
Tho' left here in the Lurch,
Where I myself look'd for that Fate,
My Ship-mate underwent,
And therefore thought to Antidate
The last I to her sent,
Thrice happy not to see these Lines,
Beholding better things,
She like a Star at present shines
Before the KING of kings.

This I sent in form of a Letter
to my Loving Friend Samuel Preston,
late Husband of Rachel Preston.
who exchang'd this World for a better the 14th day of the VIth month [August] 1716,
and was Buried at Philadelphia the 15th ditto. when my Son
John Samuel married with Hannah, (the youngest
Daughter of John) Lucken, at Germantown,
By which I was hind'red to accompany the Body of so dear
a Friend (as the sd. Rachel has been unto me,)
to its Requietorium or Resting-place,
And so could not perform to her the last office
of Love and Respect,
to my great Sorrow.

Blessed are the Dead, which die in the LORD from henceforth: yea saith the Spirit, that they may rest from their Labours; and their Works do follow them. Revel. 14:13.

This Obelisk in haste made by a sorry hand,
Serves only for a Draught, to shew, how thine should stand;
GOD's Serjeant, Death, must do, what he has in Command.   F.D.P.

Ever Esteemed Friends Hannah Hill & Mary Norris,

Henceforth but you Two, For Rachel Preston is

Ascended upon high, where She in Endless Bliss

Now and Incessantly for gladness Shouts and Sings

New Songs of Thanks & Praise to CHRIST, the KING of kings.

Ah, that our Echoing Voice to her transcendent Sound

Here in this Vale of Tears more loudly might Rebound!

However, whilst we still 'twixt Paradise and Hell,

In Mesech do Sojourn, In Kedar's Tents must dwell,[330]

Let us shun Sodom's Sins, & Egypt's Pleasures flee[331]

Let ev'ry Soul of Ours, as Rachel has been, be[332]

Viz.

Meek, Humble, Merciful, Low minded, Moderate,

Abstemious, Sober, Chaste, Content with each Estate,

Rejoycing in the Truth, with those, that were right glad,

Yet mourning bitterly with them, whom GOD made sad.

Not weary in good Works, true Love and Charity,

Obeying from the Heart, Bore all things Patiently,

Rul'd by GOD's Spirit, would Reviled not Revile,

Refraining thus her Lips, from Speaking any Guile,

Ioyn'd to the LORD, whilst here by Faith & Faithfulness,

She there the pleasant Land of Promise does possess.

Dear Ship-Mate Hannah Hill, Dear Ship-Mate Marry Norris,

(Y)Our Sister Rachel's still,* Freed from Distress and Sorrows   *Rev. 14:13.

All her Pains, Toils, Troubles and Exercises are come to a blessed End or Exit, this Twelve Month & Six days agoe, when she entered into that everlasting Rest, to which we as yet hope to come out of this tiresom & vexatious world, wherein She has been with us (to act in this Province of Pennsilvania,) as many years as David reigned in Jerusalem of Old, and as long as our dearest Lord and Saviour Jesus Christ was & visibly went

329. August 20, 1717.
330. Psalm 120:5. "Woe is me, that I sojourn in Mesech, that I dwell in the tents of Kedar!" Both Mesech (or Meshech) and Kedar were places far from Israel, among its enemies.
331. The wickedness and destruction of the proverbially sinful city of Sodom are described in Genesis 19:1–26. Though seen as a place of oppression, Egypt and its wealth also presented a temptation for abandoning the true faith.
332. In the Book of Genesis, Rachel was Jacob's favorite wife.

about in Judea and Galilee, whereof I wrote more fully unto you in my last Anniversary Paper, the Antidating[333] of which yields me great Satisfaction, seeing the same proved a-la-mi-ra of mine unto her, a Farewell Swanlike Song, sung by a Stuttering Tongue.

It's to day 34 years, since the only good God, by his all governing Arm of Power has safely landed us at Philadelphia, thereby putting a Period to our Ten-weeks Ship-Mate-Ship; During which Term I comfortably enjoyed the delightful Conversation of your ever beloved Father Thomas Lloyd, who now likewise reigns with Him, with whom he suffered; Yet for all this, going from on board of our Vessel, I was every whit as glad as the Apostle Paul's 275 Shipmates ever could have been at their Accoasting[334] in the Island Melita or Malta, whose modern bloody Inhabitants are infinitely worse than those ancient Barbarians who shewed to the said Apostle & his Companions no little kindness.[335]

But not withstanding our happy Arrival at Philadelphia, we are still Ship-mates, Fellow-pilgrims and Seafaring Travellers, on an over-worn & wrotten Ship, where Life and Death are but about 3 or 4 Inches distant, and that in the midst of the boisterous Ocean of Vanity and Wickedness: tossed with Storms, Surrounded with Pirates, and endanger'd by many Flats, Sands, Shallows and Rocks, not to mention other Ill conveniences, Difficulties and Perils, we often must struggle within the raging Deep, somewhere altogether unsailable.

Pray! what would we not have given, if Joseph Wasey, at our former crossing of the Atlantick Plain, had been able to set us ashore when (the 26th day of the 5th month 1683.[336]) mistaking a French Merchantman for a Turkish Caper, we were in a panick Fear, every Mother's Child of us, from the Cabbin-boy to the aforesaid Captain himself. Or when (the 2nd and 12th of the then next ensuing 6th month,) our Ship was covered with a multitude of huge surges, and as it were with Mountains of terrible and astonishing waves? To which Tempest that of the 9th day in the precedent 5th month was but a gentle Fore-runner, & never the less more hurtful to me than these two latter ones; as I cursorily hinted to you, Anno 1715.

Now returning to our present Journey, and last, still lasting Ship-Mate-Ship, Although we meet by the way with frightful Sea-Monsters, Mer-maids, &c. and frequently must weather the Fury of towering & merciless Billows, upon mouldy bread,

333. See note 325.
334. "Accoasting": from "to coast,"—"to sail by the sea-coast, skirt the shore; to sail in sight of land."
335. Acts 28:2 relates that the Apostle Paul and the Evangelist Luke, after being shipwrecked on the coast of the Mediterranean island of Malta, were received by "the barbarous people" with "no little kindness: for they kindled a fire, and received us every one, because of the present rain, and because of the cold." By "modern bloody Inhabitants," Pastorius probably means the Catholic Knights of Malta, who earned a bad reputation as maritime mercenaries during the seventeenth century, as opposed to their earlier renown as defenders of the faith against the Ottoman Empire.
336. July 26, 1683.

[…] Beer and stinking water, (the World's usual Provision for the Followers of Christ,) yet let us take Courage, and hold ourselves Content, It will be Better, when we come Home, into New Jerusalem, whitherwards we (as Citizens, Burgesses or Free Men and Free Women thereof,) are bound, and direct our Course, the which some finish to day, and others to morrow. Blessed are they, that without making Shipwrack of Faith & a good Conscience speedily do reach into this their desired Haven, there to receive the Crown of Righteousness, &c.

Oh, what matters of unspeakable Joy would it have been to me, if my late Sickness had minist'red an Entrance unto my never dying Soul into that magnificent heavenly City, emphatically and at large described, Rev. 21. For to tell you the Truth, I should abundantly rather like the Company of Saints, departed & among them of our dear Parents & near Relations, than of these on this Side of the Grave who still must complain to be in a strange Countrey, and Absent from the Lord; Howsoever, Passengers, (especially such, whose Fraight their Friend has paid,) ought not to leap over Board, but with Patience to wait the Master's Time, till he send his Boat, in order to fetch them, or any of them, away to their Eternal Mansions.

Mean while let us thankfully acknowledge the Goodness of our God, that he appoints us his Only Son for a Pilot or Steers-man, whose divine Grace, by the compass of his Word, & the Sea-c[h]arts of holy Writ, will surely Introduce us into the abovesaid Glorious Port of Endless Felicity, if we faint not in Well-doing, but keep our Confidence fast to the END.

He that would Happy be, and that for ever,
A Godly Life to lead ought to endeavour
Not Wealth, but Learning } makes { Mankind Compleat
Not Birth, but Vertue } makes { Us truly Great.
All Worldly things are Fading, as we See,
Here's nothing Certain but Uncertainty.
How Soon can GOD a pleasant Calm transform
Into a Hurricane, or dreadful Storm!
Let us avoid all Sin, whilst GOD gives Breath,
Least we should need to Fear, or Wish for Death.

Misspend not pretious Time, but mind to make
A quick dispatch of what you undertake.
Remember well, and ever bear in Mind,
Your Blessing you in JESUS CHRIST must find.
Now Let us seek true Wisdom to obtain,

Our present Pain will prove our future Gain.
Refuse to act to day, whereat to morrow
Repentance follows, Or Eternal Sorrow.
In all the Firmament no Sun but One,
So GOD admits no Equal on His Throne.

Repent and mend! that you to GOD may give
A glad Account, how you on Earth did live.
Consult, Believe, Obey. His Light within,
Hereby you'll Overcome the Devil, World & Sin.
Esteem unchanging Truth your chiefest Treasure,
Let knowledge Practis'd be your only Pleasure.
Pilgrims, trudge on; Yet do not trust all Friends,
Rather depend upon your Finger's Ends.
Expell all evil Thoughts, or keep them Low,
So more and more of GOD's Will you will know.
The Sun of Righteousness for ever shines
On upright Peoples ♥♥, and these combines:
None but Sweet JESUS them to Him inclines.

These next foregoing 33 lines of other Men's Composition I was willing to adopt, and then send them to you as mine own,[337] 1st that, for as much as at this very Instant a sort of Scotomy, Megrim, Vertigo, Dizziness, or Swimming of the head renders me [. . .] quite unfit for Meditation & Poetry; this Sheet may still be fill'd up there with. 2dly that by the number of so many Letters, as Spell the three most amiable Female Names in the whole Scripture you should always know without Books how many years dear Rachel has been with us in America, and 3dly that some of your Children, & the Children's Children of her, might have a few Rhythmical Copies [. . .] [. . .]. Neither would it be amiss, if our loving Friend Samuel Preston had the Perusal thereof, because his quondam Comfort and help-meet and Second-Self was mostly in the Eyes of him that scribbl'd them, to wit, of your ever Obliged F.D.P. who within twice 3 weeks will be twice 33 years old.

337. Pastorius did not include the lines he borrowed from other writers in the extant copy he made of the anniversary poems sent to the Lloyd sisters.

Worthy and Eternally Beloved Friends & Ship-Mates Hannah Hill & Mary Norris,

I made bold these four years running (or rather run, elaps'd and gone,) to send you some annual petty and pitiful Memorandums on the above mentioned Date, which was in 1683, the fortunate day of our arrival at Philadelphia, then consisting of 3 or 4 little cottages, all the Residue being only Woods, Underwoods, Timber and Trees, where among I several times have lost myself, travelling no farther than from the waterside to the house (now of our Friend William Hudson,[339]) then allotted to a Dutch Baker, whose Name was Cornelis Bom.[340] What my Thoughts were of such a renowned City, (I not long before having seen London, Paris, Amsterdam, Gandt, &c.) is needless to rehearse unto you here; But what I think now of the same I dare Ingenuously say, viz. that God omni-benevolent has made of a desert and wilderness an enclosed and well-watered GARDEN, & the Plantations about it a fruitful Field. If the owners thereof neglect Thankfully to acknowledge the Lord's great Bounty towards them, His long-suffering hand will certainly place it on their Account, He hating nothing worse than Ingratitude & Idolatry. Rom. 1:21. Col. 3:5. &c. However let others do as they please, we and our Families ought to praise & magnify Him, who most graciously preserved us these 35 years in this Province, which Term being Compleated today puts an End to a sort of a Climacterick, (5 times 7 is 35) commonly somewhat dangerous to old people, as it proved to me, and still keeps mine Outward man very low & weak, in so much, that I made no Reckonning to Survive this our Anniversary Festival, and therefore prepared nothing a fresh for so dearly Esteemed & well-deserving Friends. Nevertheless (not withstanding the trivial or trifling School,[341] I of late am occupied in again,) shall find a piece of cold Meat, Cheese and Apple-pye, for to satisfy you both, and so beg your Favour, to feed heartily upon it, there being no more than 35 Distichs[342] for each, because I'm unwilling to go beyond the number of the 35 years we spent in this Countrey, (you in Philadelphia aforesaid, & I at Germantown, the one as well as the other being denominated from Brother- & Sister-hood,) or above the 35 cubits height of the two pillars, which Solomon, the Superlative wise king of Israel erected before the Temple in Jerusalem. Out of what Quarrie he digged his Materials,

---

338. August 20, 1718.

339. William Hudson (1664–1742) was an early Quaker settler in Philadelphia, where he established a tannery. Hudson would become prominent in the political and religious life of Pennsylvania.

340. Cornelius Bom (d. 1688) opened a bakery in early Philadelphia; his account of settling in Pennsylvania, *Missive van Cornelis Bom, Geschreven uit de Stadt Philadelphia in de Provintie van Pennsylvania. . .* , was published in Rotterdam in 1685.

341. The Germantown Court school, which Pastorius himself founded in 1702.

342. Frequently used in Greek and Latin elegiac verse, a "distich" consists of two successive lines, generally rhymed and self-contained in meaning.

I can't tell, mine are taken from my GARDEN-Recreations, which were the chiefest I in Pennsilvania had Externally: the Rest have been but sad and bad.

The 35 two lined verses in the last Page of this my yearly sheet are added in Remembrance of our dear Rachel Preston, who these 2 years agoe sowed her terrestrial, natural & corruptible body, in order that so noble a grain of wheat in the plenteous Resurrection-harvest shall produce an Angelical, Spiritual & Everlasting One, Shining as the Brightness of the Firmament &c. May the almighty & alone good GOD be pleased to perpetuate health, peace & prosperity in your dwellings, to your dearest husbands, children & Relations, not only the next Ensuing Twelve-Month but all the days of your Life, and then (after you have laid down your heads in Rest with Him,) that Blessing of the pure in ♥, to laud & celebrate his holy Name for Ever and Ever, is the fervent Prayer of your ancient Friend F.D.P.

I. The Origin and Progress of Plantation-Work

1. GOD having created by Power of Pow'rs	Eph. 3:9, Col. 1:16.A
numberless number of Beautiful Flow'rs,	Gen. 1:11.
2. Was pleased in Eden a Garden to plant,	Gen. 2:8, 15, 2 Esdr. 3:6.[343]
And freely to Adam the Proto plast[344] grant,	
3. To have and to hold it, & keep it from weeds,	Job 31:40.
Who hearkning to Chavah's[345] sweet Rhetorick feeds	Gen. 3:6, 12,
	1 Tim. 2:14.
4. On apples forbidden. Thus sadly does fall,	Ibid. v. 24.
And loses this primitive Garden, and all.	
5. Now nothing than Thistles and Thickets can own,	Gen. 3:18, 23.
Who of a great Monarch is turned a Clown,	
6. And all his Posterity wicked and proud	Psal. 14:3.
Disowned and Drowned, Sins crying aloud.	Gen. 7:23, 2 Peter 2:5.
7. However just Noah obtained that grace,	
To stock a new world: continue man's Race.	Gen. 6:8.
8. Soon after the Deluge (expecting to get	
some Comfort in Troubles,) a vineyard he set	Gen. 9:20, Psal. 104:15.
9. And dress'd it, no question, like Adam his Field,	Isa. 5:4.
Which therefore but dangerous Clusters could yield:	Deut. 32:32.
10. Oh! hereof poor old man redoubling a dram,	

---

343. The Second Book of Esdras, 2 Esdras, is more commonly known as the "Book of Nehemiah."

344. "Protoplast": the first thing or being of its kind; an original, an archetype; specifically, Adam as first member or progenitor of the human race.

345. The Hebrew name for Eve, Chavah means "mother of all life." Pastorius, however, seems to fall prey to Bible interpretations that blame Eve/Chavah for Adam's fall.

Was fuddel'd, his Nakedness seen by Ham.   Gen. 21:22 (Prov. 33:32).

11. But Abraham, fearing God, planted some Trees,
    To worship his Maker on bowed-down knees.   Ibid. v. 33.

12. Much profit of plough-lands to Isaac did come,   Gen. 26:12. & 24:63.
    Where musing, he walked, when weary at home.

13. Hence Jacob sent Almonds, Nuts, Spices and Balm   Gen. 43:11.
    The Anger of Pharaoh's lieutenant to calm.

14. Job's substance were Camels and Asses, yet still   Job 1:3, 14.
    His young men with Oxen his acres must till.

15. The offspring of Shelah supplied their wants,   1 Chron. 4:23.
    By Earthen-ware baking, 'mongst hedges & plants.

16. Wise Solomon Gardens of Pleasure did make,   Eccles. 2:5, 1 Kings 11:3.
    For his, and his Consorts and Concubines sake.

17. Uzziah in Carmel husbanded the Earth,   2 Chron. 26:10.
    Which lying neglected breeds Famine and Dearth.   Prov. 20:4.

18. Of Jojakim's Garden in Babel we read,   See her History
    That honest Susanna, tho' guiltless in deed,   among the Apocrypha[346]

19. Was judged, condemned, and ready to die,
    But saved by my Name-Sake, God, hearing her cry.

20. This city Semiramis closed with walls,[347]   For the rest vid. Some
    Much higher and thicker than houses and halls.   Classical Authors,

21. Whereon she made orchards, and therein did jest,   now not in my hands.
    Six coaches upon them could travel a Breast.

22. And when there poor Israel in Thraldom must toil,
    God bids them plant gardens & manure the soil,   Jer. 29:5.

23. With promise, that when they not longer should slave,
    Their proper Plantations in Jewry to have.   Amos 9:14.

24. King Cyrus of Persia[348] (oh, glorious pelf!)

346. The Apocrypha are biblical texts whose authenticity or canonicity has been a matter of debate; as one these texts, the Book of Susanna is usually added to the Book of Daniel in the Catholic Bible but not in the Protestant one. While bathing in her garden, Susanna, the wife of Joachim, is accosted by two elders who threaten to accuse her of promiscuity unless she agrees to have sex with them. When she refuses to be blackmailed, Susanna is put on trial and sentenced to death but, at the last moment, she is saved by the intercession of the wise Daniel; the plot of the elders is exposed.

347. According to the Greek historian Diodorus (fl. first century B.C.), the Assyrian Queen Semiramis, who succeeded her husband, King Ninus, restored ancient Babylon and had a brick wall built around the city. Pastorius does not repeat often told accounts of Semiramis as a harlot (Dante famously counts her among the lustful in the *Inferno*).

348. Cyrus the Great of Persia (ca. 600–530 B.C.) built gardens in his capital city of Pasargad that were designed to create a paradise on earth. Weary of his administrative roles in the Frankfurt Land Company and various public positions in Germantown, Pastorius enumerates and thus expresses his affinity for several historical or

Was howing and sowing in gardens himself.

25. Augeas, a Grecian Prince, dunged his own,[349]
Diocletian abandon'd th' Imperial Crown,

26. Exchanging the Sceptre for a weeding-hook, and
Preferring the Harrow to Clubs of Command.[350]

27. Whole Asia's Diadem, glist'ring and deft,
(Retiring to Garden-work,) Attalus left.[351]

J.W.'s Systema Agriculturae
Prefat.[352]
Saavedra's Emblems[354]
Vol. 2ᵈ p. 379.
Wᵐ Penn's N.C.N.C.
p.m. 560.[355]

28. Attilius Calatinus[353] (Dictator of Rome,

His dignity quitting, was digging at home.

29. And Carolus Quintus[356] a Frier's coarse Cowl
with Garden-tools used, to Solace his Soul.

30. Brave Cowlay but lately has plaid for the nonce
The Gard'ner and Poet near Barnelm's at once.[357] &c.

31. So, since the Almighty, and all those said men
Were Terri-Cultores,[358] what wonder you then?

32. That F.D.P. likewise here many hours spends,

And having no Money, on Usury lends

Num. 4:6.
So follow God
and good Men
is our Duty
without Quotations.[359]
Matt. 13:8.

33. To's Garden and Orchard and Vinyard such Times,
Wherein he helps Nature, & Nature his Rimes.

34. because they produce him both Victuals & Drink,

---

mythological leaders or rulers who balanced their public lives with a retreat into their gardens, who favored them over their duties as rulers—or who even retired there.

349. In Greek mythology, as owner of the largest number of cattle in the country, Augeas was infamous for never cleaning his immense stables, a task that became one of the labors of Heracles.

350. The only Roman emperor to retire from his position, Diocletian (ca. 244–311) spent much of his retirement tending to his vegetable gardens.

351. The last king of the Greek city-state of Pergamon, Attalus III (170–133 B.C.) neglected his kingdom in favor of gardening and the study of botany and medicine.

352. John Worlidge, *Systema Agriculturae, the Mystery of Husbandry Discovered* [. . .] (London, 1669), preface.

353. Aulus Atilius Calatinus (d. ca. 216 B.C.) was a consul and general in the Roman Republic.

354. Diego de Saavedra Fajardo (1584–1648) published a book of emblems relating the ideal of the Christian prince, titled *Epresas Políticas. Idea de un Príncipe Político Cristiano* (1640).

355. William Penn, *No Cross, No Crown* (London, 1682).

356. Charles V (1500–1558), Holy Roman Emperor and King of Spain. Late in life, Charles abdicated and retired to a monastery, where he took up gardening as a friar.

357. In 1663, the English poet Abraham Cowley (1618–1667) moved to a house in Barn Elms, historically an open parkland right outside London.

358. "Cultivators of the earth."

359. Pastorius is poking fun here at his own predilection for excessive marginal quotations.

Both Med'cine & Nose-gays, both Paper and Ink* *Tumerick and Elderleaves ⎫

35. Moreover beholding his Mother, the Dust,   of which my scribbling

                         hand receives ⎬

He after his Heav'nly Father does last. Red and Green, As here is seen.[360]

Flos Dos, Post hortum Fessus Desidero Portum.[361]   Verte.[362] ⎭

II. The Improvement of Ourselves on Plantations

1. When Mundanists[363] let Crawl & Sprawl their Thoughts upon the Ground,

                          Phil. 3:19.

 To God on High I mine do raise, and Heaven-wards have bound; Col. 3:1.

2. Some times it seems mine Eyes & Hands to Earthly Objects bow, 2 Thess. 3:12.

 And yet my Spirit, ♥ and Mind by no means stand below. Phil. 3:20.

3. All Trees, Shrubs, Herbs, Flowr's, Plants & Weeds are but my Microscope,

                          Psal. 19:2.

 To spy God's Wisdom and Great Pow'r, when Moles and blind men grope.

                          Rom. 1:20.

4. As many Grasses I look in Meadows, Orchards, Fields, Matt. 6:28, 30.

 They all are living Letters, and each one, a Syllable yields, Isa. 42:11, 12.

5. By which, as in a Primmer, I do spell, Praise e the Lord, Psal. 148.

 Praise ye His blessed, holy name: Praise Him with one Accord! Acts 4:24.

6. Then whether I base Mushrooms see, or Oaks and Cedars tall,

 I read, you've both your Growth of Him, who worketh all in all. Psal. 104:14.

7. Beholding now a Mustard-bush, I 'dmire its Fruitfulness, Matt. 13:32.

 And read, an Apple-tree bears much, yet I do bear no less. Mark 12:41.

8. Next sitting in the shadow of a Plane-tree, Elm or Lime, Isa. 30:2.

 I read, we're barren & make men here Idly spend their Time. Ezek. 16:49.

9. However, some may bring forth Fruits, and still be empty Vines, Hosea 10:1.

 Because they with Demetrius make only Idol-Shrines Acts 19:24.

10. Worse is the Field of Slothful Folks, with Mettles Over-grown, Prov. 24:30.

 Whereon I read, Those are stark mad, who thus neglect their Own, Cant. 1:6.

11. And do not, when they should, destroy the Catter-pillars Nest, Psal. 137:9.

360. The words "Tumerick," "Elderleaves," "Red," and "Green" are underlined with red and green ink made from tumeric and elder leaves.

361. "Flower gift[;] worn out after [working in] the garden, I desire a port [haven]." Pastorius seems to envision, for the conclusion of the first section of this poem, a scene of himself returning to his home with a flower gift, perhaps for his wife, while longing for some respite from the tiring work—which, of course, means both gardening and writing poetry. "Portum" could also be a pun on port wine a glass of which he desires for his relaxation.

362. "Turn [the page]"; the next section started on the next manuscript page.

363. "Mundanists": those who value the pragmatic and material elements of the world above the spiritual and religious.

Nor cut the suckers off the Roots; But fold their hands and rest.   James 1:21.

12. The Exit of which Laziness is blasting Poverty,   Prov. 9:15 and 24:ult.[364]

    The Bridwell[365] or the Hospital, and endless Misery.   Matt. 25:12, Isa 1:28.

13. With goodly Gard'ners 't is not so, they can endure no Tares,   Gal. 5:24.

    No Brambles, Thorns, nay nothing, which with good Stuff interferes.

        2 Tim. 4:18.

14. They keep their gardens close & clean, well fenc'd, well dung'd & free,

        Num. 24:6.

    It yields all profit or delight, whatever you there see.   Jer. 31:12, Ezek. 36:35.

15. The poisonning Toads & hurtful Beasts therein can find no place,   Ezek. 34:25.

    No Wolfbane,[366] Hemlock,[367] or what else annoys, may have increase;

        Mark 16:18.

16. For, they remember very well, what of Christ's Church is said,   Isa. 58:11.

    How that should be, & what they do in holy Scriptures read.   Eph. 5:27,

        Phil. 2:15

      1 Peter 3:13 & 2 Peter 3:14 &c.

17. Our Lord & Master Jesus Christ would frequently Compare   Matt. 13:2,

        John 15:1.

    God to a Planter, who of his does take the utmost Care.   Isa. 5:2.

18. And he himself did oftentimes meet with his little Flock   John 18:1.

    In Mountains, Gardens, Wastes & Fields, (to follow whom Priests mock.)

        Matt. 5:17 & 2 Tim. 3:6.

19. His bloody Sufferings He began within Gethsamene's Plain,   Matt. 26:36.

    That He to fallen mankind might lost Paradise regain.   Gen. 3:24, Col. 1:20.

20. Near Golgatha a Garden was, in which they buried Him,   John 19:41.

    Here He the Lord did lie between Cherub- and Seraphim.   John 20:12.

21. And after He victoriously out of the Grave arose,   Col. 2:15, Exod. 15:1.

    He plaid the homely Gardener, as Mary did suppose.   John 20:15.

22. We, that by Him are call'd must be like He was in this World,   1 John. 4:17.

    Of Satan & his Instruments afflicted, toss'd and hurl'd.   John 16:33.

23. Bad Lawyers, Pharisees & Scribes have done, and do their best,   Luke 11:45.

    Or rather worst, that Lillies may by Briers be opprest.   Cant. 2:2, 2 Tim. 3:12.

24. They can not cease to persecute Christ, & those of his School,   1 Thess. 2:15.

---

364. "Last," here the last verse of Proverbs 24, that is, Proverbs 24:34.

365. Bridewell: house of correction for prisoners; place of forced labor.

366. Wolfbane (*Aconitum lycoctonum*), is a poisonous plant with dull yellow flowers, occurring in mountainous regions in Europe.

367. Hemlock (*Conium maculatum*), a poisonous plant having finely divided leaves and small white flowers, was used medicinally as a powerful sedative.

Nickname Emmanuel Beelzebub,[368] & the most wisest Fool.   Matt. 10:25,
John 10:20.

25. How be't, when these are burnt with Heat, & blacken'd by the Sun,   Job 30:30.
The Heav'nly Dew refreshes them; they smell like Libanon.   Hosea 14:5.

26. With Wicked-Ones 't is otherwise, they for a while here flow'r;   Psal. 103:15,
Job 8:13.

But wither unexpectedly, & perish in one hour.   Prov. 6:15, Rev. 18:19.

27. They fall, & never are no more, except there in that Lake,   Ezek. 28:19.
The which with Fire & Brimstone flames, made for the Devil's sake.
Matt. 25:41.

28. God's Children know their Origin: their Bodies of the Dust,   Gen. 3:19,
Job 14:2.

Here having Bloom'd and Fructifi'd to th' Earth return they must.   Eccles. 12:7.

29. Their Spirits coming down from God, in God perpetuate,   1. John 1:3 & 3:24.
As Branches in the Vine abide: Thrice blest and happy State!   John 15:4.

30. Thrice blest & happy souls! that are, and shall for Ever be   John 11:52.
Like Scions, grafted into that high-Zion's Olive-tree.   Rom. 11:17.

31. Whose Root the Root of Jesse is, continually green & fresh,   Isa. 11:10,
Luke 23:31.

And He himself it's Offspring too, according to the Flesh: Rev. 22:16.

32. The Flesh, (well call'd the Flow'r of Grass,) which fadeth & decays,   1 Peter 1:24.
None but the Rose of Sharon can be blossoming always.   Cant. 2:1.

33. At last, though we be Buried, as Seeds are in the ground,   1 Cor. 15:36, 37.
Which rotten, moulder'd, putrifi'd, are hardly to be found;   Ibid.

34. Yet at that Day of days we're sure, that all again shall rise,   John 6:40.
Some Strong, that here were Weakness, & Some others otherwise.   Phil. 3:21.

35. Dear Shipmates, Let us press therefore to this our highest Price,   Ibid. v. 14.
Laid up for Heav'nly-minded-Ones, who worldly Trash despised.   v. 8.

III. The Extent & Produce of the Inward Spiritual Farm.

1. Whereas Ecclesiasticus
The Fear of GOD a Pleasant Garden calls,   chap. 40:27.

2. My Muse is paraphrasing thus
A multitude of Plants are in its Walls.   Isa. 5:2.

3. As, first of all, the choisest Vine,

368. The oxymoronic name Emmanuel Beelzebub contains at once Emmanuel (Hebrew for "God is with us"), which appears in the Book of Isaiah and is usually interpreted in Christianity as a foreshadowing and a name of Christ, and Beelzebub (Hebrew for "Lord of the Flies"), the name of one of the main devils of Christian demonology.

By God's own Hand, is placed in the Midst,   John 15:1.

4. Which yields us the New Kingdom's Wine,
    Wherof, O Lord, to buy, thou all men bidst!   Matt. 26:29, Isa. 55:1.

5. Next True Love this Vine Surrounds,
    And spreads its noble Fruits above the Stars,   Matt. 22:37.

6. So that it still beneath abounds
    In Charity to all, which nothing bars.   2 Thess. 1:2, 1 Cor. 13.

7. Then Wisdom (Divine Wisdom) springs,
    Illuminating man's dark Heart and Soul,   James 3:17, Prov. 8.

8. Whereby it his affection brings
    To chuse the Clean, and to abhor the Foul.   3 John v. 11.

9. Lo! afterwards, how Righteousness
    Most sweetly here in ev'ry corner grows,   Jer. 33:15, Isa. 32:17.

10. Which Peace does as her Sister kiss,
    Whence Wealth and Substance flows.   Psal. 85:10, Prov. 3:6.

11. Now Meekness and Humility
    In that low place, as in a Valley stands,   1 Tim. 6:11, Col. 3:12.

12. Obedience keeps close thereby,
    And duly executes what God commands.   2 Cor. 10:5, 6, 1 Sam. 15:22.

13. Faith of a Diverse Growth & Size
    In Beds and Paths is ramping up and down,   Rom. 1:17 & 4:12, Luke 17:5.

14. Some tall, some small; some blunt, some nice,
    And, as it seems, each Countrey has its own.   Matt. 6:30, Rom. 1:8,
       2 Thess. 1:3.

15. Behold you on that Top good Hope,
    Weak, Joy-like, supported by a Post,   1 Peter 1:3, Heb. 6:19.

16. Till lastly it obtains its Scope,
    By Trusting in the Lord ne're ought is lost.   Rom. 5:5, Jer. 17:7.

17. There rises Courage near the same,
    Which with the Truth will live, and for it die,   Prov. 28:15, Acts 21:13.

18. And matters neither shame nor Flame,
    Its aim is War, Triumph and Victory.   Acts 5:41, Phil. 3:14.

19. Moreover Patience lurks behind
    This prickly Rose-tree here, opprest with Cares,   Rev. 14:12, Matt. 13:22.

20. And without any change of mind
    All changes of the world bears, and forbears   1 Thess. 3:3, James 1:4.

21. Hence Temperance stands not far off
    Whereby we're made good Hus$\underset{\text{wives}}{\overline{\text{bands}}}$, Sober, Chaste,   Gal. 5:23, John 6:12.

22. As Modesty lets no man scoff,

So Circumspection stops us to make haste.	Prov. 29:8, Isa. 28:16, Eccles. 5:2 & 7:9.

23. There at the Back-door I espy
    That Virtue, without which the Rest is vain,   Rom. 6:2.

24. To wit unweari'd Constancy,
    When all is done, then this the Crown does gain   Eph. 6:18, James 1:12.

25. Now, if I would in this poor Rime
    Relate what more that Garden does produce   Job 40:4.

26. I should want Paper, Words and Time,
    It's Plants are too too many, and too Spruce   Psal. 39:19.

27. No Tongue is able to express
    The Endless Joys, the Tree of Life does give   1 Cor. 2:9, Rev. 2:7.

28. With Grace & perfect Holiness,
    To those who of that feed, and in this live: Acts 15:11, 1 Tim. 2:15.

29. As Rachel Preston did, whilst here
    She an Inhabitant thereof was own'd,   Tota est Ecclesia testis.[369]

30. Now in a more exalted Sphere
    With Immortality and Glory Crown'd.   Rom. 2:7.

31. And though her Faith & Hope may cease,
    Her Patience too be come unto an End,   Rom. 8:24, 25, 2 Cor. 5:7, Rev. 24:4.

32. Yet does her Love God-wards increase,
    And still it self from Pole to Pole extend.   1 Cor. 13:8.

33. Dear Ship Mates, let us not forget
    Our Sister's eminent good Qualities,   Psal. 112:6, 2 Tim. 1:5.

34. But as a tried Pattern set
    With that of CHRIST, and Job's before our Eyes,   James 5:11, 1 Peter 2:21.

35. Thus we once shall arrive, where She now is,
    To GOD on high: To Ever-lasting Bliss!
       Amen, So be it! Amen.   (Id quod F.D.P. optat.)[370]

369. "The whole Church is a witness."
370. "That is what F. D. P. wishes."

<u>Germantown the 20th of the VIth month 1719.</u>[371]

For Hannah Hill and Mary Norris These from their ancient Friend Pastoris,
Which he sends as a New-Year's Letter,   And wishes, that it might be better.[372]

Ever well Respected and entirely Beloved Ship-mates **H. Hill & M. Norris.**

Seeing the Conceits & Opinions of People are as various and different as their Faces, and the predominant Customs & Constitutions of the sundry countries in this vain and fickle world as distant & contrary one to another, as the divers Climates thereof, it is Proverbially & well said,

Many men, many minds,
Many Nations, many Fashions.

Of this I shall give you one Instance for my present Purpose: The Arabians, Abysines,[373] and Moscovites commence their year in Autumn; The Germans, English and other Inhabitants of Europe, with those of Peru in Winter; The Armenians, Persians, Chineses, Japonians and Mexicans in Spring, as also the Hebrews who then went out of Egypt, to Serve the Lord elsewhere; the Greeks began theirs in Summer, and so (me thinks) should we Three do likewise, either on the 20th of the VIth month [August], being the day of our happy arrival at Philadelphia, Or on the 10th of the IVth month[374] which was that of our departing from Deal towards this promised land. Promised, I say, because I am sure, that the most part of the first adventurers thereinto, since it bore the Name of Penn Silvania by a mutual covenant between them & God Almighty, promised that they & their children would Serve Him in the same, only for Bread and Raiment: And He per Contra[375] putt his Seal to it in their Hearts, that they and their Seed should be the Blessed of the Lord above all Families of the Earth, If they would walk in His Way undefiled. Now, must we not Confess that He has been as good as His Word, and in very deed blessed us, even beyond Expectation, Outwardly and Inwardly, with Temporal and Spiritual Blessings. For number numberless, more than we can express? Praised and Magnified be His holy Name for Ever and Ever! Amen.

It therefore coming last Seventh-day-night into my Thoughts, that our above mentioned New Year was approaching about the End of the Week, and that I usher'd it in these Six year past with a few Rimes, as Remembrancers of our American Pilgrimage, I considered, what acceptable Gift I should present you with all at the Entrance of this Instant. The prime Idea that offer'd herself was to send you a List or Bill of Mortality, that is, to lay before your View the Names of such my Fellow-Mortals, whom I had the

---

371. August 20, 1719. Because 1719 is the last year of Pastorius's life, this is the last anniversary poem he wrote.
372. In the original, this inscription is located in the left-hand margin.
373. Abyssinians, inhabitants of Ethiopia.
374. June 10th.
375. "On the opposite side," on the other hand.

honour and unhappiness to Survive these XXXVI years of our Abode in this Province, Intending further to rank them in four Classes: the 1st, whereof should shew those supereminent Persons, who only granted me the Priviledge (of Dogs & Cats, in their Courts,) to look upon them, viz. the Roman Emperour Leopold the Ist as also Charles the II, James the I. William the IV, Mary the II and Anne the I, kings & queens of Great Britain. Item Lewis the XIV Tyrant of France.

In the 2nd I would have placed such men of high Birth, Degree & Quality to whom I durst speak, how be it with much Aw, Reverence & Submission. Dukes, Bishops, Princes, Earls, Baronets, Captains, Gentlemen, Drs. and Professors, &c. The 3d might have contained a Cloud & Croud of those I intimately was acquainted with, especially in the time of my blooming & youthful age; But forasmuch as some of my quondam School-fellows and Companions were none of the best, I formed already the 4th order, into which none should have been admitted, that were not truly Wise and Vertuous. Here your ever well Esteemed Father, Thomas Lloyd, Mordecai & Thomas Junr. your Brethren, Rachel Preston, your never forgotten Sister, John Delaval and Hannah Hill husband & daughter of the Eldest of you Two, Samuel Carpenter, Griffith Owen and William Penn, together with other good Friends of approved Integrity would have had their Encomiums more at large, pursuant to their desert & respective Characters. But this Theme or Subject seeming too too Melancholick for the present Occasion, and of a farther Extent, than to be duly compassed within three or four days, threw the Project quite aside, betaking myself to an other shift, whereby I hope to come off with more credit than by the former Emprise; For upon observation, that you both are Lovers of Gardens (the One keeping the finest I hitherto have seen in the whole countrey, filled with abundance of Rarities, physical and metaphysical: th' other a pretty little Gardeken, much like unto mine own, producing chiefly Cordial Stomachial & Culinary herbs) and moreover that you relish'd my last annual paper indifferent well, though stuffed with nothing but Rural Meditations, I resolved to entertain you for this Bout again with somewhat of the same Stamp and Complexion to wit XXXVI Paragraphs, Treating of Gardening Flowers, Shrubs & Trees, The Fruits whereof do feed Men, Beasts & Bees.

In Case either of you will cast a favourable smile only on the ninth part of the subsequent Verses, I thankfully shall acknowledge your Benignity, and in token of due Gratitude heartily wish you a long life, good health & omnifarious Prosperity from Him, who alone has it all in his hands to dispense of according to the good pleasure of his will Four years added to these of our pristine Commoration[376] in this colony makes Forty, or the full Term, the Confined to their Eating of Manna, Of which more in its proper Season. Here I only shall prefix Three times Twelve is thirty Six. And so many

---

376. "Commoration": dwelling.

years have we, (Thanks to God for Ever be!) In brave Pennsilvania been kept alife, and meanwhile Seen, Six & Thirty, in a Plain, By the Men of Ai slain,[377] &c.

	In Garden Recreations.	In Alveario.[378]
1. The first of Gardens &c.	num. 181.	num. 221
2. When I in my Garden walk,	139.	
3. Whereas I do never want,	164.	
4. Good God most full of Grace,	170.	
5. Jehova God of Gods.	169.	
6. Hosanna! oh Hosanna!	168.	
7. Lord! break the heads,	184.	
8. Christ thou glorious Prince,	236.	
9. Jesus, Lover of poor men,	229.	
10. As often as somewhere,	151.	
11. The Reliques of the Paradise,	212.	
12. The Bleeding heart,	160.	
13. Job's Tears not always flow,	121.	
14. As the Garden's Turn-sole,	102.	
15. Extract the Quint Essence,	46.	
16. Jonah's kikajon,[379]	45.	
17. You first-rate men,	179.	162.
18. Now the first-born,	124.	138.
19. True Love,	94.	
20. Since Lovage does,	126.	
21. Christ's disciples,	230.	
22. God is the Sun,	146.	
23. My Garden, which	156.	
24. God's Kingdom within man	227.	
25. What plants these lands	161.	
26. Among the English Doctors	147.	
27. God's goodness	182.	
28. Sun, Moon and Stars	159.	
29. If thou wouldst the Roses Scent	108.	
30. The Marvels of Peru,	61.	

377. Joshua 7:5: "And the men of Ai smote of them about thirty and six men: for they chased them from before the gate even unto Shebarim, and smote them in the going down: Wherefore the hearts of the people melted, and became as water."

378. Rather than copying these poems again for his own record, Pastorius refers to the poems he copied from two of his manuscripts, the *Deliciæ Hortenses, or Garden Recreations* and his "Alvearialia."

379. Mentioned only in the Book of Jonah, the Hebrew word *kikayon* is translated in the King James Version as "gourd"; it is more commonly translated now as "castor oil plant."

Dearly welcome Friends H.H. and M.N.[380] Because you took at once three Dozen of mine odd threadbare ware, I shall give you this in the Bargain:

As by the diff'rent Fruits, &c. In my Garden Recr. Num. 228. In Alveario:

Jotham,[381] after he made his Trees confabulate together 2954 years before mine ever open'd their mouths, ran away & fled; Judges 9: from v. 7 to 22. But should such a man as I go into a place of Refuge, because of some Satyrical, yet veritable expressions that dropt from my pen to save my life? I will not go in, Nehem. 6:11, rather earnestly entreat the Mercy of my Shipmates, to put a charitable Construction upon the harshness of Sound & Sense in this my rhythmical New-Years Gift, where (to be the less prolix & tedious,) I made Choice of the shortest 99 I could pick out of my delicÿs hortensibus, Copying them (as you see) in Post haste. Such as they are I leave to their perusal, and Courtesie, Recommending them both, & all theirs, to the Divine Preservation, and myself to their & their dearest husbands good Favour, and Constant affection, who am, & unalterably desire to be & remain until death, Your (not by form of Compliment but in Reality & truth) ancient, much Indebted & most willing friend & Shipmate, F.D.P.

[. . . . .]382

---

380. Hannah Hill and Mary Norris.

381. In the Second Book of Kings, Jotham was King of Judah.

382. Author's note on the bottom of the page illegible.

6 🙢

Letters and Correspondence

Letters from Pastorius's "Letterbook"

INTRODUCTION TO THE TEXT

Transcribed and annotated from Francis Daniel Pastorius, "Copies of Letters [Letterbook]," MS 8631, Pastorius Papers and Digital Library, Historical Society of Pennsylvania, the letters in this section have never before been published. They were selected to provide insight into the range of Pastorius's correspondents (most of whom were residents of colonial Pennsylvania), their relationships, and their topics of conversation. The recipient and date (when known) are given in square brackets at the head of each letter, with a horizontal line added between letters to clearly indicate where one letter ends and the next begins. Letters written entirely in French or Latin are presented in both the original language and in English translation in the main text; translations of French and Latin passages in letters written primarily in English are provided in the notes.

Pastorius followed a common early modern practice of keeping records or copies of letters written and sent to correspondents near and far in letterbooks. The copies in such books served as backups in case the original letters were lost—a frequent occurrence before a formal postal system was established in America and at a time when transatlantic shipping was frequently disrupted by war, piracy, and inclement weather. Pastorius would sometimes have to reconstruct the contents of a letter in writing his "Letterbook" copy after having sent the original; he would sometimes also note the specific circumstances for a letter on its copy, such as who had delivered a letter for him.

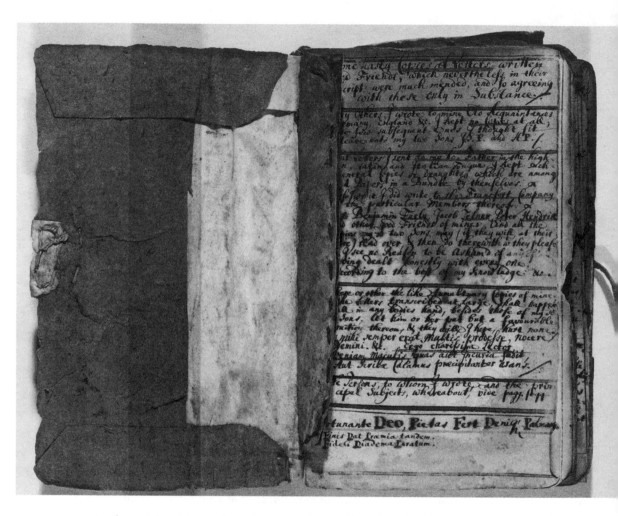

Fig. 7 | Francis Daniel Pastorius, title page and binding from "Letterbook." MS 8631, Francis Daniel Pastorius Papers, Historical Society of Pennsylvania.

The letters presented here are primarily those Pastorius wrote in the latter half of his life to friends in Pennsylvania, especially prominent Quakers such as William Penn, James Logan, Isaac Norris, several members of the Hill family, Samuel Carpenter, and the young Lloyd Zachary, who would become Pastorius's favorite correspondent in the last three years of his life. The members of this circle included the friends to whom he sent the "Ship-Mate-Ship" poems, as well as their spouses, children, and other kin. In these letters, Pastorius plays a range of roles, from intellectual equal in his letters to Logan, to grateful beneficiary in his correspondence with prominent public friends like Richard Hill and Isaac Norris (who helped him recover Germantown lands lost in a fraudulent land deal), to teacher and mentor in his many letters to younger correspondents such as Elizabeth Hill, Lloyd Zachary, and Lydia Norton. Thus his letters provide us with glimpses not only into Pastorius's mind but also into the intellectual and literary world of elite Quaker circles in early Pennsylvania. They make clear that Pastorius was part of a community of manuscript producers and circulators and that the books accompanying their letters were sent as tokens of friendship and shared edification from one trusted friend and fellow Quaker to another. Pastorius's use of French and Latin in several of the letters demonstrates the cosmopolitan urbanity cultivated by prominent Quakers in this period—despite Quaker admonitions against the excesses of higher learning.

THE TEXT

[Prefatory Reflections]
Some hasty Copies of Letters written
To good Friends, which nevertheless in their
Transcripts were much mended, and so agreeing with these only in Substance.
Of Many Others I wrote to mine Old Acquaintances
In Germany, England &c. I kept no Copies at all;
But the few subsequent Ones I thought fit
to leave unto my two Sons J.S.P. and HP.[1]
Of what Letters I sent to my loving Father[2] in the high-
German, Latin, and Italian Tongue I kept such-
Like General Copies or Draughts, which are among
my old Papers in a Bundle by themselves.[3]

1. John (Johann) Samuel and Henry (Heinrich) Pastorius.
2. Melchior Adam Pastorius.
3. Although there is no evidence of an extant collection of Francis Daniel's manuscript letters to his father, some were printed in *Umständige Geographische Beschreibung* (1700).

As also of what I did write <u>to the Francfort Company</u>,[4]
and the particular Members thereof.
Item to Benjamin <u>Furly</u>, Jacob <u>Telner</u>, Peter <u>Hendrik</u>,[5]
And other good Friends of mine[.] And all the
said Copies my said two Sons may (if they will, at their
Leisure) read over, & then do therewith what they please;
For I see no Reason to be Ashamed of any of 'em,
having dealt honestly with everyone,
according to the best of my knowledge. &c.
If these or other the like tumultuary Copies of mine,
Or the Letters transcribed at large, shall happen
to fall in any bodies hand, besides those of my said
two Sons him or her put but a favourable
Instruction thereon, & they will, I hope, hurt none.
Mens mihi semper erat multis prodesse, nocere
Nemini. &c. <u>Ergo charissime Lector,</u>
<u>Da veniam maculis</u> quas aut Incuria fadit,
Aut Scribæ Calamus præcipitanter arans.[6]
The Persons, to whom I wrote, and the
principal Subjects, whereabout, vide pagg. seqq.[7]
Fortunante Deo, Pietas Fert Deniquam Palmam.[8]
Finis Dat Præmi tandem,
Fideli Diadema Paratum.[9]

---

4. Founded by the Frankfurt Pietists as the German Society, then reorganized and renamed in 1686, the Frankfurt Land Company served as a vehicle for purchasing and administering land in Pennsylvania. At first, the Frankfurt Pietists hoped to settle on this land as a group, but eventually they cast aside that hope—to the great disappointment of Pastorius, who served as agent for the company until 1700.

5. Living in Rotterdam, the English Quaker Benjamin Furly coordinated William Penn's promotion of Pennsylvania on the Continent and served as a liaison for dissident Protestants from Germany and Holland traveling to America. The Quaker merchant Jacob Telner of Amsterdam temporarily settled in Germantown but relocated to London in the 1690s. The Dutch Quaker button maker Peter Hendrik or Hendricks also of Amsterdam, like Furly, actively supported Dutch and German Quaker groups, such as the Krefelders, both in their endeavors to find more tolerant places to live in Europe and in immigrating to Pennsylvania.

6. "My mind was always helpful to many, hurt / no-one, &c. Therefore, dear reader, / pardon the faults that are either from a lack of attention / or from the writer's pen plowing on headlong."

7. "See the following pages."

8. "God's favor and love finally carry the prize."

9. "The end at last gives the prize. / For the faithful the crown is prepared."

[To William Penn, February 19, 1701]

Guillaume Penn,

Noble & Bien-aimé Gouverneur.[10]

Il y a un an depuisque quelques uns des écoliers Philadelphiens, qui s'appellent Jean, ayant pris la liberté de témoigner la Joye qu'ils concevoient alors par la heureuse Naissance de Ton Fils cadet, le Quasi modò genitus leur Synonime, s'en sont allé[s] Te feliciter sur ce sujet aussi bien un Rime qu'en Prose. Ces lignes se retrouvantes l'autre Jour, quand Je furetai entre mes Papiers brouillars, Je les ay releu tout à l'heure, & j'y ay àjouté quarante & quatre Remarques de la méme Categorie.

Cela fait, J'ay été en suspens, si Je devois user dela hardiesse de les produire devant Toi, sachant tres bien, que Tes yeux l'accoutumerent à regarder des matieres plus relevées & plus importantes: des Traités qui enseignent ou la Pratique d'approcher au ciel, ou pour le moins celle de bien gouverner le monde.

Mais afin que Tu ne sois pas necessité aux viandes rechauffées & a telles qu'on apporte la seconde fois a la Table, J'ay marqué ce qui est frais & nouveau, mettant une petite Etoile au Commencement du Paragraph.

Et comme cela, Je Te prie, d'avoir pour agreable le pauvre Traitément que ie suis capable à faire, & d'excuser la Temerité, dont je me confesse coulpable. C'est avec cette esperance que Je prens mon congé, & que je supplie tres humblement la Bonte de Dieu, qu'il veuille departir & distribuer toutes sortes de Benedictions d'en haut à Toi méme, à Ta Femme, à Tes Enfans & à toute Ta Famille; specialement à Luy qui en est le plus Jeune. O que Tu le puisse voir Croitre de jour à autre comme ces Observations qui suivent se sont augmentées en peu de Tems! Voila le sincere Souhait de Ton ami dans la Verité

Francis Daniel Pastorius.

A Germantown le 19me. du XIIme mois 1700/01.

[Translation][11]

William Penn, Noble and well-liked Governor,[12]

It has been a year since each of the Philadelphian school children who are called John have taken the liberty to show the joy they had received then by the happy birth of your youngest son, almost as if they had begotten a reflection of themselves, to congratulate you both in rhyme as well as in prose on the subject.[13] Coming across

---

10. The spelling of Pastorius's French compositions was modernized or standardized where necessary to aid comprehension. As he mentioned in his letters to Elizabeth Hill and Lloyd Zachary (see later in this section), he had rarely used the French language since he arrived in Pennsylvania; thus some of the idiosyncrasies of his French spelling and grammar may be entirely his own.

11. Translation by Nathan Michalewicz.

12. After attending to legal battles in London for years after the founding of Pennsylvania, William Penn returned to his colony in late 1699 and remained there until 1701.

13. While teaching at the Quaker school in Philadelphia, Pastorius had the students who were named "John" produce a manuscript book entitled "Genetliacum or an hearty Congratulation," with verse and prose compositions reflecting on famous or important people in history named "John," calling them "onomastical

these lines the other day, when I was perusing the papers of my waste book,[14] I reread them all right then, and I added forty-four remarks from the same category.

This done, I have been in suspense, if I must be bold to produce them in front of you, knowing very well, that your eyes are used to looking at higher and more important matters: treatises that teach or practices to get closer to heaven, or at least that of governing the world well.

Always considering the benign reception that you have made of the onomastic observations that have arrived in before these, I am encouraged to present to you this grouping with the clusters that I already offered last year. But so that you are not compelled to [eat] reheated meat and such as one brings the second time to the table, I have marked those that are old and new, marking a small star at the beginning of the paragraph.

And as such, I beg you, be kind of the poor treatment that I am able to do, and to excuse the boldness, of which I confess I am culpable. It is with this hope that I take my leave, and I very humbly beg for God's loving kindness to divest and distribute all sorts of blessings to you from above, the same to your wife, to your children, and to all your family, especially to your youngest. Oh, that I could see him grow from one year to the next as these observations that follow are increased in little time! That is the sincere wish of your true friend,

At Germantown, 19th of the 12th month 1700/01[15]   Francis Daniel Pastorius

---

[To Samuel Jennings, February 26, 1703]

Samuel Jennings[16]   Philadelphia 26th of 12th month 1702.[17]

Dear & Esteemed Friend, Thine of the 17th Instant I received, and delivered the Inclosed unto Dan. Falkner,[18] who after the perusal thereof, told me, that he was sorry to have

considerations," Pastorius enlarged upon these, adding some of his own in his manuscript volume "A few Onomastical Considerations" and sent it together with copies of his *Four Boasting Disputers* and *New Primmer* as a gift to William Penn, who must have preserved the volume since it is today preserved at Friends' House Library in London.

14. His "Alvearialia" manuscript, where Pastorius collected notes and drafts of poems before revising them and carrying them over to other, more finished manuscript books, such as the "Bee-Hive."

15. February 19, 1701.

16. Samuel Jennings (d. 1708) was a prominent Pennsylvania Quaker and an ardent opponent of George Keith during the Keithian controversy.

17. February 26, 1703. See note 43 to chapter 3.

18. The Lutheran Pietist Daniel Falckner first arrived in Pennsylvania in 1694 with Johannes Kelpius's group of mystics. During a return visit to Germany, Falckner received the power of attorney from the Frankfurt Land Company to administer its lands in Pennsylvania beginning in 1700 but, troubled by alcoholism, he seriously mismanaged the company's funds. Pastorius's letter to Jennings testifies to Francis Daniel's ongoing efforts to protect the affairs of the Germantown community.

paid 15 £ to dear Edward Penington,[19] & that he is not willing to pay any farthing more, ere & before the lines of the land, (for the Surveying whereof the money is due,) be rectified. Now concerning the Interest I have in the matter, or favour towards the said Daniel Falkner, they are both but small, & not of such weight, that I should not rather desire, that he (who is at present the attorney of that Company, I near 18 years long have faithfully served,) might pay all Just Debts & Dues; and thou mayst be sure, I never shall harbor any hard thoughts, if thou proceed according to thine Intention, declared unto him in thy said Letter. No more for this time but my sincere Love and Salutation to thee and thy dear wife in him, who loved us first, before we were capable either of that supreme affection we owe unto him, or of the Subordinate one unto an other, I rest, F.D.P.

[To John Penn, October 6, 1710]

To my loving Friend <u>John Penn</u>[20] now at London or Bristol, or somewhere else in Great Britain.

John Penn,   Germantown the 6th of October, 1710.

Tenderly beloved Friend; for such thou ever hast been unto me from the very day of thy birth, when I welcom'd thy dear person by a few Doggrels, into this painful world. And though hitherto I was somewhat shie to declare the sincerity of my good will; yet seeing of late thy worthy & well Esteemed Father in a letter of his to me most kindly calls thyself my John Penn, I make bold to construe this Expression in the favourablest Sense viz. that he thereby in a manner would either put thee under my Pedagogie, or else a greater obligation upon me, to increase mine Inclinations, not withstanding the same be already next to the Superlative Degree. Therefore, if these lines be the first that are sent unto thee out of thy Native Countrey,[21] I (a frank-hearted Franconian,[22] not fully acquainted with the English tongue,) for all the Indearments & reasons aforementioned do beseech thee, to take this in the better part, to excuse my forwardness and to admit at present the here posted brief, candid & cordial lessons, to wit Imprimis,[23] to Fear & to love the Lord thy Creator above all, continually & in every place and Company whatsoever, so thou canst not but be sure **never** to offend his heavenly Majesty & ever to do those things which are agreeable in his sight having their Reward along with them.

19. Brother-in-law of William Penn (through Penn's first wife, Gulielma Maria Springett, the stepdaughter of Isaac Penington), the English Quaker Edward Penington arrived in Pennsylvania in 1698, where he later became surveyor general.

20. The only son of William Penn to be born in America (1700), John Penn would become proprietor of Pennsylvania—along with his brothers, Thomas and Richard.

21. In October 1710, John Penn was living with his parents in England again.

22. Having been born in Sommerhausen, Franconia, Pastorius liked to pun on the connection between the English word "frank" and "Franconia."

23. In the first place, especially.

Secondly, to honour thy good & godly Parents by true & due obedience that thou mayst be long liv'd in this the land which God will give thee on these his own Terms. But NB.[24] I speak of both, the one like as the other, To please thy Father, do not cross thy Mother. Read Prov. 1:8 & 15:20 together with a deal of Texts of that Tendency, collected in the Common-place-book to the holy Bible printed in 4° 1697.[25] As also in that Enchiridion Intitled Fruits of Solitude in 24°[26] § 162, 163, &c.

Thirdly, to live in Unity with bretheren & sisters, decorat Concordia Fratres. Peruse, when left at leisure, Psal. 133, Gen. 13:8, Acts 7:26, Hebr. 13:1, Rom. 12:10, 1 Peter 1:22, concluding with 1 John 3:16, for whosoever hateth his brother, is a Murderer, like Cain, Esau, Abimelech, &c. in the afore quoted Common-place-book p. 145 & in the 2ᵈ part of the Fruits of Solitude §293. &c. thou wilt find sufficiently to the purpose.

Fourthly to spend the Instant Time & Prime of thy youth in acquiring of those arts & parts, which may prove useful unto thee in thy approaching years of more Maturity, & shall not need to be forgotten, no, not in thine old age, whereof I can't but commend/enumerate the Chiefest, namely to learn of Christ (& such as follow his sacred Steps,) Humility, Meekness, Temperance, Patience, & the rest of divine Vertues: and of men endued with literal knowledge some of the dead & living Languages, & tantum quantum[27] of all necessary & commendable Sciences, ex.gr.[28] Arithmetick, Geometry, Navigation, Histories, Medicine, Husbandry, &c. In short, all what thou oughtest to understand of the things in the Macrocosm without, and in thy proper Microcosm, or little island of thyself; which sort of Instructions, if I might be as happy as to communicate unto thee that little I do enjoy thereof, I should, me thinks, (by watering) promote the growth of a very helpful & promising plant. Therefore, my dear John Penn, pray! endeavour as much as in thee lieth, to prompt & stir up by all lawful means the generous Genitor, to speed his Journey hitherward, where his Presence will be to adventagious, and unquestionably redount[29] to his Interest & private Profit, as well as to the publick good & felicity of the whole (still his hereditary) province, and to the universal rejoycing of all right-spirited men & women, dwelling therein, & in the adjacent neighbouring colonies.

May it be the determination of the Almighty, safely to conduct him & his family, (and among them thine own self) unto us, and I shall let thee see what a hard task thou hast occasion'd to so weak a quill as that of mine, viz. to write onomastical Remarks, which beyond expectation accrew already to above 1160 Paragraphs. Here thou wilt

---

24. *Nota bene* (note well).

25. John Locke, *A Common-place book to the Holy Bible* (London, 1697).

26. Pastorius here refers John Penn to a book by John's father: William Penn, *Fruits of Solitude* (London, 1693). An enchiridion is a handbook or manual.

27. "So much as."

28. For example; such as.

29. Redound.

meet with abundance of Johns, Emperours, Popes, Kings, Bishops, Dukes, Generals, Princes, Priests, Doctors, Champions, Lawyers, Lyers, Historiographers, Botanicks, Linguists, Poets, Magicians, Conjurers, &c. &c. Johns of all kinds and ranks, good & bad, rich & poor. too many to be rehearsed in several sheets of paper.

Now, for a conclusion I kindly desire, to remember my respectful & unfeigned Love to thy noble Parents as able to thy Brethren & Sisters, especially the two eldest of 'em, William and Letitia; for the youngest I have not yet had within the reach of my bodily Eyes, although therse ten years past I did believe & wish (even in a few lines to thy dear Father,) that God from time to time would add a more numerous Issue to the foregoing, &c. So committing & recommending thy abovesaid well-esteemed Parents, together with all theirs & thyself to the Lord's glorious Protection, humbly begging of his divine Bounty the Continuation of your good health & Prosperity with my hearty Entreaty unto thee to pardon this my hardiness & prolixity of writing of one, whom thou Impossibly canst call to mind, and yet hast seen him many times, and been often in his arms, in the Town of thy Nativity, Quae de Fraterno nomen amore trahit,[30] and still frequently in his Thoughts, who subscribes himself thine affectioned & devoted Friend, F.D.P.

NB. This letter, somewhat alter'd and enlarg'd about our good success in the New Election of Assemblymen; and what I scribbled on the backside of the late printed Friendly Advice to the Inhabitants of Pennsilvania;[31] Item, what I prefixed to the above cited Commonplacebook, I sent by the hands of P.E.[32] but had no answer to it, which with other reasons, makes me suppose that it was not delivered.

[To Samuel Carpenter, no date]

<u>Samuel Carpenter</u>[33]

Loving & Respected Friend, As I can't but acknowledge myself Highly Indebted to thee on divers Accounts, So more especially for thy generosity in communicating so many a good book to my perusal; and having returned the most of the former with either a couple of sorry Rimes, scribbled on any vacant page thereof, or a small letter (like this) besides: I now at present sending hereby back the Historical Relation of the Charity Schools & Orphan-house &c. at Glaucha before Hall in Saxony,[34] thought it

---

30. "Which draws its name from brotherly love" (Philadelphia).

31. Isaac Norris, *Friendly advice to the inhabitants of Pensilvania* (Philadelphia: Andrew Bradford, [1710?]).

32. Probably Peter Evans (see note 69 below).

33. One of the most influential citizens of Pennsylvania, the wealthy merchant Samuel Carpenter held many important positions, including treasurer and deputy governor. He helped Pastorius secure title to lands lost during several land frauds committed by Pastorius's successors as administrators of the Frankfurt Land Company.

34. The work Pastorius is referring to here is probably the one he cites in his "Bee-Hive" bibliographies of non-Quaker writings: August Hermann Francke, *Pietas Hallensis: or a public demonstration of the foot-steps of a divine being yet in the world: in an historical narration of the orphan-house* (London, 1705).

my duty, to accompany the same with these few lines thereby to forward the Continuation of this thy favour against the instant long Winter-Nights, if the Lord be pleased to spare Life & health if I do not here subjoyn so large Thanks, as are suited to the merit of the Treatise, it is, because I know, that thou doest not look for a deal of grateful expressions, but art obliging thy Friends freely, i.e. sending, & expecting nought for it. However, could I but find time, to run over mine own Itinerary,[35] I might, me thinks, make some Requital, not altogether disagreeable. First, I should tell thee of many brave & princely (and some even Charity) Schools I have seen in the world, ex.gr. that near Naumburg, at Heilsbron, at Francfort, &c. Item[36] the several excellent Orphan-houses ex. gr. at Amsterdam, one for either sex, where at that time have been 900 fatherless children. Item the many hospitals as well for sick as for poor people, ex.gr. that of St. Lewis in one of the suburbs of Paris [...] herein 10000 persons very conveniently may be lodged. It has an apothecary shop to it like that at Glaucha, & perhaps more richly stuff'd. An other at Ryssel[37] (which City cost ours very dear [...] year,)[38] founded by Count Balduin,[39] into which all [...] and diseased from the whole Countrey are to be fetched on a mule with silver shoes always kept to this purpose. Item for maimed souldiers, decrepit Seamen &c. [...] at Paris aforesaid, at Enkhuysen, where Sir William Temple gave an alms to one, whom afterwards he celebrated as the only rich man he saw in all his life.[40]

Secondly, I doubtlessly could find one or other Instance of such [...] Buildings, which by miraculous means were begun and finished, ex. gr. that of S. Sophia at Constantinople, which the mighty Emperour Constantinus[41] could never have Completed, had he not by an unexampled Providence found the greatest treasure imaginable, &c.

However, after a considerate perusal of thy abovementioned book, I confess the erecting of the Charity Schools & Orphan-house at Glaucha (commenced & hitherto continued upon no visible Stock or Subscription, but meerly upon the admirable & adorable Providence of him, on whom we are advised to cast our burden and to trust,

35. The extensive journal Pastorius kept during his travels in Europe is now lost, except for some excerpts he copied into the "Bee-Hive."

36. "Likewise," "also."

37. "Ryssel" is the Flemish name for the city of Lille in northern France.

38. Pastorius is probably referring to the siege of Ryssel by King Louis XIV in 1667, which made Ryssel/Lille French (and Catholic).

39. Count Baldwin V of Flanders (1012–1067), who founded Lille (although not the hospital that Pastorius is speaking of in the same sentence). The hospital was founded by Countess Jeanne of Flanders (1199?–1244) in 1236.

40. In his *Observations upon the United Provinces of the Netherlands* (London, 1693), Sir William Temple, ambassador to the United Provinces, recounted visiting an old people's home in the city of Enkhuizen. Apparently, an old sailor had refused a tip from Temple, claiming that the home where he lived provided everything he needed.

41. According to one tradition, Emperor Constantine the Great (ca. A.D. 272–337) began the first church structure that eventually became the Hagia Sophia of Constantinople.

Psal. 55:22, Job 35:14, is extreme[ly] remarkable, & a Token or Sign for us of lesser Faith; But seeming this is a gift of God, we ought earnestly to pray for.

Meanwhile it would be well, if those several plausible Essays of John Beller about the Poor, Manufactures, Trade, Plantations & Immorality, printed in 4° 1699,[42] as also what Thomas Tryon[43] proposed to the Lord Major & Court of Aldermen &c. of the City of London, for the building of 20 free schools in the poor Parishes, &c. Item, how they might weekly raise at least 15000 for the support of the needy, & no body be the worse for it, [the same] were proportionally put in Execution here. Yet if all those good Counsels be disregarded, as too too far fetcht from beyond the Sea, let the advice of our once well beloved friend Thomas Butt in his Good Order Established in Pensilvania & New Jersey, printed in 4° 1685[44] have placed amongst us; or finally, in case this likewise be rejected as the product of a whimsical Brain, pray then let the Laws & Acts of this Province be obeyed. For, that publick Schools are of an absolute necessity, (to have the children of the poor taught as well as those of the rich,) thou thyself art most sensible, otherwise thou wouldst not have taken that care about your Philadelphian 7 years School,[45] wherein I was concern'd as Pedagogue, as thou hast done. To speak true, without flattery, (which would be madness itself between us, who Intimately have been acquainted about 26 years from the very Infancy of this Province,) thou approvedst thyself unto Philadelphia what that faithful Centurion Luke 7[46] was to the Jews of Capernaum, in building a School house, &c. But to pass by all what's past, Schools, Orphanotrophies[47] & Bridwells[48] are still a wanting in Pensilvania and it lies at the door of you Common-wealth men, to erect and establish as many as you can; I, who as yet go twice to School every day, (the last of the week only excepted, like that old Ludi magister[49] at Minden, whom a scoffing Gentleman asked whither he was going, and upon his answer, To School, replied Sir, you must needs be a dull &

42. John Bellers, *Essays about the poor, manufactures, trade, plantations, & immorality, and of the excellency and divinity of inward light demonstrated from the attributes of God, and the nature of mans soul, as well as from the testimony of the Holy Scriptures* (London, 1699).

43. The English merchant Thomas Tryon (1634–1703) was the author of several early self-help books, as well as an early advocate of vegetarianism and animal rights.

44. Thomas Budd, *Good Order Established in Pennsilvania & New Jersey in America* . . . ([Philadelphia], 1685). Budd (Butt) became a follower of George Keith during the Keithian controversy and thus fell out of favor with Pastorius, Samuel Carpenter, and other "orthodox" Quakers.

45. The Philadelphia Friends' School, where Pastorius taught from 1698 to 1700, after which he taught at the Germantown Court school from 1702 until shortly before his death.

46. According to Luke 7:2–10 and Matthew 8:5–13, a Roman centurion asked Jesus for help because his servant boy was ill. When Jesus offered to come to his house, the centurion argued that he was not worthy to receive him but that a word from Jesus would be sufficient. Jesus told the centurion that, because of his faith, it would be so, and the servant boy was healed.

47. Hospitals or hostels for orphans.

48. Bridewells: reform schools for petty offenders.

49. A teacher at an ancient Roman school, the "Ludi magister" was responsible for the first few years of Roman education, from age 6 to 10. Pastorius thus refers to a teacher at a school akin to the present-day elementary school.

blockish devil, that you go yet thither; for I went only to that tedious place of whipping & weeping till eleven years old, &c.) can Contribute no more to your Endeavours than mine earnest prayers for the speedy Success-thereof, wherewith I ever remain.

[To Caspar Hoodt, no date]

Loving Friend Caspar Hoodt,[50]

Altho' I took my leave of thee but yesterday morning, yet hast thou been since often in my thoughts, It rising unexpectedly in my mind, how thou mayst very profitably spend those tedious days on Shipboard, viz. in translating into our Mother tongue William Penn's Primitive Christianity revived in the faith & practice of the people called Quakers. in 8° 1696[51] containing but 122 pages, and so thou mayst easily within less than 3 weeks and presently at thine arrival at Amsterdam print the same, if not already published in that language and then spread so useful a Treatice as that is, in our Native Countrey to the general good of many, as we should be glad to hear after thy happy return. So Dear Caspar, adieu, and when in the dark places of Idolatrous Germany, keep thou to the Light of Christ within, whom I devotedly pray to be thy Guide and Preserver in this dangerous Journey, that thou mayst not enter into any of the great & manifold Temptations which thou needs will meet withal by the way, thou now doest set thy foot into.

To him & his holy and wholsome Grace, I commend thee with mine own Soul, & thus bidding thee once more fare well, I remain.

[To James Logan, January 22, 1715]

<u>James Logan</u>   Germantown 22ᵈ of the 11ᵗʰ month 1714/5[52]

Esteemed Friend, Being come home last night from Philadelphia and remembering thou askedst me, whether or no I kept a copy of those odd verses, I once presented to thee, beginning Audi Poli, audi Soli, audi Mundi Gloria![53] I forthwith open'd my Silvulam Rhytmorum Germanopolitanorum,[54] & at the first view met with a bipartite Dialogue,[55] the one very sweet & th' other extreme soure, which I thought would

---

50. Originally from Hesse, Germany, Caspar Hoodt (Hoet) had moved to Germantown from New York in the early 1690s (see Duffin, *Acta Germanopolis*, 12n.). Tailor by trade, Hoodt served as a recorder on the Germantown General Court, in which role he and Pastorius had frequent interactions. Interestingly, Pastorius addressed Hoodt in English, even though both were German.

51. William Penn, *Primitive Christianity Revived in the Faith and Practice of the People Called Quakers* (London, 1696); the German translation Pastorius refers to does not seem to be extant. and there is no evidence that Pastorius's translation was printed.

52. January 22, 1715.

53. "Hear the many, hear the One, hear the Glory of the world."

54. Miscellany of Pastorius's own poetry in his "Bee-Hive" manuscript book (see chapter 5 of this reader).

55. The opening argument of the "Silvula" pro and contra poetry can be read as a dialogue: the "pro" side is sanguine or "sweet" about the uses of poetry, whereas the "contra" side is negative or "sour" (see "Bee-Hive," p. 68).

not be altogether unpleasant to thee (a Neogamus,)[56] who but lately hast changed thy condition from good to better, i.e. to that which Plato calls Officinam holum, Seminarium Re ipsi[57] &c. and some worse Philosophers than he a Bow-net, a Cage, a Labyrinth, &c. But the apostle most modestly a Yoke, unde derivamus Conjugium, Conjurgium.[58] However, I don't believe, that either thou or thy dear wife ever use hard words Interchangeably each towards other; yet for as much as there is hardly any woman, but may be some times a little out of order, the best advice in the case is, to practice what the Initial letters of our Names admonish us to do. Faemina Donis Pacatur, Fac Dona Propines,[59] and Impart Liberally; mind what Erasmus [of] Rotterdam saith in his Moria,[60] p.m. 178. viz. Novi ego quondam mei nominis, qui novae nuptae gemmas aliquit adulterinas dono dedit, persuadens, (ut erat facundus nugator,) eas non medo versa ac nativas esse, verum etiam singulari atq. inaestimabili pretio. Quaeso, quid intererat puello, cum vitro non minus jucunde pasceret & oculos et animam nugas perinde ut eximium aliquem thesaurum conditas apsud se servaret? Maritus interim & sumptus effugiebat, & uxoris errore frucbatur, nec eam tamen sibi minus habebat devinctam, quam si magno empta donasset.[61] So with my hearty Congratulations, and sincere wishes of all imaginable prosperity to you both, I send thee the abovesaid Dialogues, in pagg. seqq. with this Proviso never the less, that thou do not shew them to any, who love to be offended without a Cause. I am and always remain thy F.D.P.

Formosae Tulipae Deniq. Prætereunt[62]

[To James Logan, February 1, 1715]

Ad Eundem[63] the 1st of the 12th month 1714/5[64]

The Inclosed Botanick Rimes have been in thy house at the beginning of last week, but thou being gone to Burlington the bearer thereof (one of my Countreymen,)

56. Bridegroom, male newlywed.

57. "'The vegetable workshop [or] nursery garden itself.'" Although Pastorius is quoting Plato, the specific reference is unclear.

58. "From which we derive marriage, wrangling." Pastorius is not only linking marriage (*conjugium*) to struggle or strife (*conjurgium*) here but also alluding to a popular contemporary book about marriage: William Seymar, *Conjugium Conjurgium, or Some Serious Considerations on Marriage Wherein (by Way of Caution and Advice to a Friend) its Nature, Ends, Events, Concomitant Accidents &c. Are Examined* (London: Bancks, 1673).

59. "Women are subdued by gifts; gifts create accord."

60. Erasmus's *Moriae Encomium* (1509; *In Praise of Folly*).

61. "I once knew someone of my name, who gave a gift of some false gems to a new bride, convincing (since he was an eloquent joker) that they were not only true and natural, but also of a singular and inestimable price. I ask, what does it matter to the woman, when she could no less joyfully feed both her eyes and her soul on a mirror, if she would preserve some trifles hidden for herself as though a great treasure? In the meanwhile, the husband both fled the cost and benefited from his wife's mistake, since he held her as no less devoted to himself than if he had given [gifts] bought for a great price."

62. "Beautiful tulips finally pass."

63. "At the same [place]" (Germantown).

64. February 1, 1715.

wanting so much wit as to leave 'em there, brought the same to me again. So that I'm resolv'd to send them the second time, with the following addition, ut si Forsan Displiceant Primi, Iocularia Laudes Carmina.[65]

In the Inclosed I desire thee to accomplish the division of the land, and to have a care of Sprögel's deceitfulness & Tricks, whereof he is so full, and now at Philadelphia.[66] So submitting the management of the whole business to thyself, &c. rest thine obliged Friend F.D.P.

[To Isaac Norris, no date]

Isaac Norris my rare & real Friend,

According to the old saying a Friend In Need is a Friend IN deed, The letter which I gladly received from thy hand the night before yesterday abounding in such cherishing & refreshing Terms, seem'd little inferior to me, than if thou hast personally visited thy poor friend. Thou therein tellest me of thy readiness to contribute all what's in thy power, for getting the Patent to my Satisfaction, and, not only so but according didst write to J.L.[67] who prefixed a day, when it shall be done. I acknowledge myself, my wife & two sons extremely obliged unto thee on that account; But still must beg one favour more of thee & thy brother Hill,[68] to be pleased (when the Patent is brought unto you for signing,) carefully to read it over, so that after the great Seal is putt to it, there may be no Error about the Location, as also about the proprietary's quitrent viz. One English Silver Shilling for one thousand Acres of land. A few days agoe I never thought to have troubled my head so much in this fading & transitory Sport of the world; however, since upon the Instance of my youngest Son it is so far begun, let it (God willing,) be finished. Concerning P. Evans'[69] bill of charges, I paid my share, to wit 15 Shillings, &c.

I heartily sympathize with thy lameness, and for as much as I collected out of several experienced authors, many good Remedies against bodily distempers,[70] let me know (if thou please,) what you properly call it, & I shall very willingly translate what I find in

---

65. "So that if perhaps at first it displeases, you may praise the jocular songs."

66. The son of a prominent Pietist theologian in Germany, Johann Heinrich Sprögel, Anglicized as "John Henry Sprogel," came to Pennsylvania around 1702, where he became instrumental in defrauding the Germantown residents of lands they had purchased from the Frankfurt Land Company. For Pastorius, who was trying to regain title to his own land with help from powerful English Quakers such as Isaac Norris, Richard Hill, and Samuel Carpenter, Sprögel was the archschemer.

67. James Logan.

68. Richard Hill and Isaac Norris were brothers-in-law, having married Mary and Hannah Lloyd, the daughters of Pastorius's dear friend and shipmate Thomas Lloyd.

69. The lawyer Peter Evans (d. 1745) became sheriff of Philadelphia County in 1708 and then registrar general, being responsible for recording vital records, in 1713.

70. Pastorius is alluding to his manuscript collection of herbal and alchemical medicine, folk cures, and more modern chemical medicine entitled "Talia Qualia Medicinalia, Artificialia & Naturalia" (see chapter 7 of this reader), which excerpted from Nicholas Culpeper's *The English Physician* (London, 1652), among other English-language titles as well as from many German-language titles.

my book, not as to play the Doctor or Surgeon, but to lay before thee the advice of my Dutch Authors, in order to chuse thyself what thy good Genius indites, or inclines to. Of what thou wrotest as touching my retired life, & your hurry of publick affairs and Concernments, I can only at present say this, that the happiness lies rather at your door, for as much as the great God in his universal Oeconomy of this world employs you to what he will not leave unrewarded in the day of retribution, & I dare not undertake to enlarge either on this or any other subject for fear of Impairing the little grain of health yet left, having the most part of this day spent on a letter to H. Hill's lovely Daughter Elizabeth, &c. My sickness continues much the same, afflicting me with a cough and tough ugly phlegm. &c.

The great Physician of Value, I question not at all, will direct it to mine everlasting Well-being & therefore to him I resign myself entirely, Soul, body & Spirit, Committing thee & thy dear wife[71] (my quondam chearful Shipmate,) Children & family into his powerful Protection, and remaining thine ever assured friend until death   F.D.P.

[To Richard and Hannah Hill, Samuel Preston, Isaac and Mary Norris, January 23, 1717]

Germantown the 23rd of the 1st month 1716/7[72]

Richard & Hannah Hill, Samuel Preston, Isaac & Mary Norris.

Dear, real & singular Friends! Thus I may call you without any hyperbole & flattery; For though in this world most Friendships be contracted by reason of outward by-ends, especially of riches & wealth, as wise Solomon in his book of proverbs ch. 14:20. & 19:4. plainly intimates; yet know you that ours stands on a surer bottom, having even for its unmoveable basis or foundation that everlastingly New Commandment of our Lord & Master C. J.,[73] John 13:34 & 15:12, 17. And as you at your Side, (whom the Lord has blessed with a sure Store of these worldly goods,) have opened your hands wide unto me in distributing & Communicating to my Necessities, according to Deut. 15:7, and have not despised a poor Friend; but in a quite opposite Sense to that of the Apostle, 1 Cor. 11:22, shamed him by the Excess of your Bounty, in not only personally Visiting him in his sickness, but in overheaping him with such liberalities of yours, that he could not receive them without tears & astonishment: So now at his side (having recollected himself a little,) finds nothing to return unto you for a requital but hearty thanks in bare & unpolished words; And this grateful Acknowledgement with sincere desires to Him, who is the righteous Rewarder, yea & the exceeding great Reward itself

---

71. Mary Norris, daughter of Thomas Lloyd and sister of Hannah Hill and Rachel Preston. Beginning in 1714, Pastorius dedicated a series of anniversary poems (entitled "Ship-Mate-Ship") to these three Lloyd daughters (in memory of their late father) to commemorate their joint passage to Pennsylvania on the ship *America* in 1683 and their lives in the young colony since then.

72. March 23, 1717.

73. Christ Jesus.

unto faithful Abraham his seed, to recompense & repay you for all your large benefits, bestowed upon you weak friend, at the resurrection of the Just, must Satisfy you at present whether you will or will not.

Moreover, that sometimes the Lives of certain persons, the which God was ready to cut off, upon earnest Intercession of other good & pious men & women, have been prolonged, is pretty plain to me by Gen. 18:25, 26, Acts 27:24. And does not the holy Scripture in many places certify, that our God hears & regards the prayers of his servants, & that the same (if fervent,) are effectual and much availing with him? Now I am thorowly perswaded, that the Lord in my late Sickness, (wherein by his free Grace, Mercy & Goodness he made myself sufficiently ready to depart & to be with him for ever,) would graciously have been pleased to put a period to my natural & transitory life, had not some of his people (both in the Dutch & English Nation) retarded, as if it were, the Dissolving of my earthly house, or Tabernacle of Clay, and thus delayed to an other time the Entry of my Soul into the glorious & eternal mansions on habitations in the heavens; It being not evident, that we have no certain dwelling place here. &c.

Dear well beloved Friends, I can't chuse but believe, that you with honest Griffith Owen,[74] no doubt were some of the chief, who thus far prevailed with God, as to grant me a little more time upon the Stage of this World, And therefore kindly request of you, to entreat Him in your nearest approaches before His footstool (with my own self,) that he may enable me to spend it to his honour, & to the best advantage of my Neighbour, whom to love as ourselves, is the fulfilling not only of the Law, Rev. 19:8, but also of the holy Command of that our great Prophet, whom every Soul ought to hear, Acts 3:22, Mark 12:31. And as mine unfeigned Love & Cordial Salutation is unto you all and your children, (the hopeful offspring of my quondam Intimate Ship-Mate Thomas Lloyd,)[75] so I could wish from my whole ♥, that I might be any wise serviceable unto them, or any of them, during my further Stay in this low region of a tiresom world, and therefore expecting your Orders on that behalf I remain your highly obliged and thankful friend   F.D.P.

NB: In this my foregoing Sickness (Sleeping, but few hours at night,) I wrote pretty much in Rime & prose to several of my Friends, especially to Griffith Owen, whereof some in their answers expressed, they were well pleas'd therewith, But of most I kept no copies.

---

74. The Welsh Quaker Griffith Owen (1647–1717), who came to Pennsylvania in 1684, was an active supporter of William Penn and a longtime member of the General Assembly and the Provincial Council. He was also a physician and a close friend of Pastorius.

75. Thomas Lloyd and Francis Daniel Pastorius arrived in Pennsylvania on the same ship on August 20, 1683. The collection of anniversary poems entitled "Ship-Mate-Ship," especially the first poem "A Token of Love and Gratitude," explores the bond of friendship established between Lloyd and Pastorius during their time together on board the *America*.

[To Rowland Ellis, January 25, 1717]

Rowland Ellis[76] having accompanied Griffith O. & John S.[77] in their Journey towards New England as far as to Francfort, at their request came to visit me the 23rd of the 1st month and after some discourse desired me to write some lines to him, which he would answer. Whereupon I wrote the 25th of the aforesaid first month 1717. But having likewise kept no Copy of my Letter, I think, it was much so to this Effect.[78]

Dear friend R.E.,

For as much as last 7th day of the week upon the Incitement of our worthy friends G.O. and J.S. thou camest to visit me in my Sickness, & at thy departing desiredst me to write some lines to thee in order of being from henceforth more nearly acquainted together, I herewith for an Introduction shall say somewhat of the words Friend & FrienDshiP, than which there's hardly any other more frequently used and abused all the World over. We the people called Quakers, say of one that is of the same profession with us, he is a friend, & per Contra he is no friend, &c. Now as no friend can be where there's no Friendship, even as a godly man not without godliness, the basis of our being really friends is true friendship, not of the world (which is direct enmity with God, but of Christ, consisting in the performance of his Commandments, especially of that which never grows old, viz. to love one another, for hereby the law & prophets are fulfilled, & hereby all men may know, that we are the disciples of him, who out of meer & undeserved Love laid down his life for us.

William Penn in his Fruits of Solitude has very fine reflections upon this Subject, which I shall not mention here, the little book being in many ones hands; This I only shall add of mine own, that as the outwardness of friendship deceives many simple hearted, so true, substantial & Christian friendship seeks at all times & in all places the good of our fellow mortals. A real Christian man helps when and where he can, &c. This band of reciprocal amity is not broken neither by distress, poverty, Imprisonment, Sickness nor death itself, &c. And true friends will never flatter nor dissemble, their policy consists in being franc & plain, evermore speaking the truth one to another &c. – Of the Old Romans we read, that they had their 1st, 2nd, & 3rd rate friends, admitting some only into the court yard or hall, others into the anti chamber or parlour; but their privados into their Closets & bed-rooms. So me thinks we may do the same with a blameless partiality. The Welsh & Dutch &c. may endear those of their own Nation

76. The Welsh Quaker Rowland Ellis (1650–1731) first arrived in Pennsylvania in 1687 and settled there permanently in 1697. As a leading Pennsylvania Quaker, Ellis was actively involved in provincial politics in support of Penn's proprietary government.

77. The English Quaker preacher John Salkeld (1672–1739) settled in Chester County, Pennsylvania, in 1705. He accompanied Griffith Owen on a missionary journey to New England in 1700 and again in 1717, shortly before Owen's death.

78. Pastorius would later reconstruct from memory the contents of his March 25, 1717, letter to Ellis.

more than either French or Danes like as the apostle was deeplier affected with his countrymen.

Such kind of stuff I sent to our friend R.E. to the best of my remembrance.

[To Elizabeth Hill, no date]

Dear Child <u>Elizabeth Hill,</u>

whom I affectionedly love as well for the hopeful good temper of thine own, as also for thy well respected Parents sake, yea & on the account of thy grandfather (honest Thomas Loyd, whose Memory is blessed for ever with the blessed of the Lord, The Orange, or golden apple, as we call 'em in Latin, which thou didst send last second day by the hands of thy dearly esteemed father, I received as a Token of thy Love, with due thankfulness, which I thought to signify in those few lines.

That a word, spoken reasonably & seasonably, makes as fine a shew as apples of gold in pictures (or picture–worked Vials) of Silver, thou mayst read Prov. 15:11. Now for thy apple of gold, I [. . .] would make thee some return of a fit word, as the English Translation has it and pray! what fitter word can I find than that of thine own Surname viz. Hill, which is the same as a little Mountain. Hence the holy Hill & Mount of Sion are synonymous in the Scriptures of Truth.

These the eternal God immoveably has founded

Here thou and I and all ought firmly to be grounded

But to go on & to play, if it were, the Schoolmaker with thee, (which I hope thou wilt not take amiss,) I shall tell thee further, that if we take the Initial letters of our names, we may make some Onomastical devices,[79] of a deep Impression on our minds ex.gr. if thy dear father by **R. H.**[80] should speak thus

Rear up my ♥ Lord Heavenward, Refresh it that it grow not Hard, &c.

Or if thy dear mother **H. H.**[81] say –

Be Honour & glory to the Holy one,

And Halle-lu-yahs sound to Him alone.

So therefore, when thou seest thine own to wit **E. H.**

always remember the Everlasting Hills, Item Establish me my God of perfect Holiness,

Eject the Hethites, who fain would our land possess.

This only for a Pattern, Endeavour thou thy self to make above 600 of thy Name, as I have done with mine in Latin, high- & low Dutch, French, Italian & English, of which

---

79. Onomastics is the branch lexicology that studies the forms and origins of proper names. In what he calls "onomastical devices," "exercises," or "considerations," however, Pastorius takes the first and last names or initials of familiar individuals and inserts them into wise or moral sayings.

80. Richard Hill.

81. Hannah Hill.

last sort I shall annex some &c. &c. which if they seem Insipid, it is because they are not of **E. H.** but of **F. D. P.** who is her cordial Friend, & desires to approve himself so not only in words for her orange, but in deed & reality, if it should please the Lord, to add a few days to his life. F.D.P.

[To Elizabeth Hill, April 11, 1717]

Ma tres chere <u>Elizabeth Hill</u>,   Germantown le 11me d'Avril 1717
Ayant entendu par un de tes Condisciples, que tu apprens François che N. N. j'ai pris d'abord la resolution de te feliciter du bon dessein de ton Pere, de t'avoir instruite dans le principes de cette belle Langue; car quoy que beaucoup de François le plus souvent ne sont pas les meilleurs, & leur langage partant est fort renommé par tout le monde, et sans cela à mon arrive en Pennsilvanie je n'eussé pû parler un seul mot avec nôtre ami Guilleaume Penn, Gouverneur dela ditte Province. Depuis ce temps là (à savoir 34 ans), je n'ai pas eu la moindre occasion de m'exercer ni en parlant, ni eu écrivant François; ainsi j'ai oublié quasi cinq parts de six, et neant [moilas?] je voudrais de tout mon Coeur contribuer quelque chose àl'apprentissage que maintenant tu fois dans [...] Ecole étrangère. Si tu n'as pas la Grammaire de Claude Mauger, (la quelle, après alla de Fr. de Fenne, est preferable à toutes les autres, que j'ai veû jamais,) je te la donnerai tres volontiers aussitót que tu me manderas parole. Presentement je te fais un petit present du Maitre d'hotel, qui vient de t'enseigner, comment tu ne dois pas étre désormais si prodigue de tes oranges, que de tes donner à un, que se peut [contexter?] avec des pe[s]ches seiches, mais d'en faire des Orangade perlées, ou les Conserver & Candir, selon ton Caprice, &c. Toutes fois je t'en remercie fort Cordialement & ayant mangé le premier, je garderai le second autant que je pourai, pour me souvenir de toi le plus souvent que sera possible. Finissant la dejour, je te laisse à me répondre en Anglais ou en François, comme il te plaira: Cependant je te prie de Saluer de ma part ton pere & ta Mere tres affectionnement, & aussi le Maitre de Langue, le desirant de Corriger les fautes de cette Lettre, laquelle si tu peus lire & traduire en Anglois, je t'aimerai tant plus, & demeurerai à tonsjours ton Ami
                    Trés Fidele, Devot & Perpetuel   **FDP.**

[Translation][82]

My dear Elizabeth Hill,   Germantown, 11 April 1717
    Having heard by one of your[83] classmates, that you are learning French with N. N., I have first taken the resolution to congratulate you for the good design of your Father

---

82. Translation by Nathan Michalewicz.

83. This translation from the French does not use the typical Quaker addresses "thee," "thou," and "thy," although Pastorius often did when writing to his Quaker friends in English. His writing other Quakers in French, however, already presumed a degree of elitism that had little regard for the Quaker emphasis on "simplicity."

to have you educated in the principles of this beautiful language; for, although many French most often are not the best, their language is very famous throughout the whole world, and without it I would not have been able to speak a word at my arrival in Pennsylvania with our dear William Penn, governor of the said province. Since that time there (to wit 34 years), I have not had any opportunity to practice speaking or writing French; thus I forgot almost 5 parts out of 6, and nothing [. . .] I wish with all my heart to contribute something to the learning that you are now doing in [our?] foreign school. If you do not have the Grammar by Claude Mauger,[84] (which, after that of Fr. de Fenne,[85] is preferable to all others I have ever seen,) I will gladly give it to you as soon as you send word for it.

Presently, I make you a little present from the headwaiter,[86] just to teach you, that you should not now be so wasteful with your oranges, so that in giving you but one, you may [mix?] [it] with dried peaches,[87] or to make bubbly orangeade, or to preserve & candy it, according to your fancy, &c. In any case, I thank you very cordially, & having eaten the first, I'll keep the second as much as I can, to remember you as often as possible.[88]

As the day is coming to a close, I leave you to respond to me in English or in French, as you please: but I beg you to greet your father and your mother most affectionately, and also the master of languages, desiring him to correct the errors in this letter, that, if you can read and translate [it] into English, I will love you that much more & will always remain your friend,

Most Faithful, Devoted, and Perpetual,   FDP.

[To Lloyd Zachary, August 31, 1717]

Mon cher Ami: Lloyd Zachary   Germantown le dernier

                       Jour du Mois Sixième 1717

84. Pastorius owned two different versions of this work, Claude Mauger, *Grammaire Françoise* (London, 1688) in great octavo format and the English translation *Claudius Mauger's French grammar* (London, 1688) in octavo.

85. François de Fenne, *Institutio linguae gallicae praeceptis brevissimis suoque ordini restitutis comprehensa* (Leiden, 1680). Pastorius apparently did not own a copy of this book.

86. With "headwaiter," Pastorius is probably punning on his role as teacher or headmaster at the Germantown school and on his habit of sending gifts of books and other presents to young people among his circle of friends—such as the single orange he apparently sent with the letter to Elizabeth Hill.

87. According to Jean-Jacques (Johann Jacob) Wecker's *Le Grand Thrésor ou Dispensaire et Antidotaire* (Basel, 1610; The Great Treasury or Dispensary and Book of Antidotes), a decoction of dried peaches ("peches seiches") stops flux of the bowels or diarrhea.

88. Pastorius's point about the oranges here is both an instruction and a joke about himself. While showing Elizabeth how to do something useful with the single orange he sends her (thus also inculcating in her the Quaker value of moderation), Pastorius reveals his apparent prodigality with his own oranges, which were a luxury in early seventeenth-century Pennsylvania: having eaten one orange outright, he keeps the second as a reminder of his friend. Thus both his oranges fulfill not a utilitarian but rather a pleasant or playful purpose.

C'est avec beaucoup de Satisfaction que je recens après diner (comme un dessert tres delicat,) le peu de lignes que tu me fis l'honneur d'envoyer ce Matin. Je me rejöy d'en entendre le bon état de ta Sante, & que tu as déjà fait un tel progress dans la langue Françoise, à present fort à la mode, non seulement dans les principals Cours del'Europe, mais presque par tout le monde, où il ya des personnes de qualite, & des gens de Lettres. Et quoy que la Latine soit sans Contradiction la plus noble, & l'Angloise la plus riche, celle là (assavoir de la Gaule) par un erreur Commun est devenue la plus generale.

Neantmoins ayant raison de te remercier del avoir commence notre Commerce literaire par la premiere, je te prie de la continuer de tems en tems, & de m'arrive ta secônde en Latin & la troisie me dans ta langue maternelle; Varietas enim delectat. Si tu pren[d]s la Change de cette sorte, tu ne seras lasse jamais, & je te répondray toujours aussi bien que je puis, & pire en Françoise qu'en Anglois; Car autant que j'ay appris del'un, j'ay oublie de l'autre ces 34 ans que j'ay été en ce pais ey. J'ecrirois bien plus amplement, mais il me faut du repos: Je pren[d]s done non congé, & te prie du resaluer tres respectueusement ton oncle, ta Tante, & ta Cousine Elizabeth, & de dire à la derniere que j'attens sa réponse dans la langue qu'elle parle ou petit garçon (Mordeai Lloyd,) à qui j'offre mes Services de même qu' à tout le reste chez vous, & demoure à jamais,   Ton affection amy, Qui s'appelle F.D.P.

[Translation][89]

My dear Friend: Lloyd Zachary,[90]   Germantown, thc last day
of the sixth month 1717[91]

It is with much satisfaction that I received after dinner (like a very delicious dessert) the few lines that you did me the honor of sending this morning. I am glad to hear the good condition of your Health, & that you have made such progress in the French language, which is at the moment very fashionable, not only in the principal courts of Europe, but almost everywhere, where there are people of quality and people of letters. And even though Latin is without question the more noble, and English the richer language, this one (to wit, the French) has, by common error, become the most general.[92]

Nevertheless, having reason to thank you for beginning our literary exchange, I beg you to continue it from time to time, and from me will arrive a second letter in Latin and a third in your mother tongue; for variety pleases. If you make this kind of

89. Translation by Nathan Michalewicz.

90. Grandson of Thomas Lloyd and son of Daniel and Elizabeth Zachary, Lloyd Zachary (1701–1756) studied medicine in London and, after returning to Pennsylvania, established a large and profitable practice. Zachary was only sixteen when he began his lengthy and very intellectual correspondence with the much older Pastorius; he would become one of the original trustees of the Philadelphia Academy, along with James Logan.

91. August 31, 1717.

92. Pastorius, in other words, disapproved of French as the lingua franca of the Age of Enlightenment, preferring either Latin, the language of humanism, or English, the language of the British Empire. In the "Bee-Hive," Pastorius explained that English was the richest language because of the wealth of words from languages across the world that it had incorporated in the course of its history.

change, you never get tired, and I will answer you always as good as I can, and worse in French than in English. For all that I have learned of the one, I have forgotten of the other during the 34 years I have been in this country. I would write more extensively, but I need the rest: I therefore take my leave, and I ask you to greet very respectfully your uncle, your aunt, and your cousin Elizabeth, and tell the latter that I received her response in the language she speaks with a little boy (Mordecai Lloyd), to whom I offer my services as wells the rest of you, and humbly remain,

   Your affectionate friend Who calls himself, F.D.P.

[To Lloyd Zachary, July 20, 1718]

<u>Dear & Worthy friend L. Z.</u>[93]   Germantown the 20th of Quintilis 1718.[94]

 A Dram[95] of good Learning is better than an Ounce of Zecchins.[96]

 I have good reason to rejoyce of my pitching upon thee for a more intimate Correspondent, not only because thy letters (French, Latin & English) are 1st of a very fair, legible & flourishing hand, so that one that runs or rides the Post, may read them; but chiefly 2nd of an exact Orthography, (a few words only excepted,) and 3dly (which exceeds all the former,) that they are full of Matter & good Sense.

 The last of thine written this day a week I received, and in answer thereonto shall take Notice of two things, wherein we seemingly disagree, which is a certain means to continue our Epistolary discourse. In the first place I said, & still maintain that Typography was Invented by a Souldier, & thou tellst me to have been Informed that he was a Priest. Now to determine this difference, we ought to (mind as well how we hear, as what we hear, &c.) alledge our authorities & see which is the best. I for my part shall go no further than to Daniel Leeds'[97] Chronologies in his Almanacks printed for the years 1693, 1694, 1695, 1696, 1700, 1710, 1711, 1712, in all which thou wilt find: Since the invention of Guns by a Monk, & that of Printing by a Souldier; But perhaps thou mayst object, that **Daniel Leeds** was a **Devilish Liar**, Ergo not to be Credited. Whereat I make this reply, Concedendo totum argumentum,[98] As far as he speaks of his own. Yet when he crowds something into his yearly leafing Pamphlets out of more authentick men's writings, we are to Acquiesce therewith.[99] And to be sure, I find in

93. Lloyd Zachary.
94. July 20, 1718. "Quintilis" was the Roman fifth month, before Julius Caesar renamed it after himself, "Julius" (July).
95. A dram, though one-sixteenth of an ounce in its literal sense, here most likely is meant simply as a (quite) small amount.
96. "Zecchins": zecchini, or sequins (in both older and modern senses), were former gold coins of Venice and Turkey.
97. Daniel Leeds (1652–1720), an almanac publisher in early Philadelphia.
98. "Conceding the entire argument."
99. Pastorius is here urging Lloyd Zachary to discern between the reliability of the publisher (in this case, Leeds) and the authenticity of the original source.

Philo-laindey's[100] rhytmical Chronology annexed to his new-fashioned Almanack for 1709[:] A Soldier first Contriv'd the Art of Printing, But Guns are Berthold Swartz,[101] a Monk's Inventing. If thou canst Cite as much for to make a Priest or Chemmarin[102] the Inventor of so advantageous an art as thou emphatically termest the same, we are reconciled in this particular, or else **Falsity Does not Prevail. Falsi Dicos Proceres Fas est Dejicere Ponte.**[103]

The next thing is, that thou canst scarce have any charitable thoughts for that poor Martyred Jew, who had been at so vast Expenses to introduce Printing among discreant Turks,[104] inveighing (if I rightly understand thee,) against that servicible subservient Art itself, calling it not only a furtherer of Controversies, but also a Spreader of heresies. To which two black Epithets thou mightest have added that of a Publisher of many foul, Jocular & Atheistical books. But what then? We know, that wheresoever God builds his Church, (his Ape) the Devil is not wanting to erect a Chappel.

Nevertheless Usus habet laudem, Crimen Abusus sit.[105] Our friends in brother-love-Town[106] do not refuse a glass of the sweetest wine, which still turns to the tartest vinegar: Nor we pitiful Scholars (among whom I must needs Class myself, (Seeing I at Present teach School again,) have not the lesser Esteem for the Bible & other good writings because some make a wrong use of those divinely inspired Scriptures, even quite contrary to the end & purpose they were given forth for (exprest in), the which we're not oblig'd to Imitate no more than to read ex cerandum illum librum de tribus impostoribus,[107] Pomoerium Sermonum Quadragesimalium, Legenda aurea, Alcoranum Franciscanorum,[108] the refined & enlarged Coffeehouse Jests, Wit's Cabinet,

100. "Philo-laindey" is probably a playful coinage combining "philomath" (lover of learning), which Daniel Leeds called himself on the cover of his almanacs, and "philander." Thus Pastorius may be deriding Leeds as simply a "compulsive lover."

101. Berthold Schwarz (Schwartz), legendary German alchemist credited in early modern literature with the invention of gunpowder.

102. "Chemmarin": with his (mistaken) singular of *chemarim*, Pastorius is invoking the idolatrous priests of the Old Testament (the correct singular would be *komer*) in contrasting the clerical dress of Roman Catholic priests with the plain dress preferred by Quakers.

103. "False leaders say it is right to cut down a bridge."

104. David and Samuel Ibn Nahmias established the first printing press in the Ottoman Empire in 1493 in Istanbul. For religious reasons, Muslim Turks were prohibited from printing until the eighteenth century.

105. "'The use of it is praiseworthy, only the abuse of it is an object of reproach.'" The motto is from the classical Roman play *Octavia*, usually attributed to Seneca, and was often applied by early modern Protestants to the use of books or other things whose value depended on their use.

106. Philadelphia.

107. "From the pool of those books from the tribe of impostors."

108. Here Pastorius lists two works that he and, more generally, European Protestants, considered fabrications or just plain humbug: *Pomerium Sermonum Quadragesimalium* (1499) by Hungarian Franciscan writer and preacher Pelbartus Ladislaus of Temesvár (1430–1504); and *Legenda Aurea* (*Golden Legend*), a widely popular medieval collection of hagiographies (stories of the lives of Christian saints), as well as Erasmus Alber's *Alcoranus Franciscanus* (1531), a mocking attack on a third such work, Bartholomew of Pisa's *De Conformitate Vitae B. P. Francisco ad Vitam Domini Nostri Jesu Christi* (1399), the authoritative chronicle of the life of Saint Francis and the Franciscan order. *Alcoronus Franciscanus* (Franciscan Koran) mocks the idea that Barthomew's classic was

Wit's Interpreter, the pretty Conceit of John Splinter's Last Will & Testament, &c. and others of the like truth, or as I may stile'm Bastards & spurious products of the Press.

To wind up our present Subject of the primitive[109] author of Printing & the genuine use thereof, it is believed by me, tho' not as an article of our Christian Faith, that this noble & useable art was invented Anno Domini 1440 by John Gutenberg (in English, good Mountain, which questionless will stand until the Conflagration of the World: by John Gutt. I say a Souldier in the army of Uladislaus, King of Poland & Hungeria.)[110] testibus[111] Palmerio, Guilandino,[112] Vignerio,[113] Bibli andro Munstero, Penenfeldero, Polydoro Virgilio,[114] aliisquam quam pluribus, notwithstanding that Scriverius endeavours with a deal of Specious Arguments to make Laurentium Johannem Aedituum[115] the Contriver thereof, and Mariangelus Accursius[116] assigns it to John Faust,[117] a Citizen of Mentz. If I were as happy as to be elected umpire, I would jot this final end to the debate that Aedituus or Kuster has laid the foundation or first rudiments of the said art at Harlem in Holland; and that Gutenberg has trim'd & dress'd it more curiously at Strassburg; but that Faust brought [it?] into that Method as nowadays used & abused. For this mine Award & Arbitrament[118] the Staten Generael der Vereenighde Nederlanden[119] would, no doubt, give me many Millions of their Ducatons, & make me Chief Pensionary besides.

Having already admonished thee in my foregoing, to buy the most exquisit books thy purse gives thee leave to procure, seeing they are in our Age (especially when sold by way of vendue[120]) oftentimes dog-cheap, & moreover correcter than Transcripts. I remember what that brave & learned fellow Erasmus Roterodamus[121] complained in a

---

written with the same divine inspiration as the Islamic holy book (which, of course, early modern Christians rejected as well).

109. First or original.

110. Unclear why Pastorius now refers either to Ladislaus IV of Hungary or perhaps to Ladislaus V of Poland.

111. "As witnessed by." Pastorius lists the names of several authorities who confirmed that Gutenberg was the inventor of book printing.

112. Melchiorre Guilandino or Melchior Wieland (ca. 1520–1589), a German physician and botanist, who lived and worked in Italy.

113. Jérôme Vignier (1606–1661), a Roman Catholic priest of the Oratory of Jesus, also known as the "French Oratory" (Congregation of the Oratory of Jesus Christ and Mary Immaculate) in Paris.

114. Polydore Virgil or Polydorus Vergilius (ca. 1470–1555), an Italian scholar and priest, who lived mostly in England.

115. "Laurentium Johannem Aedituum": Latinized name (here in accusative case) of Laurens Janszoon Coster (ca. 1370–1440), also known as "Aeditus," a printer in Haarlem, Netherlands, who many Netherlanders believe invented book printing before Gutenberg.

116. Mariangelo Accorso or Accursio (ca. 1490–1546), an Italian humanist writer.

117. Johann Fust or Faust (ca. 1400–1466), early business associate of Johannes Gutenberg and later his rival as printer.

118. Decision.

119. The States General (bicameral legislature) of the United Netherlands or Dutch Republic.

120. Public sale or auction.

121. The Dutch scholar, humanist, Roman Catholic priest, and theologian Erasmus of Rotterdam or Desiderius Erasmus Roterodamus (1466–1536) was one of the foremost models of the learning in Renaissance Europe.

certain place, saying, Minoris arbitror Hieronymo constitisse libros Conditos a nobis restitutos. Et in praefatione ad opa Augustini, Vix in alterius tam Impie quam in hujus sacri Doctoris Voluminibus lusit ociosorum temeritas.[122] However even in printed books there's a great diversity of the several Editions, & those to be chosen which are truest, ex. gr. in the first Impression of the historical works of J. A. [....?] (an impartial Frenchman in deed,) there are many remarkable things which afterwards were left out in the succeeding; the Jesuits getting their hands thereinto. Vice versa Jac Usserii Antiquitates Ecclesiarum Britannicarum[123] are mended & augmented almost in every leaf, yet out of that honest book's own Original.[124] I shall not detain thee longer from thine ordinary business but (after I've told thee that at the very same time when Printing was invented, there flourished one Alphonsus Tostatus, who hardly 40 years old had already compounded 14 large volumes, of whome it has been said, Hic Stupor e[st] mundi qui Scibile discutit omne[125]) desire thee to tender my Respects to thy dear Uncle & Aunt, and my kind Love to thy Cousins E. & M. and thereupon subprint myself thy real Friend to serve thee in what I can. Featherfew. Dill. Pimpinella.[126]

[To Richard and Hannah Hill, December 7, 1718]

To <u>Richard H. and Hannah H.</u> whom God has Joyn'd together, & no man shall put asunder, at Philadelphia.

Dearly Esteemed Friends,   Germantown the 7th of December 1718.

Your Nephew (my well-beloved Correspondent)[127] and I keep our Accounts in a pretty equal balance, so that neither of us owes any thing unto the other[128] but Love, a debt unpayable as well in this world, as in that to come; Would to God, I could say, that the Case stands so between us; But alas! I'm thus deep in your book, that I now

122. Pastorius first cites Erasmus's preface to the works of Hieronymus: "'Hieronymus's books cost him less pains in the making than me the mending,'" then goes on to say, "And in the preface to the works of Augustine [again quoting Erasmus]: 'There is scarcely any author in whose work the shameless and lazy have played fast and loose so disrespectfully as in the books of this sacred Doctor of the church.'" (More often known as "Saint Jerome," Eusebius Sophronius Hieronymus [347–420] was an early Church Father and the fourth-century translator of the Bible into Latin.) In 1528–29, Erasmus published a complete collection of the writings of Saint Augustine; the passage Pastorius cites is from a letter Erasmus wrote to Archbishop Alfonso Fonseca of Toledo, which served as the preface to Erasmus's edition of Augustine, *The Correspondence of Erasmus: Letters 2082–2203*, trans. Alexander Dalzell (Toronto: University of Toronto Press, 2012), letter 2157. Pastorius is thus highlighting the problem that not all printed books necessarily provide a reliable and authentic rendering of a writer's original words.

123. James Ussher, *Britannicarum Ecclesiarum Antiquitates* (Dublin, 1639).

124. Printing errors were corrected through referencing the original manuscript.

125. "'Here lies he who astounded the world discussing all things knowable.'" Pastorius is quoting the epitaph of Alonso Tostado (ca. 1400–1455), bishop of Ávila, at his tomb in Ávila, Spain. Tostado was famous for his voluminous writings and ascetic piety, something that would have appealed to Pastorius and other Pietists.

126. Pastorius closes with these three plant names, of course, because their first letters are "F D P." For herbal details on *Pimpernella* and featherfew, see notes 71 and 131 to chapter 7.

127. Lloyd Zachary.

128. Pastorius and Zachary had a reciprocal correspondence, with regular replies back and forth.

live greatly Indebted to you both, and doubt I shall dye in that State. Oh! how more blessed is it to give than to receive! And seeing I still would fain find room among the blessed of the Lord, I herewith in a few words, & abundance of tenderness & affection give you hearty thanks for those several good things, you were pleased to send me; the which, though a very pitiful return, I beseech you to receive until I may perhaps be enabled to make a more agreable requital, If not I supplicate the Almighty to recompense your Liberality, to whose gracious Protection I recommend us all, remaining with a my respects & love,   Your, your ever obliged & thankful Friend F. D. P.

[To Richard Hill, December 10, 1718]

Well Respected Friend R. Hill.   Germantown the 10th day
of the 10th month 1718.[129]

In a grateful Sense of the excessive love & kindness, thou and thy dear wife Hannah have all along shewed unto me, & particularly of late by your sending of wine, to refresh my sometimes [. . .][130] with other good stuff, to regain my lost Stomach, or rather Appetite, and moreover, that thou of thy own accord didst go & pay the Doctors bill for me, as I am informed by my loving Friend Lloyd Zachary, I can not but reiterate my hearty & unfeigned Thanks unto you both, happily made One. And as [for] these extraordinary Obligations, you were pleased so liberally, above the least of my desert, to lay upon me, constrained me to look about for some Requital or other, I must ingenuously confess mine Inability, and find nothing but the herein included true Copy of a warrant for a Lot in your City, [and] the 200 Acres in Germantown being then in Course surveyed for me) which our quondam and generous friend William Penn out of his meer superabundant affection has granted these 35 years past, the which Lot's not taking up was mine own Neglect, I not minding so carefully my Self-Interest, as I might, & perhaps ought to have done. If my Right to the said Lot may be worth of thine Acceptation, I herewith do freely proffer the same unto thee; But if thou doest think it will turn to no better Account unto thee, than hitherto did unto me, pray send it back, that it may further rest among mine odd papers as a living remembrance of that now deceased noble Friend's well-intended favour.

And let me know, by what other means I shall endeavor to declare my thankfulness toward thee & thine, as also how much I am to reimburse of what thou paidst for physick, or else I shall scruple to have any more fetcht. My son had money with him, & would have satisfied the doctor, had he not bid him to let it alone. This is, what I at present shall interrupt thy more serious & and needful affairs withal, & therefore with my cordial love to thyself, to thy said dear wife, mine ever esteemed shipmate, they only

129. December 10, 1718.
130. Illegible line.

beloved daughter Elizabeth and nephew Lloyd, I conclude & under Divine Protection & Assistancc remain thy deeply obliged Friend F.D.P.

P.S. It was resolv'd upon in my bosom council to write also a couple of lines to the said L. Z. but having begun these to thee when most people were already gone to the market he must excuse me nolens volens[131] this time, and the next post, when it stands with his leisure & pleasure begin himself, for we are now upon even terms, though his health be somewhat better than mine, whereof I am very glad & in hope, since maybe ere long I come to be justly called good again, God willing, to whom resign all.

[To Lloyd Zachary, December 20, 1718]

Germantown the 20th of the 10th month, 1718.[132]

To my Choice & Superlatively singular Friend L. Z.

quam prae ter centum millibus unam digner Amicitiâ

Clamo é Palamo à meâ,[133] living with his loving Uncle,

Or, as it were, with his Patre secundo,[134] R. Hill at Phila.

Then when Mount **Lebanon**

& **Zion**'s Hill do perish,+

The **FrienDshiP** will have done

Which in my Breast I cherish

Towards **Loyd Zachary**, Fix'**D** on **Philo**-logy.*[135]

+ Isa. 60:13. Psal. 2:6. & 125:1.

* i.e. the Love of the WORD.

Diligo te Loydi! Tu vero dilige VERBUM,

E qui, Fonte bono, Commoda verba fluunt.[136]

Dearly beloved Friend, It seems to me by thine of late, especially by thy two last Letters, that thou endeavourest to approve thyself a follower of that Mercurius-like eloquent Apostle,[137] Acts 14:12, whose Epistles are weighty & powerful, 2 Cor. 10:10, and he, having been crafty, (though no fisherman, yet an excellent fisher of men,) caught some with guile, chap. 12:16.[138] even whole Troups of Gentiles in the net of the Gospel

---

131. "Whether willing or not."
132. December 20, 1718.
133. "Whom I call and proclaim more than three hundred thousand times a worthy friend."
134. "Second father."
135. The friendship between Pastorius and Zachary was based on their mutual love of words (philology) as well as the Word of God.
136. "I love you, Lloyd! You truly love the WORD, / from which, good source, useful words flow."
137. Apostle Paul.
138. 2 Corinthians 12:16.

unto the Christian Faith & Obedience, whereof doubtless many of our progenitors were then blessed participants.

I am well pleased with the elegancy of thy superfine expressions, and upon thine Inquiry, whether I have the Wise & Ingenious Companion French & English[139] &c.? I answer, No, and never heard of it before, but there are among my small books the Golden Annotations of Franciscus Heerman,[140] which is a collection of the noblest acts & notablest sayings of the most Illustrious & learned persons, both ancient & modern, with very suitable Morals or Doctrines, dedicated to William Prince of Orange, & afterwards King of Great Britain, &c. It is only a 12.°[141] and in the low Dutch tongue: If thou couldst read the same, I would communicate it with all my ♥. For the present I shall recommend unto thee an other little book, published by J. Hill, 1687, & Intitled the Young Secretary's Guide.[142] I think, thou toldest me that it may be had at the Printer's shop in Philadelphia. It's really worth one's frequent perusal, that would write competently well on what theme or subject soever. I prefited the following doggrel Rimes there unto: of this Secretary—More than ordinary, &c. Item: Now having well peruse'd &c. [Mitte mihi Fiens, cum sie tam charus amicus][143] Item, Temple,[144] L'Estrange,[145] &c. what I further subjoyn'd concerning these 3 Epistolographers is more than I at this Instant, and in so streight a space of place, can insert.

Thou further addest in thine of the last 4th days Post that if any edifying Book or books thou wilt take all possible care; To this I say, that those few I have thou art free & welcome to borrow. I in deed did read, pick & cull several hundreds, whilst in this Countrey, and yet bought none, but they were lent me by loving friends as et. gr. by W. Penn, S. Carpenter, J. Morris, R. Preston, Gr. Owen, &c. to whom (tho' most of 'em deceased,) I still am Obliged for their kindness.[146]

---

139. Abel Boyer, *The wise and ingenious companion, French and English, or, A collection of the wit of the illustrious persons, both ancient and modern containing their wise sayings, noble sentiments, witty repartees, jests and pleasant stories: calculated for the improvement and pleasure of the English and foreigners* (London, 1700). This book was printed with English and French on opposing pages.

140. Franciscus Heerman, *Guldene Annotatien* [. . .] (Amsterdam, 1699).

141. In duodecimo format.

142. John Hill, *The Young Secretary's Guide* [. . .] (London, 1687).

143. "Send me aloft, with so very dear a friend." Latin words within square brackets are, of course, also those of Pastorius, who is imagining his rhymes, along with the book he is sending, to fly to Zachary.

144. Sir William Temple, *Letters written by sir W. Temple, Bart., and other ministers of State, both at home and abroad, containing an account of the most important transactions that passed in Christendom from 1665 to 1672, in two volumes* (London, 1700).

145. The British pamphleteer and journalist Sir Roger L'Estrange (1616–1704) supported the Royalist cause during the English Civil War and Commonwealth period.

146. This passage testifies to the active borrowing and circulation of books among elite Friends in early Pennsylvania.

However I, herewith send & lend thee 1st the Writing Scholar's Companion,[147] wherein thou wilt meet with a world of my Manuscript Remarks,[148] & some thereof not altogether useless or unpleasant, 2nd a merry piece of Edw. Blount's, Inscribed Micro-Cosmographie in Essays & Characters.[149] 3rd my Melliotrophium Sententiarum,[150] a hasty and uncompleat by me begun, (yea and only begun,) these 20 years since, when I was teaching School in Town. Thou mayst run this soon over, and if there be any sentence therein yet unknown to thee, receive it as from thy best friend's hand, & if thou art acquainted already with 'em all, remember, quod Lectio lecta placet, decies repetita placebit[151] In case thou wilt be so good as to augment the so defective Manuscript with some that occur unto thy memory, those that henceforth shall see the same, Nunq. cessabant Loidio benedicere docto.[152]

Now after thou hast done with these three, and return'd them home again, (the sooner, the better,) I may Impart per adventure other things more agreeable, being ambitious to promote thy laudable Studies in what I can, not by way of complement, but in Sincerity & Truth,

thy constant & faithful Friend F.D.P.

Fare est Doctrinae Philo Logia Saine[153]

P.S. By thy P.S. I understand, that thou hast received my french answer; but that the pacquet directed to thy dear Uncle was not yet delivered by Edward Farmer's carter,[154] for which I am very sorry, because I inclosed a certain warrant, granted in 1683, by Governor Penn unto me for the taking of a Lott in Philadelphia, which I never did, & therefore now requested thy said Uncle's acceptance thereof, as to whom is due thankfulness for his many benefits & in a sort of requital I have freely profer'd my right unto the said Lott, &c. I shall not omit to rescue the letter from the wicked bearer thereof, as soon as he comes through Germantown, Or else write a couple of lines to his said

---

147. Anon., *The writing scholar's companion: or, Infallible rules for writing true English with ease and certainty* (London, 1695).

148. Along with the printed books the Pennsylvania Friends circulated among themselves, letters and manuscript commentaries served to situate larger worlds of knowledge in the specific, local "Republic of Letters" they had created.

149. John Earle and Edward Blount, *Micro-cosmography; or, A piece of the world discovered; in essays and characters* (London, 1628).

150. Although Pastorius nowhere else mentions a manuscript book with this name, his characterizing it as a hasty collection of phrases points toward his manuscript miscellany entitled "Alvearialia," selections from which can be found in chapter 4 of this reader.

151. "'A lesson that pleased the first time it was read, still pleases when repeated ten times.'" The sentence Pastorius is quoting seems to have appeared first in James I of England, "Speech in the Star Chamber, June 20, 1616." It is probably adapted from Horace's *De Arte Poetica*, "Haec placuit semel, haec decies repetita placebit" (The one pleases but once, the other will still please if ten times repeated).

152. "Shall never cease to speak well of their teacher Lloyd."

153. "It said that teaching philology is sensible."

154. Though here Pastorius simply seems to mean someone who drives a cart, "carter" could also mean a rude, uncultured man, a clown.

Master to have it brought forth: Mean while, I beg the pardon of they dear Uncle for having been thus **Foolish** & **Dull-Pated**, as to Intrust a Justice's Waggoner with a letter for so eminent a friend, when within less than an hour after it ran up & down in my Mind, that the wretched Fool would not deliver it; Qui quod sit,[155] it's firmly sealed up & shall (I hope) at length re-appear so that none besides us do know the contents thereof. Vale feliciter mi zucharia, & me quoquam à morbo indies convalescere tuis nuncia, cum seriâ ad precatione omnigenal Salutis.[156]

There is a kind of Plant-animal growing (as reported,) only under the Sea-rocks of the Island Samos, which we call in Latin Spongiam, and in English Spunge, & being dried sold very cheap in Germany, &c. If thou canst procure one for me in Philadelphia I shall repay thee whatever price thou mayst give for it, & acknowledge myself obliged to thee for thy pains-taking. Im Umbschlag[157]—

All Trades must live: the Paper-maker says,

And Welcome he! that Current Silver pays:

Inclosing his in empty Coverlets,

Whereof non else, but I, a penny gets.

L. Z. If thou canst handsomly & honestly come at the largest brown Sheet or Sheets, wherein some goods are brought over from Old England, I would satisfy thee for it when I pay for the Spunge mentioned within. F.D.P.

[To Lloyd Zachary, April 18, 1719]

To mine Incomparable good Friend L. Z. at Philadelphia

L.Z. my dear Friend: Germantown 18th of 2nd month 1719.[158]

Les bonnes Intentions ne produisent pas tujours des bons SucreZ.[159] that is to say, I was entirely resolved to send thee this morning a large answer to thine almost too concise Epistle of last week, as well to express my thankfulness for the vermillion, and late visit, thou was pleased to honour me withall, as also to signify unto thee, that I formerly read J. W. P.'s Letter to some divines in the high German tongue and that he the said John William Petersen is one of the Francfort Company, a true Pietist in deed, & such is likewise his wife Eleonora,[160] with whom I have been most Intimately

---

155. "In any case."
156. "Farewell, my sweet, and I daily recover from illness through your messages, with serious prayer for all kinds of health."
157. "In the envelope."
158. April 18, 1719.
159. "Good intentions do not always produce good sugar." The first and last letters of Pastorius's French remark form, of course, the initials "LZ," for Lloyd Zachary.
160. Johann Wilhelm Petersen (1649–1727) and his wife Johanna Eleonora Petersen (née von Merlau; 1644–1724) were both theologians, mystics, and leaders of radical Pietism and Philadelphianism in Germany. Pastorius met them both in Frankfurt at the meetings of the Pietist conventicle founded by Philipp Jakob Spener. Unfortunately, none of the letters Pastorius mentions seem to be extant.

Acquainted these 40 years past, and received letters from them since my voluntary Exile into this wilderness Province, &c. Of this kind of stuff I intended to entertain thee at least with half a sheet; But some of Horsam[161] employ'd me all yesterday in drawing a long deed of Sale, five Bonds and other legal writings, and my Son goes to your Market ere Sun-rise, therefore I must (as thou didst) beg thine Excuse for falling short of my purpose, Never the less am in hopes to have a deal of time to myself next week, & consequently to Impart part of it to my best & most esteemed Correspondent. Our friend Thomas Ellwood[162] in the preface to his Davideis says that having one winter clean health, he had more Leisure than before, and thus is it with me, after my Recovery; yet would I not be so sick again, (if I can help it) for all the gold & silver in my possession! My kind Salutation to all those that remember their Love unto me, & more Individually to thine own self from thy loving Semper Eodem[163]   **FDP.**

P.S. Gave me leave to find fault with thy complemental subscription, viz. Thine to command & serve L. Z. If so, why then doest thou never command? That thou art over willing to serve, I know by Experience; & now expect of thee to put in use the first Member of this thy conclusion, that I may be occasion'd to retaliate thy good turns[164] according to my weak Capacity.

[To Matthias van Bebber, April 17, 1717]

Matthias van Bebber,[165]   Germantown, 17th of 2nd month 1717[166]

Loving Friend, my youngest son H. P.[167] taking just now his leave of me, in order to go down to G. Creek,[168] and to visit his cousin M. James,[169] from whence (perhaps) he may make an Excursion into your quarters, I thought it convenient, to accompany him with this Epistolium as far as to thy house, that if he should be by any look'd upon as a Run-away, thou for our old acquaintance sake, & the Respect I always bore unto thee & thine, mayst be pleased to defend him on that account against all persons whomsoever

---

161. Pastorius probably means Horsham Township in present-day Montgomery County, Pennsylvania, founded in 1717.

162. The English Quaker Thomas Ellwood (1639–1713) was author of the religious poem *Davideis* (1712) about the life of King David.

163. "Always the same."

164. By "turns," Pastorius most likely means "returns," referring to Zachary's responses to his letter.

165. Matthias van Bebber (d. ca. 1730) was the son of Jacob Isaacs van Bebber (ca. 1640–1705), one of the original Germantown settlers from Krefeld. Matthias became a merchant, living in Philadelphia, and eventually moved to Cecil County in Maryland, where Henry Pastorius seems to have traveled repeatedly. Francis Daniel served as van Bebber's attorney in a number of legal transactions.

166. April 17, 1717.

167. Henry Pastorius. Along with Pastorius's November 25, 1714, letter to Henry, this April 17, 1717, letter underscores the elder Pastorius's struggle with his younger son's apparently peripatetic lifestyle.

168. St. Georges Creek in Newcastle County, Delaware, which had a Quaker meeting at the time and was close to Cecil County, Maryland, where Matthias van Bebber lived.

169. "M. James" (first name not known) was apparently the child of Anna (Enneke) Pastorius's niece Mary and her second husband, John James, who also lived at Duck Creek, located near present-day Smyrna, Delaware.

by these presents; which, I hope will find thee & dear Relations in that State of perfect health & prosperity, I heartily wish unto you all. We heard some Months agoe, that thy brother Isaac departed his transitory life; but the News wanting confirmation, I take it as a presage of his long Continuance here in this low region of a vexatious world.[170]

As touching myself, It was the good Will of him, who kills & makes alive, to bring me of late to the very brink of the Grave; how be it, I mend, (as the English phrase has it,) from day to day, and without a Relapse, or unless I grow worse again, I still may remain a little, (for it can't be but a little, I going towards my 66th) in this Tabernacle of Clay, and so see thee once more with us, to fetch a deal of current Silver Money of Pensilvania down to Maryland: However, It being thy Just due, I do not begrudge thy happiness, but rather wish thee a large Increase thereof, and so with my kind Salutation to thyself, & brother Isaac, and your alter Ego's or bed-fellows, I rest thine affectionate friend F.D.P.

P.S. If the bearer hereof my said Son H. should want thine Assistance, I earnestly request to do for him, what thou canst, I shall with all possible thankfulness acknowledge it as done to mine Own self.

NB: This Lettre was not delivered, because when H. P. came to Matthias van Bebber's Plantation, ditto M. v. B. was here in Germantown.

[To Lydia Norton, August 24, 1718]

Dear & well-beloved Friend, <u>Lydia Norton</u>.[171] Germantown, the 24th of the 6th month 1718.[172]

Thus far I have faithfully copied on less than 44 Pages the 44 Leaves, which are in thine old book, within four days, & some parts of three Nights.) Had the Rest of thy Barbadian Journal been there, it should be likewise here in this hasty Transcript; Not withstanding I was almost wearied with the frequent Repetitions of (after Meeting went to such or such a house, dined there, lodged there that Night, and Stayed there the next day, &c.) which being not very Material or Edifiable, takes up a deal of Paper as well as time, which both might (as I think,) be more profitably bestowed else where. If the Evangelist Luke, in the Acts of the Apostles (being the first Ecclesiastical History of about 29 or 30 years after the Resurrection of our Lord & Saviour J. C.) had used the same method, what a Bulk would that Book be? However, in Chapter 16 last verse he takes Notice, that Paul & Silas, coming out of the Prison at Thyatira, entered into the

170. Matthias's brother, Isaac Jacobs van Bebber (1661–1723), who would indeed live well past the year 1717, when Pastorius wrote the letter.

171. Lydia Norton was an itinerant Quaker preacher from Salem, Massachusetts, and a member of the Monthly Meeting there. She went on several missionary journeys along the Eastern Seaboard and the Caribbean islands, including a trip south in 1717. She probably met Pastorius during that journey.

172. August 24, 1718.

house of Lydia, the Purple-Seller, But why he mentions this particular Circumstance appears clearly by v. 15.

Journals, that contain only remarkable Passages, (in mine Eyes) are the best, seeing we can the sooner peruse 'em and the things therein related will stick the more firmly in our Memory. I do not hint this to thee, as if I was any ways displeased with Thine; but Simply, because now a days most Readers loath superfluities in all Sorts of Writings, and much more those, to whose Task it falls to Copy or transcribe them. Thou seest hereby, (and as I hope, wilt not take it amiss,) that I deal plainly, being by Birth a Franconian, and measurably by Regeneration a Free-man of the Lord C. J.

So in the Incomprehensible and Endless Love, where with our heavenly Father has loved us, I take my kind Leave of thee, heartily desiring Him, from whom all our Blessings come, to be graciously pleased from henceforth; further more to Conduct and Protect thine own self to the very Conclusion of thy days here on Earth, and then (in the World to Come) to be thy great Reward (as He doubtless will be to the faithful offspring of faithful Abraham). So as to Shine like a glistening Star in the Firmament of God's Eternal Power, for Ever & Ever. Amen.

Francis Daniel Pastorius

P.S. I wafer'd this accelerated Leaf here into this thy Book thus, that thou mayst easily tear it out, (& in pieces too,) when thou pleasest.

Fare well, dear Lydia, Fare well!

saith my Soul, & the Souls of many,

who were Comforted & Refreshed

by thy lovely Visit.

Letter to James Logan, Samuel Carpenter, Isaac Norris, and Richard Hill

INTRODUCTION TO THE TEXT

The following is a transcription and annotation of Francis Daniel Pastorius, "Letter to James Logan, Sam. Carpenter, Isaac Norris & Richard Hill the present Commissioners of Property in the Province of Pennsilvania &c. Germantown the 28th day of the Third mo: 1713," MS Society Collection, Historical Society of Pennsylvania, an unpublished letter not included in Pastorius's "Letterbook."

Written to some of his most influential Quaker friends, this letter provides a glimpse of one of the darkest periods of Pastorius's life in Pennsylvania, when, facing the fraud perpetrated on the Frankfurt Land Company and the Germantown residents who had purchased land from it, he struggled to regain legal title to his lands.

Though he would eventually succeed, through the intercession of his friends, the letter reveals Pastorius's deep disillusionment over the inability of Pennsylvania's civic leaders to safeguard Penn's peaceful and holy experiment. To gain greater sympathy from his influential correspondents, Pastorius suggests sending his sons back to Germany (even at the risk of their being captured by French pirates). And, indeed, the return voyage to Europe—a kind of reverse migration—would become a common theme in American literature, expressing many immigrants' realization of the sometimes great disparity between their utopian aspirations and the dystopian realities of life in colonial America.

Pastorius had for several years before he wrote this letter petitioned the Pietist leaders to release him from his obligations as their attorney, having come to see that his connection to the Pietists no longer served his larger spiritual goal and that the Frankfurt Land Company only supported the financial goals of its investors. When they did release him in 1700, however, the company's investors and their heirs unwisely transferred power of attorney to three radical Pietist immigrants who had arrived in Pennsylvania in 1694—Daniel Falckner, Johannes Kelpius, and Johannes Jawert. After Kelpius resigned his role to pursue his mystical eremitic life outside Germantown, and after Jawert moved to Maryland, Falckner mismanaged the company's funds, and, having incurred excessive personal debt, was eventually thrown into debtor's prison. At this juncture, the land speculator Johann Heinrich Sprögel (ironically, the son of a prominent Pietist pastor in Germany) retained the powerful Quaker lawyer David Lloyd, ostensibly to bail out Falckner, and through a variety of legal tricks wrested all of the Frankfurt Land Company's landholdings from their rightful owners—including Pastorius. When the remaining members of the company declined to file an official countersuit, Pastorius sought individual redress with James Logan, Samuel Carpenter, Isaac Norris, and Richard Hill—his personal friends and commissioners of property in Pennsylvania. With their help, he was able to regain his share fully in 1714 (Pastorius's personal correspondence with them, recorded in his "Letterbook," testifies to his profound gratitude for their assistance). The following letter is part of Pastorius's sustained but deeply jarring struggle to seek restitution of his misappropriated lands. Along with the divisive events of the Keithian controversy in the 1690s, the protracted misery of the Frankfurt Land Company fraud in the 1710s most likely drove Pastorius to turn away from public affairs and to dedicate himself even more intensively to the private studies and more intimate correspondence that constitute his literary output during this period.[173]

173. The Frankfurt Land Company affair, Pastorius's struggles with Falckner, and Sprögel's land fraud are, of course, much more complex than laid out in this introduction or in the letter to follow—included to provide a sense of the worldly disappointments Pastorius experienced late in his life in Pennsylvania and the tremendous

Well Esteemed Friends,

Having of late produced before you the Original deeds of Lease & Release of our honourable Proprietary, bearing date the 18th & 19th of January 1682 whereby Johan Wilhelm Uberfelt[174] hath purchased of Him One thousand Acres of land in the said Province; As also the Deed of Sale, by which the said Uberfelt Conveyed the same unto me under the hand & Seal of a Publick Notary besides his own, dated the 11th of July 1683. You are well assured of my Right to so much. And seeing there were One hundred & Seven Acres formerly Granted & Confirmed to the said Uberfelt, his heirs & Assigns in the Germantownship by the Patent thereof, bearing Date the 3rd day of the Second month 1689, there remains still 893 Acres to be taken up on his account. And though it may be said, that Daniel Falkner & his Co-Attornies[175] have taken up this Remainder for the Francfort Company in that Tract of land near Manatawny-Creek,[176] Yet for as much [1st—in left hand margin] as neither the said Uberfelt nor I have not signed & sealed the Contract of Society made by the said Francfort Company, And [2dly—in left hand margin] neither he nor I have not Impow'red or Authorized Daniel Falkner & his Co-Attornics, to take up any land for us, As also [3dly—in left hand margin] It is no where mentioned in the Manatawny-Patent, that they had any Power from either of us, to meddle with the said Remainder, And [4thly—in left hand margin] Not one Acre is Granted or Confirmed in the said Patent neither to the above said Uberfelt nor to me; So that none of us both can lay any Claim to any land in the afore mentioned Tract, and therefore I think it most Convenient to Renounce by the Inclosed Writing all my reputed Right, Title & Interest to any land whatsoever in the said Manatawny Tract, and to desire a Warrant of You the present Proprietary Deputies to take up those 893 Acres (for which I have paid the said Uberfelt and he the said Proprietary these almost thirty years agoe) in such a place or places, where they may be had in the abovesaid Province.

significance of his friendship with some of the leading Quakers there. For the best concise treatment of the Frankfurt Land Company affair, see Duffin, *Acta Germanopolis*, 1–53.

174. Johann Wilhelm Überfeldt was one of the original Frankfurt Pietist purchasers of land in Pennsylvania. When he decided not to settle in Pennsylvania, Überfeldt's land was signed over to Pastorius.

175. In 1700, Pastorius was relieved of his duties as attorney for the Frankfurt Land Company. The company transferred the power of attorney to Daniel Falckner, Johannes Kelpius, and Johannes Jawert; Kelpius, a mystical hermit with no interest in business affairs, assigned his power of attorney to Jawert in 1701; and Jawert moved away to Maryland, thus leaving Falckner as the de facto sole administrator of the company's assets.

176. Manatawny Creek is a small tributary of the Schuylkill River in southeastern Pennsylvania. The Manatawny tract mentioned here was a large stretch of land originally purchased by the Frankfurt Land Company and subsequently acquired fraudulently by Johann Heinrich Sprögel. Though Pastorius technically owned some of this land, he hoped to regain title to a different tract to avoid his sons' having to establish their own farms as neighbors to his implacable enemy Sprögel.

Concerning the Proposal, which One of you was pleased to make, when I last addressed myself to you, viz. to Assist me for to recover my said Remainder of land in the Manatawny-Tract by Course of Law, I have this to say, Where the Lawyers pervert all Equity, (as the Scripture Phrase is,) and plead only for Money, Meticulosa res. est, ire ad Judicem;[177] Moreover, I want no land for mine own Settlement; my two Sons, who are now both of age, intend to work upon it, and to make Plantations for themselves according to the manner of this Countrey.[178] But I would as lieve have them go over Sea to my Relations in Germany, or by the way fall into the hands of French Privateers, than thus cast them away to be a Prey of wicked Sprogel,[179] that Land-pirate, who now lives at Manatawny and bears a bitter grudge and mortal hatred against me & my poor Children. If you knew him so well as I, you would never advise me to make my two Lads his so near Neighbours; A little of his Portrait you may see (when at Leasure,) in the Letter of Benjamin Furly[180] and his Book keeper, therefore I shall not detain you any longer with this my declared Enemy, whom I wish, God Almighty might Convert.

Dear & Respected Friends,

My Design is not to be troublesome or tedious, but as short as possible. However, the old Proverb says that Dumb Folks get no Land, and in Case Falkners treachery & horrible Betraying of his Trust had not untied my Tongue, I should perhaps still keep my Peace, and Continue in that defect & neglect of Caring for those of mine own house, &c. But whereas now Divine Providence seems to Care for them more than I hitherto have done, by ordering things thus, that the said Falkner got no land granted nor Confirmed for me in the aforesaid Manatawny-Patent, that Natural Love, which Parents owe to their Offspring, constrains me to Intreat you once more for a Warrant to have my 893 Acres laid out in such Places of the Province as are not yet taken up; The which, no question, you can do very well, (if you will) and easily answer it to our worthy Proprietary & Governor, not only because I was the first of all the Dutch,[181]

177. "'What a frightful thing it is to go to law.'" The full saying by the Roman playwright Plautus (ca. 254–184 B.C.) is "Nescis tu quam meticulosa res sit ire ad judicem" (You little know what a frightful thing it is to go to law).

178. It would have been impossible in the seventeenth century to find unsettled land and establish a new plantation in the German states of that time. Instead, depending on the region, sons had to split any land they inherited, thus resulting in ever smaller parcels, or the oldest son inherited it all. Either situation resulted in a growing number of men who could no longer support themselves and their families, which often led to emigration as the only solution.

179. Son of a prominent Pietist minister in Germany, Johann Heinrich Sprögel colluded with Daniel Falckner and the English Quaker David Lloyd to defraud the Frankfurt Land Company of their land holdings.

180. Before traveling to America, Sprögel had apparently duped Benjamin Furly—Penn's representative on the Continent—into making him his agent in Pennsylvania.

181. Germans. Pastorius is using the misnomer "Dutch" commonly used by American English speakers for German immigrants because of the word's similarity with "Deutsch."

that came over under his Government in Anno 1683 bringing Several Servants with me, and many more being sent soon after,[182] whereof I in consideration of every Poll could have demanded 50 Acres, pursuant to the then printed Books; but likewise because he himself[183] not many days before his last Departure for England, told me and my wife (taking our Leave of him,) that Our two Sons, when they should live so long as to Settle any land, should have some of his, with a deal of kind Expressions, which I am fully perswaded, were Sincere and Cordial. So in expectation that you will Grant this my Righful Request, and thereby Oblige me & mine to you and yours above what we are already, I presume to subscribe myself

Germantown the 28th day
    of the Third month 1713.

Your loving & thankful Friend
Francis Daniel Pastorius.

𝕩

Letter to Son Henry

INTRODUCTION TO THE TEXT

The following is a transcription and annotation of Francis Daniel Pastorius, "Letter to Son Henry. Germantown the 25th of November 1714," MS, Arch Misc. Doc., Box 2, Folder 4, Item 1, Germantown Historical Society, an unpublished letter not included in Pastorius's "Letterbook." In a particularly moving instance of Pastorius's worries for Henry's welfare, this letter shows the apparently strained relationship between father and younger son.

Pastorius seemed to be of two minds in raising his sons, John (Johann) Samuel (1690–1722) and Henry (Heinrich; 1692–1736). On the one hand, in keeping with Quaker calls for a practical education, Pastorius had John Samuel and Henry trained as weavers (Henry later took up shoemaking on his own), and he apparently considered English to be his sons' primary language. On the other hand, however, Pastorius also fostered their broader academic training: in a letter to their grandfather in Germany, later printed as part of Pastorius's *Circumstantial Description of Pennsylvania* (*Umständige Geographische Beschreibung Der zu allerletzt erfundenen Provintz Pensylvaniæ*; 1700), his sons mentioned going to school in Philadelphia (the Quaker school where Pastorius taught) eight hours every day. And, in dedicating the "Bee-Hive" manuscript to his sons, he writes that his "*Desire, Last Will and Testament is*, that my Two Sons John Samuel and Henry Pastorius shall have &

---

182. This is perhaps the only instance where Pastorius uses his status as leader of German-speaking immigration to Pennsylvania to gain a personal favor.
183. William Penn.

hold the same with the Rest of my Writings . . . to themselves & their heirs for ever, and not to part with them for any thing in this World; but rather to add thereunto some of their own, &c. Because the price of Wisdom is above Rubies and cannot be Valued with the precious Onyx or Sapphire: And to get Understanding is rather to be chosen than Silver and Gold, &c."

Yet Henry seemed to have little interest in his father's religious and intellectual idealism. From around 1714, he made repeated trips to Maryland, returning to Germantown only sporadically. Pastorius was greatly concerned both about Henry's well-being and about his financial as well as spiritual future. A note to his "Res Propriæ" manuscript made in 1716 mentions that Henry had fallen off a horse at the May fair in Philadelphia and hurt himself so badly he was at first believed to be dead. In a caustic remark, Pastorius hopes that Henry's near brush with death will teach him to "improve himself in righteousness." Ironically, Henry's desire to escape from what this letter reveals to have been the overbearing influence of his father merely mirrors Francis Daniel's desire to escape from his own father's dominance. Henry would eventually return to Germantown and settle there permanently, marrying Sarah Boutcher of Bristol Township, some 20 miles away, in 1721. He appears as the writer and signer of a petition presented sometime around 1732 to proprietor Thomas Penn to revive the Corporation of Germantown, which had been dissolved in 1707. Finally, Henry Pastorius is recorded in the "Bee-Hive" as the son passing down the manuscript book his father had treasured so highly to generations of Pastorius descendants. In the end, Henry honored his father's legacy and helped preserve his writings for posterity.

THE TEXT

Loving Son Henry,   Germantown the 25th of November 1714
Our Cousin Marieke[184] having been here of late, we sent thee word by her, that both I and thy Mother would not have thee to launch out far into Maryland,[185] which has

---

184. Henry Pastorius did not have any actual cousins living in America. His father, Francis Daniel, and his mother, Ennecke Klostermanns, had both immigrated to America alone, and none of their family members moved there later. Thus all of Henry's actual cousins would have lived in Germany (or elsewhere in Europe). However, Henry's brother John Samuel married Hannah Lucken, the sister of Mary (Marie) Lucken, in 1716. Quite possibly, the Pastorius and Lucken families were already quite close long before then. In fact, Francis Daniel was most likely already a good friend of Mary and Hannah's father, Jan Lucken, before their children married: both men held important offices for the Corporation of Germantown from the 1690s forward. Since Francis Daniel and Jan Lucken thought of each other as brothers, Jan's daughter "Marieke"—a diminutive form of Marie, the German version of Mary—and Francis Daniel's son Henry were like first cousins.

185. In his April 17, 1717, letter to Matthias van Bebber (see main text above), Pastorius also mentions his son Henry going to Maryland.

been the Ruin of John Smith and others;[186] But advise thee for thy own best to live for some time with Matthis Keurling[187] and there to perfect thyself in the Shoemaker Trade. We perceive that at present thou art at work at the Mill-race upon Duck-Crick,[188] and thereby mayst earn good Wages in Case the man who employs thee does honestly pay; For we hear that he is much Indebted, and so perhaps after thy work is done will let thee go without Pay. They say, that if John Swift[189] had hired thee himself, thou mightest be more sure of it than now. Therefore endeavour to get thy Pay for what thou labourest in that place, or else do not spend thy time and work in vain, but rather betake thyself to Matthis Keurling and if before thy going thither thou thinkst it convenient to see us, we shall make thee as wel-come as we can. Thy brother does his duty very bravely at home, and so we desire thee to mind thy business as long as thou art abroad, that no just blame may be made against thee. We are all in health as we use to be, and our kind love and Salutation (as also that of Chris. Witt[190]) is unto thee, and so I remain thy affectionate, and loving father

F. D. Pastorius

P. S. Caspar Hoodt[191] was the day before yesterday at our house, and told us, that a fortnight agoe he has been at friends Meeting on Duck-Crick, and there did see our abovesaid Cousin, but not thee. Pray! do not neglect to meet with God's people and there to wait upon the Lord, of whose hands all our Blessings, both Temporal & Spiritual, must come.

An seinem Segen ist alles gelegen,
Und wer den erlangen will, muß auf Jesu warten in der Still.[192]

186. John Smith was an early Germantown settler, who shows up in the Germantown Court Book (Raths-Buch), but it is unclear what happened to him after he went to Maryland.

187. Matthis or Mathias Keurling or Keürlis was the son of Peter Keurling/Keürlis; they belonged to the thirteen families from Krefeld who became the first settlers of Germantown. Matthis was a shoemaker, and Henry Pastorius had apprenticed with him.

188. A Monthly Meeting of the Quakers was established at the Duck Creek millrace in the winter of 1705–6.

189. John Swift (d. 1733) was one of the earliest settlers arriving in Pennsylvania with William Penn. He was later a member of the Pennsylvania General Assembly during the same time as Francis Daniel Pastorius, which is most likely where they met (a 1691 letter from the Assembly to William Penn is signed by both Swift and Pastorius). Swift represented Southampton in Bucks County. It is unclear what job Swift would have given Henry Pastorius.

190. Pastorius's neighbor in Germantown, Christopher Witt (1675–1765), was trained as a physician in England, joined Johannes Kelpius's mystical group in 1704, but moved to Germantown upon the disbanding of that group in 1708.

191. Caspar Hoodt was from Hesse in Germany and settled in Germantown in the early 1690s. As a recorder on the Germantown General Court, he had frequent interactions with Pastorius.

192. "Everything depends on His grace, / and who wants to reach it has to wait upon Jesus in quietude."

7 ⤳

Practical Advice on Gardening, Agriculture, and Medicine

"The Monthly Monitor"

INTRODUCTION TO THE TEXT

Transcribed and annotated from Francis Daniel Pastorius, "The Monthly Monitor Briefly Showing When Our Works Ought to be Done in Gardens, Orchards, Vineyards, Fields, Meadows, and Woods. 1701," MS 8243, Pastorius Papers and Digital Library, Historical Society of Pennsylvania, the following excerpts have never before been published. Organized as a monthly advice manual for farmers, gardeners, vintners, and beekeepers, Pastorius's "Monthly Monitor" is one of his most practical manuscript books and was in frequent use, as evidenced by the worn and tattered appearance of the archived original. Each monthly section contains information on many topics, ranging from seeds to be sown, fields to be tilled, and crops to be harvested to the relationship between diet and human health, the improvement of the soil, and the impact of planetary movements on plant development; the book also contains separate units on specific themes such as viticulture and beekeeping. The excerpts below are a sampling of both the monthly installments and the longer, thematic units.

"The Monthly Monitor" provides a fascinating glimpse of the variety of plants known and cultivated in early America, but its sources range from classical writers such as the Roman natural philosopher Pliny the Elder to early modern contemporaries such as the German physician and alchemist Johann Joachim Becher, whose work is considered an important precursor of modern chemistry. Even though Pastorius himself was an avid gardener and beekeeper, he clearly could not have tested all the advice he presents or observed all the phenomena he describes in the manuscript. Like his commonplace books, "The Monthly Monitor" thus provides a record of knowledge transmission both from antiquity to his own age and from Europe to America.

Showing that classical, magical-hermetical, alchemical, and modern scientific concepts both competed and coexisted in Pastorius's time in practical applications such as gardening and agriculture, "The Monthly Monitor" helped readers, for example, gauge the influence of stars and planets on human health by displaying a table called "Tabula Planetarum horaria; Or what hour of day and Night each Planet doth Govern all the Week long." And it even told them on which day and hour, given the planetary positions, they should harvest certain medicinal herbs to capture the herbs' full potency. If, at certain places in the "Monitor," Pastorius seems steeped in magical-hermetical traditions, at other places, he turns toward the empirical approaches of the "New Science" and its practitioners, such as Francis Bacon. Thus, changing his mind about arranging "plants, which nourish themselves with the same Juice" (use the same nutrients) together in the same bed, Pastorius disregards "whatever the ancient Naturalists prate" and instead accepts how "Francis Bacon (Lord Chancellor of England) explains the whole Mystery thus, that two plants, who are nourished by the same sort of Juice, do extremely hurt each other by too near a Vicinity; [. . .] On the contrary two plants that for their aliment require Juices wholly different, vegetate & flourish perfectly well together: and this is [. . .] Sympathy or Imaginary Friendship." His gardening taught him an important lesson about the production and transmission of knowledge: when properly arranged, different knowledge systems or epistemologies could thrive at the same time, perhaps even in the same soil. Pastorius saw ancient and new ways of understanding nature as "sympathetic" plants that drew on different ways of seeing, thinking, perceiving, and knowing.

<u>The Monthly Monitor</u>[1]
briefly shewing
when our works ought to be done
in Gardens, Orchards, Vineyards,
Fields, Meadows & Woods.
& also in our Houses, Kitchins, Cellars, Garners, Barn, Stable
all the year round.
See Tho: Tusser's Husbandry for every Month in Rimes.[2]

<u>Omnia Tempus habent: Tempore cuncta suo.</u>[3]
To every thing there is a Season
And a Time to every purpose under heaven
A Time to plant & a Time to pluck up
that which is planted. &c. <u>Eccles. 3:1.</u>
These are the very words of wise King Solomon
Tho' near three thousand years agoe is dead and gone
But he does nowhere tell when your works should be done
In Orchards, Gardens, Fields: Therefore my Friends look on
This Monthly Monitor; he is my firstborn son
Of <u>Husbanderia</u>: A Youth so stout that none
For him can have their Rust by him be let alone
Till they do yield & say: The prize of Sloth is none.
<u>Tandem Solertia vicit.</u>[4]
<u>1701.</u>

[5]

---

1. All underlining, whether single or double, reflects Pastorius's in the original.

2. The English poet and farmer Thomas Tusser (1524–1580) is best known for his poem "A Hundreth Good Pointes of Husbandrie," first published in 1557.

3. "'To everything there is a season: everything in its time.'" Pastorius is quoting a contraction of Ecclesiastes 3:1 and 3:11.

4. "At last skill prevails."

5. Horizontal lines added to indicate original page breaks in the prefatory material.

And tho' a [. . .] laborious [. . .][6]
Yet they that make not knot, must often lose [. . .]
From whence this Caution here as in a [. . .]
That ev'ry one who plows, who hows, who sows, who mows
Should fit their business always to Clime & Time
And when God prospers them, praise him in Prose & Rhyme
For he is worthy still most worthy of Renown,
Whatever he does give is evermore his own.
To God be Glory, Thanks and Honour
The only good and gracious Donour,
The Giver of all perfects Gifts.
Halle lu Jah! Halle lu Jah!
DEO soli Gloria,
In sempiterna Sæcula.[7]
Cuncta DEO soli Gloria, Laus et Honor.[8]
Gott allein die Ehr, und sonst keinem mehr;
Denn seine Güt und Treü ist alle Morgen neü.[9]

Renown and Praise to the Lord,
Glory to him alone;
His Name by all men be ador'd
Till Time itself is done:
And then to all Eternity
Will men & Angels sing
Triumphal-hymns to God their King
With one accord, uncessantly.

In the XIth Month called January.[10]

For here's the <u>vulgar beginning</u> of the Year; which more properly should commence from the 25th day of the 1st month, the world then being created, & Christ Jesus conceived in the Virgin's womb. &c.

6. Verses on back of title page, some suffering from damage, are omitted here.
7. "Glory to God alone, / in all the ages."
8. "All the Glory, Praise and Honor is to God alone."
9. "All honor to God and no-one else / for his grace and faithfulness are every morning new."
10. See note 43 to chapter 3. This entry begins the section of monthly advice for garden, field, and housework in Pastorius's "Monthly Monitor."

This month is the <u>rich mans</u> Charge, & the poor mans Misery.

The trees, meadows & fields now being cloathed in white.

After Rain or Snow a North-West will blow. But if the South wind blow hard, & the Earth be not frozen, it's a Sign of following Sicknesses.

Now the Sun enters Aquarium, an äereal Sign. The old year ends, the new begins, Begin new lives shake off old sins.

When <u>days lengthen</u>, Cold does strengthen. It now increaseth even like the days do. Days longer, Cold stronger. A stock of wood will do you good.

Beware of taking <u>Cold</u>; & use <u>meats</u> that are moderately hot, for the best Physick[11] at this time of the year is good Diet & warm Clothes. Let no blood, nor go to the Apothecaries Shop, unless great Necessity require it. Remember that it's hurtful to fast long, […] […]. A Cup of Cider or other excellent Liquors. Wholesom. Why should honest Clowns[12] not enjoy the fruit of their bypast labors, eating a Surloin of beef, a souced[13] pig, a marrow pye & what else their cook-room affords.

Better to <u>work in the barn</u>, than in the Ordinary,[14] viz. […]. Nevertheless some begin the year with mirth & good Cheers.

Make use of Spices, Pepper, Ginger, Cloves, Sage, Fennel, Annis[15] seed, Penny royal,[16] &c. and in the morning of a draught of Wormwood wine.[17]

[. . . . .][18]

---

11. Medicine or medical substance.
12. Here "clowns" means rustics or peasants.
13. Soused: pickled.
14. Inn, public house, tavern.
15. Anise.
16. Pennyroyal is a small-leaved, creeping mint.
17. Wine prepared from the proverbially bitter plant wormwood (*Artemisia absinthium*).
18. Illegible lines.

Wedding & <u>ill wintering</u> tames both man & beast, and although you are to distribute your <u>Co[a]rse hay</u> [. . .] first & save the best till Spring; yet drench <u>weak, sick kine</u>[19] with verjuice[20] & horses with water & ground mault sodden with a little grass.

[. . . . .][21]

In January drink no dregs, Eat hens with short legs, whether a rain, a hail, a freeze or snow, from the fire do not go.

<u>Uncover the roots</u> of your Fruit trees as early as [. . .].

<u>Lop & prune</u> superfluous branches therefrom. Now season is good to lop or fell wood.

<u>Lance</u> young Trees, which have a thick bark.

<u>Rid</u> grass of bones, of sticks, and stones.

<u>Set all kind of Quick-sets</u>[22] in the New of the Moon, and when the ground is frozen <u>transplant</u> old Fruit trees.

<u>Cart dung & the dirt</u>, which you heaped up last 3rd month, into vineyards & fields; bring also some thereof to your fruit trees, yet have care that the dung do not touch the roots.

<u>Sow in hot beds</u>, radishes, lettuce & other Salading.

<u>Lay Wallnuts, hazelnuts</u>, the Stones of Almonds, apricocks[23] in a good sandy mould, let them spring or sprout out in a warm place; afterwards in the 2nd month[24] plant them in your garden beds, both at the increase of the Moon.

<u>Fell Timber</u> in the decrease, especially in the last Quarter of the Moon, as occasion requires, & it will be more durable and not subject to worms; from the 12th of the 9th

---

19. Archaic plural of "cow."
20. Acidic juice expressed from green or unripe grapes, crab apples, or other sour fruit, once widely used in cooking.
21. Illegible lines.
22. Single cuttings or young plants, especially hawthorn, usually taken and grown for making hedges.
23. Apricots.
24. April.

to the 12th of the 11th month, the moon being in ☿, ♂, and ♃ and ♄[25] in a good aspect. Firewood in the first quarter, the ☽ in ♃ or ♀.[26]

<u>Split likewise Rails</u> for your fences, Pipe-staves, firewood, & the next Snow fetch them home upon a Sled.

<u>Hunt Rabbits</u>, Rackoons, Squirrils &c. the Moon having been [. . .].

<u>Turn up your Beehives</u>, & sprinkle them dexterously with a little wax & sweet wort. You may also remove them.

Keep Sheep out of briers, & beast out of mires.

<u>No Contention all the year twixt Man & Wife ought to appear.</u>

<u>Lo further</u> as in November ☉ & December #. ∆.[27]

Still Mattock[28] in hand, & break up thy land.

In the XIIth Month called February

If this month prove <u>wet</u> 'tis not unseasonable; however <u>cold rains</u> are bad for poor beasts: <u>warm weather</u> not very profitable to fruit trees. Fevrier le plus court & le pire de tous.[29] February fills the dike either with black or white.

Now the Sun enter Pisces, Signum Aqueum.[30] The pinching cold makes women scold. The charity of men refrigerates extremely with the weather, both being as cold as . . .[31]

<u>The warm air</u> is not lasting, but oft deceives us to our prejudice.

25. Mercury, Mars, and Jupiter and Saturn.
26. Moon in Jupiter or Venus.
27. Pastorius uses these special characters to cross reference certain repeated tasks listed in other months. "☉" in the entry for November (not included in this selection) references: "Sow ashes, hens & pigeon's dung over the <u>Meadows & Grassplots</u> & rake it gently under [. . .]"; "#" in the entry for December (not included in this selection) references: "put good mould & a deal of Snow thereon, & when this is all melted, level it again in the XIIth month [February]"; "∆" in the entry for December references: "Take the nests of <u>Palmer (or Canker) worms</u> from your fruit trees, & straight way burn them."
28. Tool similar to a pick but with a point or chisel edge at one end of the head and an adze-like blade at the other, used for breaking up hard ground, grubbing up trees, and the like.
29. "February is the shortest (month) and the worst of them all."
30. "Water sign."
31. Ellipsis in original.

If necessity urge, you may <u>let blood</u>; but be sparing in <u>Physick</u> and prevent taking of Cold through Carelessness.

Eschew as enemies to health slimy fish, milk, the like that opilate[32] & stop the liver & veins, & thicken the blood.

Hard <u>labour</u> in cold weather's good, to cause our food to breed good blood.

Now cold Turky-pyes, roasted Ducks, a Bacon Chine[33] with some Mustard.

Poor Planters do <u>long Winters</u> fear, Some think they're longer ev'ry year: And have but little hay to spare.

<u>Make still use of</u> Spices, & sour Meats: Put agrimony in thy drink especially in good old wine. Apples boil'd & prepar'd with hony are now very wholsom.

Now we are not troubled with Wasps, as such as lie buzzing and scolding womens tongues. Now warm thy nose or't [. . .]

Both young and old now feel the Cold.

Winter for <u>Cattle</u> is half gone in the Freshes, not in Salts.

If thou have money, drink Muscadine, Choose a young wench, & give her wine, for she that's over worn & old, makes no good musick in a month so cold.

Winter spends, What Summer lends, This Makes the [. . .] look very poor.

Men & time spend one another; viz. <u>Time spends men</u>.

<u>Bare the roots</u> of your fruit trees, and if the weather [. . .], lay dung to them.

<u>Shave, prune & trim</u> all Sorts of fruit trees from moss, canker, rank twigs or sprigs & all needless branches; for if you do it near the Spring, they will bleed, which is prejudicial to their growth and if it be done already last month so much the better.

---

32. "Oppilate": to stop or block up, fill with obstructive matter, obstruct.
33. Backbone and immediately adjoining flesh of a bacon pig that remains when the sides are cut off for bacon curing.

Im Zwilling u. in der Waage pflanzt man [...]-baüm, pfopft, saübert, schneitet, curiert, u. wartet sie gedreülich, nicht aber im Löwen, Stier, Widder,[...].[34]

Remove or transplant Grafts of young trees in the last & [...], the Moon being in Ariel, Libra or Scorpio. Thiemen[35] p. 664 saith in ♉, ♏, and ♑, the ☽in good aspect with ♄[36]

'Tis held good to Cut Scions[37] & stick them in the ground a month before you graft, that they may take to grow the better.

The Moon decreasing and in [Libra] or [Aquarius] the weather being mild, dig your garden and set great Beans, & Gourd-Seed for Calabashes.

Sow also hardy Pot herb-seeds as Spinage, Beets, Chervil, Lettuce, Onions, Parsnips, Carrots, Borage, Cardibened,[38] Dill, NB: Cole-seed, as soon as you can get in the ground.

In the New Moon: Hops

But the Moon increasing: Cabbages, Parsley, Smallage,[39] Purslane,[40] Sorrel,[41] Asparagus, Garlic, Mustard, Coriander, Tobacco,

Item Nuts & kernels of apples, pears, prunes, quinces, apricocks &c. Set the sharp end of fruit stones upwards.

Plant potatoes in the worst ground, saith Geo. Parker in Alm[anack]. 1700.[42]

Destroy your Ant hills at the decrease of the Moon.

---

34. "In Gemini and in Libra, one plants [...] trees, grafts, cleans, prunes, heals, and cares for them faithfully. But not in Leo, Taurus, and Aries [...]."

35. Johann Christoph Thieme, *Haus- Feld- Arzney- Koch-Kunst und Wunder-Buch* (Nuremberg, 1682).

36. Taurus, Scorpio, and Capricorn, the Moon in good aspect with Saturn.

37. Slips for grafting, grafts.

38. *Cardo benedito,* Spanish name for Saint Benedict's or blessed thistle (*Cnicus benedictus*), commonly used to treat the bubonic plague in the Middle Ages and also used in herbal medicine to promote lactation in nursing mothers.

39. Any of several kinds of parsley or celery, especially wild celery (*Apium graveolens*), smallage was formerly used medicinally and to flavor food.

40. Any of low-growing succulent plants in the purslane family, widely grown (chiefly in warmer regions) as a salad vegetable or herb.

41. Any of small perennial plants belonging to the genus *Rumex*, characterized by their sour taste, sorrel was once cultivated for culinary purposes.

42. George Parker, *An ephemeris of the coelestial motions, heliocentrick and geocentrick, the year of our Lord, 1700* (London, 1700).

Make a Store of <u>Birchen brooms</u>, before these trees put forth leaves.

[…] to prevent & <u>destroy Earth flees</u> see [below, "Additional Observations," Num. 15].

About the middle of this month dig a Circle about your fruit trees, to destroy the grass, that the sun, air & rain may penetrate with more ease.

At the end of this month the weather being warm & suitable restore the liberty of laborious <u>Bees</u> by half opening their hives' passages. How ye may likewise remove them.

In the 1st month, called March

Which commonly cometh in like a Lion, & goes out like a Lamb: Cold & <u>turbulent</u> March weather, with extraordinary high winds; Nevertheless After Rain Fair again.

About the 10th of this month Oesters[43] Aries (Signum Igneum)[44] equalizing days & nights all the habitable world over. A time for all things, as the wise man says. The Nights this month are equal with the Days.

This month & the next <u>Physick</u> may be used to great advantages of health; Purge & let blood.

Use <u>meats</u> of good digestion, & such as afford nutriment to the body. Viz. Neats[45]-tongues, Udders, Rabbits, Pyes of Lamb-stones,[46] &c.

In Lent despise not batter'd fish, 'Tis farc as good as heart can wish.

This month in all the year The best to brew good <u>Beer</u>.

We yearly wish an <u>early Spring</u>, But often get no such like thing.

The weather being now very fickle, brings some to the Bed, & some to the Grave.

---

43. With "Oesters," Pastorius is referring both to Easter and to the Norse goddess of the dawn, Eostre or Ostara. Aries, or the astrological sign of the ram, begins March 21st, when it marks the vernal equinox.
44. "Fire sign."
45. Now rare, "neat" refers to any domestic bovine animal, such as a cow or an ox.
46. "Lamb-stones": testicles of a lamb.

Make still use of Spices, & Purl;[47] of Sage, rue,[48] penny royal, garlick, rhadish, lovage;[49] Item[50] of Mead & other sweet Drink.

Walk warm in chamber & hall, March no too fast for fear of fall:

Better is the dust, how ere the wind lies, under your feet than in the eye.

This month is best when dry; For, <u>March dust</u> is worth gold. Good to be sold. [..]51

To thy Sheep now go & look, For Dogs will have vittels by hork[52] & by [...]

Long Winters poor <u>Cattel</u>. Now planters wish the winter gone, for fodder's either scarce or none.

[..]53

<u>Cover the roots of your</u> fruit trees (opened in the 9th, 10th, & 11th months) with fat mould.

<u>Take off the Webs & Caterpillars</u> from the tops of twigs, &c.

<u>Set all Sort of kernels</u> & stony Seeds.

<u>Cut your Scions</u> before the buds sprout in the fall of the moon.

<u>Uncover & Pole your Vines</u>. Prune them of superfluous roots & shoots, which you find in the face of the ground.

<u>Early Planting & Sowing</u> sometimes yields twice so much Increase as late ones; Therefore as soon as possible <u>Set & Sow</u>:

47. "Purl": alcoholic drink made by infusing ale or beer with wormwood or other bitter herbs.
48. Any of various southern European dwarf shrubs of the genus *Ruta*, especially common or garden rue (*Ruta graveolens*), with bitter, strongly scented feathery leaves, formerly much used for medicinal purposes.
49. A perennial southern European herb, lovage (*Levisticum officinale*) was once commonly used as flavoring for food and as a domestic remedy, especially for urinary ailments.
50. "Likewise," "also."
51. Lines illegible.
52. Although no seventeenth- or eighteenth-century examples defining "hork" could be found, it most likely means "vomit" here.
53. Lines illegible.

<u>In the Full Moon</u>: Clove gilliflowers, Violets, Marigolds, [...], Lettuce, Endive,

<u>In the Decrease of the Moon</u>: English & French beans, Indian peas, [...], Cucumbers, Squashies, Cashavies,[54] Pompions,[55] Musk melons, [...] melons, Potatoes & those manner of garden Seeds you have not sow'd in the foregoing month.

<u>In the Increase of the Moon</u>: Annis seed, Sweet Marjoram, Basil, Sperage or Asparagus, Scurvigrass,[56] Burnet,[57] Sage, rue,[58] hyssop, thyme, rosemary, lavender, penny royal, worm- & Southernwood, hops, [...] in wet, marshie places.

<u>In the last Quarter</u>: hemp, flax, oats, barley, millet, rice, lentils, chick-peas, summer-wheat. <u>See set out</u>: Cabbages, Colewort,[59] Parsnips, Carrots, Onion, Parsley, [...] [...].

[..][60]

In the II[d] month, called April.

A <u>dripping</u> April is natural & hopes begin to master doubts & now the <u>Peach-trees</u> make a most beautiful show.

<u>Variable weather</u>, Fair& Foul together. This month's showers do not hinder the growing of grass. Am Aprillen Regen ist viel gelegen.[61]

Now the Sun enters Taurum, Signum Terreum.[62]

<u>Purge and Bleed.</u>

54. Cassavas are extensively cultivated in the West Indies, the tropical Americas, and Africa. Although, as largely tropical food plants, their cultivation in colonial Pennsylvania would have been highly unlikely, that Pastorius includes cassavas here among more likely food plants for his region reflects his interest in combining tropical American with European and North American food sources in his horticulture.
55. Pumpkins.
56. As its name clearly suggests, scurvy grass (*Cochlearia officinalis*) was once used to prevent or treat scurvy.
57. Any of perennial herbs or small shrubs in the rose family belonging to the genus *Sanguisorba*, especially salad or garden burnet (*Sanguisorba minor*), formerly used as a domestic remedy.
58. See note 48.
59. General name for any plant of the cabbage family.
60. Lines illegible.
61. "Much depends upon April's rain."
62. "Earth sign."

Milk & homeny is harmless <u>Diet</u>, but so is not fresh nor salt fish, therefore let good housewives mind their Dairies & white meats, and dish up Lumber-pyes,[63] a roasted haunch of venison, Lamb, Veal & bacon. Abstain from <u>Wine</u> the *Causa sine qua non*[64] of many diseases. Make <u>Diet-drink</u> of last year's dryed herbs to purge the blood.

Keep warm clothes on till this month's gone. Now cold again with wind, and rain. Now a times the weather is foul and fair together. Simul pluit atque serenat.[65]

This month the pores of the body being open & so most apt for Medicines, endeavour to remove & prevent all causes of sickness, praying to God for his blessing: this being the best time for remedying Extremities.[66]

NB: The more people use themselves to a mean & <u>spare Diet</u>, the less need they'll have of Physick.

Now shallops bringing <u>Salt</u> provide for the whole year; For if you stay to pag. 21 you may happen to pay 10 or 12 shillings for what now you can have for half a crown.[67]

Buy also <u>Rice</u>, <u>Melassus</u>,[68] Train—whale or <u>Lamp oil</u>,[69] by the hogshead & barrel, some of the neighbours joyning together.

<u>Make still use of Purl</u> or Wormwood wine and in the morning of rue, fennel-seed, betony,[70] and & bibernell[71] temper'd with hon[e]y, or boil'd in wine. *Item est*[72] Mint, lambs-meat, young chickens & bach-fischlein.[73] And of bodily Exercise or Motion many ways.

---

63. Savory pies made of meat or fish and eggs.
64. "The essential cause."
65. "It rains and clears at the same time."
66. By "extremities" here, Pastorius means extravagant opinions, behaviors, or expenditures.
67. Pastorius is referring to the November entry of "The Monthly Monitor" (not excerpted in this chapter), where he advises his readers on how best to preserve various foods with salt. Here he advises them to buy salt early and in bulk, for later in the year they may have to pay four or five times as much. Half a crown was worth 2 shillings and 6 pence (2½ shillings). Shallops were small, shallow-draft sailboats used for coastal navigation.
68. Molasses.
69. Especially as obtained by boiling the blubber of the right whale.
70. The perennial grassland herb betony (*Stachys betonica*) was formerly known for its medicinal and magical virtues.
71. Any of several plants of the genus *Pimpinella*, which includes anise (*Pimpinella anisum*), once used to treat menstrual cramps, and burnet saxifrage (*Pimpinella saxifraga*), which though neither burnet nor saxifrage, was, like true burnet and lovage, formerly used as an herbal remedy and was once thought to protect against bubonic plague and other contagious diseases.
72. "And also."
73. "Brook fish": any fish caught in a creek or other moving body of water.

[. . . . .]⁷⁴

<u>Cleanse & Clear</u> your fruit trees from Moss.

<u>Summer-stir</u>⁷⁵ <u>your fallow ground</u> when the Trees begin to blossom, the [. . .] being pretty old: Plow deep & narrow furrows.

Altho' <u>Barley</u> as well as other Summer Corn may be sown the latter end of last month, yet seeing it's more tender than the rest & kill'd above ground if Frost come after't is sprung up, its sowing is best deferred until the middle of this month.

Sow barley & oats any time, this month on land subject to weeds.

<u>Plant Indian Corn</u> in old land; but for new land next month will do swell enough, we commonly having cold rains in the forepart thereof. A matter of 10 or 12 days after it comes up, begin to how⁷⁶ it.

<u>How your Vineyard</u> the second time; <u>Plash</u>⁷⁷ or prune the Vines & <u>pour the Tears</u>⁷⁸ or water which then drops from the fresh wound in small viols or vessels.

<u>Set & Sow all</u> kinds of garden herbs. Cauliflower, Lettuce, Basil, Marjoram &c. Item⁷⁹ Turnips, Ricinus.⁸⁰

<u>Slip Artichokes</u>, Sage, &c. <u>But never do this Riddle forget, To Sow when dry, & set when wet.</u>

Towards the middle of the month <u>Plant forth your Melons</u> & Cucumbers.

<u>Gather Nettles & other good weeds</u>, dry them, & next winter mix them with the fodder of your Cattel.

74. Lines illegible.
75. Plow, prepare for sowing.
76. Hoe.
77. Interlace in a trellis, support or train against a wall (growing branches, vines, etc.).
78. Reference to "tears of the vine" (*lacrima vitis*, lit. "tear of the vine"), mentioned by Pliny the Elder in his *Natural History*, sap exuded from the grapevine thought to possess medicinal properties.
79. "Also."
80. Castor oil plant (*Ricinus communis*).

Dig up for future uses Elicampane,[81] horseradish.

At the expiration of this month: Leave off Grasing in your Winter Corn-fields.

In dry weather Let your Meadows see water if you can, donet sat prata biberunt,[82] then harrow them over with iron tines.

Gather up Worms & Snails all Summer after Evening Showers.

Bark Trees for Tanners.

Open the doors of your Bee hives, & look carefully to them, for now they hatch, and even some years begin to swarm.

A good Season to Catch Eels.

[..]

Some Additional Observations

Num. 1. To prevent the Freezing of the blossoms on your fruit trees, tie woolen- or straw-bands about them, to let the ends of the bands hang into water, Or sprinkle water to the trees roots, keeping them always moist & wet; or rather make in the 1st month a little trench about the trees, & fill it with water: Thus they will not be hurt neither by hoar nor other frost.

Num. 2. To lay open the roots of old fruit trees prevent the frost from killing the fruit; & covered again with good mould, they bear well & are less liable to blast.

[..]

Num. 10. Flowers & herbs and seeds which you gather to keep dry for Physical & huswifery uses ought to be gathered at the full Moon when full ripe. Take heed of cutting them with a knife but rather pick them with your fingers. Dry them rather in the

---

81. Elecampane or horse-heal (*Inula helenium*) is a perennial herb formerly used as a tonic and stimulant.
82. "'Until the meadows have drunk enough.'" Pastorius is loosely quoting from Virgil, *Eclogues*, book 3, line 111, which reads in full: "Claudite iam rivos, pueri: sat prata biberunt" (Close the sluices now, boys: the meadows have drunk enough).

Shade than in the Sun, which too much exhaleth their Vertue; yet to avoid corruption, let this great Luminary look a little upon them, & then put them in Paper-bags, &c.

Num. 15. There's a certain Insect called <u>Earth-fleas</u>, which in dry weather do feed upon & destroy your tender Cabbages, turnips, cresses, mustard, etc. just when they're springing; To prevent this mischief, some old women will tell you, you must sweep your house, (chamber & kitchin, they mean) & sift these sweepings over your garden-beds, whereon you have sow'ed the aforementioned seeds. Others say, Light Galbanum[83] & smoke round about your said beds. Others again bid you to fetch an Ant- (nest or) hill & sow it over your beds. But in case you suspect the first as superstitious & can't have the second, nor like the third, (as I do not,) I shall impart better Remedies, and the best of 'em at last.

As soon as you perceive these unbidden guests," <u>sprinkle</u> your plants several mornings with cold water, & immediately pick these fleas off. Item[84] Sprinkle your said plants with water in which drawn fishes (their bowels taken out) have been washed: Or in which 3 Crabs have been lying 9 or 10 days. Item strew <u>ashes</u> of Oakwood, or Gerberloh, oder Kohlengestüb[85] with a moderate hand over your said plants. Item Pulverize hens or hogs dung & strew it over 'em in manner aforesaid. Item small horse-dung; Item the chaff, whereon children do lie in their cradles. Now I come to M. John Peschelius his Experiment,[86] Pound says he, or cut very small, <u>Garlick</u>, pour water on it, let it soak well, then strain this water upon your seed and after it stood a good while, drie it again & sow it, being sure that the abovesaid Insects will not touch your plants, neither need you to fear, that your Turnips, Cabbages, &c. will smell like garlick, for the Ground takes all the stinking property to itself.

NB: Sow your Cabbage-seeds on such a place of your garden, where the sun does not shine till evening; for this trouble-som Insect delights most upon warm ground.

[. . . . .]

---

83. Gum resin obtained from certain Persian species of the genus *Ferula*.
84. "Also."
85. "Tanbark [derived from oak] or coal [bottom] ash."
86. Pastorius is referring to *Garten-Ordnung* (Leipzig, 1597; Garden Order or Garden Design) by the German Lutheran pastor and garden designer Johannes Peschelius or Johann Peschel (1535–1599).

Num. 19. A brief Description of the Lamp-Oil-Tree.[87]

There's a certain Shrub, called in Elisha Coles's Dictionary[88] <u>Palma Christi</u> & by the French <u>Main de Dieu</u>, which two names as well as several others of Popish herbalists, are both equally blasphemous, signifying in plain English the hand of God & Palm of Christ. The Spaniards call it <u>Figuera de Inferno</u>,[89] or hellish Fig. The Latin word for it is <u>Ricinus</u>, because the fruit thereof resembles a Tick in Cattel. The Germans give it the name of <u>Wunderbaum</u>, i.e. Wonderful Tree, being a matter of admiration to them, that from so small a kernel there should rise in one Summer a Tree, which, if the Soil be suitable & delightsome to it, exceeds the Stature of a man & a half, as their dialect is. (Yea & Carolus Clusius[90] makes mention of an American Wondertree, & saith he himself has seen some in Spain ad Fretum Herculeum,[91] which were as thick as a man; as high as a three men: adding that, one (or but half a) kernel thereof would purge any body very vehemently up- & downwards. Now altho' one might think this Shrub to have names enough already, yet I shall give it one more viz. that of Lampoil tree; the reason why it will appear at the bottom of the next side. But mind for an Imprimis,[92] that this marvellous plant requires a pretty rich garden mould to grow in, & the seed must be set in the 2nd month, April. The root of it is hardly a span long, full of fibres, not reaching deep in the Earth; The Stem blewish, & where somewhat brown, there it looks as if it were strewn over with Meal. The leaves are large & stand upright when it rains, gathering & holding, if it were, in the hollows of their hands the water 2 or 3 days, laging[93] it up for dry weather to come. The blossoms of this strange tree some are yellow, & some red: the knops[94] of the first drop & fall away fruitless, but the buds of the latter, Safron-Colored ones turn to prickly three partite husks, in which the Tick-like or hand-palm'd beans do lye.

> And tho' some Authors say, that Moles or Wants[95]
> Will flee the places where Lamp-Oil-tree stands;
> Yet these blind animals love dunged land.
> And we may see their hills close by our plant.

87. Castor oil plant (*Ricinus communis*).
88. The English lexicographer Elisha Coles (ca. 1608–1688) is best known for his *An English Dictionary: Explaining the Difficult Terms that are used in Divinity, Husbandry, Physick, Philosophy, Law, Navigation, Mathematicks, and Other Arts and Sciences* (1676).
89. And the Portuguese call this same plant "figueira do inferno," it having been discovered on the Portuguese island of Madeira.
90. Carolus Clusius or Charles de l'Écluse (1526–1609) was an influential Flemish botanist and horticulturalist.
91. "Near the Strait of Gibraltar."
92. For an especial reason.
93. Lagging, here meaning "saving" or "storing."
94. Flower buds.
95. (Also) moles.

Concerning the Medicinal Vertues &c. Ricinus is hot & dry in the 3ʳᵈ degree. As for the does, Dioscorides[96] bids us take 30 kernels, but others are of opinion, he means but 3. Mesue[97] allows 15 & Fernelius[98] only 8. Adding, that it is an yrksom & tedious Physick; however, the said kernels being first rosted, & then either mixt with fennil and annis-seed, or candied with Sugar, cause no Vomit at all. The leaves laid fresh on womens breasts increase the suck and upon the clefts, chaps or chinks thereof do quickly heal 'em. Again the said leaves being pound & bruised & applied to the swoln hard breasts of child-bed-women will take off their swelling together with the pain; and putting some vinegar thereunto, they cure Inflammations, der Rothlauf.[99] The Oil made of the kernels is a good Remedy against Tetters,[100] Scabs, Scurf of the head, & Inflammations of the Podes[101] or Fundament.

But my chief design is not to play the doctor; only you may hereby know, that this abovementioned shrub grows naturally or unplanted in Egypt, & that there they make their <u>Lampoil</u> of its fruit; and so may we here in Pennsilvania planting the kernels, as in the foregoing page is directed, they being almost nothing else but oil. For a proof, lay the same after you've shell'd them on a hot Iron, & they'll melt quite away. Or stick a Pin in one of these naked kernels, kindle it, & it burns & casts a flame like a little Candle. Those who know how to plant & tend Indian corn, may in like manner proceed with the Lamp-Oil-Tree.

The Character & Names of the 12 <u>Zodiacal Signs</u>, together with the Moon[']s Dominion over the several parts of mans body, as she passeth the said 12 Constellations.

♈	Aries or Ram governs the head & face.	♉	Taurus, neck & throat.
♊	Gemini, arms and shoulders.	♋	Cancer, brest & stomach.
♌	Leo, the heart & back.	♍	Virgo, bowels & belly.
♎	Libra, reins[102] & loins.	♏	Scorpio, secret members.
♐	Sagittarius, thighs & hiPs.	♑	Capricorn, the knee.
♒	Aquarius, the legs.	♓	Pisces, the feet.

96. Pedanius Dioscorides (ca. A.D. 40–90) was the author of *De materia medica*, an encyclopedia of herbal medicine influential throughout the Middle Ages and well into the early modern period.

97. The Nestorian Christian physician Mesue the Elder or Masawaiyh (777–857) was director of the Baghdad hospital and author of several medical treatises.

98. The French physician Jean François Fernel or Fernelius (1497–1558) coined the term "physiology" for the study of the functions of the body.

99. "Erysipelas": a skin infection.

100. "Tetters": general term for any pustular eruptions of the skin.

101. "Feet." Pastorius probably derived "Podes" through backformation from "antipodes."

102. Kidneys, the region of the kidneys or loins.

A Sign is an Arch of the heavens containing 30 degrees, or the 12th part of the whole circle.

In the Almanacks you find against every day of the month the Sign or place of the ☽, which governs the members above mentioned.

NB. It's held extreme dangerous to bleed when the moon is in that sign which ruleth the member where the vein is to be opened [Best to purge when the ☽ is in a watery sign, vz. ♋, ♏ or ♓.]

But an Ointment or Plaister[103] is best applied when the moon is in the same sign that ruleth the member to which it is applicable.

NB. Von Baumzucht sind ♓ und ♎ die bequemste und fruchtbarste Zeichen. Der Löw, Stier, Widder, Jungfrau u. Schütz aber taugen gar nicht.[104]

[..]

Gather your herbs, flowers & seeds in the Planetary hour, i.e. let the planet that governs the herb be angular, & the stronger the better. In herbs of Saturn, let Saturn be in the ascendant, if you can. In herbs of Mars, let Mars be in Mid-heaven, for in those houses they delight: Let the Moon apply to them by good aspect, & let her not be in the houses of her enemies. If you cannot well stay till she apply to them, let her apply to a planet of the same triplicity, & if you cannot wait that time neither, let her be with a fixed Star of their Nature. Haec Culpepper pro Studiosis Astrologia.[105] Further he bids you dry them well in the Sun, & not in the Shadow,[106] &c. Then put them up in brown Papers, &c. NB. Herbs full of Juice dry in the Sun, others in the Shadow.

Some herbs lose all their Vertue when dryed, as Lettuce, Purslane, Beet, Arach,[107] Cole, Cresses, &c. Others, tho' they may be dryed, yet are best used when green or fresh, as Wormwood, Southern wood, rue, mint, &c. these being dryed do heat too much. Whatever you will dry, gather them in their prime, & mind that their full maturity is

---

103. Plaster, poultice.
104. "For arboriculture, Pisces and Libra are the most convenient and fertile signs. Leo, Taurus, Aries, Virgo, and Sagittarius, however, are not at all suitable."
105. "Here is Culpeper for students of astrology." Nicholas Culpeper's *English Physician Enlarged: An Astrologo-Physical Discourse of the Vulgar Herbs of This Nation* (1652; enlarged ed., London, 1695).
106. Shade.
107. Orach, also called "mountain spinach" (*Atriplex hortensis*), a once-popular potherb used like spinach.

a beginning of their decay. Item by clear & fair weather, void of rain, wind, mist, dew. Otherwise they are subject to mouldiness & corruption.

<u>Dried Flowers</u> seldom keep good above one year, except those of Chamomil.

<u>Dry your Roots</u> just before they spring and sprout, or else about a months time after their seed has been ripe. Vide omnino Culpepper's English Physician Enlarged.[108]

[. . . .]

<u>In the woods & marshes &c. of Pennsilvania are [found] of their own self growing:</u> chestnuts, black wallnuts, haselnuts, galls or gallnuts, acorns, oakapples, mulberries, wild grapes, myrtle or blackberries, strawberries, wild roses, sumack, tumerick, St. John's wort, Cinqfoil,[109] Fern, Agrimony,[110] Centory,[111] Hops, Thorn-apples, Burdock, Quick grass, Honeysuckle, Knotgrass, Mullein,[112] Plantane,[113] Arsmart,[114] Watercresses, Scurvygrass, calmus,[115]

<u>Planted in Orchards & Gardens:</u> Apple – Pear – Quince – Plum – Apricock – Peach – Cherry – Mulberry – Wallnut - Medlar[116] – Cornel[117] – Hasel – Filbearts[118] – Eldar

---

108. Here follows a long list of "herbs," that is, all garden vegetables, fruits, lettuces, and what we commonly call "herbs" to be harvested best under the influence of a specific "planet," whether Saturn, Jupiter, Mars, the Sun, Venus, Mercury, or the Moon. Again, Pastorius refers to Culpeper's *English Physician Enlarged* as his main source.

109. Cinquefoil, a flowering perennial herb (*Potentilla reptans*) in the rose family, used in herbal medicine.

110. Any of the flowering perennial herbs of the genus *Agrimonia* in the rose family; agrimony is native chiefly to temperate areas of the Northern Hemisphere.

111. Centaury, any of the flowering herbs of the genus *Centaurium* in the gentian family, whose medicinal properties were said to have been discovered by Chiron the Centaur.

112. Any of the flowering herbs of the genus *Verbascum* in the figwort family; mullein leaves were used in herbal medicine.

113. Plantain, any of low-growing herbs of the genus *Plantago*, once used in herbal remedies.

114. Arsesmart, also called "water pepper" (*Polygonum hydropiper*), a pungent herb sometimes used as a spice.

115. Calamus or sweet flag (*Acorus calamus*), a perennial marsh herb in the arum family. Pastorius left considerable space at the end of this list to allow for additions. The much longer list of cultivated plants immediately following demonstrates his greater interest in horticulturally and agriculturally useful plants occurring elsewhere in the world than in those occurring naturally in Pennsylvania.

116. Allied to the hawthorn, the medlar (*Mespilus germanica*) is a small deciduous tree native to southeast Europe and western Asia and naturalized elsewhere in Europe.

117. Dogwood, or any of the flowering shrubs or trees of the genus *Cornus*.

118. Filberts, hazelnuts. The fruit or nuts of the cultivated hazel (*Corylus avellana*); the trees bearing them.

– Currant – Barberry – Box-trees. (Juniper-trees are still wish'd for, Item willows, withies,[119] or sallow-trees,[120] sloetrees)[121]

Blackberry – bramble – raspberry – gooseberry – bushes. Savine,[122] white (or haw-) thorns, Eglantine[123] or Sweet brier.

Hops & Vines, in order to preserve humidum radicale.[124]

Angelica, Asparagus.
[. . .], Burnet or Pimpinell.
Carraway & Cumin, Catmint, Celardine,[125] Chamomil, Cives & other sorts of Crush-leeks, Clary,[126] Columbines, Comfry,[127] Cowslips, Constantines,
Daisies, Dracuneulus,[128]
Elicampane,[129] Earthnuts.[130]
Featherfew,[131] Fennil,
Gentle mint, Gilliflowers,[132]
Hartichocks,[133] holiehocks, horseradish, houseleek, hyssop,
Leek, white Lillies, Lovage.

---

119. Willows of any species of the genus *Salix*.
120. See note 119.
121. Sloes or blackthorns. A deciduous large shrub or small tree in the rose family, the blackthorn (*Prunus spinosa*) is native to Europe, western Asia, and northwestern Africa and locally naturalized in eastern North America.
122. Savin, a small bushy juniper (*Juniperus sabina*) native to Europe and western Asia.
123. Eglantine rose, sweetbriar.
124. The *humidum radicale* or "radical moisture" was linked in the Middle Ages to the life force that one was not able to replenish through food or medicine. Perhaps Pastorius is satirizing this notion by suggesting that beer and wine might in fact be able to sustain this force. See also note 311 to chapter 5.
125. Celandine, common name of three distinct flowering species in three different genera and two different families, the greater celandine and celandine poppy being in the poppy family and the lesser celandine in the buttercup family.
126. A biennial or short-lived perennial plant native to southern Europe, the clary (*Salvia sclarea*) was cultivated in English gardens as a potherb.
127. Comfrey, a perennial herb (*Symphytum officinale*) in the forget-me-not family, formerly esteemed for its curative powers in healing wounds.
128. Pastorius is most likely referring to green dragon (*Arisaema dracontium*), a perennial flowering herb of the arum family native to North America.
129. See note 81.
130. Any of various plants having edible roots, tubers, or other underground parts, such as peanuts or truffles.
131. A perennial wildflower and herb in the daisy family, featherfew, also called "feverfew" or "bachelor's buttons" (*Tanacetum parthenium*), is used in herbal medicine to treat fevers, headaches, stomachaches, toothaches, insect bites, infertility, and problems with menstruation and with labor during childbirth.
132. Carnations or clove pinks.
133. Artichokes.

Winter Marjoram, Mint, (Marvel of Peru,[134])

Nep see Catmint, nettles.

Garden patience, Penny royal, Piony, Primrose,

Rosemary, Rue,

Sage, winter Savory, Savin, Scurvygrass, Sorrell, Southernwood, Succory,[135] Sperage
see Asparagus,

Tansie,[136] Thyme, wild thyme.

Violets, Dames violets,

Wormwood.

The Trees, Shrubs & Plants of the foregoing Page are Perennantest,[137] & need not to
be sown & set every year, But the following you must yearly set or sow, viz.

Garlick, Tobacco, Mustard, Dill, Coriander, Carduus benedictus,[138] Ladies-thistle,
Marigold, Mallows,[139] Cabbage Coleworts,[140] Burrage,[141] Great garden (or Rouncival)
peas,[142] Calabashes, Annis Seed, Guinny pepper, bastard Saffron, Gith,[143] Savory, Poppy,
Turnsole,[144] Lampoiltree,

Parsly, Chervil, Selery or Smallage, Spinage, Purslane, Orach or Arage, white & red; Beet
white & red; Parsnips, Carrots, Onions, Potatoes, Musk & Water Melons, Pumpions,
Lettuce, Cabbage-lettuce, Crisped Lettuce, Cresses, Basil, Sweet Marjoram,

Pisa gratiosa, Sugar peas, Indian peas,

Beans, french beans, welsh beans.

Rhadish, Winter Endive, Corn Salad,

---

134. Also called "four o'clock flower," the marvel of Peru (*Mirabilis jalapa*) is said to have been first imported
from Peru in 1540.

135. Chicory. A plant with bright blue flowers, common chicory (*Cichorium intybus*) is found wild in England,
especially by roadsides; its leaves and roots have been used medicinally and as food.

136. Tansy, a perennial flowering herb (*Tanacetum vulgare*) native to Europe and Asia and naturalized in North
America, once used to treat worms and other intestinal problems, fevers, and sores.

137. "Perennial."

138. Saint Benedict's or blessed thistle. See note 38.

139. European flowering plants of waysides and waste places, especially common mallows (*Malva sylvestris*).

140. See note 59.

141. Borage. Common British plant having prickly hairs and bright blue flowers, borage (*Borago officinalis*)
was formerly much esteemed in making a cordial.

142. These large peas are said to be the first garden variety cultivated in Europe.

143. Any plant of the genus *Nigella*, especially black caraway (*Nigella sativa*).

144. Common heliotrope (*Heliotropium arborescens*), a plant in the forget-me-not or borage family whose
flowers turn to follow the sun; by extension, any plant whose flowers or leaves do so.

Small peas, chick (or three cornered) pea, summer-wheat & rye, Oats, barley, Spelt, Indian Corn, Rice, Millet, Lentil, Vetches, hemp, flax, buckwheat & turnips belong into the fields.

[...]

Several ways of Meliorating[145] the Ground

Some Boors & Bumkins are of opinion that the very <u>dung</u> imparts the feracity[146] to their fields; But Philosophers do not ascribe the same to the dung itself, informing us, that it is the Salt (full of Nitre) which sculking or lying hidden therein makes all plants live, grow & flourish. Yea and most every clumperton[147] knows, that if the Piss, which is part of the dung & has Sal acidum[148] in it, be not well purged of its Saltish & biting Sharpness by rain & dew, the dung (poor dung!) does more Injury to their fields than good. In short, the Reason why dung makes the Earth fruitful is because it is Salt; & tempering the Moisture & Coldness of the land, makes the same fertile; Vita enim consistit in humido & calido.[149] Plinius[150] saith, If you do not dung your fields, they wax cold, & if you dung 'em too much, they're burnt. Hence you may perceive, that dry & hot ground ought not to be burdened with dung, but that a coldish & wet one is thereby reduced to a fruitful medium. And prudent husbandmen always dung their lands in the Spring & Fall of the year, being the two Seasons, wherein the then usual Rains do best dissolve & mix the Saltish parts of the dung with the Earth, which by dry weather can't be expected.

Columella, Lib. 2, Cap. 15.[151] Makes this <u>difference amongst dung</u>, viz. that the best of all comes out of dove coats, hen houses, turkey coops & other poultrey-yards; the dung of water fowls, ex. gr.,[152] geese, ducks, &c. for ever excepted, the which parching the ground is good for nothing. The next place he gives to Mans dung, but nevertheless will have it mingled with some other stuff. The third he assigns to that which drops from four footed creatures, under the following graduation, or priority: Imprimis[153] he

145. Fertilizing or improving.
146. Fruitfulness, productiveness.
147. Clodhopper, bumpkin.
148. "Acid salt."
149. "Life indeed consists of moisture & heat."
150. The Roman naturalist and natural philosopher Pliny the Elder (A.D. 23–79), like Pastorius, tried to collect much of the knowledge of his time.
151. Lucius Junius Moderatus Columella (A.D. 4–ca. 70) was the foremost writer on agriculture in Roman antiquity. Pastorius is referring here to Columella's *De re rustica*, book 2, chapter 15.
152. For example.
153. Above all.

commends the dung of Asses, by reason that this beast eats very slowly & digests well, therefore their dung may forthwith be carried into the field. The nearest in goodness is that of Sheep & Goats trattles.[154] Further that of horse stables, and finally the worst from hogs sties.

Moreover, the said Columella & Palladius[155] too do say that all dung gathered in due season is best after it has lain <u>one year</u>, to promote the fruitfulness of the seed; the order it grows, the less serviceable.[156]

[..]

14. The last but not the least thing I here shall impart to make your Lands good & well bearing by is **MARL**,[157] which Plinius lib. 17. Cap. 6. saith to be adeps terrae, ibi densante se Pinguedinis Nucleo, &c.[158] The French call it Marne, & the afore quoted Sir de Serres[159] tells us that some do Justly term it Manne, i.e. a dew & gift from heaven. It is of several Colours, white, gray, blewish, reddish; Item some clayish, some sandy, some fat, some hard, some pumice stony; Some is but indifferent & must be strewed pretty thick over the ground; some again so good that you ought to sow it thinner than Seed-Corn: Some better for Fields and the other for Meadows. If you lay that which naturally is hard too thick, it burns the soil &c. Marls if of more profit to clayie & tough land than dung; but sandy land is nothing the better for being marled. Vines & hops are quite spoil'd thereby.

Marl is commonly found where Marshes & Fens have been dried up & covered with earth; and these places, when dew falls, or when after a drought rain comes, do cast an ill brimstony scent: Item Rushes & Willows grow there higher & fatter than ordinary, but on the other hand the grass very thin & sour, notwithstanding the mould seems to be black and good. Marl lies most par in sour Meadows where the Mole-hills are

---

154. Rounded animal droppings.

155. The A.D. fourth-century Roman author Rutilius Taurus Aemilianus Palladius is known for his writings on agriculture, chiefly his *Opus agriculturae*.

156. Here follow specific sections detailing types and uses of animal dung as well as how and when to apply it.

157. Lime-rich mud or mudstone, marl was used as a soil conditioner.

158. "'The fat of the earth, there thickening itself like fatty kernels.'" Pastorius is quoting a condensed snippet from a larger passage of Pliny the Elder's *Naturalis Historia* (*Natural History*), book 17, chapter 6, which reads in full: "Spissior ubertas in ea intellegitur et quid terrae adipes ac velut glandia in corporibus, ibi densante se pinguitudinis" (This soil is looked upon as containing a greater amount of fecundating principles, and acts as a fat in relation to the earth, just as we find glands existing in the body, which are formed by a condensation of the fatty particles into so many kernels). Pliny described marl as commonly found in both Britain and Gaul (France).

159. The French writer and soil scientist Olivier de Serres (1539–1619) was especially known for his techniques on soil conditioning.

full of small Snail-shells. When you have dig'd your Marl, lay it on heaps, that it may drie, be season'd, get more Strength & wax lighter for carriage. Yea and after you have brought it on your fields, you must not presently plow it under, but let it lie a while in small heaps that it be impregnated, tenter'd[160] & tempered by the Sun, night dews & rain, but more especially by the Winter frost. Then spread it & incorporate the same with the ground by Plowing; thus it surpasses the best of dungs, warming the ground exceeding well, in so much that the corn does not prove at the like rate the very first year as it will the subsequent 10 or 12 years, be it less or more; For Plinius asserts, that the white & rush-coloured Marl, which is found in fountenous places, remains still fructifying even to its 50th year. &c.

To End this head, I shall only adjoin what Johann Joachim Becher saith in his Physica Subterranea[161] fol. 87 viz. that it is manifest by an universal Experience that wherever there are Fountains & Well-heads, though they may spring even out of hard rocks & Mountains, there's also a blewish clay or ground to be had, either shallower or deeper; the which if you distill with the softest fire you can, the most subtil-ascending Spirit will thus heat your Lembick,[162] that you dare not touch it with your bare hands, yea & make now & then glanses or cast beams as brandy does, notwithstanding there's nothing else in the recipient but an unsavory & tasteless water whereon our Galenists[163] would look as on an Inutile[164] phlegm;[165] but it is both in Metallical & Medicinal Operations of great power, & especially as to the purpose in hand not one thing in all the world more prevalent & efficacious to stir up & promote the vegetation & augmenting of all sorts of plants; because one single drop of this dungs better than ten care-loads of Muck. In a word, it is the Mercurius of Vegetables, and the Gas of renowned Helmont: For a proof, there is such a Sympathy or mutual Concord & Inclination between this Liquor & Wine, that a whole hogshead of this is strengthen'd & preserved by a very little of the other. &c. &c.

[. . . .]

160. Thinned out.
161. In the passage that follows, Pastorius is paraphrasing from the *Physica subterranea* (1669) of Johann Joachim Becher (1635–1682), a German physician and alchemist, considered an important figure in the transition from alchemy to modern chemistry.
162. Alembic: apparatus used by alchemists for distilling.
163. Followers of the ancient Roman physician Galen (A.D. 129–ca. 213). Although here Pastorius seems to be championing the chemiatric (chemical healing) practices of the Swiss physician Paracelsus (ca. 1493–1541), who vigorously rejected Galen, as well as the teachings of the Flemish alchemist and radical religious reformer Franciscus Mercurius von Helmont (1614–ca. 1699), elsewhere in his writings, he remains indebted to Galenic medicine.
164. Useless.
165. Phlegm: in alchemy, any watery, odorless, and tasteless substance obtained by distillation, especially of plant material; an aqueous solution; water, especially as one of the five principles of matter.

<u>Concerning the best Improvement of our Fields.</u>[166]

[. . . . .]

By the preceding Leaves it's manifest that the great hinge or axle-tree upon which Agriculture does turn is a Sul or Plough; For <u>Plowing or Tilling</u> (according to Columella[167]) is nothing else but to resolve the mould or earth, making it meet for fermentation; & this be best effected in hot & cold Seasons, seeing both heat & frost are of a boiling & tempering quality; Hence Solomon's Sluggard Prov. 20:4[168] who refused to plow in the very Winter, was condemned to beg in harvest; those Lazy Scotch-men, who suffered their lands overrun with weeds, by their King Kenneth his Law of Maneleta,[169] each of them was fined or amerced for an Ox, &c. Our Lord & Saviour (whose husbandry & labourers we are) parabolizing heavenly concerns with terrestrial & visible ones will not have his Plow-men so much as to look to those things they left behind. Luke 9 and Ecclesiastes forbids us to hate Husbandry, because (saith he) the most High has Created it. A most excellent and useful Creature! And in old times many brave men have not been ashamed to hold the Plough-handle, whenas nowadays many wretched fellows are too proud not only to till the ground, but even to tread upon barefoot & bareleg'd, &c.

So to wind up these present Rural Observions,[170] I would desire you to <u>Consider</u>, that difficult things are pleasant at the End to which we ought Continually to have a due regard. <u>Next</u> that such Arts & Secrets, as out of some authentick Authors are here permitted, may easier be tried or practis'd in gardens & small spots of ground, than in wide & unfathomed fields. <u>Again</u>, that most Clowns love their Country-fashion best, and that Custom Joyn'd with their Own <u>humour</u> is beyond all Reason whatsoever. <u>Further</u>, that if everyone should Improve his land after the foregoing Rules & Directions, there would be no room left to Carry our dung unto. <u>Moreover</u> that many new-fangled Singularities proceed from spungy Beans,[171] & when brought to the Test do prove ineffectual, vain & naughty.[172] <u>At last</u>, that great Plantations

> Are Incantations
> and hinderance to Rest;
> A little & well-tilled Field
> Does yield what large ones do not yield:

166. This section treats mechanical improvements of the soil, such as by plowing.
167. See note 151.
168. Proverbs 20:4: "The sluggard will not plow by reason of the cold; *therefore* shall he beg in harvest, and *have* nothing."
169. The "law of maneleta," enacted by King of Scots Kenneth II (r. 971–995), ordered that anyone who allowed harmful weeds to grow on his freshly sown land be fined one ox for the first offense and ten oxen for the second, and that he be removed from his land for the third offense.
170. Observations.
171. Spongy brains.
172. Bad, inferior, substandard, worthless.

Small & Content is best.   <u>F.D.P.</u>

Deep Plowing is most advantagious, and yields a far better crop than shallow plowing, saith Dan. Leeds in his Almanack 1703.[173]

Plowing is best from the new to the Full of the Moon.

[. . . .]

Observationes propriae Vineales.[174]

Having a little Book by itself, wherein I set down mine own Remarks concerning Bees; an other concerning Gardening, &c. But none wherein to take singular Notice of my little Vineyard,[175] (not Imagining there will be much of this Subject,) I shall do it here, and make only these following Memorandums,

    I. that after I planted a master of 30 Vines Anno 1706, the same began to bear 1710 some 2, 3, 4 & 5 Grapes.

    II. that 3 years together I planted Cabbages and Coleworts among them, and the 4th Indian beans, growing all very well. However next Summer I think they shall have no such like Company. Nil nisi Botror, Atque perambulatorum vestigia cernes.[176]

    III. Anno 1710 the 5th day of the 2nd month[177] I laid in above 100 cuttings with a dibble[178] perpendicularly downwards, & they grew fast & well.

    IV. that 1710 at the end of the 5th month[179] I counted 24 young Grapes, the berries whereof were less than pinn-heads; (the reason of this Superfetation[180] I ascribe to my much pruning and trimming of these but young Stocks). In the midst of the 6th month[181] they began to blossom, & got berries to the bigness of great Rounceval pees,[182] But were nipp'd by September's Frost. However, Spes in meliora.[183]

---

173. Even though publisher Daniel Leeds (1652–1720) promoted the ideas and positions of George Keith in his almanacs, Pastorius cited them both here and elsewhere, which, of course, in no way prevented him in his other writings from attacking the Keithians in general and Leeds in particular.

174. "My Own Vineyard Observations."

175. None, that is, except for detailed directions on viticulture (including monthly instructions as well as remarks about his own vineyard) in "The Monthly Monitor," which preceded the account given here.

176. "Nothing but [bare] grape stalks, but you see the footsteps that led there." Here Pastorius is engaging in wordplay either on the tracks left by a grape thief or on how the bare stalks can teach one the steps that led to their failure to bear fruit.

177. April 5, 1710.

178. Hand tool used to make holes in the ground for seeds, bulbs, or young plants.

179. July.

180. In botany, a second conception occurring before the development of fruit from the first; by extension, a superfluous addition. Pastorius is probably satirizing his own overeager care of and excessive hope for these few vines and the grapes they might produce.

181. Mid-August.

182. See note 142.

183. "Hope for the better."

They more clearly than Lyra,[184] or any other Glossator[185] could do, expounded to me time of the first ripe grapes, at which Moses sent out his Spies, Num. 13:17. Tempore Sol nostro BIS, ut olim, percoquit UVAS, <u>Gaudete Sodales</u> Bumastos Anno Sol Bis maturat eodem;[186] Non opis est nostre dignas persolvere grates.[187]

I. 1710 the 6th month:[188] I digged a Garden-Bed full 2 foot deep, carried the clay out, and fill'd it with good black mould, to serve hereafter as a Nursery, for to set my Cuttings in.

II. 1710. The 20th of the 6th month: (being the anniversary day of mine arrival in Philadelphia Anno 1683)[189] I with my wife and 2 Sons did eat of the first-ripe-grapes in my said Vineyard. Thanks be to God for all his Mercies & Blessings which he these 27 Years past in Pennsilvania, and almost 32 years more spent in divers parts of Europe, most graciously has been pleased to bestow upon me poor Worm; Praises belong to his holy Name for Evermore. Unto him let these them ascend throughout all succeeding Generations from the hearts, mouths & conversation of his Sanctified Ones for Ever & Ever. Amen.

III. That before the 7th month[190] all my Grapes were fully ripe; For the 26th of the 6th month[191] I gather'd & hang'd em upon Strings, having dip'd their Stalks in melted Rosin, a few laid in a Calabash under Millet seed & the former under Buckwheat after some dry'd down.

IV. Anno 1715: My Grapes were worth but little, and Anno 1716 good for nothing. Spes alit agricolas, me mea ferme necat.[192] Oh! who would toil In such a Soil?

<u>A Scriptural Observation:</u>[193] God the Creator & Upholder of all, is called in the holy writ a householder or husbandman whose right hand has planted a Vineyard in a very fruitful hill with the choicest Vine (<u>Christ Jesus</u>). It's said of him, that he gathered the

184. The French Franciscan teacher and biblical exegete Nicholas of Lyra (ca. 1270–1349), whose *Postillae perpetuae in universam S. Scripturam* (Commentary notes to the universal Holy Scripture), comprising fifty volumes, would become in 1471 the first Bible commentary to be printed.

185. Any of the eleventh- and twelfth-century scholars in Italy, France, and Germany who conducted detailed studies of legal texts, producing extensive explanations.

186. "In our time, as formerly, the Sun TWICE ripens the GRAPES. Rejoice, friends, the Sun twice a year matures the same."

187. "'It is not in our power to pay you sufficient thanks.'" Pastorius reverses the order of Aeneas's words to Dido in Virgil's *Aeneid*, book 1, lines 600–601, which read: "Grates persolvere dignas non opis est nostrae" (To pay you sufficient thanks is not in our power), although the meaning remains the same.

188. August.

189. Pastorius arrived in Philadelphia on August 20, 1683.

190. September.

191. August 26.

192. "Hope sustains the farmer, but mine almost kills me."

193. In this section, Pastorius paraphrases the parable of the tenants in Matthew 21:33–41, but he also turns it into an extended allegory for early Pennsylvania. For example, the reference to those who "said they would go, but went not" alludes to Pastorius's friends among the Frankfurt Pietists who had promised they would follow him to Pennsylvania but failed to do so.

Stones out of it, made a fence hedge & wall round about, built a Tower in the midst, and also digged a Wine press therein; doing further, whatever could be done. The dry & fruitless branches he took away, and pruned & purged the rest, that they might bear the better. He moreover hired labourers and sent them to work in this his Vineyard from morning till Evening, whereof some said they would go, but went not; others would have had more wages than they agreed for, &c. Finally he let it to certain keepers, who proved worse than those of Solomon's vineyard at Baal-hamon,[194] leaving scarce a cottage therein to the daughter of zion. Now, after this said Vineyard received the early & latter rain, the good husbandman patiently waiting for the precious Fruit, looked that it should bring forth sweet & pleasant grapes; But alas! Behold sowre & wild ones, just like them in the wilderness, Hosea 9:10. Yea, these evil men,[195] as they did eat up (or burn the Lord's vineyard & laid his choicest Vine waste,) so they kept not their own; their Vine became that of Sodom and of the fields of Gomorrah; their grapes full of gall & their clusters bitter: their Wine the poison of dragons, and the cruel venom of asPs. Has ever any man planted a Vineyard, & eats not of the fruit thereof? Judge therefore the Inhabitants of Jerusalem and men of Judah, should not these keepers be ashamed, whose Vine is thus dried up? Is it not a righteous Punishment from God upon them, that their branch shall never be green no more; no gathering of grapes, the unripe ones shaken off, their Vintage to fail, & the shouting thereof to cease, with an Everlasting Lamentation for the noble and fruitful vine? And will not at last the Lord of this Vineyard say, as Luke 13:7[196] Cut it down! why cumbreth it the ground? Item, thrust in thy sharp sickle, &c. Rev. 14:18.[197] The grapes are fully ripe! Some of the Lord's servants that came for to receive fruit, the aforesaid keepers did beat, kill & stone; And when the Landlord sent even his own beloved Son, they cast him out of the Vine-Yard, slew him, & now crucify the same afresh. Wherefore he for Justice sake, can not but miserably destroy those wicked men according to what they themselves have judged between the Lord & his Vineyard.

However, he will let his Vineyard out unto others, which shall render him the fruits in their seasons; a remnant will be left, as the grape-gleanings of the Vintage, or the

194. Song of Solomon 8:11.

195. In terms of the allegory on Pennsylvania, by "these evil men," Pastorius most likely means the Keithians, whom he never neglected to attack, if not always directly.

196. In the parable of the barren fig tree in Luke 13:6–9: "A certain *man* had a fig tree planted in his vineyard; and he came and sought fruit thereon, and found none. Then said he unto the dresser of his vineyard, Behold, these three years I come seeking fruit on this fig tree, and find none: cut it down; why cumbereth it the ground? And he answering said unto him, Lord, let it alone this year also, till I shall dig about it, and dung *it*. And if it bear fruit, *well*: and if not, *then* after that thou shalt cut it down."

197. Revelation 14:18: "And another angel came out from the altar, which had power over fire; and cried with a loud cry to him that had the sharp sickle, saying, Trust in thy sharp sickle, and gather the clusters of the vine of the earth; for her grapes are fully ripe."

harvest-over: In these clusters the new wine of the kingdom will be found; clusters of camphire, in the vine-yards of Eu-gedi![198] Tender grapes, which give a good smell in the nostrils of the husbandman, For which they shall be called Plants of holiness & of Renown, whom the Lord will bless & make to grow, that through the scent of the water of Life they may bud, & bring forth boughs; In the uppermost tops, whence there will be 2 or 3 berries, & in the outmost branches 4 or 5. So the Lord will purge 'em as aforesaid, that they may bring forth more fruit; they shall be prosperous & fruitful in every good work. Not casting their grapes before the time, neither are the foxes, the little foxes, to spoil them any longer. The Lord himself doth keep it night & day and water it every moment; he is as the dew unto Israel, &c. and even the Sons of the alien must be their vinedressers, & everlasting joy shall be unto them; their threshing will reach to the Vintage, & this to the Sowing-time &c. &c. they shall sit every man under his Vine & under his fig-tree and none shall make them afraid, Micah 4:4.[199] No, not the ro[a]ring lions of the Vineyards of Timnath, Judg. 14:5.[200] Then shall men not look to the Altars, the works of their hands, neither respect that which their fingers have made; they lift up their Eyes & Voices; they shall sing for the Majesty of the Lord, they shall cry aloud, & glorify him from the uttermost part of the Earth, to the very end of the Sea, to whom all Glory, Praise, honour & Thanks-giving doth belong for Ever & Ever.   Amen.

[. . . . .]

This foregoing Disposition or Ordering of my Garden-beds, I once thought to be the very **Best**; But now am of Opinion, that those plants, which nourish themselves with the same Juice, (containing either Saline, sulphureous, mercurial, bituminous, vitriolous, tartarous or metallick particles,) should not stand near together; Therefore I shall hereafter avoid to set in the same place the Aromatick or Cathartick plants, and always part the bitter &c. For, whatever the ancient Naturalists prate concerning the mutual Love or Sympathy and reciprocal aversion or Antipathy of Plants, yet Francis Bacon (Lord Chancellor of England,) explains the whole Mystery thus, that two plants, who are nourished by the same sort of Juice, do extremely hurt each other by too near a Vicinity; To share between them the food, that's sufficient but for one, throws both into a languishing condition: and this is the Antipathy. On the contrary two plants that

198. Engedi. Song of Solomon 1:14. In modern translations "clusters of camphire" is translated "clusters of hanna blossoms."
199. Micah 4:4: "But they shall sit every man under his vine and under his fig tree; and none shall make *them* afraid: for the mouth of the LORD of hosts hath spoken *it*."
200. In Judges 14, Samson goes to Timnath to find a wife, and when, in a vineyard he comes upon a young lion threatening him, he kills it with his bare hands.

for their alimement[201] require Juices wholly different, vegetate & flourish perfectly well together: and this is Philosophorum plebeiorum[202] <u>Sympathy</u> or Imaginary Friendship.

So between Rosemary, Lavender, Thyme & Marjoram there is an Antipathy, because when planted together, they all requiring the like nourishing Juices, Impair, prejudice, and even starve one an other; But between Garlick & Roses there's Sympathy, because the one requiring a stinking & the other an odoriferous Juice, they do not quarrel about their food, but thrive in the same ground, and are as good Neighbours helpful to one another, the Rose here bearing the sweeter Flowers. The good Intelligence between the Fig tree & Rue, because the Juice which agrees with the first, suits not the Palate of the last.

<u>There is a raging Antipathy</u> between cabbages and (Vines) Cyclamens, Hemlock and Rue; Reeds & Fern.

[. . . . .]

[Section on zodiacal signs and their influence on climate, weather and health]

Hence it appears the Old Saying to be true, **Astra cient Meteora**,[203] by means whereof all things upon the whole face of the Earth, are <u>Influenced</u> by the Stars, Job 38:31. Psal. 8:3. &c. **Attamen Astra Inclinant, Non Necessitant.**[204] Serviunt, Non Saeviunt.[205] Astra regunt homines, sed regit Astra DEUS.[206]

Therefore, and also because some Ephemerides[207] are misprinted, or calculated for an other Climate, Our <u>Almanack-makers</u> in their annual Pamphlets give us nothing but their Random-Predictions, wild Guesses, May be's, uncertain Conjectures, certain Untruths, impudent Impostures, & the like black and abominable Stuff, by which they do not only dry shave the Purses, & abuse the Credulity of Simple-hearted people to worse things, but even without all fear of punishment bely Sovereign Princes, the heavens and God (the Ocean of all Goodness) himself.

> To Cross the Stars, they set to work their Brain,
> Foretelling Rain, when fair; And Fair, when for Rain.

---

201. Aliment, nutriment, nourishment.
202. "According to the common philosophy."
203. "The stars beget meteors."
204. "However the stars incline, they do not determine."
205. "They serve, they do not rave."
206. "The stars govern men, but GOD governs the stars."
207. Tables showing the predicted or tabulated positions of a heavenly body for every day during a given period.

If one had so much Time to misspend, as to bring all their horrid lies in predicting War & Peace, health & sickness, happy or unhappy days to take Physick, bleed, cut hair & nails &c. into One Volume it would be larger than Atlas Major,[208] or Theatrum Europaeum.[209]

208. Compiled by Joan Blaeu (1596–1673), the final Latin-language edition of *Atlas Maior* (1662–65), often considered the largest book printed in the seventeenth century, comprised eleven volumes and 3,368 pages.
209. History of the German-speaking lands of Europe in twenty-one volumes comprising all issues of the journal *Theatrum Europaeum* published between 1633 and 1738.

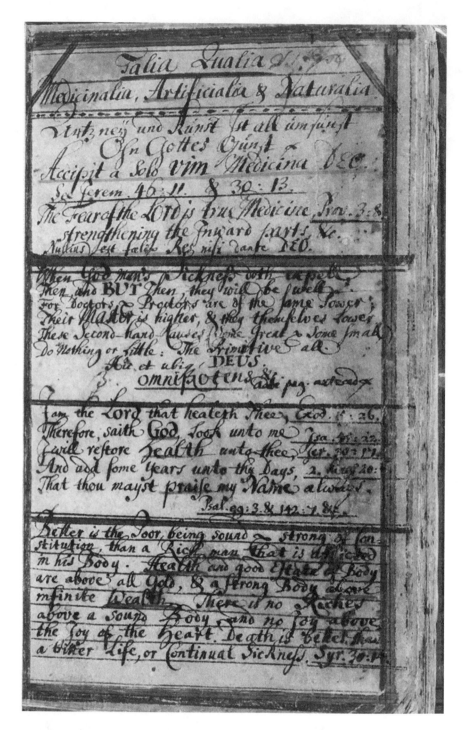

Fig. 8 | Francis Daniel Pastorius, title page from "Talia Qualia Medicinalia, Artificialia & Naturalia, [or] Artzneÿ ist all umsunst ohn Gottes Gunst." MS 8801. Francis Daniel Pastorius Papers, Historical Society of Pennsylvania.

❧

"Talia Qualia Medicinalia, Artificialia & Naturalia"
(Such Things As Relate to Medicine, Artificial & Natural)

INTRODUCTION TO THE TEXT

Transcribed and annotated from Francis Daniel Pastorius, "Talia Qualia Medicinalia, Artificialia & Naturalia. Artzneÿ und Kunst ist all umsunst ohn Gottes Gunst," MS 8801, Francis Daniel Pastorius Papers, Historical Society of Pennsylvania, the following excerpts have also never before been published. The selections include Pastorius's several title pages to this manuscript book since they reflect—as do the "Bee-Hive" title pages—Pastorius's philosophical approach, motivation, and goals in assembling the collection, as well as samples of his remedies and the list of authors and their writings from which he collected them.[210]

"Talia Qualia Medicinalia," Pastorius's medical handbook, was evidently among his most used and popular manuscripts, along, of course, with "The Monthly Monitor." This collection of medical remedies provides an intriguing early modern record of the coexistence of various competing approaches to medicine, health, and the natural world more broadly speaking, as does "The Monthly Monitor" the coexistence of competing approaches to agriculture and gardening. Including both artificial and natural ("Artificialia & Naturalia") remedies, the handbook strives to reconcile traditional approaches that relied on herbal remedies heavily infused with mystical beliefs in plant properties, on the one hand, with scientific approaches that relied on chemical pharmaceuticals, on the other.

Showing family continuity in the transmission of medical and natural history knowledge within larger intellectual traditions, Pastorius first cites a no longer extant manuscript book of remedies collected by his father, Melchior Adam. Francis Daniel's list of sources for "Talia Qualia Medicinalia" includes German herbals of the early Renaissance, alchemical treatises from seventeenth-century England, and even works by the proponents of the new scientific method. Thus he cites Balthasar Schnurr's *Kunst und Wunderbüchlein* (Frankfurt: Rötel, 1643; Small Book of Art and Miracles) and even Johann Staritz's Rosicrucian work *Neu-vermehrter Heldenschatz* (1685; Newly Enlarged Heroes' Treasure), which, along with herbal remedies for diseases, offered herbal potions for wealth, love, and protection against enemies. But Pastorius's favorite source overall was the mid-seventeenth-century English botanist, physician, and astrologer Nicholas Culpeper's *English Physician Enlarged* (1698 [1652]). Culpeper's goal was

---

210. Our selections from "Talia Qualia Medicinalia" are much less extensive than those from "The Monthly Monitor" because of the fragile condition of the original manuscript and the poor legibility of many of its passages and pages.

to provide cheap and accessible remedies, which he based on his study of plants and their medicinal value, to a broad section of the population. Yet Pastorius also turned toward authors we would consider early proponents of Enlightenment science, such as the chemist, natural philosopher, and physicist Robert Boyle, whose *Experiments* (1696) Pastorius excerpted on several pages.

Readers from various backgrounds could find remedies in Pastorius's handbook that might suit their convictions and whose ingredients would be available locally. Indeed, on one of its title pages, he explicitly identifies the content of his book as "Medicamina Delecta, Das ist Auserlesene Artzneymittel, Deren Ingredientia in Pennsilvanien und Dergleichen neubegonnenen Colonien zu bekommen sind" (Selected Medicines Whose Ingredients Are Available in Pennsylvania and Other Such Newly Established Colonies).

THE TEXT

Artzneÿ und Kunst
ist all umsunst
ohn Gottes Gunst.[211]
Si Deus tibi non esse curæ,
cur te curet Incuriose?[212]
Cura igitur, non tantum, ut valeas,
sed etiam, ut <u>bene</u> valeas,
ut aeternum valeas!
VALE![213]
<u>ut sit</u>
<u>In Sano MENS CORPORE sana;</u>[214]
<u>faciunt Ethicus & Medicus.</u>[215]
Muth und Blut.
geht vor Guth.[216]

211. "Medicine and art / is all in vain / without the favor of God." "Art" here refers to both medical skill and artificial or chemical medicine devised by humans to cure diseases that ultimately only God can heal.

212. "If God is not your cure, / why do you neglect to cure yourself?" A rhetorical question suggesting that, of course, humans are unable to cure themselves without God's grace.

213. "Therefore, take care not only that you are well, / but also that you are righteously well, / that you are forever well. FAREWELL!" Pastorius expands upon a set Latin expression, "Cura et valeas," which basically just means "Take care" but more specifically means "Take care so that you are well."

214. "And thus 'in a healthy BODY a healthy MIND.'" Pastorius is quoting, in reverse order, from Juvenal's *Satires*, satire 10, line 356, which reads in full: "Orandum est ut sit mens sana in corpore sano" (One should pray to have a healthy mind in a healthy body).

215. "They make virtue and health."

216. "Fortitude and blood [vigor] / comes before wealth."

<u>Talia Qualia</u>
<u>Medicinalia, Artificialia & Naturalia.</u>[218]
Artzneÿ und Kunst Ist all umsunst
Ohn Gottes Gunst.[219]
<u>Accipit a Solo vim Medicina DEO.</u>[220]
<u>See Jer. 46:11. & 30:13.</u>
The Fear of the Lord is true Medicine, <u>Prov. 3:8.</u>
strengthening the Inward parts, &c.
Nullius est felix Res, nisi dante DEO.[221]
When God men's Sickness doth repell,
Then, and BUT Then, they will be well.
For Doctors & Proctors are of the same Power;
Their Master is higher, & they themselves Lower.
These Second-hand Causes (some great & some small,)
Do Nothing or Little: The Primitive all.
Hic et ubiq. DEUS.
<u>OMNIPOTENS</u> &c.   adde pag. anteced.[222]

I am the Lord that healeth Thee,	<u>Exod. 15:26.</u>
Therefore, saith **God**, Look unto me	<u>Isa. 45:22.</u>
I will restore **Health** unto thee,	<u>Jer. 30:17.</u>
And add some Years unto thy Days,	<u>2 Kings 20:6.</u>
That thou mayst **praise** my Name always.	<u>Psal. 99:3. & 142:7 &c.</u>

<u>Better is the Poor, being sound & strong of Constitution, than a Rich man that is</u>
<u>afflicted in his Body.</u> **Health** <u>and good Estate of Body are above all Gold, & a strong</u>
<u>Body above infinite</u> **Wealth.** <u>There is no Riches above a sound Body, and no Joy above</u>
<u>the Joy of the Heart. Death is better than a bitter Life, or Continual Sickness. Jesu</u>
<u>Sirach [Ecclesiasticus] 30:14.</u>

---

217. Horizontal line signifies the beginning of another title page; page breaks beyond the title pages are not indicated.
218. "Such Things As Relate to / Medicine, Artificial & Natural."
219. "Medicine and art [skill] are all for naught / without God's grace."
220. "The only effective medicine [is the one] received from GOD."
221. "Nothing is fruitful, but what is given by GOD."
222. "Here and everywhere [is] GOD / ALMIGHTY &c." "Add [to the] previous page."

Ingenuum est fateri per Quos profeceris. Pliny.[223]

Die Authores, aus welchen diß Büchlein colligiert[224]

vide infra. pag. 202.[225]   Non quot, sed quales.[226]

[written vertically in left-hand margin:]

The Compiler of this little Manuscript is of Melancholy-Colerick Complexion, and therefore juxta Culpepper*p. 194[227] gentle, given to Sobriety, Solitary, Studious, doubt-ful, shame-faced, timorous, pensive, constant & true in action, of a slow wit, with obliviousness: &c. If any does him wrong, He can't remember long.

Jeremiah Love in his Clavis Medicinae, or Practice of Physick Reformed,[228] saith that The Headach proceeds from many Causes; 1. From heat; 2. from Cold; 3. from Fulness, &c. when men live Idly, & fill their bodies excessively, as like a bladder blown up; 4. from filthy Corrupt humours abounding in the body; 5. from the fume of corrupt humours, & not from the humours themselves; for the Corruption lying long in the Stomach, casteth up to the brain evil Vapours, which offend it, it being of all Parts most sensible; 6. from the Excrements tarrying too long in the body, for when thou hast taken thy dinner or the like, first Nature takes to its self for its Nourishment the thin & purest part, & leaves the rest as gross & corrupt; & then these Excrements tarrying longer than usual, send noisom vapours to the brain; So that he that is much Costive, can never be long in health. Hui e refert[229] red, sore watery Eyes, Apoplexies, Palsies, Epilepsies, Incabus, Frenzy, Lethargy, &c.

223. "'It is honorable to acknowledge the sources through which you have derived assistance.' Pliny." Pastorius repeated this motto from Pliny the Elder's Natural History (Naturalis Historia) whenever he listed the sources from which he compiled a manuscript. Thus it also appears at the beginning of his much longer list of Quaker and non-Quaker writings from which he compiled the "Bee-Hive." See note 272 to chapter 4.

224. "The authors, from whom this little book has been collected."

225. "See below on page 202." The actual list of authors is not on this title page but on page 202 of the "Talia Qualia Medicinalia" manuscript. Pastorius wrote the first two lines of this title page as well as the lines inserted vertically in the left-hand margin to frame an open space on the page. Presumably, he had reserved this space for the sources but decided later that he needed more space for this purpose. Owners of the manuscript would inscribe their names there in 1847.

226. "Not how many, but which ones."

227. "According to Culpeper, p. 194." Pastorius here still seems to subscribe to the prevalent belief in Hippocratic medicine that human bodies and personalities were defined by the preponderance or mixture of one or several of the four "humors," which were black bile, yellow bile, phlegm, and blood. Thus the resulting four temperaments in human beings were, according to the Greco-Roman physician and philosopher Galen: sanguine, choleric, melancholic, and phlegmatic. Judging from his own self-characterization as "melancholy-colerick," Pastorius's personality would have been dominated by a mixture of black and yellow bile.

228. Jeremiah Love, Clavis medicinæ: or, The practice of physic (London, 1674).

229. "Here is referred to."

The <u>Face</u> is often greatly disgraced with <u>redness, pimples, morphew & other the like</u> <u>blemishes,</u> which some have **1.** from their Parents; **2.** by drinking & sotting; **3.** from the Inflammation of the Liver; **4.** by being mighty bashful, & their blood corrupt withal: So the blood has oft recourse to their faces, as a Witness to testify, & returning a way suddenly leaves some gross Corruption behind, which Nature casteth out.

Some are troubled with the <u>Itch & Scabs, Biles, Scurffs, scald heads, Leprosie, small</u> <u>Sop or Measles, &c.</u> **1.** by Nature from their Parents; **2.** by bad Diet; **3.** by Infection, keeping Company with those that are unclean. The abovesaid Author is against the common cure of first purging, then bleeding, & afterwards using some Mercurial or Antimonial Ointment. &c.

The <u>Cough</u> is caused **1.** by a humour distilling from the head to the Trachea Arteria, & Sharpness only of the Cuticle of Trachea Arteria going about within; **2.** through cold & flegm descending upon the Lungs; **3.** through heat dissolving the superfluous matter of the Brain, & so by a catarrhal distillation. Adde infra pag. 208.[230] * Concerning <u>Shortness of breath, Entring into a Consumption, & Surfeits by taking heat and cold.</u>

Those who are troubled with <u>heart burning,</u> (as most people call it) a disease, which belongs not to the heart, but only the stomach, are commonly at ease after they have eaten but after digestion they feel a continual heat or bitterness in the mouth of their Stomachs; they are often belching & sometimes inclined to vomit. It continues long in some and in others it comes every foot, especially by eating [. . .] salt & Cholerick Meats. For Cure, Forbear those Meats after which thou art most troubled, they'le not make good blood, & Nature itself doth not like them, for if good diet will help thy Distemper, never take Physick for the same.[231] But if thy long evil Diet has laden thy Stomach with hot, salt & colerick humours which cause this heart-burning, (as 'tis named,) thou must not eat Chalk, or take some cooling Juleps, or such Slops, which do more hurt than heal, but Cleanse thy Stomach perfectly with the said Jer. Love's Apozeme,[232] which he avouches to thee a speedy Cure.

<u>The Cholick & Wind, Gnawing of the Stomach & Guts</u> proceed [from?] corrupt & filthy slimy humours, which stick to the Inner part of the Stomach & Intestines. To Cure this, the Apozeme will do without Clisters, Issues, Pills or Elixirs & To prevent those diseases, avoid all windy & slimy [. . .]. Jer. Love further saith, that it is meer madness to boil [?] these distempers Pepper, Ginger & other hot Spices or [. . .] in some wine;

230. "Add below page 208."
231. In other words, if a different diet fixes the ailment, do not take medicine for the problem.
232. Decoction or infusion.

all which are proper to warm a cold Stomach & make it apt to digest, being moderately [used?] to wit, in Old people that have their Natural heat decayed. Our Physicians follow this Road; First an emollient & Carminative[233] Clister[234] is to be administered, then a Cordial for to cause rest, & likewise Diaphoretical[235] [...] & then for some days a Mass of Pills; and if this do [not?] [...] the work, make a fontinel[236] in the Leg, & then in a [...] little time as bad as before.[237]

Surfeiting[238] either by over-eating, when one being very [hungry?] comes to dainty fare, eats over much, & so cloyeth[239] [...] that She refuseth any digestion; as a man having a burthen too heavy for him to bear, does not so much [...] offer to lift it: This proceeds from quantity.

Or when one eats Meat not well roasted, fresh herrings, fat Pyes, heavy Cake-bread, & the like of evil Quality. For the cure of these, If the matter of the disease lodges still in the Stomach, give him a draught of warm water with two Spoonfuls of Sallet Oil,[240] which will cause him to vomit; if it work not quickly, let him help it with thrusting his finger into his throat; & after vomiting give him some hot broath,[241] & that he for 3 or 4 days eat not much, but only what's hot, & of good digestion. But if this matter has passed the Stomach without Vomiting, [&?] there be little or no digestion, then burn half a pint of Canary-wine[242] with a Sprig of Rosemary & some mace,[243] [&?] put in it 2 drams of London-Treacle,[244] & some Sugar, drink it off in a morning hot, & sweat 3 or 4 hours in your bed, according to the Strength of the Patient, & [...] his Sweat let him drink posset-drink hot. This will make a perfect digestion through the whole body, of whatsoever he did surfeit of.

[..]

245

---

233. Drug or herbal means for relieving flatulence.
234. Clyster, known today as "enema."
235. Inducing or promoting perspiration.
236. Fontanel, here meaning an artificial ulcer or a natural opening for the discharge of humors of the body.
237. Pastorius is clearly being sardonic here, trying to convince his readers that a change in diet can work much better than the torturous treatments applied by physicians.
238. Excessive indulgence.
239. Cloying.
240. Salad oil.
241. Broth.
242. Sweet fortified white wine produced in the Canary Islands.
243. Aromatic spice derived from the fleshy seed covering of the fruit of the nutmeg tree (*Myristica fragrans*), mace is dried and used chiefly in powdered form to flavor savory dishes, sauces, and so on. As an herbal remedy, like nutmeg, mace has been used to treat diarrhea, nausea, stomach spasms and pain, and intestinal gas.
244. One-quarter fluid ounce of London treacle, a fluid dram being equal to one-eighth of a fluid ounce. Also called "Plague Water" by those touting it as a miraculous cure for the plague, London treacle was a potent mixture of wine, herbs, spices, honey, and opium.
245. The following section is introduced by another title page, announcing a new focus on cures and ingredients to be found in Pennsylvania.

Medicus Dilectus[246] vid. Col. 4:14 &c.
Medicamina Delecta[247] Jesu Sirach [Ecclesiasticus] 38:4
Das ist
Auserlesene Artzneÿmittel,
Deren Ingredientia in Pennsilvanien und
Dergleichen neübegonnenen Colonien
Zu bekommen sind.[248]
Vor sich und seinen Nächsten, vid. Lukas 10:36, Markus 12:3,
Aus verschiedenen Authoren Zusammen getragen
Von Franc. Daniele Pastorio
Anno 1695. Etc.[249]
Quiete & Abstinentia
Multi magni morbi curantur. Corn. Celsus.[250]
Crudelem Medicum intemperans aeger facit. Publ. Syr.[251]
The best Physicians are Doctor Diet, Doctor Merrima[252]
And Doctor Quiet.
Freüde, Mäßigkeit und Ruh
Schleüßt dem Arzt die Thüre zu.[253]
[inserted in margin:]
Mäßig doch nicht müßig.[254]
Ratio et Experientia faciunt Medicum.[255]

---

246. "Beloved physician."

247. "Selected medicines."

248. "That is, / selected medicines, / whose Ingredients are available in Pennsylvania / and other such newly established colonies."

249. "For himself and fellow man, see Luke 10:36, Mark 12:3, / gathered from various authors / by Francis Daniel Pastorius, / In the Year 1695. Etc." Since the first title page also includes the date 1695, Pastorius apparently designed these sections as separate entities—one focusing more on ailments and medicines generally and the other on locally or regionally specific remedies.

250. "'Through rest and abstinence many serious diseases can be healed.' Cornelius Celsus." The Roman encyclopedist Aulus Cornelius Celsus (ca. 25 B.C.–ca. A.D. 50) was especially known for his *De Medicina*. The Latin motto Pastorius loosely quotes is present in *De Medicina* but in a different form: "Satisque est uti quiete et abstinentia" (It suffices to rest and fast).

251. "A disorderly patient makes the physician cruel.' Publilius Syrus." A Syrian writer brought to Italy as a slave, Publilius Syrus (fl. 85–43 B.C.) became educated and known for his *sententiae* (moral sayings).

252. "Doctor Joy."

253. "Joy, moderation, and rest / keeps the doctor away [lit., shuts the door to the doctor]."

254. "Moderately but not idly." The German idiom relies for much of its pithiness on the alliteration, which is lost in the English translation.

255. "Reason and experience make the physician."

Anzeigung der Authoren, aus welchen diß Büchlein colligirt ist.[256]

   1. Ein klein geschrieben Büchlein meines lieben Vatters <u>Melch. Ad. Pastorÿ</u>.[257]

   2. <u>Staricÿ</u> Heldenschatz, gedruckt 1658.[258]

   3. Johann Tallat Artzneÿ Büchlein.[259]

   4. Leonard Thurneißerns Kräuterbuch in fol. 1575.[260]

   5. Martin <u>Schmuckens</u> Schatzkästlein in 8°.[261]

   6. L. M. S. L. De occulta magico- Magnetica morborum quorundam curatione naturali, in 8°. 1652.[262]

   7. Wolff Helmhard Freÿherrn von Hohberg Georgica Curiosa in fol. 1682.[263]

   8. Lazari Riverÿ Observationes medicæ in 8° 1646.[264]

   9. Het kleÿn Vroet wÿfs Boeck gedruck t' Amsterdam in 8°.[265]

   10. Petri Nylandts Nederlandtse Herbarius in 12° 1673.[266]

256. "List of authors from [whose works] this small book has been collected."

257. "A little manuscript book by my dear father Melchior Adam Pastorius." One, however, that does not seem to be extant.

258. Many different editions of Johann Staricius's *Heldenschatz* exist, but none of them was published in 1658. Most likely, Pastorius meant this 1685 edition: Johann Staricius [Staritz], *Neu-vermehrter Heldenschatz: d. i. naturkündliches Bedencken über und bey vulcanischer, auch natürlich-magischer Fabrefaction und Zubereitung der Waffen der Helden Achillis in Griechenland daraus neben vielen secretis zu vernehmen, was zu martialischer Ausrüstung eines Kriegshelden vornehmlich gehörig...* ([Frankfurt?], 1685).

259. Johann Tallat von Vochenberg, *Artzney Büchlein der kreutter* (Erfurt: Sachse, 1532).

260. Leonhardt Thurneysser zum Thurn, *Archidoxa: darin der recht war Motus, Lauff und Gang auch Heimligkeit, Wirckung und Krafft, der Planeten, Gestirns, und gantzen Firmament Mutierung, und Ausziechung aller Subtiliteten, und das Fünffte Wesen, auß den Metallen, Mineralien, Kreytren, Wurtzen, Seften, Steinen, und aller andren wesentlichen Dingen... sampt dem Auszug, und Verstandt des Astrolabÿ und aller Zirckeln Caracter und Zeichen* (Berlin, 1575). Pastorius most likely described Thurneyser's work as simply a "Kräuterbuch" (herbal) here because, apart from its herbal remedies, it seems far more inclined toward alchemy, esotericism, and even the dark arts, and acknowledging this would make the book scandalous for Pastorius to own.

261. Martin Schmuck, *Secretorum naturalium, chymicorum & medicorum, thesauriolus: oder, Schatzkästlin, darinnen 20 natürliche, 20 chymische, und 20 medicinische Secreta und Kunststücklein zu befinden* (Nuremberg: Dümler, 1652).

262. L. M. S. L. [Martin Schmuck], *De occulta magico-magnetica morborum quorundam curatione naturalii tractatus: das ist, wie man auff verborgene natürliche weise... vielerley Kranckheiten... heilen soll. Ein kurtzes Tractätlein... durch L.M. S. L.* (Schleusingen, 1636).

263. Wolfgang Helmhard von Hohberg, *Georgica curiosa, das ist... Bericht- und... Unterricht vn dem Adelichen Land- und Feld-Leben, auf alle in Teutschland... Wirthschafften gerichtet, etc.* (Nuremberg, 1682).

264. Lazare Rivière, *Observationes medicæ et curationes insignes. Quibus accesserunt, Observationes ab aliis communicatæ* (Paris: Piquet, 1646).

265. Eucharius Rösslin, *Het kleyn vroetwyfs-boeck: of Vermeerderden Roosengaert, vande bevruchte vrouwen, ende hare secreten, ontfanginge, baringe, vrouwen ende mannen raedt te gheven die onvruchtbaer zijn...* (Amsterdam: Broer Jansz, 1645).

266. Peter Nyland, *De Nederlandtse herbarius, of Kruydt-boeck: beschryvende de geflachten, gedaente, plaetse, tijt, oeffening, aert, krachten, en medicinael gebruyck van alderhande boomen, heesteren, boom-gewassen, kruyden, en planten, die in de Nederlanden in 't wilde gevonden, en in de hoven onderhouden worden...* (Amsterdam: Doornick, 1673).

11. **NB**. Culp. oder auch nur ein groß C. bedeüdt Nic. Culpper. English Physician enlarged, Printed at London in 8° 1698, welches treffliche buch ein überaus schlecht Register hat.[267]

12. Johannis Coleri Oeconomiæ Ruralis & domesticæ. Andern Theil, oder Haus-Artzneÿ, gedruckt zu Maÿntz in fol 1645.[268] so ebenfalls von gemeine unstudierte leüt sehr dienstig, & in diesem Büchlein mit Col. allegirt ist.[269]

13. Auch ist hierin referiert Zu meinem Calendario Calendariorum in 8°[270]

14. Christopher Wirsung sein Artzneÿ Büch in fol. 1568.[271]

15. Balthasar Schnurr von Lendsidel sein Kunst u. Wunderbuch in 8°.[272]

16. Johann Christoph Thiemen Haus-Feld-Artzneÿ &c. buch in 4° 1700.[273]

17. Vorstelick Geschenck, dat is Een Medecyn boeck &c in grooter weerden gehouden in den Vorstelicken huyse van Nassouwen ende Princen van Orangien t'Amstelredam in 8° 1662.[274]

18. Georgÿ Hornÿ Arca Mosis, in 12°. 1668.[275]

19. Philippi Theophrasti Bombasts Paracels. Opera in Zweÿ theilen, fol. 1603, gedruckt zu Straßburg, und cod. anno in in 4° zu Franckfurt am Maÿn.[276]

20. William Mather's the Young Man's Companion, in 12°. 1695.[277]

267. "'NB: Culp. or also just a capital C.' means 'Nicholas Culpepper [Culpeper,] *English Physician enlarged*, Printed at London in 1698,' which superb book has an exceedingly poor index."

268. Johannes Coler, *Oeconomiæ Rvralis Et Domesticæ, Ander Theil* (Mainz: Heyl, 1645).

269. "Which [work] is also very useful for common uneducated people and is in this little book ["Talia Qualia"] designated with 'Col.'"

270. "Also there are references in here [this book] to my 'Calendario Calendariorum' in octavo." A no longer extant manuscript.

271. Christopher Wirtzung, *Artzney Buch, Darinn werden fast alle eusserliche und innerliche Glieder des Menschlichen leibs, mit ihrer gestalt, aigenschaffi und würckung beschriben, Darbey auch vom Haupt an biss zun fersen verzaichnet, was jedes sonderlich oder inn gemain für Kranckheiten und gebrechen angreiffend: mit sondrem fleiss aus den berümptesten Artzten, so wol der newen als der alten geschribnen Bücher, und sonderbarer erfarung zusamen getragen* (Heidelberg, 1568).

272. Balthasar Schnurr, *Kunst und Wunderbüchlein: Darinnen allerhand nützliche Sachen unnd Kunststücke verfasset und begriffen . . . Kunststücken und Magischen Sachen* (Frankfurt: Rötel, 1643).

273. Johann Christoph Thieme, *Haus-, Feld-, Artzney-, Koch-, Kunst- und Wunder-Buch. Das ist: Ausführliche Beschreib- und Vorstellung, Wie ein kluger Haus-Vatter und sorgfältige Haus-Mutter, wes Standes und Würden sie auch immermehr seyn mögen, mit vortrefflichem Nutzen und ersprießlichem Nahrungs-Aufnehmen, ihr Haus-Wesen führen, und, durch Gottes reichen Seegen, auf ihre Nachkommen höchst-glücklich fortpflantzen möge: Alles, um richtiger Ordnung willen, in Zwantzig Abtheilungen enthalten. . .* (Nuremberg: Hofmann & Streck, 1700).

274. [Johannes van Ravesteyn, printer], *Vorstelick geschenck, dat is, een medecynboeck, inhoudende vele geproefde ende goet gevonden medecijn-stucken. . .* (Amsterdam: Ravesteyn, 1662).

275. George Horn, *Arca Mosis; sive, Historia mundi. Quae complectitur primordia rerum naturalium omniumque artium ac scientiarum* (Leiden and Rotterdam: Ex Officina Hackiana, 1668).

276. Paracelsus, *Aureoli Philippi Theophrasti Bombasts von Hohenheim Paracelsi [. . .] Opera Bücher und Schrifften [. . .]* (Strassburg, 1616).

277. William Mather, *The Young Man's Companion* (London, 1695).

21. Robert Boyle's Medicinal Experiments, in 12° 1696 & the third volume, 1698. He was Fellow of the Royal Society.[278]

22. James Cooke's Mellificium Chirurgiæ in 12°. 1648.[279]

23. William Salmon's Polygraphice, or the Arts of Drawing, Limning, Painting, Engraving, Etching, Dying, &c. in 8° 1684.[280]

24. Jeremiah Love's Clavis Medicinae, or Practice of Physick reformed, in 8° 1674.[281]

278. Robert Boyle, *Medicinal experiments, or, A collection of choice and safe remedies: for the most part simple and easily prepared: very useful in families, and fitted for the service of country people* (London: Samuel Smith, 1696–98).

279. James Cooke, *Mellificium chirurgiæ. Or The marrow of many good authors* (London, 1648).

280. William Salmon, *Polygraphice: or The arts of drawing, engraving, etching, limning, painting, washing, varnishing, gilding, colouring, dying, beautifying and perfuming* (London, 1685).

281. Jeremiah Love, *Clavis medicinæ: or, The practice of physic* (London, 1674).

Fig. 9 | Gerret Hendericks, Derick up de Graeff, Francis Daniell [sic] Pastorius, [and] Abraham up den Graef, first page from "Quaker Protest Against Slavery in the New World, Germantown (Pa.) 1688." Manuscript Collection 990 B-R, Quaker and Special Collections, Haverford College.

8 ❧

Legal and Civic Writings

"Quaker Protest Against Slavery in the New World"

INTRODUCTION TO THE TEXT

The text below is a complete transcription and annotation of Gerret Hendericks, Derick up de Graeff, Francis Daniell [*sic*] Pastorius, [and] Abraham up den Graef, "Quaker Protest Against Slavery in the New World, Germantown (Pa.) 1688," Manuscript Collection 990 B-R, Quaker and Special Collections, Haverford College.[1] As a hallmark document in the history of antislavery thought and abolitionism, written in the hand of and, in all likelihood, composed by Francis Daniel Pastorius, the "Quaker Protest Against Slavery in the New World" constitutes an indispensable part of this reader, even though it has been reproduced and printed before.

Indeed, the Germantown Friends' "Protest" is generally understood to be the first public protest against slavery and the slave trade in North America, initiating a long

---

1. In the Haverford Quaker and Special Collections online facsimile of the "Protest" (http://triptych .brynmawr.edu/cdm/ref/collection/HC_QuakSlav/id/5837), damage makes some parts of the text unreadable. In order to recover the parts obscured by this damage, we turned to the facsimile reproduced in Marion Dexter Learned's *Life of Francis Daniel Pastorius* (Philadelphia: Campbell, 1906), unnumbered page following 262. Learned may have received his facsimile copy at a time before some of this damage occurred. Considered lost twice, the "Protest" was most recently rediscovered at the Arch Street Meeting House in Philadelphia in 2005. Unfortunately, the transcription on the Haverford Quaker and Special Collections website does not explain what source was used to fill in the illegible or missing passages. But, in comparing the Learned facsimile with the online Haverford original, it becomes evident that someone, in imitation of Pastorius's hand, filled in a few already existing gaps, some of which, however, deviate from the original. Our transcription here attempts to create the best possible version in consultation with the facsimile of the online original and the facsimile printed by Learned in 1906. In making it, we spelled out double consonants wherever Pastorius indicated these by drawing a horizontal line over particular consonants.

tradition of Quaker abolitionism in the British colonies and later in the United States. Although Quaker founder George Fox had, as early as 1671 during his visit to Barbados, warned Quakers of the moral depravity resulting from the keeping of slaves and had enjoined his fellow Friends who owned slaves to at the very least treat them with Christian charity, he had provided no clear and consistent injunction against the practice. As scholars from Jean Soderlund to Katharine Gerbner and Brycchan Carey have shown, Quakers in the American colonies continued to hold and trade in slaves in clear violation of their faith's prohibitions against keeping and trading in stolen goods and of the more fundamental Quaker doctrines of peacefulness and brotherly love. Rejecting the assumption that any human being could be held as property, the "Protest" argues that not only did slavery violate the Quaker prohibitions against keeping and trading in stolen goods; but what was more important, it also violated the Golden Rule.

Along with fellow Germantown Quakers Abraham and Dirck op den Graeff and Gerret Hendericks (spellings of their names vary greatly), Pastorius submitted the "Protest" at the Germantown Meeting on April 18, 1688, as a petition to be presented to the Monthly Meeting at Dublin (today known as "Abington"), some 10 miles to the north. On April 30, the Dublin Meeting commented that the matter was "so weighty that we think it not expedient for us to meddle with it here, but rather commit it to the consideration of the Quarterly Meeting; the tenor of it being nearly related to Truth." On June 4, the Quarterly Meeting at Philadelphia referred the "Protest" to the Yearly Meeting, explaining that it was "of too great a weight for this meeting to determine." And, finally, on September 5, 1688, the Yearly Meeting, gathering at Burlington, West Jersey, concluded: "It was adjudged not to be so proper for this Meeting to give a Positive Judgment in the Case, It having so General a Relation to many other P[a]rts, and therefore at present they forbear It." In the Society of Friends, matters of policy were only decided and instituted as binding if all members of a given Quaker Meeting agreed. Because none could reach a unanimous consensus, the Pennsylvania Quaker Meetings at all levels neither accepted nor rejected the Germantown petition and sought instead to preserve the principles of love and unity among their members—only to have that unity shattered by the Keithian controversy three years later. Nevertheless, the "Quaker Protest" conveyed a powerful moral argument against slavery that reverberated throughout abolitionist literature.

This is to the Monthly Meeting hold at Rigert Worrells.[2]

These are the reasons, why we are against the traffick of men body, as followeth: Is there any that would be done or handled at this manner? viz, to be sold or made a slave for all the time of his life? How fearfull & fainthearted are many on sea when they see a strange vassel. being afraid it should be a Turck, and they should be taken, and sold for Slaves into Turckey.[3] Now what is this better done as Turcks doe? yea, rather is it worse for them which say they are Christians, for we hear, that the most part of such Negers are brought heither[4] against their will & consent; and that many of them are stollen. Now, tho' they are black, we can not conceive there is more liberty to have them slaves, as it is to have other white ones. There is a saying, that we shall doe to all men, licke as we will be done our selves; making no difference of what generation, descent or Colour they are. And those who steal or robb men, and those who buy or purchase them, are they not all alike? Here is liberty of Conscience, which is right & reasonable; here ought to be lickewise liberty of the body, except of evildoers, which is an other case. But to bring men hither, or to robb and sell them against their will, we stand against. In Europe there are many oppressed for Conscience sacke; and here there are those oppressed which are of a black Colour.[5] And we, who know that men must not committ adultery, some doe commit adultery in others, separating wifes from their housbands, and giving them to others. and some sell the children of those poor Creatures to other men.[6] Oh! doe consider well this things, you who doe it; if you would be done at this manner? and if it is done according Christianity? You surpass Holland and Germany in this thing.[7] This mackes an ill report in all those Countries of Europe, where they hear off, that the Quackers doe here handel men, licke they handle there the cattle. and for

2. Richard Worrell Jr., as corroborated by *Hazard's Register of Pennsylvania*, vol. 7 (February 1831), 117: "At a monthly meeting at Cheltenham, the 31st of 1st month, 1687, it was agreed that the monthly meeting be held at the house of Richard Worrell, jr. henceforward [...]. The monthly meeting appears to be kept at the house of Richard Worrell aforesaid from the said 31st of 1st month, 1687, to the 29th of 1st month, 1702, where and when it was agreed to be kept at Abington, and has so continued ever since."

3. Many Europeans in the seventeenth century feared the very real possibility of their ships being seized by Turkish pirates, who would then sell the white Christian passengers into slavery in the Muslim world.

4. Hither.

5. The "Protest" points out the hypocrisy of Pennsylvanians in granting "liberty of conscience" (freedom of religion) to white people but denying it to people of color.

6. Anticipating an argument frequently made by abolitionists in later years—that slavery violated the sanctity of marriage so dearly prized by white colonists and by American citizens after them—the "Protest" underscores the peculiar cruelty of slavery in sundering families, a rhetorical emphasis that would be shared by those later abolitionists.

7. The "Protest" here alludes to Germantown's Dutch and German settlers, most of whom were religious dissidents recruited by Pennsylvania's English Quakers. It again points to the hypocrisy of these Quakers, who recognized and indeed inveighed against the immorality of religious persecution in Holland and Germany, but who turned a blind eye to the immorality of their own buying, selling, and keeping slaves in Pennsylvania.

that reason some have no mind or inclination to come hither.[8] And who shall maintaine this your cause or plaid[9] for it? Truely we can not do so, except you shall inform us better hereoff, viz: that christians have liberty to practise this things. Pray! What thing in the world can be done worse towards us, then if men should robb or steal us away, & sell us for slaves to strange Countries, separating housband from their wife & children. Being now this is not done at that manner we will be done at,[10] therefore we contradict & are against this traffick of men body. And we who profess that it is not lawfull to steal, must lickewise avoid to purchase such things as are stollen, but rather help to stop this robbing and stealing if possibel; and such ought to be delivered out of the hands of the Robbers, and mad[e] free as well as in Europe.[11] Then is Pennsilvania to have a good report, in stead it hath now a bad one for this sacke in other Countries. Especially whereas the Europeans are desirous to know, in what manner the Quakers doe rule in their Province, & most of them doe loock upon us with an envious eye. But if this is done well, what shall we say, is don evill?

If once these Slaves; (which they say are so wicked and stubbern men) should joint themselves, fight for their freedom and handel their masters & mastrisses, as they did handel them before; will these Masters and mastrisses tacke the sword at hand & warr against these poor slaves, licke we are able to bclive, some will not refuse to doe?[12] Or have these Negers not as much right to fight for their freedom, as you have to keep them slaves?

Now consider well this thing; if it is good or bad? and in case you find it to be good to handel these blacks at that manner, we desire & require you hereby lovingly that you may informe us here in, which at this time never was done, viz. that Christians have such a liberty to do so. To the end we shall be satisfied in this point, & satisfie lickewise

8. The "Protest" cleverly asserts that the many promotional tracts published by William Penn and others in order to attract settlers to Pennsylvania would be for naught if the truth were ever known—that the colony's condoning of slavery negated all of its many advantages. Indeed, none of the extant promotional tracts on Pennsylvania distributed in Holland and Germany makes any mention of slavery, and thus the Germantown settlers may have felt deceived about the true nature of this "utopian" society.

9. Plead.

10. That is, slavery is not a practice we would tolerate having done to ourselves. In other words, in its very essence, the Golden Rule prohibits slavery.

11. The Quaker prohibitions against trading in or keeping stolen goods—and thus also slaves—were among the faith's earliest guiding principles. That Pennsylvania Quakers either engaged in or condoned slavery was one of the key reasons for the itinerant Quaker merchant John Woolman (1720–1771) to begin his own antislavery crusade.

12. Here the "Protest" invokes another fundamental Quaker principle—the "peace principle" or prohibition against all violence, even in defense of one's own life—to warn other Friends against a logical consequence of slavery. Should there be a slave rebellion, the "Protest" predicts, many seemingly peace-loving Quakers might feel compelled to take up arms and possibly to kill in order to defend themselves and their families.

our good friends & acquaintances in our natif Country, to whose[13] it is a terrour, or fairfull[14] thing that men should be handeld so in Pennsilvania.

This is from our Meeting at Germantown hold[15] the 18. of the 2. month, 1688,[16] to be delivered to the Monthly Meeting at Richard Warrell's.   gerret hendericks

derick up de graeff

Francis daniell Pastorius

Abraham up Den graef[17]

at our monthly meeting at Dublin, the 30 – 2 month 1688[18] we having inspected the matter above mentioned & considered of it we find it so weighty that we think it not Expedient for us to meddle with it here but do Rather commit it to the consideration of the Quarterly meeting the tennor of it being nearly Related to the truth.[19]

on behalf of the monthly meeting signed P. Jo: Hart[20]

This Abovementioned was read in our quarterly meeting at Philadelphia the 4th of the 4th month '88[21] and was from thence recommended to the Yearly Meeting and the abovesaid Derick[22] and the other Two mentioned therein[23] to present the same to the abovesaid meeting, it being a thing of too great A wayt[24] for This meetting to determine.[25] Signed by ord[er] themeetting Anthony Morris[26]

At a Yearly Meeting held at Burlington the 5th day of the 7th month, 1688.[27]

13. Whom.

14. Fearful.

15. Held.

16. April 18, 1688.

17. See "List of People and Places" toward the end of this reader for brief biographical information about Pastorius's co-signers.

18. April 30, 1688.

19. This note reveals how seriously these Quaker Meetings took the "Protest" and its import: a matter of "truth" was a fundamental principle of the Quaker community, requiring a unanimous agreement of the members.

20. John Hart was an early Quaker arrival from England, where he received a "Certificate of Removal" from his meeting on April 10, 1682. Hart had purchased 10,000 acres from William Penn and was a member of the Pennsylvania General Assembly in 1683 and 1684.

21. June 4, 1688.

22. Dirck op den Graeff, who signed the "Protest" as "derick up de graeff."

23. It is possible that this meeting miscounted the signers because the first, Gerret Hendericks, signed his name contiguous with the end of the text; the next three signed their names in separate lines below. Someone not looking at the document closely might easily count only the three individuals who signed in separate lines; of those three, Dirck op den Graeff, who signed his name as "derick up de graeff," was indeed the first, making it seem like the two below him were his *two* cosigners.

24. Weight.

25. The note from the Dublin Meeting of April 30, 1688, and the note from Philadelphia Quarterly Meeting of June 4, 1688, were both written at the bottom of the original manuscript of the "Protest."

26. Anthony Morris was an English Quaker who first settled in Burlington, West Jersey (present-day New Jersey), and then moved to Philadelphia in 1687, where he frequently served as clerk of the Quaker meetings.

27. September 5, 1688.

A Paper being here presented by some German Friends Concerning the Lawfulness and Unlawfulness of Buying and keeping Negroes, It was adjudged not to be so proper for this Meeting to give a Positive Judgment in the Case, It having so General a Relation to many other Parts, and therefore at present they forcbear It.[28]

---

28. The note from the the Philadelphia Yearly Meeting of September 5, 1688, was *not* written on the "Protest" itself but is transcribed from the Yearly Meeting's records.

Fig. 10 | Francis Daniel Pastorius, title page from "The Young Country Clerk's Collection." UPenn MS Codex 89, Rare Book and Manuscript Library, University of Pennsylvania.

"The Young Country Clerk's Collection"

INTRODUCTION TO THE TEXT

The following transcribed and annotated selections are excerpted from Francis Daniel Pastorius, "The Young Country Clerk's Collection of the Best Presidents of Bills, Bonds, Conditions, Acquittances, Releases, Indentures, Deeds of Sale, Letters of Attorney, Last Wills & Testaments &c. With many other necessary and useful Forms of such like Writings as are vulgarly in use between Man and Man," UPenn MS Codex 89, Rare Book and Manuscript Library, University of Pennsylvania.

Pastorius compiled his "Young Country Clerk's Collection" from the 1690s through the first decade of the eighteenth century. It is probably the first legal guide written in British North America and, like much of Pastorius's work, was designed with a very practical purpose in mind. Thus it contains forms for legal transactions (contracts for the sale and mortgaging of land and the sale of goods, labor contracts, wills) as well as forms for criminal prosecutions and for the settlement of civil disputes through arbitration—but no forms for civil lawsuits, despite the litigious nature of early Pennsylvanians. Pastorius seemed to be creating a practical legal guide for country clerks that was in keeping with his skepticism about civil lawsuits, a guide that likely reflected his desire to limit these and to settle civil disputes outside of court.

"The Young Country Clerk's Collection" draws heavily upon three English form books published from the 1640s to the 1690s: Richard Hill's *Young Clerk's Guide* (London, 1649), Edward Cocker's *Young Clerks Tutor* (London, 1680), and John Hill's *Young Secretaries Guide* (London, 8th ed., 1697) and also upon Pastorius's own forms and those of others in Pennsylvania and neighboring areas. In the body of the text, he cites the *Young Clerks Tutor* nearly forty times, the *Young Secretaries Guide* more than thirty times, and the voluminous *Young Clerk's Guide*, the most comprehensive and sophisticated of the three, nearly thirty times.

It is unclear why "The Young Country Clerk's Collection" was never published. The manuscript runs to several hundred pages and has several comprehensive indexes, which suggests that Pastorius was preparing it for extensive use and even publication. We have included eight of the forms or examples that Pastorius contributed to his guide: a form for holding property in trust for a Quaker Meeting; a will; a petition regarding the Pennsylvania charter; a contract for the sale of part of a mill; a lease of a plantation; an application form for serving as a magistrate; a license to keep an ale house; and a form to instruct a magistrate in a neighboring county to hold a man in custody on the allegation that he fathered a child outside of marriage (a critical form for advancing the legal process). Together, the forms and examples presented here give a sense of the breadth of issues that Pastorius's legal guide dealt with, of how the Pennsylvania economy was becoming involved in sophisticated commercial transactions. and of how the law was being used to maintain order at the time.

THE TEXT

The <u>Young Country Clerk's Collection</u> of the best Presidents of Bills, Bonds, Conditions, Acquittances, Releases, Indentures, Deeds of Sale, Letters of Attorney, Last Wills & Testaments, &c. With many other necessary and useful Forms of such like Writings as are vulgarly in use between Man and Man.

[...]

Declaration of Trust

To all People to whom these Presents shall come We AB CD all of the County of Pha[29] in the Province of Pn yeomen send Greeting. Whereas H of G in the said County husbandman by his deed poll duely executed bearing date the day next before the date of these Presents for the Consideration therein mentioned did grant & Convey unto us the said AB CD a certain tract of land Scituate &c Containing &c To hold the said piece of land with the appurtenances unto usu the said AB CD out heirs & ass. forever, as by the said deep poll may at large appear which said land & Premises were so as aforesaid Conveyd unto us by the direction & appointment of the Inhabitants of Germn aforesaid belonging to the Monthly Meeting of the People of God called Quakers in the township of Dublin in the said County of Pa and the above recited Deed poll was so made or Intended to us in Trust to the Intent only that we or such or so many of us as shall be & continue in unity & religious fellowship with the said People & remain members of the said Monthly Meeting (whereunto we now belong) should stand & be seized of the said land & Premises in & by said Deed poll granted to the uses & Intents herein after mentioned & declared and under the Conditions Provises & Restrictions herein after limited & expressed and to no other use Intent or Purpose whatsoever, that is to say, for the benefit use & behoof of the poor of the said People called Quakers in Germn aforesaid for ever and for a place to erect a meeting house for the use & service of the said People, and (if need shall so require) for a place to bury their bead. Provided always that neither we nor any of us nor any other person or persons succeeding us in this Trust who shall be declared by the Members of the said

29. All idiosyncratic abbreviations in this section (apart from "sd" for "said" and "aforesd" for "aforesaid") have been retained to reflect Pastorius's practice of creating legal forms for use in a specific setting.

Monthly Meeting for the time being to be out of unity with them shall be capable to execute this Trust or stand seized to the uses aforesaid nor have any Right or Interest in the said Premises while we or they shall so remain. But that in all such cases as also which any of us or others succeeding us in the Trust aforesaid shall happen to depart this life, then it shall & may be lawful to & for the said Members in their said Monthly Meeting as often as occasion shall require to make Choice of others to manage & execute the said Trust in stead of such as shall so fall away or be deceased. And upon this further Trust & Confidence that w & the Survivor of us & the heirs of such Survivor should upon the Request of the said Monthly Meeting either assign over the said Trust or Convey & settle the said Messuage piece of land & premises to such person or persons as the said Meeting shall order or appoint to and for the uses, Interests & Services aforesaid. Now have ye that the said ABCD do hereby acknowledge that use a renomination in the said recited deed poll by & on the behalf of the said People called Qrs and that we are therein trusted only by & for the Members o the said Monthly Meeting and that we do not Claim to have any Rights or Interest in the said Land & premises or any part thereof to our own use & benefits by the said deed or conveyance so made (as aforesaid or otherwise) howsoever, But only to & for the use Intent & Service herein before mentioned under the Limitation & Restrictions above expressed & rescued, and to no other use, Intent or Service whatsoever. In Witness whereof we have hereunto set our hands & Seals. Dated the thirtieth day of November in the year of our Lord One thousand Seven hundred & five.

John Dumpling's Testament

I[,] JD of Phila[delphia] merchant being sick of body, but of sound & disposing mind, memory & Judgment do make my last Will and Testmt as follows. [First] I will that all my Just Debts and funeral expenses be duely paid by my Executr after named with all expedition after my decease. Secondly I do give bequeth & devise to my wife W all and singular my clear real & personal Estate and the profits thereof during her widouity or widowhood; But in case the said my wife should marry again then I only give bequeth & devise to her the Just & equal Moity & half part of my said clear Estate real and personal and the other Just moity and half thereof. I do give & devise to my brother A and my sister MD in Holland their heirs & assigns for ever equally between them share and share alike. And in case my said Wife should dye before marriage then and in that Case I give bequeth & devise my said clear estate both real & personal to the said A and MD my brother and Sister, and to SB and their heirs, Execrs, admrs and assigns equally between them share and share alike that is to say One Just and equal third part thereof to each one of them. I do also order and appoint that my Executrix or Executor afternamed shall sell and dispose of my real and personal Estate to such persons as they shall think Convenient, and that they or any one of them do sign, Seal & deliver Deeds of Sale for the same to the Purchasers and acknowledge the same in Open Court with all Solemnities requisite. And of this my last Will and Testament I make my said Wife Executrix during her lifetime and after her decease I make VI of Philada baker my executor whom I desire to be assistant to me said Wife and Overseer of this my Last Will and Testament, to whom for his Trouble I give ten pounds. Witness my hand and Seal this 14th Septem[ber] 1699.

[...]

Humble Petition Regarding Pennsylvania Charter

Humbly showeth that with great grief we apprehending ourselves under a necessity of making this our address to the king being deeply sensible of the severe circumstances which threatened us by a bill brought into Parl, last sessions, for dissolving Charter Govrmts in America & annexing them to the Crown, & having upon the Credit & Incouragement of a Grant from King Charles the Second to our Propertary & Govr transplanted ourselve & families into this remote wilderness where with much charge, Hazard & Labour we have added another Colony to the English Empire therein without the least Charge to the Crown, and humbly conceiving if such a law should pass against us, these following Inconveniences would probably by the Consequence thereof, vizt

[...]

5[th]ly this will Inevitably discourage the better peopleing of the Province & Consequently the further Improvements thereof, which must needs sink the value of our present Estates & also hereby lessen Trade & the Interest of the Crown.

Wherefore we most humbly pray the king to take the Premises witho out annexed Case into his Princely consideration and permit us to the Manifest Inconveniences which will attend disdoing our Proprietary & Governmts Charter, Especially since not only he but some of us are yet greatly in disburse for the settlemt of this Province.

[...]

One Selling the 4th Part of his Mill

This Indenture made Before A and B of the other part, Whereas the said A by force & vertue of some good Conveyance or conveyances, assurance or assurances in Law now is & standeth lawfully seized in his demeane as of the fee of and in all those two water corn mills or grist mills under one roof commonly called or known by the

name of P Mills, with the appurtenances, scituate lying & being in the said Township
of & and of & in all that piece or parcell of land on part where the said mills now stand
Beginning &c containing &c and running thence down the several courses of the said
millrace, viz North, &c to the first mentioned stake, containing in the whole &c part
of &c as by an Indenture duly exccuted & acknowledged in Court by __ may at large
appear. Now this Ind witnesseth that the said A as well for the Consideration of 200£
Currt money of Pens to him paid by the said B, the Receipt whereof &c as for other
divers good causes & consids him the said A specially moving hath granted, sold ./.
unto the said B One full, equal & undivided fourth part of all the said piece or parcel of
land, whereon the said Mills stand containing by Estimation __ acres scituate, bounded
& being as is herein above set forth & described and also one full equal fourth part of
all the Toll & profits of the said Mills, together with one full & equall part of all the
headwaters, mill ponds with the soil thereof and also of all & singular the mill pools,
mill dams, banks, ponds, streams, waters, watercourses, millraces, creeks, fishings, ways,
freebords, passages, easements, advantages, enoluments and appurtenances whatsoever
to the said Mills, lands & premises belonging or in any wise appertaining, or therewith
now, or at any time heretofore held used, occupied or enjoyed, and the reversions &
remainders, rents, issues & profits of the said one fourth part of the said Mills, land &
premises, and true Copies of all Deeds, Evidences, writings concerning the same to be
had & made at the proper Costs & charges of the said B. To have & to hold the said
full, equall & undivided fourth part of all & singular the said Mills, land & other the
premises hercby granted or mentioned or intended to be granted with their appurtenances unto the said B & his heirs to the use & for ever—Under the proportionable
part of the quitrent hereafter accruing for the same to the Lord of the fee thereof and
the said A & his heirs the [?] one full, equall fourth part & all & singular the said mills,
land & other the premises hereby granted or mentioned or Intended to be gr. with their
app. unto the said B his heirs & ass. agt him the said A his heirs & ass & agt all other
persons whatsoever lawfully claiming or to the claim by, from, or under him, them or
any of them shall & will war[rant]— and the said A, for himself, his heirs Execrs Adms
doth Covenant promise & grant & with the said B his heirs & ass by these presents
that he the said B his heirs & ass shall & lawfully may from time to time & at all times
for ever hereafter, freely, quietly & peaceably have hold & enjoy the said fourth part
of the aforesaid mills, land, hereditaments and all other the premises hereby granted
or mentioned to be granted & every part thereof with the app. without any Lett[?],
Suit, trouble or molestation of the said A his heirs or ass or any other person or persons
whatsoever, and free & clear & freely & clearly acquitted & is charged of & from all
& all manner of former & other bargains, Seals, gifts, grants, feoffments, Jointures,
Dowers, Intails, Mortgages, Estatcs, rights, Titles, Debts, Charges, troubles, forfeitures
& Incumbrances whatsoever had, made donw, acknowledged & suffered by the said

A or any other person or persons whatsoever, by or with his means, privit, consent or procurment and that he the said A & his heirs & all and every other person or persons whatsoever having or lawfully Claiming any stake, right, title or Interest of, in & to the said fourth part of the said Mills & prem. hereby granted or any part hereof shall & will at any time hereafter upon the reasonable request, Costs & charges in Law of the said B his heirs or ass. make, execute & acknowledge or cause so to be all & every such further & other reasonable act or acts, Deed or Deeds, device or devices in Law for the further & better assurance & Confirmation of the said fourth part of the said Mills & Land and all other the premises hereby granted with the appurts unto the said B his heirs & ass as by him or them or by his or their Council learned in the Law shall be reasonably deo[?] adv & reqred, In Witness &c A.

[...]

A Lease of a Plantation for half the Increase

AB of the County of PH yeoman for the Consideration herein aftermentioned hath & hereby doth grant, demise, set & to farm let unto C of the said County husbandman a certain plantation & tract of land in ./. with the dwellinghouse, buildings, Improvements & appurtenances (:exception & reserving only unto the said AB his Execs adms & assigns one hald of the meadow, being the upper end there between the barn & the Creek,) and also two horses & Cows & calves, one heifer three sows, one plough & Irons & goats suitable[?], three bells & collars, To hold all & singular the hereby demised premises with the appurtenances unto the said C his Execs admins & ass. during the full Term of 6 years from the 25th day of May instant, In considno of which said grant & demise the said C his heirs Excess adms or ass shall give & pay unto the said AB his ./. one half part of all the wheat, rye & barley, the produce of the said Plantation yearly during the said Term, and one half to be taken out of before decision all the Corn to be divided after winnowing the said AB assisting to Carry all the Corn to the Mill and the said AB shall have one half of the yearly Increase of the Stock and whereas the said AB now leaves on the premises about 10 acres of wheat & rye in the ground, the quantity & value thereof with the Stock & Implements of husbandry being at the Comencmt of the Term view'd & valu'd by Impartial & Judicious men the said C at the expiration of the said Term shall make good unto the said AB the like value in quantity & quality Excepting only that if any of the Stock dye or miscarry accidentally (and not thro' negligence & defect of the said C) the said parties shall equally bear such Loss and at the expiration the premises shall be yielded up unto the said AB or Order in good repair and well Conditioned, and the said C shall have the liberty of keeping on the premises a breeding mare & sow of his own. For the true performance of all which said Covenants & agreemnts the said parties mutually bind & oblige themselves with one[?] to the other in the penal sum of 100 pounds lawful money of America firmly by these presents, witness the hands & seals of the said parties Interchangeably putt hereunto, dated the 18th of May anno Domni 1714.

Sealed & delivered in the presence of __

[..]

After Inserting the additional Clause before Signing It's mutually agreed between the avoce parties, that the said C shall also keep a Cow of his own on the premises, and to sow an acre of flax & hemp yearly, & to plant an acre or two of Indian Corn yearly, and whatever land the Tenant clears he shall be paid 20 shill. an acre for every acre so cleared out of the first Crop of such land, out of the Landlords share, and the said Tenant shall yearly sow with winter Corn as many acres as he possibly can without neglecting that business to sow Flax, hemp or Indian Corn above the aforsaid quantity, or follow any other business but what is unavoidably necessary besides the plantation work. Griffith Pritchard AB.

This is John Cadwalader's drawing, to which he added on the same sheet a Bond of Performance.

[..]

A Licence to keep an alehouse

For as much as good & Credible report has been made unto us A & B Justices &c by divers honest persons that C is a man made to keep a Common alehouse in the house where he had dwelleth We do by these Presents license allow & admit the said C to keep a common alehouse for one whole year next ensuing the Date hereof, that the said C suffer not any unlawful games to be used in his said house nor any evil & rude or disorder of the same During the time of his License. For the using of which License accordingly we have bound the said C by Recognizance with Surities & the Kings use in __ Ls a piece that he shall maintain good Rule and further to do & behave himself therein in all things according to the Laws &c in that behalf made & provided. In Witness where we have hereunto set our hands & Seals dated #

[..]

Power to Qualify Magistrates

Pensylvia John Evans Esq. by her Maties Roall approbation Liet Governour of the Province of Pensylvia & Counties of New Castle, Kent & Sussex upon Delaware To Geo Lowther Gent. Whereas I am willing that Justice should be done unto the Inhabitants

of Germantown pursuant to their Charter & to the end they may be qualified according to Law who are to administered the same both Provincial & ministerial officers I
therefore hereby give unto you full Power authority to administer unto Thomas Rutter
Bayliff, Casper Hood Recorded for Daniel Pastorius Clerk & all others the Justices &
Officers of the same Corporacon such oaths or affimacons as by Law they ought to take
for their due Qualification. Given under my hand & seal at Philadeia the Eighteenth
day of March Anno Dno 1706.

[. . . . .]

A Mittemus of the reputed Father of a bastard child
I send you herewithal the body of A of &c brought before me this present day &
charged by B of &c to have gotten her with Child; and for that the said A refuseth
to put in Security for his appearance at the next Court & to the end that he may be
forthcoming whence Order shall be taken for the relief & discharging of the said care,
and for the keeping of the said Child (when he shall happen to be born:) according
to the statute in that case provided: these are therefore in the kings behalf to charge
& command you that immediately you receive the said A and him safely keep in your
goal until such time as he shall be from thence delivered by due order of Law. And
hereof faithfully.

N.B. In every Mittimus the Cause of the Commitment is to be set down to the
end it may appear whether the Prisoner be bailable. In the manner of the offence, how
long time the offender is to be kept in Prison for it.

List of People and Places

Below are the names of Pastorius's family members and contemporaries he met and mentioned in his writings and significant places where he lived or visited, or that were otherwise significant to him. The entries briefly identify and provide background for each person or place and describe Pastorius's connection to each. Although this explanatory list is meant primarily as a reference tool, readers may first wish to look it over to gain a sense of Pastorius's transatlantic community before proceeding to the selected texts.

Altdorf. Town near Nuremberg in Franconia (present-day Bavaria), where Pastorius attended the university from 1668 to 1670, in 1672, and again from 1675 to 1676, when he completed his doctorate in law.

Bom, Cornelius (Cornelis). Dutch baker who first settled in Philadelphia, then relocated to Germantown, where he bought land in 1685. Pastorius mentions meeting Bom at his bakery after getting lost on the way from the Delaware riverfront. Bom wrote an account of Pennsylvania and Germantown, *Missive van Cornelis Bom. Geschreven uit de Stadt Philadelphia in de Provintie van Pennsylvania*, that was published in Rotterdam in 1685.

Bowyer, Thomas. One of the four Keithians who disrupted a Quaker Meeting at Burlington in 1696, Bowyer drew the ire of Pastorius, who roundly derided him in his 1697 pamphlet *Four Boasting Disputers*.

Bradford, William. Arriving from England in 1685, Bradford became the first printer of colonial Pennsylvania, where he was promised by the Quaker leadership the guaranteed purchase of 200 copies of everything he printed with their approval. However, when he printed unauthorized pamphlets for the Keithians, the Quaker authorities shut down his press. After a brief incarceration for libel, Bradford left Pennsylvania to work for the governor of New York, although he continued to print writings by the Pennsylvania Quakers, including Pastorius's *Four Boasting Disputers* (1697) and *A New Primmer* (1698). Bradford famously appears in Benjamin Franklin's *Autobiography*: when the young Franklin approached him for employment in New York, the elder printer sent Franklin to work for his son Andrew in Philadelphia, helping to launch Franklin's career there.

Budd (Butt), Thomas. Early Quaker settler in Pennsylvania who praised the civic accomplishments of the new colony in a 1685 promotional tract, *Good Order Established in Pennsilvania & New Jersey in America*. During the Keithian controversy, however, Budd sided with George Keith and repudiated the Pennsylvania Quaker leadership, becoming the target of Pastorius's ire in several of his poems and other writings on the controversy.

Burlington. Town founded by Quaker settlers in 1677 and the capital of West Jersey until 1702 (when it became part of the crown colony of New Jersey). The Society of Friends' Yearly Meeting was established at Burlington in 1681; from 1685 to 1760, it met alternately at Burlington and Philadelphia. In 1688, the Yearly Meeting at Burlington, after considering the protest against slavery co-signed by Pastorius and three other Germantown Quakers, stated that the matter was too complex to decide.

Carpenter, Samuel. Originally from Sussex, England, Carpenter became a Quaker in the 1670s and moved to the British colony of Barbados, where he and other Quakers came into conflict with local authorities for condemning slavery and refusing to make military contributions. Settling in Pennsylvania in 1683, he entered colonial politics and became first treasurer, then deputy governor of Pennsylvania. As one of Pastorius's most influential Quaker friends, Carpenter helped him recover some of the lands lost during the Frankfurt Land Company fraud perpetrated by Daniel Falckner and Johann Heinrich Sprögel in collusion with David Lloyd.

Davis, William. English Quaker immigrant to Pennsylvania who, with fellow Keithians Thomas Rutter, Thomas Bowyer, and Heinrich Bernhard Köster (Henry Bernhard Koster), disrupted a Quaker Meeting at Burlington in 1696. Together, the four men then formed a faction that broke away from the Keithian Quakers to embark on a short-lived communitarian experiment. Pastorius condemned both the disruption and the faction's experiment in his 1697 pamphlet *Four Boasting Disputers*. In 1700, Davis published a pamphlet of his own, *Jesus The Crucified Man*, strongly defending his decision to renounce Quakerism for its alleged heresy of denying Christ's physical suffering and resurrection.

Deal. Town on the English Channel northeast of Dover and an important shipping port for Britain's overseas colonies. Pastorius would depart for Pennsylvania from Deal on June 7, 1683, as he wrote in a letter of that date to his father and family.

Dilbeck, Isaac. Employee of the German Society (later the Frankfurt Land Company) who, with his wife, Marieke, and two sons, Abraham and Jacob, accompanied Pastorius to Pennsylvania in 1683 to establish the infrastructure for the settlement where his Frankfurt sponsors originally hoped to relocate.

Ellis, Rowland. Leading Welsh Quaker who settled permanently in Pennsylvania in 1697. As a prominent Friend, Ellis was well known to Pastorius, and they communicated with each other both in person and through letters.

Erfurt. City in Thuringia, sixty miles southwest of Leipzig, and birthplace of Pastorius's father, Melchior Adam. An important city in the Holy Roman Empire, Erfurt was one of the first German cities to adopt the Protestant faith during the Reformation; its university was a premier center of humanist education.

Falckner (Falkner), Daniel. As sons of a Lutheran pastor in Saxony, Falckner and his brother Justus were both slated for the ministry. Daniel studied theology at the University of Erfurt, where he became a student of August Hermann Francke, the Pietist founder of the Francke Foundations (Franckesche Stiftungen) in Halle. Traveling through Germany, Daniel met with and joined the group of celibate mystics around Johannes Kelpius. He would move with them to Pennsylvania in 1694 but then be expelled from their community for fathering a child out of wedlock. On a return visit to Germany in 1700, Falckner (along with Kelpius and Johannes Jawert) was granted power of attorney by the Frankfurt Land Company to administer the company's interests in Pennsylvania. After mismanaging company funds and incurring excessive personal debt, however, he was thrown into debtor's prison. Not long after his release, Falckner would collude with land speculator Heinrich Sprögel and Philadelphia attorney David Lloyd to defraud the company—and its hapless land purchasers, including Pastorius himself—of their lands. He eventually moved to New Jersey, where he became a Lutheran minister.

Frankfurt am Main. One of the most important cities of the Holy Roman Empire, located in Hesse, Germany, Frankfurt was also an economic, intellectual, and religious center, attracting free-spirited individuals like the Pietists, who assembled at the Saalhof, and who would become Pastorius's sponsors through the German Society (later the Frankfurt Land Company). The city's relative toleration of religious differences, however, may have been a key reason the Frankfurt Pietists decided not to follow Pastorius to Pennsylvania.

Furly, Benjamin. Prominent English Quaker living in Rotterdam, where Pastorius would meet him before departing for Pennsylvania in 1683. As the linchpin in William

Penn's efforts to recruit dissenting Protestants on the Continent for settlement in Pennsylvania, Furly established an information network across Europe that distributed printed and manuscript tracts on Pennsylvania to groups like the Frankfurt Pietists and the Krefeld Quakers. He also arranged land sales in the new colony to radical Protestants wishing to immigrate there and assisted them in their immigration. More cosmopolitan than mainstream Quakers, Furly amassed a vast and eclectic library, and his home served as an early modern salon for intellectuals from across Europe.

Gasper, Thomas. One of the employees of the German Society (later the Frankfurt Land Company) who traveled with Pastorius to Pennsylvania in 1683 to establish a settlement there, whom Pastorius mentions in his first published description of Pennsylvania, *Sichere Nachricht* (1684; Certain News).

Germantown. Often described as the first permanent German settlement in North America, Germantown was formally established on October 12, 1683, with William Penn's grant of a six-thousand-acre tract to the Quaker immigrants from Krefeld and the German Society (later Frankfurt Land Company). Pastorius's naming of Germantown (which he also sometimes called "Germanopolis") reflected his hope to create a settlement specifically dedicated to German immigrants.

Halle (Hall). City in Saxony and home to the Francke Foundations (Franckesche Stiftungen), established by the Pietist minister and theologian August Hermann Francke in Halle's suburb of Glaucha in 1698. These combined a progressive pedagogy and exemplary Christian charity to remedy the social ills of the day and included a famous orphanage as well as schools, gardens. teaching workshops, a hospital, and a pharmacy. Deeply impressed by the accounts he collected, Pastorius recommended the Halle institutions to Samuel Carpenter as a model for civic development in Pennsylvania.

Hendericks, Gerret. After immigrating to Pennsylvania from Kriegsheim in the Rhenish Palatinate in 1685, Hendericks settled in Germantown and became a member of its Quaker Meeting. He would join Pastorius and the op den Graeff brothers Abraham and Dirck in signing and submitting the 1688 Germantown Friends' "Protest" against slavery in 1688.

Hill, Elizabeth. Second daughter of Richard and Hannah Hill, Elizabeth was also the granddaughter of Thomas Lloyd, with whom Pastorius had forged a lifelong friendship on his passage to Pennsylvania in 1683. As her mentor, Pastorius exchanged books, poetry, and letters with Elizabeth, who would become, in his judgment, one of the most educated young women in Pennsylvania.

Hill, Hannah, Jr. First daughter of Richard and Hannah Hill, Hannah Jr. died in 1714 at age 11 of a "violent fever and flux." Family members collected the pious words she uttered during her illness and published them as *A Legacy for Children, being some of the last Expressions & Dying Sayings of Hannah Hill Junr* in 1717. Pastorius expressed his regret for not being able to attend Hannah's funeral (which took place on the wedding day of his older son, John Samuel) in one of his "Ship-Mate-Ship" poems.

Hill, Hannah, Sr. One of ten children of the prominent Welsh Quakers Thomas and Mary Lloyd, Hannah Sr. arrived on the *America* with Pastorius in 1683. After the early death of her first husband, John Delaval, in 1693, she married the wealthy Pennsylvania merchant and politician Richard Hill. From 1714, the year her daughter Hannah Jr. died, until 1716, the year her sister Rachel died, Pastorius sent Hannah Sr. and her sisters Mary and Rachel a series of anniversary poems commemorating the day of their arrival in Philadelphia on August 20, 1683, a series he would continue with Hannah Sr. and Mary until 1719, the year of his own death.

Hill, Richard. Connected to Pastorius through his wife, Hannah Sr., the daughter of Pastorius's friend and shipmate Thomas Lloyd, Richard Hill was one of the most influential men of early colonial Pennsylvania. He served on the Provincial Council and in the General Assembly (three times as its speaker); he was mayor of Philadelphia for four terms and a justice on the Pennsylvania Supreme Court. Pastorius repeatedly expressed his gratitude to Hill for helping him regain title to the lands he had lost in the land fraud perpetrated by Daniel Falckner and Johann Heinrich Sprögel in collusion with the Quaker lawyer David Lloyd.

Hoodt (Hood, Hoet), Caspar. Tailor by trade, Hoodt had immigrated to New York from Hesse, Germany, but moved to Pennsylvania and settled in Germantown in the early 1690s, where he and Pastorius became neighbors and friends, and where he would serve as recorder for the Germantown General Court. When Francis Daniel's son Henry took to traveling to Maryland in later years, Pastorius asked Hoodt to check up on him.

Horb, Johann Heinrich. Brother-in-law of Philipp Jakob Spener, considered the father of German Pietism, the Pietist theologian Horb served as a Lutheran pastor in Windsheim from 1679 to 1685, where he met Pastorius. Horb introduced him to the Pietist circle in Frankfurt and would become an important influence on Pastorius's spiritual development.

Hoskens (Hoskins), Jane Fenn. According to her own account, nineteen-year-old Jane Fenn followed an inner voice that told her, "Go to Pennsylvania!" in 1712. She worked as an indentured servant and housekeeper for several years before embarking with several other Quaker women on numerous missionary trips across North America and Europe. She married a wealthy Quaker merchant, Joseph Hoskins, in 1738. Her autobiographical writings *The Life and Spiritual Sufferings of that Faithful Servant of Christ Jane Hoskens* were published in 1771. Hearing of her literary skills when Fenn was still a young woman working in the households of prominent English Quakers, Pastorius gave her advice on writing poetry and praised her as being in line with other female poets such as Anne Bradstreet, although none of the manuscripts of Fenn's poetry seems to be extant.

Jena. Located not far from Erfurt, the Thuringian city of Jena became an important center of higher learning with the founding of its university in 1558; it was also an early proponent of Martin Luther's religious reforms. Pastorius transferred from Altdorf to the University of Jena in 1672; he studied law under Heinrich Linck and the Italian language there until 1674.

Jones, Griffith. English Quaker and early purchaser of land in Pennsylvania, where he would become a successful merchant and tavern owner. Jones belonged to a circle of prominent Quakers with whom Pastorius exchanged books and manuscript writings.

Keith, George. Early convert to Quakerism and one of its leading figures in seventeenth-century Scotland and England, Keith traveled with other prominent Friends such as George Fox, William Penn, and Robert Barclay on a mission trip to Germany in 1677. After a brief period as surveyor-general in East Jersey, Keith moved to Philadelphia in 1688, where he served as headmaster at the Friends' Public School. Soon, however, he became dissatisfied with the state of the Quaker orthodoxy in the new colony. Claiming that most Pennsylvania Quakers knew little of Christian doctrine and that their spiritualist notions amounted to denying the physical suffering and sacrifice of Jesus Christ, Keith was held chiefly responsible for the schism among Pennsylvania Friends that resulted from what was called the "Keithian controversy." On his return to England in 1694, Keith converted to Anglicanism, but he continued to criticize Quaker views. In the communal memory of early Pennsylvania Quakers and especially in Pastorius's writings about the controversy, Keith was an archnemesis, whose vociferous attacks on Quaker doctrine breached the principles of peace and harmony central to the Friends' spiritual and social lives.

Kelpius, Johannes. Born in a German-speaking enclave in Transylvania, Kelpius studied theology at several German universities and later became acquainted with Johann Jakob Zimmermann, a dissenting Lutheran minister. Kelpius joined a group of forty mystical seekers around Zimmermann planning to immigrate to Pennsylvania and there await an apocalyptic event and the establishment of a New Jerusalem. When Zimmermann died in Rotterdam, however, Kelpius became the leader of the group. On arriving in Pennsylvania in 1694, he established a mystical community of celibate hermits just outside Germantown; its members engaged in mystical speculations, hymn composing and singing, and efforts to educate local children. Whereas some of his followers, such as Heinrich Bernhard Köster and Daniel Falckner, left the community and became embroiled in religious disputes, Kelpius continued to live as a mystical hermit until his death in 1708 at age forty-one. Pastorius embraced the basic tenets of Kelpius's Pietist mysticism but had no use for his complete renunciation of worldly affairs.

Köster, Heinrich Bernhard (Henry Bernhard Koster). University-educated theologian who traveled to Pennsylvania with the group of mystical Pietists around Johann Jakob Zimmermann and Johannes Kelpius. Rather than follow Kelpius's eremitic example, however, Köster preached to the larger Pennsylvania community in both German and English. He became embroiled in the Keithian controversy and, together with three English renegade Quakers, disrupted a Friends' Meeting in Burlington in 1696, after which he set up a communitarian group modeled after the Baptists. In his 1697 pamphlet *Four Boasting Disputers*, Pastorius denounced Köster's religious views (which attacked the supposedly rampant heresies among Pennsylvania Quakers in a no longer extant German-language tract) and mocked his communal experiment, which Pastorius was certain would only end in Babel-like confusion.

Krefeld. Town on the lower Rhine, home to a group of Mennonites seeking religious toleration in the mid-seventeenth century. When some of the Mennonites met with outright hostility after forming a Quaker Meeting, however, they decided to immigrate to America. On his way from Frankfurt to Pennsylvania, Pastorius visited the Krefeld Quakers and agreed to represent them regarding land they wished to purchase there. Sailing on the ship *Concord*, thirteen families from Krefeld and surrounding areas reached America in October 1683 to become the first group of settlers in Germantown. Pastorius would live and work among these Krefelders, whose low-German dialect was more akin to Dutch than his High German, but since Pastorius also spoke Dutch, he managed quite well.

Kriegsheim. Town in the Rhenish Palatinate, home to a sizable Quaker community in the seventeenth century. Pastorius visited the Friends' Meeting in Kriegsheim before he left for America, and several Quaker families from Kriegsheim, including the family of Jacob Schumacher, would later join him in immigrating to Pennsylvania.

Leeds, Daniel. Quaker settler in colonial New Jersey who published a yearly almanac printed by William Bradford in Philadelphia. Joining the Keithians, Leeds waged an acerbic pamphlet war against the Pennsylvania Quaker establishment, especially Caleb Pusey, long after George Keith had returned to England. Pastorius scoffed at Leeds's involvement with the Keithians, regularly lampooning him in his manuscripts, and at the unreliability of almanacs even as he cited Leeds's.

Leeds, Titan. Son of Daniel Leeds, Titan began publishing his father's almanac in 1714 at age 15, even while his father was still alive—a situation Pastorius made fun of in one of his mocking "Bee-Hive" entries about the Leeds family. This, in turn, may have prompted Benjamin Franklin to carry out his famous hoax on Titan Leeds, announcing the death of his young rival almanac publisher in the first edition of *Poor Richard's Almanack* when, of course, Titan was very much alive.

Linck, Heinrich. Professor under whom Pastorius studied law at the University of Jena from 1672 to 1674. When Linck moved to the University of Altdorf, Pastorius followed him there to complete his law degree in 1675.

Logan, James. Arriving in Pennsylvania as William Penn's secretary in 1699, Logan quickly rose to become one of the most influential, intellectual, and wealthy men in the colony. He held offices ranging from commissioner of property, mayor of Philadelphia, and member of the Provincial Council to chief justice of the Pennsylvania Supreme Court and acting governor, while assembling one of the largest libraries in the American colonies. Logan's immense learning and book collection helped make him a favorite correspondent of Pastorius, and the two bibliophiles would exchange letters, books, and witty banter for many years.

Lloyd, David. Powerful Quaker lawyer and politician who served as chief justice of the Pennsylvania Supreme Court from 1717 until his death in 1731 and as William Penn's lawyer in earlier years. From Pastorius's perspective, however, Lloyd was the epitome of a scheming, self-serving politician devoid of any ethical constraints. Leader of the anti-proprietary faction in the Pennsylvania Assembly, Lloyd resented the special privileges (like self-government) that Penn had granted the Germantowners; in 1707, when the Corporation of Germantown Charter came under attack, then Speaker Lloyd refused to help them. And, in 1708–9, he colluded with Daniel Falckner and Johann Heinrich Sprögel to defraud the Frankfurt Land Company of their Germantown holdings by bribing Pennsylvania Attorney General Thomas Clarke to turn a blind eye to Falckner and Sprögel's specious legal maneuvers.

Lloyd, Mordecai. Son of Thomas and Mary Lloyd, who came over to Pennsylvania with Pastorius on the *America* in 1683. Mordecai would die in 1694 at age twenty-five and is mourned in Pastorius's "Ship-Mate-Ship" poetry, dedicated to Mordecai's sisters Hannah, Rachel, and Mary.

Lloyd, Thomas. Welsh physician, prominent Quaker, and one of the most important friends Pastorius made on his passage to America. Thomas Lloyd (no relation to Chief Justice David Lloyd) was a close confidant of William Penn, who appointed him president of the Provincial Council and lieutenant governor from 1690 to 1693. During the Keithian controversy, Lloyd sided with the orthodox Quakers against George Keith and his followers. After Lloyd's death and that of his son Mordecai in 1694, Pastorius remained in close contact with Lloyd's surviving children, especially his daughters Hannah Hill, Rachel Preston, and Mary Norris; he dedicated his series of anniversary poems, entitled "Ship-Mate-Ship," to Lloyd and his family commemorating their joint passage on the *America* on the anniversaries of their landing in Philadelphia.

New Castle. Located at the mouth of the Delaware River, the first town Pastorius saw from his ship upon arriving in America. Originally settled by the Dutch West India Company, New Castle became part of Pennsylvania when Penn received his charter from King Charles II in 1681 and colonial capital of Delaware after it split away from Pennsylvania in 1704.

Norris, Isaac. Steadfast supporter of William Penn and proprietary interests in colonial Pennsylvania and one of the colony's wealthiest and most influential men. Norris served as member of the General Assembly, justice for Philadelphia County, and mayor of Philadelphia. With his marriage to Mary Lloyd, he became connected to another influential family of early Pennsylvania and through the Lloyds befriended Pastorius, with whom he would exchange letters, books, and even home remedies. Along with Samuel Carpenter, Richard Hill, and James Logan, Isaac Norris used his influence to help Pastorius regain title to the lands he lost during the defrauding of the Frankfurt Land Company.

Norris, Mary. Third daughter of Welsh Quakers Thomas and Mary Lloyd, who came to Pennsylvania in 1683 on the same ship as Pastorius. He fondly called Mary and her family his "ship-mates" and their friendship "ship-mate-ship" in a collection of manuscripts honoring the anniversaries of their arrival in Philadelphia. As the wife of Isaac Norris, Mary was matriarch of one of the most influential Quaker families in colonial Pennsylvania.

Norton, Lydia. Originally from Massachusetts, Norton was part of a larger movement of itinerant Quaker women preachers like Elizabeth Ashbridge and Jane Fenn Hoskens who revolutionized the Quaker faith in the eighteenth century by publicly testifying to the working of the Inner Light. She most likely met Pastorius during her brief stop in Philadelphia in 1717. As evidence of his interest in the literary aspirations of Quaker women, Pastorius borrowed Norton's diary of her missionary trips and copied much of it into his own notebooks.

op den Graeff (Graef), Abraham. With Pastorius, Abraham's brother Dirck, and Gerret Hendericks, one of the four co-signers of the 1688 Germantown Friends' "Protest" against slavery. Abraham and his brothers Dirck and Herman had come to Pennsylvania in 1683 with the first thirteen families from Krefeld. Although Pastorius appears to have been good friends with the Krefeld settlers, when Abraham took George Keith's side during the Keithian controversy, it may well have chilled relations between the two of them.

op den Graeff (Graef), Dirck (Derick). Original Germantown settler from Krefeld who, along with his brother Abraham, Gerret Hendericks, and Pastorius, signed the 1688 Germantown Friends' "Protest" against slavery, most likely authored by Pastorius.

op den Graeff (Graef), Herman (Hermann). Original Germantown settler from Krefeld and brother to Abraham and Dirck op den Graeff. Herman received the prize for the first piece of linen woven in Pennsylvania in 1685. In *Sichere Nachricht* (1684; Certain News), Pastorius reports that Herman's mother was the only Krefeld settler who had died up to that point.

Owen, Griffith. Prominent Welsh Quaker and physician who came to Pennsylvania in 1684. Holding numerous public offices, from coroner and member of the Provincial Council and Pennsylvania General Assembly to justice of the peace and commissioner of property, Owen also made frequent trips as a missionary for the Society of Friends. Pastorius was both Owen's patient and his personal friend; he speaks fondly of him in several of his manuscript poems, and he deeply mourned Owen's passing in 1717.

Pastorius, Anna (Ennecke). Born Ennecke Klostermanns in 1658 in the town of Mühlheim an der Ruhr in Westphalia, Anna came to Pennsylvania in 1685. She married Pastorius in 1688, and the couple had two sons, John (Johann) Samuel and Henry (Heinrich). Pastorius seldom mentions her in his manuscript writings.

Pastorius, Henry (Heinrich). Second son of Francis Daniel, born in Germantown in 1692. Pastorius dedicated his magnum opus, the "Bee-Hive," to his sons, Henry and John Samuel. True to his critique of the vain pursuit of academic advancement among the social elites of Europe, Pastorius ensured that his sons, growing up in Pennsylvania, learned both English and practical skills. In keeping with Germantown's main industry, both became weavers, but Henry later took up shoemaking as well. The relationship between Henry and his father was strained. As Henry came to spend more and more time in Maryland, the elder Pastorius asked friends to watch out for his well-being there and reminded him to stay in touch with his faith. Henry later returned to and settled in Germantown. He married Sarah Boutcher in 1721, and they had five children.

Pastorius, John (Johann) Samuel. First son of Francis Daniel, born in Germantown in 1690. As a boy, John Samuel studied under his father at the Friends' Public School in Philadelphia along with his younger brother, Henry. As a grown man, he took up weaving and settled in Germantown, marrying Hannah Lucken in 1716. The couple had two children. He died in 1722 at the age of thirty-two.

Pastorius, Magdalena. Mother of Francis Daniel, born Magdalena Dietz in 1607. Already forty-four when she gave birth to Pastorius in Sommerhausen in 1651, Magdalena would die six years later, in 1657, leaving her son a half orphan. Whatever his memories of her, Pastorius mentions his mother only once in his writings, in a poem he wrote especially about her.

Pastorius, Melchior Adam. Father of Francis Daniel, born in Erfurt, Thuringia, in 1624. As both a reflection of his personal piety and a step toward career advancement, Melchior Adam converted from Catholicism to the Lutheran faith of his new employer, the Count of Limpurg in Sommerhausen in 1649, which set the elder Pastorius on a path through several high government offices in the imperial city of Windsheim. Providing some precedent for his son Francis Daniel, Melchior Adam was a lawyer and a writer in both poetry and prose. He also promoted his son's work and reputation in Germany by collaborating with the Frankfurt Pietists to publish Francis Daniel's accounts and letters. He survived his first wife and Francis Daniel's mother, Magdalena, by nearly half a century, until his death in 1702.

Penn, John. Only son of William Penn to be born in America, in 1700, John would become proprietor of Pennsylvania with his brothers Thomas and Richard. Pastorius took special interest in the young Penn, whose birth during William Penn's second visit to the colony seemed to promise a rebirth of the Quaker idealism that had inspired his father's "holy experiment." Pastorius wrote several letters to John and, with his students at the Philadelphia Friends' Public School, produced a manuscript book dedicated to him.

Penn, William. Born into privilege in 1644 as the son of English Admiral William Penn, who played a key role in restoring the monarchy to England in 1660. As payment for debts he owed Penn's father, King Charles II awarded the younger Penn the charter for the lands the king named "Pennsylvania" in 1681. Soon traveling to his new colony, William Penn hoped to set up a model community characterized by religious liberty, political freedom, and social harmony among citizens from many ethnic backgrounds. In 1683, he met with Pastorius and granted the landowners of the German Society (later the Frankfurt Land Company) the 6,000-acre tract they desired to build a separate German-speaking settlement Pastorius would name "Germantown." Penn's proprietorship of Pennsylvania was beset by antiproprietary factionalism in the General Assembly, a border dispute with Lord Baltimore, proprietor of Maryland, and economic and legal troubles in England, which drew him back. When Penn returned on his second visit to Pennsylvania in 1699, Pastorius greeted him with a welcome poem entitled "Epibaterium" to celebrate his arrival. During this second visit, in 1701, Penn would sign the important Charter of Liberties, a constitution that gave Pennsylvanians wide personal freedoms (and stayed in effect until 1776). All hopes to the contrary, he was obliged that same year to return once more to England, where he would remain until his death in 1718.

Philadelphia. Founded by William Penn in 1682, Philadelphia was built on land that belonged to the indigenous Lenape people. Dutch and Swedish colonists fought over this area beginning in the early seventeenth century. Penn hoped to bring previous residents and newcomers, indigenous and European people, and Protestants of various stripes together in a city of harmony and, as its name suggested, "brotherly love." But when Pastorius arrived in Philadelphia in August 1683, he described Philadelphia's humble abodes on the Delaware riverfront as "cave dwellings," perhaps exaggerating the city's wilderness appearance to impress readers in Germany.

Petersen, Johann Wilhelm. University-educated theologian who early in his career came into contact with Philipp Jakob Spener and his Pietist ideas for reforming Protestant Christianity. Petersen would develop more mystical and millenarian beliefs than Spener and would marry the prominent Frankfurt mystic and noblewoman Johanna Eleonora von Merlau in 1680, about the time Pastorius was in Frankfurt. After meeting Petersen and his wife, Pastorius hoped they would later join him in Pennsylvania, but the couple chose to remain in Germany, with Petersen pursuing his theological studies and eventually becoming pastor in the city of Lüneburg in Saxony, a position he would lose in 1692 for his radical Pietist views.

Preston, Rachel. Second daughter of Welsh Quakers Mary and Thomas Lloyd, who came to Pennsylvania in 1683 on the same ship as Pastorius. Like her sisters, Rachel married a prominent Pennsylvania Quaker, the jurist and merchant Samuel Preston. And along with her sisters Hannah and Mary, Rachel was the recipient of Pastorius's anniversary poems commemorating their arrival in Philadelphia. When she died in August 1716, Pastorius's anniversary poem for that year included a memorial poem in Rachel's honor.

Pusey, Caleb. English Quaker and early investor in Pennsylvania, who arrived in the new colony in 1682. Pusey built grist- and sawmills on Chester Creek, of which several were destroyed by floods; he became involved in a pamphlet war with Daniel Leeds over lingering doctrinal issues relating to the Keithian controversy.

Rotterdam. Dutch city whose location on the Rhine delta and North Sea made it an important trading and shipping center. Many German immigrants to Pennsylvania, Pastorius among them, passed through Rotterdam. It was here that Pastorius met with Benjamin Furly, Penn's agent in Europe, before traveling via London and Deal to America.

Rutter, Thomas. English Quaker who arrived in Philadelphia in 1684 as a personal employee of William Penn. Blacksmith by trade, Rutter would pioneer iron manufacturing in Pennsylvania. When, however, he joined the Keithians in the early 1690s and, along with Henry Bernhard Köster (Koster), William Davis, and Thomas Bowyer, disrupted a Quaker meeting in Burlington in 1696, he drew the ire of Pastorius, who lambasted him in his 1697 pamphlet *Four Boasting Disputers* and in some of his manuscript poems.

Schumacher (Shoemaker), Jacob. One of the employees of the German Society (later Frankfurt Land Company) who traveled with Pastorius to Pennsylvania in 1683 and settled in Germantown.

Schumberg, Tobias. Rector of the Windsheim Latin School, which Pastorius attended from 1659 to 1668. Originally from a German-speaking minority in Hungary, Schumberg impressed Pastorius with his learning and piety, and he would dedicate a Latin poem to him, later printed in Pastorius's 1700 description of Pennsylvania, *Umständige Geographische Beschreibung*.

Sommerhausen. Small town on the Main near Würzburg in Franconia (present-day Bavaria) and Pastorius's birthplace in 1651. His father, Melchior Adam, had moved to Sommerhausen in 1649 to find employment with the Count of Limpurg, a Lutheran Protestant nobleman in an otherwise Catholic area. The house where Pastorius lived before he moved with his family to Windsheim in 1659 is still standing and part of a winery; it bears a prominent plaque and other inscriptions commemorating Pastorius.

Spener, Philipp Jakob. Father of German Pietism and a Lutheran pastor in Frankfurt when he published one of the early Pietist manifestos, *Pia Desideria* (1675). Pastorius met Spener in Frankfurt in 1679 and became part of his small Pietist group meeting there, away from the city's established Lutheran church structures and institutions. Known as the "Saalhof Pietists" (after the hall where they met), the group would later embrace separation from the orthodox Lutheran Church under the leadership of the lawyer and lay theologian Johann Jakob Schütz.

Sprögel, Johann Heinrich. Son of a prominent German radical Pietist pastor by the same name, who arrived in Pennsylvania in 1700. The younger Sprögel incurred debts he endeavored to repay by traveling back to Germany in 1706 to get help from his father. On his return to America, exploiting the fragile state of the Frankfurt Land Company's finances under Pastorius's successor, Daniel Falckner, Sprögel would induce Benjamin Furly to make him his company agent in Pennsylvania. Acting in that capacity, he colluded with Quaker lawyer David Lloyd to defraud Pastorius and other Germantowners of the lands they had purchased from the company. Only through the intercession of several influential Quaker friends did Pastorius regain title to his land. He was especially bitter about his countryman Sprögel, whom he called a "land pirate."

Strasbourg (Strassburg). Cosmopolitan city on the Rhine, located between French- and German-speaking regions. Pastorius studied law and the French language in Strasbourg (which he sometimes called by its German name, "Strassburg") for nearly two years, from 1670 to 1672.

Telner, Jacob. Wealthy Quaker merchant from Amsterdam who settled in Germantown in 1684. Telner became a prominent Germantown citizen and was deeply involved in its civic life. In 1696, upon his departure for Europe, he gave Pastorius a substantial amount of fine European writing paper, which Francis Daniel used to form the beginning of his "Bee-Hive" manuscript book.

Tinicum (Dunicum). Township and island southwest of Philadelphia, which Pastorius mentions seeing from his ship before arriving in Philadelphia. Tinicum was the site of the first Swedish settlement in Pennsylvania, founded in 1643.

Tunesen (Tunis, Tünics), Abraham. Quaker, original settler of Germantown from the Krefeld area, and farm tenant of the German Society (later the Frankfurt Land Company). As reported in *Sichere Nachricht* (1684; Certain News), Tunesen's wife, Beatrix, recuperated in Pastorius's house from an unspecified illness during their first year in Pennsylvania.

Upland. Small town and disembarkation point 15 miles downriver from Philadelphia. In *Sichere Nachricht* (1684; Certain News), Pastorius advised passengers crossing the Atlantic to pay for passage all the way to Philadelphia to avoid the rigors of the overland trip from Upland to the city.

van Bebber, Matthias. Son of an original Germantown settler from Krefeld, Jacob Isaacs van Benner, and a client of Pastorius, who served as his attorney in a number of legal transactions. Matthias would become a merchant in Philadelphia, eventually moving from there to Maryland.

von Merlau, Johanna Eleonora. One of the most influential figures in German Pietism from the 1680s to the 1710s. Born to impoverished German nobility, von Merlau became a lady-in-waiting to improve her chances for social mobility. But she then escaped her would-be courtly life to become a prominent leader among the Saalhof Pietists in Frankfurt, where she met William Penn and several other traveling Quaker missionaries in 1677. In Frankfurt, von Merlau drew the ire of the city's authorities by preaching publicly to both women and men. It was here that she met and married the Pietist minister Johann Wilhelm Petersen in 1680, and here that she would also meet Pastorius, who hoped the couple would join him and other Saalhof Pietists in Pennsylvania. The Petersens decided to remain in Germany, however, where they would collaborate on several theological books.

Wasey (Vasey), Joseph. Captain of the ship *America*, which brought Pastorius, his retinue of company employees, and the Lloyd family to Pennsylvania in 1683.

Wertmüller, Georg. Employee of the German Society (later the Frankfurt Land Company) who came with Pastorius on the *America* in 1683. Originally from Switzerland, Wertmüller would write a brief account of Pennsylvania, published in Dutch with another such account by Cornelius Bom as *Twee Missiven geschreven uyt Pensilvania* in Rotterdam in 1684.

Windsheim. Town in Franconia, forty miles west of Nuremberg. Windsheim (present-day Bad Windsheim in Bavaria) was where Pastorius's father, Melchior Adam rose through the ranks of public administration and where Pastorius lived from 1659 to 1668, when he left for the University of Altdorf.

Witt (De Witt, deWitt), Christopher. English physician who came to Pennsylvania in 1704, where he became a clockmaker, organ builder, expert in herbal medicine, and botanist. Witt joined the group of mystics around Johannes Kelpius and translated the German manuscript hymns written by Kelpius into English. When the mystics disbanded after Kelpius's death in 1708, Witt came to reside in Germantown as a next-door neighbor to Pastorius. The two men shared a passion for gardening and plants. Witt was also known as a mentor to the early American botanist John Bartram.

Worrell, Richard, Jr. English Quaker immigrant to Pennsylvania, who was one of the first settlers to buy land from William Penn. In 1688, Gerret Hendericks, Dirck op den Graeff, Francis Daniel Pastorius, and Abraham op den Graeff submitted their "Protest" against slavery to the Germantown Quaker Meeting held at Worrell's house.

Zachary, Lloyd. Nephew of Richard and Hannah Hill. Having studied medicine in London, Zachary established a successful medical practice in Philadelphia, where he became one of the original trustees of the Philadelphia Academy. Around 1717, Pastorius began a lively correspondence with the sixteen-year-old Zachary, which Pastorius maintained until his death in late 1719.

Bibliography

Primary Sources by Francis Daniel Pastorius—Alone and with Others

Listed here are all works written by Francis Daniel Pastorius, including later editions, translations, and original manuscript sources, as well as the archive or rare book repository where original sources are located and digital or online databases (both open and restricted access) for some of Pastorius's writings. The Historical Society of Pennsylvania (HSP) Digital Library, which contains the Pastorius Papers, can be found at http://digitallibrary.hsp.org (open access). The University of Pennsylvania Rare Book and Manuscript Library's "Bee-Hive" digitization project (open access) can be found at http://dla.library.upenn.edu/dla/medren/detail.html?id=MEDREN_2487547 (see "Penn in Hand: Selected Manuscripts").

Hendericks, Gerret, Derick up de Graeff, Francis Daniell [*sic*] Pastorius, [and] Abraham up den Graef. "Quaker Protest Against Slavery in the New World, Germantown (Pa.) 1688." Manuscript Collection 990 B-R. Quaker and Special Collections, Haverford College.

Pastorius, Francis Daniel. "An Act to enable his Majesties Natural born Subjects to Inherit the Estate of their Ancestors, either Lineal or Collateral, notwithstanding their Father or Mother were Aliens. November 16, 1699." Manuscript copy with German translation on reverse. Society Collection: Aug. 20, 1698; Mar. 28, 1713. HSP.

———. "Alvearialia, Or such Phrases and Sentences which in haste were Booked down here, before I had Time to Carry them to their respective proper Places in my English-Folio-Bee-hive." MS 8845. Pastorius Papers and Digital Library, HSP.

———. "Bee-Hive." *See* Pastorius, Francis Daniel. "His Hive, Melliotrophium Alvear or, Rusca Apium, Begun Anno Domini or, in the year of Christian Account, 1696."

———. *Circumstantial Geographical Description of Pennsylvania*. Translated by Gertrude Selwyn Kimball. In *Narratives of Early Pennsylvania, West New Jersey and Delaware*, edited by Albert Cook Myers. Vol. 11 of *Original Narratives of Early American History*, edited by Franklin J. Jameson, 353–448. New York: Scribner's, 1912.

———. "Commonplace Book." *See* Pastorius, Francis Daniel. "F. D. P. Francis Daniel Pastorius [Commonplace Book]."

———. *Copia der Germantownischen Charters; Gesetz, Ordnungen, und Statuta der Gemeinden Zu Germantown; the laws of the Province of Pennsilvania antecedent to the sd Charter & By Laws.* 1693. MS 7205. Pastorius Papers and Digital Library, HSP (bound with *Lex Pennsylvaniensis* and *Leges Pennsilvaniæ*).

———. "Copia, eines von einem Sohn an seine Eltern auss America, abgelassenen Brieffes, sub dato Philadelphia, den 7 Martii 1684." Photographic reproduction of a printed original in the Zentralbibliothek Zürich (Zurich Central Library), in Marion Dexter Learned, *The Life of Francis Daniel Pastorius*, unnumbered page following 124. Philadelphia: Campbell, 1908.

———. "Copia, eines von einem Sohn an seine Eltern auss America, abgelassenen Brieffes, sub dato Philadelphia, den 7 Martii 1684." Photostat copy of printed original in *Letters Relating to the Settlement of Germantown in Pennsylvania 1683–4 from the Könneken Manuscript in the Ministerial-Archiv of Lübeck*, translated and edited by Julius Friedrich Sachse, 2. Lübeck and Philadelphia: For the author, 1903.

———. "Copies of Letters [Letterbook]." MS 8631. Pastorius Papers and Digital Library, HSP.

———. "Copy of a Letter sent from America by a Son to his Parents. Philadelphia, March 7, 1684." Translated by Julius Friedrich Sachse. In *Letters Relating to the Settlement of Germantown in Pennsylvania 1683–4 from the Könneken Manuscript in the Ministerial-Archiv of Lübeck*, translated and edited by Julius Friedrich Sachse, 3–6. Lübeck and Philadelphia: For the author, 1903.

———. *Deliciæ Hortenses or Garden-Recreations* and *Voluptates Apianæ*. Edited by Christoph E. Schweitzer. Studies in German Literature, Linguistics, and Culture 2. Columbia, S.C.: Camden House, 1982.

———. "Description of the Map of Germantown, 1688." In Marion Dexter Learned, *The Life of Francis Daniel Pastorius*, 298. Philadelphia: Campbell, 1908.

———. "Disputatio Inauguralis, De Rasursa Documentorum, Quam, Divina Suffragante Gratia, Auctoritate Magnifici Ictorum Ordinis in Incluto Noribergensium Athenæo, pro Licentia Summos in Utroquo Jure Honores ac Privilegia Doctoralia, more Majorum, rite capessendi, *Publico Eruditorum Examini* sistit Franciscus Daniel Pastorius, Windtsheimensis. D. 23 Novembr. A. ab. incarnatione J. C. 1676. Altdorff: Literis Henrici Maieri, Univ. Typogr., 1676.

———. "Eulogy on Thomas Lloyd, July 1692." Ferdinand J. Dreer Autograph Collection MS 163:2 (Philanthropists). HSP.

———. "F. D. P. Francis Daniel Pastorius [Commonplace Book]." MS 8864. Pastorius Papers and Digital Library, HSP.

———. "A few Onomastical Considerations, enlarged From the Number of Sixty Six to that of One Hundred; and Presented or rather Re-presented to William Penn, Proprietary and Governour of Pennsilvania, & Territories thereunto belonging. Patri Patriæ, The Father of this Province, and lately also the Father of John Penn, an innocent & hopeful Babe, by whose Nativity & Names sake they were first contrived." MS AM 1.3. German Society of Pennsylvania Joseph Horner Memorial Library. Photostat copy of the original held at Friends' House, London.

———. *Four Boasting Disputers. See* Pastorius, Francis Daniel. *Henry Bernhard Koster, William Davis, Thomas Rutter & Thomas Bowyer, four Boasting Disputers Of this World briefly REBUKED. . . .*

———. Frankfurt Company Papers. MS 8917. Pastorius Papers and Digital Library, HSP.

———. *Geographisch-statistische Beschreibung der Provinz Pensylvanien, von Fr. Dan. Pastorius. Im Auszug mit Anmerkungen.* Memmingen: Andreas Seyler, 1792.

———. "Germans' Petition to John Evans for naturalization. May 15, 1706." [Signed by Pastorius and 155 others.] Misc. Papers of Philadelphia County. MS Am. 3841-f52 ½. HSP.

———. "Grund- und Lager-Buch aller und jeden unbeweglichen Güter, geklärt- und ungeklärten Landes, in der gantzen German Township Durch Ordre Einer daselbstigen Generalen Court angefangen Francisco Daniele Pastorio." MS Am 3713/Am 3714. HSP.

———. *Henry Bernhard Koster, William Davis, Thomas Rutter & Thomas Bowyer, four Boasting Disputers Of this World briefly REBUKED. And Answered according to their Folly, which they themselves have manifested in a late Pamphlet, entituled, Advice for all Professors and writers.* New York: William Bradford, 1697.

———. "His Hive, Melliotrophium Alvear or, Rusca Apium, Begun Anno Domini or, in the year of Christian Account, 1696." UPenn MS Codex 726. Rare Book and Manuscript Library, University of Pennsylvania.

———. "Invitation to wedding." Manuscript handwriting of F. D. P. Signed D. P. Swarthmore Friends' Historical Library. No date.

———. *Kurtze geographische Beschreibung der letztmahls erfundenen Americanischen landschafft Pensylvania, mit angehenckten einigen notablen Begebenheiten und Bericht-schreiben an dessen hrn. Vattern, Patrioten und gute Freunde.* Nuremberg, 1692. Bound with Melchior Adam Pastorius, *Kurtze Beschreibung der Reichs-stadt Windsheim.* Nuremberg, 1692.

———. *Leges Pennsilvaniæ, h. e. The Great Law of the Province of Pennsylvania.* 1690. Bound with *Lex Pennsylvaniensis in Compendium redacta* and *Copia der Germantownischen Charters.* MS 7205. Pastorius Papers and Digital Library, HSP.

———. "Letterbook." *See* Pastorius, Francis Daniel. "Copies of Letters [Letterbook]."

———. "Letter to Isaac Norris. Germantown, March 12, 1716/7." MS. George W. Norris Papers. HSP.

———. "Letter to Isaac Norris. Germantown, March 15, 1716/7." MS. George W. Norris Papers. HSP.

———. "Letter to James Logan, Sam. Carpenter, Isaac Norris & Richard Hill the present Commissioners of Property in the Province of Pennsilvania &c. Germantown the 28th day of the Third mo: 1713." MS. Society Collection, HSP.

———. "Letter to Phineas Pemberton, April 12, 1698." MS. Etting Collection, HSP.

———. "Letter to Son Henry. Germantown the 25th of November 1714." MS. Arch. Misc. Doc. Box 2, Folder 4, Item 1. Germantown Historical Society.

———. *Lex Pennsylvaniensis in Compendium redacta: h.e. The Great Law of Pennsylvania abriged, for the particular use of Francis Daniel Pastorius.* 1693. Bound with *Leges Pennsilvaniæ* and *Copia der Germantownischen Charters.* MS 7205. Pastorius Papers and Digital Library, HSP.

———. "The Matter of Taxes & Contributions briefly Examined by plain Scripture-Testimonics & Sound Reason." MS Vol. 340, n.d. Swathmore Friends' Historical Society.

———. "The Monthly Monitor Briefly Showing When Our Works Ought to be Done in Gardens, Orchards, Vineyards, Fields, Meadows, and Woods. 1701." MS 8243. Pastorius Papers and Digital Library, HSP.

———. *A New Primmer or Methodical Directions To attain the True Spelling, Reading & Writing of ENGLISH. Whereunto are added, some things Necessary & Useful both for the Youth of this Province, and likewise for those, who from forreign Countries and Nations come to settle amongst us.* New York: William Bradford, 1698.

———. "A Particular Geographical Description of the Lately Discovered Province of Pennsylvania, Situated on the Frontiers of this Western World, America." Translated by Lewis H. Weiss. *Memoirs of the Historical Society of Pennsylvania* 4, part 2 (1850): 83–104.

———. "Petition To Charles Gookin Esqr. Lieutenant Governr. of the Province of Pennsilvania, &c. and his honourable Council. The earnest Petition of Francis Daniel Pastorius. March 1, 1708/9." Logan Papers. MS Vol. 4, p. 56. HSP.

———. "Petition to Council for a Road to Germantown." 18 November 1701. Logan Papers. MS Vol. 3, f. 31, 32. HSP.

———. "Petition to William Penn. By Order of a general Court held at German Town the 28th day of the 4th month 1701" [signed by Pastorius]. Logan Papers. MS Vol. 3, f. 16, HSP.

———. "Poetry from *The Beehive* (MS)." In *Seventeenth-Century American Poetry*, edited by Harrison T. Meserole, 293–304. Garden City: Anchor, 1968.

———. "Positive Information from America, concerning the Country of Pennsylvania, from a German who has migrated thither; dated Philadelphia, March 7, 1684." Translated by Gertrude Selwyn Kimball. Vol. 11 of *Original Narratives of Early American History*, edited by Franklin J. Jameson, 392–411. New York: Scribner's, 1912.

———. "Positive News from America, About the Province of Pennsylvania, from a German who has Journeyed hither, *de dato*, Philadelphia, March 7, 1684." Translated by Julius Friedrich Sachse. In *Letters Relating to the Settlement of Germantown in Pennsylvania, 1683–4. From the Könneken Manuscript in the Ministerial-Archiv of Lübeck*, translated and edited by Julius Friedrich Sachse, 7–29. Lübeck and Philadelphia: For the author, 1903.

———. "Release of 1000 acres in the German tract to Wm Penn. July 22, 1713." MS. Gratz Misc. Case 8 Box 15. HSP.

———. "Res Propriæ." MS 8842. Pastorius Papers and Digital Library, HSP.

———. "Selections from the *Bee-Hive*." Edited by Marion Dexter Learned. *Americana Germanica* 1, no. 4 (1897): 67–110; 2, no. 1 (1898): 33–42; 2, no. 2 (1898): 59–70; 2, no. 4 (1898): 65–79.

———. *Ein Send-Brieff Offenhertziger Liebsbezeugung an die so genannte Pietisten in Hoch-Teutschland*. Amsterdam: Jacob Claus, 1697.

———. "Ship-Mate-Ship. An Omer full of Manna, For Mary, Rachel, Hannah, The Daughters of brave Lloyd, By brave Men now enjoy'd. [Composition Book]." MS 8846. Pastorius Papers and Digital Library, HSP.

———. *Sichere Nachricht auß America, wegen der Landschafft Pennsylvania, von einem dorthin gereißten Teutschen, de dato Philadelphia, den 7 Martii 1684*. Photographic reproduction of the original in the Zentralbibliothek Zürich (Zurich Central Library). MS S 190, 114a (Dr. 31). In Marion Dexter Learned, *The Life of Francis Daniel Pastorius*, 128–29. Philadelphia: Campbell, 1908.

———. "Talia Qualia Medicinalia, Artificialia & Naturalia. Artzneÿ und Kunst ist all umsunst ohn Gottes Gunst." MS 8801. Pastorius Papers and Digital Library, HSP.

———. "To Peter Evans, Germantown, 23th. of the 5th mo: 1716." MS 705. Haverford Quaker Collection.

———. *Umständige Geographische Beschreibung Der zu allerletzt erfundenen Provintz Pensylvaniæ, In denen End-Gräntzen Americæ In der West-Welt gelegen*. Frankfurt and Leipzig: Andreas Otto, 1700.

———. *Vier kleine Doch ungemeine Und sehr nutzliche Tractätlein*. Germantown, 1690.

———. "The Young Country Clerk's Collection of the Best Presidents of Bills, Bonds, Conditions, Aquittances, Releases, Indentures, Deeds of Sale, Letters of Attorney, Last Wills & Testaments, &c. With many other necessary and useful Forms of such Writings as are vulgarly in use between Man and Man." UPenn MS Codex 89. Rare Book and Manuscript Library, University of Pennsylvania.

———. "Zwei unbekannte Briefe von Pastorius." Edited by Julius Goebel. *German American Annals* 2, n.s. (1904): 492–503.

Pastorius, Francis Daniel, et al. "The General Court Records of the Corporation of Germantown, oder, Raths-Buch der Germantownischen Gemeinde." Germantown, 1691–1707. MS Am 3711, HSP; no pagination.

Primary Sources by Other Authors

Listed here are primary works that are either directly connected to Francis Daniel Pastorius's life and work (e.g., his father's writings) or are relevant for understanding his context and writings (e.g., William Penn's promotional texts on early Pennsylvania).

Andreæ, Johann Valentin. *Fama Fraternitatis* (1614); *Confessio Fraternitatis* (1615); *Chymische Hochzeit: Christiani Rosencreutz. Anno 1459* (1616). Edited by Richard Van Dülmen. Stuttgart: Calwer, 1973.

Bacon, Francis. *The Essayes or Counsels, Civill and Morall.* 1625. Edited by Michael Kiernan. Reprint, Oxford: Oxford University Press, 1985.

Bom, Cornelius. *Missive van Cornelis Bom, Geschreven uit de Stadt Philadelphia in de Provintie van Pennsylvania Leggende op d' vostzyde van de Zuyd Revier van Nieuw Nederland Verhalende de groote Voortgank van deselve Provintie Waerby komt de Getuygenis van Jakob Telner van Amsterdam.* Rotterdam: Pieter van Wijnbrugge, 1685.

Bom, Cornelius, and Georg Wertmüller. *Twee Missiven geschreven uyt Pensilvania, d'Eene door een Hollander, woonachtig in Philadelfia, d'Ander door een Switser, woonachtig in German Town, Dat is Hoogduytse Stadt Van den 16 en 26 Maert 1684.* Rotterdam: Pieter van Alphen, 1684.

Budd, Thomas. *Good Order Established in Pennsilvania & New Jersey in America* [. . .]. [Philadelphia], 1685.

Culpeper, Nicholas. *English Physician Enlarged: An Astrologo-Physical Discourse of the Vulgar Herbs of This Nation.* 1652. Enlarged ed., London, 1698.

Davis, William. *Jesus the Crucified Man, the Eternal Son of God.* Philadelphia, n.p., 1700.

Duffin, J. M., ed. *Acta Germanopolis: Records of the Corporation of Germantown, Pennsylvania, 1691–1707.* Philadelphia: Genealogical Society of Pennsylvania, 2008.

Ellwood, Thomas. *Truth defended and the friends thereof cleared from the false charges, foul reproaches, and envious cavils, cast upon it and them by George Keith.* London, 1695.

Falckner, Daniel. *Curieuse Nachricht von Pensylvania in Norden-America, welche, Auf Begehren guter Freunde, Uber vorgelegte 103. Fragen, bey seiner Abreiß aus Teutschland nach obigem Lande Anno 1700. ertheilet, und nun Anno 1702 in den Druck gegeben worden. Von Daniel Falcknern, Professore, Burgern und Pilgrim allda.* Frankfurt and Leipzig: Andreas Otto, 1702.

———. *Daniel Falckner's Curieuse Nachricht from Pennsylvania: the book that stimulated the great German immigration to Pennsylvaina [sic] in the early years of the XVIII century.* 1702. Translated by and annotated by Julius Friedrich Sachse. Lancaster, Pa.: Pennsylvania German Society, 1905.

Fox, George. *Instructions for right-spelling, and plain directions for reading and writing true English: With several delightful things, very useful and necessary, both for young and old, to read and learn.* 1683. Reprint, Philadelphia: Reiner Jensen, 1702.

Frankfurt Land Company. *Im Nahmen und zur Ehre Gottes!* . . . [agreement of the Frankfurt Land Company of 1686]. Frankfurt, 1686.

Furly, Benjamin. *Bibliotheca Furliana: Sive Catalogus librorum Benjamin Furly.* Rotterdam: Fritsch and Bohm, 1714.

Hill, Hannah[, Jr.] *A Legacy for Children, Being some of the last expressions, and dying sayings of Hannah Hill, Junr. Of the City of Philadelphia, in the Province of Pensilvania, in America, aged eleven years and near three months.* Philadelphia: Andrew Bradford, [1717].

Hoskens [Fenn], Jane. *The Life and Spiritual Sufferings of That Faithful Servant of Christ Jane Hoskens, A Public Preacher among the People called Quakers. Never before printed.* Philadelphia: William Evitt, 1771.

Jennings, Samuel. *The State of the Case, Briefly but Impartially given betwixt the People called Quakers, in Pensilvania, &c. in America, who remain in Unity; and George Keith* [. . .]. London: T. Sowle, 1694.

Keith, George. *An Appeal from the Twenty Eight Judges to the Spirit of Truth & true Judgment. In all Faithful Friends, called* Quakers, *that meet at this Yearly Meeting at Burlington, the 7 Month, 1692.* [Philadelphia: William Bradford, 1692.]

———. *An Exhortation & Caution to Friends Concerning buying or keeping of Negroes.* [New York: William Bradford, 1693.]

———. *The Heresie and Hatred Which was falsely Charged upon the Innocent Justly returned upon the Guilty. Giving some brief and impartial Account of the most material Passages of a late Dispute in Writing, that hath passed at Philadelphia betwixt John Delavall and George Keith, With some intermixt Remarks and Observations on the whole.* Philadelphia: William Bradford, 1693.

———. *A Plain short Catechism for Children & Youth, That May be Servicable to such Others who need to be instructed in the first principles and Grounds of the Christian Religion. To which is added, A short paraphrase or opening, by way of meditation on that prayer which our Lord Jesus Christ taught his disciples, Commonly call'd the Lord's Prayer. By G. K.* Philadelphia: William Bradford, 1690.

———. *Truth and Innocency Defended Against Calumny and Defamation, In a late Report spread abroad concerning the Revolution of Humane Souls, With a further Clearing of the Truth, by a plain Explication of my Sence, &c.* [Philadelphia: William Bradford, 1692.]

Keith, George, and Thomas Budd. *An Account of the Great Divisions, Amongst the Quakers in Pensilvania.* London: John Gwillim, 1692.

Keith, George, et al. *The Judgment Given forth by Twenty Eight Quakers Against George Keith, and his Friends*[. . .]. Philadelphia: William Bradford, 1693.

Leeds, Daniel. *The American Almanack for the Year of Christian Account 1713.* Philadelphia: William Bradford, 1712.

Norris, Isaac. "Letter to Francis Daniel Pastorius. Philadelphia, March 13, 1716/7." MS. George W. Norris Papers. HSP.

Ockanickon. *A True Account of the Dying Words of Ockanickon, an Indian King, Spoken to Jahkursoe, His Brother's Son, whom he appointed King After Him.* London: Benjamin Clark, 1682.

Paskell, Thomas. *An Abstract of a Letter from Thomas Paskell of Pennsylvania to his friend J. J. of Chippenham.* London: John Bringhurst, 1683.

Pastorius, Johann [John] Samuel. "Certificate of Marriage of Samuel Pastorius and Hannah Lucken. Philadelphia, June 15, 1716." MS 950. Quaker Collection, Haverford College.

Pastorius, Melchior Adam. *Des Melchior Adam Pastorius Leben und Reisebeschreibungen von ihm selbst erzählt und nebst dessen lyrischen Gedichten als Beitrag zum deutschen Barock*. Edited by Albert R. Schmitt. Reprint, Munich: Delp'sche Verlagsbuchhandlung, 1968.

————. *Liber Intimissimus Omnium Semper Mecum*. [1697–1701]. MS. Pastorius Papers and Digital Library. HSP.

————. *Römischer Adler, oder Theatrum Electionis et Coronations* [. . .]. Frankfurt: Aegidio Vogel, 1657.

"Pastorius House." Image. 705. Charles Roberts Autograph Collection, Haverford College.

Penn, William. *An Account of William Penn's Travels in Holland and Germany* [. . .]. London: J. Sowle, 1694.

————. *Beschreibung der in America neu-erfundenen Provinz Pensylvanien* [. . .]. [Hamburg]: Henrich Heuss, 1684.

————. *A Brief Account of the Province of Pennsylvania, Lately Granted by the King, Under the Great Seal of England, to William Penn and his Heirs and Assigns*. London: Benjamin Clark, 1681.

————. "For Thomas Holmes Surv. Gen. Warrant of Survey of City Lots to Francis Daniel Pastorius on behalf of the German Purchasers." 16 d. 5 mo. 1684. MS. Penn Papers. Phila. Land Grants. Vol. 7. HSP.

————. *A Further Account of the Province of Pennsylvania*. [London, 1685].

————. *A letter from William Penn proprietary and governour of Pennsylvania in America: to the committe of the Free Society of Traders of that Province, residing in London . . . To which is added, an account of the city of Philadelphia*. [London]: A. Sowle, 1683.

————. *Eine Nachricht wegen der Landschaft Pennsilvania in America*. Amsterdam: Christoff Cunraden, 1681. 2nd ed., Frankfurt, 1683.

————. *The Papers of William Penn*. Edited by Richard S. Dunn and Mary Maples Dunn. Philadelphia: University of Pennsylvania Press, 1982.

————. *Some Account of the Province of Pennsilvania in America; Lately Granted under the Great Seal of England to William Penn, &c. . Together with Priviledges and Powers necessary to the well-governing thereof. Made publick for the Information of such as are or may be disposed to Transport themselves or Servants into those Parts*. London: Benjamin Clark, 1681.

————. *Some Fruits of Solitude in Reflections and Maxims*. London: n.p., 1682.

Saavedra Fajardo, Diego de. *The Royal Politician represented in one hundred Emblems, written in Spanish by Van Diego Saavedra, done into English by Sir James Astry, two volumes*. 1640. London, 1700.

Schnurr. Balthasar. *Kunst und Wunderbüchlein: Darinnen allerhand nützliche Sachen unnd Kunststücke verfasset und begriffen: Als I. Von Zubereitung mancherley Confecten/ Fisch/ und Vogelfang . . . II. Ein vortreffliches Kochbuch . . . III. Von pflantzung der Würtz/ Küchen und Baumgarten . . . IV. Probierbüchlein . . . mit vielen Alchimistischen Künsten . . . V. Distillier: und Artzeneybuch . . . VI. Frawenbuch . . . VII. Mahlerbüchlein . . . VIII. Roßartzeneybüchlein. IX. Und dan[n] endlich ein Wunderbuch von . . . Kunststücken/ und Magischen Sachen*. Frankfurt: Rötel, 1643.

[Seelig, Johann Gotfried.] *Copia Eines Send-Schreibens auß der neuen Welt, betreffend Die Erzehlung einer gefährlichen Schifffarth, und glücklichen Anländung etlicher Christlichen Reisegefehrten, welche zu dem Ende diese Wallfahrt angetretten, den Glauben an Jesum Christum allda außzubreiten. Tob. XII. 8. Der Könige und Fürsten Rath und Heimlichkeiten soll man verschweigen, aber Gottes Werck soll man herrlich preisen und offenbaren. German-don in Pennsylvania Americæ d. 7 Aug. 1694.* [Halle?], 1695.

———. "Copy of a Report from the New World, being an Account of the dangerous Voyage and happy Arrival of some Christian Fellow-travelers, who undertook their Pilgrimage to the end of spreading the Belief in Jesus Christ. Job xxi 8. Printed in the year 1695." Translated by Oswald Seidensticker. *Pennsylvania Magazine of History and Biography* 11 (1887): 427–41.

Spener, Philipp Jakob. *Briefe aus der Frankfurter Zeit, 1666–1678.* Edited by Johannes Wallmann. 4 vols. Tübingen: Mohr Siebeck, 1992–2005.

———. *Pia Desideria.* 1675. Translated by Theodore G. Tappert. Reprint, Philadelphia: Fortress Press, 1964.

Staricius [Staritz], Johann. *Neu-vermehrter Heldenschatz: d. i. naturkündliches Bedencken über und bey vulcanischer, auch natürlich-magischer Fabrefaction und Zubereitung der Waffen der Helden Achillis in Griechenland daraus neben vielen secretis zu vernehmen, was zu martialischer Ausrüstung eines Kriegshelden vornehmlich gehörig. . . .* [Frankfurt?], 1685.

Thomas, Gabriel. *Continuatio Der Beschreibung der Landschafft Pennsylvaniæ An den End-Gräntzen Americæ* [. . .]. Frankfurt and Leipzig: Andreas Otto, 1702.

Secondary Sources

Listed here are scholarly and nonscholarly works both about Pastorius and about his historical, religious, literary, and intellectual context.

Albrecht-Birkner, Veronika, and Udo Sträter. "Die radikale Phase des frühen August Hermann Francke." In *Der Radikale Pietismus: Perspektiven der Forschung*, edited by Wolfgang Breul et al., 57–84. Göttingen: Vandenhoeck & Ruprecht, 2010.

Amory, Hugh, and David D. Hall, eds. *The Colonial Book in the Atlantic World.* Cambridge: Cambridge University Press, 2000.

Bauman, Richard. *For the Reputation of Truth: Politics, Religion, and Conflict Among the Pennsylvania Quakers, 1750–1800.* Baltimore: Johns Hopkins University Press, 1971.

———. *Let Your Words Be Few: Symbolism of Speaking and Silence Among Seventeenth-Century Quakers.* Cambridge: Cambridge University Press, 1983.

Becker-Cantarino, Barbara. "Martin Opitz." In *German-Baroque Writers, 1580–1660, Dictionary of Literary Biography*, vol. 164, ed. James Hardin, 256–68. Detroit: Gale, 1996.

Beiler, Rosalind J. "Bridging the Gap: Cultural Mediators and the Structure of Transatlantic Communication." In *Atlantic Communications: The Media in American and German History from the Seventeenth to the Twentieth Century*, edited by Norbert Finzsch and Ursula Lehmkuhl, 45–64. Oxford: Berg, 2004.

———. "Distributing Aid to Believers in Need: The Religious Foundations of Transatlantic Migration." In "Empire, Society, and Labor: Essays in Honor of Richard S. Dunn," special supplemental issue of *Pennsylvania History: A Journal of Mid-Atlantic Studies* 64 (Summer 1997): 73–87.

———. "From the Rhine to the Delaware Valley: The Eighteenth-Century Transatlantic Trading Channels of Caspar Wistar." In *In Search of Peace and Prosperity: New German Settlers in Eighteenth-Century Europe and America*, edited by Hartmut Lehmann et al., 172–88. University Park: Pennsylvania State University Press, 2000.

——. "German-Speaking Immigrants in the British Atlantic World, 1680–1730," *OAH Magazine of History* 18, no. 3 (April 2004): 19–22.

——. *Immigrant and Entrepreneur: The Atlantic World of Caspar Wistar, 1650–1750*. University Park: Pennsylvania State University Press, 2008.

——. "Migration and the Loss of Spiritual Community: The Case of Daniel Falckner and Anna Maria Schuchart." In *Enduring Loss in Early Modern Germany: Cross Disciplinary Perspectives*, edited by Lynne Tatlock, 369–95. Leiden: Brill, 2010.

Benzendörfer, Udo, and Wilhelm Kühlmann, eds. *Heilkunde und Krankheitserfahrung in der frühen Neuzeit*. Tübingen: Max Niemeyer, 1992.

Berns, Jörg Jochen. "Utopie und Medizin: Der Staat der Gesunden und der gesunde Staat: Utopische Entwürfe des 16. und 17. Jahrhunderts." In *Heilkunde und Krankheitserfahrung in der frühen Neuzeit*, edited by Udo Benzendörfer and Wilhelm Kühlmann, 55–93. Tübingen: Max Niemeyer, 1992.

Beyreuther, Erich. *Geschichte des Pietismus*. Stuttgart: Steinkopf, 1978.

Binder-Johnson, Hildegard. "The Germantown Protest of 1688 Against Negro Slavery." In *Pennsylvania Magazine of History and Biography* 65 (1941): 145–56.

Bittinger, Lucy Forney. *The Germans in Colonial Times*. New York: Russell & Russell, 1968.

Bowden, James. *The History of the Society of Friends in America*. 2 vols. 1850. Reprint, New York: Arno Press, 1972.

Braithwaite, William. *The Beginnings of Quakerism*. 2nd ed. Cambridge: Cambridge University Press, 1961.

——. *The Second Period of Quakerism*. 2nd ed. Cambridge: Cambridge University Press, 1961.

Brecht, Martin, ed. *Der Pietismus vom siebzehnten bis zum frühen achtzehnten Jahrhundert*. Vol. 1, *Geschichte des Pietismus*. Göttingen: Vandenhoeck & Ruprecht, 1993.

Brendle, Thomas Royce, and Claude W. Unger. *Folk Medicine of the Pennsylvania Germans: The Non-Occult Cures*. New York: Kelley, 1970.

Bronner, Edwin B. "The Quakers and Non-Violence in Pennsylvania." *Pennsylvania History* 35 (1968): 1–22.

Brophy, Alfred L. "Francis Daniel Pastorius." In *The Multilingual Anthology of American Literature: A Reader of Original Texts with English Translations*, edited by Marc Shell and Werner Sollors, 12–15. New York: New York University Press, 2000.

——. "'Ingenium est Fateri per quos profeceris:' Francis Daniel Pastorius' *Young Country Clerk's Collection* and Anglo-American Legal Literature, 1682–1716." *University of Chicago Law School Roundtable* (1996): 637–734.

——. "The Intellectual World of a Seventeenth-Century Jurist: Francis Daniel Pastorius and the Reconstruction of Pietist Thought." In *German? American? Literature?: New Directions in German-American Studies*, edited by Winfried Fluck and Werner Sollors, 43–63. New York: Peter Lang, 2002.

——. "The Quaker Bibliographic World of Francis Daniel Pastorius." *Pennsylvania Magazine of History and Biography* 122, no. 3 (July 1998): 241–91.

Browning, Robert M. *German Baroque Poetry, 1618–1723*. University Park: Pennsylvania State University Press, 1971.

Burkhart, John, and Ralph West, eds. *Better Than Riches: A Tricentennial History of William Penn Charter School, 1689–1989*. Philadelphia: William Penn Charter School, 1989.

Butler, Jon. *Awash in a Sea of Faith: Christianizing the American People*. Cambridge, Mass.: Harvard University Press, 1990.

———. "'Gospel Order Improved': The Keithian Schism and the Exercise of Ministerial Authority in Pennsylvania." *William and Mary Quarterly*, 3ʳᵈ ser., 31 (1974): 431–52.

———. "Into Pennsylvania's Spiritual Abyss: The Rise and Fall of the Later Keithians, 1693–1703." *Pennsylvania Magazine of History and Biography* 101 (1977): 151–70.

———. "Magic, Astrology, and the Early American Heritage, 1600–1760." *American Historical Review* 84 (1979): 317–46.

———. "Power, Authority, and the Origins of American Denominational Order: The English Churches in the Delaware Valley, 1680–1730." *Transactions of the American Philosophical Society* 68, no. 2 (1978): 32–39.

———. "The Records of the First 'American' Denomination: The Keithians of Pennsylvania, 1694–1700." *Pennsylvania Magazine of History and Biography* 120 (1996): 89–105.

Canup, John. "Cotton Mather and 'Criolian Degeneracy.'" *Early American Literature* 24, no. 1 (1989): 20–34.

Carey, Brycchan. *From Peace to Freedom: Quaker Rhetoric and the Birth of American Antislavery, 1657–1761*. New Haven: Yale University Press, 2012.

Chartier, Roger. *The Order of Books: Readers, Authors, and Libraries in Europe Between the Fourteenth and Eighteenth Centuries*. Translated by Lydia G. Cochrane. 1992. Reprint, Cambridge: Polity Press, 1994.

———. "Reading Matter and 'Popular' Reading: From the Renaissance to the Seventeenth Century." In *A History of Reading in the West*, edited by Guglielmo Cavallo and Roger Chartier, translated by Lydia Cochrane, 269–83. 1995. Reprint, Amherst: University of Massachusetts Press, 1999.

Cody, Edward. "The Price of Perfection: The Irony of George Keith." *Pennsylvania History* 39 (1972): 1–19.

Crain, Patricia. *The Story of A: The Alphabetization of America from "The New England Primer" to "The Scarlet Letter."* Stanford: Stanford University Press, 2000.

Cremin, Lawrence A. *American Education: The Colonial Experience, 1607–1783*. New York: Harper & Row, 1970.

Davis, Garold N. *German Thought and Culture in England, 1700–1770; A Preliminary Survey Including a Chronological Bibliography of German Literature in English Translation*. Chapel Hill: University of North Carolina Press, 1969.

de Capua, A. G. *German Baroque Poetry: Interpretive Readings*. Albany: State University of New York Press, 1973.

Deppermann, Andreas. *Johann Jakob Schütz und die Anfänge des Pietismus*. Beiträge zur historischen Theologie 119. Tübingen: Mohr Siebeck, 2002.

Deppermann, Klaus. "Pennsylvanien als Asyl des frühen deutschen Pietismus." In *Pietismus und Neuzeit: Ein Jahrbuch zur Geschichte des Neueren Protestantismus*. Vol. 10, *Schwerpunkte Friedrich Christoph Oetinger*, 190–226. Göttingen: Vandenhoeck & Ruprecht, 1984.

Derounian-Stodola, Kathryn Zabelle, ed. *Early American Literature and Culture: Essays Honoring Harrison T. Meserole*. Newark: University of Delaware Press, 1992.

Dunn, Mary Maples. *William Penn: Politics and Conscience*. Princeton: Princeton University Press, 1967.

Dunn, Richard S., and Mary Maples Dunn, eds. *The World of William Penn*. Philadelphia: University of Pennsylvania Press, 1986.

Endy, Melvin B. *William Penn and Early Quakerism*. Princeton: Princeton University Press, 1973.

Engelbert, Arthur F. "Francis Daniel Pastorius in his Literary Activities." Ph.D. diss., University of Pittsburgh, 1935.

Erben, Patrick M. "Educating Germans in Colonial Pennsylvania." In *"The Good Education of Youth": World of Learning in the Age of Franklin*, edited by John H. Pollack, 122–49. New Castle, Del.: Oak Knoll Press, 2009.

———. *A Harmony of the Spirits: Translation and the Language of Community in Early Pennsylvania*. Chapel Hill: University of North Carolina Press for the Omohundro Institute of Early American History and Culture, 2012.

———. "'Honey-Combs' and 'Paper-Hives': Positioning Francis Daniel Pastorius's Manuscript Writings in Early Pennsylvania." *Early American Literature* 37, no. 2 (2002): 157–94.

———. "Promoting Pennsylvania: Penn, Pastorius, and the Creation of a Transnational Community." *Resources for American Literary Study* 29 (2003–4): 25–65.

———. "Writing and Reading a 'New English World': Literacy, Multilingualism, and the Formation of Community in Early America." Ph.D. diss., Emory University, 2003.

Faust, Albert Bernhardt. *Francis Daniel Pastorius and the 250th Anniversary of the Founding of Germantown*. Philadelphia: Carl Schurz Memorial Foundation, 1934.

———. *The German Element in the United States, with Special reference to Its Political, Moral, Social and Educational Influence*. New York: Houghton, 1927.

Ferlier, Louisiane. "Building Religious Communities with Books: The Quaker and Anglican Transatlantic Libraries, 1650–1710." In *Before the Public Library: Reading, Community, and Identity in the Atlantic World, 1650–1850*, edited by Mark Towsey and Kyle B. Roberts, 34–51. Leiden: Brill, 2018.

Fisher, Elizabeth. "'Prophesies and Revelations': German Cabbalists in Early Pennsylvania." *Pennsylvania Magazine of History and Biography* 109 (1985): 299–333.

Foster, Leonard. "Neo-Latin Tradition and Vernacular Poetry." In *German Baroque Literature: The European Perspective*, edited by Gerhart Hoffmeister, 87–108. New York: Ungar, 1983.

Frost, J. William. *The Keithian Controversy in Early Pennsylvania*. Norwood, Pa.: Norwood Editions, 1980.

———. "Quaker Books in Colonial Pennsylvania." *Quaker History* 80, no. 1 (Spring 1991): 1–23.

———. *The Quaker Family in Colonial America: A Portrait of the Society of Friends*. New York: St. Martin's Press, 1973.

———. "Religious Liberty in Early Pennsylvania." *Pennsylvania Magazine of History and Biography* 105, no. 4 (1982): 419–52.

———. "Unlikely Controversialists: Caleb Pusey and George Keith." *Quaker History* 64, no. 1 (1975): 16–36.

Galinsky, Hans. *Amerika und Europa: Sprachliche und sprachkünstlerische Wechselbeziehungen in amerikanischen Sicht*. Berlin: Langenscheidt, 1968.

———. "Three Literary Perspectives on the German in America: Immigrant, Homeland, and American Views." In *Eagle in the New World. German Immigration to Texas and America*, edited by Theodore Gish and Richard Spuler, 102–31. College Station: Texas A&M University Press, 1986.

Gerbner, Katharine. "Antislavery in Print: The Germantown Protest, the *Exhortation*, and the Seventeenth-Century Quaker Debate on Slavery." *Early American Studies* 9, no. 3 (2011): 552–75.

———. "'We Are Against the Traffik of Men-Body': The Germantown Quaker Protest of 1688 and the Origins of American Abolitionism." *Pennsylvania History: A Journal of Mid-Atlantic Studies* 74, no. 2 (2007): 149–72.

Gillespie, Gerald. *German Baroque Poetry*. New York: Twayne, 1971.

Grafton, Anthony. "The Humanist as Reader." In *A History of Reading in the West*, edited by Guglielmo Cavallo and Roger Chartier, 179–212. Amherst: University of Massachusetts Press, 1999.

———. "The Republic of Letters in the American Colonies: Francis Daniel Pastorius Makes a Notebook." *American Historical Review* 117, no. 1 (February 2012): 1–39.

———. *Worlds Made by Words: Scholarship and Community in the Modern West*. Cambridge, Mass.: Harvard University Press, 2009.

Green, James N. "The Book Trade in the Middle Colonies, 1680–1720." In *The Colonial Book in the Atlantic World*, edited by Hugh Amory and David D. Hall, 199–223. Cambridge: Cambridge University Press, 2000.

Greenblatt, Stephen. *Marvelous Possessions: The Wonder of the New World*. Chicago: University of Chicago Press, 1991.

Hoffmeister, Gerhart, ed. *German Baroque Literature: The European Perspective*. New York: Ungar, 1983.

Horle, Craig, et al., eds. *Lawmaking and Legislators in Pennsylvania: A Biographical Dictionary*. Vol. 1, *1682–1709*. Philadelphia: University of Pennsylvania Press, 1991.

Hull, William I. *William Penn and the Dutch Quaker Migration to Pennsylvania*. 1935. Reprint, Baltimore: Genealogical Publishing Company, 1970.

Jantz, Harold. "German-American Literature: Some Further Perspectives." In *America and the Germans: An Assessment of a Three-Hundred-Year History*, edited by Frank Trommler and Joseph McVeigh, 283–93. Philadelphia: University of Pennsylvania Press, 1985.

———. "Pastorius, Intangible Values." *American-German Review* 25, no. 1 (1958): 4–7.

Jehlen, Myra. *American Incarnation: The Individual, the Nation, and the Continent*. Cambridge, Mass.: Harvard University Press, 1986.

Johns, David L. "Convincement and Disillusionment: Printer William Bradford and the Keithian Controversy in Colonial Pennsylvania." *Journal of the Friends' Historical Society* [Great Britain] 57, no. 1 (1994): 21–32.

Jones, Howard Mumford. "The Colonial Impulse: An Analysis of the 'Promotion' Literature of Colonization." *Proceedings of the American Philosophical Society* 90, no. 2 (1946): 131–61.

Jones, Rufus M. *The Quakers in the American Colonies*. 1911. Reprint, New York: Russell & Russell, 1962.

Juterczenka, Sünne. *Über Gott und die Welt: Endzeitvisionen, Reformdebatten und die europäische Quäkermission in der frühen Neuzeit*. Göttingen: Vandenhoeck & Ruprecht, 2008.

Kashatus, William C. "Franklin's Secularization of Quaker Education." In *"The Good Education of Youth": World of Learning in the Age of Franklin*, edited by John H. Pollack, 55–21. New Castle, Del.: Oak Knoll Press, 2009.

———. *A Virtuous Education: Penn's Vision for Philadelphia Schools*. Wallingford, Pa.: Pendle Hill, 1997.

Kirby, Ethyn Williams. *George Keith (1638–1716)*. New York: Appleton-Century, 1942.

Könneken, Jaspar [Caspar Köhn]. MS fol. 356–72. "Geistliches Ministerium" [1683–84]. Archiv der Hansestadt Lübeck, Germany.

———. *Letters relating to the Settlement of Germantown in Pennsylvania, 1683–4: From the Könneken Manuscript in the Ministerial-Archive of Lübeck*. Translated and edited by Julius Friedrich Sachse. Lübeck and Philadelphia, 1903.

Lambert, Margo M. "Francis Daniel Pastorius: An American in Early Pennsylvania, 1683–1719/20." Ph.D. diss., Georgetown University, 2007.

Lindholdt, Paul J. "The Significance of the Colonial Promotion Tract." In *Early American Literature and Culture: Essays Honoring Harrison T. Meserole*, edited by Kathryn Zabelle Derounian-Stodola, 57–72. Newark: University of Delaware Press, 1992.

Learned, Marion Dexter. "From Pastorius's Bee-Hive or Bee-Stock." *Americana Germanica* 1, no. 4 (1897): 67–73.

———. *The Life of Francis Daniel Pastorius.* Philadelphia: Campbell, 1908.

Mack, Rüdiger. "Franz Daniel Pastorius, sein Einsatz für die Quäker." In *Pietismus und Neuzeit: Ein Jahrbuch zur Geschichte des neueren Protestantismus.* Vol. 15, *Schwerpunkt: Die Gemeinschaftsbewegung*, 132–71. Göttingen: Vandenhoeck & Ruprecht, 1989.

Martin, Clare J. L. "Controversy and Division in Post-Restoration Quakerism: The Hat, Wilkinson-Story and Keithian Controversies and Comparisons with the Internal Divisions of Other Seventeenth-Century Non-Conformist Groups." Ph.D. diss., Open University, 2003.

McNeely, Ian F., and Lisa Wolverton. *Reinventing Knowledge: From Alexandria to the Internet.* New York: W. W. Norton, 2008.

Meid, Volker. *Barocklyrik.* Stuttgart: Metzler, 1986.

Meserole, Harrison T. "Francis Daniel Pastorius." In *American Poetry of the Seventeenth Century*, 293–94. University Park: Pennsylvania State University Press, 1985.

Minardi, Margot. "The Boston Inoculation Controversy of 1721–1722: An Incident in the History of Race." *Willian and Mary Quarterly*, 3rd ser., 61, no. 1 (2004): 47–76.

Monaghan, Jennifer E. *Learning to Read and Write in Colonial America.* Amherst: University of Massachusetts Press; Worcester: American Antiquarian Society, 2005.

Moore, Rosemary. *The Light in Their Consciences: Early Quakers in Britain, 1646–1666.* University Park: Pennsylvania State University Press, 2000.

Moss, Ann. "Commonplace-Rhetoric and Thought-Patterns in Early Modern Culture." In *The Recovery of Rhetoric: Persuasive Discourse and Disciplinarity in the Human Sciences*, edited by R. H. Roberts and J. M. M. Good, 49–60. Charlottesville: University Press of Virginia, 1993.

———. *Printed Commonplace-Books and the Structuring of Renaissance Thought.* Oxford: Clarendon Press, 1996.

Murphy, Andrew R. *Conscience and Community: Revisiting Toleration and Religious Dissent in Early Modern England and America.* University Park: Pennsylvania State University Press, 2001.

Myers, Albert Cook. *Narratives of Early Pennsylvania, West New Jersey and Delaware.* Vol. 11 of *Original Narratives of Early American History*, edited by Franklin J. Jameson. New York: Scribner's, 1912.

Nash, Gary B. *Quakers and Politics, Pennsylvania, 1681–1726.* 1968. Reprint, Boston: Northeastern University Press, 1993.

Palmieri, Brooke. "'What the Bees Have Taken Pains for': Francis Daniel Pastorius, The Beehive, and Commonplacing in Colonial Pennsylvania." Undergraduate Humanities Forum 2008–9: Change. University of Pennsylvania, 2009.

Pennypacker, Samuel Whitaker. *The Settlement of Germantown and the Beginning of German Emigration to North America.* 1899. Reprint, New York: Blom, 1970.

Peters, Kate. *Print Culture and the Early Quakers.* Cambridge: Cambridge University Press, 2005.

Peterson, Mark A. "The Selling of Joseph: Bostonians, Antislavery, and the Protestant International, 1689–1733." *Massachusetts Historical Review* 4 (2002): 1–22.

Riley, Lyman W. "Books from the 'Beehive' Manuscript of Francis Daniel Pastorius." *Quaker History* 83, no. 2 (1994): 116–29.

Roeber, Gregg A. "German and Dutch Books and Printing." In *The Colonial Book in the Atlantic World*, edited by Hugh Amory and David D. Hall, 298–313. A History of the Book in America 1. New York: Cambridge University Press, 2000.

———. "The Migration of the Pious: Methodists, Pietists, and the Antinomian Character of North American Religious History." In *Visions of the Future in Germany and America*, edited by Norbert Finzsch and Hermann Wellenreuther, 25–47. Oxford: Berg, 2001.

———. "Der Pietismus in Nordamerika im 18. Jahrhundert." In *Der Pietismus im achtzehnten Jahrhundert*. Vol. 2., *Geschichte de Pietismus*, edited by Martin Brecht and Klaus Deppermann, 666–99. Göttingen: Vandenhoeck & Ruprecht, 1995.

Rosenberg, Nancy. "The Sub-textual Religion: Quakers, the Book, and Public Education in Philadelphia, 1682–1800." Ph.D. diss., University of Michigan, 1991.

Rosenmeier, Rosamund. "Francis Daniel Pastorius." In *American Colonial Writers, 1606–1709*, edited by Emory Elliott, 245–47. *Dictionary of Literary Biography* 24. Detroit: Gale, 1984.

Sachse, Julius Friedrich. *The German Pietists of Provincial Pennsylvania, 1694–1708*. 1895. Reprint, New York: AMS Press, 1970.

Sammons, Jeffrey L. *Angelus Silesius*. New York: Twayne, 1967.

Scheiding, Oliver. "The Poetry of British America: Francis Daniel Pastorius, 'Epibaterium, Or a hearty Congratulation to William Penn' (1699) and Richard Lewis, 'Food for Criticks' (1731)." In *A Handbook of American Poetry: Contexts—Developments—Readings*, edited by Oliver Scheiding, 23–36. Trier: Wissenschaftlicher Verlag Trier, 2014.

Schneider, Hans. *German Radical Pietism*. Translated by Gerald T. MacDonald. Lanham, Md.: Scarecrow Press, 2007.

———. "Der radikale Pietismus im 17. Jahrhundert." In *Der Pietismus vom siebzehnten bis zum frühen achtzehnten Jahrhundert*. Vol. 1, *Geschichte des Pietismus*, edited by Martin Brecht, 391–437. Göttingen: Vandenhoeck & Ruprecht, 1993.

Schöberl, Ingrid. "Franz Daniel Pastorius and the Foundation of Germantown." In *Germans to America: 300 Years of Immigration, 1683–1983*, edited by Günter Moltmann, 16–24. Stuttgart: Institute for Foreign Cultural Relations, 1982.

Schramm, Karen. "Promotion Literature." In *The Oxford Handbook of Early American Literature*, edited by Kevin J. Hayes, 69–91. Oxford: Oxford University Press, 2008.

Schweitzer, Christoph E. "Excursus: German Baroque Literature in Colonial America." In *German Baroque Literature. The European Perspective*, edited by Gerhart Hoffmeister, 178–93. New York: Ungar, 1983.

———. "Francis Daniel Pastorius, the German-American poet." *Yearbook of German-American Studies* 18 (1983): 21–28.

———. Introduction to *Deliciæ Hortenses or Garden-Recreations* and *Voluptates Apianæ* by Francis Daniel Pastorius, edited by Christoph E. Schweitzer, 1–6. Studies in German Literature, Linguistics, and Culture 2. Columbia, S.C.: Camden House, 1982.

Seidensticker, Oswald. "Francis Daniel Pastorius: Pennsylvania's First Poet." In *German Day Celebration*, 62–65. Philadelphia, 1892.

———. "Pastorius und die Gründung von Germantown." *Der Deutsche Pionier* 3 (1871–72): 8–12, 56–58, 78–83.

Shantz, Douglas H. *An Introduction to German Pietism: Protestant Renewal at the Dawn of Modern Europe*. Baltimore: Johns Hopkins University Press, 2013.

Showalter, Shirley Hershey. "'Herbal Signs of Nature's Page': A Study of Francis Daniel Pastorius' View of Nature." *Quaker History* 71, no. 2 (1982): 89–99.

Smith, Nigel. *Perfection Proclaimed: Language and Literature in English Radical Religion, 1640–1660.* Oxford: Clarendon Press, 1989.

Soderlund, Jean R. *Quakers and Slavery: A Divided Spirit.* Princeton: Princeton University Press, 1985.

Stievermann, Jan, and Oliver Scheiding, eds. *A Peculiar Mixture: German-Language Cultures and Identities in Eighteenth-Century North America.* University Park: Pennsylvania State University Press, 2013.

Stoeffler, F. Ernest, ed. *Continental Pietism and Early American Christianity.* Grand Rapids, Mich.: Eerdmans, 1976.

———. *German Pietism During the Eighteenth Century.* Leiden: Brill, 1973.

———. *Mysticism in The German Devotional Literature of Colonial Pennsylvania.* Allentown, Pa.: Schlechter's, 1950.

———. *The Rise of Evangelical Pietism.* Leiden: Brill, 1971.

Strom, Jonathan, Hartmut Lehman, and James Van Horn Melton. *Pietism in Germany and North America, 1680–1820.* Burlington, Vt.: Ashgate, 2009.

Thomas, Andrew L. "Francis Daniel Pastorius and the Northern Protestant Transatlantic World." *Acta Comeniana* 28 (2014): 95–126.

Tinkcom, Harry M., Margaret B. Tinkcom, and Grant Miles Simon. *Historic Germantown: From the Founding to the Early Part of the Nineteenth Century; A Survey of the German Township.* Philadelphia: American Philosophical Society, 1955.

Tolles, Frederick B. *Meeting House and Counting House: The Quaker Merchants of Colonial Philadelphia, 1682–1763.* Chapel Hill: University of North Carolina Press, 1948.

———. "'Of the Best Sort but Plain': The Quaker Aesthetic." *American Quarterly* 9 (1959): 484–502.

———. *Quakers and the Atlantic Culture.* New York: Macmillan, 1960.

Toms, DeElla Victoria. "The Intellectual and Literary Background of Francis Daniel Pastorius." Ph.D. diss., Northwestern University, 1953.

Towsey, Mark, and Kyle B. Roberts, eds. *Before the Public Library: Reading, Community, and Identity in the Atlantic World, 1650–1850.* Leiden: Brill, 2018.

Turner, Beatrice Pastorius. "William Penn and Pastorius." *Pennsylvania Magazine of History and Biography* 57 (1933): 66–90.

Wallmann, Johannes. *Der Pietismus.* Göttingen: Vandenhoeck & Ruprecht, 1990.

Weaver, John David. "Franz Daniel Pastorius (1651–c.1720): Early Life in Germany with Glimpses of his Removal to Pennsylvania." Ph.D. diss., University of California, Davis. 1985.

Wellenreuther, Hermann. *Glaube und Politik in Pennsylvania, 1681–1776: Die Wandlungen der Obrigkeitsdoktrin und des Peace Testimony der Quäker.* Kölner Historische Abhandlungen 20. Cologne: Böhlau, 1972.

———. "The Political Dilemma of the Quakers in Pennsylvania, 1681–1748." *Pennsylvania Magazine of History and Biography* 94, no. 2 (1970): 135–72.

———. "The Quest for Harmony in a Turbulent World: The Principle of 'Love and Unity' in Colonial Pennsylvania Politics." *Pennsylvania Magazine of History and Biography* 107 (1983): 537–76.

Wiggin, Bethany. *Germanopolis, 1683–1763: Postcolonial Figures in Colonial American History.* Philadelphia: Pennsylvania State University Press, forthcoming.

Wilson, Renate. *Pious Traders in Medicine: A German Pharmaceutical Network in Eigh-teenth-Century North America.* University Park: Pennsylvania State University Press, 2000.

Wokeck, Marianne S. "Francis Daniel Pastorius." In *Lawmaking and Legislators in Pennsylva-nia: A Biographical Dictionary.* Vol. 1, *1682–1709,* edited by Craig Horle et al., 586–90. Philadelphia: University of Pennsylvania Press, 1991.

———. *Trade in Strangers: The Beginning of Mass Migration to North America.* University Park: Pennsylvania State University Press, 1999.

Wolf, Edwin. *The Book Culture of a Colonial American City: Philadelphia Books, Bookmen, and Booksellers.* Oxford: Clarendon Press, 1988.

———. *The Library of James Logan, 1674–1751.* Philadelphia: Library Company, 1974.

Wolf, Stephanie Grauman. *Urban Village: Population, Community, and Family Structure in Germantown, Pennsylvania 1683–1800.* Princeton: Princeton University Press, 1976.

Woody, Thomas. *Early Quaker Education in Pennsylvania.* 1918. Reprint, New York: Arno Press,1969.

Wright, Luella M. *The Literary Life of the Early Friends, 1650–1725.* New York: Columbia Univer-sity Press, 1932.

Index

This index includes authors Pastorius cited frequently, such as Francis Bacon, Nicholas Culpeper, and William Penn, but not every writer listed in his extensive bibliographies. The index also includes general references to the Bible but not every direct Scriptural reference.

manuscript, 27, 137, 140, 145–53, 213–14, 233, 239, 327, 344–45, 378, 385–86

printed, 31, 61, 73, 83, 231, 245, 260, 277, 329, 340, 349, 403

Quaker, 87, 156–90

See also commonplace books; education; knowledge; learning; libraries; reading

botany. *See* plants

Bradford, William (pilgrim), viii

Bradford, William (printer), xxv, 10, 66–67, 79, 91, 93, 411

bridewells, 305, 323

Burlington (New Jersey), xxiv–xxv, 5, 18, 68, 71, 325, 397, 400, 411–12, 417, 423

Carpenter, Samuel, xxvi, 310, 315, 321–24, 340, 345–49, 412

Catholicism, xxii, 2, 8, 48, 78, 81, 88, 125, 168–69, 180, 184, 194, 270, 288, 421, 424

cattle, 6, 50, 55, 359, 361, 398, 408–9

censure. *See* critics

Certain News from America, xxii, xxiv, 26, 43–60

charity. *See* love

Christianity, 2–4, 9, 18–19, 65–67, 73, 78, 88, 228, 324, 398, 422

church(es), 80, 84, 108, 116, 122–25, 260, 335

discipline, 2, 67

corrupt, 1–5, 66–78, 81, 88, 123

heavenly, 295, 305

Pietist critique of, 1–5, 79–90, 210

Circumstantial Geographical Description, xxv, 26, 60–65, 349

climate, 15, 250, 309, 355, 382

clothing, 57, 64, 125, 356, 364

Comenius, Jan Amos, xi, 7, 9, 32, 194

commemoration. *See* memory

commonplace book(s),

"Alvearialia," 113–26

"Bee-Hive," 92, 127–50, 151–207, 208–13, 213–78

circulation, 21–24, 321

in Europe, 11, 13, 20–21

in Pennsylvania, ix, xiii, xvii, xxv, 11, 13–21, 24–25

in Renaissance, 8, 11, 14

See also book(s); education; knowledge

community, xii–xiii, 208, 279

building, viii, ix–x, 5–7, 27–29, 32, 92

education, 7–11

failure of, 17–20

immigrant, 68

knowledge, xviii, 11–17, 21–24, 315

religion, xxiv, 1–5, 29–31, 68–79, 80–90

conflict, xxii, xxv, 4–5, 30–32, 66–79, 396–402

confusion. *See* conflict

conscience, 25, 59–60, 64, 86–87, 109, 123, 126, 230, 231, 292, 298, 398

contentiousness. *See* conflict

contentment, 26, 28, 53, 133, 232, 235, 296–98, 378

correspondence, ix, xiii, xxvi, 5, 22–23, 82, 313–51, 426

See also "Letter-Book;" manuscript circulation

court(s), xxii, xxiii, xxv, 6–7, 10, 62, 64, 131, 157, 166, 176, 181, 185, 209, 310, 323–33, 403–10, 415, 418, 425

Crefeld. *See* Krefeld

critics, 8, 115, 136–37, 262

cross (Creutz, Kreutz), 3, 86, 87, 136, 179, 222, 269

Culpeper, Nicholas, 117, 119, 164, 195, 370–71, 385–86, 388

deafness (taub, Taubheit), 253–4

death (Tod), ix–xxvi, 10, 22, 29, 30–31, 75, 83–86, 162, 204, 212, 219, 221–22, 235, 245, 252–255, 264–66, 291, 295, 297–98, 312, 329, 350, 387

debt, xxv, 271, 312, 319–21, 337–38, 346, 351, 405–7, 413, 422–24

devil, 64, 70, 75, 84–86, 99, 123–24, 158, 171, 183, 190, 195, 199, 201, 204, 233–34, 236, 260, 266, 275, 299, 306, 334–35

devotion, 63, 92, 127

Diderot, Denis, 12, 20

diet, 6, 16, 25, 47, 50, 59, 108, 114, 149–50, 284, 352–74, 382–94

discernment, ix–x, 14, 17–20, 123, 144, 215, 229, 246, 259, 397, 401, 405, 414

disciple(s), 31, 53, 64, 86, 101, 311, 329

Hill, Richard, xxvi, 22, 315, 326–28, 337–39, 345–49, 415
honey, xiii, 11, 73, 115, 128, 134–35, 138, 140–45, 147–49, 154, 232, 238–39, 242
honeycombs, 128, 135–38, 144, 148, 151, 154, 239
Hoodt, Caspar, 324, 351, 415
Horb, Johann Heinrich, xxiii, 1, 172, 415
Hoskens, Jane. *See* Fenn, Jane
humanism, x, xii, 7–11, 14, 21, 25, 413
  See also education

index, 20–21, 129–30, 147, 154, 208, 403
ingratitude, 70, 73, 283, 300
Inner (Inward) Light, 2, 5, 11, 22–24, 67–68, 415, 420

Jawert, Johannes, xxv–xxvi, 346, 413
Jennings, Samuel, 67, 173, 318–19
Jesus Christ, 4, 31, 98, 101, 107, 124, 144, 222–30, 256, 274
  atonement of, 64, 83, 85, 229, 246
  commandment(s) of, 53, 228, 247–48, 262–63, 275, 329
  divinity of (*see* Jesus Christ: nature of)
  incarnation of (*see* Jesus Christ: nature of)
  life of, 31, 82, 87, 296–97, 305
  light of, 263, 324
  love of, 269, 311
  members of, 82, 263, 270
  name(s) of, 210, 275, 294, 311
  nature of, 2, 29, 67–68, 73–79, 84–86, 219, 281, 296–97, 299, 308, 320, 355, 379
  presence, 2, 143, 228, 273, 279, 284, 298
  as redeemer (*see* Jesus Christ: atonement of)
  servants of, 64, 83, 86, 275, 277, 291, 298, 305
  son of God (*see* Jesus Christ: nature of)
  suffering and death of, 26, 85, 87, 210, 221–22, 251, 305, 412, 416
  spirit of, 88–89
  spouse of, 210, 305
  witnesses of (*see* Jesus Christ: servants of)
journey. *See* transatlantic passage
judgment
  divine, 1, 19, 53, 67, 97, 144
  human (*see* discernment)

Keith, George. *See* Keithian controversy
Keithian controversy (schism), xii, xxv, 4–5, 346, 397, 411–12, 416–20, 423
  publications on, 66–90, 93, 173–74, 181–83
  in poetry, 30–31, 225–29, 267–68, 287, 291
Kelpius, Johannes, xxv, 4, 68–71, 80–90, 346, 351, 413, 416–17, 426
Kircher, Athanasius, xi, 12, 174
knowledge
  circulation of, x, 23, 45, 61, 91, 153
  collection of, viii–xiii, xvii, xxv, 8, 10–24, 27, 31–32, 113–14, 127–29, 139–40, 147, 150 154, 208, 214, 240, 320, 326, 340, 385–86, 403–4, 414–15
  loss of, xviii–xix, 14
  production of, 10–24, 31–32, 113–14, 127–29
  retrieval of, 10–24, 31–32, 113–14, 127–29
  storage of, x, xiii, 10–24, 31–32, 113–14, 127–29
  testing of, ix, xiii, 17–20, 32, 115, 140, 353, 377
  transfer of, x, xix, 8, 10–24, 30, 127
Könneken, Jaspar, 44–45
Koster (Köster), Henry (Heinrich) Bernhard, xxv, 5, 66–90, 93, 412, 417, 423
Krefeld, xxiv, 4, 46–47, 53–54, 55–56, 60, 68, 414, 417, 420, 425

land, 25, 123, 144, 252, 255, 266–67, 274, 281, 283, 302, 311, 320, 326, 347–49, 407, 411
  Native ownership, 4, 17, 60
  purchase, xxiii–xxvi, 6–7, 26, 43–45, 54–56, 63, 70–73, 315, 319, 326, 345–47, 403–5
  quality of, 11, 16, 26, 43, 46, 49, 51, 55, 57, 60, 246, 284, 287, 296, 309, 358, 365, 368, 374–77, 404–5, 409
language(s), ix–x, 2–4, 7–11, 13, 16–17, 26, 29, 31–32, 52, 63–64, 68, 78, 84, 92, 100, 133, 147, 209, 313, 320, 324, 332–34, 348–49
Latin (language), xii, xxii, 7–8
law, viii, xiii, xviii, xxii–xxiii, 5–7, 18, 26, 58, 62–63, 77, 81, 98, 101, 118, 122–24, 149, 231–32, 254–55, 305, 323, 328–29, 348, 377, 399, 401, 403–10
learning. *See* education
Leeds, Daniel, 183, 200, 236, 264, 334, 378, 418
Leeds, Titan, 200, 264, 418
Lenape. *See* Native Americans